International Rare
Book Prices

SCIENCE &
MEDICINE

1988

International Rare Book Prices

SCIENCE & MEDICINE

Series Editor: Michael Cole

1988

Picaflow Ltd., York

ISBN 1 870773 04 7

North America

Spoon River Press, P.O. Box 3635
Peoria, Illinois 61614, U.S.A.

Cover illustration by courtesy of Ken Spelman, York, England
Typesetting by Maxiprint, York, England
Printed and bound by Unwin Brothers Ltd., Woking, England

Contents

Introduction and Notes

Science & Medicine is the fourth title in the annual series *International Rare Book Prices*. The other titles are *The Arts & Architecture, Early Printed Books, Modern First Editions, Voyages, Travel & Exploration.*

IRBP was established in 1987 so as to provide annual records of the pricing levels of out-of-print, rare or antiquarian books within a number of specialty subject areas and to give likely sources and suppliers for such books in Britain and the United States of America.

Sources of information:

The books recorded each year in the various subject volume of *IRBP* have been selected from catalogues of books for sale issued during the previous year by numerous bookselling firms in Britain and the United States. These firms, listed at the end of this volume, range in nature from the highly specialized, handling books solely with closely defined subject areas, through to large concerns with expertise across a broad spectrum of interests.

Extent of coverage:

IRBP concentrates exclusively on books published in the English language and, throughout the series as a whole, encompasses books published between the 16th century and the 1970s.

The specific titles recorded in the annual volumes of *IRBP* vary greatly from year to year although naturally there is a degree of overlap, particularly of the more frequently found titles. Consecutive annual volumes do not, therefore, merely update pricings from earlier years; they give substantially different listings of books on each occasion. The value of the *IRBP* volumes lies in providing records of an ever-increasing range of individual titles which have appeared for sale on the antiquarian or rare book market.

Emphasis is placed on books falling within the lower to middle range of the pricing scale rather than restricting selection to the unusually fine or expensive. In so doing, *IRBP* provides a realistic overview of the norm, rather than the exception, within the booktrade.

Further details of the scope of the individual titles in the series are given on the final page of this volume.

Authorship and cross-references:

Authors are listed alphabetically by surname.

Whenever possible, the works of each author are grouped together under a single form of name irrespective of the various combinations of initials, forenames and surnames by which the author is known.

Works published anonymously, or where the name of the author is not recorded on the title-page, are suitably cross-referenced by providing the main entry under the name of the author (when mentioned by the bookseller) with a corresponding entry under the first appropriate word of the title. In cases of unknown, or unmentioned, authorship, entry is made solely under the title.

Full-titles:

Editorial policy is to eschew, whenever possible, short-title records in favour of full-, or at least more complete and explanatory, titles. Short-title listings do little to convey the flavour, or even the content, of many books - particularly those published prior to the nineteenth century.

Descriptions:

Books are listed alphabetically under each author's name, using the first word of the title ignoring, for alphabetical purposes, the definite and indefinite articles *the, a* and *an*. Within this alphabetical grouping of titles, variant editions are not necessarily arranged in chronological order, i.e., a 2nd, 3rd or 4th edition might well be listed prior to an earlier edition.

Subject to restrictions of space and to the provisos set out below, the substance of each catalogue entry giving details of the particular copy offered for sale has been recorded in full.

The listings have been made so as to conform to a uniform order of presentation, viz: Title; place of publication; publisher or printer; date; edition; size; collation; elements of content worthy of note; description of contents including faults, if any; description and condition of binding; bookseller; price; approximate price conversion from dollars to sterling or vice versa.

Abbreviations of description customary within the booktrade have generally been used. A list of these abbreviations will be found on page *x*.

Collations:

Collations, when provided by the bookseller, are repeated in toto although it should be borne in mind that booksellers employ differing practices in this respect; some by providing complete collations and others by indicating merely the number of pages in the main body of the work concerned. The same edition of the same title catalogued by two booksellers could therefore have two apparently different collations and care should be taken not to regard any collation recorded in *IRBP* as being a definitive or absolute record of total content.

Currency conversion:

IRBP lists books offered for sale priced in either pounds sterling (£) or United States dollars ($). For the benefit of readers unaccustomed to one or other of these currencies, an approximate conversion figure in the alternative currency has been provided in parentheses after each entry, as, for example, "**£100 [≈ $180]**", or, "**$60 [≈ £33]**". The conversion is based upon an exchange rate of £1 sterling ≈ US $1.80 (US $1 ≈ £0.556 sterling), the rate applicable at the date of going to press.

It must be stressed that the conversion figures in parentheses are provided merely as an indication of the approximate pricing level in the currency with which the reader may be most familiar and that fluctuations in exchange rates will make these approximations inaccurate to a greater or lesser degree.

Acknowledgements:

I am indebted to those booksellers who have provided their catalogues during 1987 for the purposes of *IRBP*. A list of the contributing booksellers forms an appendix at the rear of this volume.

This appendix forms a handy reference of contacts in Britain and the United States with proven experience of handling books within the individual specialist fields encompassed by the series. The booksellers listed therein are able, between them, to offer advice on any aspect of the rare and antiquarian booktrade.

Many of the listed books will still, at the time of publication, be available for purchase. Readers with a possible interest in acquiring any of the items may well find it worth their while communicating with the booksellers concerned to obtain further and complete details.

Caveat:

Whilst the greatest care has been taken in transcribing entries from catalogues, it should be understood that it is inevitable that an occasional error will have passed unnoticed. Obvious mistakes, usually typographical in nature, observed in catalogues have been corrected. I have not questioned the accuracy in bibliographical matters of the cataloguers concerned.

Michael Cole
Series Editor IRBP

Abbreviations

advt(s)	advertisement(s)	jnt(s)	joint(s)
addtn(s)	addition(s)	lge	large
a.e.g.	all edges gilt	lea	leather
a.l.s.	autograph letter signed	lib	library
altrtns	alterations	ltd	limited
Amer	American	litho(s)	lithograph(s)
bibliog(s)	bibliography(ies)	marg(s)	margin(s)
b/w	black & white	ms(s)	manuscript(s)
bndg	binding	mrbld	marbled
bd(s)	board(s)	mod	modern
b'plate	bookplate	mor	morocco
ctlg(s)	catalogue(s)	mtd	mounted
chromolitho(s)	chromo-lithograph(s)	n.d.	no date
ca	circa	n.p.	no place
cold	coloured	num	numerous
coll	collected	obl	oblong
contemp	contemporary	occas	occasional(ly)
crnr(s)	corner(s)	orig	original
crrctd	corrected	p (pp)	page(s)
cvr(s)	cover(s)	perf	perforated
dec	decorated	pict	pictorial
detchd	detached	port(s)	portrait(s)
diag(s)	diagram(s)	pres	presentation
dw(s)	dust wrapper(s)	ptd	printed
edn(s)	edition(s)	qtr	quarter
elab	elaborate	rebnd	rebind/rebound
engv(s)	engraving(s)	rec	recent
engvd	engraved	repr(d)	repair(ed)
enlgd	enlarged	rvsd	revised
ex lib	ex library	roy	royal
f (ff)	leaf(ves)	sep	separate
facs	facsimile	sev	several
fig(s)	figure(s)	sgnd	signed
fldg	folding	sgntr	signature
ft	foot	sl	slight/slightly
frontis	frontispiece	sm	small
hand-cold	hand-coloured	t.e.g.	top edge gilt
hd	head	t.l.s.	typed letter signed
ill(s)	illustration(s)	unif	uniform
illust	illustrated	v	very
imp	impression	vell	vellum
imprvd	improved	vol(s)	volume(s)
inscrbd	inscribed	w'engvd	wood-engraved
inscrptn	inscription	w'cut(s)	woodcut(s)
iss	issue	wrap(s)	wrapper(s)

Science & Medicine
1987 Catalogue Prices

Aaron, Charles H.
- A practical treatise on testing and working silver ores. San Francisco: Dewey, 1876. 1st edn. 12mo. 114,vi advts pp. Text ills, diags. Notes & sgntrs on endpapers. Lib stamp. Orig cloth, extremities rubbed, hd of spine a bit chipped. *(Heritage)* **$60 [≃£33]**

Abbott, Maude E.
- Atlas of congenital cardiac disease. New York: 1954. Facs reprint of 1936 edn. One of 1500. Folio. 62 pp. 25 plates.
(Scientia) **$75 [≃£41]**

Abell, Irvin
- Two addresses: a retrospect of surgery in Kentucky ... N.p., 1926. 8vo. 64 pp. 29 plates. Front free endpaper cut neatly away. Orig cloth. *(Pollak)* **£20 [≃$36]**

Abercrombie, John
- Inquiries concerning the intellectual powers and the investigation of truth. Edinburgh: Waugh & Innes, 1830. 1st edn. 8vo. Orig cloth, ptd paper label, spine faded, front jnt reprd, uncut edges. Author's inscrptn on half-title. *(Traylen)* **£225 [≃$405]**
- Inquiries concerning the intellectual powers and the investigation of truth. Boston: 1841. 8vo. 284 pp. Light foxing. Lea, sl scuffed & stained. *(Elgen)* **$35 [≃£19]**
- Pathological and practical researches on diseases of the stomach ... the liver, and other viscera of the abdomen. Edinburgh: Waugh, 1830. 2nd edn, enlgd. 8vo. 424 pp. Old qtr calf, somewhat worn. *(Oasis)* **$65 [≃£36]**
- Pathological and practical researches on diseases of the stomach ... the liver, and other viscera of the abdomen. Phila: 1830. 1st Amer edn. 416 pp. Some waterstains. Orig cloth-backed paper-cvrd bds. *(Fye)* **$75 [≃£41]**
- Surgical observations on injuries of the head and on miscellaneous subjects. Phila:

Dobson, 1811. 1st Amer edn. 8vo. 162 pp. Engvd frontis (browned). Orig paper-cvrd bds, spine worn, hinges reprd with tape.
(Oasis) **$250 [≃£138]**

Abernethy, John
- Surgical observations on the constitutional origin and treatment of local diseases; and on aneurisms. London: 1814. 3rd edn. 8vo. xii,315 pp. Orig bds, front cvr loose, spine somewhat defective. *(Hemlock)* **$175 [≃£97]**
- Surgical observations on the constitutional origin and treatment of local diseases; and on aneurisms. London: Longman ..., 1825. 8th edn. xii,346 pp. Half-title discarded. Half calf gilt, spine ends & crnrs worn. Vol 1 of 'Surgical Works'. *(Pollak)* **£30 [≃$54]**
- Surgical observations on the constitutional origin and treatment of local diseases; and on aneurisms. Vol. 1 [all published]. London: 1828. 10th edn. xii,346 pp. Orig paper cvrd bds, spine sl defective, bds worn at edges.
(Whitehart) **£40 [≃$72]**

Abraham, James Johnston
- Lettsom, his life, times, friends and descendants. London: 1933. 1st edn. Lge 8vo. x,498 pp. 144 text ills, extndg pedigree. Author's pencilled inscrptn on half-title. Orig buckram, faded, lower cvr marked.
(Bow Windows) **£40 [≃$72]**
- Lettsom, his life, times, friends and descendants. London: Heinemann, 1933. 1st edn. Lge 8vo. 498 pp. Ills. Orig cloth.
(Oasis) **$75 [≃£41]**
- Lettsom, his life, times, friends and descendants. London: 1933. 8vo. 498 pp. Ills. Orig cloth. *(Goodrich)* **$60 [≃£33]**

Abraham, R.M.
- Surveying instruments: their design, construction, testing and adjustment. London: [1926]. 8vo. ix.309 pp. Frontis, ills,

diags. Orig cloth.   *(Weiner)* **£20 [≃ $36]**

Abrahams, Harold J.
- Extinct medical schools of nineteenth-century Philadelphia. Phila: 1966. 580 pp. Binding spotted.   *(Goodrich)* **$45 [≃ £25]**

Abt, Isaac A. (ed.)
- Pediatrics, by various authors. Phila: [1923-26]. 1st edn. 8 vols (ex 9, lacks general index vol). Lge thick 8vo. Many cold plates, diags. Orig cloth, cnr of vol 2 cvr dampstained.   *(Elgen)* **$175 [≃ £97]**
- Pediatrics, by various authors. Phila: [1923]. 1st edn. 9 vols inc index vol. 8vo. Ills. Orig cloth.   *(Oasis)* **$250 [≃ £138]**

Account ...
- An account of several new inventions ... See Hale, Thomas
- An account of some new microscopical discoveries ... See Needham, John Turbeville
- Descriptive and historical account of the cotton manufacture of Dacca in Bengal. London: John Mortimer, 1851. 8vo. xvi pp. Text w'cuts. Orig blind-stamped cloth, some dusting.   *(Taylor)* **£25 [≃ $45]**

Accum, Friedrich
- A practical treatise on gas-light ... with remarks on the utility, safety, and general nature of this new branch of civil economy. London: for R. Ackermann, 1815. 2nd edn. Roy 8vo. 7 full-page & fldg cold plates. Orig bds, new paper spine, uncut edges.
         (Traylen) **£250 [≃ $450]**
- A practical treatise on gas-light ... apparatus and machinery ... for illuminating streets, houses ... with coal gas ... London: R. Ackermann, 1816. 3rd edn. Imp 8vo. x,[vi], xi-xvii, 194,6 advts pp. 7 hand-cold plates (2 fldg). Contemp half calf, reprd at ft.
         (Gough) **£265 [≃ $477]**
- A treatise on adulterations of food ... London: Longman ..., 1820. 2nd edn. [2],xxiv,360 pp. Uncut, orig bds.   *(Goodrich)* **$250 [≃ £138]**

Ackernecht, E.H.
- Medicine at the Paris Hospital 1794-1848. Balt: 1967. 8vo. 242 pp. Orig cloth, dw.
         (Goodrich) **$35 [≃ £19]**

Acland, Harold J.
- The Harveian Oration. London: 1865. 85 pp.
         (Goodrich) **$45 [≃ £25]**

Acret, G.S.
- A treatise on hernia, explaining its varieties, situations, symptoms, and causes   ...

construction and application of the most approved mechanical remedies. London: 1835. [ii],120 pp. 7 plates. Sl staining in some margs. New cloth.   *(Whitehart)* **£40 [≃ $72]**

Acton, Eliza
- Modern cookery in all its branches. London: Longman ..., 1847. 6th edn. 8vo. Engvd frontis, 7 plates, half-title, 32 pp inserted advts. Orig cloth, spine gilt, sl worn, inner hinges cracked.   *(Sanders)* **£85 [≃ $153]**

Adam, C.
- Ophthalmoscopic diagnosis based on typical pictures of the fundus of the eye ... Translated ... New York: 1913. 4to. 229 pp. 86 cold plates. Cloth.   *(Goodrich)* **$75 [≃ £41]**

Adam, Neil Kensington
- Physical chemistry. Oxford: [1958]. 1st edn, 2nd imp. 8vo. xii,658 pp. Ills. Cloth, dw. Ex lib.   *(Elgen)* **$50 [≃ £27]**

Adami, J. George
- Inflammation. An introduction to the study of pathology. London: Macmillan, 1907. 3rd edn. 8vo. xvi,240 pp. 19 figs. Orig cloth, spine faded, partly unopened.
         (Pollak) **£25 [≃ $45]**
- Medical contributions to the study of evolution. London: 1918. 8vo. xviii,372 pp. Ills. Cloth.   *(Rittenhouse)* **$37.50 [≃ £20]**

Adams, A.
- The Western Rajputana States. A medico-topographical and general account of Marwar, Sirohi and Jaisalmir. 1899. 1st edn. 8vo. xi,455 pp. Port frontis, 77 ills. Orig cloth, sl marked, lower bd damaged, sm split in lower jnt.   *(Old Cinema)* **£65 [≃ $117]**

Adams, George
- Astronomical and geographical essays. London: 1812. 6th edn, crrctd & enlgd by William Jones. 8vo. Frontis, 16 fldg plates. Tree calf, rebacked. *(Argosy)* **$200 [≃ £111]**
- Geometrical and graphical essays   ... description of ... mathematical instruments ... [with] Plates to the ... essays ... London: 1813-03. 4th & 3rd edns. xii,534 pp. 24 pp ctlg, 34 fldg plates. Text vol cloth, stained, loose; plates vol calf, worn, cvr detchd.
         (Weiner) **£125 [≃ $225]**

Adams, George, Jr.
- Essays on the microscope; containing a practical description of the most improved microscopes ... London: for the author, 1787. 1st edn. 2 vols. 4to & obl folio. Frontis, 4 pp

ctlg of instruments, atlas of 32 engvd plates. Contemp tree calf, gilt spines.
(Traylen) **£1,200 [≈ $2,160]**
- Essays on the microscope; containing a practical description of the most improved microscopes ... London: for the author, 1787. 1st edn. 2 vols. 4to & obl folio atlas. Frontis, 32 engvd plates. Bds.
(Halewood) **£240 [≈ $432]**

Adams, George, Sr.
- Micrographia illustrata: or the microscope explained. London: for the author, 1771. 'Fourth' (i.e. 3rd) edn. 8vo. [12],lxi, [1],325 pp. 72 engvd plates, many fldg. Some spotty foxing. Contemp diced calf, rebacked.
(Antiq Sc) **$650 [≈ £361]**
- Micrographia illustrata: or the microscope explained. London: 1771. 4th edn. lix,325 pp. 72 copper plates. Frontis reprd. Mod qtr lea, mrbld bds.
(Scientia) **$575 [≈ £319]**

Adams, H.C.
- The sewerage of sea coast towns. London: 1911. 1st edn. 8vo. viii,134,34 advts pp. 5 extndg plates, other ills. Inscrptn on half-title. Orig cloth.
(Bow Windows) **£36 [≈ $64]**

Adams, John Couch
- Lectures on the lunar theory. Cambridge: University Press, 1900. 1st sep edn. 8vo. [4],88 pp. Orig cloth. *(Antiq Sc)* **$110 [≈ £61]**

Adams, Joseph
- Memoirs of the life and doctrines of the late John Hunter, founder of the Hunterian Museum ... London: 1817. 10,[2],284 pp. Errata. Calf, jnts cracked.
(Goodrich) **$275 [≈ £152]**
- Observations on morbid poisons, phagadaena, and cancer ... on the laws of the venereal virus ... London: for J. Johnson, 1795. 1st edn. 8vo. [4],iv,328,[2] pp. Contemp half mor. Wellcome lib withdrawal stamp. *(Rootenberg)* **$500 [≈ £277]**
- A philosophical treatise on the hereditary peculiarities of the human race: with notes illustrative of the subject, particularly in gout, scrofula, and madness. London: 1815. 2nd edn. 125,24 pp. Pub ctlg. Contemp mrbld bds, rebacked with paper spine.
(Scientia) **$325 [≈ £180]**

Adams, R.D., et al.
- Diseases of muscle. A study in pathology. 1962. 2nd edn. xvi,735 pp. Frontis, num ills. Orig cloth, sl stained.
(Whitehart) **£25 [≈ $45]**

Adams, W.H. Davenport
- The healing art; or, chapters upon medicine, diseases, remedies, and physicians ... London: 1887. 2nd edn. 2 vols. 8vo. viii,316; 377 pp. Orig cloth, badly waterstained near foreedges, 1 back bd bowed. *(Weiner)* **£30 [≈ $54]**

Addison, Joseph
- The evidences of the Christian religion ... with a preface, containing the sentiments of Mr. Boyle, Mr. Lock, and Sir Isaac Newton. London: Tonson, 1730. 1st edn. Sm 8vo. Marg wormhole. Contemp calf, jnts worn.
(Marlborough) **£40 [≈ $72]**

Addison, Thomas
- A collection of the published writings. London: 1868. 8vo. 242 pp. 1st edn. Orig cloth. *(Fye)* **$250 [≈ £138]**
- A collection of the published writings of the late ... London: New Sydenham Soc., 1868. 8vo. xxxi,239 pp. Plates. Orig cloth, top of spine sl chipped. Ex lib.
(Rittenhouse) **$90 [≈ £50]**
- On the constitutional and local effects of disease of the supra-renal capsules. London: Highley, 1855. 1st edn. 4to. viii,43 pp. 11 cold litho plates. Minor marg stains, Wellcome lib stamp on title verso. Orig cloth, spine restored, preserved in qtr mor box.
(Rootenberg) **$13,500 [≈ £7,500]**

Adelmann, H.B.
- Marcello Malpighi and the evolution of embryology. Ithaca, New York: 1966. 1st edn. 5 vols. Lge 4to. 11 fldg plates in red & black, fldg map. Boxed.
(Elgen) **$250 [≈ £138]**

Adolph, E.F.
- The regulation of size as illustrated in unicellular organisms. London: 1931. 233 pp. Diags. Orig cloth, faded.
(Weiner) **£30 [≈ $54]**

Aerostatics ...
- Aerostatics or, a history of balloons ... aerial voyages, observations and discoveries ... art of constructing, inflating, navigating ... For the author, 1802. 3rd edn. Hand-cold fldg engvd frontis, title, 3-55 pp. Sl foxing. 19th c pebble cloth, sl faded. *(Edwards)* **£950 [≈ $1,710]**

Agassiz, L. & Gould, A.A.
- Outlines of comparative physiology, touching the structure and development of the race of animals ... Edited ... London: 1851. Sm 8vo. xxiv,442 pp. Cold frontis, 390 figs. Polished brown calf, gilt, by Westerton.
(Bow Windows) **£75 [≈ $135]**

Agassiz, Louis

- Contributions to the natural history of the United States. Boston: 1857-62. 1st edn. 4 vols. 4to. 643; 301,26; 380,12 pp. 62 plates. Mod cloth & endpapers.
(Scientia) **$275 [≃ £152]**

Agricola, G.A.

- The experimental husbandman and gardener ... to which is now added an appendix, containing a variety of experiments ... by R. Bradley. London: 1726. 2nd edn. 4to. [xxiv],314,[4] pp. 22 plates (13 double-page). Contemp calf, trifle worn.
(Wheldon & Wesley) **£150 [≃ $3,106]**

Agriculture & Rural Affairs ...

- Essays relating to agriculture and rural affairs ... See Anderson, James

Aikin, J.

- A manual of materia medica ... account of all the simples directed in the London and Edinburgh Dispensatories ... Yarmouth printed: Downes & March, 1785. 1st edn. 8vo. ix,194,viii index,[i advt] pp. Title laid down, spotted, ink-mark at ft. 19th c cloth.
(Gough) **£80 [≃ $144]**

Aikin, John

- Biographical memoirs of medicine in Great Britain from the revival of literature to the time of Harvey. London: 1780. 8vo. 12,338 pp, 6ff index, advt leaf. Cloth.
(Halewood) **£150 [≃ $270]**

Ainslie, John

- The gentleman and farmer's pocket companion and assistant ... Edinburgh: for T. Brown ..., 1802. 1st edn. Sm sq 8vo. [iv],xxxvi,180 pp. Contemp calf, minor rubbing. *(Burmester)* **£75 [≃ $135]**
- The gentleman and farmer's pocket companion and assistant: Directions for finding the contents of any piece of land by pacing, or by dimensions ... Edinburgh: 1802. Sq 16mo. 180 pp. Orig calf.
(Argosy) **$50 [≃ £27]**

Air, Weather ...

- A general chronological history of the air, weather, seasons ... See Short, Thomas

Aird, I.

- A companion in surgical studies. Edinburgh: 1949. 8vo. viii,1060 pp. Orig cloth, sl marked & faded, back inner hinge cracked but firm.
(Whitehart) **£25 [≃ $45]**

Airy, G.B.

- An elementary exposition of the principal perturbations in the solar system. 1834. 1st edn. xxiii,215 pp. Orig watered silk bds, rebacked. *(Whitehart)* **£25 [≃ $45]**
- Mathematical tracts on physical astronomy, the figure of the earth ... designed for the use of students in the University. Cambridge: Deighton, 1826. 1st edn. viii,180 pp. Erratum leaf, 4 fldg plates of figs (1 dampstained in marg). Contemp calf rebacked. *(Hinchliffe)* **£30 [≃ $54]**
- Mathematical tracts on the lunar and planetary theories ... and the undulatory theory of optics. Cambridge: 1842. 3rd edn. viii,390 pp. 5 fldg plates. New cloth, mrbld edges. *(Whitehart)* **£35 [≃ $63]**

Aitken, W.

- The science and practice of medicine. London: 1866. 4th edn, revsd. 2 vols. 8vo. xxxviii,963; xxxvi,1010 pp. 54; 33 figs. Orig cloth, dust-stained, new endpapers, vol 2 rebacked, orig spine laid down.
(Whitehart) **£35 [≃ $63]**

Alanson, Edward

- Practical observations on amputation and the after-treatment ... an account of amputation above the ankle ... London: 1782. 2nd edn, greatly enlgd. 8vo. 31,296 pp. Half calf.
(Halewood) **£90 [≃ $162]**

Albinus, Bernhard Siegfried

- Tables of the skeleton and muscles of the human body. Translated ... London: for John & Paul Knapton, 1749. 1st edn in English, Lge folio. 48 ff. 40 engvd plates, 12 in outline. Some browning, mainly marginal, title soiled. Mod half mor.
(Pickering) **$4,250 [≃ £2,361]**
- Tables of the skeleton and muscles of the human body. Edinburgh: for Andrew Bell, 1777-78. 2nd English edn. 2 parts in 1 vol. Folio. Engvd title vignettes, 28 engvd, 13 outline plates. Some offsetting & spotting. Contemp mrbld bds, rebacked in mor.
(Quaritch) **£550 [≃ £305]**

Alcott, William A.

- Vegetable diet as sanctioned by medical men and by experience in all ages. Boston: 1838. 8vo. 276 pp. Orig cloth, faded.
(Goodrich) **$75 [≃ £41]**

Alison, William

- Observations on the management of the poor in Scotland, and its effect on the health of the great towns. Edinburgh: William Blackwood,

1840. 123 pp. Disbound.
(C.R. Johnson) **£45 [≈ $81]**

Alison, William P.
- Outlines of pathology. Edinburgh: Blackwood, 1833. xv,333 pp. Contemp bds, rebacked, uncut.   *(Goodrich)* **$75 [≈ £41]**

Allbutt, Thomas C.
> The historical relations of medicine and surgery to the end of the sixteenth century. London: 1905. 125 pp. Orig cloth.
(Goodrich) **$60 [≈ £33]**
- The historical relations of medicine and surgery to the end of the sixteenth century. London: 1905. 8vo. xvi,125 pp. Orig cloth.
(Weiner) **£25 [≈ $45]**

Allbutt, Sir Thomas Clifford
- Diseases of the arteries including angina pectoris. 1915. 1st edn. 2 vols. 8vo. xi,534; vi,559 pp. A few anntns & pencil notes. Orig cloth, dampstained, hds of spines sl defective & reprd, spines faded.
(Whitehart) **£80 [≈ $144]**
- Diseases of the arteries including angina pectoris. London: 1915. 1st edn. 2 vols. 8vo. xiii,534; 559 pp. Cloth, sm tears at spine ends & back jnts. Ex lib.   *(Elgen)* **$90 [≈ £50]**
- Diseases of the arteries including angina pectoris. London: Macmillan, 1915. 1st edn. 2 vols. 8vo. 534; 559 pp. Orig cloth, spines dulled, extremities worn. Terence East's copy with his b'plate & sgntrs.
(Oasis) **$250 [≈ £138]**

Allchin, W.H. (ed.)
- A manual of medicine. 1900-03. 5 vols. Each approx 400 pp. Plates, text ills. Some pencil underlining. Orig cloth, dust-stained & marked.   *(Whitehart)* **£25 [≈ $45]**

Allen, R.L.
- The American farm book; or compend of American agriculture ... soils, grain, fruit, cotton, tobacco, sugar cane ... New York: 1854. Cr 8vo. Over 100 text ills. Orig cloth.
(Halewood) **£48 [≈ $86]**

Allen, Z.
- Philosophy of the mechanics of nature, and the source and modes of action of natural motive-power. New York: Appleton, 1852, Thick roy 8vo. 797. Orig cloth, spine ends worn.   *(Xerxes)* **$40 [≈ £22]**

Allestree, Richard
- A discourse concerning the period of humane life: whether mutable or immutable. London:

J.R. for Enoch Wyer, 1677. 2nd edn crrctd. Sm 8vo. [x],134 pp. Contemp sheep, backstrip defective. New Wing A1111.
(Blackwell's) **£65 [≈ $117]**

Alleyne, James
- A new English dispensatory, in four parts. London: Tho. Astley, 1733. 1st edn. 8vo. xiv,646,[56] pp. Prelim & final advt leaf. Contemp calf.   *(Spelman)* **£160 [≈ $288]**

Allingham, W.
- The diagnosis and treatment of diseases of the rectum. Edited and revised ... 1888. 5th edn. xvi,366 pp. 53 diags. Orig cloth.
(Whitehart) **£25 [≈ $45]**

Allsop, F.C.
- Induction coils and coil making, a treatise on the construction and working of shock, medical and spark coils. London: Spon, 1914. 2nd edn. 12mo. 172 pp. 125 ills, some fldg. Orig cloth.   *(Xerxes)* **$50 [≈ £27]**
- Practical electric bellfitting. A treatise on fitting-up and maintenance of electric bells ... London: Spon, 1890. Sm 8vo. 170 pp. Ills.
(Xerxes) **$50 [≈ £27]**

Alvarez, Walter C.
- The mechanics of the digestive tract. New York: 1922. 8vo. 192 pp. Orig cloth.
(Goodrich) **$65 [≈ £36]**
- The mechanics of the digestive tract. New York: 1928. 2nd edn. 447 pp. Orig cloth.
(Fye) **$50 [≈ £27]**

American Pharmaceutical Association
- The national formulary of unofficinal preparations. 1888. 1st iss. 8vo. 176 pp. Qrig cloth, worn, inner hinges cracked.
(Elgen) **$75 [≈ £41]**

Amory, Robert
- A treatise on electrolysis and its applications to therapeutical and surgical treatment in disease. New York: 1886. 1st edn. 307 pp. Num w'cuts. Orig cloth.   *(Fye)* **$50 [≈ £27]**

Amos, William
- The theory and practice of drill husbandry; founded upon philosophical principles and confirmed by experience ... London: for G.G. & J. Robinson, 1794. 1st edn. 4to. Advt leaf, 9 fldg engvd plates. Orig blue-grey bds, lacking spine, uncut edges.
(Traylen) **£295 [≈ $531]**

Anatomy & Physiology ...
- A system of anatomy and physiology with the

comparative anatomy of animals compiled from the latest and best authors .... Edinburgh: Creech, 1795. New edn. 3 vols. 8vo. Frontis, 20 copperplates. Contemp calf, worn, jnts weak.   *(Goodrich)* **$175 [≃ £97]**

Anatomy ...
- The anatomy of humane bodies epitomized ... See Gibson, Thomas

Anderson, C.L.G.
- Arizona as a health resort. [N.p.: 1890]. 4 pp. Stiff pict wraps, wraps darkened.
    (Reese) **$95 [≃ £52]**

Anderson, James
- Essays relating to agriculture and rural affairs ... by a farmer. Edinburgh: for T. Cadell, London, 1775. 1st edn. 2 pts in 1. 8vo. xxxiii,[i],196; [v],200-472 pp. 24 ills on 3 fldg engvd plates. Contemp calf, minor split on top of spine.   *(Burmester)* **£240 [≃ $432]**

Anderson, William K.
- Malarial psychoses and neuroses. London: 1927. 1st edn. Sm 4to. 395 pp. 4 cold plates, ills. Cloth, spine ends sl frayed.
    (Elgen) **$50 [≃ £27]**

Andral, G.
- Medical clinic: diseases of the chest. Translated ... Phila: 1843. 8vo. iv,408 pp. Lea, spine somewhat scuffed, upper hinge sl weak.   *(Rittenhouse)* **$45 [≃ £25]**
- Medical clinic: diseases of the chest. Phila: 1843. 1st Amer edn. 408 pp. Orig binding.
    (Fye) **$100 [≃ £55]**

Andral, Gabriel
- Pathological hematology: an essay on the blood in disease. Translated ... Phila: Lea & Blanchard, 1844. 8vo. 129,30 pub ctlg pp. Sl browned. Orig cloth, worn.
    (Oasis) **$450 [≃ £250]**

Andrews, Frederick W., et al.
- Diptheria; its bacteriology, pathology and immunology. London: 1923. 1st edn. Orig cloth, top & bottom of spine & edges of bds rubbed, inner hinges cracked.
    (Scientia) **$95 [≃ £52]**

Andrews, William
- The doctor in history, literature, folk-lore, etc. Hull: 1896. 8vo. 287 pp. Frontis, ills. Orig cloth, sl discold.   *(Weiner)* **£35 [≃ $63]**

Andry, Felix
- A manual of diagnosis of diseases of the heart.

Translated from the "Western Lancet" ... Cincinnati: Robinson & Jones, 1847. 8vo. iv,9-144 pp. Old mrbld wraps.
    (Antiq Sc) **$75 [≃ £41]**

Angerstein, E. & Eckler, G. (eds.)
- Home gymnastics for the well and the sick. Translated ... Boston: 1893. 8vo. ix,94 pp. 55 text w'cuts. Lge fldg chart in pocket (minor tears at fold). Orig pict cloth.
    (Elgen) **$50 [≃ £27]**

Ansted, David Thomas
- An elementary course of geology, mineralogy, and physical geography. London: Van Voorst, 1850. 1st edn. 8vo. xxvii,584, [vi] pp. Ills & tables in text. Uncut in orig cloth, some wear to extremities. *(Frew Mackenzie)* **£28 [≃ $50]**
- Geology; introductory, descriptive and practical. London: John Van Voorst, 1844. 1st edn. 2 vols. 8vo. Text engvs. Contemp half calf, gilt panelled spines.
    (Traylen) **£65 [≃ $117]**
- Geology; introductory, descriptive and practical. London: 1844. 2 vols. 8vo. Text figs. Orig cloth, sl used.
    (Wheldon & Wesley) **£25 [≃ $45]**
- The gold-seeker's manual. London: Van Voorst, 1849. 2nd edn. 12mo. [4],172,[5 advts dated June 1848] pp. Half mor, upper third of spine missing, hinges cracking, extremities rubbed. Armorial b'plates inc that of W.E. Gladstone.   *(Heritage)* **$85 [≃ £47]**
- The great stone book of nature. 1863. 1st edn. Sm 8vo. xxvii,309 pp. 5 plates. Lib blind-stamp on title. Orig cloth, worn at top of spine, lib number on upper cvr.
    (Bickersteth) **£20 [≃ $36]**
- Scenery, science and art. Being extracts from the notebook of a geologist and mining engineer [in France, Germany, Africa, America, &c.]. 1854. 1st edn. 8vo. viii,323 pp. 4 lithos, 21 text w'cuts. Endpapers sl stained. Embossed cloth, spine chipped.
    (Edwards) **£100 [≃ $180]**

Appleton
- Appleton's cyclopaedia of applied mechanics. New York: 1880. 2 vols. 8vo. 960; 959 pp. Nearly 5000 engvs, many full-page plates. 3/4 lea, scuffed, mrbld bds, outer jnt vol 1 starting.   *(Elgen)* **$95 [≃ £52]**

Appleton, John Howard
- Chemistry: developed by facts and principles drawn chiefly from the non-metals. Providence: 1884. 8vo. 232 pp. Ills, 14 cold litho plates (1 with shabby edges). Cloth, sl shaken.   *(Elgen)* **$75 [≃ £41]**

Arago, D. Francois J.
- Popular astronomy. Translated from the original and edited by Admiral W.H. Smyth ... London: Longman, Brown ..., 1855-58. 1st of this trans. 2 vols. 8vo. xlviii,707; xxxii,846 pp. 25 plates, some fldg, 358 other ills. Contemp calf.   *(Fenning)* £65 [≈ $117]
- Popular astronomy. Translated ... and edited by Admiral W.H. Smyth ... London: 1855-58. 2 vols. 8vo. xlviii,707; xxxii,846 pp. 25 plates, some fldg (duplicate plate 1 in place of plate 2). Orig cloth, shaken, 1 backstrip torn.   *(Weiner)* £35 [≈ $63]

Arago, F.
- Historical eloge of James Watt. Translated ... 1839. ix,261 pp. Port. [Bound with] Reid, H. Remarks on certain statements regarding the invention of the steam engine in [this same work]. Glasgow: 1840. 68 pp. Qtr mor, spine gilt, a.e.g.   *(Whitehart)* £65 [≈ $117]

Arbuthnot, John
- An essay concerning the effects of air on human bodies. London: for J. Tonson, 1733. 1st edn. 8vo. Half-title. Contemp calf, rebacked, crnrs worn.
            (Chaucer Head) £340 [≈ $612]
- Tables of the Grecian, Roman and Jewish measures. London: Smith, n.d. [?1705]. 1st edn. Obl 4to. Title, 13ff. Engvd throughout. Contemp red mor gilt, refurbished.
            (Marlborough) £350 [≈ $630]

Aretaeus
- The extant works of Aretaeus, the Cappadochian. Edited & translated by Francis Adams. London: Sydenham Society, 1856. 1st edn in English.
            (Scientia) $135 [≈ £75]

Ariens Kappers, Cornelius U., et al.
- The comparative anatomy of the nervous system of vertebrates including man. New York: 1936. 1st edn. 2 vols. Dws, in orig box.
            (Scientia) $250 [≈ £138]

Aristotle
- The works of Aristotle. The famous philosopher ... directions for midwives. London: n.d. [ca 1840]. 286 pp. Browned. Orig cloth, worn & shaken.
            (Goodrich) $30 [≈ £16]

Armstrong, John
- Facts, observations, and practical illustrations, relative to puerpereal fever, scarlet fever ... Phila: 1826. 2nd Amer edn. [Bound with] Practical illustrations of the scarlet fever ... Orig lea, worn.
            (Rittenhouse) $75 [≈ £41]
- Facts, observations, and practical illustrations, relative to puerpereal fever, scarlet fever ... Hartford: 1823. 1st Amer edn. Some foxing. Orig lea, some wear, hd of spine sl chipped.   *(Rittenhouse)* $135 [≈ £75]
- Practical illustrations in typhus and other fevers: Of pulmonary consumption, measles ... Boston: 1829. 8vo. 559 pp. Sgntr on title. Cvrs v shabby, hinges weak, endpapers discold.   *(Rittenhouse)* $55 [≈ £30]
- Practical illustrations of typhus fever ... and of inflammatory diseases. New York: Duyckink ..., 1824. 1st Amer edn. xi,432 pp. Old waterstain affecting final 50 pp. Contemp calf, rubbed.   *(Karmiole)* $100 [≈ £55]
- Practical illustrations of typhus fever ... and of inflammatory diseases. London: Baldwin, 1819. 3rd edn. 8vo. 566 pp. Lib stamps on title, occas staining. Half calf, rebacked.
            (Oasis) $60 [≈ £33]

Armstrong, John (1709-1779)
- The art of preserving health: a poem. London: 1774. Sgntr on title erased. Orig calf, top bd & endpapers detchd.
            (Rittenhouse) $75 [≈ £41]

Arnaud de Ronsil, G.
- A dissertation on hernias or ruptures ... London: 1748. vii pp, 4ff, 412 pp. Pp 413-439 (vocabulary of terms) omitted by binder. Endpapers sl stained. Orig lea, worn, rebacked.   *(Whitehart)* £65 [≈ $117]

Arnold, John P.
- Origin and history of beer and brewing ... Chicago: 1911. 8vo. xvi,411 pp. Ills. Orig green & orange dec cloth.
            (Weiner) £75 [≈ $135]

Arnott, Neil
- Elements of physics, or natural philosophy, general and medical, explained independently of technical mathematics ... Phila: Carey, Lea ..., 1829. 1st Amer edn. 8vo. 532 pp. Num w'cuts. Qtr calf, lightly rubbed, hinges weak.   *(Argosy)* $50 [≈ £27]
- Elements of physics, or natural philosophy. Written for general use, in plain or non-technical language. London: Longman, 1864-65. 2 vols (2 pts). 8vo. Some spotting of prelims. 19th c half calf, spine gilt, red & green mor labels.   *(Hughes)* £65 [≈ $117]
- Elements of physics, or natural philosophy, general and medical. First American edition with additions by Isaac Hays. 1829. Stamp on title & edges. Sheep.   *(Allen)* $20 [≈ £11]

- On the smokeless fire-place, chimney-valves, and other means, old and new, of obtaining healthful warmth and ventilation. London: 1855. 1st edn. 8vo. 232,24 advts pp. Text diags. Orig diced cloth.
(Halewood) **£68 [≃ $122]**
- On the smokeless fire-place, chimney-valves, and other means, old and new, of obtaining healthful warmth and ventilation. London: Longman ..., 1855. 1st edn. 8vo. xii,232,24 pub advts pp. Text ills. Lib stamp on title. Orig cloth (soiled). *(Rootenberg)* **$150 [≃ £83]**

Arrhenius, Svente
- Theories of solution. New Haven: 1912. 1st edn. xx,247 pp. Cloth.   *(Elgen)* **$35 [≃ £19]**

Art of Cookery ...
- The art of cookery, in imitation of Horace's art of poetry ... See King, William

Aschoff, Ludwig
- Lectures on pathology delivered in the United States, 1924. New York: Hoeber, 1924. 1st edn. 365 pp. Orig cloth, cvrs spotted.   *(Goodrich)* **$45 [≃ £25]**
- Lectures on pathology delivered in the United States, 1924. New York: Hoeber, 1924. 8vo. xi,[i],365, [v] pp. 35 ills. Pub bndg.   *(Pollak)* **£30 [≃ $54]**

Asgis, Alfred J.
- Professional dentistry in American Society. New York: 1941. 175 pp. Cloth, spine sl faded, hinge sl weak.
(Rittenhouse) **$30 [≃ £16]**

Ashhurst, John (ed.)
- International encyclopaedia of surgery ... by authors of various nations. New York: 1881-86. 1st edn. 6 vols. 35 chromolitho plates, num text w'cuts. Sheep, rubbed & scuffed, jnts cracked on 2 vols.
(Elgen) **$200 [≃ £111]**

Ashton, T.J.
- A treatise on corns, bunions and ingrowing of the toe-nail; their cause and treatment. London: 1852. 82 pp. 5 plates. Orig cloth, spine chipped.   *(Goodrich)* **$45 [≃ £25]**

Ashurst, Frederick
- Memoirs of a young surgeon. London: Digby, Long, [1898]. 8vo. [vi],124,15 ctlg,[i] pp. 6 ills. Orig dec cloth.   *(Pollak)* **£20 [≃ $36]**

Aston, F.W.
- Isotopes. 1922. 1st edn. x,276 pp. 21 ills. Cloth, sl marked.   *(Whitehart)* **£60 [≃ $108]**

- Isotopes. London: Arnold, 1922. 1st edn. 8vo. Ills. Orig cloth.
(Chaucer Head) **£130 [≃ $234]**
- Mass spectra and isotopes. 1942. 2nd edn. x,276 pp. 12 plates, 48 text figs. Orig cloth, dw.   *(Whitehart)* **£40 [≃ $72]**
- Mass spectra and isotopes. London: 1933. 1st edn. 248 pp. 8 plates. Orig cloth.
(Oasis) **$45 [≃ £25]**
- Mass spectra and isotopes. New York: Longmans, & London: Arnold: 1933. 1st edn. 8vo. xi,[1],248 pp. 8 h/t plates. Orig cloth.
(Antiq Sc) **$85 [≃ £47]**

Astronomical Catechism ...
- An astronomical catechism, for the instruction of young gentlemen and ladies. By a minister in the country for the use of his own children. London: T. Wilkins, 1792. 53pp plus table. Stabbed pamphlet as issued, enclosed in early wraps.
(C.R. Johnson) **£50 [≃ $90]**

Astronomy ...
- Physical astronomy; or the system of nature delineated. In a letter to the Royal Society of London. Liverpool: for W. Willian ..., n.d. [early 19th c]. 8vo. Endpapers spotted. Half calf, worn, jnts cracked. *(Hughes)* **£25 [≃ $45]**

Atkinson, E. Miles
- Intracranial suppuration. London: [1932]. 1st edn. 8vo. 127 pp. Errata slip tipped-in. Cloth. Ex lib.   *(Elgen)* **£65 [≃ £36]**

Atkinson, Frederick R.B.
- Acromegaly. London: 1932. 1st edn. 260 pp. Spine faded.   *(Scientia)* **$95 [≃ £52]**

Atlee, Walter
- Notes of M. Bernard's lectures on the blood; with an appendix. Phila: 1854. 1st edn. 224 pp. Spine faded.   *(Scientia)* **$350 [≃ £194]**

Atticus (pseud.)
- Hints on the subject on interments within the City of Philadelphia addressed to the ... Members of Councils ... and citizens generally. Phila: 1838. 8vo. 22 pp. A little pencilling. Disbound.
(Rittenhouse) **$60 [≃ £33]**

Aub, Joseph C. & Hapgood, Ruth K.
- Pioneer in modern medicine, David Linn Edsall. [Cambridge:] 1970. 1st edn. Orig cloth, dw.   *(Rittenhouse)* **$35 [≃ £19]**

Austin, J.A.
- Ambulance sermons. being a series of popular

essays on medical and allied subjects. London: 1887. xvi,384 pp. A little foxing. Orig cloth, sl marked & worn.
(Whitehart) **£25 [≃ $45]**

Austin, James G.

- A practical treatise on the preparation, combination and application of calcareous and hydraulic limes and cements ... useful recipes for various scientific ... purposes. Trubner, 1862. 1st edn. 8vo. 181,vi pp. Advt leaf, 3 plates. Orig cloth.
(Spelman) **£65 [≃ $117]**

Austin, R.

- Early American imprints 1668-1820. Washington: 1960. 8vo. 240 pp. Orig cloth.
(Goodrich) **$50 [≃ £27]**

Awsiter, John

- An essay on the effects of opium considered as a poison. London: G. Kearsly, 1763. 1st edn. 8vo. vii,70 pp. Uncut & sewn as issued. Preserved in a cloth box.
(Rootenberg) **$650 [≃ £361]**

Axon, William E.A.

- On the plague of caterpillars ... at Clitheroe. Not published, 1881. 7 pp. Contemp cloth wraps. *(C.R. Johnson)* **£20 [≃ $36]**

Ayres, John

- Arithmetick made easie for the use and benefit of trades-men ... London: for Tho. Norris ..., 1716. 13th edn. 12mo. A little browned, sm repr to crnr of last leaf, frontis marg reinforced. Contemp sheep, rebacked.
(Charles Cox) **£50 [≃ $90]**

Ayrton, Hertha

- The electric arc. London: [1902]. 1st edn in book form. 8vo. 479,20 pub ctlg pp. 146 ills. Cloth, sm scratch on spine.
(Elgen) **$50 [≃ £27]**

Ayscough, James

- A short account of the eye and nature of vision. The sixth edition. Printed for John Gilbert, n.d. [1760?]. 8vo. Fldg engvd frontis. Mod mrbld bds, calf spine, red mor label.
(Bickersteth) **£225 [≃ $405]**

Baas, J.H.

- Outlines of the history of medicine and the medical profession. New York: 1889. 8vo. 1171 pp. Cloth, sl shelfwear, hinges a little weak. *(Rittenhouse)* **$60 [≃ £33]**

Babb, Lawrence

- Elizabethan malady. A study of melancholia in English literature from 1580 to 1642. Mich State College Press, 1951. 8vo. ix,[iii], 206,[ii] pp. Pub bndg, dw. *(Pollak)* **£20 [≃ $36]**

Babbage, Charles

- The ninth Bridgewater treatise. A fragment. London: Murray, 1838. 2nd edn. 19th c half calf, cloth sides, mrbld endpapers & edges. Endpapers lightly spotted, some light rubbing. *(Frew Mackenzie)* **£205 [≃ $369]**
- On the economy of machinery and manufactures ... London: Charles Knight ..., 1832. 1st edn. 8vo. [ii],xvi, 320, [2 advts] pp. Engvd title with vignette. Tear across text of B2 reprd without loss, title foxed. Contemp green half calf, mrbld bds.
(Pickering) **$800 [≃ £444]**
- On the economy of machinery and manufactures ... London: Charles Knight ..., 1833. 3rd edn, enlgd. 8vo. 32mo in 8's. Engvd title (waterstained), xxiv,392,[2 advts] pp. Orig moire grained buff cloth.
(Pickering) **$600 [≃ £333]**
- On the economy of machinery and manufactures. London: Charles Knight, 1832. 1st edn. 12mo. Engvd title. Without the 2 leaves of advts at end. Mod half polished calf, mrbld bds.
(Chaucer Head) **£280 [≃ $504]**
- Passages from the life of a philosopher. London: Longman ..., 1864. 1st edn. 8vo. xii,496, 24 pub advts pp. Frontis. Orig cloth. *(Rootenberg)* **$950 [≃ £527]**
- Passages from the life of a philosopher. London: Longman, Green ..., 1864. 1st edn. 8vo. xii,496 pp. W'engvd frontis. Mod half brown crushed mor, cloth sides, gilt spine, in mrbld bd slipcase.
(Pickering) **$1,000 [≃ £555]**
- Passages from the life of a philosopher. London: 1864. 1st edn. 8vo. xii,496 pp. W'engvd frontis. Pencilled notes on rear endpaper & blank, some minor spots & sm marks. Prize calf (Harrow School).
(Bow Windows) **£450 [≃ $810]**

Babington, William, et al.

- A syllabus of a course of chemical lectures read at Guy's Hospital. London: Royal Free School Press, 1811. 8vo. ii,[i],142,[ii] pp. Interleaved with blanks. Orig bds, crude lea reback, crnrs a bit worn.
(Pollak) **£130 [≃ $234]**

Bacon, Sir Francis

- Baconiana. Or certain genuine remains ... now for the first time faithfully published.

London: for Richard Chiswell, 1679. 1st edn. 8vo. Old calf, rebacked, new endpapers.
(Charles Cox) **£50 [≃ $90]**
- Baconiana. Or certain genuine remains ... in arguments civil and moral, natural, medical ... for the first time faithfully published. London: Richard Chiswell, 1679. 1st edn. Cr 8vo. Lacks port & 2nd divisional title. Contemp calf, worn, jnt cracked.
(Stewart) **£100 [≃ $180]**
- The historie of life and death with observations natural and experimental for the prolonging of life. London: 1638. 12mo. 323 pp. Title reprd. Old calf, rebacked.
(Goodrich) **$225 [≃ £125]**
- Novum organum or true suggestions for the interpretation of nature. London: Pickering, 1844. 1st Pickering edn. 8vo. [iv],336 pp. Black & red title & half-title. Occas offsetting. Prize calf, spine edges & crnrs a little worn.
(Pollak) **£40 [≃ $72]**
- Of the advancement and proficience of learning ... interpreted by Gilbert Wats. Oxford: for Rob. Young ..., 1640. 1st edn in English. Folio. Port (laid down), engvd title. Later panelled calf, rebacked, new endpapers. STC 1167.
(Charles Cox) **£275 [≃ $495]**
- Of the advancement and proficience of learning, or the partitions of sciences ... interpreted by Gilbert Wats. Oxford: for Rob. Young ..., 1640. 1st edn of this trans. Folio. 19ff, 477 pp, 10ff. Sl waterstained. Contemp calf, jnt mended. STC 1167.
(Argosy) **$750 [≃ £416]**
- Of the advancement and proficience of learning, or the partitions of sciences ... interpreted by Gilbert Wats. London: Thomas Williams, 1674. Sm folio. Port frontis. Contemp calf, recased. Wing B312.
(Argosy) **$300 [≃ £166]**
- Sylva sylvarum: or, a natural historie. In ten centuries ... London: for William Lee, 1635. 4th edn. Folio. [xx],260, [xxxii],47,[i] pp. Engvd frontis, addtnl title. Lacking 1 leaf of "Magnalia naturae". Old calf, later rebacking, worn, loose in binding. *(Clark)* **£60 [≃ $108]**
- The two bookes of Francis Bacon. Of the proficience and advancement of learning, divine and humane. London: for Henrie Tomes, 1605. 1st edn. 4to. Early engvd port mtd to face title. Some light waterstains & early underlining. Early 19th c calf. STC 1164,
(Charles Cox) **£650 [≃ $1,170]**
- The works ... in four volumes. London: A. Millar, 1740. Folio. Lge paper. 4 engvd frontis, 4 vignette titles, 2 fldg tables. Sporadic dampstaining, insignificant worming towards end of vol 2. Contemp calf, worn, calf pitted & defective in parts, jnts cracked.
(Clark) **£130 [≃ $234]**

- The works ... London: A. Millar, 1765. 5 vols. 4to. Red & black titles with vignettes, 4 port frontis, 2 fldg tables. Contemp calf, gilt, light rubbing, jnts cracked but holding. B'plates. *(Frew Mackenzie)* **£240 [≃ $432]**
- The works ... London: R. Gosling ..., 1730. 4 vols. Folio. 4 engvd frontis. Contemp speckled calf, gilt, rebacked, mor labels, gilt.
(Traylen) **£250 [≃ $450]**
- The works ... London: R. Gosling ..., 1730. 4 vols. Sm folio. 4 engvd frontis. Mottled calf, early rebacking, jnts worn.
(Book Block) **$175 [≃ £97]**

Badcock, John
- Conversations on conditioning. The groom's oracle, and pocket stable directory. For the author ..., 1829. 1st edn. 8vo. xii,274,[iv advts] pp. Fldg hand-cold aquatint frontis, half-title (with sm stain). Orig qtr green cloth, grey bds, a little soiled.
(Blackwell's) **£105 [≃ $189]**

Badger, John
- A collection of remarkable cures of the King's Evil, perfected by the Royal Touch, collected from the writings of many eminent physicians and surgeons, and learned men. London: Cooper, 1748. Half-title. 64 pp. Some foxing & underlining. New bds.
(Goodrich) **$135 [≃ £75]**

Baikie, R.
- Observations on the Neilgherries ... effects of the climate on the European constitution ... Calcutta: 1834. One of 500. Lge 8vo. xiv,[ii],136 pp. Num maps & plans, 11 lithos (10 cold). A little worming at inner marg. Contemp mor, a little rubbed.
(Morrell) **£1,700 [≃ $3,060]**

Bailey, Benjamin F., et al.
- Present state of pediatrics. 1896. Sm 8vo. x,304 pp. Advts.
(Rittenhouse) **$27.50 [≃ £15]**

Bailey, J. & Culley, G.
- A general view of the agriculture of the County of Northumberland, with observations on the means of its improvement. Newcastle: Sol. Hodgson, 1800. 1st edn. 8vo. Fldg engvd map, 11 engvd plates (some fldg), Text w'cuts. Uncut, orig bds, worn, new spine. *(Hughes)* **£85 [≃ $153]**

Bailey, Pearce
- Diseases of the nervous system resulting from accident and injury. New York: 1907. 627 pp. Orig cloth. *(Goodrich)* **$95 [≃ £52]**

Bailey, Percival
- Intracranial tumours. Springfield: 1948. 2nd edn. xxiv,478 pp. Frontis, 16 plates, num text ills. Orig cloth, recased with new endpapers.
(Whitehart) **£40 [≃$72]**

Baillie, J.
- Advice to mothers, on the best means of promoting the health, strength, beauty ... of their offspring ... Newcastle-upon-Tyne: Mackenzie ..., 1812. 1st edn. 8vo. 318 pp. Engvd title. Some browning & spotting. Contemp calf, rebacked, crnrs rubbed.
(Burmester) **£85 [≃$153]**

Baillie, Matthew
- The morbid anatomy of some of the most important parts of the human body. Albany: Thomas Spencer, 1795. 1st Amer edn. 8vo. [2],viii, 248,[12] pp. Some waterstaining & browning. Contemp calf, lower front jnt broken.
(Antiq Sc) **$185 [≃£102]**
- The morbid anatomy of some of the most important parts of the human body. London: 1818. 5th edn. 8vo. xliii,482 pp. Orig half mor, mrbld bds, sl worn.
(Rittenhouse) **$75 [≃£41]**
- The morbid anatomy of some of the most important parts of the human body. London: 1797. 2nd edn. 8vo. xxxvi,460 pp. Lacking cloth spine, bds detchd or nearly so.
(Rittenhouse) **$150 [≃£83]**

Baillie, Thomas
- A solemn appeal to the public ..., London: for Captain Baillie, 1779. Sole edn. Folio. [8],xliv, 190,[6] pp. Index, errata, dedn. Contemp red mor, elab gilt dec.
(Rootenberg) **$550 [≃£305]**

Bain, A.
- The emotions and the will. 1888. 3rd edn. xxxxii,604 pp. Orig cloth, lib label on inside cvr.
(Whitehart) **£25 [≃$45]**
- The senses and the intellect. 1894. 4th edn. xxxii,702 pp. 3/4 mor, sl marked & worn.
(Whitehart) **£35 [≃$63]**

Baker, Richard T. & Smith, Henry G.
- A research on the eucalypts, especially in regard to their essential oils. Sydney: 1920. 2nd edn. Roy 4to. Ills throughout in colour & b/w. Orig cloth, cvrs a little used. Authors' inscribed pres copy. *(Sotheran)* **£85 [≃$153]**

Baker, T. Thorne
- Wireless pictures and television, a practical description of the telegraphy of pictures, photographs and visual images. London:

1926. 8vo. x,188 pp. Ills, diags. Orig cloth, orig pict dw.
(Weiner) **£85 [≃$153]**

Baker, Walter
- The chocolate plant (Theobrama Cacao) and its products. Dorchester, Mass: 1891. 1st edn. 4to. 40 pp. Ills. Cloth. *(Jenkins)* **$75 [≃£41]**

Bakewell, J.R.
- An introduction to the study of mineralogy; or, student's pocket companion. London: 1829. 1st edn. 12mo. 2 hand-cold plates. Orig linen-backed bds. *(Halewood)* **£58 [≃$104]**

Bakewell, Robert
- Travels, comprising observations made during a residence in the Tarentaise, and ... the Grecian and Pennine Alps, and ... Auvergne in ... 1820, 1821 and 1822. London: 1823. 1st edn. 2 vols. 8vo. 2 cold aquatint views. Contemp half calf, gilt dec spines. *(Traylen)* **£295 [≃$531]**

Baldwin, F.G.C.
- The history of the telephone in the United Kingdom. London: n.d. [1925 or 1938]. Thick 8vo. xxvi,728 pp. Plates, ills, tables. Orig pict cloth, gilt. *(Weiner)* **£75 [≃$135]**

Balfour, F.M.
- A treatise on comparative embryology. 1885. 2nd edn. 2 vols. xi,583, xxii; xi,792, xxiv pp. Cloth, vol II v sl worn.
(Whitehart) **£50 [≃$90]**

Balfour, George W.
- The senile heart; its symptoms, sequelae and treatment. New York: 1894. 1st Amer edn. 300 pp. Foxed. *(Scientia)* **$75 [≃£41]**
- The senile heart; its symptoms, sequelae and treatment. London: 1896. 2nd edn. 308 pp.
(Scientia) **$60 [≃£33]**
- The senile heart; its symptoms, sequelae and treatment. London: 1894. 8vo. ix,300 pp. Ills. Pencil markings. Orig cloth, hd of spine torn.
(Weiner) **£25 [≃$45]**

Ball, J.M.
- The sack-'em-up men. An account of the rise and fall of the modern resurrectionists. Edinburgh & London: 1928. 8vo. xxxi,216 pp. 61 plates. Orig cloth.
(Weiner) **£50 [≃$90]**

Ball, Sir Robert
- The causes of the ice age. 1891. 1st edn. Sm 8vo. xv,180 pp. Frontis, text figs. Cancelled blind lib stamp on title. Orig cloth, lib number on upper cvr.

(Bickersteth) **£20 [≃ $36]**
- Reminiscences and letters. Edited by his son ... Cassell, 1915. Sole English edn. 8vo. xv,406 pp. Frontis, 8 plates. Orig dark blue cloth, gilt.   *(Blackwell's)* **£40 [≃ $72]**

Ballance, Sir Charles
- The Bradshaw lecture on the surgery of the heart. London: 1920. 8vo. 154 pp. Cloth.
(Goodrich) **$95 [≃ £52]**

Ballantyne, J.W. (ed.)
- Encyclopaedia medica. Edinburgh: W. Green, 1915-25. 2nd edn. 13 vols. Orig buckram, final vol faded & jnts weak, occas strained jnt.   *(Pollak)* **£60 [≃ $108]**

Ballenger, W.L.
- Diseases of the nose, throat, and ear, medical and surgical. 1914. 4th edn. 1080 pp. 536 ills, 33 cold plates. Orig cloth, marked & dust-stained.   *(Whitehart)* **£25 [≃ $45]**

Bancroft, F.W. & Pilcher, C.
- Surgical treatment of the nervous system. Phila: 1946. 8vo. 534 pp. 5 cold plates, 293 ills. Orig cloth.   *(Goodrich)* **$45 [≃ £25]**

Banfield, T.C.
- The statistical companion for 1854. London: Longman, 1854. Sm 8vo. Orig cloth.
(Marlborough) **£45 [≃ $81]**

Banks, Sir J.
- A short account of the cause of the disease in corn, called by the farmers the blight, the mildew and the rust. 1805. 1st edn. 8vo. 31,4 pub advts pp. Fldg engvd plate, half-title. Untrimmed in mod half mor.
(Edwards) **£135 [≃ $243]**

Banting, William
- Letter on corpulence, addressed to the public. Third edition. London: Harrison, 59 Pall Mall, 1864. 50 pp. Mod wraps.
(C.R. Johnson) **£25 [≃ $45]**

Barber, H.
- The aeroplane speaks. New York: 1929. 9th edn, revsd & enlgd. Tall 8vo. [5]ff,148 pp. Ills, 50 plates. Cloth.   *(Elgen)* **$40 [≃ £22]**

Barclay, A.W.
- A manual of medical diagnosis: being an analysis of the signs and symptoms of disease. 1858. 2nd edn. xxiv,616 pp. 1 or 2 minor ink underlinings, light foxing on edges. Orig blindstamped cloth, sl dust-stained, inner hinge cracked.   *(Whitehart)* **£25 [≃ $45]**

- A manual of medical diagnosis: being an analysis of the signs and symptoms of disease. Phila: 1864. 3rd Amer edn. 8vo. xx,451 pp. Sgntr on front endpaper, lib pouch on inside back cvr.   *(Rittenhouse)* **$25 [≃ £13]**

Barclay, William
- Callirhoe; commonly called the Well of Spa ... what diseases may be cured by drinking of the well ... Aberdeen: Burnett & Rettie, 1799. 12mo. 26,[2] pp. W'cuts arms & ms notes on title verso. Uncut in old bds, cloth spine.
(Burmester) **£30 [≃ $54]**

Barcroft, Joseph
- The respiratory function of the blood. Part I. Lessons from high altitudes. Cambridge: 1925. 1st edn. 8vo. Half-title, ix,207 pp. Ills. Front flyleaf lacking, some marg ink marks & notes. Cloth.   *(Elgen)* **$75 [≃ £41]**

Bard, Samuel
- A compendium of the theory and practice of midwifery. New York: Collins & Perkins, 1808. 1st edn, 2nd iss. Sm 8vo. 239,[1 pub advt] pp. 19 w'cuts in text. Some light browning, few minor tears to foremargins. Contemp calf, minor wear.
(Antiq Sc) **$500 [≃ £277]**

Barker, Fordyce
- On sea sickness. New York: Appleton, 1870. 8vo. 36 pp. Limp bds, a.e.g., stained.
(Goodrich) **$85 [≃ £47]**

Barker, Llewellys
- The nervous system and its constituent neurones. New York: 1899. 1st edn. 11132 pp. Orig cloth.   *(Fye)* **$300 [≃ £166]**
- The young man and medicine. New York: 1928. 8vo. 202 pp. Orig cloth. Author's pres copy.   *(Goodrich)* **$65 [≃ £36]**

Barlow, John
- On man's power over himself to prevent or control insanity. London: 1849. 2nd edn, enlgd. Sm 8vo. viii,123, 10 pub ctlg pp. Paper cvrs & spine labels (labels sl chipped).
(Elgen) **$100 [≃ £55]**

Barlow, Nora (ed.)
- The autobiography of Charles Darwin 1809-1882. With original omissions restored. London: Collins, 1958. 253,[i] pp. Frontis, 3 plates. Pub bndg, frayed dw.
(Pollak) **£20 [≃ $36]**

Barlow, Peter
- A new mathematical and philosophical

dictionary ... terms and principles of pure and mixed mathematics ... London: 1814. 1st edn. Sm 4to. vii,386ff. 13 plates. Amateurishly bound in grey bds. *(Whitehart)* **£150 [≈ $270]**

- A new mathematical and philosophical dictionary ... terms and principles of pure and mixed mathematics ... London: 1814. vii,[771] pp. Errata leaf, ills, 13 engvd plates. Buckram. Ex lib. *(Elgen)* **$125 [≈ £69]**

Barlow, W.F.
- On fatty degeneration. London: 1853. 8vo. 92 pp. Orig cloth, spine worn. Partially unopened. Author's pres inscrptn on front blank. *(Goodrich)* **$55 [≈ £30]**

Barnes, Ernest William
- Scientific theory and religion: the world described by science and its spiritual interpretation. New York: 1933. 8vo. xxi,685 pp. Cloth. *(Elgen)* **$30 [≈ £16]**

Barnes, R.
- A clinical history of the medical and surgical diseases of women. 1878. 2nd edn. xix,918 pp. 181 diags. Cloth, faded & worn. *(Whitehart)* **£40 [≈ $72]**

Barnesby, Norman
- Medical chaos and crime. London: 1910. 1st edn. 384 pp. Orig cloth, upper hinge sl weak. *(Rittenhouse)* **$35 [≈ £19]**

Barron, A.F.
- Vines and vine-culture. London: Journal of Horticulture, 1883. 8vo. 30 plates, 49 text engvs. New half calf. *(Cooper Hay)* **£48 [≈ $86]**

Barrough, Philip
- The method of physick, containing the causes, signes, and cures of inward diseases in mans body from the head to the foote. London: 1610. 4th edn. Sm 4to. 8ff, 477,7 pp. Inconspicuous worming in last 30 leaves. Rec calf. *(Hemlock)* **$650 [≈ £361]**

Barrow, Isaac
- Euclide's elements; the whole fifteen books compendiously demonstrated ... a brief treatise of regular solids. By Thomas Haselden. London: for Daniel Midwinter, 1732. 8vo. Port frontis, text figs. Lacking final endpaper. Contemp calf, sl rubbed, jnts cracked. *(Stewart)* **£100 [≈ $180]**
- Euclide's elements; the whole fifteen books compendiously demonstrated ... and a brief treatise of regular solids. London: 1714. Contemp lea, rebacked. *(Whitehart)* **£80 [≈ $144]**

- Euclide's elements; the whole fifteen books compendiously demonstrated. London: For E. Redmayne, 1705. Sm 8vo. [vi],366 pp. Advt leaf, num w'cut diags in text. Crnr torn from 1 leaf, just touching page numeral. New qtr calf, mrbld bds. *(Bickersteth)* **£160 [≈ $288]**
- The usefullnesse of mathematical learning explained and demonstrated ... London: 1734. 1st edn. xxxii,440,[23] pp. Port frontis, fldg plate. Contemp calf, rebacked, spine gilt, crnrs worn. *(Whitehart)* **£150 [≈ $270]**

Barry, Edward
- The Aesculapian monitor; or faithful guide to the history of the human species, and most important branches of medical philosophy. London: Longman, 1811. 1st edn. 8vo. xii,xx, 170,[ii] pp. Untrimmed in orig bds, new paper spine. *(Bennett)* **£125 [≈ $225]**
- Observations historical, critical and medical on the wines of the ancients ... principles and qualities of water ... particular those of Bath. London: 1775. 4to. xii,479,[i] pp. Engvd frontis, engvs on title. Old calf, v worn, rebacked. *(Weiner)* **£325 [≈ $585]**
- A treatise on three different digestions, and discharges of the human body ... London: A. Millar, 1759. 1st edn. 8vo. xvi,434 pp. 1 text ill. Marg repr to lower edge of title. Qtr calf. *(Rootenberg)* **$275 [≈ £152]**

Barry, P.
- The fruit garden; a treatise ... physiology of fruit trees, the theory and practice of all operations ... New York: Moore, 1858. 8vo. xvi,398,18 advts pp. profusely illust. Orig green blindstamped & gilt cloth. *(Karmiole)* **$40 [≈ £22]**

Bartholow, Roberts
- Medical electricity. A practical treatise on the application of electricity to medicine and surgery. Phila: 1881. 8vo. 262 pp. Ills. Orig cloth. *(Goodrich)* **$75 [≈ £41]**

Bartlett, Thomas
- The young man's companion or, book of knowledge ... the latest discoveries and improvements in science and art. London: Thomas Kelly, [1837]. 1st edn. 8vo. xvi,752 pp. Frontis (mtd), 9 plates (1 fldg). Contemp tree calf. *(Claude Cox)* **£30 [≈ $54]**

Bartlett, William
- An elementary treatise on optics, designed for the use of the United States Military Academy. New York: Wiley & Putnam, 1839. 1st edn. 8vo. vi,231 pp. Orig cloth. Ex lib. *(Antiq Sc)* **$85 [≈ £47]**

Bascombe, E.
- A history of epidemic pestilences from the earliest ages ... with researches into their nature, causes, and prophylaxis. London: 1851. 8vo. vii,250 pp. Orig cloth, short tear at hd of spine. Inscrbd by author.
(Weiner) **£50 [≈ $90]**

Bassler, Anthony
- Diseases of the stomach and upper alimentary tract. Phila: Davis, 1910. 1st edn. 8vo. 836 pp. 56 plates, some in color, 15 radiographs, num text ills. Orig cloth. *(Oasis)* **$40 [≈ £22]**

Bastion, H. Charlton
- The modes of origin of lowest organisms: including a discussion of the experiments of M. Pasteur, & a reply to some statements by Professors Huxley and Tyndall. London: 1871. 109,47 ctlg pp. Orig cloth. Author's pres copy. *(Goodrich)* **$95 [≈ £52]**
- Studies in heterogenesis. 1903. 8vo. ix,354,xxxvii pp. 19 fldg plates. Cancelled blind lib stamp on title. Half mor, reprd.
(Bickersteth) **£38 [≈ $68]**

Bate, George
- Pharmacopoeia Bateana: or, Bate's dispensatory ... containing his choice and select recipes ... London: Innys, 1713. 4th edn. 8vo. [16],744,[16] pp. Double column. Lacking front endpaper. Contemp panelled calf, rear hinge split.
(Hemlock) **$200 [≈ £111]**

Bateman, Dr.
- A short treatise of ... Dr. Bateman's pectoral drops ... See Okell, Benjamin

Bateman, Thomas
- Delineations of cutaneous diseases exhibiting the ... principal genera and species comprised in the classification of the late Dr. Willans ... London: 1849. New edn. Folio. viii pp. 72 hand-cold engvd plates each with leaf of explanation. Half mor, sl rubbed.
(Hemlock) **$600 [≈ £333]**
- A practical synopsis of cutaneous diseases, according to the arrangement of Dr. Willans ... Phila: 1818. 8vo. xxiv,348 pp. Frontis. Sgntr on title, ms notes on endpapers, some occas foxing. Orig bds, rebacked.
(Rittenhouse) **$275 [≈ £152]**

Bateman, William
- Magnacopia; or, a library of useful and profitable information for the chemist and druggist, surgeon-dentist, oilman, and licensed victualler. London: Churchill, 1837.

2nd edn. 12mo. xii,286,[ii advts] pp. Orig cloth-backed bds, faded & a trifle worn.
(Pollak) **£45 [≈ $81]**

Bateson, Beatrice
- William Bateson, F.R.S. Essays and addresses, together with a short account of his life. Cambridge: 1928. 1st edn. 473 pp. Sm tear in spine reprd. *(Scientia)* **$85 [≈ £47]**

Bateson, William
- Materials for the study of variation treated with especial regard to discontinuity in the origin of species. London: 1894. 1st edn. 598 pp. *(Scientia)* **$225 [≈ £125]**
- Mendel's principles of heredity. A defence. Cambridge: University Press, 1902. 1st edn. Sm 8vo. xiv,[2],212 pp. Half-title, port frontis. Orig cloth.
(Rootenberg) **$350 [≈ £194]**
- Mendel's principles of heredity. Cambridge: University Press, 1909. 8vo. xiv,[2],396 pp. Half-title, 3 photo ports, 1 full-page & 5 double-page cold plates, num text figs. Orig cloth, spine reprd.
(Rootenberg) **$250 [≈ £138]**
- Mendel's principles of heredity. [With translations of the papers on Hybridisation and on Hieracium]. Cambridge: University Press, 1909. 1st edn thus. Lge 8vo. xv.396 pp. Owner's name on f.e.p. Orig blue-grey buckram, gilt. *(Blackwell's)* **£250 [≈ $450]**
- Mendel's principles of heredity. A defence. Cambridge: University Press, 1902. 1st edn. 212 pp. *(Scientia)* **$300 [≈ £166]**
- The methods and scope of genetics. Cambridge: University Press, 1908. 1st edn. 12mo. [2],49,[1] pp. Orig cloth.
(Antiq Sc) **$65 [≈ £36]**
- Scientific papers of ... Edited by R.C. Punnett. Cambridge: 1928. 1st edn. 2 vols. 452; 503 pp. Upper crnr rear cvr vol 1 bumped with resultant creasing to pages.
(Scientia) **$250 [≈ £138]**

Battley, Harry
- Single finger prints. A new and practical method of classifying and filing single finger prints and fragmentary impressions. 1930. 1st edn. 8vo. Ills. Orig cloth.
(Robertshaw) **£18 [≈ $32]**

Bauer, Louis H. (ed.)
- Seventy-five years of medical progress 1878-1953. Phila: 1954. Cloth, spine faded.
(Rittenhouse) **$35 [≈ £19]**

Bauer, Max
- Precious stones. London: 1904. 1st English

edn. Lge 8vo. 627 pp. 20 plates in 8 chromolithos. Orig half mor, extremities worn, v shaken.   *(Oasis)* **$75 [≈ £41]**

Baxter, Andrew

- An enquiry into the nature of the human soul; wherein the immateriality of the soul is evinced from the principles of reason and philosophy. London: [1733]. 1st edn. 4to. [6]ff,376 pp. Orig calf, worn.
(Elgen) **$125 [≈ £69]**

- Matho: or, the cosmotheoria puerilis; in ten dialogues ... phaenomena of the material world ... principles of natural religion ... London: for A. Millar, 1765. 3rd edn. 2 vols. 12mo. 2 fldg engvd tables. Contemp calf, spines gilt, 2 jnts sl cracking.
(Burmester) **£45 [≈ $81]**

Baxter, J.

- The library of agricultural and horticultural knowledge. Lewes: Sussex Agricultural Press, 1832. 2nd edn. 8vo. Engvd port frontis. Some marg damage to lower crnrs of last few leaves. Mod qtr calf.   *(Waterfield's)* **£125 [≈ $225]**

Bayle, A.L.J.

- A manual of general anatomy, containing a concise description of the elementary tissues of the human body. From the French ... [translated] by S.D. Gross. Phila: Grigg, 1828. 8vo. x,272 pp. Light foxing. Calf.
(Goodrich) **$150 [≈ £83]**

Bayle, Pierre

- The dictionary, historical and critical. London: 1734-38. 2nd edn. 5 vols. Folio. Red & black titles, engvd port. Old calf, worn & shabby.   *(Hemlock)* **$250 [≈ £138]**

- The dictionary, historical and critical. London: J.J. & P. Knapton, 1734. 2nd English edn. 5 vols. Folio. Half-titles in each vol, red & black titles. Contemp tan calf, vol 1 jnts cracked, others beginning to split at hd & tail, some crnrs bumped.
(Frew Mackenzie) **£360 [≈ $648]**

- An historical and critical dictionary ... Translated into English ... London: C. Harper ..., 1710. 1st edn in English. 4 vols. Folio. 4 title vignettes. Some minor marg worming vols 1-3, occas light dampstaining. Contemp calf, old rebacking, worn.
(Clark) **£165 [≈ $297]**

Bayliss, William

- Principles of general physiology. 1918. 2nd edn, revsd. xxiv,858 pp. 261 text ills. Half-title reprd along inner edge. Cloth.
(Whitehart) **£25 [≈ $45]**

- Principles of general physiology. 1915. 1st edn. 850 pp. Orig cloth. *(Fye)* **$125 [≈ £69]**

Bayma, Joseph

- The elements of molecular mechanics. London: Macmillan, 1866. 1st edn. 8vo. [2 advts],xviii, 266,[2 advts] pp. 3 fldg plates. Orig cloth.   *(Fenning)* **£65 [≈ $117]**

Baynard, Edward

- Health, a poem shewing how to procure, preserve, and restore it. To which is annex'd The Doctor's Decade. London: J. Roberts, 1740. 48 pp. Half-title.
(C.R. Johnson) **£65 [≈ $117]**

Beach, W.

- The family physician, or, the reformed system of medicine: On vegetable or botanical principles. New York: 1846. 7th edn. Thick 8vo. xlviii,782 pp. Ills. Occas v light foxing. Orig lea cvrs.   *(Rittenhouse)* **$26 [≈ £14]**

Beale, Lionel S.

- How to work with the microscope. London: 1865. 3rd edn. 8vo. xvi,272 pp. Actual photo frontis, 56 plates. Orig cloth.
(Weiner) **£35 [≈ $63]**

- How to work with the microscope. London: 1868. 4th edn. 8vo. xix,383 pp. Actual photo frontis, 69 plates. Orig cloth, a little grubby & worn.   *(Weiner)* **£25 [≈ $45]**

- How to work with the microscope. 1868. 4th edn. xix,383 pp. Actual photo frontis, 69 full-page plates. New cloth.
(Whitehart) **£35 [≈ $63]**

- The microscope in its application to practical medicine. Phila: 1867. 3rd edn. Half-title, xxii,320,4 advts pp. 59 engvd plates, over 400 ills. Light foxing. Cloth, cvrs stained, spine ends v worn.   *(Elgen)* **$50 [≈ £27]**

- On the structure and growth of the tissues and on life. ten lectures delivered at King's College, London. London: Hardwicke, 1865. 8vo. vii,226,[ii advts] pp. Frontis. Pub bndg, jnts a bit slack. Author's pres inscrptn.
(Pollak) **£30 [≈ $54]**

Bealey, Adam

- Dr. Kennion's observations on the medicinal springs of Harrogate, London: 1869. 7th edn. 8vo. 56 pp. Orig limp cloth. Author's pres inscrptn on title.   *(Oasis)* **$35 [≈ £19]**

Beard, G. & Rockwell, A.D.

- The medical use of electricity with special reference to general electricization as a tonic in neuralgia ... New York: 1867. 8vo. 65 pp. Some leaves a bit brittle. Orig cloth, ex lib.

(Goodrich) **$45 [≈ £25]**

Beard, George
- The home physician; a new and popular guide to the art of preserving health and treating disease ... New York: 1869. 1st edn. 1066 pp. Sheep, lightly rubbed.
(Scientia) **$85 [≈ £47]**

Beasley, Henry
- The druggist's general receipt book; comprising a copious veterinary formulary; numerous recipes in patent and proprietary medicines ... London: John Churchill, 1854. 3rd edn. Sm 8vo. viii,483 pp. Contemp half calf, spine sl rubbed & chipped at hd.
(Spelman) **£50 [≈ $90]**

Beaufoy, Mark
- Nautical and hydraulic experiments, with numerous scientific miscellanies. Vol. 1 [all published]. Henry Beaufoy, 1834. 1st edn. Lge 4to. iv,cxix,688 pp. Engvd pres leaf, engvd port, 16 engvd plates (dampstained), 8 fldg tables. Orig cloth, rebacked.
(Antiq Sc) **$275 [≈ £152]**
- Nautical and hydraulic experiments. Vol. 1 [all published]. South Lambeth: Privately printed, 1834. 4to. [x],688 pp. Port frontis, 16 engvd plates (foxed), 2 engvd vignettes. Orig blind-stamped cloth, recased, crnrs worn.
(Pollak) **£75 [≈ $135]**

Beaumont, R.
- Woollen and worsted. The theory and technology of the manufacture of woollen, worsted and union yarns and fabrics. 1919. 3rd revsd edn. xxxi,x,716 pp. 42 plates, num text figs, 18 tables. Orig half rexine, edges worn, back stained. *(Whitehart)* **£35 [≈ $63]**

Beaumont, William
- Experiments and observations on the gastric juice, and the physiology of digestion: Boston: Lilly, Wait, 1834. 1st edn, Boston iss. 8vo. 280 pp. Text w'cuts. Light foxing. Orig cloth-backed bds. Waterstain on upper crnr rear cvr extending to some leaves.
(Antiq Sc) **$750 [≈ £416]**
- Experiments and observations on the gastric juice, and the physiology of digestion: Edinburgh: Maclachlan & Stewart, 1839. 1st British edn. xx,319 pp. Half-title. Orig bds, soiled, headpiece worn.
(Goodrich) **$495 [≈ £275]**
- The physiology of digestion, with experiments on the gastric juice. Burlington: 1847. 2nd edn. V light & occas foxing, v light browning on last 2 leaves. Orig cloth, minor wear at extremities.

(Rittenhouse) **$400 [≈ £222]**
- The physiology of digestion, with experiments on the gastric juice. Burlington: 1847. 2nd edn. 8vo. 303,[1] pp. Foxing. Orig blindstamped cloth, ends of spine bruised, split in upper front hinge.
(Hemlock) **$375 [≈ £208]**
- The physiology of digestion, with experiments on the gastric juice. Burlington: 1847. 2nd edn. 304 pp. Orig cloth, rebacked, part of orig spine laid down.
(Fye) **$400 [≈ £222]**

Beck, Conrad
- The microscope. A simple handbook. London: Beck, 1923. 2nd edn. 8vo. 144 pp. 131 figs. Pub bndg. *(Pollak)* **£15 [≈ $27]**

Beck, Richard
- A treatise on the construction, proper use, and capabilities of Smith, Beck, and Beck's achromatic microscopes. London: 1865. Lge 8vo. v,144 pp. 29 plates (1 cold), ills. Orig cloth. Author's daughter's pres inscrptn on endpaper. *(Weiner)* **£110 [≈ $198]**

Beck, T.R. & J.B.
- Elements of medical jurisprudence. London: Longman ..., 1836. 8vo. xviii,1010 pp. Some text figs. Occas finger & dust marks. Requiring rebinding. *(Barbary)* **£18 [≈ $32]**

Beckmann, John
- A history of inventions, discoveries, and origins. London: J. Walker, 1814. 2nd edn. 4 vols. 8vo. Some browning & spotting. Contemp half calf, mrbld sides, spines gilt.
(Frew Mackenzie) **£260 [≈ $468]**
- A history of inventions and discoveries. London: R. Lea, 1814. 2nd edn, enlgd by a 4th vol. 4 vols. 8vo. Contemp half calf, mrbld bds. *(Chaucer Head)* **£250 [≈ $450]**
- A history of inventions, discoveries, and origins ... London: 1846. 4th edn. 2 vols. 8vo. 2 engvd port frontis. Orig blue cloth, gilt, lib labels on spines, spines sl faded.
(Hughes) **£25 [≈ $45]**
- A history of inventions, discoveries, and origins ... London: 1846. 4th edn. 2 vols. Sm 8vo. xxiii,518; xii,548 pp. Frontis, ports. Orig dec blindstamped cloth, sl worn.
(Weiner) **£35 [≈ $63]**

Beclard, P.A.
- Elements of general anatomy: translated ... by Robert Knox. Edinburgh: 1830. xxvii,399 pp. Title dampstained. Orig bds, worn. Translator's pres copy.
(Goodrich) **$195 [≈ £108]**

Beddoes, Thomas

- Observations on the medical and domestic management of the consumptive ... and on the cure of scrophula. Troy, New York: O. Penniman, 1803. 12mo. 162,2 advts pp. Frontis. Foxing. Contemp calf, lightly rubbed.   *(Karmiole)* **$150 [≈ £83]**
- Observations on the medical and domestic management of the consumptive; on the powers of digitalis purpurea and on the cure of scrofula. London: 1801. 8vo. 172 pp. Lacking front endpaper. Orig lea, rebacked with cloth. Ex lib.
            (Rittenhouse) **$195 [≈ £108]**
- Observations on the nature and cure of calculus, sea scurvy, catarrh, and fever: together with conjectures upon several other subjects of physiology and pathology. London: 1793. 8vo. xvi,278 pp. Errata. Half mor, 2 b'plates. *(Rittenhouse)* **$375 [≈ £208]**
- Observations on the nature and cure of calculus, sea scurvy, catarrh, and fever: together with conjectures upon several other subjects of physiology and pathology. Phila: 1797. Sgntr on title. 1st Amer edn. Orig lea, worn.   *(Rittenhouse)* **$350 [≈ £194]**

Bedell, Arthur J.

- Photographs of the fundus oculi. A photographic study of normal and pathological changes seen with the opthalmoscope. Phila: 1929. 1st edn. 4to. 317 pp. 95 plates of num photos, inc 272 stereos. A few pp with pencil underlining. Orig cloth, lightly worn.   *(Elgen)* **$250 [≈ £138]**

Bedford, W.K.R. & Holbeche, Richard

- The Order of the Hospital of St. John of Jerusalem ... a history of the English Hospitallers of St. John. London: Robinson, 1902. 8vo. x,227,[i] pp. Frontis, 24 plates, 5 text ills. Orig dec cloth. *(Pollak)* **£25 [≈ $45]**

Bedingfield, James

- A compendium of medical practice, illustrated by interesting and instructive cases, and by ... observations. Greenfield, Mass: 1823. 1st Amer edn. 8vo. 192 pp. Sgntr on title. Bds almost detchd.
            (Rittenhouse) **$55 [≈ £30]**

Bedlington, John

- An address to the proprietors of collieries, on the Rivers Tyne and Wear, on the subject of ventilation. Newcastle: 1814. Sm 8vo. 8 pp. Disbound.   *(Halewood)* **£40 [≈ $72]**

Beecroft, George

- Companion to the iron trade, etc ... in a series

of comprehensive tables ... Leeds: Y.F. Knight, 1851. 3rd edn. 8vo. Plate, double-page trade advt at end. Contemp calf, sl rubbed. Editor's pres copy.
            (Stewart) **£45 [≈ $81]**

Beekman, Fenwick

- Hospital for the ruptured and crippled. New York: privately printed, 1939. 8vo. 157 pp. Ills, ports. Ex lib. [With] Seventy-five years of pioneering service. New York: 1939. 63 pp. Orig pict wraps, worn. Ex lib.
            (Elgen) **$35 [≈ £19]**

Beeton, Isabella

- The book of household management. Beeton, 1861. 1st edn in book form, 1st iss. Cold frontis, extra title, 12 cold plates, num w'engvs in text. Well thumbed, num sm chips & reprs. Mod half mor. *(Ash)* **£500 [≈ $900]**

Beissel, Dr.

- Thermal springs of Aix-la-Chapelle and Brocette. Aix-la-Chapelle: 1883. 12mo. Fldg map. Orig flexible cloth, front cvr broken. Ex lib.   *(Argosy)* **$40 [≈ £22]**

Belfield, William T.

- Diseases of the urinary and male sexual organs. New York: 1884. 1st edn. 8vo. vii,351 pp. Text ills. Cloth.   *(Elgen)* **$30 [≈ £16]**

Bell, Benjamin

- A treatise on gonorrhea virulenta and lues venerea. Phila: 1795. 1st Amer edn. 2 vols in 1. 220,250, index, contents pp. Lea.
            (Scientia) **$275 [≈ £152]**

Bell, Charles

- The anatomy and philosophy of expression, as connected with the fine arts. London: John Murray, 1844. 3rd edn. Roy 8vo. 4 engvd plates, text ills. Orig blindstamped cloth.
            (Chaucer Head) **£220 [≈ $396]**
- The anatomy and philosophy of expression, as connected with the fine arts. London: 1872. 6th edn. 275 pp. 4 plates. Orig cloth, rebacked, orig spine laid down.
            (Scientia) **$95 [≈ £52]**
- The anatomy and philosophy of expression, as connected with the fine arts. London: Murray, 1847. 4th edn. 8vo. 275 pp. 4 plates. Calf, crnrs worn.   *(Oasis)* **$80 [≈ £44]**
- Engravings of the arteries; illustrating the second volume of the anatomy of the human body ... London: 1806. 2nd edn. 76 pp. 11 hand-cold plates (1 fldg, trimmed & loosely inserted). Later half lea. *(Fye)* **$250 [≈ £138]**
- An essay on the forces which circulate the

blood ... the difference of the motions of fluids in living and dead vessels. London: 1819. 1st edn. 12mo. [ii],viii, 83,[1] pp. Lacking half-title, ms notes on front flyleaf, stamps on title & p 1. Contemp half calf.
(Hemlock) **$400 [≃ £222]**

- A familiar treatise on the five senses, being an account of the conformation and functions of the eye, ear, nose, tongue, and skin. London: Henry Washbourne, 1841. 2nd edn. Sm 8vo. 20 cold plates. Title torn & reprd, some spotting. Orig cloth, spine relaid.
(Chaucer Head) **£55 [≃ $99]**

- The hand; its mechanism and vital endowments, as evincing design. London: Pickering, 1834. 3rd edn. 8vo. 348 pp. Ills. Orig cloth, spine label a little worn.
(Oasis) **$350 [≃ £194]**

- The hand; its mechanism and vital endowments, as evincing design. London: William pickering, 1834. 3rd edn. 8vo. xvi,348 pp. 52 engvd text figs. Random spots & dustmarks, sm paper fault in 1 blank crnr with loss. Contemp prize calf (Trinity College, Dublin).
(Bow Windows) **£105 [≃ $189]**

- The hand; its mechanism and vital endowments, as evincing design. London: 1852. 5th edn, revsd. 428 pp. Half lea, mrbld bds. *(Scientia)* **$125 [≃ £69]**

- Illustrations of the great operations of surgery ... London: Longman, Hurst, 1821. 1st edn. Obl folio. viii,134 pp. 20 hand-cold engvd plates. Ownership inscrptn on title, light browning. Uncut. Orig bds a little worn.
(Rootenberg) **$1,850 [≃ £1,027]**

- Letters concerning the diseases of the urethra. Boston: 1811. 1st Amer edn. 156 pp. 6 plates (foxed). Piece torn from top of front blank. Lea. *(Scientia)* **$175 [≃ £97]**

- Letters concerning the diseases of the urethra. Boston: Wells & Wait, 1811. 1st Amer edn. 8vo. 155,[8] pp. 6 engvd plates. Light unif browning. Orig ptd bds, uncut, lacking most of backstrip. *(Antiq Sc)* **$275 [≃ £152]**

- A series of engravings, explaining the course of the nerves with an address to young physicians on the study of the nerves. Phila: 1818. 1st Amer edn. Sgntr inside front cvr. Half mor, mrbld bds.
(Rittenhouse) **$285 [≃ £158]**

- A series of engravings, explaining the course of the nerves with an address to young physicians on the study of the nerves. Phila: 1818. 1st Amer edn. 4to. xxi-71 pp. Half-title, 9 plates. Foxing. Qtr sheep, jnts cracked.
(Goodrich) **$895 [≃ £497]**

Bell, E.T.
- The development of mathematics. McGraw Hill, 1945. 2nd edn, 4th imp. xiii,637 pp. Orig cloth. *(Hinchliffe)* **£20 [≃ $36]**

Bell, F. Dillon & Young, Frederick
- Reasons for promoting the cultivation of New Zealand flax. London: Smith, Elder, 1842. 34,2 pp. Sewn pamphlet as issued.
(C.R. Johnson) **£65 [≃ $117]**

Bell, Jacob & Redwood, Theophilus
- Historical sketch of the progress of pharmacy in Great Britain. London: for the Pharmaceutical Soc., 1880. 8vo. [iv],415,[i] pp. Some foxing at front. Orig cloth, crnrs & spine ends bumped. *(Pollak)* **£55 [≃ $99]**

- Historical sketch of the progress of pharmacy in Great Britain. London: 1880. 8vo. 415 pp. Orig cloth, sm lib label on spine.
(Weiner) **£35 [≃ $63]**

Bell, James B.
- The homeopathic therapeutics of diarrhoea, dysentery, cholera ... New York: 1875. Sm 8vo. iv,168 pp. Cloth, spine a little loose.
(Rittenhouse) **$20 [≃ £11]**

Bell, John
- Engravings explaining the anatomy of the bones, muscles, and joints. Edinburgh: 1794. 4to. [iv],xxii, 191,[i] pp. 2 extra leaves 37* & 109*. 32 plates (4 outline), 2 text engvs. A poor copy, 2 plates loose, frayed. Contemp calf, rubbed. *(Pollak)* **£150 [≃ $270]**

- Engravings of the bones, muscles, and joints. Part second containing engravings of the muscles and joints. Phila: 1816. 4to. 123 pp. Half-title. 16 plates. Foxing. Binding worn.
(Goodrich) **$495 [≃ £275]**

- Engravings of the bones, muscles, and joints. Part second. Containing engravings of the muscles and joints. Phila: 1816. 1st Amer from 2nd London edn. 4to. Sgntrs on inside front cvr, some v light foxing. Mor-backed bds. *(Rittenhouse)* **$200 [≃ £111]**

Bell, John & Bell, Charles
- The anatomy and physiology of the human body. New York: 1827. 5th Amer edn. 2 vols. 584; 475 pp. Engvd plates. Extremities of binding worn, vol 1 front hinge cracked.
(Fye) **$200 [≃ £111]**

- The anatomy and physiology of the human body. New York: 1817. 3rd Amer from 4th English edn. 3 vols. Sgntrs on titles, some occas light browning, foxing on endpapers. Unif lea, worn. *(Rittenhouse)* **$95 [≃ £52]**

- The anatomy of the human body. London:

Longman ..., 1811. 3rd edn. 3 vols. 8vo. 36 engvd plates, num text engvs. Orig qtr calf, mrbld bds, some shelf wear.
(Goodrich) **$295 [≈ £163]**

Bell, John & Condie, D. Francis
- All the material facts of the history and treatment of the epidemic cholera, from its appearance in India in 1817 ... Phila: 1832. 8vo. 127 pp. Bds, uncut.
(Goodrich) **$95 [≈ £52]**

Bell, John
- Report of the importance and economy of sanitary measures to cities. New York: 1859. 8vo. 243 pp. Orig cloth.
(Goodrich) **$65 [≈ £36]**

Bell, John
- A treatise on baths; including cold, sea, warm, hot, vapours, gas, and mud baths. Phila: 1850. 8vo. 658 pp. Blindstamped cloth, crnrs worn, top of spine chipped. Ex lib. Author's pres inscrptn.
(Rittenhouse) **$35 [≈ £19]**

Bell, L.
- The telescope. New York: 1922. viii,287 pp. 190 ills. Cloth.   *(Whitehart)* **£25 [≈ $45]**

Bell, Thomas
- The anatomy, physiology, and diseases of the teeth. London: Highley, 1835. 2nd edn. 8vo. xv,[i],332 pp. Frontis, 10 plates. 8 pp advts at front, 4 pp advts at end. Plates sl foxed. Orig cloth, faintly spotted, spine ends soft.
(Pollak) **£160 [≈ $288]**

Bell, W.B. (ed.)
- Some aspects of the cancer problem. 1930. xiv,543 pp. 90 plates. Cloth.
(Whitehart) **£25 [≈ $45]**

Bell, Walter G.
- The Great Plague in London in 1665. London: 1924. 1st edn. 8vo. 374 pp. Cloth.
(Rittenhouse) **$65 [≈ £36]**

Bellows, John G.
- Cataract and anomalies of the lens. London: Kimpton, 1944. 624 pp. 4 cold plates. 208 ills. Pub bndg.   *(Pollak)* **£20 [≈ $36]**

Bemis, George
- Report of the case of John W. Webster ... Doctor of Medicine at Harvard University ... indicted for the murder of George Parkman, Master of Arts ... Boston: C.C. Little ..., 1850. Thick 8vo. Engvd frontis, 7 plates &

plans. Half blue mor, gilt.
(Cooper Hay) **£45 [≈ $81]**

Bemiss, Elijah
- The dyer's companion. In two parts ... many useful recipes for dying, staining, painting, &c. New York: 1815. 2nd enlgd edn. Rubber-stamp on title & sev other leaves, marg stain on a few leaves at end. Sheep, base of spine chipped.   *(Allen)* **$100 [≈ £55]**

Benas, Baron Louis
- £ S D; or pounds, shillings, and pence, still retained; a plan for the decimalization of British coinage. London: Effingham Wilson, 1868. 22 pp. Orig ptd wraps.
(C.R. Johnson) **£20 [≈ $36]**

Benedict, Francis G.
- The composition of the atmosphere with special reference to its oxygen content. Washington, DC: 1912. 8vo. 114 pp. Frontis, tables. Orig cloth. Author's pres inscrptn to Sir William Ramsay.   *(Weiner)* **£35 [≈ $63]**

Benjamin, Park
- The intellectual rise in electricity, a history. London: 1895. 8vo.611 pp. Ports, ills. Orig cloth.   *(Weiner)* **£50 [≈ $90]**

Bennett, H.
- The chemical formulary, a condensed collection of valuable, timely, practical formulae for making thousands of products ... Volumes I-V. Brooklyn or London: 1933-41. 5 vols. About 600 pp per vol. Ex lib, cloth (not matching).   *(Weiner)* **£65 [≈ $117]**

Bennett, James Risdon
- Cancerous and other intra-thoracic growths ... 1872. viii,189 pp. 5 plates. Cancelled lib stamps on title. Orig cloth, spotted. Author's pres inscrptn on half-title.
(Bickersteth) **£20 [≈ $36]**

Bennett, Samuel
- A new explanation of the ebbing and flowing of the sea, upon the principles of gravitation. New York: for the author, 1816. 1st edn. 8vo. 79 pp. Fldg engvd plate. Mod stiff wraps.
(Antiq Sc) **$150 [≈ £83]**
- A new explanation of the ebbing and flowing of the sea, upon the principles of gravitation. New York: privately printed, 1816. 8vo. 79 pp. Fldg diag. Some light foxing, some pp frayed. New mrbld bds.
(Whitehart) **£35 [≈ $63]**

Berdoe, Edward
- The origin and growth of the healing art. A popular history of medicine in all ages and countries. 1893. xii,509 pp. 5 plates. Pub stamp on title, sgntr & label on endpaper. Cloth.   *(Whitehart)* **£25 [≃ $45]**
- The origin and growth of the healing art. A popular history of medicine in all ages and countries. London: Swan Sonnenschein, 1893. 8vo. xii,509,[iii] pp. Frontis, 4 plates. Pub bndg.   *(Pollak)* **£40 [≃ $72]**
- The origin and growth of the healing art. London: 1893. 8vo. 509 pp. Orig cloth.
                              (Goodrich) **$35 [≃ £19]**

Bergh, Augustus
- An essay on the causes of distant alternate periodic inundations over the low lands of each hemisphere ... London: Ridgway, n.d. [ca 1861]. 8vo. [iv],46,[ii] pp. Fldg table. Orig cloth.   *(Pollak)* **£30 [≃ $54]**

Bergman, Torbern
- A dissertation on elective attractions. London: Murray, and C. Elliot, Edinburgh, 1785. 1st edn in English. 8vo. xiv,[2], 382,[1 errata] pp. 3 extra-lge fldg tables, 4 fldg engvd plates. Contemp speckled calf.
                         (Antiq Sc) **$475 [≃ £263]**

Bergson, Henri
- Creative evolution. London: Macmillan, 1911. 1st edn in English. 8vo. Orig cloth.
                      (Chaucer Head) **£55 [≃ $99]**

Berkeley, George
- An essay towards a new theory of vision. Dublin: 1709. 2nd edn. 8vo. xiv,198 pp. Contemp lea, back hinge broken.
                         (Argosy) **$100 [≃ £55]**
- Siris: a chain of philosophical reflexions and inquiries concerning the virtues of tar water ... Dublin printed, London re-printed: 1744. 2nd edn, imprvd & crrctd.
                          (Traylen) **£70 [≃ $126]**
- Siris: a chain of philosophical reflexions ... Dublin printed, London re-printed: 1744. [Bound with] Prior, Thomas - An authentick narrative of the success of tar-water in curing ... distempers. 1746. Contemp mottled calf. Ex Signet Library.
                      (Waterfield's) **£135 [≃ $243]**
- Siris: a chain of philosophical reflexions and inquiries concerning the virtues of tar water ... Dublin printed, London re-printed: 1744. [Bound with] Anti-Siris, or English wisdom ... For M. Cooper, 1744. Repr to top of 1st title. Contemp half calf.
                      (Waterfield's) **£185 [≃ $333]**

- The works ... To which is added, an account of his life ... London: for Richard Priestley, 1820. 3 vols. 8vo. [viii],lxxv,411; [iv],455; [vi],476 pp. Fldg engvd plan in vol I. Some foxing at the ends, dusty in top margs. New paper bds.   *(Pollak)* **£120 [≃ $216]**

Berkenhout, Dr. John
- A volume of letters [on mathematics, botany, geography, &c., &c.] ... to his son at the University. Cambridge: for T. Cadell, 1790. 8vo. [iv],iv,374, [ii] pp. Final errata leaf. Contemp speckled calf, rebacked, crnrs rubbed.   *(Clark)* **£100 [≃ $180]**

Berliner, M.L.
- Biomicroscopy of the eye. New York: 1943. 2 vols. Orig cloth. *(Rittenhouse)* **$75 [≃ £41]**
- Biomicroscopy of the eye: slit lamp microscopy of the living eye. New York: Hoeber, 1949. 2 vols. 8vo. 1515 pp. 82 col ptd plates, num text ills. Orig cloth.
                              (Oasis) **$150 [≃ £83]**

Bernard, Claude
- An introduction to the study of experimental medicine. Translated ... New York: 1927. 8vo. 226 pp. Orig cloth.
                          (Goodrich) **$55 [≃ £30]**
- Notes on M. Bernard's lectures on the blood; with an appendix ... Phila: 1854. 1st edn. 224 pp. Orig binding.   *(Fye)* **$300 [≃ £166]**

Bernutz, Gustave & Goupil, Ernest
- Clinical memoirs of the diseases of women. Translated and edited ... London: New Sydenham Soc, 1866. 2 vols. 8vo. xiv,276; xii,270,59 list of members pp. Orig cloth. Ex lib.   *(Rittenhouse)* **$35 [≃ £19]**

Berry, James
- The story of a Red Cross Unit in Serbia. London: Churchill, 1916. 8vo. xvi,293 pp. 29 ills. Dec cloth.   *(Zeno)* **£17.50 [≃ $30]**

Berthollet, C.L. & A.B.
- Elements of the art of dyeing ... the art of bleaching ... London: 1824. 2 vols. 8vo. xxvii,408; vii,453 pp. 9 plates, some fldg. Old sgntr on 1 title & elsewhere. Uncut in mod qtr lea.   *(Weiner)* **£175 [≃ $315]**

Bettany, G.T.
- Eminent doctors: their lives and their work. London: John Hogg, 1885. 2nd edn. 2 vols. 8vo. viii,[ii];311; vi,318,24 ctlg pp. Orig cloth, gilt, sm dent on 1 bd.
                            (Pollak) **£35 [≃ $63]**
- Eminent doctors: their lives and their work.

[1887]. 2nd edn. 2 vols. 24 pp advts. Orig green cloth, vol 2 back cvr marked.
(Halewood) **£35 [≈ $63]**

Beverley, Robert Mackenzie
- The Darwinian theory of the transmutation of species examined by a graduate of the University of Cambridge. London: James Nisbet, 1868. 2nd edn. 8vo. viii,[ii], 386,[ii] pp. Orig cloth, spine worn at ends.
(Pollak) **£60 [≈ $108]**

Bhagavantam, S.
- Scattering of light and the Raman effect. Waltair, India: 1940. Lge 8vo. x,333 pp. Diags. Orig cloth.   *(Weiner)* **£25 [≈ $45]**

Bianchi, Leonardo
- The mechanism of the brain and the function of the frontal lobes. Edinburgh: 1922. 1st edn in English. 348 pp. Orig cloth, spine faded.
(Scientia) **$175 [≈ £97]**

Bibby, George H.
- The planning of lunatic asylums. London: 1896. 8vo. lxxxix advts, 132 pp. Orig ptd cloth-backed bds.   *(Weiner)* **£50 [≈ $90]**

Bickerton, Thomas H.
- A medical history of Liverpool ... to the year 1920. London: Murray, 1936. xx,313,[iii] pp. Port frontis, 8 maps & plans, 73 ills. Occas foxing. Orig cloth, uncut, sm snag in ft of spine.   *(Pollak)* **£45 [≈ $81]**
- A medical history of Liverpool ... to the year 1920. London: 1936. 4to. xx,313 pp. Ports, plans, maps (2 fldg & mtd on linen). Orig cloth.   *(Weiner)* **£30 [≈ $54]**

Biegel, Hermann
- The human hair; its structure, growth, diseases and their treatment. London: Renshaw, 1869 1st edn. 8vo. Sm w'cuts. New cloth.   *(Oasis)* **$35 [≈ £19]**

Bieglow, Henry J.
- Medical education in America. Cambridge: 1871. 1st edn. 83 pp. *(Scientia)* **$100 [≈ £55]**

Bierman, William
- The medical applications of the short wave current. Baltimore: 1938. 1st edn, 3rd printing. 8vo. xvii,379 pp. 25 plates, text ills. Cloth.   *(Elgen)* **$30 [≈ £16]**

Bigelow, Henry J.
- Fragments of medical science and art. An address before the Boylston Medical Society ... Boston: Ticknor, 1846. 1st edn. 8vo. 54

pp. Orig ptd wraps. Author's pres copy.
(Antiq Sc) **$85 [≈ £47]**
- Orthopedic surgery and other medical papers. Boston: Little, Brown, 1900. 1st coll edn. 8vo. ix,[3],373 pp. Sev plates & text figs. Orig cloth, t.e.g., spine faded.
(Antiq Sc) **$65 [≈ £36]**

Bigelow, Jacob
- Nature in disease, illustrated in various discourses and essays. To which are added miscellaneous writings chiefly on medical subjects. Boston: 1854. 8vo. 391 pp. Cloth worn.   *(Goodrich)* **$75 [≈ £41]**
- A treatise on the materia medica, intended as a sequel to the pharmacopoiea of the United States ... Boston: 1822. 1st edn. 424 pp. Lea, scuffed.   *(Scientia)* **$175 [≈ £97]**

Bigg, Heather
- Caries of the spine. Being an advance chapter of the spine, its deformities, debilities, and deficiences. London: Churchill, 1902. 8vo. 82 pp. 11 figs. Orig cloth. *(Pollak)* **£20 [≈ $36]**

Bilguer, Johann Ulrich von
- A dissertation on the inutility of the amputation of the limbs ... Now first translated into English ... London: for R. Baldwin ..., 1764. 1st edn in English. 8vo. xvi,100 pp. Disbound.
(Burmester) **£120 [≈ $216]**

Billard, C.M.
- A treatise on the diseases of infants, founded on recent clinical observations and investigations in pathological anatomy ... New York: 1839. 1st edn in English. 620 pp. Mod qtr lea, mrbld bds, new endpapers.
(Scientia) **$375 [≈ £208]**

Billing, Archibald
- Practical observations on diseases of the lungs and heart. London: S. Highley, 1852. 1st edn. 8vo. Some advts on rear endpapers. Orig black binder's cloth, gilt. Author's pres inscrptn on title.   *(Hughes)* **£25 [≈ $45]**
- Practical observations on diseases of the lungs and heart. London: 1852. 8vo. 138 pp. Diag. Inscrbd by author on title, pub ctlg at end. Binder's cloth.   *(Weiner)* **£50 [≈ $90]**

Billings, John S. & Hurd, Henry
- Suggestions to hospital and asylum visitors. Phila: 1895. 1st edn. 48 pp. Orig cloth.
(Fye) **$75 [≈ £41]**

Billings, John Shaw
- Description of the Johns Hopkins Hospital.

Balt: 1890. 1st edn. 4to. 116 pp. 56 plates. Embossed stamp on title. Rebacked, orig spine laid down, new endpapers.
(Scientia) **$600 [≃ £333]**
- The principles of ventilation and heating and their practical application. London: 1884. 1st London edn. 216 pp. Cloth, recased, new endpapers.   *(Scientia)* **$150 [≃ £83]**

Billroth, Theodor
- General surgical pathology and therapeutics. In fifty-one lectures ... New York: Appleton, 1883. 8vo. xvi,835 pp. Cloth, rubbed.
(Goodrich) **$65 [≃ £36]**
- Lectures on surgical pathology and therapeutics. Translated ... London: 1877. 2 vols. 8vo. 438; 543 pp. Cloth, spines worn & spotted, 1 hinge & 1 spine cracking. Ex lib.
(Rittenhouse) **$45 [≃ £25]**

Binet, Alfred
- The psychic life of micro-organisms, a study in experimental psychology. Chicago: 1910. 8vo. xii,121 pp. Diags. Orig cloth.
(Weiner) **£21 [≃ $37]**

Bingley, William
- Animal biography; or, authentic anecdotes of the lives, manners. and economy, of the animal creation. London: Phillips, 1805. 3rd edn. 3 vols. 8vo. xxiv,502; [2],557; [2],606 pp. Advt leaf. Some age-browning at end. Contemp speckled calf, lacking 2 labels.
(Claude Cox) **£38 [≃ $68]**

Binz, C.
- Lectures on pharmacology for practitioners and students. London: New Sydenham Soc, 1895-97. 2 vols. 8vo. vi,389; 451,[1] pp. Orig cloth.   *(Whitehart)* **£25 [≃ $45]**

Bion, M.
- The construction and principle uses of mathematical instruments ... London: 1723. 1st English edn. Folio. viii,264 pp. 26 fldg plates. A few pages at rear sl torn & reprd, light waterstain top outer crnr, a few pages grubby. Contemp panelled calf, rebacked.
(Whitehart) **£380 [≃ $684]**

Birch, John
- An essay on the medical application of electricity. London: J. Johnson ..., 1803. 1st edn (?). 4to. iv,57,[3] pp. Light dampstain to inner marg of last gathering. Uncut. Contemp wraps, spine worn & chipped.
(Rootenberg) **$300 [≃ £166]**

Birch, Thomas
- The history of the Royal Society of London for improving of natural knowledge ... 1756-57. 1st edn. Vols 1-3. 4to. Fldg plates, text diags. A little foxing. Contemp bds, late 19th c mor backed. *(Halewood)* **£300 [≃ $540]**

Bird, Anthony & Hallows, Ian
- The Rolls-Royce Motor Car. London: Batsford, 1966. 2nd edn. 320 pp. Frontis, 242 ills. Pub bndg, dw.   *(Pollak)* **£35 [≃ $63]**

Bird, S. Dougan
- On Australasian climates and their influence in the prevention and arrest of pulmonary consumption. London: 1863. 8vo. vii,168 pp. Orig cloth, spine defective, crnrs bent. Ex lib.
(Rittenhouse) **$50 [≃ £27]**

Biringuccio, Vannoccio
- The pirotechnia, translated from the Italian with an introduction and notes by Cyril Standley Smith ... Amer Inst of Mining & Metall Eng., 1942. 4to. One of 1000. xxvi,476 pp. Re & black title. Orig cloth.
(Weiner) **£60 [≃ $108]**

Birks, Thomas Rawson
- On matter and ether or the secret laws of physical change. Cambridge: 1862. 8vo. vii,216 pp. Pub ctlg. Cancelled blind lib stamp on title. Orig cloth, worn at top of spine.   *(Bickersteth)* **£22 [≃ $39]**

Birnbaum, R.
- A clinical manual of the malformations and congenital diseases of the foetus. Translated ... Phila: 1912. 1st edn in English. 8vo. xiv,379 pp. 8 plates, 58 text ills. Cloth.
(Elgen) **$65 [≃ £36]**

Birth ...
- The birth of man-kinde ... See Roesslin, Eucharius

Bishop, John
- On articulate sounds; and on the causes and cure of impediments of speech ... London: Samuel Highley ..., 1851. 1st edn. 8vo. vii,9-79 contents, [1],40 advts pp. Frontis. Orig cloth, blindstamped sides, worn, jnts split.   *(Pickering)* **$120 [≃ £66]**
- On articulate sounds; and on the causes and cure of impediments of speech ... London: Highley, 1851. 8vo. 79 pp. Frontis, Light dampstaining. Orig cloth, rubbed.
(Goodrich) **$65 [≃ £36]**

Bishop, John George
- The Brighton chain pier ... its history from 1823 to 1896 ... Brighton: 1897. 4to. [vi],74,xxv pp. Fldg double-page frontis, many plates. Orig bevelled gilt & black pict embossed plum cloth, a.e.g., minor damp-faded area on bottom crnrs.
(Weiner) **£110 [≃ $198]**

Bjerre, A.
- The psychology of murder. A study in criminal psychology. Translated ... 1927. xi,164 pp. Endpapers sl discold. Cloth sl dust-stained.   *(Whitehart)* **£18 [≃ $32]**

Black, G. Vardiman
- A work on special dental pathology devoted to the diseases and treatment of the ... tissues of the teeth and the dental pulp. Chicago: 1915. 1st edn. 489 pp. 518 ills. Sm piece of cloth missing from crnr of rear cvr.
(Scientia) **$100 [≃ £55]**

Black, John Janvier
- Forty years in the medical profession, 1858-1898. Phila: 1900. 1st edn. 8vo. 498 pp. Cloth. Author's pres copy.
(Elgen) **$25 [≃ £13]**

Black, Joseph
- Lectures on the elements of chemistry... Edinburgh: ... William Creech, 1803. 1st edn. 2 vols. 4to. lxxvi (misnumbered lxvi), 4],556; [2],762 pp. Port, 3 engvd plates. Without the 20pp index. Waterstaining 1st few leaves, occas foxing. Contemp tree calf.
(Pickering) **$3,500 [≃ £1,944]**

Blacker, C.P.
- Eugenics. Galton and after. London: Duckworth, 1952. 8vo. 349,[i] pp. 4 plates, 4 text figs. Pub bndg, dw. *(Pollak)* **£20 [≃ $36]**

Blackfan, K.D. & Diamond, L.K.
- Atlas of the blood in children. New York: 1944. 8vo. 320 pp. 70 cold plates. Orig cloth, rubbed.   *(Goodrich)* **$60 [≃ £33]**

Blackham, G.E.
- On angular aperture of objectives for the microscope, read before the Microscopical Congress, at Indianapolis, 1878. New York: 1880. 21 pp. 18 fldg diags. Light waterstains on edge. Orig cloth, sl wear.
(Weiner) **£35 [≃ $63]**

Blackley, Charles H.
- Experimental researches on the causes and nature of catarrhus aestivus (hay-fever or hay-

asthma). London: 1873. 1st edn. 8vo. Half-title, vii,[ii],202 pp. 7 w'cut plates, 2 fldg tables. Occas foxing. Cloth. George M. Beard's copy with his inscrptn.
(Elgen) **$400 [≃ £222]**
- Hay fever; its causes, treatment and effective prevention. Experimental researches. London: 1880. 2nd edn, revsd & enlgd. 281 pp. Cloth, rebacked, orig spine laid down, new endpapers.   *(Scientia)* **$295 [≃ £163]**

Blackwell, Elizabeth
- Pioneer work in opening the medical profession to women; autobiographical sketches. London: 1895. 1st edn. 265 pp. Cloth.   *(Scientia)* **$150 [≃ £83]**

Blair, David (pseud.)
- An easy grammar of natural and experimental philosophy ... See Phillips, Sir Richard

Blair, William
- The soldier's friend ... instructions to the loyal volunteer ... and military men in general on the preservation of their health; wounds and casualties ... prevention of diseases; hospitals and nursing. London: Murray, 1804. Orig blue bds, paper spine, uncut.
(C.R. Johnson) **£90 [≃ $162]**

Bland, M.
- Algebraical problems, producing simple and quadratic equations, with their solutions ... Cambridge: 1832. 6th edn. viii,438 pp. A few insignificant stains. Orig bds, rebacked in lea.
(Whitehart) **£35 [≃ $63]**

Bland-Sutton, Sir John
- Selected lectures and essays. Including ligaments, their nature and morphology. London: Heinemann, 1920. 4th edn. 8vo. xi,[i],320 pp. 111 ills. Pub bndg, sl faded.
(Pollak) **£20 [≃ $36]**

Bliss, Arthur Ames
- Blockley days: memories and impressions of a resident physician, 1883-1884. Privately printed, 1916. 1st edn. 94 pp. Untrimmed. Cloth.   *(Elgen)* **$50 [≃ £27]**

Blogg, M.W.
- Bibliography of the writings of Sir William Osler ... revised and enlarged with an index. Balt: 1921. 8vo. 96 pp. Cloth.
(Goodrich) **$85 [≃ £47]**

Bloomfield, Robert
- Good tidings; or news from the farm. A poem ... [on smallpox & vaccination]. Parnassian

Press, for Vernor & Hood, 1804. 1st edn. 4to.
37,[1] pp. Contemp sgntr on title, early
inscrptn on half-title. Contemp crimson
straight grained mor, spine sl rubbed.
(Pickering) **$650 [≈ £361]**

Blount, Sir Thomas Pope
- A natural history: containing many not
common quotations: extracted out of the best
modern writers. London: for R. Bentley ...,
1693. 1st edn. 12mo. [xvi],469,3 advts] pp.
Some browning. Old panelled calf, crnrs
worn, rec rebacking, new endpapers. Wing
B3351.   *(Bow Windows)* **£275 [≈ $495]**

Blumenbach, Johann Friedrich
- Elements of physiology, translated ... to
which is subjoined ... an appendix ... of the
existing discoveries relative to ... animal
electricity. Phila: Thomas Dobson, 1795. 1st
edn in English. 2 vols in 1. 8vo. xvi,229 pp;
1f, 247 pp. Contemp calf.
(Offenbacher) **$500 [≈ £277]**

Blyth, Alexander Wynter
- Poisons: their effects and detections. A
manual for the use of analytical chemists and
experts. London: 1895. 3rd edn, revsd &
enlgd. 8vo. xxxii,724 pp. 2 or 3 leaves a little
creased, back inner hinge a little weak. Orig
cloth, tips of crnrs rubbed.
(Bow Windows) **£42 [≈ $75]**
- Poisons: their effects and detections. A
manual for the use of analytical chemists and
experts. New York: Wood, 1885. 1st edn. 2
vols. 333; 668 pp. Tables, ills. Orig cloth.
(Xerxes) **$80 [≈ £44]**

Boase, H.S.
- A treatise on primary geology. London: 1834.
8vo. xi,399 pp. Contemp calf, edges rubbed,
rebacked.   *(Wheldon & Wesley)* **£50 [≈ $90]**

Bock, C.E.
- Atlas of human anatomy, with explanatory
text. New York: 1881. Folio. 38 cold plates.
Light pencil & ink marks on some plates. Orig
cvrs.   *(Rittenhouse)* **$75 [≈ £41]**

Boddington, George
- An essay on the treatment and cure of
pulmonary consumption. Reprinted, with a
preface by Dr. Arthur E. Bodington. 1906.
xv,60 pp. 2 associated a.l.s. & 3 photographs
in pocket at rear. *(Rittenhouse)* **$125 [≈ £69]**

Boerhaave, Herman
- Aphorisms: concerning knowledge and cure
of diseases. London: 1755. 3rd edn. 8vo.
xvi,444 pp. Index. Names, dates & a b'plate

on front endpaper. Orig binding, hinges
weak.   *(Rittenhouse)* **$195 [≈ £108]**
- Aphorisms: concerning knowledge and cure
of diseases. London: 1735. 8vo. [14],444 pp.
Index. Contemp lea.
(Rittenhouse) **$225 [≈ £125]**
- A new method of chemistry ... the history,
theory and practice of the art ... London:
Longman, 1741. 2nd edn. 2 vols. 4to.
xxx,593, [i]; [i],410, [xxxviii index] pp. 41
fldg engvd plates on 25 sheets. Occas
spotting. Contemp calf, jnts & extremities
reprd.   *(Frew Mackenzie)* **£450 [≈ $810]**
- A new method of chemistry including the
theory and practice of that art ... London: for
J. Osborn & T. Longman, 1727. 1st edn. 4to.
Contemp calf, jnts cracked.
(Waterfield's) **£450 [≈ $810]**
- A new method of chemistry including the
theory and practice of that art ... London: for
J. Osborn ..., 1727. 1st edn. 4to. 2 pts in 1 vol.
2 engvd plates. 18th c calf, rebacked.
(Chaucer Head) **£620 [≈ $1,116]**

Boghurst, William
- Loimographia; an account of the Great
Plague of London in the year 1665 ... Edited
by J.F. Payne. London: 1894. 1st edn. 99 pp.
(Scientia) **$125 [≈ £69]**

Bohr, Niels
- The theory of spectra and atomic
constitution. Three essays. Cambridge:
University Press, 1922. 1st coll edn, 1st edn
in English. 8vo. x,126 pp. Text figs. Orig
cloth.   *(Antiq Sc)* **$150 [≈ £83]**

Boivin, Mme. Veuve & Duges, A.
- A practical treatise on the diseases of the
uterus and its appendages. Translated from
the French. London: 1834. 8vo. xliv,559 pp.
Rec buckram.   *(Rittenhouse)* **$27.50 [≈ £15]**
- A practical treatise on the diseases of the
uterus and its appendages. Translated from
the French. London: 1834. 1st edn in
English. 559 pp. Mod qtr lea, mrbld bds, new
endpapers.   *(Scientia)* **$375 [≈ £208]**

Bolton, H.C.
- A select bibliography of chemistry.
1492-1892. Washington: 1893. 1st edn. 8vo.
1212 pp. Unopened. Orig wraps. [with] First
Supplement 1492-1897. Published 1899. 489
pp. Cloth. Ex lib.   *(Oasis)* **$100 [≈ £55]**
- A select bibliography of chemistry.
1492-1892. With the 2 supplements (to 1902).
Washington: 1893-1904. 4 vols. 8vo. Approx
2700 pp. 3 vols orig cloth, 4th vol new
buckram.   *(Weiner)* **£150 [≈ $270]**

Bompass, Charles Carpenter

- An essay on the nature of heat, light and electricity. London: Underwood, 1817. Sole edn. 8vo. x,266,[2 blank] pp. Lib cloth, with lib b'plate.   *(Offenbacher)* **$285 [≃ £158]**

Bonnet, Charles

- The contemplation of nature. London: 1766. 1st edn in English. 2 vols. 256; 230 pp. Sm section cut from 1st blank in each vol. Lea.
          (Scientia) **$350 [≃ £194]**
- Interesting views of Christianity being a translation of part of ... Recherches Philosophiques sur les Preuves de Christianisme. Dublin: P. Byrne, 1798. A few leaves browned & fragile, faint pencil marks throughout. Contemp sheep, worn.
          (Waterfield's) **£45 [≃ $81]**

Bonnycastle, John

- An introduction to algebra ... for the use of schools and places of public education. 1788. 2nd edn. x,[1],208 pp. Light marg waterstaining on a few pp. Contemp lea, sl worn, hinges cracked.
          (Whitehart) **£50 [≃ $90]**
- An introduction to algebra. New York: Dean, 1831. Sm 8vo. Foxed. Binding worn, front bd loose.   *(Xerxes)* **$35 [≃ £19]**
- An introduction to mensuration and practical geometry. London: for J. Johnson, 1812. 11th edn. 8vo. xii,276 pp. Vignette title. Lacking half-title. Orig sheep, hinges cracked.
          (Claude Cox) **£20 [≃ $36]**
- Treatise on algebra in practice and theory. London: J. Johnson, 1813. 2 vols. 406; 428 pp. 3/4 lea. Ex lib.   *(Xerxes)* **$30 [≃ £16]**

Bontius, Jacobus

- Bontius on tropical medicine. An account of the diseases, natural history and medicines of the East Indies [1769]. Amsterdam: 1931. lxix,459 pp.   *(Scientia)* **$85 [≃ £47]**

Book of Trades ...

- The book of trades. Or library of useful arts. The fourth edition (Parts I and II). For Tabart & Co., 1810-11. 2 vols. 12mo. [iv],210,[2 advts] ; [iv],188 pp. 23 & 24 copper plates. Some soiling & dustmarks, a few short tears. Contemp half mor, defective.
          (Barbary) **£55 [≃ $99]**
- The boy's book of trades and the tools used in them. London: Routledge, n.d. [ca 1880]. 1st edn (?). Sm 4to. 326 pp. 700 w'cut ills. Orig pict green cloth.   *(Gough)* **£85 [≃ $153]**

Boole, George

- A treatise on the calculus of finite differences.

Cambridge: Macmillan, 1860. 1st edn. 8vo. [6],248 pp. Orig green cloth.
          (Rootenberg) **$600 [≃ £333]**
- A treatise on the calculus of finite differences. Cambridge: 1860. 1st edn. 8vo. 248 pp. Ink underlining on 3 pages. Orig cloth, rebacked, old spine laid down.   *(Weiner)* **£50 [≃ $90]**

Booth, Charles

- The aged poor in England and Wales. London: Macmillan, 1894. 8vo. vi,[ii],527, [i] pp. Orig cloth, front jnt pulled, mostly unopened.   *(Pollak)* **£40 [≃ $72]**

Borden, W.C.

- The use of the Roentgen ray by the Medical Department of the United States Army in the war with Spain. Washington: 1900. 1st edn. 4to. 98 pp. 38 X-ray plates. Orig cloth, spine spotted, rear outer hinge torn, spine lettering faded.   *(Fye)* **$200 [≃ £111]**

Borlase, William

- The natural history of Cornwall. The air, climate, waters, rivers ... tin and the manner of mining ... Oxford: for the author, 1758. 1st edn. Folio. xix,426,[1 errata, 1 directions] pp. 29 plates inc extndg map. Minor dust marks. Contemp calf, rebacked.
          (Bow Windows) **£350 [≃ $630]**
- The natural history of Cornwall. Oxford: 1758. Folio. xix,326,[2] pp. Double-page map, 28 engvd plates. A little minor foxing, sm tears in map & 1 plate reprd, occas ms crrctns in text. Contemp calf, jnts cracked,
          (Wheldon & Wesley) **£250 [≃ $450]**

Born, M.

- Natural philosophy of cause and chance. being the Waynflete Lectures ... Hilary Term 1948. Oxford: 1949. 1st edn. viii,215 pp. A few text diags.   *(Whitehart)* **£35 [≃ $63]**

Born, Max

- The constitution of matter, modern atomic and electron theories. London: 1923. 8vo. vii,80 pp. Diags. Orig cloth.
          (Weiner) **£30 [≃ $54]**
- Einstein's theory of relativity. 1924. 1st English edn. vii,293 pp. Port frontis, 135 text figs.   *(Whitehart)* **£25 [≃ $45]**
- The mechanics of the atom. 1927. 1st edn in English. xvi,317 pp. Fldg chart. Orig cloth.
          (Whitehart) **£40 [≃ $72]**
- Problems of atomic dynamics. Cambridge, Mass: M.I.T., 1926. 1st edn. 8vo. xiv,[2],200 pp. Orig cloth.   *(Antiq Sc)* **$185 [≃ £102]**

Bossut, Charles
- A general history of mathematics ... to the middle of the eighteenth century ... London: 1803. 1st English edn. 8vo. xxvi,540 pp. Double-page table. Mod buckram.
(Weiner) £50 [≃ $90]

Boucher, J.N.
- William Kelly: a true history of the so-called Bessemer process. Greensburgh, Pa: the author, 1924. 8vo. xvii,258 pp. Ports, plates. Orig cloth. *(Weiner)* £35 [≃ $63]

Bouillon-Lagrange, J.B.
- A manual of a course of chemistry; or, a series of experiments and illustrations ... London: J. Cuthell ..., 1800. 1st edn. 2 vols. 8vo. 17 engvd plates. Contemp tree calf, occas surface damage to sides.
(Frew Mackenzie) £250 [≃ $450]
- A manual of a course of chemistry; or, a series of experiments and illustrations ... London: 1800. 1st English edn. 2 vols. xx,488 pp, 9ff; vii,457 pp, 9ff. 17 engvd plates, 1 double-page. Contemp half calf, mrbld bds, vol 2 rebacked. *(Whitehart)* £220 [≃ $396]

Bousfield, E.C.
- Guide to the science of photo-micrography. 1892. 2nd edn. xv,174 pp. Frontis, 34 ills.
(Whitehart) £20 [≃ $36]

Boutcher, William
- A treatise on forest-trees ... best methods of their culture ... new and useful discoveries ... Edinburgh: R. Fleming, 1775. 1st edn. 4to. Author's authentication, sgnd, on title verso. Contemp calf, rebacked with orig spine, gilt.
(Traylen) £120 [≃ $216]
- A treatise on forest-trees ... best methods of their culture ... new and useful discoveries ... Edinburgh: for the author, 1778. 2nd edn. 4to. xlviii,259,[5] pp. Contemp calf-backed mrbld bds, spine rubbed, hinges starting.
(Karmiole) $200 [≃ £111]

Bowden, Ambrose
- A treatise on dry rot ... causes of that diseases in ships, houses, mills, &c., with methods of prevention and cure ... London: for Burton & Brigg, 1815. 1st edn. 8vo. 2 hand-cold plates. Contemp diced calf, gilt borders, mrbld edges. *(Traylen)* £240 [≃ $432]

Bowditch, Nathaniel Ingersoll
- A history of the Massachusetts General Hospital. Second edition, with a continuation to 1872. Boston: 1872. 734 pp. Engvd plates. Orig cloth. *(Fye)* $200 [≃ £111]

- Memoir of Nathaniel Bowditch. By his son. Boston: Little & Brown, 1840. 2nd edn. 4to. 172 pp. 2 plates (light waterstain to lower crnr of each). Orig cloth, faded & somewhat worn.
(Argonaut) $225 [≃ £125]

Bowlby, A.A.
- Surgical pathology and morbid anatomy. London: 1895. 3rd edn. 8vo. 640 pp. 183 text figs. Sev finger marks. Orig cloth.
(Bow Windows) £25 [≃ $45]

Bowles, R.L.
- A method for the treatment of the apparently drowned. Together with remarks in discussion on the phenomena attending death from drowning. London: 1904. 8vo. 14 pp pamphlet. Plates. *(Goodrich)* $50 [≃ £27]

Bowring, Sir J.
- The decimal system in numbers, coins and accounts ... decimalisation of the currency and accountancy of the United Kingdom. 1854. Port frontis (sl marked), plates in text. Lib stamps on plate versos & elsewhere. Orig cloth, rebacked. *(Whitehart)* £18 [≃ $32]

Boyce, R.W.
- Health progress and administration in the West Indies. London: 1910. 8vo. xv,350 pp. Map, plates. Orig cloth. *(Weiner)* £35 [≃ $63]

Boyle, Robert
- Certain physiological essays and other tracts written at distant times ... a discourse upon the absolute rest in bodies. London: for H. Herringman, 1669. 2nd edn (1st of 2nd part). 2 pts in 1. Contemp calf, rebacked, mor label, gilt. Wing B3930. *(Traylen)* £495 [≃ $891]
- Certain physiological essays and other tracts ... London: for H. Herringman, 1669. 2nd enlgd edn. 4to. Collation as in Fulton, with the final blank. 18th c sgntr on title scored through, some browning. Contemp calf, rebacked, orig spine preserved. Wing B3930.
(Pickering) $850 [≃ £472]
- Medicina hydrostatica: or, hydrostaticks applyed to the materia medica. London: Smith, 1690. 1st edn. 12mo. [20],217,[7], t.p., 14 [ctlg with title dated 1690] pp. Half-title, engvd frontis. A few crnrs strengthened. Contemp speckled calf, early rebacking.
(Antiq Sc) $2,100 [≃ £1,166]
- Medicinal experiments, or a collection of choice remedies. London: Smith, 1692. 1st edn. 12mo. [10],88 pp. Imprim leaf & 17 pp pub ctlg. Crnr torn from p 5 with loss of a few letters, headlines closely shaved, some pages worn at crnrs. Old calf, rebacked.
(Oasis) $225 [≃ £125]

- The origine of formes and qualities ... illustrated by considerations and experiments. Oxford: 1667. 2nd edn, 1st iss. 8vo. Contemp calf, rebacked. Wing B4015.
(Argosy) **$500 [≈ £277]**
- The philosophical works; abridged, methodized and disposed under the general heads of physics ... and medicine. London: Innys, 1725. 1st edn. 3 vols. 4to. [iv],xliii, 730; xx,726; [iv],xv,756 pp. 21 fldg engvd plates. Contemp calf, some jnts splitting, rubbed. *(Frew Mackenzie)* **£780 [≈ $1,404]**
- Some considerations touching the usefulnesse of experimental natural philosophy ... Oxford: 1664-71. 2 vols in 1. 4to. 2nd edn vol 1; 1st edn vol 2. Complex collation, complete, with all blanks, &c. Contemp blindstamped calf. *(Hemlock)* **$900 [≈ £500]**
- Some considerations touching the usefulnesse of experimental natural philosophy ... A second edition ... Oxford: for Ric. Davis, 1664-71. 2 vols in 1. 8vo. Lacking ddd4 (label title). Contemp panelled calf, rebacked. Wing B4029 & B4030.
(Waterfield's) **£700 [≈ $1,260]**
- The works ... In five volumes. To which is prefixed the life of the author. London: A. Millar, 1744. 1st edn. 5 vols. Folio. Engvd port frontis, red & black titles, 24 engvd plates on 15 fldg sheets. Contemp calf, gilt, jnts & extremities restored.
(Frew Mackenzie) **£1,300 [≈ $2,340]**
- The works ... In six volumes. To which is prefixed the life of the author. London: for F. & J. Rivington, 1772. New edn. 6 vols. 4to. Engvd port frontis, 24 plates on 16 leaves, 6 engvd vignette titles. Contemp calf, worn, crnrs reprd, rebacked, mor labels.
(Traylen) **£1,100 [≈ $1,980]**
- The works ... To which is prefixed the life of the author. London: A. Millar, 1744. 5 vols. Folio. Port frontis, 22 plates, subscribers' list. Contemp calf, 3 jnts cracking.
(Waterfield's) **£650 [≈ $1,170]**

Boyles, John
- Table calculated to shew the contents (in feet and twelfth parts of a foot) of any sled load or cart load of wood. Boston: John Boyles, 1771. 16 mo. 7 pp. 3 leaves torn without loss, contemp ink notes in margs. Disbound.
(Xerxes) **$200 [≈ £111]**

Braasch, William F. & Hager, B.H.
- Urography. Phila: 1927. 2nd edn, revsd & enlgd. 8vo. 480 pp. 750 roentgenograms. Cloth. *(Elgen)* **$35 [≈ £19]**

Bracken, Henry
- The traveller's pocket-farrier: or a treatise upon the distempers and common incidents happening to horses upon a journey ... London: B. Dod, 1743. 1st edn. 12mo. [6],151,[9] pp. Red & black title. Contemp calf, cvrs loose. *(Rootenberg)* **$175 [≈ £97]**

Bradford, E.H. & Lovett, Robert W.
- A treatise on orthopedic surgery. New York: 1890. 8vo. viii,783 pp. 789 w'engvs. Cloth.
(Rittenhouse) **$37.50 [≈ £20]**

Bradford, Thomas L.
- History of the Homeopathic Medical College of Pennsylvania ... Phila: 1898. 1st edn. 8vo. xvii,904 pp. Port frontis, num plates, ports. Cloth, sl shelf wear. *(Elgen)* **$125 [≈ £69]**

Bradley, Richard
- A complete body of husbandry, collected from the practice and experience of the most considerable farmers in Britain. Woodman, 1727. 1st edn. 8vo. [i],xi,392 pp, 2ff pub advts. 4 fldg engvd plates. Light dust-soiling. Contemp calf, rebacked, recrnrd.
(Frew Mackenzie) **£190 [≈ $342]**
- New improvements of planting and gardening, both philosophical and practical London: 1739. 7th edn. 8vo. [xvi],608,[23] pp. Engvd frontis, 13 engvd plates. Mod half calf. *(Wheldon & Wesley)* **£70 [≈ $126]**

Bradshaw, Watson
- The anatomy of dyspepsia ... derangements of the organs of digestion ... hints to tropical invalids ... London: 1864. 8vo. 267 pp. Errata slip, 4 pp advts, engvd frontis. Marg staining. Orig embossed cloth, faded.
(Elgen) **$25 [≈ £13]**

Bragg, Lawrence
- The history of X-ray analysis. London: 1943. 8vo. 25 pp. 4 plates, ills. Orig ptd wraps.
(Weiner) **£20 [≈ $36]**

Bragg, Sir William
- An introduction to crystal analysis. London: Bell, 1928. 1st edn. 8vo. vii,[i],168 pp. 8 plates, 105 text figs. Pub bndg.
(Pollak) **£40 [≈ $72]**

Bragg, William Henry
- Studies in radioactivity. 1912. x,196 pp. 70 figs. Orig cloth, sl waterstained in 1 crnr.
(Whitehart) **£25 [≈ $45]**

Bragg, William Henry & Bragg, William Lawrence

- X-rays and crystal structure. London: Bell, 1915. 1st edn. 8vo. vii,[1],228,[1] pp. 4 plates, text figs. Orig cloth, light edge wear.
(Antiq Sc) **$250 [≃ £138]**
- X-rays and crystal structure. London: Bell, 1916. 2nd edn. 8vo. vii,[i],228,[iv] pp. 4 plates, 75 text figs. Pub bndg.
(Pollak) **£35 [≃ $63]**

Bragg, William Lawrence

- Atomic structure of minerals. Ithaca: 1937. 1st edn. xiii,292 pp. Port frontis, 9 plates, 144 text figs. *(Whitehart)* **£25 [≃ $45]**
- Atomic structure of minerals. Ithaca: 1950. 2nd printing of 1937 edn. 8vo. xiii,[i],292 pp. Frontis, 144 text figs. Pub bndg.
(Pollak) **£20 [≃ $36]**

Braid, James

- Neurypnology; or, the rationale of nervous sleep, considered in relation to animal magnetism. London: John Churchill, 1843. 1st edn. 8vo. xxii,265,[3] pp inc half-title, errata & 2 pp pub advts. Inscrbd & dated by author. Orig cloth, upper hinge reprd.
(Rootenberg) **$2,000 [≃ £1,111]**
- Neurypnology; or, the rationale of nervous sleep, considered in relation to animal magnetism ... New edition, edited by A.E. Waite. London: 1899. 8vo. Orig cloth, sl rubbed, dampmark on spine, stamp on endpaper. *(Robertshaw)* **£25 [≃ $45]**

Braithwaite, R.B.

- Scientific explanation: a study of the function of theory, probability and law in science. Cambridge Univ Press, 1953. 1st edn. 8vo. 376 pp. Orig cloth, spine sl faded.
(Oasis) **$75 [≃ £41]**

Bramble, Charles A.

- The ABC of mining: a handbook for prospectors ... Chicago & New York: Rand, McNally, [1898]. 1st edn. 12mo. 183 pp. Text ills. Lib stamp on endpaper. Orig red cloth, gilt-lettered. *(Heritage)* **$125 [≃ £69]**

Bramwell, Byrom

- Atlas of clinical medicine ... Edinburgh: 1892-96. 1st edn (2nd imp vol I). 3 vols. Folio. viii,184; viii,128; viii,149 pp. 100 h/t & chromolitho plates, w'engvs in text. Orig blue cloth, gilt lettering, gilt tops.
(Pickering) **$550 [≃ £305]**
- Diseases of the spinal chord. Edinburgh: 1884. 2nd edn. 359 pp. Num chromolitho ills. Orig cloth. *(Fye)* **$75 [≃ £41]**

- Studies in clinical medicine. A record of some of the more interesting cases observed ... at the author's out-patient clinic in the Edinburgh Royal Infirmary. Volume first. Edinburgh: 1890. xi,344 pp. 104 ills. Ex lib.
(Whitehart) **£35 [≃ $63]**
- Treatment of the diseases of the heart. Edinburgh: 1895. 24 pp pamphlet. Lacks wraps. *(Goodrich)* **$25 [≃ £13]**

Brande, William Thomas

- A manual of chemistry. 1836. 3 vols. xx,514; 515-868; 869-1317 pp. Errata leaf. Contemp half roan, rebacked. *(Whitehart)* **£85 [≃ $153]**
- A manual of chemistry. London: Murray, 1821. 2nd edn. 8vo. 3 vols. 470; 546; 350,88 index, 8 pub ctlg pp. 3 fldg plates, text ills. Spines split, cvrs detchd.
(Oasis) **$125 [≃ £69]**
- A manual of chemistry. To which are added notes and emendations ... New York: G. Long, 1821. 1st Amer edn. 3 vols in 1. 8vo. viii,638,[2] pp. 3 engvd plates (2 fldg), text w'cuts & tables. Spotty foxing. Contemp tree calf, a bit rubbed. *(Antiq Sc)* **$100 [≃ £55]**

Brande, William Thomas & Cauvin, Joseph

- A dictionary of science, literature and art. New York: 1843. Half lea.
(Allen) **$25 [≃ £13]**

Brannt, William T.

- Petroleum: its history, origin, occurrence ... chemical technology ... occurrence and uses of natural gas ... Phila: 1895. Thick 8vo. xxvii,715 pp. Many ills & diags, few maps. Orig cloth, sl discold on crnrs.
(Weiner) **£60 [≃ $108]**

Braune, Wilhelm

- An atlas of topographical anatomy after plane sections of frozen bodies. Phila: Lindsay & Blakiston, 1877. 1st Amer edn. 4to. xii,200 pp. 34 photo plates, text w'cuts. Orig cloth, worn at edges. *(Antiq Sc)* **$175 [≃ £97]**

Bray, William

- Memoirs illustrative of the life and writings of John Evelyn. London: Colburn, 1818. 2nd edn. 2 vols. 4to. 671; 678 pp. 10 engvd plates (1 double-page), map, fldg table. Rec qtr calf, mrbld bds. *(Oasis)* **$200 [≃ £111]**

Brera, Valerian Lewis

- A treatise on verminous diseases, preceded by the natural history of intestinal worms, and their origin in the human body. Boston: 1817. 8vo. 367 pp. 5 fldg plates. Blank portion of

title cut away, foxed. New cloth.
(Goodrich) **$125 [≈ £69]**

Brett, W.R.
- A short history of some common diseases. By divers authors. London: OUP, 1934. 8vo. xii,211,[i] pp. Pub bndg. *(Pollak)* **£20 [≈ $36]**

Brewster, D.
- A treatise on magnetism. Edinburgh: 1838. [3],363 pp. Fldg map, 106 text figs. Orig blindstamped cloth, dust-stained, spine sl defective at top. *(Whitehart)* **£25 [≈ $45]**

Brewster, David
- Letters on natural magic, addressed to Sir Walter Scott. London: John Murray, 1832. 1st edn. 12mo. xi,351 pp. Num w'engvd ills, a few with overlays. Contemp calf, rebacked. *(Burmester)* **£35 [≈ $63]**
- Letters on natural magic, addressed to Sir Walter Scott. London: 1832. xi,351 pp. Sl foxing on endpapers. Orig cloth, sl marked & dust-stained. *(Whitehart)* **£25 [≈ $45]**

Brewster, Sir David
- The life of Sir Isaac Newton. London: Tegg, 1858. Sm 8vo. xv,384 pp. Engvd port frontis, vignette title, text ills. Contemp polished calf, gilt, some wear to joints.
(Frew Mackenzie) **£35 [≈ $63]**
- The life of Sir Isaac Newton. London: Tegg ..., 1858. 2nd edn. 8vo. xvi,384 pp. Engvd port, w'engvd vignette on title, text ills. Contemp polished calf, gilt, spine rubbed, jnts nicked. *(Pickering)* **$150 [≈ £83]**
- Memoirs of the life, writings, and discoveries of Sir Isaac Newton. Edinburgh & London: 1855. 1st edn. 2 vols. 8vo. xxxii,[ii], 478,[2 blank]; xii,564,[4 advts] pp. W'engvd text ills. Port frontis & title vol I foxed. Gathering S vol I duplicated. Orig cloth.
(Pickering) **$600 [≈ £333]**
- Memoirs of the life, writings, and discoveries of Sir Isaac Newton. London: 1855. 1st edn. 2 vols. 8vo. Frontis, text ills. Contemp calf, hinges reprd. *(Argosy)* **$200 [≈ £111]**
- Memoirs of the life, writings, and discoveries of Sir Isaac Newton. Constable, 1855. 1st edn. 2 vols. 8vo. xxxii,[i],478; xi,564,4 advts pp. Port frontis vol I. Text ills. Uncut in orig cloth. *(Frew Mackenzie)* **£160 [≈ $288]**
- The stereoscope - its history, theory and construction. London: Murray, 1856. 1st edn. Sm 8vo. iv,235,[4 pub advts], 15 ctlg,32 pub ctlg pp. Num text w'cuts. Lacking endpaper, a little worn & chipped. Orig cloth, gilt. *(Antiq Sc)* **$275 [≈ £152]**

Bridge, B.
- A treatise on the elements of algebra. London: 1821. 5th edn. [vii],227 pp. Sl foxing on endpapers & title. Contemp 3/4 lea, sl worn, mrbld bds & endpapers.
(Whitehart) **£28 [≈ $50]**

Bridge, Edward M.
- Epilepsy and compulsive disorders in children. New York: McGraw-Hill, 1949. 1st edn. 8vo. 670 pp. Ills. Orig cloth.
(Oasis) **$35 [≈ £19]**

Brierre de Boismont, Alexandre
- Hallucinations; or, the rational history of apparitions, visions, dreams, ecstasy, magnetism and sonambulism. Phila: 1853. 1st Amer edn. 8vo. xx,553 pp. Lacking front free endpaper. Orig embossed cloth, worn. Ex lib.
(Elgen) **$95 [≈ £52]**

Briggs, Charles F. & Maverick, Augustus
- The story of the telegraph and the history of the Great Atlantic Cable. New York: Rudd & Carleton, 1858. 1st edn. 255 pp, 5 pp advts. Port frontis, num text ills, fldg map. Orig blindstamped cloth. *(Argonaut)* **$125 [≈ £69]**

Briggs, L. Vernon
- Occupation as a substitute for restraint in the treatment of the mentally ill. A history of the passage of two bills through the Massachusetts legislature. Boston: 1923. 8vo. 205 pp. Plates. Author's pres copy.
(Goodrich) **$65 [≈ £36]**

Bright, Dr.
- Clinical memoirs on abdominal tumors and intumescence. London: 1860. 8vo. xviii,326 pp. Orig blindstamped cloth, hd & ft of spine chipped. Ex lib. *(Rittenhouse)* **$70 [≈ £38]**

Bright, Richard
- Original papers of Richard Bright on renal disease. Edited by A.A. Osman. London: 1937. 1st edn thus. 172 pp. Cloth, sl warped.
(Scientia) **$95 [≈ £52]**

Brillat-Savarin, Anthelme
- The handbook of dining or corpulency and leanness scientifically considered. Comprising the art of dining on correct principles consistent with easy digestion ... London: Longman ..., 1864. 2nd English edn. 8vo. Orig cloth.
(Chaucer Head) **£120 [≈ $216]**

Brillat-Savarin, J.A.
- The physiology of taste; or meditations on

transcendental gastronomy. London: Peter Davies, 1925. One of 750. Sm folio. xviii,326 pp. Orig qtr vellum, mrbld bds. Printing error pp xvii & xx with 2 pp transposed.
(Gough) £60 [≃ $108]

Brinkley, John
- Elements of plane astronomy. Dublin: 1836. 8vo. xxiv,287 pp. 6 fldg plates. Old half calf, worn.   *(Weiner)* £25 [≃ $45]

Bristowe, J.S.
- A treatise on the theory and practice of medicine. London: 1876. xxxiii,1166 pp. 10 diags. Sl foxing & pencil anntns in margs. Orig cloth, dust-stained & worn.
(Whitehart) £35 [≃ $63]

Bristowe, John S.
- The physiological and pathological relations of the voice and speech. London: Bogue, 1880. 8vo. viii,[1],147 pp. Orig cloth, rubbed.
(Goodrich) $125 [≃ £69]

British Wines ...
- British wines. Approved receipts and directions for making wines, shrubs, &c. from English fruits, flowers, &c. Lancaster: W. Minshull, 1816. 1st edn. Sm 8vo. viii,39,[1] pp inc half-title. Mod half calf.
(Rootenberg) $350 [≃ £194]

Broadbent, William
- The pulse. London: 1890. 1st edn. 312 pp. 59 sphygmographic tracings. Sgntr on title. Half lea.   *(Scientia)* $175 [≃ £97]

Broadbent, William & John
- Heart disease, with special reference to prognosis and treatment. London: 1897. 1st edn. 331 pp. Pub ctlg. Cloth.
(Scientia) $225 [≃ £125]

Broca, Paul
- On the phenomena of hybridity in the genus homo. London: Longman ..., 1864. 1st edn in English. 8vo. xiv,119,[1] pp. Orig cloth.
(Antiq Sc) $90 [≃ £50]

Brock, Alan St. H.
- A history of fireworks. London: 1949. 8vo. 280 pp. 40 plates (8 cold). Orig cloth.
(Weiner) £45 [≃ $81]
- A history of fireworks. London: Harrap, 1949. 1st edn. 8vo. Cold frontis, cold & b/w plates, text ills. Title sl fingered. Orig cloth, rubbed. Ex lib.   *(Hughes)* £18 [≃ $32]

Brock, Arthur J.
- Greek medicine ... medical writers from Hippocrates to Galen. London: 1929. 255 pp. Cloth, ex lib. *(Goodrich)* $45 [≃ £25]
- Greek medicine being extracts illustrative of medical writers from Hippocrates to Galen. London: Dent, 1929. 8vo. xii,256 pp. Pub bndg, dw.   *(Pollak)* £25 [≃ $45]

Brock, S.
- The basis of clinical neurology. The anatomy and physiology of the nervous system in their application to clinical neurology. Baltimore: 1945. 2nd edn. xiii,393 pp. 72 diags. Cloth, v sl worn.   *(Whitehart)* £18 [≃ $32]

Brockbank, William
- Ancient therapeutic arts. The Fitzpatrick Lectures ... 1950 and 1951. London: Heinemann, 1954. 8vo. 162,[ii] pp. Num ills. Pub bndg, dw.   *(Pollak)* £25 [≃ $45]

Brodie, Sir Benjamin Collins
- Clinical lectures on surgery. Delivered at St. George's Hospital. Phila: 1846. 1st Amer edn. 8vo. 352 pp. Foxed. Orig bds, jnts weak.
(Goodrich) $65 [≃ £36]
- Lectures illustrative of certain local nervous affections. London: for Longman, Rees, [etc], 1837. 1st edn. 8vo. iv,88 pp. Lib stamps on title verso & first leaf of text. Uncut in orig bds, new paper spine.
(Pickering) $350 [≃ £194]
- Lectures on the diseases of the urinary organs. London: Longmans, 1849. 4th edn. 8vo. vii,[i],392 pp. Title dust-soiled. New cloth.   *(Pollak)* £30 [≃ $54]
- The works ... with an autobiography. London: Longmans, Green ..., 1865. 1st edn. 3 vols. 8vo. xxvi,659; vi,680; viii,698,[2 advts] pp. 3 frontis. Sgntrs on titles. Orig purple sand grain cloth, blindstamped, spine faded.   *(Pickering)* $500 [≃ £277]

Brokesby, Francis
- The life of Henry Dodwell; with an account of his works ... to which is added, a letter to Robert Nelson from Dr. Edmund Halley ... London: Geo. James, 1715. 1st edn. 8vo. [xxviii],638 pp. Engvd port. Early 19th c panelled calf.   *(Bennett)* £75 [≃ $135]

Brookes, R.
- An introduction to physic and surgery. Containing I. Medical institutions ... II ... anatomy ... London: Newbury. 1754. 1st edn. 8vo. vii,556 pp. Later qtr calf.
(Goodrich) $150 [≃ £83]

Brookes, Samuel
- An introduction to the study of conchology ... John & Arthur Arch, 1815. 1st edn. Tall 4to. vii,164 pp. 11 plates (9 hand-cold). Contemp calf, rebacked, sides worn, crnrs bumped.
(Frew Mackenzie) **£410 [≈ $738]**

Brooks, Alfred H., et al.
- Reconnaissance of Cape Nome and the adjacent gold fields of Seward Peninsula, Alaska in 1900. Washington: 1901. 222 pp. Lge fldg map, maps, num ills from photos. Ptd wraps, lightly stained.
(Argonaut) **$100 [≈ £55]**

Brotherston, J.H.F.
- Observations on the early public health movement in Scotland. London: 1952. 8vo. xi,119 pp. Port frontis, map, diags. Cloth.
(Elgen) **$35 [≈ £19]**

Brougham, Henry, Lord
- The circle of the sciences, with an introductory discourse ... Edited by James Wylde. London: [1862-67]. 2 vols. 4to. 2 port frontis, 61 plates, num text ills. Contemp half calf, gilt.
(Traylen) **£60 [≈ $108]**

Broughton, Charles
- Memoir respecting a new theory of numbers. Part First [all published]. Edinburgh: for Archibald Constable ..., 1814. 4to. Half-title, tables. Contemp half calf, mrbld bds, rebacked. Author's pres copy to Signet Lib.
(Chaucer Head) **£150 [≈ $270]**

Broussais, Francois J.V.
- History of chronic phlegmasiae, or inflammation, founded on clinical experience and pathological anatomy. Phila: 1831. 2 vols. 497; 403 pp. Scattered foxing. lea, vol 2 binding damp-warped, lacking labels.
(Fye) **$75 [≈ £41]**
- A treatise on physiology applied to pathology. Translated ... Phila: 1826. 1st edn in English. 559 pp. Foxed. Lea, scuffed, hinges cracked.
(Scientia) **$95 [≈ £52]**

Brown, Basil J.W.
- Astronomical atlases, maps and charts. An historical and general guide. London: 1932. 4to. 20 collotype plates. Orig brown vellum, gilt, uncut edges. *(Traylen)* **£60 [≈ $108]**
- Astronomical atlases, maps and charts. An historical and general guide. London: 1932. 1st edn. 4to. Ills. Bds, worn dw.
(Tooley) **£48 [≈ $86]**

Brown, Christopher
- Itinerarium Novi Testamenti: or, the sacred history ... of the New Testament ... added, a supplement describing the universe, the calculation of time ... regulation of the seasons ... London: the author, 1753. 3rd edn. 8vo. Frontis, 9 plates. Contemp roan.
(Chaucer Head) **£35 [≈ $63]**

Brown, E.W.
- The inequalities in the motion of the moon due to the direct action of the planets ... Cambridge: Univ Press, 1908. 1st edn. Lge 8vo. xii,92 pp. Orig cloth.
(Bow Windows) **£45 [≈ $81]**
- An introductory treatise on the lunar theory. Cambridge: Univ Press, 1896. 1st edn. Lge 8vo. xvi,292 pp. Some spotting, endpapers browned. Orig cloth.
(Bow Windows) **£48 [≈ $86]**

Brown, H.T.
- Five hundred and seven mechanical movements ... in dynamics, hydraulics, pneumatics ... horology, and miscellaneous machinery. New York: 1884. 14th edn. Cloth dull & sl worn. *(Whitehart)* **£25 [≈ $45]**

Brown, Isaac B.
- On some diseases of women admitting of surgical treatment. Phila: 1856. 8vo. 276,32 advts pp. 24 text engvs. Cloth.
(Goodrich) **$125 [≈ £69]**

Brown, J.C.
- A history of chemistry from the earliest times to the present day. London: 1913. 8vo. xxix,543 pp. Port frontis (detchd), ills. Orig cloth, sl shaken. *(Weiner)* **£21 [≈ $37]**

Brown, O.P.
- The complete herbalist; or the people their own physicians ... London: 1879. Cr 8vo. 504 pp. Port. Orig cloth, sl used.
(Wheldon & Wesley) **£18 [≈ $32]**

Brown, Richard
- A history of accounting and accounts. Edinburgh: for the Chartered accountants of Scotland, 1905. 1st edn. Lge 8vo. Port frontis, plates. Orig qtr mor, gilt, rubbed.
(Hughes) **£75 [≈ $135]**

Brown, Robert
- The miscellaneous botanical works. London: for the Ray Society, 1866-67-68. 1st edn. 2 vols 8vo, folio plate vol. viii,[2],612; viii,[2],786; 15 pp. 38 engvd plates, 11 fldg. A bit worn & chipped. Text vols, orig cloth;

plate vol, orig cloth & bds. Ex lib.
(Antiq Sc) **$450 [≃ £250]**

Brown, Samuel
- Lectures on the atomic theory and essays scientific and literary. London: 1858. 2 vols. 8vo. x,357; 384 pp. Orig cloth.
(Weiner) **£40 [≃ $72]**

Browne, J. Ross & Taylor, James W.
- Reports upon the mineral resources of the United States. Washington: GPO, 1867. 1st edn. 360 pp. Orig cloth, gilt-lettered spine.
(Argonaut) **$90 [≃ £50]**
- Reports upon the mineral resources of the United States. Washington: 1867. 8vo. 360 pp. Orig cloth.
(Wheldon & Wesley) **£36 [≃ $64]**

Browne, John
- Myographia nova: or, a graphical description of all the muscles in the humane body ... London: 1697. 3rd edn. 4to. [xl],109 pp. Engvd port frontis, 40 engvd plates (tear in 1 without loss). 17th c b'plate. Sl browning. Contemp calf, rebacked. Wing B5128.
(Pickering) **$850 [≃ £472]**

Browne, Lennox
- The nose and throat and their diseases. Phila: 1893. 4th edn. 8vo. xx,734 pp. 120 cold ills, 235 engvs. Orig cloth.
(Rittenhouse) **$37.50 [≃ £20]**
- The throat and other diseases, including associated affections of the nose and ear. 1887. 2nd edn. xvi,614 pp. 15 plates, 200 ills. Light foxing on prelims, ink inscrptn facing title. Orig cloth, dust-stained, spine faded.
(Whitehart) **£25 [≃ $45]**

Browne, Montague
- Artistic and scientific taxidermy and modelling. A. & C. Black, 1896. 1st edn. 8vo. xii,463 pp. 22 b/w plates, 11 diags. Foxed at fore-edges. Orig buckram, faded.
(Gough) **£75 [≃ $135]**

Browne, O'Donel T.D.
- The Rotunda Hospital 1745-1945. Edinburgh: Livingstone, 1947. 8vo. xx,296 pp. Frontis, 43 plates, graph. Pub bndg, torn dw.
(Pollak) **£30 [≃ $54]**

Browne, Sir Thomas
- Certain miscellany tracts ... London: Mearne ..., 1684. 1st edn, 2nd iss. x,215,6 pp. Engvd port. Contemp calf, rebacked.
(Goodrich) **$295 [≃ £163]**
- Hydriotaphia: Urn-buriall, or a discourse of

the sepulchrall urnes lately found in Norfolk. London: for Hen. Brome ..., 1658. 1st edn. 4to. 4ff, 73 pp. 2 engvd plates. [Bound with, in mod cloth] Pseudodoxia Epidemica. London: 1658. 4th edn. 2nd work lacking title.
(Argosy) **$750 [≃ £416]**
- Pseudodoxia epidemica: or, enquiries into very many received tenets ... Urn-Burial ... Garden of Cyrus ... London: E. Dod, 1658. 4to. [xvi],468 (440), [xvi],[xii],73,[iii] pp. 3 engvs, longitudinal title. Contemp calf, backstrip worn, jnt cracked. Wing B5762.
(Clark) **£160 [≃ $288]**
- Religio medici ... with annotations never before published ... London: for Andrew Crook, 1656. 4th edn. Cr 8vo. Engvd frontis (crnr torn), 4 pp advts. B6 reprd, marg wormhole, old names on title. Contemp calf, crnrs worn, rebacked. *(Stewart)* **£60 [≃ $108]**
- The works. London: Bassett ..., 1686. 1st collected edn. Folio. Engvd port. Contemp calf, rebacked. *(Goodrich)* **$295 [≃ £163]**
- The works. London: Pickering ..., 1836. 4 vols. 8vo. Engvd plates. later half mor, jnts weak. *(Goodrich)* **$195 [≃ £108]**
- The works ... edited by Simon Wilkin. London: Bohn, 1852. 3 vols. 8vo. Contemp half calf, mrbld bds, ft of spine of Vol I reprd.
(Pollak) **£125 [≃ $225]**
- The works ... edited by Charles Sayle. London & Edinburgh: 1904-07. 3 vols. 8vo. Orig paper bds, buckram spines, t.e.g., uncut, new labels. *(Pollak)* **£75 [≃ $135]**
- The works. Edited by Charles Sayle. Edinburgh: 1927. 3 vols. 8vo. Port, frontis, 2 plates. Orig cloth-backed bds, dws.
(Elgen) **$95 [≃ £52]**
- The works ... edited by Geoffrey Keynes. London: Faber & Gwyer, 1928-31. 6 vols. 8vo. Orig blue cloth, spines sunned, uncut.
(Goodrich) **$145 [≃ £80]**
- The works ... edited by Geoffrey Keynes. London: 1928-31. 6 vols. One of 210, sgnd by Keynes. Vellum. *(Fye)* **$400 [≃ £222]**

Brownell, L.W.
- Photography for the sportsman naturalist. New York: Macmillan, 1904. 1st edn. One of 100 lge paper. 84 photo ills. 3/4 blue mor, raised bands, gilt ruled panels, inlaid designs, uncut. *(Argonaut)* **$225 [≃ £125]**

Browning, William
- Medical heredity: distinguished children of physicians ... Baltimore: 1925. 1st edn. 8vo. 250 pp. Cloth, sl worn. *(Elgen)* **$40 [≃ £22]**

Brownlow, John
- The history and design of the Foundling

Hospital, with a memoir of its founder. London: Warr, 1858. 8vo. [iv],144 pp. Frontis, 2 plates. Orig cloth, gilt, front jnt weak.   *(Pollak)* £55 [≈ $99]

Bruff, P.
- A treatise on engineering field work, comprising the practice of surveying, levelling ... connected with engineering ... Levelling. Simpkin, Marshall, 1842. 1st edn. 128 pp. 4 fldg plates, figs & tables. Orig blindstamped cloth. Single vol of larger work.
                    (Hinchliffe) £25 [≈ $45]

Brunton, T. Lauder
- Lectures on the actions of medicines. New York: 1899. 1st Amer edn. 673 pp. Orig cloth.   *(Fye)* $75 [≈ £41]

Brunton, T.L.
- Text-book of pharmacology, therapeutics and materia medica. London: 1887. 3rd edn. Thick 8vo. Cloth, spine damaged with damp.
                    (Rittenhouse) $27.50 [≈ £15]

Bryant, Joseph D.
- Manual of operative surgery. New York: Appleton, 1890. 2nd edn. 8vo. 530 pp. 800 text ills. Pub ctlg dated May, 1893. Orig binding, sl worn.   *(Oasis)* $50 [≈ £27]

Bryant, W.W.
- A history of astronomy. London: 1907. 8vo. 355 pp. Fldg frontis, many plates. Orig cloth.   *(Weiner)* £20 [≈ $36]

Buchan, William
- Domestic medicine; or, the family physician ... Edinburgh: Balfour ..., 1769. 1st edn. 8vo. xv,[i],624 pp. Occas foxing, 1 leaf lacking portion of lower marg, marg tear reprd, some tips creased. Contemp calf, rebacked, crnrs worn.   *(Pollak)* £250 [≈ $450]
- Domestic medicine; or, the family physician: being an attempt to render the medical art more generally useful ... Edinburgh: Balfour ..., 1769. 1st edn. 8vo. 624 pp. Some thumbing. Contemp calf, rebacked.
                    (Goodrich) $750 [≈ £416]
- Domestic medicine ... The ninth edition: to which is now added, an additional chapter on cold bathing ... London: for A. Strahan ..., 1786. 8vo. Contemp speckled calf, jnts cracked but sound.   *(Sotheran)* £78 [≈ $140]
- Domestic medicine ... London: 1792. 13th edn. Light foxing. Contemp calf, rebacked with simulated lea spine.
                    (Goodrich) $115 [≈ £63]
- Domestic medicine; or, a treatise ... with

observations concerning sea-bathing, and the use of mineral waters ... London: Cadell, 1807. 20th edn. Calf, rebacked, in slipcase.
                    (Goodrich) $125 [≈ £69]
- Domestic medicine ... Exeter: 1839. 22nd edn. Some darkening. Contemp lea, much marked.   *(Rittenhouse)* $45 [≈ £25]
- Observations concerning the prevention and cure of the venereal disease ... to which is added a supplement ... A pharmacopeoia syphilitica ... London: Cadell, 1803. 3rd edn. xvi-300,civ pp. Qtr calf, rebacked.
                    (Goodrich) $95 [≈ £52]
- A treatise on sea bathing with some remarks on the use of the warm bath. London: Cadel & Davies, 1810. 2nd edn. 8vo. xxxvi,292 pp. Light foxing. Orig bds, worn, uncut.
                    (Goodrich) $85 [≈ £47]

Buchanan, Joseph
- Outlines of lectures on the neurological system of anthropology ... Cincinnati: 1854. 8vo. 384 pp. New bds.
                    (Goodrich) $95 [≈ £52]

Buchius, Paulus
- The Divine Being and its attributes philosophically demonstrated from the Holy Scriptures and original nature of things ... London: Randal Taylor, 1693. With a1 (blank). 18th c panelled calf. Wing B5299.
                    (Waterfield's) £200 [≈ $360]

Buchoz, Pierre Joseph
- The toilet of flora; or a collection of the most simple methods of preparing baths, essences ... perfumes ... cosmetics of every kind ... take off the appearance of old age and decay. London: Nicoll, 1772. 8vo. [16],272 pp. Contemp calf, hd of spine chipped.
                    (Spelman) £300 [≈ $540]
- The toilet of flora; or a collection of the most simple methods of preparing baths, essences ... perfumes ... cosmetics of every kind ... London: for J. Murray, 1779. New edn, imprvd. [xii],342 pp. Frontis. Orig sheep, crnr worn, upper hinge cracked.
                    (Claude Cox) £120 [≈ $216]

Buck, Albert (ed.)
- A reference handbook of the medical sciences ... topics belonging to the entire range of scientific and practical medicine. New York: 1885. 1st edn. 8 vols. Thousands of w'cuts, many cold plates. Lea.   *(Fye)* $200 [≈ £111]

Buck, Albert H.
- Diagnosis and treatment of ear diseases. New York: Wood's Library, 1880. 1st edn. 8vo.

411 pp. 1 leaf torn without loss. Orig cloth.
(Oasis) **$45 [≈ £25]**

Buckland, William

- Geology and mineralogy, considered with reference to natural theology. London: Pickering, 1837. 2nd edn. 2 vols. 8vo. 86 plates (3 double-page, 5 fldg inc 1 cold). Contemp calf, rebacked, orig mor labels, gilt.
(Traylen) **£50 [≈ $90]**
- Geology and mineralogy, considered with reference to natural theology. 1836. 1st edn. 2 vols. 8vo. xvi,600; vii,128 pp. 87 engvd plates (1 fldg & hand-cold, some fldg, some double-page, a very few foxed). Diced calf, backstrips gilt.   *(Edwards)* **£110 [≈ $198]**
- Geology and mineralogy, considered with reference to natural theology. London: 1836. 2 vols. 8vo. 87 engvd or litho plates (sev double-page or fldg, 1 extending & hand-cold). Some foxing, sgntr & date on flyleaves. Contemp half calf by Winstanley, sl rubbed.
(Bow Windows) **£125 [≈ $225]**
- Reliquiae diluvianae; or, observations on the organic remains contained in caves, fissures and diluvial gravel ... London: 1823. 1st edn. 4to. viii,303 pp. Fldg table, 27 plates & maps (3 cold). Contemp russia, gilt, rebacked.
(Wheldon & Wesley) **£220 [≈ $396]**

Buckler, Helen

- Doctor Dan [D.H. Williams], pioneer in American surgery. Boston: [1954]. 1st edn, 2nd ptg. 8vo. xiv,381 pp. Port frontis, ills. Cloth, dw. Author's pres copy.
(Elgen) **$40 [≈ £22]**

Bucknill, Sir John C. & Tuke, Daniel Hack

- A manual of psychological medicine. London: John Churchill ..., 1858. 1st edn. 8vo. [iv],viii,562 & [2],32 advts pp. Litho frontis. Orig ribbed cloth.
(Pickering) **$1,000 [≈ £555]**

Budd, George

- On diseases of the liver. Phila: Blanchard & Lea, 1857. 3rd Amer edn. 8vo. 499 pp, 32 pp pub ctlg. 4 litho plates. A little foxed. Orig cloth, a little worn.   *(Oasis)* **$45 [≈ £25]**

Budd, William

- Typhoid fever; its nature, mode of spreading and prevention. New York: 1931. One of 800. 184 pp. Boxed.   *(Scientia)* **$75 [≈ £41]**

Budge, Sir Ernest Alfred Wallis

- The divine craft of the herbalist. London: Soc of Herbalists, 1928. 8vo. ix,[i],96 pp. 13 plates. Orig cloth, faded, dw.
(Pollak) **£30 [≈ $54]**

Buhl, Ludwig

- Inflammation of the lungs; tubercolosis and consumption. Translated ... New York: 1874. 1st edn in English. 161 pp. Cloth, top & bottom of spine frayed, crnrs of cvrs torn.
(Scientia) **$85 [≈ £47]**

Bulkley, L.D.

- Syphilis in the innocent Clinically and historically considered with a plan for the legal control of the disease. New York: 1894. xvi,398 pp. Orig cloth, sl worn.
(Whitehart) **£25 [≈ $45]**

Bullar, Joseph & Henry

- A winter in the Azores; and a summer at the baths of the Furnas. 1841. 2 vols. 8vo. xiv,375; ix,391,2 advts pp. 2 hand-cold frontis, text ills. Half calf, mrbld bds, rebacked.   *(Edwards)* **£120 [≈ $216]**
- A winter in the Azores; and a summer at the baths of the Furnas. London: 1841. 1st edn. 2 vols. 8vo. Cold plates, text ills. Cloth-backed mrbld bds. *(Halewood)* **£100 [≈ $180]**

Bulloch, William

- The history of bacteriology. London: OUP, 1938. 8vo. xii,422,[ii] pp. 16 plates, 36 ills. Pub bndg.   *(Pollak)* **£35 [≈ $63]**
- The history of bacteriology. London: 1938. 8vo. xiii,422 pp. Plates. Orig cloth.
(Weiner) **£30 [≈ $54]**

Burbank, Luther

- Luther Burbank, his methods and discoveries and their practical application. New York: 1914. 12 vols. Over 1200 mtd col photo prints. Full green levant, backs uniformly faded, gilt panelled backs & sides, t.e.g.
(Elgen) **$375 [≈ £208]**

Burbank, W.H.

- The development of gelatine dry plates. Brunswick, Maine: Burbank, 1890. 1st edn. 8vo. 93 pp. Text figs. Orig cloth.
(Antiq Sc) **$95 [≈ £52]**

Burke, Richard M.

- A historical chronology of tubercolosis. Springfield: [1938]. 1st edn. 8vo. viii,84 pp. V lge fldg chart. Cloth, dw. *(Elgen)* **$35 [≈ £19]**

Burket, Walter C.

- Bibliography of William Henry Welch. Baltimore: 1917. Lge 8vo. 47 pp. 335 items. Port. Lib stamp on endpaper. Orig cloth.
(Weiner) **£30 [≈ $54]**

Burks, James W.
- Wire brush surgery in the treatment of certain cosmetic defects and diseases of the skin. Springfield: [1956]. 8vo. xvi,154 pp. Ills. Cloth. Ex lib.   *(Elgen)* **$25 [≈ £13]**

Burnell, G.R.
- Letter to ... Viscount Palmerston ... in reply to the report of the ... Board of Health on the Nuisances Removal and Diseases Prevention Act. From 1848 to 1854. 15 pp. Disbound.
          (C.R. Johnson) **£25 [≈ $45]**

Burness, Alexander G. & Mavor, F.J.
- The specific action of drugs on the healthy system. London: Bailliere ..., 1874. 8vo. x,184,28 ctlg pp. Lib bndg, spine faded, ends & crnrs worn.   *(Pollak)* **£15 [≈ $27]**

Burnet, T.
- The theory of the earth ... A review of the theory of the earth. London: Norton, 1684-90. 1st edns. 2 vols. Folio. 2 engvd frontis, 12 engvs, 3 plates (2 fldg), advt leaf. Minor repr to vol 2 title, a few sm lib stamps. Contemp calf, spines gilt. Wing B5950/1.
          (P & P) **£195 [≈ $351]**

Burnet, Thomas
- The sacred theory of the earth ... with copious notes on the wonders of nature ... from the writings of the most learned divines. London: [1826]. 4to. 716 pp. Extra engvd title, frontis, plates. Light foxing, crnr of a few leaves stained. Old calf, crnrs worn.
          (Weiner) **£50 [≈ $90]**

Burns, John
- Observations on an abortion containing an account of the manner in which it takes place, the causes which produce it ... Springfield: Isaiah Thomas, jun, 1809. 2nd Amer edn. 12mo. 138 pp. Foxed. Contemp calf.
          (Goodrich) **$75 [≈ £41]**

Burrage, Walter
- A history of the Massachusetts Medical Society. Boston: 1923. 8vo. 505 pp. Cloth.
          (Goodrich) **$35 [≈ £19]**
- A history of the Massachusetts Medical Society ... 1781-1922. Norwood: privately printed, 1923. 8vo. 505 pp. 42 plates. Orig cloth.   *(Oasis)* **$35 [≈ £19]**

Burrows, George
- On disorders of the cerebral circulation ... London: for Longman, Brown ..., 1846. 1st edn. 8vo. xvi,220,16 advts pp. 6 hand-cold litho plates. Orig cloth, a little worn, hd of spine torn.   *(Pickering)* **$450 [≈ £250]**

- On disorders of the cerebral circulation and on the connection between the affections of the brain and diseases of the heart. Phila: 1848. 1st Amer edn. 214 pp. 6 hand-cold plates. Some smudging. Orig cloth.
          (Scientia) **$300 [≈ £166]**

Burt, John G.M.
- Illustrations of surgical anatomy, with explanatory references. Glasgow: Blackie, [1833]. 2nd edn. 4to. Engvd title, ptd dedn leaf, preface leaf, 16 engvd plates (lightly spotted) each with facing page of letterpress. Orig half calf, mrbld bds, rubbed.
          (Bickersteth) **£80 [≈ $144]**

Burton, Robert
- The anatomy of melancholy ... in three partitions. New York: 1889. 3 vols. 500; 467; 514 pp. Cloth, t.e.g.
          (Rittenhouse) **$75 [≈ £41]**
- The anatomy of melancholy ... To which is now first prefixed, an account of the author. London: for Vernor, Hood ..., 1800. 9th edn crrctd. 2 vols. 8vo. 2 engvd frontis. Contemp polished calf, hinges cracked.
          (Chaucer Head) **£80 [≈ $144]**
- The anatomy of melancholy ... London: Henry Cripps. 1662. 7th edn. Sm folio. Argument leaf & engvd allegorical title. Foxing. Contemp calf, rubbed.
          (Goodrich) **$450 [≈ £250]**
- The anatomy of melancholy. London: 1827. 13th edn crrctd. 8vo. 2 vols. 606;612 pp. Frontis. Orig cloth-backed bds, sl worn, partly unopened.   *(Oasis)* **$150 [≈ £83]**
- The anatomy of melancholy. Oxford: for Henry Cripps, 1624. 1st folio edn. Sm folio. [iv],64,[iv], 189-332, [ii],333-557, [vii] pp. Paper fault on 1 leaf, pen markings on prelims & some margs. Later calf, mrbld sides, rebacked. STC 4160.
          (Frew Mackenzie) **£600 [≈ $1,080]**
- The anatomy of melancholy. What it is, with all the kinds, causes ... and several cures of it. Oxford printed: for Henry Cripps. 1632. 4th edn. Sm folio. Prelim leaf mtd, engvd title frayed, lacking final index leaf. Calf, rebacked.   *(Goodrich)* **$195 [≈ £108]**

Butler, William
- Exercises on the globes ... designed for the use of young ladies. 1800. 2nd edn. 8vo. 200 pp. Contemp sheepskin, worn.
          (Old Cinema) **£15 [≈ $27]**

Butschli, O.
- Investigations on microscopic forms and on protoplasm ... directed towards a solution of

the question of ... the phenomena of life. London: 1894. xvi,379 pp. 12 plates, diags. Orig cloth, faded & shaken.

(Weiner) **£40 [≃ $72]**

Buxton, Thomas Fowell
- An inquiry whether crime and misery are produced or prevented by our present system of prison discipline. Edinburgh: Constable, 1818. Sm 8vo. Orig ptd wraps, worn.

(Marlborough) **£65 [≃ $117]**

Byers, Horace
- The thunderstorm. Washington, DC: GPO, 1947. 1st edn. 4to. 287 pp. Charts, photos.

(Xerxes) **$35 [≃ £19]**

Byrne, John O.
- Compendium of Irish sanitary law, ... relating to workshops, common lodging houses, bakehouses, and the adulteration of food and drink ... Dublin: William McGee, 1870. 1st edn. Cr 8vo. x,[1],277 pp. Orig cloth, gilt.

(Fenning) **£14.50 [≃ $25]**

Byrne, Oliver
- The first six books of the elements of Euclid in which coloured diagrams and symbols are used instead of letters ... London: Pickering, 1847. 1st edn. 4to. xxix,268 pp. Half-title. Illust throughout in 3 colours & black. Insignificant browning. Orig cloth.

(Rootenberg) **$1,850 [≃ £1,027]**
- The first six books of the elements of Euclid in which coloured diagrams and symbols are used ... London: Pickering, 1847. 1st edn. Sm 4to. xxix,268 pp. Lacking half-title. Diags throughout in 3 colours & black. Some foxing. Later half parchment.

(Frew Mackenzie) **£825 [≃ $1,485]**

Badcock, William
- A touch-stone for gold and silver wares; or, a manual for goldsmiths, and all other persons ... London: for Bellinger & Bassett, 1677. 1st edn. Sm 8vo. 26,115,[11] pp. Engvd frontis, engvd plate. Prev owner's sgntr. Contemp calf, spine reprd. Wing B382.

(Rootenberg) **$850 [≃ £472]**

Cabanes, Dr.
- Curious bypaths of history being medico-historical studies and observations. Paris: Charles Carrington, 1898. One of 500. 8vo. Engvd frontis, red & black title. Orig black cloth, gilt, rubbed, edges chafed.

(Hughes) **£24 [≃ $43]**

Cabot, Richard
- Differential diagnosis presented through an

analysis of 363 cases. Phila: 1911. 1st edn, 2nd ptg. 8vo. 753,16 pub ctlg pp. Ills, plates. Cloth.

(Elgen) **$45 [≃ £25]**
- Differential diagnosis presented through an analysis of 363 cases. Phila: 1911. 1st edn. 753 pp. Orig cloth.

(Fye) **$50 [≃ £27]**
- Differential diagnosis. Phila: 1920. 2nd edn, revsd. 8vo. 709 pp. Num ills. Cloth.

(Elgen) **$35 [≃ £19]**

Cadogan, William
- A dissertation on the gout, and all chronic diseases ... addressed to all invalids. London: Dodsley, 1771. 7th edn. 8vo. 100 pp. Half-title. Contemp calf-backed mrbld bds, some worming to hd of spine, extndg to last gathering, extremities rubbed.

(Frew Mackenzie) **£130 [≃ $234]**

Calculations ...
- Calculations deduced from first principles ... See Dale, W.

Calderwood, Henry
- The relations of mind and brain ... London: Macmillan, 1879. 1st edn. 8vo. xvi,456 pp. W'engvd text ills. Univ of Edinburgh prize copy in polished calf, jnts reprd, prize label sgnd by author. *(Pickering)* **$100 [≃ £55]**

Calkins, Marshall
- Thoracic diseases: their pathology, diagnosis, and treatment. Phila: 1858. 8vo. xxiv,546 pp. Blindstamped cloth, sl worn.

(Rittenhouse) **$27.50 [≃ £15]**

Calmet, Augustine
- The phantom world: or, the philosophy of spirits, apparitions, &c. London: R. Bentley, 1850. 1st English edn (?). 2 vols. 12mo. xxxii,378; vi,362 pp. 19th c half calf, mrbld bds, rubbed. *(Karmiole)* **$65 [≃ £36]**

Calonne, Charles Alexandre de
- Museum Calonnianum. Specification of the various articles of natural history collected by M. de Calonne. London: George Humphrey, 1797. 8vo. 84 pp. 1,439 lots. Added engvd port. Old wraps, dusty.

(Marlborough) **£250 [≃ $450]**

Calvert, John
- The gold rocks of Great Britain and Ireland, and a general outline of the gold regions of the world, with a treatise on the geology of gold. 1853. 8vo. Orig cloth, a little soiled. Author's pres inscrptn. *(Farahar)* **£100 [≃ $180]**

Calwell, William, et al.
- A textbook of treatment. London: Appleton, 1908. 1st edn. 8vo. Cloth.
(Emerald Isle) £20 [≃ $36]

Camac, C.N.B.
- Counsels and ideals from the writings of William Osler. Oxford: 1906. 2nd imp. 8vo. 276 pp. Orig gilt cloth, uncut.
(Goodrich) $45 [≃ £25]
- Counsels and ideals from the writings of William Osler. Oxford: Frowde, 1905. 1st edn. 8vo. Orig gilt cloth.
(Oasis) $100 [≃ £55]

Cameron, Alexander M.
- Light as the interpretation of the law of gravity. Sydney: Angus & Robertson, 1895. vi,54; 6 pp. Orig blue cloth.
(Karmiole) $50 [≃ £27]

Cameron, Sir Charles A.
- History of the Royal College of Surgeons in Ireland, and of the Irish Schools of Medicine. Dublin: 1886. 8vo. 757 pp. Half calf, gilt, a.e.g.
(Goodrich) $75 [≃ £41]

Cammidge, P.J. & Howard, H.A.H.
- New views on diabetes mellitus. London: 1923. 8vo. Cold frontis, 189 diags. Half mor, rebacked, orig spine laid down, gilt. Pres copy, sgnd by Cammidge on half-title.
(Traylen) £60 [≃ $108]

Campbell, D.
- Arabian medicine and its influence on the Middle Ages. London: 1926. 2 vols. 8vo. Orig cloth, dws.
(Goodrich) $135 [≃ £75]

Campbell, J. Menzies
- A dental bibliography. British and American 1682-1880. London: 1949. 63 pp. Slipcase
(Goodrich) $60 [≃ £33]

Camper, Petrus
- The works ... connexion between ... anatomy and the arts of drawing, painting ... London: Dilly, 1794. 1st English edn. 4to. xxiii,[i errata], 175,[i] pp. Port frontis, 17 fldg plates (foxed), 7 outline plates. Dampstained. Later half calf, spine worn at ends.
(Pollak) £400 [≃ $720]

Canavan, Myrtelle
- Elmer Ernest Southard and his parents. A brain study. Cambridge: 1925. Lge 4to. 29 pp. 6 plates. Ex lib. Stanley Cobb's copy with his sgntr.
(Goodrich) $75 [≃ £41]

Candler, C.
- The prevention of consumption. London: 1887. 8vo. 240 pp. Pub ctlg. Orig cloth, spine defective, crnrs worn. Ex lib.
(Rittenhouse) $85 [≃ £47]

Canine Madness ...
- Report from the Committee on the Bill to prevent the spreading of canine madness. London: 1830. Folio. 34 pp. Disbound.
(Weiner) £60 [≃ $108]

Cannon, Walter B.
- The mechanical factors of digestion. London: 1911. 1st edn. 227 pp.
(Scientia) $175 [≃ £97]

Canton, Edwin
- On the arcus senilis, or, fatty generation of the cornea. London: 1863. 8vo. 228 pp. Sgntr on title, some pages carelessly opened. Orig cloth, hinges weak. Ex lib.
(Rittenhouse) $25 [≃ £13]

Carey, George C.
- Chemistry as it is, compared with what it was ... the present state of chemistry, with its application to the mechanical arts. London: William Coe, 1825. 1st edn. 8vo. [2],340, [6],104 pp. Engvd frontis (dampstained in margs), browning. Orig bds, rebacked.
(Antiq Sc) $200 [≃ £111]

Carey, Mathew
- A short account of the malignant fever, lately prevalent in Philadelphia ... to which are added accounts of the plague in London and Marseilles ... Phila: for the author, 1794. 8vo. 4th edn. Wraps. *(Farahar)* £225 [≃ $405]

Carlson, Anton
- The control of hunger in health and disease. Chicago: 1916. 1st edn. 319 pp. Stamp on title. Cloth. *(Scientia)* $75 [≃ £41]

Carmoly, E.
- History of the Jewish physicians ... See Dunbar, John

Carpenter, William B.
- The microscope and its revelations. 1868. 4th edn. xxviii,796 pp. 25 plates, 412 text ills. Scattered foxing. 3/4 lea, rather rubbed, inner hinges cracked. Ex lib.
(Whitehart) £25 [≃ $45]
- The microscope and its revelations. New York: Wood's Library, 1883. 6th edn. 8vo. 388; 354 pp. 26 plates, 500 text ills. Orig cloth, front cvr vol II soiled affecting spine.

(Oasis) **$45 [≈ £25]**
- The microscope and its revelations. London: 1891. 7th edn. 1099 pp. Pub ctlg dated 1895. Cloth, inner hinges cracked.
(Scientia) **$125 [≈ £69]**
- The microscope and its revelations. London: 1901. 8th edn. 2 vols in 1. 8vo. 22 plates (8 cold). A little minor foxing. Orig cloth, trifle used.   *(Wheldon & Wesley)* **£50 [≈ $90]**
- Nature and man. Essays scientific and philosophical. London: Kagan Paul, 1888. vi,483 pp. Frontis. Pub bndg.
(Pollak) **£40 [≈ $72]**
- Principles of comparative physiology. London: 1855. 5th edn. Thick 8vo. xxiv,960 pp. 3 plates, ills. Ex lib, sl wear.
(Weiner) **£35 [≈ $63]**
- Principles of human physiology, with their chief applications to psychology, pathology, therapeutics, hygiene and forensic medicine. Phila: 1866. Lge 8vo. 902 pp. 261 text w'cuts. Sheep, rubbed & scuffed. *(Elgen)* **$45 [≈ £25]**

Carpue, Joseph Constantine
- An introduction to electricity and galvanism; with cases, shewing their effects in the cure of diseases ... London: A. Phillips, 1803. 1st edn. 8vo. viii,112 pp. 3 fldg plates. Sgntr on front blank, prelims & last leaves foxed. Contemp calf-backed mrbld bds.
(Rootenberg) **$950 [≈ £527]**

Carribber (pseud.)
- See Gibb, Sir Donald

Carrington, Charles
- Untrodden fields of anthropology ... being a record by a French Army Surgeon of thirty years' experience in Asia, Africa, America and Oceania. Paris: Charles Carrington, 1898. 2nd English edn. 2 vols. Roy 8vo. Cold pict title, 23 plates. Orig half vell.
(Chaucer Head) **£160 [≈ $288]**

Carus, Paul
- The soul of man. An investigation into the facts of physiological and experimental psychology. Chicago: Open Court, 1900. 2nd ed,. 8vo. xviii,482,[iv] ctlg pp. Frontis, 182 ills. Orig cloth, gilt.   *(Pollak)* **£20 [≈ $36]**

Case, Robert Hope
- A theory of the universe. New York: Wynkoop, 1868. Tall 8vo. 91 pp. Orig green cloth, gilt-stamped spine.
(Karmiole) **$125 [≈ £69]**

Casper, J.L.
- A handbook of the practice of forensic

medicine. London: New Sydenham Soc, 1861-65. 4 vols. 8vo. Cloth.
(Goodrich) **$195 [≈ £108]**

Castellani, A. & Chalmers, A.J.
- Manual of tropical medicine. 1919. 3rd edn. x,2436 pp. 909 ills. Cloth.
(Whitehart) **£25 [≈ $45]**

Caswell, Alexis
- Smithsonian contributions to knowledge. meteorological observations made at Providence R.I. Washington: 1860. 4to. Mod cloth-backed bds, orig wraps bound in. Author's pres copy.   *(Argosy)* **$125 [≈ £69]**

Catalogue ...
- A catalogue of the collection of mammalia and birds in the Museum of the Army Medical Department, at Fort Pitt, Chatham. Chatham: for James Burrill, 1838. 1st edn. 8vo. x,48 pp. Disbound.
(Burmester) **£35 [≈ $63]**

Catalogues
- For catalogues of equipment, instruments, &c., See Trade catalogue ...

Catechism of Mineralogy ...
- A catechism of mineralogy ... See Pinnock, Wm.

Cathell, D.W.
- Book on the physician himself and things that concern his reputation and success. Phila: 1890. 9th edn. 8vo. 298 pp. Pub ctlg. Cloth.
(Rittenhouse) **$37.50 [≈ £20]**

Catlin, George
- The breath of life or mal-respiration and its effects upon the enjoyment of man. London: Trubner, 1862. 2nd edn. 75,[vii blank] pp. 25 text ills. Orig pts paper bds, recased, new cloth spine & endpapers. *(Pollak)* **£50 [≈ $90]**

Cavendish, Henry
- The electrical researches ... written between 1771 and 1781., edited ... Cambridge: University Press, 1879. 1st edn. Lge 8vo. lxvi,454,32 pub advts pp. Prelims lightly foxed. Orig cloth. Univ of Camb pres b'plate to the Bishop of Sydney.
(Rootenberg) **$450 [≈ £250]**
- The electrical researches of the Honourable Henry Cavendish, F.R.S. Written between 1771 and 1781. Edited ... by J. Clerk Maxwell. Cambridge: Univ Press, 1879. 1st edn. 8vo. 3 plates. Orig plum cloth, lettered in gilt.   *(Chaucer Head)* **£180 [≈ $324]**

Cayley, Arthur
- An elementary treatise on elliptic functions. London: Bell, 1895. 2nd edn. 8vo. xii,[ii],386 pp. Orig cloth.   *(Pollak)* **£20 [≈ $36]**

Cazeau, Paulin
- A theoretical and practical treatise on midwifery. ... diseases of pregnancy and parturition. Phila: 1877. 6th Amer edn. Lge 8vo. 1124 pp, 40 pub ctlg pp. 175 w'cuts. Sheep, black lea spine label.
          (Elgen) **$55 [≈ £30]**

Celebrated Receipts ...
- Celebrated receipts, or the arts of life; being the universal instructor and economist. Adapted to merchants, householders, servants, and others. London: Henry Beesley, 1844. 1st edn. 12mo. 48 pp. Outer leaves a bit soiled & frayed, crnrs dog-eared. Rec cloth.
          (Burmester) **£38 [≈ $68]**

Century of Progress ...
- The official pictures of a century of progress. Exposition Chicago, 1933. Chicago: Donnelly, 1933. Folio. 10,[148 plates] pp. Over 350 photos. Blue cloth, stamped in silver, in chipped slipcase.
          (Karmiole) **$60 [≈ £33]**

Chadwick, Edwin
- Report ... into the sanitary conditions of the labouring population ... [with] A supplementary report ... into the practice of interment in towns. London: HMSO, 1842-43. 1st edn. 2 vols. 8vo. 21 plates, 2 fldg cold maps. Orig cloth, gilt, spines faded.
          (Traylen) **£750 [≈ $1,350]**

Chadwick, J.
- Radioactivity and radioactive substances. An introduction to the study ... London: Pitman, 1921. 1st edn. 8vo. xii,111,[i], [viii ctlg] pp. 30 text figs. Orig dec cloth.
          (Pollak) **£75 [≈ $135]**
- Radioactivity and radioactive substances. An introduction to the study ... London: Pitman, 1923. 2nd edn. 8vo. xii,111,[i], [xii ctlg] pp. 32 figs. A few marg notes. Orig cloth.
          (Pollak) **£25 [≈ $45]**

Chalmers, Thomas
- On the power, wisdom and goodness of God as manifested in the adaptation of external nature to the moral and intellectual constitution of man. London: Pickering, 1834. 3rd edn. 2 vols. 8vo. Orig cloth, lightly spotted.   *(Cooper Hay)* **£30 [≈ $54]**
- On the power, wisdom and goodness of God as manifested in the adaptation of external nature to the moral and intellectual constitution of man. London: Pickering, 1834. 3rd edn. 2 vols. 8vo. Some browning. Uncut & unopened in orig cloth.
          (Bow Windows) **£60 [≈ $108]**

Chambers, Ephraim
- Cyclopaedia: or, an universal dictionary of arts and sciences. London: Rivington, 1786-84-81-83. 5 vols (vol 5 of plates, without title). Folio. 143 engvd plates, 10 pp printing types, fldg plate of printing types. Contemp tree calf, 1 jnt splitting.
          (Frew Mackenzie) **£850 [≈ $1,530]**
- Cyclopaedia: or, an universal dictionary of arts and sciences ... Fourth edition ... London: 1741. 2 vols. Lge thick folio. Fldg frontis, 19 (ex 20?) plates, some fldg. [with] A supplement. 1753. Folio. 2 vols. 12 plates. Old calf, rebacked.   *(Weiner)* **£200 [≈ $360]**
- Cyclopaedia: or, an universal dictionary of arts and sciences ... with the supplement and modern improvements incorporated in one alphabet by Abraham Rees. 1786-91. 5 vols. Folio. Frontis, 169 plates. Contemp half calf, very worn, bds detached.
          (Weiner) **£300 [≈ $540]**
- Cyclopaedia: or, an universal dictionary of arts and sciences ... With the Supplement ... by Abraham Rees. London: Rivington, 1786. New edn. 4 vols. Folio. 144 engvd plates, 6ff printing types (2 fldg). Contemp tree calf, rebacked, orig spines laid down.
          (Gough) **£650 [≈ $1,170]**
- Cyclopaedia: or, an universal dictionary of arts and sciences. London: Rivington, 1786-79-81-83. 5 vols inc plate vol. Lge folio. 141 (ex 145) engvd plates, 8 pp folio type specimen. Occas spots & stains, 3 short tears. Contemp reversed calf, hinges cracked.
          (Claude Cox) **£250 [≈ $450]**

Chambers, G.F.
- Descriptive astronomy. Oxford: Clarendon Press, 1867. 1st edn. Lge thick 8vo. [xl],816,[16 advts] pp. 224 figs inc 37 plates, some with colour. 1 or 2 finger marks. Orig cloth.   *(Bow Windows)* **£48 [≈ $86]**

Chambers, Robert
- Vestiges of the natural history of creation. London: John Churchill ..., 1844. [with] Explanations: a sequel to 'Vestiges ...' Churchill, 1845. 1st edn of each vol. 2 vols. 8vo. vi,390; viii,198,8 advts pp. Sl foxing vol II. Orig cloth, spines sl rubbed.
          (Pickering) **$1,000 [≈ £555]**
- Vestiges of the natural history of creation. London: 1844. 1st edn. Cr 8vo. vi,390 pp.

half calf, gilt.
(Wheldon & Wesley) **£200 [≃ $360]**
- Vestiges of the natural history of creation.
London: 1844. 2nd edn. 8vo. vi,394 pp. New
qtr calf.   *(Weiner)* **£150 [≃ $270]**
- Vestiges of the natural history of creation.
London: 1860. 11th edn. 8vo. iv,286,lxiv pp.
Ills. Orig green dec blindstamped cloth, little
worn, bookplate removed from front
pastedown.   *(Weiner)* **£75 [≃ $135]**

Chambers, Thomas
- Digestion and its derangements. The
principles of rational medicine applied to
disorders of the alimentary canal. New York:
1856. 1st Amer edn. 441 pp. Orig cloth.
          (Fye) **$50 [≃ £27]**

Chance, Burton
- Ophthalmology. New York: 1939. 1st edn.
8vo. xvii,240 pp. Frontis, 5 plates. Cloth.
Postcard from author laid in.
          (Elgen) **$35 [≃ £19]**
- Ophthalmology. New York: Hoeber, 1939.
8vo. xvii,[i],240 pp. 6 plates. Pub bndg.
          (Pollak) **£25 [≃ $45]**

Channing, W.F.
- Notes on the medical application of
electricity. Boston: Davis, 1849. 8vo. 199 pp.
8 text engvs. Stamps on title. Orig cloth,
rebacked.   *(Goodrich)* **$75 [≃ £41]**
- Notes on the medical application of
electricity. Boston: 1852. 3rd edn. 200 pp.
Sev ills. Orig cloth.   *(Fye)* **$75 [≃ £41]**

Channing, William
- The reformation of medical science,
demanded by inductive philosophy. New
York: 1839. 1st edn. 59 pp. Some
underlining. Half mor.
          (Jenkins) **$125 [≃ £69]**

Chapman, Nathaniel
- Lectures on the more important diseases of
the thoracic and abdominal viscera. Phila:
Lea & Blanchard, 1844. 1st edn. 8vo. 383,[1
errata] pp. Spotty foxing. Contemp sheep, a
bit scuffed.   *(Antiq Sc)* **$125 [≃ £69]**
- Lectures on the more important diseases of
the thoracic and abdominal viscera. Phila:
1844. 8vo. vi,383 pp. Errata & ctlg. Some
foxing. Cvrs scuffed.
          (Rittenhouse) **$37.50 [≃ £20]**

Charaka Club
- The Proceedings of the Charaka Club.
Volumes 1-10, 1902-1941. Rebound in blue

buckram, lib call numbers on spines.
          (Fye) **$650 [≃ £361]**

Charcot, J.M.
- Clinical lectures on diseases of the nervous
system. Vol 3. London: New Sydenham Soc,
1889. 1st edn in English. 8vo. 438 pp. Text
ills. Orig cloth.   *(Oasis)* **$85 [≃ £47]**
- Clinical lectures on senile and chronic
diseases. Translated by William S. Tuke.
London: 1881. 8vo. xvi,307 pp. 6 plates,
some with color. Lacking spine cloth, hinges
weak.   *(Rittenhouse)* **$80 [≃ £44]**
- Clinical lectures on the diseases of old age.
New York: 1881. 1st English translation. 280
pp. Orig cloth.   *(Fye)* **$75 [≃ £41]**
- Lectures on Bright's disease of the kidneys.
New York: W. Wood, 1878. 1st edn in
English. 8vo. x,100 pp, errata slip. 2
chromolitho plates, text w'cuts. Some
dampstains. Orig cloth, spine faded.
          (Antiq Sc) **$185 [≃ £102]**
- Lectures on Bright's disease of the kidneys.
New York: 1878. 1st edn in English. 8vo. 100
pp. 2 cold lithos, sev w'cuts. Orig cloth.
          (Fye) **$100 [≃ £55]**
- Lectures on the localisation of cerebral and
spinal diseases ... Translated and edited ...
London: New Sydenham Soc, 1883. 1st edn
in English. 8vo. xxxii,341 pp. Text w'cuts.
Rebound in cloth, orig cloth panels laid
down.   *(Elgen)* **$150 [≃ £83]**

Charleton, Walter
- Natural history of the passions ... In the
Savoy [London], for James Magnes ..., 1674.
1st edn. 8vo. [xlviii],188 pp. W'cut device on
title, anntns on 1 page, sm rust holes &
dampstains on 1 or 2 leaves. Contemp
mottled calf, rebacked.
          (Pickering) **$650 [≃ £361]**

Charras, Moses
- The Royal Pharmacopoeia, Galenical and
chymical, according to the practice of the
most eminent and learned physicians of
France ... London: John Starkey ..., 1678.
[viii],272, 245,[xv] pp. Sm folio. 4 (ex 6)
plates. Contemp calf, worn at top of spine.
          (Goodrich) **$250 [≃ £138]**

Chatley, H.
- The force of the wind. London: 1909. 8vo.
viii,83 pp. Diags. Ex lib. Inscrbd by author
on half-title.   *(Weiner)* **£20 [≃ $36]**
- The problem of flight: a text-book of aerial
engineering. London: 1907. 8vo. x,119 pp.
Ills (some full-page), diags. Orig cloth.
          (Weiner) **£40 [≃ $72]**

Cheatle, George & Cutler, Max
- Tumours of the breast: their pathology, symptoms, diagnosis and treatment. Phila: 1931. 1st Amer edn. 4to. 596 pp. Cloth.
(Scientia) **$135 [≈ £75]**

Chelius, J.M.
- A system of surgery. London: Renshaw, 1847. 1st edn in English. 2 vols. 814; 1009 pp. Vol I title with short tear. Old half calf, mrbld bds.
(Oasis) **$125 [≈ £69]**

Chemical Gazette
- The Chemical gazette, or journal of practical chemistry, in all its applications to pharmacy, arts and manufactures. Vols 1-17 (all published). London: 1842-59. Approx 500 pp per vol. Some pages & sections loose. Old cloth-backed bds, v worn & soiled. Ex lib.
(Weiner) **£260 [≈ $468]**

Chemistry ...
- Chemistry, theoretical, practical and analytical as applied to the arts and manufactures by writers of eminence. N.d. [ca 1880]. 8 vols. 1008 pp. Many full-page plates (some fldg), text ills. Orig pict cloth. gilt, 1 spine torn & reprd. *(Whitehart)* **£40 [≈ $72]**
- Chemistry, theoretical, practical and analytical as applied to the arts and manufactures. London: n.d. [ca 1876]. Bound in orig 8 divisions. Lge 8vo. 1048; 1008 pp. 53 engvd plates. Orig gilt dec cloth. 1 or 2 spine ends fingered.
(Bow Windows) **£165 [≈ $297]**

Chenevix, Richard
- Observations on mineralogical systems. Translated from the French ... To which are now added, remarks by Mr. Chenevix on the reply of M. d'Auboisson ... London: J. Johnson, 1811. 8vo. viii,138 pp, 1f. Some foxing, lib b'plate. Contemp bds, rebacked, uncut. *(Offenbacher)* **$375 [≈ £208]**

Cheselden, William
- The anatomy of the human body. London: Cliff, Jackson & Innys, 1713. 1st edn. 23 fldg plates, advt leaf at end. Some stains & discoloration, 1 plate torn, contemp ink inscrptns on title & another leaf. Half mod calf, gilt, mrbld bds.
(John Smith) **£175 [≈ $315]**
- The anatomy of the human body. Boston: J. White, S. Hall ..., 1795. 1st Amer edn. 8vo. vi,350 pp. 40 engvd plates (browning & offsetting). 1 sgntr sl sprung. Contemp tree calf. *(Antiq Sc)* **$325 [≈ £180]**
- The anatomy of the human body. London:

1792. 13th edn. 8vo. Frontis, engvd title, 40 engvd plates. Qtr calf.
(Halewood) **£98 [≈ $176]**
- Cheselden's plates of the human bones, correctly reduced from the original copy ... Edinburgh: 1816. Sm 8vo. 32 pp. 13 plates with text leaves. Half-title. Contemp bds, rebacked. *(Goodrich)* **$125 [≈ £69]**
- Osteographia, or the anatomy of the bones. London: [Bowyer], 1733. 1st edn. Lge paper. Lge folio. Engvd frontis, engvd vignette on title, engvd arms, 56 engvd plates each in 2 states. Some marg soiling, inscrptn on title. Uncut in contemp bds, worn, rebacked.
(Quaritch) **$3,750 [≈ £2,083]**

Cheyne, George
- The English malady, or, treatise of nervous diseases of all kinds ... in three parts ... London: for G. Strahan ..., 1733. 1st edn. 8vo. [vi],xxxii,370, [vi advt] pp. Divisional titles. Some light browning in some margs. Contemp mottled calf.
(Barbary) **£230 [≈ $414]**
- An essay of health and long life. London: 1724. 1st edn. 8vo. Panelled calf.
(Halewood) **£85 [≈ $153]**
- An essay of health and long life. London: 1724. 1st edn. Contemp calf, jnts cracked.
(Goodrich) **$295 [≈ £163]**
- An essay of health and long life. London: 1725. 4th edn. 232 pp. Title wrinkled & stained, old careless repr of tear. Rec qtr lea.
(Fye) **$150 [≈ £83]**

Cheyne, John
- An essay on cynanche trachealis or croup. Phila: 1913. 8vo. 110 pp. Orig wraps, uncut.
(Goodrich) **$145 [≈ £80]**

Cheyne, W.W.
- Manual of the antiseptic treatment of wounds. New York: 1885. 1st Amer edn. 8vo. 151 pp. Text ills. Orig cloth.
(Oasis) **$30 [≈ £16]**

Chomel, J.B.L.
- An historical dissertation on a particular species of gangrenous sore throat ... translated from the French ... London: 1753. 8vo. xvi,128 pp. Welcome Historical Lib stamp on title verso. Linen-backed bds.
(Hemlock) **$225 [≈ £125]**

Chomel, Noel
- Dictionnaire oeconomique: or, the family dictionary ... Done into English [husbandry, rural crafts, medicine, &c.]. Dublin: J. Watts ..., 1727. 2 vols. Folio. Many w'cut ills. Occas

browning. Contemp calf, rebacked, crnrs reprd, calf a little pitted.
(Clark) **£380 [≃ $684]**

Christison, Robert
- A treatise on poisons, in relation to medical jurisprudence, physiology and the practice of physic. Edinburgh: 1836. 3rd edn. 876 pp. Buckram. *(Fye)* **$75 [≃ £41]**

Church, A.H.
- Colour. London: Cassell, Petter & Galpin, [1872]. 12mo. 112 pp. Cold frontis. Orig cloth. *(Xerxes)* **$45 [≃ £25]**

Church, Archibald
- Diseases of the nervous system. New York: 1910. 8vo. 1205 pp. Ills. Cloth.
(Goodrich) **$65 [≃ £36]**

Churchill, C.H.
- Theory and practice of the electric telegraph: a manual for operators and students. Oberlin, Ohio: 1875. 1st edn. 144,[2] pp. Orig cloth over bds. *(Jenkins)* **$35 [≃ £19]**

Churchill, Fleetwood
- Researches on operative midwifery, etc. Dublin: 1841. 1st edn. 8vo. xiii,360 pp. Half-title, 19 fldg engvd plates. Orig cloth, spine ends frayed, jnts & crnrs worn.
(Elgen) **$125 [≃ £69]**

Clanny, W.R.
- A history and analysis of the mineral waters situated at Butterby near Durham. Durham: L. Pennington, 1807. 1st edn. 12mo. [iv],60 pp. Ink inscrptn at hd of title. Uncut in orig blue wraps, lightly soiled.
(Frew Mackenzie) **£160 [≃ $288]**

Clanny, William Reid
- Practical observations on safety lamps for coal mines. Sunderland: 1816. 1st edn. Sm 8vo. 8 pp. Plate. Disbound.
(Halewood) **£75 [≃ $135]**

Clapp, Herbert C.
- A tabular handbook of ausculation and percussion. Boston: 1878. 8vo. vii,101 pp. Ex lib with b'plates.
(Rittenhouse) **$37.50 [≃ £20]**

Claridge, John
- The shepherd of Banbury's rules to judge the changes of the weather, grounded on forty years experience ... London: W. Bickerton, 1744. 8vo in 4's. viii,43 pp. A bit cropped at ft. Old qtr mor, rubbed. *(Clark)* **£32 [≃ $57]**

Claridge, R.T.
- Hydropathy or the cold water cure as practised by Vincent Priessnitz. London: Madden, 1842. 2nd edn. 8vo. 318 pp. Frontis. Spine faded. Orig cloth.
(Oasis) **$75 [≃ £41]**

Clark, Daniel Kinnear
- The steam engine. London: 1891. Sm 4to. 2 vols in 4 as issued. 22 plates, 1026 ills. Cloth. Ex lib. *(Elgen)* **$90 [≃ £50]**

Clark, G.N.
- Science and social welfare in the age of Newton. Oxford: Clarendon Press, 1937. 8vo. [viii],159,[i] pp. Pub bndg.
(Pollak) **£20 [≃ $36]**

Clark, George L.
- Applied X-rays. New York: McGraw Hill, 1940. 3rd edn. 8vo. xvii,[i],674,[ii] pp. 342 ills. Pub bndg. *(Pollak)* **£25 [≃ $45]**

Clark, J.
- Observations on the diseases which prevail in long voyages to hot countries, particularly ... the East Indies; ... the same diseases ... in Great Britain. Volume I [all published]. London: 1792. 2nd edn. xxii,252 pp. Orig bds, spine defective, hinges cracked.
(Whitehart) **£40 [≃ $72]**

Clark, James
- The influence of climate in the prevention and cure of chronic diseases ... London: Murray, 1830. 2nd edn. 8vo. Author's pres copy. Uncut in orig cloth, spine faded.
(Quaritch) **£350 [≃ £194]**
- The sanative influence of climate. London: 1846. 4th edn. 8vo. 412 pp. Orig cloth.
(Oasis) **$100 [≃ £55]**
- The sanative influence of climate: with an account of the best places of resort for invalids in England, the South of Europe, &c. Phila: 1841. [Bound with] Changes of the blood in disease. Translated from the French of M. Gibert. Phila: 1841. Lea.
(Rittenhouse) **$35 [≃ £19]**
- Treatise on pulmonary consumption ... an inquiry into the causes, nature, prevention and treatment of tuberculous and scrofulous diseases in general. London: 1835. 1st edn. 8vo. 399 pp, advts. Orig cloth, inner hinges mended, back chipped.
(Argosy) **$85 [≃ £47]**
- Treatise on pulmonary consumption ... an inquiry into the causes, nature, prevention and treatment of tuberculous and scrofulous diseases in general. Phila: 1835. 1st Amer

edn. 296 pp. Pub ctlg. Cloth, spine extremities frayed. *(Scientia)* **$95 [≈ £52]**

Clark, John Willis & Hughes, Thomas McKenny
- The life and letters of the Reverend Adam Sedgwick. Cambridge: Univ Press, 1890. 1st edn. 2 vols. 8vo. [xiv],539; viii,640 pp. Ports, maps (1 cold). Sgntr on flyleaves. Orig cloth.
  (Bow Windows) **£110 [≈ $198]**

Clark, Samuel
- The British gauger: or, trader and officer's instructor ... rules of vulgar and decimal arithmetic ... London: for J. Nourse, 1765. 2nd edn. Sm 8vo. [iv],v,[i], 432, *433-*448, 433,[1],x pp. 6 fldg engvd plates (1 hand-cold). Sl browning at end. Rec qtr calf.
  (Burmester) **£240 [≈ $432]**

Clark, Sir Andrew, et al.
- Fibroid diseases of the lung, including fibroid phthisis. London: 1894. 8vo. viii,199 pp. Pub advts. Cloth. Ex lib.
  (Rittenhouse) **$35 [≈ £19]**

Clark-Kennedy, A.E.
- The art of medicine in relation to the progress of thought. Cambridge: Univ Press, 1945. 1st edn. Slim 8vo. Orig ptd wraps.
  (Chaucer Head) **£28 [≈ $50]**

Clarke, Arthur
- The mother's medical assistant containing instructions for ... the treatment of the diseases of infants and children. London: 1820. 8vo. 148 pp. Uncut.
  (Goodrich) **$75 [≈ £41]**

Clarke, Edward H.
- Sex in education; or, a fair chance for girls. Boston: 1873. 1st edn. 181 pp. Cloth, crease in front cvr. *(Scientia)* **$95 [≈ £52]**
- Visions: a study of false sight (pseudopia) with an introduction ... by Oliver Wendell Holmes. Boston: 1878. 1st edn. 315 pp. Orig cloth. *(Fye)* **$100 [≈ £55]**

Clarke, Edward, et al.
- A century of modern medicine. Phila: Lea, 1876. 1st edn. 8vo. 366 pp. 12 pp pub ctlg. Orig cloth. *(Oasis)* **$150 [≈ £83]**

Clarke, H.
- A dissertation on the summation of infinite converging series with algebraic divisors. London: for the author, 1779. 4to. xx,222 pp. 2 fldg plates. Contemp bds, roan spine gilt, v sl rubbed & little worn.
  (Whitehart) **£60 [≈ $108]**

Clausius, Rudolf
- The mechanical theory of heat, with its applications to the steam-engine and to the physical properties of bodies. London: Van Voorst, 1867. 1st edn in English. 8vo. xvi,376,[2] pp. Text figs. Blindstamp on title. Orig cloth, rebacked, orig spine laid down.
  (Antiq Sc) **$275 [≈ £152]**

Clay, Rotha Mary
- The mediaeval hospitals of England. London: Methuen, 1909. 8vo. xxii,357, [i],[iv advts], 48 ctlg pp. Frontis, 30 plates, 37 text ills. Orig cloth, gilt. *(Pollak)* **£25 [≈ $45]**
- The mediaeval hospitals of England. [London:] 1966. 8vo. xxii,357 pp. Num ills, plates. Cloth, dw. *(Elgen)* **$30 [≈ £16]**

Clemow, Frank
- The cholera epidemic of 1892 in the Russian Empire with notes upon treatment and methods of disinfection ... London: 1893. 8vo. 123 pp. Fldg plates & maps. Ex lib.
  (Goodrich) **$35 [≈ £19]**

Clerk, Dugald
- The gas engine. London: 1886. Sm 8vo. v,279 pp. Ills. Rear endpaper damaged. Cloth, spine edges frayed, tear at lower jnt.
  (Elgen) **$30 [≈ £16]**

Clerke, Agnes M.
- A popular history of astronomy during the nineteenth century. London: 1908. 8vo. xviii,489 pp. Mtd photo on frontis & title. Orig cloth. *(Weiner)* **£20 [≈ $36]**

Clifford, William K.
- Lectures and essays. London: Macmillan, 1879. 1st edn. 2 vols. 8vo. 340; 321 pp, 32 pp pub ctlg. Mtd photo port. Orig cloth.
  (Oasis) **$120 [≈ £66]**

Clifton, Francis
- The state of physic ancient and modern, briefly considered: with a plan for the improvement of it. London: Bowyer, 1732. 8vo. [20],192 pp. Sgntrs on title. Contemp panelled calf, rebacked.
  (Goodrich) **$195 [≈ £108]**
- The state of physic ancient and modern, briefly considered: with a plan for the improvement of it. London: Nourse, 1732. 1st edn. 8vo. 192 pp. Fldg table. Lacking front endpaper. Old calf, a little worn.
  (Oasis) **$125 [≈ £69]**

Coade, Eleanor
- A descriptive catalogue of Coade's artificial

stone manufactory ... London: 1784. [with] Etchings of Coade's artificial stone manufacture, London: n.d. [ca 1778-79]. 2 works in 1. 4to & obl folio. [ii],31 pp; 67 etched plates. Occas minor soiling. Lib binding.   *(Burmester)* **£3,500 [≃ $6,300]**

Cobb, Augustus G.

- Earth-burial and cremation. The history of earth burial ... New York: 1892. 1st edn. xi,173 pp. Engvd frontis. Cloth.
                        (Elgen) **$45 [≃ £25]**

Cobb, Jonathan Holmes

- A manual containing information respecting the growth of the Mulberry tree, with suitable directions for the culture of silk. Boston: Carter ..., 1831. 1st edn. 8vo. 68 pp. 3 engvd plates (2 hand-cold). Orig cloth-backed ptd bds.   *(Burmester)* **£110 [≃ $198]**
- A manual containing information respecting the growth of the Mulberry tree, with suitable directions for the culture of silk. Boston: Carter ..., 1831. 2nd edn. 8vo. 98 pp. 3 engvd plates (2 hand-cold). Orig cloth-backed ptd bds.   *(Burmester)* **£80 [≃ $144]**
- A manual containing information respecting the growth of the Mulberry tree, with suitable directions for the culture of silk. Boston: 1833. 12mo. 98 pp. 3 plates (2 hand-cold). Orig linen-backed ptd bds, jnts & end of spine torn.   *(Bow Windows)* **£48 [≃ $86]**

Cobbett, William

- The English gardener: or, a treatise on the situation, soil, enclosing and laying-out of kitchen gardens ... London: 1833. 8vo. Fldg engvd plate, w'cut ills. Orig bds, cloth spine, rebacked, uncut edges. *(Traylen)* **£48 [≃ $86]**
- A treatise on Cobbett's corn. London: Cobbett, 1828. 3 w'cut plates. Bds, uncut, jnts v fragile. *(Marlborough)* **£75 [≃ $135]**

Coca, Arthur, et al.

- Asthma and hayfever in theory and practice. Springfield: 1931. 1st edn. Lge 8vo. [xxiv],851 pp. Ills. Cloth, dw (torn).
                        (Elgen) **$50 [≃ £27]**

Cocker, E.

- Cocker's decimal arithmetick, wherein is shewed the nature and use of decimal fractions ... London: 1695. [16],436 pp. 2 sm contemp sgntrs on title, sm marg tear reprd, foxed. New lea. *(Whitehart)* **£120 [≃ $216]**

Codman, E.A.

- Bone sarcoma. An interpretation of the nomenclature used by the Committee ... of

bone sarcoma of the American College of Surgeons. New York: 1925.
                        (Goodrich) **$75 [≃ £41]**
- The shoulder. Rupture of the supraspinatus tendon and other lesions in or about the subacromial bursa. Boston: 1934. 2nd printing. 513 pp. Cloth. Author's pres copy with full-page inscrptn, sgnd, on blank plus postscript, also sgnd.
                        (Goodrich) **$350 [≃ £194]**
- The shoulder. Rupture of the supraspinatus tendon and other lesions in or about the subacromial bursa. Boston: 1934. 1st edn. xl,513,29 pp. Cloth. *(Scientia)* **$175 [≃ £97]**
- A study in hospital efficiency as demonstrated by the case report of the first five years of a private hospital. Boston: privately printed, 1917. 8vo. New bds, fldg sheet in pocket.
                        (Goodrich) **$125 [≃ £69]**

Coffin, Albert I.

- Medical botany: a course of lectures delivered at Sussex Hall, during 1850. W.B. Ford, [1850]. 1st edn. Lge 12mo, xi,[2],223 pp inc errata leaf. Port, 25 ills. Orig cloth.
                        (Fenning) **£28.50 [≃ $50]**

Coffin, James

- Elements of conic sections and analytical geometry. Collins, 1849. 158 pp. Some foxing, rear endpaper defective. Lea, spine worn & chipped.   *(Xerxes)* **$65 [≃ £36]**

Cohausen, Johann Heinrich

- Hermippus redivivus, or the sage's triumph over old age and the grave ... prolonging the life and increasing the vigour of man ... London: for J. Nourse, 1749. 8vo. [8],249 pp. Tear in 1 marg with loss of 5 letters. Contemp half calf, top bd nearly loose.
                        (Claude Cox) **£60 [≃ $108]**

Cohen, J. Solis

- Inhalation: its therapeutics and practice ... including a description of the apparatus employed. Phila: 1867. 8vo. xii,305 pp. Some fading on spine & cvrs. Lib b'plate.
                        (Rittenhouse) **$35 [≃ £19]**

Cohnheim, Julius

- Lectures on general pathology. London: 1889-90. 1st English translation. 3 vols. 1434 pp. Orig cloth.   *(Fye)* **$225 [≃ £125]**

Cohnheim, P.

- Diseases of the digestive canal. Phila: [1909]. xxi,373 pp. 45 text figs, orig cloth, marked, new endpapers.   *(Whitehart)* **£25 [≃ $45]**

Coker, E.G. & Filon, L.N.G.
- A treatise on photo-elasticity. Cambridge: 1931. 8vo. xviii,720 pp. Cold plates, ills, diags. Lib stamp on title verso. Orig cloth, sl worn.   *(Weiner)* **£40 [≃ $72]**

Colbatch, John
- Four treatises of physick and chirurgery ... The second edition corrected and enlarged. London: for J.D. ..., 1698. 1st coll edn. Sm 8vo. xxiii,[i], 122,86 pp, divisional title to each part. Contemp mottled calf, end of upper jnt cracked, a little rubbed.
                                   (Pickering) **$550 [≃ £305]**
- The generous physician, or medicine made easy ... the causes, symptoms, and method proper for cure of several distempers ... London: for J. Roberts, [1733]. 1st edn. 8vo. [ii],iv,90 pp. Some foxing, outer leaves a bit soiled. Disbound. *(Burmester)* **£110 [≃ $198]**

Colby, L.J.M.
- The chemical studies of P.J. Macquer, London: [1938]. 1st edn. 8vo. 132,4 pub ctlg pp. Cloth, dw.   *(Elgen)* **$35 [≃ £19]**

Cole, Grenville A.J. & Hallisy, T.
- Handbook of the geology of Ireland. London: Thomas Murby, 1924. 1st edn. Sm 4to. viii,82 pp. Geological map, 7 ills. Orig blue cloth, gilt.   *(Gough)* **£18 [≃ $32]**

Coles, A.C.
- The blood: how to examine and diagnose its diseases. London: 1898. 1st edn. 8vo. xii,260 pp. 6 cold plates. Some pencilled notes & finger marks, tiny wormholes at ft of sev leaves. Orig cloth, faded & a little rubbed.
                             (Bow Windows) **£25 [≃ $45]**

Coles, James
- Patent specifications for: Improvements in apparatus for the prevention and treatment of distortions in the spine and chest ... Patent No. 11,364. 1846. London: Eyre & Spottiswoode, 1857. 9,[i] pp. Lge fldg plate. New wraps.   *(Pollak)* **£45 [≃ $81]**

Coles, L.B.
- Philosophy of health: natural principles of health and cure; or, health and cure without drugs. Boston: 1854. 37th edn, revsd & enlgd. 8vo. 312 pp, 15 plates [with] Coles: The beauties and deformities of tobacco-using. 1854. 144 pp. Orig gilt dec cvrs.
                                   (Elgen) **$50 [≃ £27]**

Collection ...
- A collection of above three hundred receipts ... See Kettilby, Mary

Colles, A.
- Selection from the work of Abraham Colles, consisting chiefly on his practical observations on the venereal disease and on the use of mercury. New Sydenham Soc, 1881. 8vo. xvi,413 pp. Port frontis. Orig blindstamped cloth, sl worn. Ex lib with stamps.   *(Whitehart)* **£35 [≃ $63]**

Collier, Charles
- The history of the plague of Athens; translated from Thucydides. London: David Nutt, 1857. Cr 8vo. xxi,[1 erratum slip],86,[2] pp. Orig cloth, a little used. Author's pres copy to his son.
                                   (Taylor) **£22 [≃ $39]**

Collignon, Charles
- The miscellaneous works. Cambridge: Hodson, 1786. 4to. [5],345, errata leaf. Halftitle, subscribers' list. Calf, jnts weak.
                                   (Goodrich) **$145 [≃ £80]**

Collins, E. Treacher
- The history and traditions of the Moorfields Eye Hospital ... London: 1929. 8vo. xii,226 pp. 27 plates. Orig cloth.
                                   (Weiner) **£50 [≃ $90]**

Collins, F.W. (ed.)
- Disease diagnosed by observation of the eye. New Jersey: F. Collins, 1919. 2 parts. 8vo. 122 pp. 45 'charts', mostly cold plates (possibly lacking 1). Orig cloth, shaken.
                                   (Oasis) **$25 [≃ £13]**

Colloquia Chirurgica ...
- Colloquia chirurgica ... See Handley, James

Colquhoun, J.C.
- An history of magic, witchcraft, and animal magnetism. London: 1851. 1st edn. 2 vols. 8vo. Mostly unopened. Inscrptn on title. Orig cloth.   *(Argosy)* **$100 [≃ £55]**

Colton, J.J.
- The physiological action of nitrous oxide gas, as shown by experimentation upon man and the lower animals ... its safety, uses, and abuses. Phila: 1871. 32 pp. Orig paper cvrs.
                                   (Rittenhouse) **$35 [≃ £19]**

Combe, A.
- The principles of physiology applied to the preservation of health and to the improvement of physical and mental education. 1835. 3rd edn. xii,404 pp. Sm stamp on title. Orig watered silk binding, dust-stained & marked.
                                   (Whitehart) **£20 [≃ $36]**

Combe, Andrew
- The physiology of digestion considered with relation to the principles of dietetics. Edinburgh: 1841. 3rd edn, revsd & enlgd. Cr 8vo. 12 w'cuts, 10 pp advts. Orig bds, cloth spine.   *(Traylen)* **£38 [≃$68]**
- The physiology of digestion considered with relation to the principles of dietetics. Boston: 1836. 1st Amer edn. 328 pp. Orig cloth.
          (Fye) **$75 [≃£41]**

Combe, George
- Elements of phrenology. Edinburgh: 1825. 2nd edn, imprvd & enlgd. xi,240 pp. Fldg frontis, plate. Contemp half calf.
          (Spelman) **£55 [≃$99]**
- A system of phrenology. Edinburgh: 1836. 4th edn. 2 vols. 8vo. Engvd frontis, 2 engvd plates (1 cold), text ills. Orig green cloth, ptd paper labels, uncut edges.
          (Traylen) **£65 [≃$117]**

Combrune, Michael
- An essay on brewing. With a view of establishing the principles of the art. London: R. & J. Dodsley, 1758. 214 pp. Half-title, vignette title. Contemp calf.
          (C.R. Johnson) **£350 [≃$630]**

Committee on Employment of Boys ...
- Report from the Committee on Employment of Boys in Sweeping of Chimneys ... minutes of the evidence and an appendix. [London:] Ordered by the House of Commons, 1817. Folio. 51 pp. Half-title. New bds.
          (Goodrich) **$175 [≃£97]**

Compston, H.F.B.
- The Magdalen Hospital. The story of a great charity. London: SPCK, 1917. 8vo. xi,[iii], 15-237,[iii] pp. Frontis, 19 plates. Pub bndg, front jnt weak, lacking front free endpaper.
          (Pollak) **£25 [≃$45]**

Compton, Arthur H. & Allison, Samuel K.
- X-rays in theory and experiment. London: Macmillan, 1935. 8vo. xiv,828,[ii] pp. Num text figs. Orig cloth.   *(Pollak)* **£30 [≃$54]**

Comrie, John D.
- History of Scottish medicine. London: Wellcome, 1932. 2nd edn. 2 vols. Orig cloth.
          (Goodrich) **£65 [≃£36]**
- History of Scottish medicine. London: 1932. 2nd edn. 2 vols. 2 frontis (1 cold), num ports & ills. Orig cloth.   *(Weiner)* **£30 [≃$54]**

Comte, Auguste
- The positive philosophy ... freely translated and condensed by Harriet Martineau. London: 1853. 1st edn in English. 2 vols. 8vo. xxxvi,480; xvi,561 pp. Prelims marg waterstained, a few sm lib stamps. Orig cloth, little worn.   *(Weiner)* **£50 [≃$90]**
- The positive philosophy of Auguste Comte. Freely translated and condensed by Harriet Martineau. New York & London: 1853. 1st edn in English. 2 vols. 480; 561 pp. Spines faded, spine lettering dull.
          (Scientia) **$225 [≃£125]**

Condillac, Etienne Bonnot de
- Condillac's treatise on the sensations. Translated ... London: 1930. 1st edn in English.   *(Scientia)* **$125 [≃£69]**

Condorcet, M.J.A.N.
- Outlines of an historical view of the progress of the human mind ... Phila: 1796. 1st Amer edn. 12mo. 293 pp. Some foxing & browning, front flyleaf missing. Orig calf, rubbed, edge of front bd blackened. *(Elgen)* **$325 [≃£180]**

Confessions ...
- Confessions of an English opium-eater ... See De Quincey, Thomas

Congreve, Sir William
- A concise account of the origin and principles of the new class of 24 pounder medium guns ... with a variety of experiments and other deductions ... London: for J. Whiting, [1820]. 1st edn. 4to. Fldg engvd plate, num tables & diags. Half mor, a little rubbed.
          (Traylen) **£180 [≃$324]**
- An elementary treatise on the mounting of naval ordnance, shewing the true principles of construction for the carriages of every species of ordnance ... London: J. Egerton, 1811. 1st edn. 4to. 5 engvd plates (4 fldg). Half mor, gilt, a little rubbed. *(Traylen)* **£190 [≃$342]**

Constable, H. Strickland
- Fashions of today in medicine and science: a few more hints. Kingston-upon-Hull: 1879. 8vo. 300 pp. Orig cloth. *(Weiner)* **£30 [≃$54]**
- Our medicine men: a few hints. Kingston-upon-Hull: [1876]. 8vo. xi,689 pp. Orig cloth, inner jnts loose.   *(Weiner)* **£30 [≃$54]**

Conversations ...
- Conversations on conditioning ... See Badcock, John
- Conversations on mineralogy ... (and also) Conversations on chemistry ... See Marcet, Jane
- Conversations on the animal economy by a physician. London: 1827. 2 vols. 8vo. Ills.

Dampstaining. Calf. *(Goodrich)* $65 [≈£36]

Cook, Sir Theodore Andrea
- The curves of life, being the account of spiral formations and their applications to growth in nature, to science and to art; with special reference to the manuscripts of Leonardo da Vinci. New York: Holt, 1914. Roy 8vo. 479 pp. 11 plates, 415 text ills. Cloth.
(Xerxes) $125 [≈£69]

Cooke, John
- A treatise on nervous diseases. Boston: 1824. 1st Amer edn. 432 pp. Lea, scuffed.
(Scientia) $400 [≈£222]

Cooke, Josiah P.
- Elements of chemical physics. Boston: Little, Brown, 1860. 1st edn. 8vo. xii,739 pp. Num text figs. Orig cloth, spine faded, edge wear.
(Antiq Sc) $85 [≈£47]
- The new chemistry. New York: D. Appleton, 1874. 1st edn. 8vo. 326 pp. Text figs. Orig cloth, spotted. *(Antiq Sc)* $35 [≈£19]

Coolidge, Julien
- A treatise on the circle and the sphere. Oxford: 1916. 1st edn. 8vo. 602 pp. Orig cloth. *(Oasis)* $30 [≈£16]

Coolidge, Julien Lowell
- A history of geometrical methods. Oxford: [1947]. 8vo. 451 pp. Orig cloth.
(Argosy) $60 [≈£33]

Cooper, Sir Astley
- The anatomy and diseases of the breast; to which are added, his various surgical papers, now published in a collected form. Phila: 1845. 1st Amer edn. 130,63,188 pp. Lea, scuffed, top of spine chipped.
(Scientia) $200 [≈£111]
- Lectures ... on the principles and practices of surgery ... Phila: Sherman, 1826 (vols 1 & 2); Boston: Wells & Lilly, 1828 (vols 3 & 4). 157; 196; 383 pp. 6 plates. Stamps on titles, marg dampstaining. Old syle bds, uncut.
(Goodrich) $125 [≈£69]
- Lectures ... on the principles and practices of surgery. Phila: 1826. 2 vols in 1. Plates. Foxed. Lea, worn. *(Allen)* $25 [≈£13]
- Lectures on the principles and practices of surgery, as delivered in the theatre of St. Thomas's Hospital. London: Westley, 1832. 3rd edn. 8vo. viii,637,[iii] pp. Occas foxing. Orig bds, rebacked. *(Pollak)* £50 [≈$90]

Cooper, Astley & Travers, Benjamin
- Surgical essays. London: Cox, 1818; &

Longman, 1820. 2nd edn. 2 vols. 8vo. xiii,[3],291; [2],255 pp. Half-title vol I, 21 engvd plates, some fldg & some double-page (1 hand-col). Plates somewhat spotted. Contemp lea-backed mrbld bds, a bit rubbed, rebacked. *(Antiq Sc)* $525 [≈£291]

Cooper, Samuel
- The first lines of the practice of surgery ... Hanover: 1815. 2nd Amer edn. 8vo. 462 pp. 9 plates. Calf, jnts weak.
(Goodrich) $45 [≈£25]
- The first lines of the practice of surgery ... in two parts ... Boston: 1828. 3rd Amer edn. 8vo. 447 pp. 9 engvd plates. Sheep.
(Goodrich) $50 [≈£27]

Cope, Z.
- William Chesleden 1688-1752. Edinburgh: 1952. 112 pp. Cloth. *(Goodrich)* $45 [≈£25]

Copeland, Alfred James
- Bridewell Royal Hospital past and present. London: Wells Gardner, 1888. 8vo. vii,[iii], 151,[i] pp. 8vo. Frontis, plates, text ills. Orig dec cvrs. Author's inscrptn.
(Pollak) £25 [≈$45]

Corlett, W.T.
- The medicine-man of the American Indian and his cultural background. USA: 1935. 8vo. viii,369 pp. Frontis, 22 ills. Orig cloth, chipped dw. *(Snowden Smith)* £55 [≈$99]

Cormack, John Rose
- A treatise on the chemical, medicinal and physiological properties of creosote, illustrated by experiments on the lower animals ... Edinburgh: John Carfrae, 1836. 1st edn. 8vo. Orig green cloth, rebacked. Author's pres inscrptn on title.
(Traylen) £48 [≈$86]

Cornaro, Luigi (Lewis)
- Sure methods of attaining a long and healthy life: with means of correcting a bad constitution. London: for Daniel Midwinter ..., 1727. 4th edn. 12mo. xl,120 pp. Occas spotting. Mod calf. *(Young's)* £65 [≈$117]
- Sure methods of attaining a long and healthy life. Translated ... Edinburgh: A. Donaldson, 1768. 12mo. Contemp calf, jnts cracked.
(Charles Cox) £40 [≈$72]

Cornil, A. Victor & Ranvier, Louis
- A manual of pathological histology. Translated, with notes and additions ... Phila: 1880. 1st edn in English. 784 pp. Pub ctlg.
(Scientia) $95 [≈£52]

Cornish, Vaughan
- Scenery and the sense of sight. Cambridge: Univ Press, 1935. 8vo. xii,111,[i] pp. Frontis, 9 plates. Pub bndg, cvrs a little shabby.
(Pollak) £12 [≈ $21]

Corrington, Julian D.
- Adventures with the microscope. Rochester, New York: Bausch & Lamb Optical Co., 1934. ix,[i], 455,[i] pp. 352 ills. Orig cloth.
(Pollak) £35 [≈ $63]

Corti, Count
- A history of smoking. Translated by Paul England. London: 1931. 8vo. 296 pp. 64 ills. V sl discoloration on top cvr.
(Rittenhouse) $50 [≈ £27]

Councilman, William T., et al.
- Studies on the pathology and on the etiology of variola and of vaccinia. Boston: 1904. 361 pp. 29 plates. Orig ptd wraps, upper crnr front wrap missing with sl loss of text.
(Scientia) $100 [≈ £55]

Couper, Robert
- Speculations on the mode and appearances of impregnation in the human female ... Edinburgh: C. Elliott; London: Elliott & Kay, 1789. 1st edn. 8vo. 149,[1] pp. Qtr calf over mrbld bds. *(Rootenberg)* $550 [≈ £305]

Cowdry, Edmund V. (ed.)
- General cytology. A textbook of cellular structure and functions for students of biology and medicine. Univ of Chicago Press, 1925. 2nd imp. 8vo. vii,[i], 754,[ii] pp. Num ills. Faint damp mark in lower marg. Pub bndg. *(Pollak)* £25 [≈ $45]

Cowley, John Lodge
- An appendix to the elements of Euclid, in seven books. London: T. Cadell, n.d. [ca 1770]. 2nd edn. 4to. [iv],14 pp. 42 plates of cut-outs. Contemp dark calf, rebacked & recrnrd to match.
(Frew Mackenzie) £1,300 [≈ $2,340]

Cowper, William (1666 - 1709)
- Myotomia reformata: or an anatomical treatise on the muscles of the human body ... London: for Knaplock ..., 1724. 1st folio edn. [10],lxxvii, 194,[4] pp. Engvd frontis, 66 plates plus 1 in outline. Anntns in contemp hand throughout. Elab gilt dec calf.
(Rootenberg) $5,500 [≈ £3,055]

Cox, William Sands
- A memoir on amputation of the thigh at the

hip-joint. London: 1845. 1st edn. Folio. 2 cold plates, subscribers' list, advt leaf. Inner margs strengthened. Buckram.
(Halewood) £150 [≈ $270]

Coxe, James
- Lunacy in its relation to the State. A commentary on the evidence taken by the Committee of the House of Commons on lunacy law ... London: 1878. 1st edn. 49 pp. Orig pts wraps, rear wrap chipped, stamp on front. *(Scientia)* $95 [≈ £52]

Coxe, John Redman
- The American dispensatory, containing the operations of pharmacy; together with the ... history of the different substances employed in medicine ... Phila: 1806. 1st edn. 787 pp. 6 plates. Final leaf supplied in facsimile. Orig lea. *(Fye)* $200 [≈ £111]
- The American dispensatory, containing the operations of pharmacy ... Phila: 1810. 2nd edn. Plates. Lea, scuffed.
(Rittenhouse) $95 [≈ £52]
- The American dispensatory ... together with the operations of pharmacy ... principles of modern chemistry ... Phila: 1827. 7th edn. 8vo. 780 pp. Old style bds.
(Goodrich) $50 [≈ £27]
- The American dispensatory, containing the ... history of the different substances employed in medicine ... Phila: 1830. 8vo. iv,808,12 pub ctlg pp. 2 engvd plates. Scattered foxing, last 100 pp stained. Contemp calf. *(Elgen)* $65 [≈ £36]
- Practical observations on vaccination or inoculaton for the cow-pock. Phila: 1802. 8vo. 152 pp. Cold frontis. Heavy dampstaining. Calf, very worn, jnts split.
(Goodrich) $65 [≈ £36]

Cozens-Hardy, Basil (ed.)
- The diary of Sylas Neville 1767-1788. London: OUP, 1950. 8vo. xvi,357,[i] pp. Frontis, 4 plates. Pub bndg, dw.
(Pollak) £25 [≈ $45]

Cozzens, Issacher
- A geological history of Manhattan or New York Island. New York: W.E. Dean, 1843. 1st edn. 8vo. 114 pp inc subscribers' list. 8 hand-cold litho plates, 1 fldg hand-cold map. Scattered spotty foxing. Orig cloth. Author's sgnd pres copy. *(Antiq Sc)* $250 [≈ £138]

Crabb, George
- Universal technological dictionary. or, familiar explanation of the terms used in all arts and sciences, 1823. Lge 4to. 2 vols.

Approx vii,800; 600 pp. 60 full-page plates. Contemp bds, rebacked, bds sl stained.
(Whitehart) £180 [≃ $324]

Crace-Calvert, F.
- Dyeing and calico printing; including an account of the most recent improvements in ... aniline colours. Manchester: 1876. 2nd edn. 8vo. xxix,509 pp. Port frontis, fldg table, mtd dyed textile samples, ills. Bds dampstained, jnts shaken.
(Weiner) £50 [≃ $90]

Craigie, David
- Elements of general and pathological anatomy. Edinburgh: Black, 1828. 1st edn. 8vo. 816 pp. Half calf, spine gilt.
(Oasis) $125 [≃ £69]

Cramer, John Andrew
- Elements of the art of essaying metals. In two parts ... For Tho. Woodward ..., 1741. 1st edn in English 8vo. [xii],1-204, half-title, 203-208,[205]-470, viii] pp. 6 fldg engvd plates. Orig calf, upper jnt beginning to crack at hd. *(Bickersteth)* £360 [≃ $648]

Crawfurd, Raymond
- Plague and pestilence in literature and art. London: 1914. 8vo. viii,222 pp. 32 plates. Orig cloth. *(Weiner)* £38 [≃ $68]

Creech, Thomas
- The five books of M. Manilius. Containing a system of the ancient astronomy and astrology. London: for Jacob Tonson, 1697. 1st edn. Frontis, 5 plates, half-title, errata leaf. 2 leaves stained. Later half calf gilt, cloth bds. Wing M430. *(Charles Cox)* £35 [≃ $63]

Creighton, Charles
- Jenner and vaccination. A strange chapter of medical history. London: 1889. 8vo. 360 pp. Orig cloth. *(Goodrich)* $75 [≃ £41]

Cresswell, D.
- An elementary treatise on the geometrical and algebraical investigation of maxima and minima ... Cambridge: Deighton, 1817. 2nd edn. iv,298,138 pp. Text figs. Orig paper bds, backstrip a little worn.
(Hinchliffe) £25 [≃ $45]

Cresy, Edward
- An encyclopaedia of civil engineering, historical, theoretical, and practical. London: 1847. 1st edn. 2 vols in 1. 8vo. xii,1655,32 pub ctlg pp. Num w'engvs. Cloth, spine defective. *(Elgen)* $75 [≃ £41]

Crew, F.A.E. (ed.)
- Medical history of the Second World War. The Army Medical Services. London: HMSO, 1957. xxxvii,537 pp.20 plates, 66 figs. Pub bndg, dw. *(Pollak)* £25 [≃ $45]

Crile, Grace (ed.)
- George Crile: an autobiography. Phila: 1947. 2 vols. In orig box, dws.
(Rittenhouse) $35 [≃ £19]

Cripps, Ernest C.
- Plough Court, the story of a notable pharmacy, 1715-1927. London: 1927. 1st edn. 8vo. xviii,227 pp. Num half-tones. Pres copy. *(Elgen)* $30 [≃ £16]

Crisp, Sir Frank
- Mediaeval gardens: flowery medes and other arrangements of herbs, flowers and shrubs grown in the Middle Ages. London: [1924]. Ltd edn. 2 vols. 4to. Orig pict buckram, gilt.
(Argosy) $200 [≃ £111]

Crookshank, Edgar M.
- History and pathology of vaccination. London: 1889. 1st edn. 2 vols. Lge 8vo. xxiii,466; vi,610 pp. Half-title, port frontis, 22 chromolithos, 4 facs (1 fldg). Some pencil underlinings & marks. Orig cloth, worn, shaken, inner hinges cracked.
(Elgen) $195 [≃ £108]
- History and pathology of vaccination. Phila: 1889. 2 vols. 8vo. xxiii,466; 610 pp. Some foxing on frontis, sgntr on title. Orig cloth. *(Rittenhouse)* $195 [≃ £108]

Crookshank, F.G.
- The mongol in our midst, a study of man and his three faces. New York: Dutton, 1924. 1st edn. 16mo. 123 pp. Photos. Cloth.
(Xerxes) $45 [≃ £25]

Crosse, V. Mary
- A surgeon in the early nineteenth century. The life and times of John Green Crosse ... 1790-1850. Edinburgh: Livingstone, 1968. 8vo. xii,210,[ii] pp. Frontis, 19 plates. Pub bndg, dw. *(Pollak)* £25 [≃ $45]

Crothers, T.D.
- The disease of inebriety from alcohol. opium and other narcotic drugs, its etiology, pathology, treatment and medico-legal relations. New York: 1899. 8vo. xiv,400 pp. Red cloth. *(Rittenhouse)* $27.50 [≃ £15]

Crowley, Aleister
- Magic in theory and practice by the Master

Therion. [Paris:] for subscribers only, 1929. 1st edn. 4to. xxxiv,436 pp. Orig cloth, marked, snag in backstrip reprd.
(Claude Cox) £50 [≃ $90]

Crowther, J.A.
- The principles of radiography. London: Churchill, 1922. 8vo. vi,[ii],138, [xiv] advts pp. 55 ills. Orig bds.   *(Pollak)* £25 [≃ $45]

Cruveilhier, J.
- The anatomy of the human body. Edited by J.S. Pattison. New York: 1844. 1st Amer edn. 8vo. 960 pp. Light foxing. Cloth, rubbed.
(Goodrich) $85 [≃ £47]

Cullen, Thomas
- Adenomyoma of the uterus. Phila: 1908. 8vo. 270 pp. Ills. Cloth, ex lib.
(Goodrich) $95 [≃ £52]

Cullen, William
- First lines of the practice of physic. Edinburgh: for Charles Elliot, 1784. 4th edn. 4 vols. 8vo. Titles to vols 2, 3 & 4 a little grubby. New buckram.
(Pollak) £175 [≃ $315]
- First lines of the practice of physic. Phila: 1816. 2 vols in 1. Rubber stamp on title. Cvrs worn & scuffed, upper hinge broken & reprd with tape.   *(Rittenhouse)* $55 [≃ £30]
- First lines of the practice of physic. With supplementary notes ... by Peter Reid. Brookfield: 1807. 674 pp. Lea.
(Fye) $175 [≃ £97]

Culpeper, Nicholas
- The British herbal and family physician to which is added a dispensatory for the use of private premises. Halifax: n.d. [ca 1820]. 8vo. 52 hand-cold plates (2 torn), 6 anatomical plates. Worn & soiled. *(Spelman)* £40 [≃ $72]
- The complete herbal ... Thomas Kelly, 1850. New edn. 8vo. vi,398,[vi index] pp. 20 hand-cold plates. Some general foxing & occas staining. Mod qtr calf, mrbld bds.
(Gough) £175 [≃ $315]
- Culpeper's English physician and complete herbal. London: J. Adlard, 1810. 14th edn. 4to. xvi,400,256 pp. Engvd port (laid down), 29 hand-cold engvd plates, 13 anatomical plates. Contemp reverse calf, a little worn at hd & ft of spine.   *(Gough)* £195 [≃ $351]
- The English physician enlarged: with three hundred, sixty, and nine medicines made of English herbs ... London: Peter Cole, 1656. 8vo. [22],398,[16] pp. Lacking 1st blank, sl loss to title border, paper flaw in D1, some

soiling. Contemp calf, crude respining.
(Spelman) £160 [≃ $288]
- The idea of practical physick in twelve books. London: Peter Cole, 1657. Sm folio. [10],345 pp (paginated in sections, with some errors). Foxing. Rec calf. *(Goodrich)* $1,250 [≃ £694]

Culver, E.M. & Hayden, J.R.
- A manual of venereal diseases. Phila: 1891. 1st edn. 8vo. viii,294, 16 pub ctlg pp. Text ills. Cloth, inner hinges starting, spine ends sl frayed.   *(Elgen)* $25 [≃ £13]

Cumberland, Richard (1631-1718)
- A treatise of the laws of nature ... deduced from the nature of things. London: 1727. 1st edn in English. 4to. Red & black gen title. Contemp calf, rebacked.
(Chaucer Head) £300 [≃ $540]

Cummings, T.G.
- Illustrations of the origin and progress of rail and tram roads, and steam carriages ... principal railways now in use ... conveyance of passengers ... Denbigh: 1824. Thin 8vo. 64 pp. Frontis, plate. Half calf, mrbld bds, rubbed.   *(Edwards)* £350 [≃ $630]

Cumston, C.G.
- An introduction to the history of medicine. 1926. xxxii,390 pp. Frontis, 24 plates. Sl foxing. Cloth.   *(Whitehart)* £18 [≃ $32]
- An introduction to the history of medicine from the time of the Pharaohs to the end of the xviiith century. London: 1926. xxxii,390 pp. 24 plates. Orig cloth.
(Weiner) £40 [≃ $72]
- An introduction to the history of medicine. New York: Knopf, 1926. 8vo. 390 pp. 24 plates. Orig cloth.   *(Oasis)* $65 [≃ £36]

Cures ...
- The cures of the diseased in forraine attempts of the English Nation ... See Whetstone, George

Currie, James
- Medical reports on the affects of water, cold and warm, as a remedy in fever, and febrile diseases. Liverpool printed: for Cadell & Davies, London, 1797. 1st edn. x,vii,[1 errata],252,45 pp. Clean tear in 1 leaf. Contemp half calf, mrbld bds, rebacked.
(Antiq Sc) $475 [≃ £263]
- Medical reports on the affects of water, cold and warm, as a remedy in fever ... Liverpool: 1804. 2 vols. 8vo. 2nd edn vol 1; 1st edn vol 2. xxiii,379; vi,383-630, 55,xv pp. Vol 2 title supplied in photocopy & a few other defects.

Mod qtr calf, mrbld bds.
(Weiner) £75 [≃ $135]

Currie, William
- An historical account of the climates and diseases of the United States of America ... Phila: 1792. 1st edn. 409,v pp. Mod lea, new endpapers. *(Scientia)* $475 [≃ £263]

Curschmann, H.
- Typhoid fever and typhus fever. Edited, with additions by William Osler. 1905. Orig cloth, sl wear at top of spine. *(Allen)* $25 [≃ £13]

Curtis, George
- A treatise of Gunter's scale, and the sliding rule ... use of the sector, protractor ... and line of chords. Whitehall, New York: E. Adams, 1824. 1st edn. 12mo. 119 pp. 3 full-page w'cut ills. Lacking front flyleaf, outer margs sl dampstained. Contemp lea.
(Antiq Sc) $250 [≃ £138]

Curtis, John G.
- Harvey's views on the use of the circulation of the blood. New York: 1915. 8vo. 194 pp. Port frontis, plates. *(Goodrich)* $75 [≃ £41]

Curtis, John Harrison
- A treatise on the physiology and diseases of the eye: containing a new mode of curing cataract without an operation ... London: 1833. 1st edn. 222 pp. Advt leaf. Cold frontis, half-title. Orig qtr cloth, rubbed, uncut.
(Goodrich) $225 [≃ £125]
- A treatise on the physiology and diseases of the eye: containing a new mode of curing cataract without an operation ... London: 1835. 2nd edn. xvi,242,[3], [16 advts] pp. Cold frontis with flap, cold plate. Uncut in orig mrbld bds. *(Whitehart)* £120 [≃ $216]

Curtis, William
- Instructions for collecting and preserving insects ... the nets, and other apparatus necessary for that purpose ... London: for the author, 1771. 1st edn. 8vo. iv,44 pp. Engvd frontis (with old fold mark), some staining on endpapers. Old mrbld bds, calf spine.
(Burmester) £225 [≃ $405]

Curwen, J.C.
- Hints on agricultural subjects, and on the best means of improving the condition of the labouring classes. London: J.Johnson, 1809. 2nd edn, imprvd & enlgd. 8vo. Aquatint frontis, 4 plates, Half calf, mrbld bds, rebacked. *(Traylen)* £95 [≃ $171]

Curzon, H.
- The universal library: or, compleat summary of science [and arts], containing about sixty select treatises ... London: for T. Warner, 1722. 2nd edn. 2 vols. 8vo. Fldg pedigree. Contemp panelled calf, gilt panelled spines, mor labels, gilt. *(Traylen)* £250 [≃ $450]

Cushing, Harvey
- A biography. London: 1946. 1st British edn. Orig cloth, dw. *(Goodrich)* $55 [≃ £30]
- Consecratio medici and other papers. Boston: 1928. 1st edn. One of 2000. 8vo. 276 pp. Dw.
(Elgen) $90 [≃ £50]
- Consecratio medici and other papers. Boston: 1928. 1st edn. One of 2000. 8vo. 276 pp. Without dw. *(Elgen)* $65 [≃ £36]
- From a surgeon's journal. Boston: Little, Brown, 1936. 1st edn. 8vo. 534 pp. Ills. Orig cloth, spine sl dulled. *(Oasis)* $60 [≃ £33]
- The Harvey Cushing collection of books and manuscripts. New York: 1943. 1st edn. 207 pp. Orig cloth, a few stains on cvrs.
(Elgen) $100 [≃ £55]
- Life of Sir William Osler. 1940. xviii,1417 pp. Port frontis, 10 plates. Cloth, spine faded. *(Whitehart)* £35 [≃ $63]
- Life of Sir William Osler. Oxford: 1925. 2nd imp. 2 vols. 8vo. Orig cloth, dws.
(Goodrich) $195 [≃ £108]
- Life of Sir William Osler. Oxford: 1926. 2 vols. 8vo. Orig cloth, dws. Author's inscrbd pres copy. *(Goodrich)* $575 [≃ £319]
- Life of Sir William Osler. Oxford: 1925. 2nd imp. 2 vols. 8vo. Orig cloth.
(Goodrich) $125 [≃ £108]
- The medical career and other papers. Boston: Little, Brown, 1940. 1st edn. 8vo. Orig cloth.
(Oasis) $45 [≃ £25]
- Papers relating to the pituitary body, hypothalamus and parasympathetic system. Springfield, Ill: 1932. 1st edn. 8vo. Cvrs lightly spotted, dw. *(Rittenhouse)* $325 [≃ £180]
- The pituitary body and its disorders. Phila: Lippincott, 1912. 1st iss. 8vo. 341 pp. Num ills. 2 stamps erased from title verso. Orig cloth. *(Oasis)* $300 [≃ £166]
- The pituitary body and its disorders. Phila: 1912. 1st edn, 1st iss. 341 pp. Orig cloth, top & bottom of spine lightly rubbed.
(Scientia) $325 [≃ £180]
- The story of U.S. Army Base Hospital No. 5. By a Member of the Unit. Cambridge: 1919. One of 250. 118 pp. Plates. Orig ptd wraps, worn. Preserved in a box.
(Scientia) $1,000 [≃ £555]

Cushing, Harvey & Bailey, P.A.
- A classification of the tumors of the glioma group on a histogenetic basis with a correlated study of prognosis. Phila: 1928. 175 pp. Orig cloth.   *(Goodrich)* **$295 [≈ £163]**

Cushing, Harvey & Eisenhardt, Louise
- Meningiomas. Their classification, regional behavior, life history, and surgical end-results. Springfield: C. Thomas, 1938. 1st edn. 8vo. 785 pp. Num ills. Orig cloth, spine v sl dulled.   *(Oasis)* **$500 [≈ £277]**

Cutler, E.G. & Garland, G.M.
- Percussion outlines. Boston: 1882. 1st edn. 8vo. 65 pp. 9 plates on heavy paper. Cloth.   *(Elgen)* **$50 [≈ £27]**

Cuvier, G.
- A discourse of the revolutions of the surface of the globe, and the changes thereby produced in the animal kingdom ... London: 1829. 1st edn of this trans. 8vo. 261 pp. 4 plates, ills. Half calf, mrbld bds, rebacked with orig spine laid down.
          (Weiner) **£100 [≈ $180]**
- Essay on the theory of the earth with geological illustrations, by Professor Jameson. Edinburgh & London: 1827. 5th edn. 8vo. xxiv,550 pp. 11 plates. Sm lib stamp on title verso; title & frontis lightly foxed. Polished calf.   *(Weiner)* **£100 [≈ $180]**
- Essay on the theory of the earth, translated from the French ... with mineralogical notes and ... geological discoveries ... Edinburgh: 1813. 1st English edn. 8vo. xiii,265 pp. 2 plates. Half calf. Ex lib.
          (Weiner) **£100 [≈ $180]**

Da Costa, Emanuel Mendes
- Elements of conchology. London: for Benjamin White, 1776. 1st edn. viii,[iii]-vi, 318,[2 errata] pp, advt leaf. 7 fldg engvd plates, 2 fldg charts. Contemp tree calf.
          (Claude Cox) **£110 [≈ $198]**

Da Costa, J.M.
- Harvey and his discovery. Phila: 1879. 1st edn, 2nd ptg. 8vo. 57 pp. Cloth, spine ends lightly frayed.   *(Elgen)* **$45 [≈ £25]**

Da Costa, John C. (ed.)
- Handbook of medical treatment. Phila: 1919. 2 vols. 8vo. 1745 pp. Cloth.
          (Rittenhouse) **$35 [≈ £19]**

Dale, James
- Essay upon the question, Is medical science favourable to scepticism? Phila: 1839. 8vo. 22

pp. Sl foxing. Rec buckram.
          (Rittenhouse) **$20 [≈ £11]**

Dale, W.
- Calculations deduced from first principles ... by plain arithmetic, for the use of Societies instituted for the benefit of old age ... London: Ridley, 1772. Sole edn. 8vo. xcvi,[i], 247,[184] pp. Uncut & lgely unopened in orig bds.   *(Frew Mackenzie)* **£620 [≈ $1,116]**

Dalton, J.C.
- History of the College of Physicians and Surgeons in the City of New York, medical department of Columbia College. New York: 1888. 208 pp. a few ills. Cloth dull, spine marked, ex lib.   *(Whitehart)* **£35 [≈ $63]**

Dalton, John
- Topographical anatomy of the brain. Phila: 1885. 1st edn. 3 vols. 4to. 48 heliotypes, outline sketches. Orig binding.
          (Fye) **$750 [≈ £416]**

Dalton, John (1766-1844)
- Meteorological observations and essays. London: ... Pennington, 1793. 1st edn, 1st iss. 8vo in 4's. xvi,208 pp. Sev w'cut diags in the text. Uncut in orig lavender bds, a little worn, mor-backed case. Inscrbd by author to William Fothergill.
          (Pickering) **$3,000 [≈ £1,666]**
- Meteorological observations and essays. Manchester: for Baldwin & Cradock, 1834. 2nd edn. 8vo. 4 pp ctlg of books. Orig bds, rec rebacked. Author's pres copy.
          (Chaucer Head) **£250 [≈ $450]**

Dana, C.L.
- Text-book of nervous diseases. New York: 1925. 10th edn. 667 pp. Cloth.
          (Goodrich) **$90 [≈ £50]**

Dana, Charles L.
- Peaks of medical history. New York: 1926. 1st edn. 105 pp. Cloth.
          (Goodrich) **$35 [≈ £19]**
- Peaks of medical history. New York: 1926. 1st edn. 8vo. 105 pp. 40 plates, 16 text ills. Cloth.   *(Elgen)* **$40 [≈ £22]**

Dana, James D.
- Characteristics of volcanoes with contributions ... from the Hawaiian Islands. London: [1890]. 8vo. xvi,399 pp. 16 plates, text figs. Orig cloth, trifle worn.
          (Wheldon & Wesley) **£90 [≈ $162]**
- Corals and coral islands. London: 1875. 2nd edn. 8vo. xx,348 pp. Cold frontis, 76 text ills,

3 extndg charts. Contemp prize mor, gilt spine, arms of King's College London on sides, a.e.g. *(Bow Windows)* £75 [≃ $135]

- Manual of geology ... with special reference to American geological history. New York: Ivison ..., 1876. 8vo. xvi,828 pp. Num text figs, fldg cold map. Orig green cloth, gilt. *(Gough)* £40 [≃ $72]

Dana, James Freeman

- An epitome of chymical philosophy. Concord, N.H.: Isaac Hill, 1825. 1st edn. 8vo. 231,[1] pp. 4 pp table at end. Orig bds, paper label, uncut. Author's sgnd pres inscrptn. *(Antiq Sc)* $175 [≃ £97]
- An epitome of chymical philosophy. Concord, N.H.: 1825. 1st edn. 8vo. 231 pp. Errata leaf. Few pages foxed. Orig paper-cvrd bds, v worn. Author's pres inscrptn. *(Elgen)* $160 [≃ £88]

Dana, Samuel

- Manures: a prize essay. Lowell: 1844. 1st edn. 12mo. 47 pp. Mod bds. *(Argosy)* $150 [≃ £83]

Dandolo, Count

- The art of rearing silk-worms. London: Murray, 1825. 1st English edn. 8vo. 2 fldg plates, 2 fldg tables. Orig blue-grey bds, cloth spine, ptd paper label. *(Traylen)* £165 [≃ $297]

Dandy, Walter

- Benign tumors of the third ventricle of the brain: diagnosis and treatment. Springfield: 1933. 8vo. 171 pp. Ills. Cloth. Pres copy from Sidney Gross to Joseph P. Globus. *(Goodrich)* $195 [≃ £108]
- Intracranial arterial aneurysms. Ithaca: 1945. 2nd printing. 8vo. 147 pp. Fldg tables. Cloth. *(Goodrich)* $150 [≃ £83]
- Orbital tumors; results following the transcranial operative attack. New York: 1941. 168 pp. 1st edn. Cloth, crnr of front cvr roughened. *(Scientia)* $200 [≃ £111]
- Selected writings. Compiled by C. Troland and F. Otenasek. Springfield: 1957. 1st edn. 789 pp. Orig cloth, dw. *(Scientia)* $150 [≃ £83]

Danforth, I.N.

- The life of Nathan Smith Davis. 1817-1904. Chicago: 1907. 8vo. 193 pp. Ills. Orig cloth. *(Goodrich)* $65 [≃ £36]

Danson, J.T.

- On the method, and the range, of statistical inquiry, as applied to the promotion of social

science. 1859. 8 pp. Ptd wraps. *(C.R. Johnson)* £20 [≃ $36]
- Statistical observations on the growth of the human body (males) in height and weight, from eighteen to thirty years of age. London: Edward Stanford, 1881. Orig blue ptd wraps. *(C.R. Johnson)* £20 [≃ $36]

Darrach, William

- Drawings of the anatomy of the groin with anatomical remarks. Phila: 1844. 2nd edn. 8vo. 127 pp. 4 litho plates. Foxed. Cloth, worn. *(Goodrich)* $75 [≃ £41]

Darwin, Charles

- The descent of man, and selection in relation to sex. London: Murray, 1871. 1st edn. 2 vols. 8vo. viii,424,16 advts; viii,[1 postscript],[1 blank], 476,16 advts pp. Some light foxing mainly to advts. Occas pencil marginalia. Orig green cloth, a little worn. *(Pickering)* $2,000 [≃ £1,111]
- The descent of man, and selection in relation to sex. London: Murray, 1871. 1st edn, 2nd iss. 2 vols. 8vo. viii,424,16 pub ctlg; viii,475, pub list pp. Sgntr on both titles. Orig embossed green cloth. *(Hemlock)* $125 [≃ £69]
- The descent of man, and selection in relation to sex. London: Murray, 1871. 1st edn, 2nd iss. 2 vols. 8vo. viii,423,[1]; viii,475,[1], 16 pub advts (Jan 1871) in both vols pp. Foxing on prelims & at ends. Orig green cloth (lightly worn), partially unopened. *(Rootenberg)* $400 [≃ £222]
- The descent of man. London: 1875. 2nd edn (11th thousand, revsd & augmented. 8vo. xvi,688 pp. 78 text ills. Pencilled notes in margs. Orig cloth, inner hinges trifle strained, extremities sl worn. *(Bow Windows)* £35 [≃ $63]
- The descent of man, and selection in relation to sex. London: Murray, 1889. 2nd edn, revsd & augmented, 25th thousand. xvi,693 pp. Half-title, 78 text ills. Orig green cloth, gilt spine. *(Gough)* £20 [≃ $36]
- The descent of man, and selection in relation to sex. London: 1889. 2nd edn. 25th thousand. 8vo. Orig cloth. *(Wheldon & Wesley)* £30 [≃ $54]
- The descent of man and selection in relation to sex. London: Murray, 1909. 8vo. Half green mor, gilt, t.e.g. *(Traylen)* £30 [≃ $54]
- The different forms of flowers on plants of the same species. London: Murray, 1877. 1st edn. 8vo. viii,352 pp. 15 text figs, 38 tables, 32 pp pub ctlg dated March 1877 at end. Occas light pencil underlinings & marg notes throughout. Orig cloth.

(Bickersteth) **£220 [≃ $396]**
- The different forms of flowers on plants of the same species. London: Murray, 1877. 1st edn. 8vo. viii,352 pp. 32 pp pub advts dated March 1877. W'cut ills & tables in text. Light browning on prelims & at end, a few reprs. Orig green cloth. *(Rootenberg)* **$475 [≃ £263]**
- The different forms of flowers on plants of the same species. London: 1877. 1st ed. 8vo. Ills. Orig green cloth, unopened.
(Argosy) **$400 [≃ £222]**
- The effects of cross and self fertilisation in the vegetable kingdom. London: Murray, 1876. 1st edn. 8vo. viii,482 pp. Errata slip. Title a little spotted, some pale pencil underlining & neat marg notes. Orig cloth.
(Bickersteth) **£220 [≃ $396]**
- The effects of cross and self fertilisation in the vegetable kingdom. London: 1900. 2nd edn, 5th imp. Orig cloth, sl worn. Ex lib with stamps. *(Whitehart)* **£18 [≃ $32]**
- The expression of the emotions in man and animals. London: 1872. 1st edn, 2nd iss. Cr 8vo. 7 heliotype plates, 3 fldg, 4 pp advts. Orig green cloth, a little worn, lib label removed from front cvr.
(Traylen) **£90 [≃ $162]**
- The expression of the emotions in man and animals. London: Murray, 1872. 1st edn, 2nd iss. 8vo. vi,374 pp, 4 pp pub advts dated November 1872. 7 heliotype plates (3 fldg), text ills. Orig green cloth, spine strengthened. W.J. Herschel's stamp of ownership.
(Rootenberg) **$450 [≃ £250]**
- The expression of the emotions in man and animals. New York: Appleton, 1873. 1st Amer edn. 8vo. v,[3],374,[14 advts] pp. 7 heliotype plates (3 fldg). Orig cloth.
(Antiq Sc) **$175 [≃ £97]**
- The expression of the emotions in man and animals. New York: Appleton, 1873. 1st Amer edn. 8vo. 374 pp. Advts. 7 heliotype plates. Orig cloth, headpiece worn.
(Goodrich) **$175 [≃ £97]**
- The expression of the emotions in man and animals. London: 1873. 10th thousand. 8vo. vi,374 pp. 7 plates. Orig cloth.
(Wheldon & Wesley) **£55 [≃ $99]**
- Expression of the emotions in man and animals. London: 1890. 2nd edn. 8vo. 7 heliotype plates, other ills. V minor spotting & dust marks. Orig cloth, ft of spine a trifle rubbed. *(Bow Windows)* **£75 [≃ $135]**
- Expression of the emotions in man and animals. London: 1892. 11th thousand. 8vo. viii,394,32 advts pp. 7 plates, 21 text figs. Inscrptn on flyleaf. Orig cloth.
(Bow Windows) **£65 [≃ $117]**
- The formation of vegetable mould, through

the action of worms ... London: Murray, 1881. 1st edn, third thousand. vii,326,[i advt] pp. 3-line errata tipped-in. Sl spotted. Reading copy in orig rather worn cloth. Ex lib. *(Gough)* **£18 [≃ $32]**
- The formation of vegetable mould through the action of worms. London: Murray, 1882. Sixth thousand, crrctd. 8vo. vii,328 pp. Pub list. Orig dark green cloth.
(Taylor) **£26 [≃ $46]**
- The formation of vegetable mould, through the action of worms ... London: 1892. Twelfth thousand. 8vo. vii,328,[2], 32 advts pp. Figs. Endpapers foxed. Uncut & unopened in orig cloth.
(Bow Windows) **£35 [≃ $63]**
- The formation of vegetable mould, through the action of worms ... London: Murray, 1897. 8vo. Half green mor, gilt, t.e.g.
(Traylen) **£25 [≃ $45]**
- Geological observations on the volcanic islands ... visited during the voyage of H.M.S. 'Beagle'. London: Smith, Elder, 1876. 2nd edn. 8vo. xiii,647 pp. Fldg map & chart, 5 fldg plates, text w'cuts. V slight marg foxing. Orig brown cloth, spine gilt.
(Morrell) **£95 [≃ $171]**
- Insectivorous plants. London: Murray, 1875. 1st edn, 1st iss. x,462 pp. Orig green cloth, a little rubbed. *(Pickering)* **$600 [≃ £333]**
- Journal of researches into the geology and natural history of the countries visited ... London: Colburn, 1840. 1st edn, 3rd iss. [iv],vii], xiv,629,16 pub advts dated August 1839 pp. 2 lge fldg maps bound in text. Orig blue cloth, variant a; spine reprd.
(Rootenberg) **$1,500 [≃ £833]**
- Journal of researches into the natural history and geology ... during the voyage of H.M.S. 'Beagle' ... London: Murray, 1860. 10th thousand. 8vo. xvi,519, 32 [advts dated Jan 1860] pp. Orig green cloth, sl soiled.
(Pickering) **$500 [≃ £277]**
- Journal of researches ... London: Murray, 1860. 10th thousand. 8vo. xvi,519. Contemp half brown mor, mrbld bds, rather rubbed.
(Gough) **£38 [≃ $68]**
- Journal of researches into the natural history and geology ... during the voyage of H.M.S. 'Beagle' ... London: 1860. 10th thousand. 8vo. xvi,519 pp. Clean tear in p 1 without loss. Half mor.
(Wheldon & Wesley) **£60 [≃ $108]**
- Journal of researches ... London: Thomas Nelson, 1890. 8vo. x,[ii],13-615 pp. 22 plates. Half red calf, gilt, trifle rubbed.
(Wheldon & Wesley) **£30 [≃ $54]**
- Journal of researches ... London: 1893. 615 pp. Frontis, num plates & ills. Orig cloth, sl

marked & dust-stained.
(Whitehart) £18 [≈ $32]

- The movements and habits of climbing plants. London: Murray, 1876. Second thousand. 8vo. viii,208,32 pub advts pp. Half-title. Orig green cloth, spine gilt.
(Gough) £75 [≈ $135]

- The movements and habits of climbing plants. London: 1888. 3rd thousand. 8vo. x,208 pp. 13 text figs. Orig cloth.
(Wheldon & Wesley) £40 [≈ $72]

- The movements and habits of climbing plants. London: Murray, 1906. 8vo. Half green mor, gilt, t.e.g. *(Traylen)* £25 [≈ $45]

- A naturalist's voyage. Journal of researches ... London: 1890. New edn. 8vo. Port & figs. Sgntr & dated 1891 on half-title. Uncut, partially unopened in orig cloth.
(Bow Windows) £22 [≈ $39]

- On the origin of species by means of natural selection ... London: Murray, 1859. 1st edn. 8vo in 12's. ix,[1],502,32 pub advts dated June 1859 pp. (variant 3). 1 fldg plate. Orig blindstamped cloth (variant a). Minor reprs. Uncut in solander case of qtr mor.
(Rootenberg) $7,500 [≈ £4,166]

- On the origin of species by means of natural selection ... London: Murray, 1859. 1st edn. 8vo. Fldg diag. Orig cloth, binding variant a, minor strengthening of hd & tail of spine. Searles Valentine Wood's copy with his sgntr & pencil notes to text.
(Quaritch) $12,000 [≈ £6,666]

- On the origin of species by means of natural selection ... London: Murray, 1869. 5th edn, tenth thousand. xxiii,596,32 pp pub advts. Half-title. Orig green cloth, inner jnt a bit ragged. *(Gough)* £100 [≈ $180]

- The origin of species by means of natural selection ... Sixth edition, with additions and corrections. (Thirteenth thousand). London: Murray, 1872. 8vo. Plate dusty at edges, some foxing. Orig cloth, recased.
(Pollak) £75 [≈ $135]

- The origin of species by means of natural selection ... Sixth edition, with additions and corrections to 1872. (Twentieth thousand). London: Murray, 1878. 8vo. xxi,[i],458 pp. Orig green cloth, rubbed.
(Pickering) $200 [≈ £111]

- On the origin of species by means of natural selection ... New York: 1883. New edn. xxi,458 pp. Fldg table. Orig cloth.
(Whitehart) £18 [≈ $32]

- The origin of species ... London: 1895. 6th edn, 47th thousand. 8vo. xxi,432 pp. Extndg diag. Tiny spot on title, 1st lf of text a little frayed. Orig cloth, inner hinges a little strained. *(Bow Windows)* £36 [≈ $64]

- The origin of species by means of natural selection. London: Murray, 1911. 8vo. Port. Half green mor, gilt, t.e.g.
(Traylen) £30 [≈ $54]

- The power of movement in plants. London: Murray, 1880. 1st edn, 1st iss. 8vo. x,592 pp. 32 pp pub advts dated May, 1878. Text ills. A few reprs. Orig green cloth.
(Rootenberg) $475 [≈ £263]

- The variation of animals and plants under domestication. London: 1868. 1st edn, 1st iss. 2 vols. 8vo. Advts & errata as called for. Sgntr on titles, sl foxing at beginning & end of each vol. Orig green cloth, trifle used, refixed.
(Wheldon & Wesley) £180 [≈ $324]

- The variation of animals and plants under domestication. London: Murray, 1868. 1st edn, 1st iss. 2 vols. viii,411; viii,486 pp. Lacking advts. Contemp half calf, spines gilt.
(Gough) £125 [≈ $225]

- The variation of animals and plants under domestication. London: Murray, 1868. 1st edn, 1st iss. 2 vols. Roy 8vo. viii,412,32 [advts April 1867]; viii,486,[2 advts Feb 1868] pp. Minor foxing at beginning of each vol. Orig green cloth, 1 inner hinge split.
(Pickering) $850 [≈ £472]

- The variation of animals and plants under domestication. London: 1899. 8th imp of 2nd edn, revsd, 2 vols. 8vo. Orig cloth, sl marked.
(Wheldon & Wesley) £30 [≈ $54]

- On the various contrivances by which British and foreign orchids are fertilised by insects ... London: Murray, 1862. 1st edn. 8vo in 12's. vi,365, 32 pub advts dated December 1861 pp. Fldg plate, 33 text w'cuts. Orig plum cloth, gilt orchid (variant a).
(Rootenberg) $650 [≈ £361]

- The various contrivances by which orchids are fertilised by insects. London: Murray, 1877. 2nd edn, revsd. Cr 8vo. 32 pp pub ctlg January 1882 at end. Mostly unopened, orig green cloth, front inner hinge cracking, sl crease on front bd. *(Taylor)* £58 [≈ $104]

- The various contrivances by which orchids are fertilised by insects. London: Murray, 1899. 8vo. Half green mor, gilt, t.e.g.
(Traylen) £25 [≈ $45]

Darwin, Erasmus

- Phytologia; or the philosophy of agriculture and gardening. With the theory of draining morasses ... London: Bensley, 1800. 1st edn. 4to. viii,612,[12] pp. 12 engvd plates, a few with plate numbers shaved. Occas light waterstaining. Half calf, mrbld bds.
(Antiq Sc) $185 [≈ £102]

- Zoonomia or the laws of organic life. London: for J. Dodsley, 1794. 2 vols. 4to. 8 plates.

Title of each vol laid down & trimmed. Contemp half calf, rebacked.
(Waterfield's) **£300 [≈ $540]**

Darwin, Francis

- The life and letters of Charles Darwin ... London: Murray, 1888. 7th thousand, revsd. 3 vols. 8vo. x,396,[1 advts]; [iv],394,[1 advts]; iv,418,[1 advts] pp. 3 frontis, 2 plates, 2 text ills. Orig blue-green cloth, spines faded, sides a little soiled.   *(Pickering)* **$300 [≈ £166]**
- The life and letters of Charles Darwin ... London: 1887. 3rd edn. 3 vols. 8vo. 7 ills inc ports. Sl spotting & some margs browned. Orig cloth, dull, ends of spines v sl fingered.
(Bow Windows) **£90 [≈ $162]**
- The life and letters of Charles Darwin ... London: Murray, 1887. 3rd edn. 3 vols. 8vo. 3 ports. Orig cloth, Mudie's lib label on each, sl worn.   *(Stewart)* **£60 [≈ $108]**
- The life and letters of Charles Darwin ... London: Murray, 1888. 7th thousand, revsd. 3 vols. 8vo. 3 frontis. Orig green cloth, spines gilt.   *(Gough)* **£95 [≈ $171]**

Darwinian theory ...

- The Darwinian theory of the transmutation of species ... See Beverley, Robert Mackenzie

Daubeny, Charles

- An introduction to the atomic theory. Oxford: Murray, 1831. 1st edn. xv,[1],147,[1] pp. Orig bds. Joseph Henry's copy, presented to John Torrey, with sgntrs of both.
(Antiq Sc) **$650 [≈ £361]**

Daukes, S.H.

- The medical museum. Modern developments, organisation and technical methods ... London: Wellcome Museum, 1929. 8vo. 183 pp. Ills. Orig cloth.
(Goodrich) **$35 [≈ £19]**

Davenport, Charles Benedict

- Experimental morphology. New York: 1897-99. 1st edn. 2 vols. 509 pp. Orig cloth, pres stamp in vol 2.   *(Scientia)* **$95 [≈ £52]**
- Experimental morphology. New York: Macmillan, 1897-99. 1st edn. 2 vols. 8vo. xiv,280.[2]; xviii,281-509 pp. Pencil lining in margs. Orig cloth.   *(Antiq Sc)* **$175 [≈ £97]**
- Experimental morphology. New York: 1908. 8vo. xviii,509 pp. Ills. Orig cloth.
(Weiner) **£25 [≈ $45]**

Davenport, John

- Aphrodisiacs and anti-aphrodisiacs: three essays on the powers of reproduction. London: privately printed, 1869. 1st edn. Sm

4to. xii,154 pp. Advt leaf. 8 plates. Uncut in contemp mor-backed mrbld bds, rubbed.
(Claude Cox) **£35 [≈ $63]**

David, Mrs. Edgeworth

- Funafuti, or three months on a coral island; an unscientific account of a scientific expedition. London: Murray, 1899. 1st edn. 8vo. xiii,[iii], 318 pp. Half-title, map, 16 plates. Orig cloth, t.e.g., sl damp-spotted & stained.   *(Morrell)* **£75 [≈ $135]**

David, Sir T.W.

- A geological map of the Commonwealth of Australia. Sydney: 1931 [with] Explanatory notes to accompany ... Sydney: 1932. Cold map in 4 sections, 77 x 63 inches, mtd on linen. 177 pp text. Orig ptd wraps. Cloth slip case, a little worn.
(Bow Windows) **£240 [≈ $432]**

David, William K.

- Secrets of wise men, chemists and great physicians. Chicago: the author, 1889. 1st edn. Sm 8vo. 128 pp. Text ills. Orig cloth. David's patented double-disk perpetual calendar mtd inside cvr. *(Oasis)* **$40 [≈ £22]**

Davie, Oliver

- Methods in the art of taxidermy. Columbus: 1894. 4to. xiv,150,vii index, xii subscribers pp. 90 full-page engvs. Orig bds, recased, sl soiled, rubbed, new endpapers.
(Edwards) **£250 [≈ $450]**

Davies, Charles

- Elements of surveying and navigation, with descriptions of the instruments and the necessary tables. New York: Barnes, 1853. Revsd edn. 222 pp. 6 fldg engvd plates, 100 pp tables, ills. Lea.   *(Xerxes)* **$50 [≈ £27]**

Davies, E.W.L.

- Algiers in 1857 ... with especial reference to English invalids ... London: Longman ..., 1858. 1st edn. 8vo. xii,164 pp. 4 cold plates (each with sm lib stamp). Orig cloth, gilt, inner hinges cracked, faded, crnrs bumped.
(Lloyd-Roberts) **£18.50 [≈ $32]**

Davies, John

- The innkeeper's and butler's guide ... making ... British wines ... colouring and flavouring of foreign ... spirits ... Leeds: 1807. 3rd edn. [iv],200 pp. Hole in front free endpaper. Orig ptd paper bds, hinges rubbed, backstrip torn, cvrs soiled.   *(Claude Cox)* **£150 [≈ $270]**
- The innkeeper's and butler's guide ... making and managing of British wines ... managing, colouring and flavouring of foreign wines and

spirits ... Leeds: George Wilson, 1808. 11th edn. 12mo. Contemp grey bds, reversed calf spine, uncut edges. *(Traylen)* **£180 [≃$324]**

Davis, David

- Elements of operative midwifery ... new and improved powers for assisting difficult and dangerous labours. London: 1825. 4to. [4],344 pp. 20 engvd plates. Foxed, dampstained, lacking top blank portion of title & dedn leaf without loss of text. Contemp calf.   *(Goodrich)* **$125 [≃£69]**

Davis, John

- The measure of the circle. Perfected in January 1845. London: 1854. 156 pp. Text pages sl dust-stained. Orig bds, spine defective, reprd with linen.
                (Whitehart) **£25 [≃$45]**
- The measure of the circle. Perfected in January 1845. Providence: privately printed, 1854. 8vo. Ills. Orig cloth.
                (Argosy) **$45 [≃£25]**

Davis, John Staige

- Plastic surgery; its principles and practice. Phila: 1919. 1st edn. 770 pp. Cloth, top & bottom of spine sl rubbed.
                (Scientia) **$375 [≃£208]**

Davis, Joseph B.

- Thesaurus craniorum, Catalogue of the skulls of the various races on man in the collection of J.B. Davis. London: for the subscribers, 1867. 8vo. 367 pp. 2 engvd plates, num text engvs. Cloth, spine worn, jnts cracked.
                (Goodrich) **$75 [≃£41]**

Davis, Nathan Smith

- History of medicine with the code of medical ethics. Chicago: 1903. 8vo. 209 pp. Lacking front blank. Uncut, binding worn.
                (Goodrich) **$95 [≃£52]**

Davis, R.H.

- Breathing in irrespirable atmospheres and ... also under water including a short history of gas and incendiary warfare, [1948]. xi,386 pp. Num plates inc 4 cold. Cloth.
                (Whitehart) **£25 [≃$45]**

Davis, Robert H. (ed.)

- Deep diving and submarine operations. A manual for deep sea divers and compressed air workers. London: St. Catherine Press, [1935]. 4th edn. 8vo. xii,510,[ii] pp. Lge fldg frontis, cold fldg chart, profusely illus. Pub bndg, dw.
                (Pollak) **£65 [≃$117]**

Davis, Thomas

- General view of the agriculture of Wiltshire. London: for Richard Phillips, 1811. 8vo. xix,268 pp, [4 advt] ff. Port, fldg map, plate. Later half calf, gilt backstrip.
                (Claude Cox) **£65 [≃$117]**

Davis, William

- A treatise on land surveying, by the chain, cross and offset staffs ... subterraneous surveys. 1813. 5th edn. xx,393,[1] pp. List of books, engvd port, 9 fldg plates, table. Contemp bds, linen spine.
                (Whitehart) **£40 [≃$72]**

Davy, Edward

- An experimental guide to chemistry. London: George Herbert, 1836. 8vo. iv,98,17 pp. Engvd frontis, fldg plate. Orig dec cloth, ptd label on front cvr.
                (Offenbacher) **$275 [≃£152]**

Davy, Sir Humphrey

- The collected works. Edited by his brother John Davy. London: 1839-40. 1st coll edn. 9 vols. 8vo. Port, fldg facs, 35 litho plates. Lib stamp on flyleaf & 2nd title verso. Orig embossed cloth, uncut.
                (Halewood) **£275 [≃$495]**
- Elements of agricultural chemistry, in a course of lectures ... 1813. 1st edn. 4to. 323,63 appendix pp. 10 engvd plates. Mod qtr mor, uncut.   *(Edwards)* **£220 [≃$396]**
- Elements of agricultural chemistry, in a course of lectures ... 1813. 1st edn. 4to. 10 plates. A little foxing. New qtr calf.
                (Halewood) **£110 [≃$198]**
- Six discourses delivered before the Royal Society at their anniversary meetings ... London: Murray, 1827. 1st edn. 4to. xi,25; 17; 21; 19; 19; 30 pp. Final blank restored in lower crnr. Contemp sugar-paper wraps with a few reprs.   *(Blackwell's)* **£200 [≃$360]**

Davy, John

- Memoirs of the life of Sir Humphry Davy, Bart. London: Longman, 1836. 2 vols. 8vo. xii,507; viii,419,[1 errata] pp. Engvd port frontis vol 1. Uncut in orig bds, hinges split, spines with some defects.
                (Hemlock) **$170 [≃£94]**

Dawkins, W.B.

- Early man in Britain and his place in the tertiary period. 1880. xxiii,537 pp. 168 text figs. 3/4 mor, gilt, sl rubbed, sm crack in lower hinge.   *(Whitehart)* **£35 [≃$63]**

Dawson, Sir J.W.

- Life's dawn on earth ... the history of the oldest known fossil remains. and their relations to geological time ... London: Hodder ..., 1875. 2nd thousand. 8vo. xii,239 pp. 8plates, 49 ills. Orig pict green cloth, gilt. *(Gough)* £18 [≈ $32]
- Some salient points in the science of the earth. London: 1893. 1st edn. 8vo. x,[ii],499 pp. Frontis, 28 plates, 19 figs. Some finger & other marks, pencilled notes on last leaf verso. Orig cloth, a little marked, inner hinges strained. *(Bow Windows)* £20 [≈ $36]

Dawson, Warren R.

- The beginnings - Egypt and Assyria. New York: Hoeber, 1930. ix,[i],86 pp. Pub bndg. *(Pollak)* £20 [≈ $36]
- A leechbook or collection of medical recipes of the fifteenth century ... together with a transcript into modern spelling. London: 1934. 8vo. 344 pp. Orig cloth. *(Weiner)* £30 [≈ $54]
- A leechbook or collection of medical recipes of the fifteenth century ... London: 1934. 8vo. 344 pp. Orig cloth. *(Goodrich)* $50 [≈ £27]
- Manuscripta medica. A descriptive catalogue of the manuscripts in the Library of the Medical Society of London. London: 1932. 8vo. 140 pp. Orig cloth. *(Goodrich)* $35 [≈ £19]

Day, Jeremiah

- An introduction to algebra, being the first part of a course of mathematics, adapted to the method of instruction in the American colleges. New Haven: 1838. 32nd edn. viii,332 pp. 2 fldg plates. Scattered foxing throughout. Contemp lea, rubbed, worn. *(Whitehart)* £40 [≈ $72]

D'Agapayeff, A.

- Codes and ciphers. London: 1939. 8vo. 160 pp. Diags. Orig cloth. *(Weiner)* £21 [≈ $37]

D'Albe, E.E. Fournier

- The moon element: an introduction to the wonders of selenium. New York: Appleton, 1924. 1st edn. 8vo. 156 pp. Plates. Orig cloth, dw. *(Oasis)* $40 [≈ £22]

D'Aubuisson de Voisins, J.F.

- A treatise on hydraulics for the use of engineers, translated from the French ... Boston: 1852. 8vo. xxiv,532 pp. 90 figs on 4 fldg plates. Orig cloth, spine ends worn. *(Weiner)* £30 [≈ $54]

de Beer, G.R.

- Growth. London: 1924. 8vo. viii,120 pp. Plates, diags. Orig cloth. *(Weiner)* £20 [≈ $36]

de Camus, C.E.L.

- A treatise on the teeth of wheels ... for the purposes of machinery such as mill-work and clock-work. London: 1868. 8vo. vi,102 pp. 18 plates. Orig cloth. *(Weiner)* £40 [≈ $72]

De Chapman, Frederick Henry

- A treatise on ship-building, with explanations and demonstrations respecting the Architecture Navalis Mercatoria ... Cambridge: Deighton, 1820. 1st English edn. 2 vols. 4to. 2 fldg tables, 23 fldg engvd plates. Contemp russia, gilt, by Hayday. *(Traylen)* £950 [≈ $1,710]

De la Beche, H.T.

- The geological observer. London: 1851. 8vo. xxxii,846 pp. 309 text figs. Orig cloth, spine faded, trifle worn at headband. *(Wheldon & Wesley)* £50 [≈ $90]
- How to observe: Geology. London: 1836. 2nd edn. 8vo. viii,312 pp. W'cuts. Lacking front free endpaper. Orig dec cloth, a little discold. *(Weiner)* £40 [≈ $72]
- Researches in theoretical geology. London: 1834. xvi,408 pp. Frontis, plate, few ills. Orig cloth, rebacked. *(Weiner)* £60 [≈ $108]

De Mendoza y Rios, Joseph

- A complete collection of tables for navigation and nautical astronomy. London: T. Bensley, 1809. 2nd edn, imprvd. 4to. Contemp polished calf, gilt spine, mor label, gilt. *(Traylen)* £85 [≈ $153]

De Moivre, Abraham

- The doctrine of chances: or, a method of calculating the probability of events in play. London: 1718. 1st edn. Lge 4to. [2]ff, xiv,175 pp. Engvd vignettes. Orig calf, rubbed, jnts open. *(Elgen)* $750 [≈ £416]
- The doctrine of chances: or, a method of calculating the probability of events in play. London: for the author, 1718. 1st edn. Lge 4to. [6],175 pp. 2 vignettes (1 on title). Contemp calf, spine & label reprd. *(Rootenberg)* $1,500 [≈ £833]
- The doctrine of chances ... London: 1738. 2nd edn. 4to. Lge paper. [2]ff, xiv,256 pp. Engvd vignette. Title somewhat browned. Lib binding. Ex lib. *(Elgen)* $400 [≈ £222]

De Morgan, Augustus

- Arithmetical books from the invention of

printing to the present time ... London: 1847.
Lge 12mo. xxviii,124 pp. Marg of few leaves
water-stained. Orig cloth, paper label, ex lib.
(Weiner) **£35 [≈ $63]**
- A budget of paradoxes. Edited by D.E.
Smith. London & Chicago: 1915. 2nd edn. 2
vols. viii,402; 387 pp. Cloth, sl torn dws.
(Whitehart) **£35 [≈ $63]**
- The differential and integral calculus ...
London: Robert Baldwin, [1842]. 1st edn.
8vo. xx,785, [2]; 64 pp. Pres binding in full
calf.   *(Rootenberg)* **$385 [≈ £213]**
- The differential and integral calculus ...
London: Robert Baldwin, 1842. 1st edn. 8vo.
xx,785, [iii],64 pp. A little foxing at front.
Orig cloth, rebacked, old spine relaid.
(Pollak) **£40 [≈ $72]**
- Elements of algebra preliminary to the
differential calculus and fit for the higher
classes of schools ... Taylor & Walton, 1837.
2nd edn. 248 pp. Erratum leaf, ctlg leaf. Orig
cloth.   *(Hinchliffe)* **£55 [≈ $99]**
- An essay on probabilities, and on their
application to life contingencies and
insurance offices. London: Longman ...,
1838. 1st edn. 8vo. xviii,306 pp, 40 pp
appendix, 16 pp pub advts. Engvd title, text
diags. Orig cloth. *(Rootenberg)* **$275 [≈ £152]**
- Formal logic: or, the calculus of inference,
necessary and probable. London: Taylor &
Walton, 1847. 1st edn. 8vo. xvi,336 pp. Sm
dampstain on title & early leaves, occas light
spotty foxing. Orig blindstamped cloth.
(Antiq Sc) **£450 [≈ £250]**
- The globes. celestial and terrestrial. London:
Malby, 1845. 1st edn. xv,[i],147,[i] pp. Some
text w'cuts. Without the advt before title.
Orig cloth, recased.   *(Pollak)* **£65 [≈ $117]**
- Trigonometry and double algebra. London:
1849. xii,167 pp. A few diags. Sl waterstain
on a few pp. New cloth.
(Whitehart) **£35 [≈ $63]**

De Quincey, Thomas
- Confessions of an English opium-eater.
London: Taylor & Hessey, 1823. 3rd edn.
12mo. 6 pp advts at end. Orig bds backed
with glazed paper, crnrs rubbed, jnts cracked,
backstrip chipped.   *(Clark)* **£85 [≈ $153]**

De Reaumur, Rene Antoinette Ferchault
- The art of hatching and bringing up
domestick fowls of all kinds ... by means of
the heat of hot-beds or that of common fire.
London: for C. Davis ..., 1750. 1st English
edn. 8vo. 15 fldg engvd plates, 10 engvd
vignettes. Contemp calf, gilt, jnts reprd.
(Traylen) **£295 [≈ $531]**

De Vries, Hugo
- Intracellular pangenesis. Including a paper on
fertilization and hybridization. Chicago:
Open Court Publishing, 1910. 1st edn in
English. 270 pp. Orig cloth.
(Oasis) **$125 [≈ £69]**
- The mutation theory. London: Kegan Paul,
1910-11. 1st English edn. 2 vols. 8vo. 582;
683 pp. 12 cold plates. Orig cloth.
(Oasis) **$125 [≈ £69]**
- Species and varieties: their origin by
mutation. Chicago: Open Court Publishing,
1905. 1st edn. 8vo. 847 pp. Orig cloth.
(Oasis) **$200 [≈ £111]**
- Species and varieties: their origin by
mutation. Chicago & London: 1904. 8vo.
xviii,847 pp. Binder's cloth, faded.
(Weiner) **£50 [≈ $90]**

Deaver, John B.
- Enlargement of the prostrate: its history,
anatomy, setiology, pathology ... Phila:
[1922]. 2nd edn. 8vo. xiii,358 pp. Frontis,
142 ills. Cloth.   *(Elgen)* **$45 [≈ £25]**
- A treatise on appendicitis. Phila: 1900. 8vo.
300,40 pub ctlg pp. 10 cold plates, 12 b/w
plates. Orig cloth, spine ends sl frayed. Ex lib.
(Elgen) **$55 [≈ £30]**

Debeer, Sir Gavin R.
- The development of the vertebrate skull.
Oxford: 1937. xxiii,552 pp. 143 full-page
plates.   *(Whitehart)* **£40 [≈ $72]**
- Embryos and ancestors. Oxford: 1951. Revsd
edn. 8vo. xii,159 pp. Ills, plates. Orig cloth,
dw.   *(Elgen)* **£35 [≈ £19]**

Defoe, Daniel
- An historical narrative of the Great Plague at
London, 1665 ... And some account of other
remarkable plagues, ancient and modern.
London: W. Nicoll, 1769. 8vo. Some
spotting. Mod calf, in calf & cloth slipcase.
(Chaucer Head) **£180 [≈ $324]**
- History of the plague in London with suitable
reflections. Bath: S. Hazard, [1795]. 8vo.
W'cut on title. Sewn as issued. An
abridgement, Cheap Repository Tract.
(Waterfield's) **£30 [≈ $54]**
- A system of magick or a history of the black
art ... London: A. Millar, 1728. 2nd edn. 8vo.
xii,404 pp. Engvd frontis. Some soiling. New
half calf, gilt. *(Lloyd-Roberts)* **£125 [≈ $225]**

Dejerine, J. & Gauckler, E.
- The psychoneuroses and their treatment by
psychotherapy. Phila: 1915. 2nd English edn.
395 pp. Orig cloth. *(Goodrich)* **$115 [≈ £63]**

Delafield, Francis
- A hand-book of post-mortem examinations and of morbid anatomy. New York: 1872. 1st edn. 376 pp. Sgntr on title. Cloth, top of spine chipped.   *(Scientia)* **$200 [≃ £111]**

Delafield, Francis & Prudden, T. Mitchell
- A hand-book of pathological anatomy and histology. New York: 1855. 1st edn. 575 pp. Stamp on front blank. Cloth, sm tears at spine hd & ft.   *(Scientia)* **$150 [≃ £83]**

Delafield, Francis & Stillman, Charles
- A manual of physical diagnosis. New York: 1878. 1st edn. 4to. 30 pp. Cold overlay ills. Orig cloth.   *(Fye)* **$125 [≃ £69]**

Delmege, J. Anthony
- Towards national health; or, health and hygiene in England from Roman to Victorian times. New York: 1932. 8vo. Port frontis, xiv,234 pp. Num ills, ports. Orig cloth, torn dw.   *(Elgen)* **$50 [≃ £27]**

Demonologia ...
- Demonologia ... See Forsyth, J.S.

Denman, Thomas
- An introduction to the practice of midwifery. New York: Oram, 1802. 1st Amer edn. 2 vols. Old calf, worn.   *(Oasis)* **$250 [≃ £138]**
- An introduction to the practice of midwifery. New York: 1821. 8vo. vi,683 pp. 16 plates. Some browning & foxing, title, final page & endpapers waterstained. Orig lead bds.   *(Rittenhouse)* **$45 [≃ £25]**
- An introduction to the practice of midwifery. With: Aphorisms on the application and use of the forceps and vectis ... New York: 1821. 8vo. 683 pp. Half-title, 16 engvd plates (some offsetting). Contents section bound out of order. Orig lea bds, rebacked.   *(Elgen)* **$175 [≃ £97]**
- An introduction to the practice of midwifery ... with notes and emendations by John W. Francis. New York: 1829. 3rd Amer edn. 776 pp. 17 plates. Some marg staining. Calf.   *(Goodrich)* **$55 [≃ £30]**

Dent, Edward J.
- A treatise on the aneroid, a newly invented portable barometer ... [Bound with] --- A treatise on the dipleidoscope ... fourth edition. London: 1849-45. 2 vols in 1. 8vo. 34; 24 pp. Ills. Half roan, worn.   *(Weiner)* **£150 [≃ $270]**

Derham, William
- The artificial clock-maker. A treatise of watch, and clock-work. London: Knapton, 1696. 1st edn. 8vo in 4's. [12],132 pp. W'cut plate, 2 w'cut ills in text. Some waterstaining, dust-soiled throughout. Contemp panelled calf, spine chipped, rubbed. Wing D1099.   *(Pickering)* **$3,000 [≃ £1,666]**
- Astro-theology: or a demonstration of the being and attributes of God, from a survey of the heavens. London: Innys, 1715. 1st edn. 8vo. lviii,[vi], 228,[vii] pp. 3 fldg engvd plates, w'cut vignette on title. Contemp calf, sl rubbed.   *(Blackwell's)* **£150 [≃ $270]**
- Astro-theology: or a demonstration of the being and attributes of God, from a survey of the heavens. London: Innys, 1719. 3rd edn, imprvd. 8vo. [xvi],lvi, [viii],246, [x] pp. 3 fldg plates. Contemp calf.   *(Lloyd-Roberts)* **£90 [≃ $162]**

Derrick's Handbook ...
- The derrick's handbook of petroleum. A complete chronological and statistical review of petroleum developments from 1859 to 1898. Oil City, Pa: 1898-1900. 2 vols. Thick 8vo. 1062,cxxi; 18,573 pp. Advts. Orig cloth.   *(Weiner)* **£250 [≃ $450]**

Desaguliers, J.T.
- A course of experimental philosophy. London: 1734-44. 1st edn. 2 vols. 4to. 10ff, 463,12 index & pub ctlg; xv,568,8 index & ctlg pp. 78 fldg plates. 2 pp soiled, few marg stains. Mod half calf. *(Weiner)* **£500 [≃ $900]**

Desault, Pierre
- A treatise on fractures, luxations and other affections of the bones. Edited by Xavier Bichat. Translated ... Phila: 1805. 1st edn in English. 413 pp. 3 plates. Lea.   *(Scientia)* **$275 [≃ £152]**

Descour, L.
- Pasteur and his work. Translated from the French ... New York: n.d. [ca 1921]. 256 pp. Port frontis. Cloth.   *(Elgen)* **$35 [≃ £19]**

Dewees, William P.
- A treatise on the diseases of females. Phila: 1826. 1st edn. 557 pp. 13 plates. Lower crnr of 1st 200 pp stained. Lea.   *(Scientia)* **$325 [≃ £180]**
- A treatise on the diseases of the female. Phila: 1837. 6th edn, revsd. 8vo. 590 pp. 12 engvd plates. Dampstained. Calf.   *(Goodrich)* **$25 [≃ £13]**
- A treatise on the physical and medical treatment of children. Phila: 1825. 1st edn. 496 pp. Lea, scuffed, sm gouge on front cvr.   *(Scientia)* **$350 [≃ £194]**

- A treatise on the physical and medical treatment of children. Phila: 1832. 4th edn. 548 pp. Lea, backstrip chipped.
(Fye) **$125** [≃ **£69**]
- A treatise on the physical and medical treatment of children. Phila: 1834. 5th edn. 8vo. 548 pp. Light foxing. Sheep.
(Goodrich) **$25** [≃ **£13**]

Dewey, Richard
- Recollections of Richard Dewey, pioneer in American psychiatry. An unfinished autobiography ... Chicago: 1936. 8vo. 174 pp. Orig cloth, dw.   *(Goodrich)* **$35** [≃ **£19**]

Dexter, Lewis & Weiss, Soma
- Pre-eclanptic and eclanptic toxemia of pregnancy. Boston: 1941. 8vo. xviii,415 pp. Cloth. Ex lib.   *(Rittenhouse)* **$27.5** [≃ **£15**]

Dickerson, E.N.
- Joseph Henry and the magnetic telegraph. New York: Scribner's, 1885. 1st edn. 8vo. 65 pp. Orig cloth. Author's sgnd pres inscrptn.
(Antiq Sc) **$75** [≃ **£41**]

Dickinson, H.W.
- A short history of the steam engine. Babcock & Wilson, 1938. 1st edn. 8vo. xvi,255 pp. Frontis, 10 plates, 78 figs, 3 tables. Orig cloth, spine faded.
(Bow Windows) **£22** [≃ **$39**]
- A short history of the steam engine. Cambridge: 1938. 8vo. xvi,255 pp. 11 plates, ills. Orig cloth, sl discold or soiled.
(Weiner) **£25** [≃ **$45**]

Dickinson, R.L. & Bryant, L.S.
- Control of conception, an illustrated medical manual. Baltimore: 1932. 1st edn, 2nd ptg. 8vo. xii,290 pp. Ills, plates. Cloth.
(Elgen) **$20** [≃ **£11**]

Dickinson, W. Howship
- Diabetes. London: Longmans, Green, 1877. 1st edn. 8vo. 3 plates, 17 w'cuts, 24 pp pub advts. Cloth, gilt, a little stained.
(Traylen) **£30** [≃ **$54**]

Dickson, Adam
- The husbandry of the ancients. Edinburgh: for J. Dickson ..., 1788. 1st edn. 2 vols. 8vo. Half-titles. Contemp half calf, gilt.
(Traylen) **£220** [≃ **$396**]
- A treatise of agriculture. Edinburgh: for A. Kincaid ..., 1770. 2nd edn. 2 vols. 8vo. 2 fldg plates. Contemp speckled calf, gilt ribbed spines.   *(Traylen)* **£180** [≃ **$324**]

Dickson, David
- An essay on the possibility and probability of a child being born alive, and live, in the latter end of the fifth solar ... month. Edinburgh: James Watson, 1712. 1st edn. 12mo. Without half-title. Contemp panelled calf, rebacked.
(Quaritch) **$700** [≃ **£388**]

Dickson, R.W.
- Practical agriculture: or a complete system of modern husbandry ... London: for Richard Phillips, 1805. 1st edn. 2 vols. 4to. 87 plates (27 hand-cold). Contemp calf, hinges cracked or broken, some wear to crnrs.
(Claude Cox) **£250** [≃ **$450**]
- Practical agriculture: or a complete system of modern husbandry ... London: 1814. 2nd edn. 2 vols. 4to. Fldg & cold frontispieces, 85 plates (26 old). Contemp calf, rebacked.
(Traylen) **£330** [≃ **$594**]

Dickson, Samuel
- Fallacies of the faculty; with the principles of the crono thermal system. London: 1841. 2nd edn. 8vo. 328 pp. Marg pencil notes. Cloth.
(Goodrich) **£30** [≃ **£16**]

Dickson, W.E. Carnegie
- The bone-marrow. A cytological study. London: Longmans ..., 1908. 4to. xii,160 pp. 14 plates microphotos, 12 cold plates. Orig cloth, damp-spotted along fore-edge.
(Pollak) **£25** [≃ **$45**]

Dickson, Walter B.
- Poultry: their breeding, rearing, diseases, and general management. London: 1938. 1st edn. F'cap 8vo. xvi,316 pp. Engvd frontis, text vignettes. Intermittent foxing. Orig cloth, cloth partly lifted from front bd.
(Taylor) **£25** [≃ **$45**]

Dictionarium ...
- Dictionarium rusticum ... See Worlidge, John

Dictionary ...
- The modern dictionary of arts and sciences ... London: for the authors ..., 1774. 1st edn. 4 vols. 8vo. Frontis, 47 engvd plates (a few with outer margs trimmed close with loss of plate numerals). Orig mrbld bds, calf spines with sl wear, 2 jnts cracked.
(Bickersteth) **£170** [≃ **$306**]

Diday, P.
- A treatise on syphilis in new-born children and infants at the breast. Translated ... London: New Sydenham Soc., 1859. 1st edn

in English. 8vo. xii,272 pp. Orig cloth.
(Elgen) **$65** [≃ **£36**]
- A treatise on syphilis in new-born children
and infants at the breast. Translated ...
London: New Sydenham Soc, 1859. 8vo.
xii,272 pp. Ex lib.
(Rittenhouse) **$37.50** [≃ **£20**]
- A treatise on syphilis in new-born children
and infants at the breast. New York: Wood's
Library, 1883. 1st Amer edn. 8vo. 310 pp.
Cold frontis. Orig cloth. *(Oasis)* **$30** [≃ **£16**]

Difficiles Nugae ...
- Difficiles Nugae ... See Hale, Sir Matthew

Dimock, Susan
- Memoir of Susan Dimock, resident physician
of the New England Hospital for Women and
Children. Boston: 1875. 1st edn. 103 pp.
Photograph frontis. Cloth.
(Scientia) **$175** [≃ **£97**]

Dimsdale, Thomas
- The present method of inoculating for the
smallpox. London: 1767. 3rd edn. 160 pp. No
half-title (called for?). Mod qtr lea, cloth bds.
(Scientia) **$275** [≃ **£152**]

Dinsdale, Alfred
- First principles of television. London:
Chapman & Hall, 1932. 8vo. xv,[i],241,[i] pp.
38 plates, 130 text figs. Pub bndg.
(Pollak) **£50** [≃ **$90**]
- Television. With a foreword by Dr. J.A.
Fleming. London: Television Press, 1928.
2nd edn. 8vo. [xx],180,[ii advts] pp. Frontis,
32 plates, 38 text figs. Pub bndg.
(Pollak) **£50** [≃ **$90**]
- Television. With a foreword by Dr. J.A.
Fleming. London: 1928. 8vo. xx,180 pp.
Port, 32 plates. Orig cloth, dw.
(Weiner) **£75** [≃ **$135**]

Dirac, P.A.M.
- The principles of quantum mechanics.
Oxford: 1930. 1st edn. x,257 pp. Sl foxing on
half-title & blank, ink sgntr on endpaper.
(Whitehart) **£40** [≃ **$72**]
- The principles of quantum mechanics.
Oxford: Clarendon Press, 1930. 1st edn. Roy
8vo. Orig cloth, bds sl dampmarked, in dw.
(Chaucer Head) **£120** [≃ **$216**]
- The principles of quantum mechanics.
Oxford: 1930. 1st edn. x,257 pp. Crayon
markings on a few early pages. Orig cloth.
(Weiner) **£50** [≃ **$90**]

Dircks, Henry
- The life, times and scientific labours of the

Second Marquis of Worcester. London:
Quaritch, 1865. 8vo. xxiv,624 pp. Errata slip.
2 steel engvs, fldg plan, num text w'engvs.
Touch of dampstaining at beginning & end.
Orig cloth, much faded, unopened.
(Pollak) **£40** [≃ **$72**]
- The life, times and scientific labours of the
Second Marquis of Worcester ... added a
reprint of his Century of Inventions, 1663 ...
London: 1865. 1st edn. Contemp half
mor. *(Robertshaw)* **£35** [≃ **$63**]
- The life, times and scientific labours of the
Second Marquis of Worcester. To which is
added, a reprint of his century of inventions.
London: Quaritch, 1865. 1st edn. 8vo.
Frontis, steel & w'engvs. Orig cloth,
untrimmed. *(Chaucer Head)* **£110** [≃ **$198**]
- Perpetuum mobile: or, search for self-motive
power, during the 17th, 18th and 19th
centuries ... London: 1861. 8vo. xli,558 pp.
Plates, ills, diags. Elab tooled mor, gilt extra,
a.e.g. Author's pres copy with his b'plate.
(Weiner) **£150** [≃ **$270**]

Directory ...
- The homoeopathic medical directory of Great
Britain and Ireland ... to which has been
added a list of foreign physicians in
homoeopathic practice. London: Henry
Turner, 1872. 8vo. 435,viii advts pp. name
cut from title. Orig cloth, gilt, spine ends a bit
worn. *(Pollak)* **£25** [≃ **$45**]

Discourse ...
- A discourse concerning the period of humane
life ... See Allestree, Richard

Disney, A.N., et al.
- Origin and development of the microscope ...
1928. xi,303 pp. 30 plates, 36 text figs. Cloth
dust-stained, spine faded, sm nick reprd.
(Whitehart) **£45** [≃ **$81**]

Dix, Thomas
- A treatise on land surveying in seven parts.
Fourth edition, with great additions and
improvements. London: 1819. 8vo. Half-title,
fldg cold map, 18 pp advts, engvd plate, ills
in text 2 pp advts. Half red calf, gilt.
(Traylen) **£65** [≃ **$117**]

Dixon, Edward H.
- Scenes in the practice of a New York surgeon.
New York: 1855. 8vo. 407 pp. 8 ills. Old qtr
sheep, considerably worn.
(Goodrich) **$35** [≃ **£19**]

Dixon, Frederic
- The geology and fossils of the tertiary and

cretaceous formations of Sussex. London: 1850. 4to. 45 plates inc 3 cold. Some foxing. Half mor, sl worn. *(Halewood)* **£135 [≈ $243]**
- The geology and fossils of the tertiary and cretaceous formations of Sussex. London: for the author, 1850. 4to. 45 litho plates (3 cold). Contemp full black mor, gilt, gilt panelled spines, edges gilt, a little rubbed.
(Traylen) **£240 [≈ $432]**
- The geology of Sussex ... Brighton: 1878. 2nd edn. 4to. xxiv,469 pp, with 160*-167*. Extndg cold map, cold frontis, 63 litho plates (2 cold, 2 double-page). Light damp mark on last few plates, some minor spots. Rec half calf, mrbld sides.
(Bow Windows) **£175 [≈ $315]**

Dobell, Clifford
- The amoebae living in man; a zoological monograph. London: 1919. 1st edn. 155 pp. 5 plates. *(Scientia)* **$100 [≈ £55]**

Dobell, Horace
- On asthma: its nature and treatment. London: 1886. Lge 8vo. 31 pp. Ills. Cloth. Ex lib.
(Rittenhouse) **$22.50 [≈ £12]**
- On bacillary consumption: its nature and treatment in the true first stage. 1889. xi,138 pp. Cloth. Inscrbd by author.
(Whitehart) **£35 [≈ $63]**
- On coughs, consumption, and diet in disease. Phila: 1877. 8vo. 22 pp. Advts. Ex lib.
(Rittenhouse) **$22.50 [≈ £12]**
- On loss of weight, blood-spitting and lung disease. Phila: 1879. 8vo. viii,273 pp. Chart in pocket at rear. Upper hinge cracked. Ex lib. *(Rittenhouse)* **$27.50 [≈ £15]**
- On winter cough, catarrh, bronchitis, emphysema, asthma: A course of lectures ... Phila: 1872. New & enlgd edn. xii, errata, 238 pp. 2 cold plates, 4 figs. Uncut. Ex lib.
(Rittenhouse) **$37.50 [≈ £20]**

Dobson, Edward
- The student's guide to the practice of designing, measuring and valuing artificers' works. John Weale, 1852-53. 2nd edn. 8vo. xv,[i], 271,[12 advts pp. 8 fldg plates. Rather dusty in worn orig cloth.
(Spelman) **£35 [≈ $63]**

Doctor ...
- Doctor dissected: or, Willy Cadogan in the kitchen. Addressed to all invalids, and readers of a late dissertation on the gout, etc., etc. By a lady. London: T. Davies, 1771. 21 pp. Rebound in qtr mor, mrbld bds.
(C.R. Johnson) **£300 [≈ $540]**

Dodd, George
- The curiosities of industry and the applied sciences. London: Routledge, 1852. 1st edn. 8vo. [4] pp 16 parts, each with 24 pp excepting last part with 20 pp. Contemp cloth. *(Rootenberg)* **$750 [≈ £416]**
- The textile manufactures of Great Britain. London: C. Knight, 1844. 1st edn. 12mo. 232 pp. 33 ills. Contemp prize calf, gilt.
(Fenning) **£21.50 [≈ $37]**

Dodge, Raymond
- Elementary conditions of human variability ... responses to similar stimuli ... New York: 1927. Folio. 107 pp. Charts (2 fldg). Binder's cloth. Ex lib with a few marg stamps.
(Weiner) **£40 [≈ $72]**

Dodsley, Robert
- The oeconomy of human life. In two parts ... Printed at Glasgow, 1765; sold by Robert Bell, Dublin [Reprinted Dublin: ca 1765]. 12mo. [iv],xv, [i],54; iv,[ii],92 pp. Engvd frontis. Contemp mottled calf.
(Burmester) **£45 [≈ $81]**
- The oeconomy of human life. London: W. Gardiner, 1806. Lge paper proof imp. Tall 8vo. 116 pp. Vignettes. Straight grain mor, gilt, defective, hinges reprd.
(Argosy) **$250 [≈ £138]**
- The oeconomy of human life. Translated from an Indian manuscript ... London: for Harding, 1795. One of 25 lge paper. 8vo. 22,119 pp. 49 engvd vignettes. Contemp red mor, gilt, a.e.g., cvrs a little darkened in places. *(Marlborough)* **£550 [≈ $990]**

Dolbear, A.E.
- The art of projecting. A manual of experimentation in physics, chemistry and natural history with the porte lumiere and magic lantern. Boston: Lee & Shepard, 1877. 1st edn. 8vo. vi,158 pp. Text w'cuts. Orig cloth, dampstained. *(Antiq Sc)* **$75 [≈ £41]**
- The telephone: an account of the phenomena of electricity, magnetism and sound as involved in its action. With directions for making a speaking telephone. London: Sampson Low, 1878. 1st edn. 12mo. 127 pp. Text figs. Orig ptd pict bds, mod mor-spined cloth box. *(Frew Mackenzie)* **£180 [≈ $324]**

Dolby, Richard
- The cook's dictionary and house-keeper's directory. London: 1830. 1st edn. 8vo. iv,516,[2 advts] pp. Some foxing & other stains. Orig cloth, somewhat faded & a trifle rubbed. *(Bow Windows)* **£125 [≈ $225]**

Dommett, W.E.
- Aeroplanes and airships including steering, propelling and navigating apparatus ... anti-aircraft guns and searchlights. London: 1915. 8vo. 106 pp. 12 plates. Orig pict wraps, ink inscrptn on front.   *(Weiner)* **£25 [≃ $45]**

Donders, Frans C.
- On the anomalies of accommodation and refraction of the eye with a preliminary essay on physiological dioptrics. Translated ... London: 1864. 1st edn. 635 pp. Fldg eye chart.   *(Scientia)* **$300 [≃ £166]**

Donnelly, Ignatius
- Atlantis: the antediluvian world. New York: [1882]. 24th edn. 8vo. x,490 pp. Ills. Cloth, spine sl frayed.   *(Elgen)* **$45 [≃ £25]**

Donovan, Edward
- Instructions for collecting and preserving various subjects of natural history ... together with a treatise on the management of insects ... London: for the author, 1794. 1st edn. Thick paper. 8vo. [iv],86 pp. 2 engvd plates. Contemp mrbld bds, rebacked.
        (Burmester) **£225 [≃ $405]**

Donovan, Michael
- A treatise on chemistry. London: Cabinet Cyclopaedia, 1837. 4th edn. xii,407 pp. A few text diags. New cloth.
        (Whitehart) **£25 [≃ $45]**
- A treatise on chemistry. Lardner's Cabinet Cyclopaedia, 1832. Lge 12mo. [4 advts],xii,407, [3],[2 blank] pp. Addtnl engvd title, text ills. Rec bds, uncut.
        (Fenning) **£55 [≃ $99]**

Dossie, Robert
- The elaboratory laid open, or, the secrets of modern chemistry and pharmacy revealed. London: for J. Nourse, 1758. 1st edn. 8vo. Some marg browning to title & a few other pp. Contemp calf, hinges splitting, crnrs worn.   *(Chaucer Head)* **£200 [≃ $360]**
- Institutes of experimental chemistry ... an essay towards reducing that branch of natural philosophy to a regular system. London: Nourse, 1759. 1st edn. 2 vols. 8vo. xx,[viii], 491,[i]; [iv],437,[xxiii] pp. Occas light foxing. Contemp calf, gilt, rubbed.
        (Frew Mackenzie) **£200 [≃ $360]**

Douglas, James
- Myographiae comparatae specimen: or, a comparative description of all the muscles in a man and in a quadruped ... muscles peculiar to a woman. London: for George Strahan, 1707. 1st edn. 12mo. Contemp panelled calf, rebacked, mor label, gilt.
        (Traylen) **£120 [≃ $216]**
- Myographiae comparatae specimen: or, a comparative description of all the muscles in a man and in a quadruped ... London: for George Strahan, 1707. 1st edn. 12mo. Title & margs a little browned. Contemp panelled calf, spine repaired. *(Quaritch)* **$300 [≃ £166]**
- Myographiae comparatae specimen: or, a comparative description of all the muscles in a man and in a quadruped ... a new edition ... London: 1763. 8vo. xxxi,240 pp. Contemp calf, rebacked. Sgntr of "John Hunter, jr" on blank. Soc of Apothecaries b'plate.
        (Goodrich) **$195 [≃ £108]**

Downing, Carter Harrison
- Osteopathic principles in disease. San Francisco: 1935. 1st edn. Lge 8vo. xxxiii,623 pp. Num text ills. Cloth. *(Elgen)* **$55 [≃ £30]**

Drake, Daniel
- A systematic treatise, historical, etiological, and practical, on the principal diseases of the interior valley of North America ... Second series. Phila: 1854. 985 pp. Waterstain on inner marg 1st 10 ff, scattered foxing. Orig lea, inner hinges cracked.
        (Fye) **$500 [≃ £277]**

Drake, James
- Anthropologia nova; or, a new system of anatomy. London: Walford, 1707. 2 vols. Port, 81 plates (ex 83), of which 30 fldg. Lacking 2 fldg plates vol 2, a few plates with sm tears. Contemp panelled calf, jnts worn, 1 bd nearly detchd.   *(Pollak)* **£150 [≃ $270]**

Draper, John William
- Human physiology, statical and dynamical; or, the conditions and course of the life of man. New York: 1856. 1st edn. 649 pp. Nearly 300 w'cut engvs. Lacking backstrip.
        (Fye) **$75 [≃ £41]**

Dreyer, J.L.E.
- History of the planetary systems from Thales to Kepler. Cambridge: 1906. 8vo. xi,432 pp. Diags. Orig cloth.   *(Weiner)* **£50 [≃ $90]**

Dreyer, J.L.E., et al.
- History of the Royal Astronomical Society 1820 - 1920. The Society, 1923. 1st edn. Roy 8vo. Plates. Orig cloth gilt.
        (Taylor) **£32 [≃ $57]**
- History of the Royal Astronomical Society 1820 - 1920. 1923. 8vo. vii,258 pp. 12 ports. Orig dark blue cloth, gilt.
        (Blackwell's) **£45 [≃ $81]**

- History of the Royal Astronomical Society 1820 - 1920. London: 1923. 8vo. vii,258 pp. Ports. Orig cloth. *(Weiner)* **£30 [≃ $54]**

Drude, Paul
- The theory of optics. Translated ... New York: Longmans, 1902. 1st edn in English. 8vo. xxi,[1],546 pp. Text figs. Orig cloth, spine a bit chipped. *(Antiq Sc)* **$90 [≃ £50]**

Druitt, Robert
- The surgeon's vade mecum: a manual of modern surgery. London: Rensham, 1870. 10th edn. 8vo. 823 pp. 350 w'engvs. Old diced calf, rebacked. *(Oasis)* **$60 [≃ £33]**

Du Moncel, Count
- The telephone, the microphone and the phonograph. Authorised translation ... London: 1879. 1st English edn. Sm 8vo. x,363,[32 advts] pp. Orig cloth. *(Bow Windows)* **£65 [≃ $117]**

Du Moulin, Peter
- The elements of logick ... now translated into English by Joshua Ahier. Oxford: Henry Hall, 1647. 2nd English edn. Sm 8vo. [10],155 pp. Title lightly soiled. Sgntr of Richard Cope (1776-1856). Qtr calf over mrbld bds. Wing D2583. *(Rootenberg)* **$200 [≃ £111]**

Duane, William
- An epitome of the arts and sciences ... adapted to the use of schools in the United States. Phila: Duane, 1811. 2nd edn. 12mo. xiii,324 pp. 15 w'cut plates. Contemp calf, hinges rubbed. *(Karmiole)* **$65 [≃ £36]**

Dublin Hospital Gazette
- Dublin Hospital Gazette ... for the improvement of medicine and surgery. Dublin: 1854-60. Vols 1-7 [all published in this series]. 7 vols. Sm 4to. Half calf & cloth. *(Emerald Isle)* **£135 [≃ $243]**

Dubravius
- A new booke of good husbandry, very pleasaunt, and of great profite for gentlemen and yomen ... 1599. 1st edn in English. Sm 4to. Black & Roman letter. Headlines of some leaves cropped affecting a few letters. 19th c mor, gilt, a little worn. STC 7268. *(Traylen)* **£750 [≃ $1,350]**

Duchene, M.
- The mechanics of the aeroplane. A study of the principles of flight. Translated ... London: 1916. New imp. 8vo. x,230 pp. Ills.

A few pp with edge tears. Cloth, sm tear, chip at ft of jnt. *(Elgen)* **$50 [≃ £27]**
- The mechanics of the aeroplane. A study of the principles of flight. Translated ... London: 1912. 1st English edn. x,231 pp. 91 text figs. Orig cloth. *(Whitehart)* **£35 [≃ $63]**

Duchenne de Boulogne
- Selections from the clinical works ... Translated by G.V. Poore. London: 1883. 8vo. xxii,472 pp. Sl weakness in upper hinge. Ex lib. *(Rittenhouse)* **$150 [≃ £83]**

Dugdale, Sir William
- The history of imbanking and drayning of divers fenns ... and of the improvements thereby. London: Alice Warren, 1662. 1st edn. Folio. Engvd port, 11 fldg maps, red & black title, 5 addtnl leaves at end. 18th c polished calf, gilt, edges gilt. Wing D2481. *(Traylen)* **£720 [≃ $1,296]**
- The history of imbanking and drayning of divers fenns ... and of the improvements thereby. London: W. Bowyer ... 1772. 2nd edn. Folio. xii,469 pp. 11 fldg maps. Ex lib with stamps on title & throughout. Contemp calf, rubbed, rebacked, new endpapers. *(Titles)* **£225 [≃ $405]**

Duhamel du Monceau, Henri Louis
- The elements of agriculture. Translated ... and revised by Philip Miller. London: P. Vaillant, 1764. 1st English edn. 2 vols. 8vo. xx,445; [8],443 pp. 14 engvd plates. Contemp half calf, rebacked & recrnrd. B'plate of Earl Fitzwilliam. *(Spelman)* **£160 [≃ $288]**
- A practical treatise of husbandry. Wherein are contained many useful and valuable experiments and observations ... London: for C. Hitch ..., 1762. 2nd edn., crrctd & imprvd. 4to. Red & black title, 6 engvd plates (4 fldg). Contemp calf, gilt. *(Traylen)* **£140 [≃ $252]**

Duhring, Louis A.
- Atlas of skin diseases. Phila: 1876. 1st edn. 4to. 36 cold plates. Half lea. *(Scientia)* **$350 [≃ £194]**
- A practical treatise on diseases of the skin. Phila: 1883. 3rd edn, revsd & enlgd. 685 pp. *(Scientia)* **$65 [≃ £36]**

Dumas, J. & Boussingault, J.B.
- The chemical and physiological balance of organic nature. New York: Saxton & Miles, 1844. 1st Amer edn. 16mo. 174 pp. Orig cloth, soiled & chipped. *(Antiq Sc)* **$90 [≃ £50]**

Dumble, E.T.
- Geological survey of Texas, second annual report 1890. Austin: 1891. Thick lge 8vo. 756 pp. Num ills, fldg maps & plans. Lea cloth.
(Halewood) **£54 [≃ $97]**

Dunbar, John
- History of the Jewish physicians, from the French of E. Carmoly, with notes. Baltimore: n.d. [ca 1845]. 94 pp. Front endpaper torn & partly missing, waterstain in sev margs. Lea, rubbed, front hinge cracked.
(Fye) **$250 [≃ £138]**

Duncan, Andrew
- Annals of medicine for the year 1796 ... for the year 1797. Edinburgh: 1796-97. 1st edn. 2 vols. Lea, backstrips taped with black cloth, inner hinges crudely reprd. Ex lib.
(Fye) **$75 [≃ £41]**

Duncan, William
- The elements of logick. In four books: Of the original of our ideas ... Of the methods of inventions and science ... London: 1770. 12mo. 370,[2 advts] pp. Sm piece torn from 1 leaf with sl loss, free endpapers removed. Contemp calf, a little rubbed.
(Bow Windows) **£36 [≃ $64]**

Duncum, Barbara M.
- The development of inhalation anaesthesia with special reference to the years 1846-1900. London: OUP, 1947. 8vo. xvi,640 pp. Frontis, 60 ills. Pub bndg, dw.
(Pollak) **£60 [≃ $108]**

Dundonald, Earl of
- A treatise shewing the intimate connection that subsists between agriculture and chemistry ... London: 1803. New edn. 4to. Half-title. Lacking front & rear endpapers, sm lib stamp on title. Uncut in paper-cvrd bds, cloth spine, paper label.
(Robertshaw) **£75 [≃ $135]**

Dunglison, Robley
- A dictionary of medical science. Phila: 1844. 4th edn. Some loose pages frayed, preface stained. Orig cloth, v worn & loose.
(Rittenhouse) **$25 [≃ £13]**
- History of medicine from the earliest ages to the commencement of the nineteenth century. Phila: 1872. 8vo. 287 pp. Orig cloth, rubbed.
(Goodrich) **$75 [≃ £41]**
- Human health; or the influence of atmosphere and locality, change of air and climates; seasons; food ... mineral springs ... intellectual pursuits ... on healthy man ...

Phila: 1844. 2nd edn. 464 pp. Scattered foxing. Lea, lacking labels. *(Fye)* **$75 [≃ £41]**
- Human physiology. Phila: 1856. 8th edn. 2 vols. 729; 755 pp. Lea.   *(Fye)* **$50 [≃ £27]**
- The medical student; or aids to the study of medicine. Phila: 1837. 1st edn. 323 pp. Pub ctlg. Mod bds, paper spine.
(Scientia) **$125 [≃ £69]**
- New remedies: with formulae for their preparation and administration. Phila: 1856. 7th edn. 769 pp. Lea.   *(Fye)* **$50 [≃ £27]**
- On the influence of atmosphere and locality; change of air and climate ... on human health; constituting elements of hygiene. Phila: 1835. 1st edn. Lea, dry, front hinge broken, lacking label.   *(Fye)* **$125 [≃ £69]**

Dunglison, Robley (ed.)
- Medical and surgical monographs by Andral, Babbington, Beck, Bright ... and Taylor with occasional comments by the editor. Phila: 1838. Orig bds, spine dried & imperfect at top, crnrs bent. *(Rittenhouse)* **$195 [≃ £108]**

Dunkin, E.
- The midnight sky. Familiar notes on the stars and planets. 1891. New & revsd edn. 4to. xii,19-428 pp. 32 star maps & other text ills. Some light marg foxing. Orig pict cloth, t.e.g.
(Whitehart) **£35 [≃ $63]**

Dunn, C.L. (ed.)
- Medical history of the Second World War. Emergency Medical Services. London: HMSO, 1952-53. 2 vols. 8vo. xvi,460; xii,492 pp. 80 plates, 10 figs. Marg notes. Pub bndg, dws.   *(Pollak)* **£50 [≃ $90]**

Dunn, Matthias
- An historical, geological, and descriptive view of the coal trade of the North of England ... Newcastle-upon-Tyne: 1844. 8vo. ix,248 pp. Hand-cold fldg diag. Binder's cloth, front cover badly faded & cockled.
(Weiner) **£75 [≃ $135]**
- A treatise on the winning and working of collieries; including ... remarks on ventilation ... Newcastle-upon-Tyne, 1848. 1st edn. 8vo. 27 cold or partly cold plates (1 fldg), 8 pp advts. Orig embossed cloth, jnts reprd.
(Traylen) **£180 [≃ $324]**

Dunn, Samuel
- A new and general introduction to practical astronomy ... London: for the author, 1744. Roy 8vo. 30 plates & 6 engvd plates. Contemp calf, rebacked, orig spine laid down.
(Traylen) **£110 [≃ $198]**

Dunning, Edwin J.
- Remarks to the pupils at Eaglewood School, on the preservation of the teeth. February 19, 1860. New York: T. Holman, 1860. 20 pp. Orig ptd wraps, sm tear at bottom, chipped along edges.   *(Karmiole)* **$25 [≈ £13]**

Dunoyer, L.
- Vacuum practice. the practical applications of X-rays. Translated ... London: Bell, 1926. 8vo. x,228 pp. 80 figs. Pub bndg.
          (Pollak) **£25 [≈ $45]**

Duns, John
- Memoir of Sir James Y. Simpson. Edinburgh: 1873. 1st edn. 544 pp. Frontis. Top & bottom of spine lightly rubbed.
          (Scientia) **$150 [≈ £83]**

Dupuytren, Baron Guillaume
- Clinical lectures on surgery delivered at the Hotel Dieu 1832. Translated ... Boston: 1833. 1st edn. in English. 312 pp. Stamps on all fore-edges,   *(Scientia)* **$150 [≈ £83]**
- On lesions of the vascular system, diseases of the rectum, and other surgical complaints. London: 1854. Title nearly detchd. Cloth, top of spine defective, t.e.g.
          (Rittenhouse) **$50 [≈ £27]**
- On the injuries and diseases of bones. Translated ... London: 1847. 8vo. xx,459 pp. Cloth, t.e.g., b'plates.
          (Rittenhouse) **$80 [≈ £44]**

Dutton, C.E.
- Earthquakes in the light of the new seismology. 1904. xxiii,314 pp. 10 plates, 63 text ills. Lib stamps on endpapers, title & some plate versos. Cloth sl faded & marked.
          (Whitehart) **£18 [≈ $32]**

Duveen, Denis I. & Klickstein, Herbert S.
- A bibliography of the works of Antoine Lavoisier ... [with] A supplement to a bibliography ... London: 1954-65. 2 vols. 8vo. xxiii,491; xv,175 pp. Port, num plates. Orig cloth, dws.   *(Weiner)* **£95 [≈ $171]**

Dyvernois, J.L.
- A dissertation upon the sugar of milk ... great efficacy in consumptions, hectic fevers ... translated into English. London: for T. James ..., 1753. 1st edn in English. 8vo. viii,32 pp inc half-title. Outer pages a little soiled. Disbound.   *(Pickering)* **$200 [≈ £111]**

Dziobeck, Otto
- Mathematical theories of planetary motions. Translated ... Ann Arbor: 1892. 8vo. viii,294 pp. Browned. Ex lib with perf stamp on title. Orig cloth, front hinge reprd, spine ends worn.   *(Weiner)* **£35 [≈ $63]**

Eagle, John
- Notes on pharmacy in the olden time, collected and illustrated. Harrow on the Hill: ... the author, 1885. 8vo. iii,53 pp. Cold dec title, fldg w'cut facs, num facs in the text. Loose, as issued, in orig ptd wraps, spine trifle frayed.   *(Burmester)* **£40 [≈ $72]**

Eagleton, Wells P.
- Brain abcess: its surgical pathology and operative technic. New York: 1922. 1st edn. 8vo. 297 pp. Frontis, half-title, ills, plates. Cloth.   *(Elgen)* **$65 [≈ £36]**

Eastlake, Lady (ed.)
- Dr. Rigby's letters from France. etc., in 1789. Edited by his daughter ... London: 1880. 1st edn. 8vo. xviii,232 pp. Cloth.
          (Elgen) **$50 [≈ £27]**

Eaton, Mary
- The cook and housekeeper's complete and universal dictionary ... modern cookery ... baking, brewing ... family medicine ... rules of health ... Bungay: Childs, 1823. 8vo. xxxii,495 pp. Port, 4 plates. Occas light spotting. Contemp half calf, rebacked.
          (Gough) **£295 [≈ $531]**

Eckhardt, George H.
- Electronic television. Chicago: 1936. 8vo. xx,162 pp. Num ills & diags. Orig limp cloth, pict dw rather rubbed. *(Weiner)* **£75 [≈ $135]**

Eddington, Arthur Stanley
- Fundamental theory. Cambridge: 1946. 1st edn. Lge 8vo. viii,292 pp. Orig cloth, fore-edge of cvrs discold by damp.
          (Weiner) **£40 [≈ $72]**
- Fundamental theory. Cambridge: 1946. 1st edn. viii,292 pp. Contemp ink sgntr on endpaper. Orig cloth, sl marked, spine faded.   *(Whitehart)* **£45 [≈ $81]**
- The mathematical theory of relativity. Cambridge: 1924. 2nd edn. 4to. ix,270 pp. Contemp ink sgntr on endpaper.
          (Whitehart) **£40 [≈ $72]**
- The mathematical theory of relativity. Cambridge: 1923. 1st edn. ix,247 pp. Contemp ink sgntr on endpaper, some pencil anntns in margins. *(Whitehart)* **£60 [≈ $108]**
- Space, time and gravitation. An outline of the general theory of relativity. Cambridge: Univ Press, 1920. 1st edn. 8vo. vi,[ii], 218,[ii] pp. Frontis, 18 figs. Orig cloth, some ink splodges

on endpapers.   *(Pollak)* £20 [≃ $36]
- Stellar movements and the structure of the
universe. London: 1914. 1st edn. 8vo. Orig
cloth. Ex lib.   *(Argosy)* $125 [≃ £69]
- Stellar movements and the structure of the
universe. London: Macmillan, 1914. 1st edn.
8vo. xii,266 pp. 4 photo plates. Orig cloth, sm
dampstain on rear cvr. *(Antiq Sc)* $90 [≃ £50]

Eden, Williams
- Principles of penal law [including 'proposal to
subject (criminals) during their life to medical
experiments']. London: Cadell, 1771. 8vo.
xxvii,[i], 331,[i] pp. Contemp calf, spine ends
& edges worn.   *(Pollak)* £65 [≃ $117]

Edgeworth, R.L.
- An essay on the construction of roads and
carriages. 1813. 1st edn. 8vo. 4 fldg plates, 4
pp advts. Bds, uncut.
          (Halewood) £220 [≃ $396]

Edinburgh New Dispensatory
- Edinburgh New Dispensatory. Containing I.
The elements of pharmaceutical chemistry.
II. The materia medica ... III. Pharmaceutical
preparations and medicinal compositions ...
Edinburgh: 1801. 6th edn. xxxi,622 pp. 3
fldg plates. Contemp lea, worn, rubbed.
          (Whitehart) £80 [≃ $144]

Edlin, A.
- A treatise on the art of bread-making ...
London: Vernor & Hood, 1805. 1st edn.
12mo. xxiv,216,[2] pp. 5 fldg plates.
Contemp anntns on last leaf. Half calf over
mrbld bds.   *(Rootenberg)* $500 [≃ £277]

Edmonds, Emma
- Nurse and spy in the Union Army ...
adventures and experiences of a woman in
hospitals, camps and battlefields. Hartford:
1865. 1st edn. 8vo. 384 pp. 9 plates. Orig
cloth, sl worn & shaken. *(Oasis)* $50 [≃ £27]

Edwardes, E.J.
- A concise history of small-pox and
vaccination in Europe. London: Lewis, 1902.
1st edn. 8vo. 142 pp. Orig cloth, spine sl
faded.   *(Oasis)* $50 [≃ £27]

Edwards, W.F.
- On the influence of physical agents on life,
translated from the French ... Phila: 1838. 1st
Amer edn. 8vo. 228 pp. [Bound after:] Essays
on physiology and Hygiene. Phila: 1838. 240
pp. Old half calf, mrbld bds.
          (Hemlock) $175 [≃ £97]

Ehrenfest, Hugo
- Birth injuries of the child. New York: 1928.
8vo. 221 pp. Cloth.   *(Goodrich)* $35 [≃ £19]
- Birth injuries of the child. New York: 1928.
Lge 8vo. xiv,221 pp. Cloth, some shelfwear.
          (Rittenhouse) $25 [≃ £13]

Ehret, George
- Twenty-five years of brewing with an
illustrated history of American beer. New
York: 1891. 4to. 120 pp. Cold charts, ills
(some full-page). Orig gilt dec cloth, ex lib.
          (Weiner) £30 [≃ $54]

Ehrlich, P. & Lazarus, A.
- Histology of the blood. Normal and
pathological. Cambridge: 1900. xiii,216 pp. 3
plates. Cloth, sl marked.
          (Whitehart) £25 [≃ $45]

Ehrlich, Paul
- Studies in immunity. Collected and translated
by C. Bolduan. New York: 1910. 2nd edn,
revsd & enlgd. 712 pp. Stamps on title. Cloth.
          (Scientia) $195 [≃ £108]

Einstein, Albert
- Investigations on the theory of the Brownian
movement. London: Methuen, [1926]. 1st
edn in English. Sm 8vo. viii,124 pp. 3 text
figs. Orig cloth.   *(Antiq Sc)* $85 [≃ £47]
- The meaning of relativity. London: Methuen,
1922. 1st edn in English. 8vo. 123 pp. Orig
cloth. "Presentation Copy" stamp.
          (Oasis) $125 [≃ £69]
- On the method of theoretical physics. Oxford:
1933. 1st edn. 16 pp. Title & edges of text
pages sl stained. Orig ptd wraps.
          (Whitehart) £25 [≃ $45]
- Out of my later years. New York: 1950. 1st
edn. 8vo. 282 pp. Port. Orig blue cloth, sl
chipped dw.   *(Oasis)* $60 [≃ £33]
- Relativity: The special and the general
theory. London: 1920. 1st edn in English.
8vo. 138 pp. New half calf.
          (Oasis) $75 [≃ £41]
- Relativity: The special and the general
theory. London: 1920. 1st English edn. 8vo.
xiii,138 pp. Orig cloth spine faded, front
inner hinge shaken. Relevant 1919 newspaper
cutting pasted to front endpaper.
          (Weiner) £25 [≃ $45]
- The theory of relativity. London: Methuen,
1920. 1st edn in English. 8vo. 138 pp. Port
frontis. Orig cloth.   *(Oasis)* $100 [≃ £55]

Einstein, Albert & Infeld, Leopold
- The evolution of physics. The growth of ideas

from the early concepts to relativity and quanta. Cambridge: Univ Press, 1938. 1st edn. 8vo. x,319,[i] pp. 3 plates, num text figs. Pub bndg, dw.   *(Pollak)* **£25 [≈ $45]**

Einstein, Albert, et al.
- The principle of relativity, a collection of original memoirs ... London: 1923. 8vo. viii,216 pp. Orig cloth. *(Weiner)* **£45 [≈ $81]**

Elaboratory ...
- The elaboratory laid open ... See Dossie, Robert

Elements of Trigonometry ...
- The elements of trigonometry ... See Emerson, William

Ellis, Arthur J.
- The divining rod, a history of water witching. Washington: 1917. 8vo. 59 pp. Ills, 28 pp bibliography. Wraps.   *(Weiner)* **£30 [≈ $54]**

Ellis, E.S.
- Ancient anodynes, primitive anaethesia and allied conditions. London: 1946. 187 pp. Orig cloth.   *(Weiner)* **£20 [≈ $36]**

Ellis, George Viner & Ford, G.H.
- Illustrations of dissections ... original coloured plates the size of life ... London: Walton, 1867. 2 vols. Lge folio & 8vo. 58 full page cold plates. Title, 2 prelims & plates mtd (some dusty, soiled & reprd). Contemp qtr calf, rebacked. 8vo vol recased.
  (Goodrich) **$950 [≈ £527]**
- Illustrations of dissections. New York: Wood's Library, Jan 1882. 1st Amer edn. 2 vols. 8vo. 233; 226 pp. 58 full-page cold litho plates. Orig cloth.   *(Oasis)* **$150 [≈ £83]**

Ellis, Henry Havelock
- The psychology of sex. The biology of sex - the sexual impulse in youth ... A manual for students. London: Heinemann, 1933. 2nd imp. xii,322 pp. Orig cloth.
  (Pollak) **£20 [≈ $36]**
- Studies in the psychology of sex ... Phila: F.A. Davis, 1920. 1st coll edn. 6 vols. 8vo. xv,353; xi,391; xii,353; xi,270; x,285; xvi,656 pp. Orig brown cloth, worn.
  (Pickering) **$300 [≈ £166]**

Ellis, John
- The natural history of many curious and uncommon zoophytes collected from many parts of the globe ... London: for Benjamin White ..., 1786. 4to. 63 plates. Contemp half calf, lea renewed, uncut.

(Waterfield's) **£200 [≈ $360]**

Ellis, John D.
- The injured back and its treatment. Illinois: Thomas, 1940. vii,[i], 377,[iii] pp. Num ills. Pub bndg.   *(Pollak)* **£25 [≈ $45]**

Ellis, Thomas T.
- Leaves from the diary of an army surgeon; or, incidents of field, camp and hospital life. New York: 1863. 1st edn. 312 pp. Cloth.
  (Scientia) **$150 [≈ £83]**

Ellis, William
- Ellis's husbandry, abridged and methodized; comprehending the most useful articles of practical agriculture. London: for W. Nicoll, 1772. 2 vols. 8vo. Engvd frontis. Contemp calf, gilt panelled spines, jnts worn.
  (Traylen) **£130 [≈ $234]**

Elsberg, Charles A.
- Diagnosis and treatment of surgical diseases of the spinal cord and its membranes. Phila: Sunders, 1916. 1st edn. 8vo. 330 pp. 158 ills (3 in color). Orig cloth. *(Oasis)* **$160 [≈ £88]**

Elshotz, Johann Sigsmund
- The curious distillatory: or the art of distilling coloured liquors, spirits ... from vegetables ... and metals ... London: for Robert Boulter, 1677. 1st edn in English. 12mo. [xvi],111 pp. Engvd frontis & plate. Minor spotting & offsetting. 19th c half calf.
  (Burmester) **£650 [≈ $1,170]**

Emanuel, Harry
- Diamonds and precious stones: their history, value, and distinguishing characteristics. London: Hotten, 1867. 8vo. xxii,266 pp. Cold litho title, 5 litho plates. Orig dark blue cloth, gilt.   *(Burmester)* **£45 [≈ $81]**

Emerson, William
- The doctrine of fluxions: not only explaining the elements thereof, but also its application and use in several parts of mathematics and natural philosophy. London: Robinson, 1768. 3rd edn. xvi,[iv], 432,[ii errata]. 12 fldg plates. Contemp sheep, spine worn.
  (Pollak) **£80 [≈ $144]**
- The elements of optics. In four books. London: for J. Nourse, 1768. 1st edn. [with, 2nd part] Perspective: or, the art of drawing ... upon a plane. 2 pts in 1. 8vo. [ii],xii,244; vi,[ii],111 pp. 13 & 15 engvd plates. Wanting half-title. Contemp reversed calf.
  (Burmester) **£285 [≈ $513]**
- The elements of trigonometry. Containing

the properties, relations, and calculations of sines, tangents ... For W. Innys, 1749. 1st edn. 8vo. viii,186 pp. 6 fldg plates. Contemp calf, rebacked. *(Bickersteth)* £110 [≃ $198]
- The mathematical principles of geography ... [bound with] Dialling or the art of drawing dials, on all sorts of planes whatsoever ... London: Nourse, 1770. viii,ii,172; iv,164 pp. 18 fldg plates. Tree calf, spine rubbed.
(P & P) £125 [≃ $225]
- The principles of mechanics. Explaining and demonstrating the general laws of motion ... An appendix ... by G.A. Smeaton ... London: 1836. New edn, crrctd. 8vo. xxiv,[x],320 pp. 83 copper plates, num w'cut text figs. Some spots & dust marks. Rec calf, gilt.
(Bow Windows) £110 [≃ $198]
- The principles of mechanics. Explaining and demonstrating the general laws of motion ... projectiles ... construction of machines ... For J. Richardson, 1758. 2nd edn, crrctd. 4to. viii,[ii],284 pp. 43 fldg plates. Orig calf, rebacked. *(Bickersteth)* £290 [≃ $522]
- The projection of the sphere, orthographic, stereographic and gnomical. For W. Innys, 1749. 1st edn. 8vo. iv,52 pp. 12 fldg plates. Contemp mrbld bds, new calf spine.
(Bickersteth) £95 [≃ $171]
- Tracts containing I. Mechanics ... II. The projection of the sphere. III. The laws of centripetal ... force. ... Some account of the life ... of the author. London: Wingrave, 1793. New edn. 8vo. xxii,302 pp. Contemp roan, rubbed, hd of spine & crnrs chipped.
(Frew Mackenzie) £30 [≃ $54]

Emery, S.
- Switzerland through the stereoscope. A journey over and around the Alps. New York: [1901]. Booklet, fldg map, 99 stereo photos. Orig 3 vol boxed case.
(Halewood) £135 [≃ $243]

Emmet, Thomas Addis
- Incidents of my life: professional - literary - social, with services in the cause of Ireland. New York: 1911. 1st edn. One of 750. 4to. xxx,480,2 pub advts pp. Port frontis, 27 plates. Orig cloth, t.e.g Ex lib.
(Elgen) $65 [≃ £36]

Encyclopaedia ...
- The British encyclopaedia: comprising ... a dictionary of terms ... treatises illustrative of the arts and sciences ... Manchester: Russell & Allen, 1814. 5 vols. 264 plates (ex 269), some defective. Half calf, mrbld bds. A working copy. *(Pollak)* £75 [≃ $135]
- Encyclopaedia Britannica; or, a dictionary of

all arts and sciences ... 1771. 1st edn. 3 vols. 4to. 160 (ex 161) plates. Stain on lower marg of last 200 pp vol 3. Calf, all cvrs detchd, all spines broken. *(Allen)* $750 [≃ £416]
- The English encyclopaedia: being a collection of treatises ... illustrative of the arts and sciences ... 1802. 10 vols. 4to. Approx 8500 pp. Frontis to vol I, approx 400 engvd plates (lacking 2). Contemp polished calf, lacking backstrips, bds detchd.
(Weiner) £200 [≃ $360]

Engel, S.
- Lung structure. Springfield: 1962. x,300 pp. 424 ills. Inscrbd by author.
(Whitehart) £25 [≃ $45]

Engineer & Machinist ...
- The engineer and machinist's drawing book ... linear drawing, projection ... tinting and colouring, and perspective ... progressive series of lessons in drawing ... London: 1871. Folio. viii,116 pp. 71 engvd plates, 246 text figs. Contemp half calf.
(Bow Windows) £145 [≃ $261]

Englefield, Sir H.
- On the determination of the orbits of comets, according to the methods of Father Boscovitch and Mr. de la Place ... London: 1793. xi,iv,204, [26],4 pp. 4 fldg plates (2 loose). Pencil & ink notes on some pp. Later cloth. *(Whitehart)* £60 [≃ $108]

Englefield, Sir Henry C.
- A description of the ... beauties, antiquities and geological phenomena of the Isle of Wight. 1816. 1st edn. Lge paper. Folio. 46 engvd plates, 3 maps (inc 1 hand-cold geological), hand-cold aquatint panorama. Lacking port. Contemp mor, a little rubbed.
(Sotheran) £365 [≃ $657]

Ennemoser, Joseph
- The history of magic. Translated from the German ... second-sight, sonambulism, predictions, witchcraft ... spirit rapping. London: Bohn, 1854. 2 vols. 8vo. viii,xvi, 471; viii,518 pp. Occas foxing. Orig blindstamped cloth, gilt.
(Frew Mackenzie) £35 [≃ $63]

Enquiry ...
- An enquiry into the nature of the human soul ... See Baxter, Andrew

Epitome ...
- An epitome of the arts and sciences ... See Duane, William

Epps, J.
- The life of John Walker, M.D. 1832. 2nd edn. viii,342,8 pp. 2nd edn. Sl foxing. Contemp bds, rebacked.
(Whitehart) £30 [≈ $54]

Erb, William
- Handbook of electro-therapeutics. New York: Wood's Library, 1883. 1st Amer edn. 8vo. 366 pp. 39 text ills. Orig cloth.
(Oasis) $60 [≈ £33]
- Handbook of electro-therapeutics. New York: 1883. 1st English translation. 366 pp. Orig cloth. *(Fye)* $75 [≈ £41]

Erichsen, John Eric
- Observations on aneurism selected from the works of the principal writers ... London: for the Sydenham Society, 1844. 1st edn. 8vo. A few leaves sl soiled. Partially unopened in orig cloth, spine reprd. *(Quaritch)* $50 [≈ £27]
- Observations on aneurism selected from the works of the principal writers ... London: Sydenham Soc, 1844. 8vo. xii,524 pp. Orig cloth, worn. *(Goodrich)* $125 [≈ £69]

Ericksen, John Eric
- The science and art of surgery, being a treatise on surgical injuries, diseases, and operations. London: 1869. 5th edn, enlgd. 2 vols. 600 w'engvs. Sheep, rubbed.
(Goodrich) $30 [≈ £16]

Erlanger, Joseph & Gasser, Herbert S.
- Electrical signs of nervous energy. Phila: 1937. 1st edn. 221 pp. Sgntr on title. Cloth.
(Scientia) $125 [≈ £69]

Esdaile, James
- Mesmerism in India, and its practical application in surgery and medicine. London: 1846. Sm 8vo. xxxi,287 pp. Orig cloth, a little faded & worn. *(Weiner)* £400 [≈ $720]

Essay ...
- An essay on brewing ... See Combrune, Michael
- An essay on the possibility and probability of a child being born alive ... See Dickson, David
- An essay towards illustrating the science of insurance ... See Morris, Corbyn

Etheridge, Robert
- Fossils of the British islands stratigraphically and zoologically arranged. Volume I [all published]. Oxford: 1888. Lge 4to. viii,468 pp. Tables. Orig cloth. *(Weiner)* £60 [≈ $108]

Etheridge, Samuel
- Tables for the use of bankers, merchants, tradesmen and others. London: Dilly, 1773. Sm sq 8vo. Contemp tree calf, gilt.
(Marlborough) £85 [≈ $153]

Euclid
- The English Euclide being the first six elements of geometry. Translated ... by Edmund Scarburgh. Oxford: at the Theater, 1705. Folio. 6ff,282 pp. Half-title, engvd title. Lacking final blank. Sl worming in upper margs & prelims. Contemp calf, rebacked. *(Titles)* £225 [≈ $405]
- Euclides elements of geometry. The first vi books ... contracted and demonstrated by Captain Thomas Rudd ... whereunto is added. the mathematical preface of Mr. John Dee. London: Tomlins ..., 1651. 1st edn. Sm 4to. [128],254 pp. Num w'cut text ills. Disbound. *(Argosy)* $250 [≈ £138]
- See also Barrow, Isaac

Evans, A.F.
- The history of the oil engine ... from the year 1680 to ... 1930 ... London: [1932]. 8vo. xviii,318 pp. Num plates. Orig cloth, dw.
(Weiner) £40 [≈ $72]

Evans, George A.
- Hand-book of historical and geographical phthisiology. With special reference to the distribution of consumption in the United States. New York: 1888. 8vo. 295 pp. Advts, errata slip. Ex lib. *(Rittenhouse)* $45 [≈ £25]

Evans, Oliver
- The abortion of the young steam engineer's guide. Phila: for the author, 1805. 1st edn. 8vo. xii,139 pp. Title & 1st leaf with old reprd tears, lib perf & rubber stamps. Mid 19th c 3/4 lea. *(Antiq Sc)* $800 [≈ £444]

Eve, A.S.
- Rutherford. Being the life and letters of the Rt Hon Lord Rutherford. Cambridge: Univ Press, 1939. xvi,451,[i] pp. Frontis, 17 plates, 6 text figs. Pub bndg, dw.
(Pollak) £20 [≈ $36]

Evelyn, John
- Sylva: or, a discourse of forest trees, and the propagation of timber ... Pomona ... also Kaledarium Hortense ... London: for Jo. Martyn ..., 1670. Folio. 3 pts in 1. [48],247; 67; 33 pp. 5 text engvs. Contemp calf, rubbed, rebacked. Wing E3517.
(Karmiole) $350 [≈ £194]
- Sylva: or, a discourse of forest-trees, and the

propagation of timber ... Pomona ... also Kaledarium Hortense ... London: John Martyn, 1679. 3rd edn. Folio. 3 pts in 1. Engvs, errata with sl tear. Old calf, spine reprd. *(Halewood)* **£150 [≈ $270]**

- Silva: or, a discourse of forest trees. London: for J. Walthoe, 1729. 5th edn.Folio. Red & black title, 6 engvs. Contemp mottled calf, gilt, gilt spine. *(Traylen)* **£295 [≈ $531]**

- Silva: or, a discourse of forest trees ... With notes by A. Hunter. York: 1776. 1st Hunter edn. 4to. Port, 40 engvd plates (1 fldg), fldg table. Contemp calf, rebacked, orig spine laid down, mor label, gilt.
(Traylen) **£150 [≈ $270]**

- Terra; a philosophical discourse of earth ... York: for A. ward, 1778. New edn, with notes by A. Hunter. 8vo. Contemp calf, gilt.
(Traylen) **£65 [≈ $117]**

Ewald, C.A.
- The diseases of the stomach. New York: 1892. 497 pp. Orig cloth. *(Fye)* **$75 [≈ £41]**

Ewart, William
- Gout and goutiness. New York: 1898. 8vo. xii,589 pp. Errata leaf. Marg tear on 2 pp not affecting text. Orig cloth, inner hinges started, spine ends sl frayed.
(Elgen) **$75 [≈ £41]**

Ewing, James
- Causation, diagnosis and treatment of cancer. Baltimore: 1931. 1st edn. 8vo. 87 pp. Cloth, stain on front cvr. Ex lib. *(Elgen)* **$25 [≈ £13]**
- Neoplastic diseases. Phila: 1941. 4th edn. 1160 pp. Orig cloth. *(Fye)* **$60 [≈ £33]**

Ewing, Thomas
- A system of geography on a new ... plan ... including also the elements of astronomy, an account of the solar system, a variety of problems to be solved by the terrestrial and celestial globes ... Edinburgh: 1833. 14th edn. 8vo. Pub lea, rubbed. *(Tooley)* **£48 [≈ $86]**

Exhibitor ...
- The illustrated exhibitor ... the principal objects in the Great Exhibition of the Industry of all Nations. London: Cassell, 1851. xliv,556 pp. 11 lge fldg plates, num text ills. Half calf. *(Pollak)* **£50 [≈ $90]**

Experimental Chemistry ...
- Institutes of experimental chemistry ... See Dossie, Robert

Exposition ...
- An exposition of the case of the Assistant-

Surgeons of the Royal Navy. By a naval medical officer. Third edition. London: John Churchill, 1850. 39 pp. Disbound.
(C.R. Johnson) **£25 [≈ $45]**

Fagge, Charles Hilton
- The principles and practice of medicine, edited and compiled from the manuscript of the late ... 1888. 2nd edn. 2 vols. xvi,1014; xiv,1103,[16] pp. New cloth.
(Whitehart) **£35 [≈ $63]**

Fairbairn, William
- Remarks on canal navigation, illustrative of the advantages of steam, as a moving power of canals ... London: 1831. 1st edn. 8vo. 5 lge fldg litho plates. Sm lib stamp on title verso. Contemp bds, cloth spine.
(Traylen) **£295 [≈ $531]**

Fajans, Kasimir
- Radio-elements and isotopes: chemical forces and optical properties of substances. New York: 1931. 1st edn. 8vo. 125 pp. Port, ills. Cloth. *(Elgen)* **$35 [≈ £19]**

Falconer, William
- A new universal dictionary of the marine; being, a copious explanation of the technical terms and phrases usually employed ... London: for T. Cadell ..., 1815. 4to. Half-title, 25 plates, some fldg. Contemp half calf, rebacked, orig spine laid down.
(Traylen) **£330 [≈ $594]**

Falkiner, Sir Frederick R.
- The foundation of the hospital and free school of King Charles II, Oxmantown, Dublin ... Dublin: Sealy, Bryers ..., 1906. 1st edn. 8vo. vi,[1],314 pp. 9 plates. Orig cloth.
(Fenning) **£38.50 [≈ $68]**

Family Oracle ...
- The family oracle; or, the art of improving beauty ... to adorn and beautify the ladies .. how to make washes, perfumes ... powders and medicines ... Newcastle-upon-Tyne: 1828. "Eighth" edn. 8vo. 16 pp. Rather foxed & dog-eared. Orig blue ptd wraps.
(Burmester) **£50 [≈ $90]**

Faraday, Michael
- The chemical history of a candle to which is added a lecture on platinum. London: 1861. 1st edn. 8vo. 208 pp. Ills. Crnr of 1 page nicked. Orig cloth, rebacked, spine dull.
(Oasis) **$75 [≈ £41]**
- Chemical manipulation; being instructions to students in chemistry, on the methods of performing experiments of demonstration or

of research, with accuracy and success. London: W. Philips, 1827. 1st edn. 8vo. Half vellum, mor label, gilt.
(Traylen) **£285 [≃ $513]**
- A course of six lectures on the chemical history of a candle to which is added a lecture on platinum. London: Griffin, Bohn, 1861. 1st edn. Sm 8vo. Text ills. Orig blindstamped red cloth.   *(Chaucer Head)* **£120 [≃ $216]**
- Experimental researches in chemistry and physics, reprinted from the Philosophical Transactions of 1821-57 ... and other publications. London: Richard Taylor, 1859. 1st edn. 8vo. 3 fldg plates. Orig green cloth, gilt.   *(Traylen)* **£330 [≃ $594]**
- Experimental researches in chemistry and physics. London: R. Taylor & W. Francis, 1859. 1st edn. vii,496 pp. Errata slip p 445. 3 engvd plates (1 fldg), text w'cuts. Orig cloth, spine sl nicked.   *(Antiq Sc)* **£450 [≃ £250]**
- Experimental researches in chemistry and physics. London: 1859. viii,496 pp. 3 plates. B'plate, few marks on rear pastedowns. Orig gilt-lettered green dec cloth, sl wear to edge of spine.   *(Weiner)* **£180 [≃ $324]**
- Faraday's diary being the various philosophical notes of experimental investigation ... London: G. Bell, 1932-36. 8 vols inc index. Lge 8vo. Orig dws.
(Rootenberg) **$600 [≃ £333]**
- Faraday's diary. Being the various philosophical notes of experimental investigations ... during the years 1820-1862. London: Bell, 1932-36. 8 vols. Roy 8vo. Ca 450 pp per vol (except index). Num plates. Pub bndgs, dws.   *(Pollak)* **£300 [≃ $540]**

Farmer ...
- Every farmer his own land surveor. For the use of emigrants and all in way connected with land, surveying and levelling. 1856. vii,162 pp. 9 plates, some fldg. Orig cloth, v worn & faded, new endpapers.
(Whitehart) **£35 [≃ $63]**

Farrar, J.
- An elementary treatise on plane and spherical trigonometry ... from the mathematics of Lacroix and Bezout ... Cambridge, Mass: 1820. v,163 pp. 5 fldg plates. Minor discoloration & sl offsetting. Bds sl worn.
(Whitehart) **£40 [≃ $72]**
- An introduction to the elements of algebra ... Cambridge, Mass: 1821. 2nd edn. xii,216 pp. 1st few pp a little shaky in binding, final 4 pp with sm marg tear crudely reprd. Bds, rather worn, front hinge cracked.
(Whitehart) **£40 [≃ $72]**

Farrar, John
- Elementary treatise on astronomy. Cambridge: Hilliard ..., 1827. 420 pp. 8 fldg plates. Binding v worn. *(Xerxes)* **$45 [≃ £25]**
- An experimental treatise on optics. Cambridge, Mass: 1826. 1st edn. 8vo. 350 pp. 6 fldg plates. Orig bds, spine damaged.
(Oasis) **$60 [≃ £33]**

Farre, John Richard
- Pathological researches. Essay I. On malformations of the human heart: illustrated by numerous cases ... London: Longman ..., 1814. Sole edn, all published. Tall 8vo. [xv],46 pp. 5 engvd plates (4 shaved, lightly waterstained at ft). Mod cloth-backed bds.
(Hemlock) **$725 [≃ £402]**

Farriar, John
- An essay towards a theory of apparitions. London: Cadell & Davies, 1813. 1st edn. 8vo. x,[2],139,[5] pp. Qtr calf.
(Rootenberg) **$350 [≃ £194]**

Fatio de Duillier, Nicolas
- Fruit walls improved by inclining them ... whereby they receive more sun shine and heat ... London: R. Everingham, 1699. 1st edn. 4to. Engvd frontis, vignette on title & dedn leaf, 2 lge fldg engvd plates. Contemp half calf, mrbld bds, reprd. Wing F557.
(Traylen) **£390 [≃ $702]**

Faulds, Henry
- Guide to finger-print identification. Hanley: 1905. 8vo. viii,80 pp. Plates, diags. Orig ptd bds, sl worn at spine ends.
(Weiner) **£40 [≃ $72]**

Fawcett, Benjamin
- Observations on the nature, causes and cure of melancholy. Especially of that which is commonly called religious melancholy. Shrewsbury: 1780. 1st edn. Sm 8vo. A little spotting to title. Contemp half calf, mrbld bds.   *(Chaucer Head)* **£180 [≃ $324]**

Fearing, Franklin
- Reflex action: a study in the history of physiological psychology. Balt: Williams & Wilkins, 1930. 1st edn. 8vo. Plates. Orig cloth, spine dulled. Author's pres copy.
(Oasis) **$125 [≃ £69]**

Ferguson, James
- Astronomy explained upon Sir Isaac Newton's principles, and made easy to those who have not studied mathematics. London: for the author, 1757. 2nd edn. 4to.

[viii],283,[ix] pp. 13 fldg engvd plates. Occas
spotting. Contemp calf, spine restored at hd.
        (Frew Mackenzie) **£300 [≈ $540]**
- An easy introduction to astronomy, for young
gentlemen. London: for T. Cadell, 1769. 2nd
edn. 8vo. [iv],247,[5] pp. 7 fldg engvd plates.
Contemp calf, gilt spine, lacking label, 2 short
holes in upper jnt. *(Burmester)* **£100 [≈ $180]**
- Ferguson's astronomy ... upon Sir Isaac
Newton's principles with notes and ...
chapters by David Brewster. Edinburgh:
1811. 1st edn thus. 2 vols 8vo, atlas vol 4to.
Fldg plate & port vol 1, 24 plates in atlas vol.
Contemp calf, rebacked. Atlas vol in bds.
        (Chaucer Head) **£260 [≈ $468]**
- An introduction to electricity. London: 1778.
3rd edn. 8vo. 140 pp. 3 fldg plates. Old
polished calf, worn, rebacked.
        (Weiner) **£100 [≈ $180]**
- Introduction to electricity ... London: 1770.
1st edn. 8vo. 3 fldg plates. Mod wraps.
        (Argosy) **$300 [≈ £166]**
- Lectures on select subject in mechanics,
pneumatics, hydrostatics and optics ...
London: for A. Millar, 1764. [with] A
supplement ... London: 1767. 2nd & 1st edns.
4to. viii,252,[4]; 23 & 13 fldg engvd plates
(some frayed at margs). Contemp calf,
rebacked. *(Pickering)* **$425 [≈ £236]**
- Lectures on select subject in mechanics,
hydrostatics ... optics ... London: W. Strahan
..., 1770. 2nd 8vo edn. [xvi],394, [vi],48 pp.
36 fldg engvd plates. Orig calf, sl worn at ft
of spine.   *(Bickersteth)* **£110 [≈ $198]**
- Lectures on select subject in mechanics,
hydrostatics ... optics ... with the supplement.
London: Strahan ..., 1773. 4to. [viii],252, [iv
index],40 pp. 30 fldg engvd plates, some
browned. Contemp tree calf, jnts cracking,
cvrs scraped, extremities bumped.
        (Frew Mackenzie) **£250 [≈ $450]**
- Ferguson's Lectures on select subject in
mechanics, hydrostatics ... and dialing.
Edinburgh: for Bell & Bradfute ..., 1805.
New edn. 2 vols 8vo, 4to plate vol. lvi,369,[i];
ix,488,[i] pp. 48 engvd plates (2 fldg).
Contemp half calf, paper sides.
        (Frew Mackenzie) **£275 [≈ $495]**
- Select mechanical exercise: shewing how to
construct different clocks orreries and sun-
dials ... London: 1778. 2nd edn. 8vo. Port. 9
plates. Contemp calf, worn, cvrs loose.
        (Robertshaw) **£50 [≈ $90]**
- Select mechanical exercises ... London: W.
Strahan ..., 1778. 2nd edn. 8vo. [xii],xliii,272
pp. Port, 9 fldg engvd plates. Orig calf,
rebacked, new label.
        (Bickersteth) **£110 [≈ $198]**
- Tables and tracts, relative to several arts and

sciences. London: for Millar & Cadell ...,
1767, 1st edn. 8vo. xvi,328 pp. 3 fldg engvd
plates. Rebound in half calf, mrbld bd sides.
        (Pickering) **$400 [≈ £222]**
- Tables and tracts, relative to several arts and
sciences. London: Millar & Cadell, 1767. 1st
edn. 8vo. xiii,[i errata],328 pp. 3 fldg plates,
tables in text. Contemp sheep, jnts cracked,
chipped at hd & ft of spine.
        (Frew Mackenzie) **£275 [≈ $495]**

Ferguson, John
- Bibliotheca chemica: a catalogue of the
alchemical, chemical and pharmaceutical
books in the collection of the late James
Young ... Glasgow: Maclehose, 1906. Orig
edn. 2 vols. 4to. 2 ports. Orig cloth, mor
spines, gilt, uncut. *(Traylen)* **£130 [≈ $234]**

Ferguson, William
- The introductory lecture delivered at King's
College, London, on the opening of the
medical session 1848-49. London: 1848. 8vo.
32 pp. Gilt calf.   *(Goodrich)* **$45 [≈ £25]**

Ferrier, Sir David
- The functions of the brain. New York: 1886.
2nd edn, enlgd. 8vo. xxiii,498 pp. Cloth.
        (Elgen) **$350 [≈ £194]**
- On tabes dorsalis. New York: 1906. 1st Amer
edn. 8vo. 122 pp. Num ills. Sm lib stamp on
endpaper. Cloth, cvr dampstained.
        (Elgen) **$195 [≈ £108]**

Feuchtersleben, Ernst von
- The principles of medical psychology ...
Translated ... London: Sydenham Soc, 1847.
8vo. xx,392 pp. Blindstamped cloth.
        (Rittenhouse) **$37.50 [≈ £20]**
- The principles of medical psychology ...
Translated ... London: Sydenham Soc, 1847.
Tall 8vo. xx,392 pp. Orig embossed cloth, gilt
arms on cvr, t.e.g. Ex lib Fisher collection.
        (Hemlock) **$100 [≈ £55]**

Ficarra, Bernard J.
- Essays on historical medicine. New York:
1948. 1st edn. 8vo. 220 pp. Ills, ports. Cloth
stained.   *(Elgen)* **$35 [≈ £19]**

Field, B. Rush
- Medical thoughts of Shakespeare. Easton:
1885. 2nd edn, revsd & enlgd. 8vo. 85 pp.
Wraps torn, paper a bit brittle.
        (Goodrich) **$65 [≈ £36]**

Fife, Sir John (ed.)
- Manual of the Turkish bath; heat a mode of
cure and a source of strength for men and

animals, from writings of Mr. Urquhart.
London: 1865. 8vo. xiv,419 pp. Frontis
(detchd), 2 fldg plates, few ills. Orig cloth, a
little soiled. Ex lib, stamp on title & margs.
(Weiner) **£30 [≈ $54]**

Findley, A. & Mills, W.H.
- British chemists. London: Chemical Soc,
1947. 1st edn. 8vo. 431 pp. Ports. Orig cloth.
(Bow Windows) **£20 [≈ $36]**

Findley, Palmer
- Priest of Lucia. The story of obstetrics.
Boston: 1939. 1st edn, specially bound. 421
pp. Ms note on front endpaper. Sgnd by
author. *(Rittenhouse)* **$60 [≈ £33]**

Firebaugh, Ellen
- The physician's wife and the things that
pertain to her life. Phila: 1894. 1st edn. 186
pp. Orig cloth. *(Fye)* **$60 [≈ £33]**

Fischer, Alfred
- The structure and function of bacteria.
Translated ... Oxford: Clarendon Press, 1900.
1st edn in English. 8vo. viii,198 pp. Text ills.
Cloth, spine ends sl frayed.
(Elgen) **$40 [≈ £22]**

Fishbein, Morris
- A history of the American Medical
Association 1847 to 1947. Phila: 1947.
xvi,1226 pp. Photos & ills. Orig cloth.
(Whitehart) **£40 [≈ $72]**
- A history of the American Medical
Association. Phila: 1947. 1st edn. Orig cloth.
Author's sgnd inscrptn.
(Rittenhouse) **$90 [≈ £50]**
- Medical writing. The technic and the art.
Chicago: 1938. 1st edn. 8vo. 212 pp. Orig
cloth. *(Goodrich)* **$35 [≈ £19]**

Fisher, G.
- Arithmetick in the plainest and most concise
methods hitherto extant. Hitch & Hawes,
1759. 10th edn. [x],312 pp. Front free
endpaper almost detchd, ink spillage on 2 pp,
crnr torn from B1 without loss. Contemp calf.
(Hinchliffe) **£40 [≈ $72]**

Fisher, Ronald A.
- The genetical theory of natural selection.
Oxford: 1930. 1st edn. 272 pp. Cloth, cvrs sl
warped, hd & ft of spine rubbed.
(Scientia) **$150 [≈ £83]**

Fiske, Eben.
- An elementary study of the brain based on the
dissections of the brain of the sheep. New

York: 1913. 8vo. 132 pp. Photo plates. Orig
cloth. *(Goodrich)* **$35 [≈ £19]**

Fitzpatrick, T.J.
- Rafinesque. A sketch of his life with
bibliography. Des Moines, 1911. 8vo. 241
pp. Ills. Dampstaining.
(Goodrich) **$115 [≈ £63]**

Fitzwilliams, Duncan
- The tongue and its diseases. London: 1927.
1st edn. 505 pp. Orig cloth. *(Fye)* **$75 [≈ £41]**

Flamant, Adolphe
- A practical treatise on olive culture, oil
making and olive pickling. San Francisco:
Gregoire, Booksellers, 1887. 8vo. 76 pp.
Oliver wraps, sl soiled, spine chipped.
(Karmiole) **$45 [≈ £25]**

Flatters, A.
- Methods of microscopical research: vegetable
histology. London: 1905. 4to. x,116 pp. 23
cold plates. Half roan, worn.
(Weiner) **£30 [≈ $54]**

Flax-Husbandry ...
- Progress of flax-husbandry in Scotland ... See
Home, Henry, Lord Kames

Flaxman, John
- Anatomical studies of the bones and muscles.
for the use of artists. London: Nattali. 1833.
Folio. 6 ptd text leaves, 21 full-page engvd
plates, some in aquatint. Foxing. Orig bds,
worn, weak jnts. *(Goodrich)* **$795 [≈ £441]**

Fleet, John
- A discourse relative to the subject of
animation ... Boston: John & Thomas Fleet,
1797. 1st edn. 8vo. [3],25,[1] pp. Half-title,
appendix. Mod cloth.
(Rootenberg) **$350 [≈ £194]**

Fleming, Alexander & Petrie, G.F.
- Recent advances in vaccine and serum
therapy. Phila: 1934. 1st Amer edn. 463 pp.
Orig cloth. *(Fye)* **$75 [≈ £41]**

Fleming, Alexander (ed.)
- Penicillin, its practical application. London:
1946. 1st edn. 380 pp. Orig cloth.
(Fye) **$90 [≈ £50]**
- Penicillin, its practical application. London:
1946. 1st edn. 8vo. x,380 pp. Ills. Orig cloth.
(Weiner) **£30 [≈ $54]**

Fleming, J.A. (ed.)
- The electrical educator. A comprehensive,

practical and authoritative guide for all engaged in the electrical industry. 1926. 2 vols. 1556 pp. 22 plates, num photo ills & diags. *(Whitehart)* **£25 [≈ $45]**

Fleming, Peter

- Geometrical solutions to the quadrature of the circle. Montreal: 1850. Tall 4to. [8],10 pp. 6 fldg litho plates. Orig green cloth, spine gouged. *(Karmiole)* **$125 [≈ £69]**

Flexner, Abraham

- Medical education in Europe. New York: 1912. 1st edn. 357 pp. Buckram.
  (Fye) **$125 [≈ £69]**
- Medical education in Europe. New York: 1912. 1st edn. 357 pp. Orig ptd wraps. Carnegie Foundation for the Advancement of Teaching, Bulletin No. 6.
  (Scientia) **$85 [≈ £47]**
- Medical education in the United States and Canada. New York: 1910. 1st edn. 346 pp. Buckram, lacking orig ptd wraps. Carnegie Foundation for the Advancement of Teaching, Bulletin No. 4.
  (Scientia) **$135 [≈ £75]**
- Medical education in the United States and Canada. New York: 1910. 1st edn. 346 pp. Orig ptd wraps, backstrip chipped.
  (Fye) **$225 [≈ £125]**
- Medical education; a comparative study. New York: 1925. 1st edn. 334 pp. Cloth, dw worn.. *(Scientia)* **$60 [≈ £33]**

Flinn, D. Edgar

- Ireland, its health resorts and watering places ... distribution of temperature and rainfall throughout Ireland. London: Kegan Paul, 1888. 8vo. 175 pp. Frontis, fldg cold map. Rec maroon cloth. *(Emerald Isle)* **£50 [≈ $90]**

Flint, Austin

- Clinical medicine; a systematic treatise on the diagnosis and treatment of diseases. Phila: 1879. 1st edn. 795 pp. Orig cloth.
  (Scientia) **$150 [≈ £83]**
- Hand-book of physiology. New York: 1905. 8vo. 877 pp. Cloth, hinges a little loose, sl shaken. *(Rittenhouse)* **$35 [≈ £19]**
- Phthisis ... in a series of clinical studies. Phila: 1875. 1st edn. 8vo. xi,446 pp. Cloth. Ex lib. *(Rittenhouse)* **$35 [≈ £19]**
- Phthisis; its morbid anatomy, etiology, symptomatic events and complications ... treatment and physical diagnosis ... Phila: 1875. 1st edn. 446 pp. Orig cloth.
  (Scientia) **$200 [≈ £111]**
- Physical exploration and diagnosis of diseases affecting the respiratory organs. Phila: 1856.

1st edn. 636 pp. Rec cloth. *(Fye)* **$75 [≈ £41]**
- The physiology of man: designed to represent the existing state of physiological science ... New York: 1873. 8vo. 502 pp. Advts at rear. Ex lib, worn. *(Rittenhouse)* **$25 [≈ £13]**
- A practical treatise on the physical exploration of the chest, and the diagnosis of diseases affecting the respiratory organs. Phila: 1866. 2nd edn, revsd. 595 pp. Pub ctlg. Cloth spine faded & frayed at top.
  (Scientia) **$95 [≈ £52]**
- A practical treatise on the physical exploration of the chest ... Phila: 1856. 1st edn. 636 pp. Cloth. *(Scientia)* **$250 [≈ £138]**
- A text-book of human physiology; designed for the use of practitioners and students of medicine. New York: D. Appleton, 1876. 1st edn. Lge 8vo. xviii,978 pp. 3 litho plates, over 300 text figs. Orig cloth. Ex lib.
  (Antiq Sc) **$65 [≈ £36]**
- A treatise on the principles and practice of medicine. Phila: 1866. 1st edn. 867 pp. Pub ctlg. Orig cloth, rebacked, orig spine laid down, new endpapers.
  (Scientia) **$175 [≈ £97]**
- A treatise on the principles and practice of medicine. Phila: 1866. 1st edn. Title & 5 other pages stained in marg, sgntr on title, lacking endpapers, index pp dampstained. Orig lea, worn. *(Rittenhouse)* **$65 [≈ £36]**

Flint, Austin, Jnr.

- On the source of muscular power; arguments and conclusions drawn from observations ... New York: 1878. 1st edn. 103 pp. Orig cloth.
  (Scientia) **$75 [≈ £41]**

Flower, P.W.

- A history of the trade in tin; a short description of tin mining and metallurgy ... ancient and modern processes ... London: 1880. 8vo. xiii,219 pp. Plates. Orig cloth.
  (Weiner) **£60 [≈ $108]**

Floyer, Sir John

- Psykhroloysia; or, the history of cold bathing, both ancient and modern. In two parts. London: W. & J. Innys, 1722. 5th edn. [22],491,[31] pp. Orig blindstamped lea, rebacked, orig spine laid down.
  (Elgen) **$350 [≈ £194]**

Fluckiger, F.A. & Hanbury, D.

- Pharmacographia: a history of the principal drugs of vegetable origin, met with in Great Britain and British India. London: 1879. 2nd edn. 8vo. xx,803 pp. Orig qtr lea, worn.
  (Weiner) **£35 [≈ $63]**

Flugge, C.

- Micro-organisms with special reference to the etiology of the infective diseases. London: 1890. 1st English trans. 826 pp. Orig cloth.
(*Fye*) **$75 [≃ £41]**
- Micro-organisms. London: New Sydenham Soc, 1890. 1st edn in English. 8vo. 826 pp. Num text ills. Orig cloth. (*Oasis*) **$60 [≃ £33]**

Foakes, J.W.

- Gout and rheumatic gout: a new method of cure. London: 1883. 9th edn. Sm 8vo. [iv],xii, 132 pp. Orig cloth.
(*Bow Windows*) **£28 [≃ $50]**

Fontanelle, Bernard le Bovyer de

- Conversation with a lady on the plurality of worlds ... translated by Mr. Glanvill. London: for M. Wellington, 1719. 4th edn. 12mo. Frontis, fldg plate, 4 pp pub ctlg at end. Contemp panelled calf.
(*Charles Cox*) **£25 [≃ $45]**
- Conversation with a lady on the plurality of worlds ... translated by Mr. Glanvill. London: for M. Wellington, 1719. 4th edn. 8vo. Frontis, fldg plate. Some minor waterstaining affecting a few leaves. Contemp panelled calf, sm tear of back cvr.
(*Waterfield's*) **£90 [≃ $162]**
- Conversations on the plurality of worlds. Dublin: Peter Wilson, 1761. 12mo. xx,181 pp. 4 engvd fldg plates. Contemp calf, hinges starting. (*Karmiole*) **$125 [≃ £69]**
- Dialogues of the dead. London: for Jacob Tonson, 1708. liv,209 pp. Lacking frontis. Contemp unlettered panelled calf, v sl chipped at hd of spine. (*Pirages*) **$50 [≃ £27]**
- A week's conversation on the plurality of worlds ... to which is added Mr. Addison's defence on the Newtonian philosophy. London: 1737. 6th edn. 12mo. Frontis, fldg plate. Contemp calf, lacking label.
(*Robertshaw*) **£36 [≃ $64]**

Foot, Jesse

- A complete treatise on the origin, theory, and cure of the lues venerea, and obstructions of the urethra ... London: for the author, 1792. 1st edn. 4to. Lge copy, ex lib Matthew Boulton. Contemp half calf, jnts reprd.
(*Quaritch*) **$1,550 [≃ £861]**

Forbes, John

- A manual of select medical bibliography. London: 1835. 8vo. viii,403 pp. Orig cloth, worn, paper label. (*Weiner*) **£100 [≃ $180]**
- A physician's holiday or a month in Switzerland in the summer of 1848. London: Murray & Churchill, 1850. 2nd revsd edn. 8vo. vii,350,[2] pp. 4 tinted lithos inc frontis, fldg map. Orig cloth, sl soiled, hd & tail of spine bumped. (*Morrell*) **£95 [≃ $171]**

Forbes, John (ed.)

- The cyclopaedia of practical medicine: comprising treatises on the nature and treatment of diseases, materia medica and therapeutics ... Phila: 1845. 4 vols. 8vo. 788; 804; 782; 770 pp. Half lea, mrbld bds, lea dry & cracked with some defects.
(*Rittenhouse*) **$50 [≃ £27]**
- The cyclopaedia of practical medicine ... Phila: 1859. 4 vols. Pigskin.
(*Rittenhouse*) **$75 [≃ £41]**

Forbes, John

- The theory of the differential and integral calculus. Glasgow: 1837. 1st edn. 8vo. Calf, hinges reprd. (*Argosy*) **$100 [≃ £55]**

Forbes, Thomas R.

- The midwife and the witch. New Haven: Yale Univ Press, 1966. 8vo. x,[iv], 196,[iv] pp. Title vignette, 8 plates, 8 text figs. Pub bndg, dw. (*Pollak*) **£20 [≃ $36]**

Ford, Frank R.

- Diseases of the nervous system in infancy, childhood and adolescence. Springfield: [1937]. 1st edn. Lge 8vo. xxiv,953 pp. Num ills. Cloth, dw. (*Elgen*) **$50 [≃ £27]**

Ford, William W.

- Bacteriology. New York: Hoeber, 1939. 8vo. xv,[i], 207,[i] pp. 8 ills. Pub bndg.
(*Pollak*) **£25 [≃ $45]**

Fordyce, Sir William

- A new enquiry into the causes, symptoms and cure of putrid and inflammatory fevers with an appendix on the hectic fever and on the ulcerated and malignant sore throat. London: 1777. 3rd edn. 8vo. Old calf.
(*Halewood*) **£95 [≃ $171]**

Forel, Auguste H.

- Hypnotism or suggestion and psychotherapy ... from the fifth German edition ... Rebman ..., 1906. 1st English edition. 8vo. xii,370, [2 blank] pp. Orig cloth.
(*Fenning*) **£24.50 [≃ $43]**

Forman, Maurice Buxton (ed.)

- John Keat's anatomical and physiological note book. London: OUP, 1934. One of 350. 8vo. xi,[iii],68 pp. Frontis. Ex Lewis's lib. Pub bndg. (*Pollak*) **£25 [≃ $45]**

Forster, A.R.
- Theory of functions of a complex variable. Cambridge: 1900. 2nd edn. 4to. xxiv,782 pp. 125 diags. Sl foxing on endpapers. Cloth.
(Whitehart) **£35** **[≈ $63]**

Forsyth, J.S.
- Demonologia; or, natural knowledge revealed ... expose of ancient and modern superstitions ... amulets, apparitions, astrology ... witches and witchcraft. London: Bumpus, 1827. 1st edn. xvi,438 pp. Orig linen bds, extremities little worn, split in lower hinge.
(Claude Cox) **£45** **[≈ $81]**
- The farmer, maltster, distiller, and brewer's practical memorandum book ... to which is added, an abstract of the new Beer Act. London: D. Cox, n.d. [ca 1820]. Sm 8vo. Contemp bds, worn, uncut.
(Stewart) **£45** **[≈ $81]**

Forsyth, William
- A treatise on the culture and management of fruit trees. London: Nichols, 1802. 1st edn. 4to. 13 fldg engvd pates. Rec half calf, gilt.
(Traylen) **£110** **[≈ $198]**

Fort, George
- Medical economy during the Middle Ages. A contribution to the history of European morals ... New York: Bouton, 1883. 8vo. 488 pp. Uncut. *(Goodrich)* **$75** **[≈ £41]**

Fossil Fuel ...
- The history and description of fossil fuel ... See Holland, John

Foster, Michael
- Lectures on the history of physiology. Cambridge: 1901. 8vo. 304 pp. Orig cloth, a bit worn. *(Goodrich)* **£35** **[≈ £19]**
- A text book of physiology. London: 1877. 1st edn. 559 pp. Cloth, spine extremities frayed, crnrs worn. Ex lib. *(Scientia)* **$135** **[≈ £75]**
- A text book of physiology. London: 1883. 4th edn. 8vo. xv,784 pp. Cloth.
(Rittenhouse) **$45** **[≈ £25]**
- A textbook of physiology. 1893-95-90-91. 6th & 5th edns. Sgntrs on half-titles, marg anntns & underlinings. Orig cloth, sl worn.
(Whitehart) **£45** **[≈ $81]**

Foster, Samuel
- Miscellanies: or mathematical lucubrations ... Translated ... Leybourn, 1659. 1st edn. Folio. Latin & English titles (inner margs reprd), 7 ptd titles to sections, 10 engvd plates. Some pages & plates strengthened, marg waterstaining. Mod mor. Wing F1634.

Foster, William & Gaskell, J.F.
- Cerebro-spinal fever. Cambridge: 1916. 1st edn. 222 pp. Orig cloth. Inscrbd by author.
(Fye) **$100** **[≈ £55]**

Fothergill, John
- An account of the sore throat attended with ulcers; a disease which hath of later years appeared in this city ... London: for C. Davis, 1748. 1st edn. 8vo. iv,62 pp. Tear in title reprd, upper margin trimmed close. Orig calf, lower jnt reprd. *(Bickersteth)* **£480** **[≈ $864]**

Fourcroy, Antoine Francois de
- Elements of natural history, and of chemistry ... first published in 1782, and now ... translated into English. London: Robinson, 1788. 4 vols. 8vo. 9 fldg engvd tables. Contemp tree calf, occas sl surface damage to sides. *(Frew Mackenzie)* **£375** **[≈ $675]**

Fourier, Joseph
- The analytical theory of heat. Cambridge: University Press, 1878. 1st edn in English. 8vo. xxiii,[1],466 pp. Lib stamp on title. Orig cloth. *(Antiq Sc)* **$225** **[≈ £125]**
- The analytical theory of heat. Cambridge: University Press, 1878. 1st edn in English. 8vo. xxiii,466,[2] pp. 32 pp pub advts. Text diags throughout. Orig cloth.
(Rootenberg) **$400** **[≈ £222]**

Fournier, Alfred
- Syphilis and marriage. London: Bogue, 1881. 1st edn in English. 8vo. 264 pp. 30 pp pub ctlg. Half calf. *(Oasis)* **$100** **[≈ £55]**

Fovargue, Stephen
- A new catalogue of vulgar errors. Cambridge: for the author, 1767. 1st edn. 8vo. [ii],202 pp. Errata slip. Wanting half-title, 1st few leaves sl browned, a few inner margs dampstained. Rec qtr calf. *(Burmester)* **£125** **[≈ $225]**

Fowler, J.K. & Godlee, R.J.
- The diseases of the lungs. 1898. xv,715 pp. 5 plates, 154 diags. Sl foxing. Orig cloth, marked & dust-stained.
(Whitehart) **£18** **[≈ $32]**

Fox, George Henry
- Photographic illustrations of cutaneous syphilis. New York: Treat, 1881. 1st edn. Lge 4to. 106 pp. 48 hand-cold artotype plates. Orig half mor, spine a little rubbed.
(Oasis) **$450** **[≈ £250]**
- Photographic illustrations of skin diseases.

(P & P) **£560** **[≈ $1,008]**

New York: Treat, 1885. 2nd edn. Lge 4to.
208 pp. 48 hand-cold artotype plates.
Contemp half mor. sl worn.
(Oasis) **$250 [≃ £138]**
- Photographic illustrations of skin diseases.
New York: Treat, 1887. 2nd series. 208 pp.
90 hand-cold photo plates. Half lea, rebound
preserving orig bds.   *(Fye)* **$250 [≃ £138]**

Fox, Joseph
- The natural history of the human teeth ... to
which is added, an account of the diseases
which affect children during the first
dentition. London: for Thomas Cox, 1803.
4to. [ii],vii, [i],100 pp. 13 plates, 7ff text.
Some crnrs dampstained. New half calf.
(Pollak) **£300 [≃ $540]**

Fox, R. Dacre
- Bone-setting so-called and the treatment of
sprains. Manchester: John Heywood, 1883.
15,[i] pp. New wraps.   *(Pollak)* **£15 [≃ $27]**

Fox, Wilson
- An atlas of the pathological anatomy of the
lungs. London: Churchill, 1888. 4to. 286 pp.
45 cold plates. Qtr calf, recased.
(Goodrich) **$250 [≃ £138]**
- An atlas of the pathological anatomy of the
lungs. London: 1888. Lge 8vo. 286 pp. 45
full-page plates, mostly in color. Binding
broken, bds detchd. *(Rittenhouse)* **$30 [≃ £16]**

Fracastoro, Girolamo
- Syphilis or the French disease. A poem ...
with a translation ... London: Heinemann,
1935. 8vo. vii,253 pp. Errata slip. Ills. Orig
cloth, gilt.   *(Fenning)* **£35 [≃ $63]**

Francis, D.J.T.
- Change of climate considered as a remedy in
dyspeptic, pulmonary and other chronic
affections. With an account of the most
eligible places of residence for invalids in
Spain, Portugal, Algeria, &c. London:
Churchill, 1853. 8vo. xii,339,4 advts pp. Orig
cloth.   *(Pollak)* **£30 [≃ $54]**

Frankland, E.
- Experimental researches in pure, applied and
physical chemistry. 1877. xliv,1047 pp. 23
ills inc 2 fldg cold plates. Scattered foxing
throughout. Orig blindstamped cloth, spine
faded.   *(Whitehart)* **£60 [≃ $108]**

Frankland, P. & Mrs. P.
- Micro-organisms in water. Their
significance, identification and removal ...
designed for the use of those connected with

the sanitary aspects of water supply. 1894.
xi,532 pp. 2 plates, 28 text figs. Light
scattered foxing. Authors' pres copy.
(Whitehart) **£20 [≃ $36]**

Franklin, Benjamin
- The complete works ... now first collected ...
with memoirs of his early life. London:
Johnson, 1806. 3 vols. 8vo. 440; 468; 552 pp.
3 engvd port frontis (some sl soiled), fldg table. Sm marg worming
vol 2. Contemp calf, hinges cracked.
(Oasis) **$450 [≃ £250]**
- Memoirs of the life and writings of Benjamin
Franklin ... written by himself ... London:
Henry Colburn, 1833. New edn. 6 vols. 8vo.
9 engvd plates (6 fldg). Lib stamps on title &
plate versos. Contemp half calf, some spines
reprd.   *(Traylen)* **£120 [≃ $216]**
- The works ... with notes and life of the author
by Jared Sparks. Boston: 1836-40. 4to. 10
vols. 5 engvd port frontis, facs frontis, 17
engvd plates, text engvs. Occas marg foxing.
3/4 red mor, spines gilt, mrbld bds, t.e.g., by
Bradstreet.   *(Elgen)* **$350 [≃ £194]**

Frauenthal, H.W. & Manning, J.v.V.
- A manual of infantile paralysis with modern
methods of treatment ... Phila: 1914. xii,374
pp. 128 ills. Cloth. *(Whitehart)* **£18 [≃ $32]**

Frazer, J.E.
- The anatomy of the human skeleton. 1920.
2nd edn. 4to. viii,284 pp. 219 ills. Cloth.
(Whitehart) **£25 [≃ $45]**

Freeman, John
- Hay-fever, a key to the allergic disorders.
London: 1950. 1st edn. 8vo. xx,321 pp. Port
frontis, ills. Cloth, dw. *(Elgen)* **$45 [≃ £25]**

Freeman, John R.
- Report upon New York's water supply with
particular reference to the need of procuring
additional sources and their probable cost.
New York: 1900. 8vo. vii,587 pp. Fldg map
& charts, plates. Orig cloth.
(Weiner) **£40 [≃ $72]**

Freeman, W.
- Neuropathology. The anatomical foundation
of nervous diseases. Phila & London: 1933.
349 pp. 116 text figs. Some pencil
underlining. Cloth sl dust-stained.
(Whitehart) **£18 [≃ $32]**

Freeman, Walter & Watts, James W.
- Psychosurgery; intelligence, emotion and
social behavior following prefontal lobotomy

for mental disorders. Springfield: 1942. 1st edn. 337 pp. Pres copy, sgnd by both authors.
(Scientia) **$200 [≃ £111]**

Freind, J.
- The history of physick from the time of Galen to the beginning of the sixteenth century. London: Walther, 1726-27. 3rd, 2nd edns. Orig panelled calf, worn, jnts cracked.
(Goodrich) **$275 [≃ £152]**

French, C.
- A handbook of the destructive insects of Victoria, with notes on the methods to check and extirpate them. Melbourne: Bain, 1904. 1st edn. 3 vols. 8vo. 163; 222; 163 pp. 54 cold lithos (1 reprd) & ills. Orig cloth, some fading. *(Morrell)* **£170 [≃ $306]**

French, Gilbert J.
- Remarks on the mechanical structure of cotton fibre. Manchester: Charles Simms, 1857. Contemp green mor, elab gilt. Author's pres copy to his son.
(C.R. Johnson) **£65 [≃ $117]**

French, J.W. (ed.)
- Modern power generators; steam, electric and internal combustion and their application to present-day requirements. Gresham: 1908. 1st edn. 2 vols. Sm folio. many diags & ills; a series of cold composite sectional models. Orig dec cloth. *(Halewood)* **£58 [≃ $104]**

French, John
- The York-shire spaw, or a treatise of four famous medicinal wells ... causes, vertues, and use thereof ... London: for E. Dod ..., 1652. 1st edn. 8vo. [viii],124,[2 table of contents] pp. With final blank R4. Rec bds.
(Pickering) **$350 [≃ £194]**

French, Sidney J.
- Torch and crucible; the life and death of Antoine Lavoisier. Princeton: [1941]. 8vo. 285 pp. Cloth. *(Elgen)* **$30 [≃ £16]**

Frend, William
- Evening amusements; or, the beauty of the heavens displayed ... to be observed on various evenings ... during the year 1820 ... London: Mawman, 1820. 12mo. iv,219,[5 advts] pp. Engvd frontis, sev tables. Orig blue bds, uncut, rebacked. *(Karmiole)* **£65 [≃ £36]**

Frenkel, J.
- Wave mechanics, advanced general theory. Oxford: 1934. 8vo. viii,525 pp. Orig cloth.
(Weiner) **£30 [≃ $54]**

Frerichs, F.T.
- A clinical treatise on diseases of the liver. Translated ... London: 1860. 2 vols. 8vo. xxvi,402; xix,484 pp. Cloth, chipped & worn, Ex lib. *(Rittenhouse)* **$35 [≃ £19]**
- A clinical treatise on diseases of the liver. New York: 1879. 1st Amer edn. 3 vols. Orig cloth. *(Fye)* **$75 [≃ £41]**

Fresenius, C.R.
- A system of instruction in qualitative chemical analysis. London: 1855. 4th edn. 8vo. xxii,310 pp. Diced calf, gilt spine.
(Weiner) **£20 [≃ $36]**

Freud, Sigmund
- Beyond the pleasure principle. London: 1922. 1st English edn. [6],90 pp. Green cloth, lower crnr bumped. *(Karmiole)* **$45 [≃ £25]**
- Civilisation and its discontents. London: 1930. 8vo. 144 pp. Port frontis. Uncut in orig green cloth, spine wrinkled, extremities lightly rubbed. *(Frew Mackenzie)* **£30 [≃ $54]**
- Collected papers. Authorized translation under the supervision of Joan Riviere. 1957. 5 vols. Orig cloth. *(Allen)* **$100 [≃ £55]**
- Collected papers. London: Hogarth Press, 1948. Vols 1, 2, 3 & 4. Cloth. Dws.
(Rittenhouse) **$50 [≃ £27]**
- The ego and the id. London: Hogarth Press, 1927. 1st English edn. 88,[1] pp. Orig green cloth, gilt, uncut, some warping of cvrs.
(Jenkins) **$175 [≃ £97]**
- Group psychology and the analysis of the ego. London: 1922. 1st English edn. [4],134 pp. Orig gilt-stamped green cloth, sl faded.
(Karmiole) **$45 [≃ £25]**
- Group psychology and the analysis of the ego. London: 1922. 1st edn in English. 8vo. 134,[2] pp. Some underlining & finger marks. Orig cloth. *(Bow Windows)* **£48 [≃ $86]**
- Reflections on war and death. New York: 1918. 1st edn in English. 8vo. 72 pp. A few marg pencil notes. Cloth, sm stain on cvr.
(Elgen) **$90 [≃ £50]**

Frick, J.
- Physical technics; or practical instructions for making experiments in physics and the construction of physical apparatus ... Phila: 1862. 467 pp. 797 text ills. Endpapers sl foxed. Orig blindstamped cloth, spine sl faded & worn. *(Whitehart)* **£35 [≃ $63]**

Friedenwald, Harry
- The Jews and medicine, essays. Baltimore: 1944-46. 1st edn. 2 vols. 817 pp. Orig cloth, dw. *(Fye)* **$200 [≃ £111]**

Fritsch, Heinrich
- The diseases of women. New York: Wood's Library, 1883. 1st Amer edn. 8vo. 355 pp. 159 text ills. Orig cloth. *(Oasis)* **$40 [≈ £22]**

Frost, Wade Hampton
- Papers ... A contribution to epidemiological method. New York: 1941. 1st edn. Lge 8vo. viii,628 pp. Port frontis, charts, diags, fldg maps. Cloth, dw. *(Elgen)* **$35 [≈ £19]**

Fruhwald, F.
- Reference handbook of the diseases of children. Edited by T.S. Westcott. Phila: 1906. 8vo. 533 pp. Pub ctlg. Cloth. *(Rittenhouse)* **$35 [≈ £19]**

Fruit Walls ...
- Fruit walls improved ... See Fatio de Duillier, Nicolas

Fujikawa, Y.
- Japanese medicine. Translated ... New York: Hoeber, 1934. 8vo. xiii,[i], 114,[ii] pp. Ills. Pub bndg. *(Pollak)* **£30 [≈ $54]**

Fulke, William
- A most pleasant prospect into the garden of naturall contemplation, to behold the naturall causes of all kinde of meteors ... London: E.G. for William Leake, 1640. Sm 8vo. [3],71ff. Closely trimmed. Half mor over mrbld bds. *(Rootenberg)* **$400 [≈ £222]**

Fuller, Francis
- Medicina gymnastica: or a treatise concerning the power of exercise, with respect to the animal economy; and the great necessity of it ... London: 1728. 6th edn. 8vo. 271 pp. Contemp calf. *(Goodrich)* **$75 [≈ £41]**
- Medicina gymnastica: or a treatise concerning the power of exercise ... London: Knaplock, 1728. 6th edn. 8vo. [36],271,[10 advts] pp. Lower marg waterstained, title verso stamped. Rec half calf. *(Spelman)* **£55 [≈ $99]**

Fuller, Thomas (1654-1734)
- Exanthematogia: or ... a rational account of eruptive fevers, especially of the measles and small pox. London: Rivington & Austen, 1730. 1st edn. 4to. 439,[9] pp. Advt leaf. Red & black title. Titles to pts 2 & 3 dated 1729. Contemp lea-backed mrbld bds. *(Antiq Sc)* **$375 [≈ £208]**

Fuller, William
- Architecture of the brain. Grand Rapids: 1896. 1st edn. 4to. Photo ills. Orig cloth. *(Fye)* **$90 [≈ £50]**

Fulton, John F.
- Functional localization in relation to frontal lobotomy. New York: OUP, 1949. 1st Amer edn. 8vo. 140 pp. Ills. Orig cloth. *(Oasis)* **$50 [≈ £27]**
- Muscular contraction and the reflex control of movement. Balt: 1926. 1st edn. 644 pp. Cloth, dw torn. *(Scientia)* **$150 [≈ £83]**
- Physiology of the nervous system. London: OUP, 1938, reprint 1939. xv,675 pp. 94 text figs. Orig cloth. *(Whitehart)* **£25 [≈ $45]**
- Physiology of the nervous system. London & New York: OUP, 1938. 1st edn. 8vo. xv,[1],675 pp. Ills. A few pages with underlining. Orig cloth. *(Antiq Sc)* **$65 [≈ £36]**
- Physiology of the nervous system. New York: 1938. 1st edn. 675 pp. Cloth. Sgnd by author. *(Scientia)* **$150 [≈ £83]**

Fulton, John F. & Keller, A.D.
- The sign of Babinski. A study of the evolution of cortical dominance in primates. Springfield: 1932. 8vo. 165 pp. Cloth, dw. *(Goodrich)* **$65 [≈ £36]**

Fyfe, A.
- A compendium of the anatomy of the human body. Illustrated by upwards of 160 tables ... Edinburgh: 1800. 1st edn. 3 vols. 4to. profusely illust, many plates cold (lacking 3). Half calf, rebacked. *(Halewood)* **£135 [≈ $243]**

G.M.
- Cheape and good husbandry for the well-ordering of all beasts and fowles and for the generall cure of their diseases. 1653. 8th edn. 188 pp. Contemp inscrptn & anntn on 2 leaves. Rebound in calf, gilt, new endpapers. *(Edwards)* **£150 [≈ $270]**

Gabb. Thomas
- Thoughts on the creation, and on the systems of astronomy. London: Keating, Brown, 1812. 8vo. Contemp mottled calf. *(Stewart)* **£20 [≈ $36]**

Gabell, D.P., et al.
- The report on odontones by the committee appointed by the British Dental Association. 1914. ix,133 pp. 45 plates. Cloth sl worn. *(Whitehart)* **£25 [≈ $45]**

Gage, S.H.
- The microscope: an introduction to microscopic methods and to histology. Ithaca, New York: 1904. 9th edn. 8vo. vi,299 pp. Ills. Orig cloth. *(Weiner)* **£20 [≈ $36]**

Gairdner, W.T.
- Clinical medicine. Observations recorded at the bedside with commentaries. Edinburgh: 1862. xvii,741 pp. 32 diags & ills. Front blank removed. Orig cloth, sl worn.
(Whitehart) **£28 [≃ $50]**
- The physician as naturalist. Addresses and memoirs bearing on the history and progress of medicine chiefly during the last hundred years. Glasgow: Maclehose, 1889. 8vo. x,436 pp. Pub bndg.   *(Pollak)* **£30 [≃ $54]**

Gairdner, William
- On gout; its history, its causes, and its cure. London: 1849. 1st edn. 8vo. viii,232 pp. Some extensive dust marks & spotting, pencilled notes in margs. Orig cloth, rebacked, old spine preserved, lacking rear free endpaper.   *(Bow Windows)* **£48 [≃ $86]**

Gall, F.J., et al.
- On the functions of the cerebellum, by Drs. Gall, Vimont, and Brousais, translated from the French ... also answers to the objections urged against phrenology ... Edinburgh: Maclachan, 1838. 8vo. xliv,339 pp. Text ills. Rec qtr cloth.   *(Goodrich)* **$250 [≃ £138]**

Galton, Sir D.
- Observations on the construction of healthy dwellings, namely houses, hospitals, barracks, asylums, etc. Oxford: 1880. 1st edn. 8vo. xi,296,36 advts pp. Num text ills. Some underlining & finger marks. Orig cloth, inner hinges a little weak.
(Bow Windows) **£95 [≃ $171]**

Galton, Francis
- Decipherment of blurred finger prints. London: 1893. 18 pp. 16 plates.
(Scientia) **$150 [≃ £83]**
- Finger prints. London: 1892. 8vo. xvi,216 pp. 16 plates. Orig cloth, a bit faded & worn, jnts shaken. A.l.s. from Galton accepting dinner invitation loosely inserted.
(Weiner) **£180 [≃ $324]**
- Finger prints. London: 1892. xvi,216 pp. 15 plates, 34 tables. V sl foxing on endpapers. Orig cloth, sl worn, spine faded & with sm tear reprd.   *(Whitehart)* **£180 [≃ $324]**
- Finger prints. London: Macmillan, 1892. 1st edn. 8vo. xvi,216 pp. 15 plates, some cold. Lib stamp on title. Orig cloth, rebacked, orig spine laid down.   *(Antiq Sc)* **$350 [≃ £194]**
- Finger prints. London: Macmillan, 1892. 8vo. Half-title, 24 figs on 16 plates (correct, not 23 on 15 as called for in list of plates). Orig cloth, gilt.   *(Traylen)* **£350 [≃ $630]**
- Hereditary genius: an inquiry into its laws

and consequences ... London: Macmillan, 1869. 1st edn. 8vo. viii,390,[2 advts] pp. 2 fldg plates. Long inscrptn on half-title. Orig purple cloth, gilt design on upper bd, spine faded & a little worn.
(Pickering) **$600 [≃ £333]**
- Hereditary genius: an inquiry into its laws and consequences. London: 1869. 1st edn. 390 pp. Mod qtr lea, mrbld bds.
(Scientia) **$275 [≃ £152]**
- Hereditary genius ... London: Macmillan, 1869. 1st edn. 8vo. 2 fldg charts, 34 pp advts at end. Sm lib stamps on half-title & title. Orig maroon cloth, gilt.
(Traylen) **£190 [≃ $342]**
- Inquiries into human faculty and its development. London: Macmillan, 1883. 1st edn. 8vo. xii,[1],387 pp. Mtd photo frontis, 4 plates (1 cold). A few leaves carelessly opened. Orig cloth, spine faded, sl wear to edges.   *(Antiq Sc)* **$250 [≃ £138]**
- Inquiries into human faculty and its development. London: 1883. 1st edn. 8vo. xii,[1],387 pp. Frontis, 4 plates. Orig cloth, spine sl faded.   *(Whitehart)* **£200 [≃ $360]**
- Natural inheritance. London: Macmillan, 1889. 1st edn. 8vo. Half-title, 2 pp advts. Orig maroon cloth, gilt.   *(Traylen)* **£275 [≃ $495]**
- Natural inheritance. London: Macmillan, 1889. 1st edn. 8vo. ix,[5 inc errata],259 pp. Text figs. Some marg annotations. Orig cloth, a bit worn.   *(Antiq Sc)* **$275 [≃ £152]**
- Vacation tourists and notes of travel in 1862-3. London: Macmillan, 1864. 1st edn. 8vo. viii,524 pp. Some light spotting.. Contemp half-calf, mrbld sides, extremities rubbed, lacking label.
(Frew Mackenzie) **£45 [≃ $81]**

Gamow, George
- Constitution of atomic nuclei and radioactivity. Oxford: Clarendon Press, 1931. 1st edn. 8vo. viii,114,[1] pp. Fldg tables, text diags. Orig cloth.   *(Antiq Sc)* **$75 [≃ £41]**
- Constitution of atomic nuclei and radioactivity. Oxford: 1931. 8vo. viii,114 pp. Fldg table. Occas pencilling. Orig cloth.
(Weiner) **£20 [≃ $36]**
- Cosmic rays, fifteen lectures, New York: 1946. 1st English trans. 8vo. 192 pp. Diags. Orig cloth, dw.   *(Weiner)* **£40 [≃ $72]**

Ganot, A.
- Elementary treatise on physics ... for the use of colleges and schools. 1863. 1st edn. [2],780 pp. Num text ills. Orig pict cloth, inner hinges sl cracked, spine torn at ft.
(Whitehart) **£25 [≃ $45]**

Gardiner, John
- An inquiry into the nature, cause, and cure of the gout, and of some of the diseases with which it is connected. Phila: Wiliam Spotswood, 1793. 1st Amer edn. 8vo. xxv,[1], 27-216 pp. Some foxing. Contemp calf, front cvr loose, rear hinge cracked.
  (Hemlock) **$200 [≈ £111]**

Gardner, Henry A.
- Physical and chemical examination of paints, varnishes and colors. Washington: Inst of Paint & Varnish Research, 1925. 8vo. 376 pp. Charts, tables, num text ills. Orig half roan.
  (Marlborough) **£48 [≈ $86]**

Garnett, Thomas
- A treatise of the mineral waters of Harrogate. Leeds: 1804. 4th edn. Sm 8vo. 208 pp. Mod cloth.   *(Weiner)* **£35 [≈ $63]**

Garnier, Pierre
- A medical journey in California [1854] ... Translated ... Los Angeles: 1967. One of 500. 1st thus. 93 pp. Dw. *(Scientia)* **$95 [≈ £52]**

Garrigues, Henry J.
- Text-book of the diseases of women. Phila: 1898. 2nd edn, revsd. 728,32 pub ctlg pp. 4 cold plates, 331 engvs. Cloth, inner hinges starting. Ex lib.   *(Elgen)* **$40 [≈ £22]**

Garrison, Fielding H.
- An introduction to the history of medicine. 1925. 2nd edn. Thick 8vo. 905 pp. Num ports. Orig cloth, rather worn.
  (Weiner) **£25 [≈ $45]**
- An introduction to the history of medicine. Phila: 1929. 4th edn. 996 pp. New cloth.
  (Goodrich) **$55 [≈ £30]**
- An introduction to the history of medicine. Phila: Saunders, 1929. 4th edn, revsd & enlgd. 8vo. 996 pp. Many ills. Pub bndg.
  (Pollak) **£45 [≈ $81]**
- John Shaw Billings, a memoir. New York: 1915. 1st edn. 432 pp. 3 a.l.s. from Billings & 2 photos of Billings loosely inserted.
  (Scientia) **$200 [≈ £111]**

Garrod, Archibald, et al. (eds.)
- Diseases of children by various authors. London: 1913. 1st edn. 1184 pp. Orig cloth.
  (Fye) **$125 [≈ £69]**

Gask, George
- Essays in the history of medicine. 1950. 8vo. 215 pp. Ills. Orig cloth, lightly spotted.
  (Weiner) **£35 [≈ $63]**

Gaskell, Walter H.
- The involuntary nervous system. London: 1920. New edn. 8vo. 178 pp. Cloth.
  (Goodrich) **$75 [≈ £41]**

Gaskin, T.
- The solution of geometrical problems ... proposed at St. John's College, Cambridge, from Dec. 1830 to Dec. 1846. Cambridge: 1847. viii,263 pp. 8 fldg plates. Light scattered foxing. Contemp bds, cloth spine, sl worn.   *(Whitehart)* **£25 [≈ $45]**

Gassendi, Petrus
- The vanity of judiciary astrology, or divination by the stars. London: 1659. 1st English edn. 8vo. Port (sl worming). A little staining at beginning. Contemp sheep, rubbed. Wing G298.
  (Robertshaw) **£145 [≈ $261]**

Gauger, Monsieur
- Fires improv'd: being a new method of building chimneys, so as to prevent their smoaking ...the manner of making coal-fires ... 1715. 1st edn. 8vo. 161 pp, contents & 2 pp advts. 9 fldg plates (v sl dampstained). Half calf, a little worn. *(Edwards)* **£200 [≈ $360]**

Gause, G.F.
- The struggle for existence. Balt: 1934. 1st edn. 163 pp. Cloth, sm nick in rear cvr.
  (Scientia) **$100 [≈ £55]**

Gauss, Karl Friederich
- Theory of the motion of the heavenly bodies moving about the sun in conic sections. Boston: Little Brown, 1857. 1st edn in English. Folio. xvii,326,40 pp. 8 full-page plates. Pub cloth, gilt-stamped spine, spine a little worn.   *(Karmiole)* **$350 [≈ £194]**

Gaylord, H.R. & Aschoff, L.
- The principles of pathological histology. 1902. 359 pp. 81 engvs, 40 plates. Sgntr on title, 1 plate loose. Cloth sl marked & dust-stained, back inner hinge badly cracked.
  (Whitehart) **£25 [≈ $45]**

Gegenbauer, Carl
- Elements of comparative anatomy. Translated ... 1878. 1st edn in English. 8vo. xxvi,645 pp. Text figs. Cancelled blind lib stamp on title. Orig cloth, inner jnts weak, sl wear at top of spine. *(Bickersteth)* **£48 [≈ $86]**

Geikie, Sir Archibald
- The ancient volcanoes of Great Britain. London: Macmillan, 1897. 1st edn. 2 vols.

xxiv,477; xv,492 pp. Advts leaf at end vol 1, 2 advt leaves at end vol 2. 7 fldg cold maps (1 with short tear in fold). Uncut in orig green cloth.   *(Frew Mackenzie)* **£130 [≈ $234]**
- Textbook of geology. London: Macmillan, 1903. 4th edn, revsd & enlgd. 2 vols. 8vo. 1472 pp. Num text ills. Full red calf by Bickers, spines gilt.   *(Oasis)* **$125 [≈ £69]**
- Textbook of geology. London: Macmillan, 1903. 4th edn, revsd & enlgd. 2 vols. 8vo. 503 text figs. Orig green cloth, spines gilt.
                             (Gough) **£35 [≈ $63]**

Geikie, James
- Fragments of earth lore. Sketches and addresses geological and geographical. Edinburgh: 1893. 1st edn. 8vo. 428 pp. 6 cold maps. Sgntr & label on half-title, some spotting. Loose in orig cloth, spine worn at ends.   *(Bow Windows)* **£15 [≈ $27]**
- Fragments of earth lore. Sketches and addresses geological and geographical. Edinburgh: 1893. 1st edn. 8vo. viii,428 pp. 6 fldg cold maps. Orig blue cloth, spine gilt.
                             (Gough) **£35 [≈ $63]**
- Prehistoric Europe; a geological sketch. London: Edward Stanford, 1881. 1st edn. 8vo. xviii,592,[vi advts] pp. 5 tinted lithos, 12 text figs. Name cut from front free endpaper. Orig pict blue cloth, gilt.
                             (Gough) **£45 [≈ $81]**

Gelfand, Michael
- Livingstone the doctor, his life and travels. A study in medical history. Oxford: Blackwell, 1957. 8vo. xix,[i],333,[i] pp. Frontis, 18 plates, 4 maps. Pub bndg, dw.
                             (Pollak) **£30 [≈ $54]**

Genet, Edmond Charles
- Memorial on the upward force of fluids, and their applicability to several arts, sciences, and public improvements. Albany: Packard & Van Benthuysen, 1825. 1st edn. 8vo. 112 pp. 6 engvd plates, fldg table. Spotty foxing. Orig ptd bds, lower spine chipped.
                             (Antiq Sc) **$1,350 [≈ £750]**
- Memorial on the upward force of fluids, and their applicability to several arts, sciences, and public improvements. Albany: Packard & Van Benthuysen, 1825. 1st edn. 8vo. 112 pp. 6 plates, fldg table. Minor foxing. Full red mor.   *(Rootenberg)* **$1,750 [≈ £972]**

Gerard, John
- Gerard's Herball, the essence thereof distilled by Marcus Woodward ... London: Gerald Howe, 1927. One of 150. 4to. xix,303 pp. W'cut ills throughout. Orig vellum, sl darkened.   *(Gough)* **£115 [≈ $207]**

- The herball or general historie of plants. London: 1597. Folio. [xx],1392,[72] pp. Engvd title (re-margined), engvd port, 2146 w'cuts in text. last 3 leaves of index reprd with sl loss of text. Calf, rebacked, worn at jnts & edges.
                    (Wheldon & Wesley) **£1,800 [≈ $3,240]**
- The herball, or generall historie of plantes ... enlarged and amended by Thomas Johnson. London: Adam Islip, 1636. Thick folio. Engvd title (sm portion missing from crnr), num text w'cuts. Contemp calf, rebacked, mor label. STC 11752.
                             (Traylen) **£850 [≈ $1,530]**
- The herball, or generall historie of plantes ... enlarged and amended by Thomas Johnson. London: Adam Islip, 1633. 1st Johnson edn. Folio. Engvd title (sm lib stamp on verso), num text w'cuts. Full vellum, mor label. STC 11751.   *(Traylen)* **£1,200 [≈ $2,160]**

Gerber, Friedrich
- Elements of the general and minute anatomy of man and the mammalia to which is added notes and an appendix ... by George Gulliver. London: 1842. 8vo. xvi,390 pp. Atlas of 34 plates & 106 pp appendix bound in.
                             (Rittenhouse) **$45 [≈ £25]**

Gerhard, W.W.
- Lectures on the diagnosis of diseases of the chest ... Phila: 1836. 1st edn. 8vo. xv,183 pp. 2 plates. Title, dedn & 1st preface page wormed in crnr. Much browning & dampstaining. Binding worn.
                             (Rittenhouse) **$40 [≈ £22]**
- Lectures on the diagnosis of diseases of the chest ... Phila: 1846. 2nd edn. 8vo. Contemp lea, worn hinges v weak.
                             (Rittenhouse) **$25 [≈ £13]**

Gerster, Arpad G.
- The rules of aseptic and antiseptic surgery. New York: Appleton, 1891. 8vo. 365 pp. 252 text ills, 3 chromolitho plates, 64 pp illust pub ctlg. Orig half mor, sl worn & stained.
                             (Oasis) **$100 [≈ £55]**

Gesner, Abraham
- Remarks on the geology and mineralogy of Nova Scotia. Halifax, Nova Scotia: Gossip & Coade, 1836. 1st edn. 8vo. Fldg litho frontis, plate, cold fldg map, explanation slip, list of agents. Orig pink cloth, spine faded & worn, orig ptd paper label. *(Traylen)* **£285 [≈ $513]**

Gibb, Sir Donald
- Odd showers: or, an explanation of th rain of insects, fishes, and lizzards; soot, sand, and ashes ... meteoritic stones; and other bodies.

London: Kerby, 1870. 16 mo. 43 pp.
Author's pres copy, unsgnd.
(Xerxes) **$85 [≃ £47]**

Gibb, Sir George Duncan
- On the diseases of the throat, epiglottis and
windpipe. London: John Churchill, 1860. 1st
edn. 8vo. xii,182,[i advts] pp. Orig embossed
cloth, jnts reprd.   *(Barbary)* **£30 [≃ $54]**

Gibbons, Benjamin
- On the ventilation of mines; and especially of
the thick or ten-yard coal mines of South
Staffordshire. Birmingham: Wrightson &
Webb, 1847, 8vo. Half-title, 4 fldg plans.
Orig embossed red cloth, gilt.
(Traylen) **£105 [≃ $189]**

Gibbs, J. Willard
- The collected works ... New Haven: Yale
Univ Press, 1948. Reprint of 1928 edn. 2
vols. 8vo. Pub bndg.   *(Pollak)* **£45 [≃ $81]**

Gibson, Alexander George
- The physician's art. An attempt to expand
John Locke's Fragment de Arte Medica.
Oxford: Clarendon, 1933. 8vo. [viii],237,[i]
pp. A little foxing. White buckram.
(Pollak) **£20 [≃ $36]**

Gibson, John, Surgeon
- A treatise on bilious disorders and
indigestion, with the effects of quassy and
natron in these disorders. London: for
Murray & Highley ..., 1799. 1st edn. 8vo.
[iv],68 pp. Mod cloth.
(Burmester) **£45 [≃ $81]**

Gibson, Thomas
- The anatomy of humane bodies epitomized.
London: Flesher, 1682. 1st edn. 8vo.
[viii],510 pp. 13 engvd plates inc imprim leaf
before title. Cancel 2K8 at end. Sm piece torn
from upper marg P1 with sl loss, sm rusthole
in 1 lf. Contemp speckled calf. Wing G672.
(Pickering) **$950 [≃ £527]**
- The anatomy of humane bodies epitomized.
London: for Awnsham & John Churchill ...,
1697. 5th edn. 8vo. [xvi],vi,626 pp. 20 engvd
plates. Contemp calf, rebacked. Wing G676.
(Pickering) **$300 [≃ £166]**

Gibson, William
- A new treatise on the diseases of horses ...
London: A. Millar, 1751. 1st edn. 4to.
[10],464,[12] pp. Lge paper. Engvd frontis,
31 plates. Contemp ms recipes on prelim
blanks. B'plates. Contemp calf, rebacked.
(Rootenberg) **$650 [≃ £361]**

Gilbert, Samuel
- The florist's vade-mecum ... propagation,
raising ... and preserving the rarest flowers
and plants. London: 1702. 3rd edn. enlgd.
12mo. 149,[19] pp. Sev text diags. Somewhat
browned throughout, light dampstain, a few
other faults. Contemp sheep, jnts cracked.
(Bow Windows) **£65 [≃ $117]**

Gilford, Hastings
- Tumors and cancers, a biological study.
London: Selwyn & Blount, 1925. 1st edn.
Thick roy 8vo. xii,[2],703 pp. Orig green
cloth. Author's pres copy.
(Taylor) **£28 [≃ $50]**

Gill, Mrs.
- Six months in Ascension. An unscientific
account of a scientific expedition. London:
Murray, 1878. 8vo. liv,[ii],285, [i],24 ctlg pp.
Map. Sm tear in lower edge of 1 leaf. Orig
cloth, recased, new endpapers, a little faded
and worn.   *(Pollak)* **£30 [≃ $54]**

Gillespie, A. Lockhart
- The natural history of digestion. London:
1898. 8vo. 427 pp. Ills. half mor.
(Goodrich) **$45 [≃ £25]**

Gillies, Harold D.
- Plastic surgery of the face, based on selected
cases of war injuries of the face including
burns. London: 1920. 1st edn. 4to. 408 pp.
Upper crnrs of some pp chewed. Orig cloth,
rebacked, orig spine laid down.
(Scientia) **$225 [≃ £125]**

Gillmore, Q.A.
- Practical treatise on limes, hydraulic cements,
and mortars. New York: 1864. 8vo. 333 pp.
Advts. 53 text figs. Sgnd by author on half-
title, some pencilling in margs. Orig cloth,
crnrs worn.   *(Spelman)* **£35 [≃ $63]**

Girdwood, J.
- Tube teeth and porcelain rods. 1918. x,407
pp. 280 ills.   *(Whitehart)* **£18 [≃ $32]**

Givry, Grillot de
- Witchcraft, magic and alchemy. London:
1931. 4to. 395 pp. 10 cold plates, many ills.
Ex lib with stamps.   *(Weiner)* **£50 [≃ $90]**

Gladstone, R.J. & Wakeey, C.P.G.
- The pineal organ. 1940. 1st edn. xvi,528 pp.
324 figs in text. Orig cloth, new endpapers,
lib mark on spine.   *(Whitehart)* **£40 [≃ $72]**

Glaister, J.
- A text-book of medical jurisprudence, toxology and public health. Edinburgh: 1902. 1st edn. xxii,820 pp. 238 ills. Cloth.
(Whitehart) **£18 [≈ $32]**

Glaister, John
- The power of poison. London: [1954]. 1st edn. 8vo. 272 pp. 6 ports. Cloth, dw.
(Elgen) **$30 [≈ £16]**

Glanvill, Joseph
- Saducismus triumphatus: or, full and plain evidence concerning witches and apparitions. London: for J. Collins ..., 1681. 1st edn. 3 pts in 1 vol. 2 port frontis, 4 text figs. Paper fault in 1 leaf, a few crnrs defective. Contemp calf, jnts cracked, scuffed. *(Pirages)* **$325 [≈ £180]**
- Saducismus triumphatus: or, full and plain evidence concerning witches and apparitions. London: for S.L., 1689. 3rd edn. Addtnl engvd title. Sm tear in 1 marg. Contemp calf, rebacked. Wing G825.
(Waterfield's) **£250 [≈ $450]**
- Scepsis scientifica; or, confest ignorance the way to science. Edited ... by John Owen. London: Kegan, Paul, 1885.
(Waterfield's) **£20 [≈ $36]**

Glass, Samuel
- An essay on magnesia alba. Wherein its history is attempted, its virtues pointed out, and the use of it recommended. Oxford: R. Davis, & London: J. Fletcher, 1764. 1st edn. 8vo. 6,38 pp. Title dusty & with sm stain. Stitched as issued, uncut.
(Offenbacher) **$275 [≈ £152]**

Glasser, Otto (ed.)
- The science of radiology. Springfield & Baltimore: 1933. 8vo. xiii,450 pp. Ills, diags. Orig cloth.
(Weiner) **£40 [≈ $72]**

Glasstone, Samuel
- Sourcebook on the space sciences. New York: [1965]. 8vo. xviii,937 pp. Ills. Cloth, dw.
(Elgen) **$45 [≈ £25]**

Glazebrook, R.T.
- James Clerk Maxwell and modern physics. London: Cassell, 1901. 8vo. vi,[ii],[9]-224 pp. Frontis. Prize calf, a little rubbing.
(Pollak) **£20 [≈ $36]**
- Laws and properties of matter. London: Kegan Paul ..., 1893. 8vo. x,184 pp. 37 text figs. Pub bndg. *(Pollak)* **£15 [≈ $27]**

Glazebrook, Sir Richard
- A dictionary of applied physics. 1922-23. 5

vols. 1067; 1104; 839; 914; 592 pp. Num text diags. Orig cloth, t.e.g.
(Whitehart) **£65 [≈ $117]**
- Dictionary of applied physics. 1922-23. 5 vols. 8vo. Cancelled blind lib stamp on first title. Orig cloth. *(Bickersteth)* **£48 [≈ $86]**

Glover, Robert Mortimer
- On the pathology and treatment of the scrofula ... London: Churchill ..., 1846. 1st edn. 8vo. 4 litho plates at end (sl spotted). Contemp half calf, rubbed.
(Hughes) **£25 [≈ $45]**

Godfrey, W.H.
- The English alms-house, with some account of its predecessor, the medieval hospital. London: Faber & Faber, 1955. 8vo. 95,[i] pp. 48 plates. 60 text ills. Orig cloth, torn dw.
(Pollak) **£25 [≈ $45]**

Godwin, William
- Of population. An enquiry concerning the power of increase in the numbers of mankind, being an answer to Mr. Malthus's essay on the subject. London: Longman, 1820. 1st edn. 8vo. Half calf. *(Halewood)* **£650 [≈ $1,170]**

Golborne, John
- The report of ... Engineer, concerning the drainage of the North Level of the fens, and the outfal of the Wisbeach River. [Chester: ca 1769?]. Sm 4to. 11,[1 blank] pp. Lge fldg map. Old paper wraps.
(Bow Windows) **£56 [≈ $100]**
- The report of ... Engineer, concerning the drainage of the North Level of the fens, and the outfal of the Wisbeach River. N.d. [ca 1769]. Sole edn. 11 pp. Engvd fldg map, ptd in 2 sections. Contemp (orig?) grey paper wraps. *(Blackwell's)* **£120 [≈ $216]**

Goldschmidt, Richard
- The mechanism and physiology of sex determination. Translated by W. Dakin. New York: 1923. 1st Amer edn. 259 pp. Cloth.
(Scientia) **$60 [≈ £33]**
- The mechanism and physiology of sex determination. London: 1923. 8vo. viii,259 pp. Plates, some fldg, ills, diags. Orig cloth, unevenly faded. *(Weiner)* **£30 [≈ $54]**

Goldsmith, Oliver
- An history of the earth and animated nature. For J. Nourse, 1774. 1st edn. 8 vols. 8vo. 101 engvd plates. Contemp mottled calf, spines rubbed, tops of spines sl worn.
(Bickersteth) **£260 [≈ $468]**
- An history of the earth and animated nature.

London: R. Edwards, 1817. 4to. xii,812 pp. 80 plates (78 hand-cold). 2 pp torn, with some loss, 1 laid down, occas heavy browning. Rebound in calf, spine elab gilt dec.
(Gough) **£150 [≃ $270]**
- A survey of experimental philosophy, considered in its present state of improvement. London: for T. Carnan ..., 1766. 1st edn. 2 vols. 8vo. Half-title in vol I. Contemp calf, rebacked, mor labels, gilt.
(Traylen) **£335 [≃ $603]**

Golebiewski, E.
- Atlas and epitome of diseases caused by accidents. 1900. 549 pp. 40 cold plates, 143 ills. A little light foxing. Cloth, inner hinge cracked but firm. *(Whitehart)* **£28 [≃ $50]**

Gooch, Robert
- An account of some of the most important diseases peculiar to women. From the second London edition. Phila: 1836. 8vo. 326 pp. Foxing. Sheep. *(Goodrich)* **$45 [≃ £25]**

Good, John Mason
- The book of nature. London: for Longman ..., 1826. 1st edn. 3 vols. 8vo. Contemp half calf, mrbld sides, rubbed, spines scraped & darkened. *(Hughes)* **£45 [≃ $81]**
- A physiological system of nosology; with a corrected and simplified nomenclature. London: Bensley, 1817. 8vo. 548 pp. Old style bds, uncut. *(Goodrich)* **$75 [≃ £41]**

Goodell, William
- Lessons in gynecology. Phila: 1880. 2nd edn. 8vo. xiv,454 pp. 92 ills. New buckram.
(Rittenhouse) **$25 [≃ £13]**

Goodeve, T.M.
- Text-book on the steam engine with a supplement on gas engines. London: 1893. 12th edn, enlgd. 8vo. viii,357,48, [18 advts] pp. Frontis, num figs in text. Some spotting. Orig cloth, traces of old wraps on pastedowns.
(Bow Windows) **£22 [≃ $39]**
- Text-book on the steam engine. London: 1879. Cr 8vo. Frontis, text diags. Lib stamp on title. Contemp half calf.
(Halewood) **£30 [≃ $54]**

Gordon, Benjamin
- Medicine through antiquity. Phila: 1949. 8vo. 818 pp. Ills. Cloth.
(Goodrich) **$75 [≃ £41]**

Gordon, Benjamin L.
- Between two worlds, the memoirs of a physician. New York: [1952]. 1st edn. 352 pp.

Port frontis. Cloth, dw. *(Elgen)* **$30 [≃ £16]**
- Medieval and Renaissance medicine. New York: 1959. 8vo. 843 pp. Ills. Occasional pencilling. Cloth. *(Goodrich)* **$35 [≃ £19]**

Gordon, J.E.H.
- A physical treatise on electricity and magnetism. London: Sampson, Low, 1880. 2 vols. 8vo. xvii,[iii], 323,[i]; xvi,[iv], 295,[i] pp. 52 plates, 255 text figs. Orig cloth.
(Pollak) **£50 [≃ $90]**

Gordon, John
- Observations on the structure of the brain. Edinburgh: printed ... London: 1817. 1st edn. 8vo. [iv],215 pp. 2 engvd plates. A little dust soiled. Orig grey wraps, rebacked, frayed wraps mtd. *(Pickering)* **$300 [≃ £166]**

Gordon, Maurice Bear
- Aesculapius comes to the colonies. The ... early days of medicine in the thirteen original colonies. Ventnor: [1949]. 1st edn. 8vo. xiv,560 pp. Port frontis, num ports, facs, fldg broadside. Cloth, dw. *(Elgen)* **$55 [≃ £30]**

Gore, George
- The art of scientific discovery or the general conditions and methods of research in physics and chemistry. London: 1878. 8vo. xx,648 pp. Orig cloth. *(Weiner)* **£40 [≃ $72]**

Goring, C.R. & Pritchard, Andrew
- Micrographia: containing practical essays on reflecting, solar, oxy-hydrogen gas microscopes, micrometers ... &c., &c. London: 1837. 8vo. viii,231 pp. 3 plates (1 double-page), double-page advt sheet tipped-in. Orig cloth, stained, spine defective.
(Weiner) **£85 [≃ $153]**

Gosse, Philip Henry
- Omphalos: an attempt to untie the geological knot. London: Van Voorst, 1857. 1st edn. 8vo. xiv,376,[vi] pp. Orig str-grained olive cloth, spine gilt, faded, inner hinges sl cracked. *(Bennett)* **£90 [≃ $162]**

Goulard, Thomas
- Remarks and practical observations on the venereal complaints and disorders ... with the compositions of ... medicated candles for the cure of those complaints. London: Emsley, 1772. 1st edn in English. Sm 8vo. 261 pp. 1 page torn without loss. Qtr calf.
(Oasis) **$250 [≃ £138]**
- A treatise on the effects and various preparations of lead ... for different chirurgical disorders. Translated ... Dublin:

R. Moncrieffe, 1777. 6th edn. 12mo.
[8],231,[1] pp. Contemp calf.
(Elgen) **$95 [≈£52]**

Gould, Benjamin Apthrop
- Report on the history of the discovery of
Neptune. Washington City: Smithsonian,
1850. 1st edn. 8vo. 56 pp. Orig ptd wraps, a
bit stained. Author's sgnd pres inscrptn.
(Antiq Sc) **$135 [≈£75]**

Gould, G. & Pyle, W.L.
- Anomalies and curiosities of medicine ... rare
and extraordinary cases ... Phila: 1900.
"Popular edition". 8vo. 968 pp. 12 plates, 295
ills. Orig cloth, lightly shaken.
(Goodrich) **$85 [≈£47]**
- Anomalies and curiosities of medicine. Phila:
Saunders, 1900. "Popular edition". 8vo. Orig
cloth, top bd detchd, back hinge loose.
(Rittenhouse) **$90 [≈£50]**

Gowers, Sir William Richard
- The diagnosis of diseases of the spinal cord.
London: 1884. 3rd edn. 8vo. 92 pp. Cold
plate, text engv. Underlining throughout.
Cloth.   *(Goodrich)* **$95 [≈£52]**
- The diagnosis of diseases of the spinal cord.
London: 1884. 3rd edn. 92 pp. Cold plate,
pub ctlg. Sgntr & stamp on title. Cloth, spine
edges rubbed.   *(Scientia)* **$100 [≈£55]**
- Epilepsy and other chronic convulsive
diseases. New York: 1885. 1st Amer edn. 255
pp. Orig cloth.   *(Fye)* **$100 [≈£55]**
- Epilepsy and other chronic convulsive
diseases; their causes, symptoms and
treatment. New York: 1885. 1st Amer edn.
255 pp. Pub ctlg. Cloth.
(Scientia) **$125 [≈£69]**
- Lectures on the diagnosis of diseases of the
brain. London: 1885. 1st edn. 246 pp. Orig
cloth, inner hinges cracked.
(Fye) **$225 [≈£125]**
- A manual of diseases of the nervous system.
Phila: 1888. 1st Amer edn. 1357 pp. Cloth.
(Scientia) **$250 [≈£138]**
- A manual of diseases of the nervous system.
Phila: Blakiston, 1903-1893. 2 vols. 3rd &
2nd edns. 8vo. 692; 1069 pp. Pub ctlg. Mixed
bindings, vol 1 orig sheep, vol 2 orig cloth.
(Oasis) **$225 [≈£125]**
- Subjective sensations of sight and sound,
abiotrophy, and other lectures. Phila: 1904.
"Lectures on diseases of the nervous system.
2nd series". 1st Amer edn. 8vo. 250,32 pub
ctlg pp. Ills. Upper marg dampstained not
affecting text. Cloth, dampstained.
(Elgen) **$115 [≈£63]**

Goyonneau de Pambour, Comte F.M.
- A practical treatise on locomotive engines ...
the velocity at which it will draw ... a great
many new experiments and researches ...
1840. 2nd edn. 8vo. xlviii,583 pp. 5 fldg
plates, many tables. Sm stamp on title &
elsewhere. Orig cloth, recased.
(Edwards) **£250 [≈$450]**

Graham, Harvey
- Surgeons all. London: Rich & Cowan, 1939.
1st edn. Lge 8vo. Frontis, many ills. Orig
cloth.   *(Chaucer Head)* **£40 [≈$72]**

Graham, T.J.
- A treatise on indigestion. With observations
on some painful complaints ... tic doloreaux,
nervous disorders ... Phila: 1831. 1st Amer
edn. Uncut.   *(Goodrich)* **$45 [≈£25]**

Graham, Thomas
- Chemical and physical researches, collected
and printed for presentation only. Edinburgh:
Univ Press, 1876. 1st edn. Lge 8vo. lvi,660
pp. Collotype frontis, 3 double page litho
plates, half-title. Orig cloth, hinges partially
cracked, edges worn.
(Antiq Sc) **$300 [≈£166]**

Graham, Thomas J.
- Modern domestic medicine: a popular
treatise, etc. London: 1832. 5th edn. 648 pp.
Some foxing, stain in crnr of title. Rebound in
bds.   *(Rittenhouse)* **$27.50 [≈£15]**
- On the diseases peculiar to females; a treatise
illustrating their symptoms, causes, varieties,
and treatment. Including the diseases and
management of lying-in women. London: for
the author, 1834.1st edn. 8vo. Orig grey bds.
(Chaucer Head) **£55 [≈$99]**

Graham, William
- The art of making wines, of fruits, flowers,
and herbs ... a succinct account of their
medicinal virtues ... many secrets relative to
the mystery of vintners ... London: for J.
Williams ..., n.d. [ca 1760]. 2nd edn. 8vo. 42
pp. Later qtr calf, uncut.
(Argosy) **$175 [≈£97]**

Grant, Robert
- History of physical astronomy ... to the
middle of the nineteenth century ...
establishment of the theory of gravitation ...
London: [1852]. 8vo. xx,638 pp. Orig dec
blindstamped cloth, sl cockled.
(Weiner) **£35 [≈$63]**
- History of physical astronomy ... to the
middle of the nineteenth century ... London:

Bohn, 1852. 638 pp. Orig cloth, front hinge cracked, spine ends worn.
(Xerxes) **$65 [≃ £36]**

Grant, William
- An essay on the pestilential fever of Sydenham, common called the gaol, hospital, ship, and camp-fever. London: for T. Cadell, 1775. 1st edn. 8vo. [iv],ix,193 pp. Old lib inscrptn on title. Orig calf, jnts cracked, rubbed.   *(Bickersteth)* **£45 [≃ $81]**

Grantham, John
- Facts and observations in medicine and surgery: With additional memoirs. London: Churchill, 1849. 8vo. ix,283,[i] pp. Text figs. [with] Additional memoirs in medicine & surgery, A.J. Dunkin, Dartford, bound-in at end. Orig cloth, spine ends & crnrs worn.
(Pollak) **£25 [≃ $45]**

Granville, A.B.
- The spas of England and principal sea-bathing places. Midland spas. London: 1841. 8vo. ix,324 pp. Engvd frontis, vignette title, engvd text vignettes, fldg tablé. Cloth.
(Elgen) **£50 [≃ $27]**
- The spas of Germany. London: Henry Colburn, 1838. 2 edn. 8vo. lviii,[2],516 pp. 4 maps (1 lge fldg), 14 plates, 21 vignettes. Contemp half calf, mrbld paper sides, rubbed.   *(Claude Cox)* **£110 [≃ $198]**

Grasset, Joseph
- The semi-insane and the semi-responsible. New York: Funk & Wagnall, 1907. 1st edn. 8vo. 415 pp. Orig cloth. *(Oasis)* **$35 [≃ £19]**

Graves, Richard
- The invalid: with the obvious means of enjoying health and long life. By a nonogenarian. R. Phillips, 1804. Sm 8vo. x,147,[iii advts] pp. Discold, prelims sl foxed. Contemp half calf, gilt, mrbld bds.
(Blackwell's) **£60 [≃ $108]**

Graves, Robert James
- Clinical lectures on the practice of medicine. Dublin: 1864. 2nd edn. xxvii,873 pp. Orig cloth, rebacked, orig spine laid down, marked.   *(Whitehart)* **£45 [≃ $81]**
- Clinical lectures on the practice of medicine. Dublin: 1864. 2nd edn. 873 pp. Orig cloth, front bd nearly detchd, rear hinge cracked, spine defective.   *(Fye)* **£60 [≃ £33]**
- Clinical lectures on the practice of medicine. London: 1884. 2 vols. 673; 651 pp. Orig cloth.   *(Fye)* **$75 [≃ £41]**
- A system of clinical medicine. With notes and

a series of lectures by W.W. Gerhard. Phila: 1848. 3rd Amer edn. 8vo. 751 pp. Lea, front cvr detchd.   *(Rittenhouse)* **$37.50 [≃ £20]**

Gray, A.
- A treatise on gyrostatics and rotational motion. 1918. xx,530 pp. 122 ills.
(Whitehart) **£25 [≃ $45]**

Gray, Henry
- Anatomy, descriptive and surgical. Phila: 1859. 1st Amer edn. Lge 8vo. xxxii,754 pp. Half-title, 363 engvs. Contemp sheep, some scuffing & rubbing.   *(Elgen)* **$550 [≃ £305]**
- Anatomy, descriptive and surgical. Phila: 1862. 2nd Amer edn. 816 pp. Orig lea, short tear at bottom of front hinge.
(Fye) **$75 [≃ £41]**
- Anatomy, descriptive and surgical. London: Longmans, Green, 1872. 6th edn. Roy 8vo. 363 ills in text. Contemp half calf, mor label, gilt.   *(Traylen)* **£60 [≃ $108]**

Green, F.H.K. & Covell, Sir Gordon
- Medical history of the Second World War. Medical Research. London: HMSO, 1953. 8vo. xvi,387 pp. Occas marg note. Pub bndg, dw.   *(Pollak)* **£25 [≃ $45]**

Green, Horace
- Observations on the pathology of croup; with remarks on its treatment by topical medications. New York: 1849. 1st edn. 115 pp. Cloth, top of spine sl chipped.
(Scientia) **$125 [≃ £69]**
- A treatment on diseases of the air-passages; comprising an enquiry into the history, pathology, causes ... of ... bronchitis. New York: 1849. 2nd edn, revsd & enlgd. 306 pp. Pub ctlg. Ex lib.   *(Scientia)* **$85 [≃ £47]**

Green, Robert M.
- Asclepiades: his life and writings. New Haven: 1955. 167 pp. *(Scientia)* **$75 [≃ £41]**

Green, Thomas
- The universal herbal; or, botanical, medical and agricultural dictionary ... Liverpool: Nuttall, Fisher, 1816-20. 2 vols. 4to. 2 hand-cold frontis, cold engvd title to vol I, 106 hand-cold engvd plates. Contemp calf, gilt, rebacked, mor labels, gilt.
(Traylen) **£750 [≃ $1,350]**

Greenhill, Sir G.
- Notes on dynamics. HMSO, 1908. 2nd edn. Obl 4to. 221 pp. 118 diags. Ptd bds, linen spine, sl dust-stained.
(Whitehart) **£25 [≃ $45]**

Greenhill, Thomas
- Nekrokedeia: or, the art of embalming ... experiments and inventions of modern physicians ... For the author, [1705]. 1st edn. 4to. [ii],viii,v, [viii],367,[xii] pp. Frontis & fldg map (both with short tears), 13 plates (1 fldg). Contemp calf, rebacked.
(Frew Mackenzie) **£350 [≈ $630]**

Greenish, Henry George & Collin, Eugene
- An anatomical atlas of vegetable powders. Designed as an aid to the microscopical analysis of powdered foods and drugs. London: Churchill, 1904. 8vo. 287,[i] pp. 128 plates with num figs. Orig cloth.
(Pollak) **£45 [≈ $81]**

Greenwood, Major
- Some British pioneers of social medicine. The Health Clark lectures, 1946. London: OUP, 1948. 8vo. [x],118,[ii] pp. Pub bndg.
(Pollak) **£25 [≈ $45]**

Gregory, G.
- A dictionary of arts and sciences, London: Richard Phillips, 1806. 1st edn. 2 vols. [4],960; vi,[2],928 pp. 136 (ex 138) engvd plates, some foxed. Contemp half calf, mrbld sides, rubbed, newly rebacked.
(Claude Cox) **£120 [≈ $216]**

Gregory, George
- Elements of the theory and practice of physic. Phila: 1831. 3rd Amer edn. 2 vols. 535; 556 pp. Lea.
(Fye) **$75 [≈ £41]**

Gregory, Olinthus
- Elements of plane and spherical trigonometry ... heights and distances, projections of the sphere, dialling, astronomy ... London: 1816. 1st edn. x,244 pp. Orig bds, uncut.
(Whitehart) **£25 [≈ $45]**
- Mathematics for practical men: being ... principles, theorems, rules, and tables ... especially to the pursuits of surveyors, architects ... and civil engineers. London: Baldwin, 1825. 1st edn. 8vo. 3 fldg plates. Contemp calf, sl rubbed, inkstain on cvr.
(Hughes) **£25 [≈ $45]**
- Mathematics for practical men: being ... designed chiefly for the use of civil engineers, architects and surveyors. 1848. 3rd edn. xix,392,118 pp. Lge fldg table, 13 fldg plates. 3/4 lea, sl worn, a little dust-stained.
(Whitehart) **£40 [≈ $72]**
- A treatise of mechanics, theoretical, practical and descriptive. London: 1806. 1st edn. 2 vols. 8vo. Contemp half calf.
(Robertshaw) **£38 [≈ $68]**

Gregory, Samuel
- Man-midwifery exposed and corrected; or the employment of men to attend women in childbirth ... shown to be a modern invention, unnecessary, unnatural and injurious ... pernicious ... on public morality. Boston: 1848. 4th edn. 50 pp. Orig ptd wraps.
(Scientia) **$95 [≈ £52]**

Grew, Nehemiah
- Experiments in consort of the luctation arising from the affusions of several menstruums upon all sorts of bodies ... London: for John Martyn, 1678. 12mo. [xii],118 pp. Browning & marg defects on 6ff without loss. Contemp calf, rubbed.
(Wheldon & Wesley) **£200 [≈ $360]**
- Musaeum Regalis Societatis ... natural and artificial rarities belonging to the Royal Society. London: for the author, 1681. 1st edn. Folio. [xii],386,[2]; title, 43 pp. Port, 43 engvd plates. Some minor stains & dustmarks. Contemp calf, rebacked. Wing G1952.
(Bow Windows) **£495 [≈ $891]**
- Musaeum Regalis Societatis. London: for the author, 1681. 1st edn. 2 vols in 1. Folio. Port frontis, 31 engvd plates. Title smudged at bottom, minor tears, sl foxing & dampstaining. Contemp calf, rebacked, crnrs worn. *(Pirages)* **$575 [≈ £319]**
- Musaeum Regalis Societatis. London: 1681. Folio. [xii],386, [2],[ii],43 pp. Port, 31 plates. Inscrptn inked out on title. calf, reprd.
(Wheldon & Wesley) **£495 [≈ $891]**
- Musaeum Regalis Societatis. Or ... the natural and artificial rarities belonging to the Royal Society ... London: Newman, 1694. Folio. [xii],386,[ii], [iv],43 pp. 31 engvd plates (1 fldg, torn & reprd). Occas dampstaining & worming. Contemp calf. rebacked.
(Frew Mackenzie) **£265 [≈ $477]**

Grey, Messrs.
- Arithmetical excellencies adapted to the various calculations incidental to public offices, the compting-house, trade, &c. Dublin: Thomas Courtney, 1822. 1st edn. 12mo. 47 pp. Subscribers' list. Contemp half calf, spine worn. *(Burmester)* **£25 [≈ $45]**

Grey, Richard (1694-1771)
- Memoria technica, or method of artificial memory ... To which are subjoined, Lowe's Mnemonics delineated ... Oxford: W. Baxter, 1821. new edn. 8vo. xxxiii,216 pp. Uncut in orig bds, grey backstrip (defective).
(Blackwell's) **£35 [≈ $63]**

Griesinger, Wilhelm
- Mental pathology and therapeutics. London: New Sydenham Soc, 1867. 1st edn. 8vo. xiv,530 pp. Orig cloth, edges frayed. *(Antiq Sc)* **$90 [≈£50]**
- Mental pathology and therapeutics. New York: Wood's Library, 1882. Re-issue. 375 pp. Orig cloth, gilt spine. *(Oasis)* **$50 [≈£27]**

Griffin, J.
- A plain and popular system of practical navigation and nautical astronomy ... ascertaining the latitude ... 1852. 1st edn. x,234, [329,52] pp. Frontis, many ills. Orig 3/4 roan, sl rubbed & worn. *(Whitehart)* **£25 [≈$45]**

Griffith, G.W. & Henfrey, A.
- The micrographic dictionary. London: 1883. 4th edn. 2 vols. 8vo. xlvi,829 pp. 53 plates (18 cold) of 818 figs. half calf. *(Wheldon & Wesley)* **£70 [≈$126]**

Griffith, J.K.
- A general Cheltenham guide ... virtues and qualities of the mineral waters ... the modes of their application. Cheltenham: [1818]. 2nd edn. Sm 4to. [iv],[5]-217,[1 blank],[2 contents] pp. Fldg engvd map, engvd plate, engvd advts. Sl browning. Orig bds. *(Blackwell's)* **£95 [≈$171]**

Griffith, J.W. & Henfrey, A.
- The micrographic dictionary; a guide to the examination and investigation of the structure and nature of microscopic objects. London: Van Voorst, 1856. 1st edn. xl,696 pp. 41 engvd plates, some hand-cold. Contemp half lea, rebacked, orig spine rubbed, chipped. *(Antiq Sc)* **$100 [≈£55]**
- The micrographic dictionary; a guide to the examination and investigation of the structure and nature of microscopic objects. London: 1856. xl,696 pp. 41 plates, 816 w'cuts. Scattered foxing on title & elsewhere. Hinges taped. *(Whitehart)* **£35 [≈$63]**

Griffiths, William
- A practical treatise on farriery; deduced from the experience of above forty years ... Wrexham: R. Marsh, [1784]. 1st edn. 4to. [iv],iii,184,[14] pp. Aquatint frontis. Some outer margs sl stained. Contemp tree calf, spines elab gilt, jnts reprd. *(Burmester)* **£180 [≈$324]**
- A practical treatise on farriery; deduced from the experience of above forty years ... Wrexham: R. Marsh, [1784]. 1st edn. 4to. Aquatint frontis. Occas spotting. Contemp

tree calf, spines gilt, hinges cracking. *(Chaucer Head)* **£180 [≈$324]**

Griscom, John H.
- Animal mechanism and physiology. being a plain and familiar exposition of the structure and functions of the human system. New York: 1839. 357 pp. Ills. *(Rittenhouse)* **$27.50 [≈£15]**

Groenveldt, Jan
- A compleat treatise of the stone and gravel ... With an ample discourse on lithontriptick ... London: for Smith & Lintott, 1710. 1st edn. 8vo. 23 engvd plates, 3 fldg (1 with outer marg torn away without loss). Contemp calf, old spine laid down. *(Quaritch)* **$1,600 [≈£888]**

Grollman, Arthur
- The cardiac output of man in health and disease. Springfield: 1932. 1st edn. Cloth. *(Scientia)* **$100 [≈£55]**

Gross, Louis
- The blood supply to the heart in its anatomical and clinical aspects. New York: 1921. 1st edn. 171 pp. 29 plates. Ex lib with stamp on title & plates. *(Scientia)* **$65 [≈£36]**

Gross, Robert E.
- The surgery of infancy and childhood. Its principles and techniques. Phila: 1953. 8vo. 1000 pp. Ills. Orig cloth. *(Goodrich)* **$75 [≈£41]**

Gross, Samuel D.
- Autobiography ... with reminiscences of his times and contemporaries. Phila: 1893. 2 vols. 8vo. Blank removed. Cloth. *(Goodrich)* **$75 [≈£41]**
- Autobiography; with sketches of his contemporaries. Edited by his sons. Phila: 1887. 1st edn. 2 vols. 407; 438 pp. Cloth. *(Scientia)* **$200 [≈£111]**
- Elements of pathological anatomy. Phila: 1845. 2nd edn, greatly enlgd. 8vo. 822 pp. 6 cold plates. Foxed. Orig sheep, worn. *(Goodrich)* **$145 [≈£80]**
- Memoir of Valentine Mott, M.D. New York: 1868. 1st edn. 96 pp. Photograph frontis. Recased. *(Scientia)* **$175 [≈£97]**
- Memorial oration in honor of Ephraim McDowell, the father of overiotomy. Louisville: 1879. 1st edn. 77 pp. Editor's sgnd pres copy. *(Scientia)* **$170 [≈£94]**
- Memorial oration in honor of Ephraim McDowell, the father of overiotomy. Louisville: 1879. 1st edn. 77 pp.

(Scientia) **$170 [≈ £94]**
- A practical treatise on foreign bodies in the air-passages. 1854. Orig cloth, tips of spine chipped.   *(Allen)* **$25 [≈ £13]**
- A practical treatise on foreign bodies in the air-passages. Phila: 1854. 1st edn. 468 pp. Pub ctlg. Cloth, crnrs worn, top & bottom of spine sl chipped.   *(Scientia)* **$450 [≈ £250]**
- A practical treatise on the diseases, injuries, and malformations of the urinary bladder, the prostate gland ... Revised and edited by Samuel W. Gross. Phila: 1876. 3rd edn. 8vo. xvi,574 pp. Pub ctlg. Cvr crnrs worn. Ex lib.
                          (Rittenhouse) **$35 [≈ £19]**
- A system of surgery; pathological, diagnostic, therapeutic and operative. Phila: 1862. 2nd edn. 2 vols. Thick 8vo. 1227 engvs. Bindings scuffed, lacking labels.
                          (Rittenhouse) **$50 [≈ £27]**
- A system of surgery; pathological, diagnostic, therapeutic and operative. Phila: 1862. 2nd edn, revsd & enlgd. 2 vols. 8vo. xxxi,1062; xxviii,1134,32 pub ctlg pp. 1227 engvs. Contemp sheep, sl scuffed & rubbed.
                          (Elgen) **$195 [≈ £108]**
- A system of surgery; pathological, diagnostic, therapeutic and operative. Phila: Lea, 1866. 4th edn. 2 vols. 8vo. xxxi,[32]-1049, [iii],32 ctlg; xxviii, 17-1087, [iii] pp. Num figs. A few leaves a little loose at ft. Contemp Amer calf, a little worn.   *(Pollak)* **£50 [≈ $90]**

Gross, Samuel W.
- A practical treatise on impotence, sterility, and allied disorders of the male sexual organs. Phila: 1881. 8vo. vii,174 pp.
                          (Rittenhouse) **$45 [≈ £25]**

Groth, Paul
- An introduction to chemical crystallography. New York: J. Wiley, 1906. 1st Amer edn. 8vo. vii,[5], 123,[1] pp. Orig cloth. P.W. Bridgman's copy with his sgntr.
                          (Antiq Sc) **$65 [≈ £36]**

Guerini, V.
- A history of dentistry from the most ancient times until the end of the the eighteenth century. Phila: 1909. 1st edn. 8vo. 355 pp. Num plates & ills. Orig cloth.
                          (Goodrich) **$150 [≈ £83]**

Guidott, Thomas
- A discourse of Bathe, and the hot springs there ... an account of the lives ... of the physicians of Bathe. London: for Henry Brome, 1676. 8vo. [30],200 pp. Explanation leaf before title, engvd title, 4 plates (3 fldg), plan. Contemp calf, a little worn.

(Burmester) **£150 [≈ $270]**

Guillemin, Amedee
- The applications of physical forces. Translated from the French ... London: 1877. 1st edn. Lge 8vo. [xl],741,[1] pp. 4 cold, 21 engvd plates. Num figs. 1 or 2 thumb prints in margs & on verso of last lf. Contemp calf, a little rubbed, spine ends chipped.
                          (Bow Windows) **£70 [≈ $126]**

Gully, James M.
- An exposition of the symptoms, essential nature, and treatment of neuropathy or nervousness. London: 1837. 8vo. 192 pp. Errata. Contemp bds, uncut.
                          (Goodrich) **$145 [≈ £80]**

Gunter, Edmund
- The description and use of the sector, cross-staffe ... with a canon of artificiall sines and tangents. 1636. 2 pts in 1. 2nd edn. Sm 4to. Engvd & ptd titles, plate, num w'cut text diags, 2 slips with w'cuts. Some age blemishes. Contemp calf, new spine.
                          (Halewood) **£250 [≈ $450]**

Gunther, R.T.
- Early science in Cambridge. Oxford: for the author, 1937. 1st edn. 8vo. xii,513 pp. Num plates & ills. Orig cloth. *(Weiner)* **£50 [≈ $90]**

Guthrie, Douglas
- A history of medicine. London: 1945. 8vo. xvi,448 pp. 72 plates. Orig cloth.
                          (Weiner) **£25 [≈ $45]**
- A history of medicine. Edinburgh: 1948. 8vo. 448 pp. 72 plates. Cloth, dw.
                          (Goodrich) **$55 [≈ £30]**

Guthrie, G.J.
- On wounds and injuries of the abdomen and the pelvis; being the second part of the lectures on some of the more important parts of surgery. London: 1857. 8vo. 73 pp. Ex lib, spine defective.   *(Goodrich)* **$90 [≈ £50]**

Guttman, Oscar
- Monumenta pulveris pyrii: reproductions of ancient pictures concerning the history of gunpowder, with explanatory notes. Balham: Artist's Press, 1906. One of 270. Lge 4to. Tri-lingual text. 102 plates. Orig lea-backed wooden bds, hand-chased metal clasps.
                          (Weiner) **£250 [≈ $450]**

Guttmann, Paul
- A handbook of physical diagnosis. Comprising the throat, thorax and abdomen.

London: New Sydenham Soc, 1879. 8vo.
xii,441 pp. Orig brown cloth, blocked in gilt
& blind.   *(Blackwell's)* £30 [≃ $54]
- A handbook of physical diagnosis.
Comprising the throat, thorax and abdomen.
New York: 1880. 1st Amer edn. x,344 pp.
Cold frontis, 89 w'cuts. Cloth.
     (Elgen) $30 [≃ £16]

Gwathmey, James T.
- Anesthesia. New York: 1924. 2nd revsd edn.
799 pp.   *(Scientia)* $65 [≃ £36]

Hadfield, R.A.
- The work and position of the metallurgical
chemist ... references to Sheffield and its
place in metallurgy. London: 1922. 8vo. 99
pp. 34 plates, fldg tables. Orig cloth, ex lib.
     (Weiner) £25 [≃ $45]

Haeckel, Ernst
- The history of creation: or the development
of the Earth and its ancestors. 1876. 1st
English edn. 2 vols. xx,374; viii,408 pp.
Frontis, 13 plates, cold fldg map, text figs.
Orig cloth, dull, 1 hinge cracked.
     (Whitehart) £25 [≃ $45]
- The last link - our present knowledge of the
descent of man. London: Black, 1898. 1st
edn. 8vo. [4],156 pp. Orig cloth.
     (Antiq Sc) $100 [≃ £55]

Hafed, Prince of Persia
- His experiences in earth-life and spirit-life.
Being spirit communications received
through Mr. David Duguid, the Glasgow
trance-painting medium ... London: 1876. 1st
edn. 8vo. xii,580 pp. 24 plates, ills. Num
pencilled notes. Orig cloth, defective.
     (Bow Windows) £48 [≃ $86]

Haighton, Ernst
- A syllabus of the lectures on midwifery,
delivered at Guy's hospital. London: W. Cox
& Son, reprinted in the year 1814. 3rd edn (?).
8vo. 88 pp with the half-title. Interleaved
copy with contemp ms notes. Half calf,
rubbed, jnt partially cracked.
     (Antiq Sc) $200 [≃ £111]

Haldane, J.S. & Priestly, J.G.
- Respiration. Oxford: 1935. 2nd edn. xiii,493
pp. 124 text figs. Cloth, inner hinges sl
cracked but firm.   *(Whitehart)* £25 [≃ $45]

Hale, Sir Matthew
- Difficiles Nugae: or, observations touching
the Torricellian experiment ... weight and
elasticity of air. London: for W. Shrowsbury,

1674. 1st edn. 8vo. 2 fldg engvd plates (1 with
sm rust-hole), initial blank, 2 pp advts.
Contemp calf, rebacked. Wing H238.
     (Traylen) £375 [≃ $675]

Hale, Thomas
- An account of several new inventions and
improvements ... also A treatise of naval
philosophy ... by Sir Will. Petty. London:
1691. 1st edn. 2 pts in 1. 12mo. Sep titles,
licence 1f, 2 fldg charts, 2 fldg leaves. 19th c
calf, gilt, jnts worn. Wing H265.
     (Traylen) £360 [≃ $648]

Hales, Stephen
- An account of some experiments and
observations on tar-water ... London: for R.
Manby ..., 1745. 1st edn. 8vo. W'cut. Bds,
cloth spine.   *(Traylen)* £110 [≃ $198]
- An account of some experiments and
observations on Mrs. Stephen's medicines for
dissolving the stone ... to which is added, a
supplement to a pamphlet ... London: [1740].
1st edn. 66 pp. Plate. Mod bds.
     (Scientia) $175 [≃ £97]
- Philosophical experiments: containing useful,
and necessary instructions for such as
undertake long voyages at sea ... London: W.
Innys ..., 1739. [4],xxx,[2],163 pp. 6 pp
index, 2 pp advts. Plate. Rec half calf, mrbld
bds.   *(Goodrich)* $675 [≃ £375]
- Statical essays: containing vegetable staticks:
or, an account of sap in vegetables ... Also ...
an attempt to analyse the air ... London: W.
Innys, 1731. 8vo. 2nd edn. 8vo. [vi],[viii], 376
pp. 19 engvd plates. Contemp calf, hd of
spine worn, jnts cracked.
     (Hemlock) $275 [≃ £152]

Halford, Sir Henry
- Essays and orations read and delivered at the
Royal College of Physicians ... an account of
the opening of the tomb of King Charles I.
London: 1831. 8vo. 192 pp. Cloth, rubbed.
     (Goodrich) $35 [≃ £19]

Hall, Albert
- The true road to radio: Ferranti. London:
Ferranti, [1931]. 3rd edn. 8vo. 243,[i] pp. 10
plates, 135 text figs. Orig cloth, v sl wear to
spine ends.   *(Pollak)* £25 [≃ $45]

Hall, J. Sparkes
- The book of the feet. A history of boots and
shoes. With illustrations of the fashions of the
Egyptians, Hebrews, Persians, Greeks and
Romans ... also ... remedies for corns.
London: Simpkin, Marshall, [1845]. 2nd edn.
Sm 8vo. 4 hand-cold plates. Orig cloth.
     (Chaucer Head) £95 [≃ $171]

Hall, Marshall

- Commentaries principally on those diseases of females which are constitutional. London: 1830. 2nd edn. 8vo. 284 pp. 7 cold plates. Rebacked, preserving orig bds.
(Oasis) **$175 [≃ £97]**
- A descriptive, diagnostic and practical essay on disorders of the digestive organs and general health ... contrasted with some acute and insidious disorders. Keene, NH: 1823. 1st Amer edn. 8vo. 192 pp. Uncut. Orig paper-backed bds, sm chip at hd of spine.
(Elgen) **$225 [≃ £125]**
- A descriptive, diagnostic and practical essay on disorders of the digestive organs and general health ... Keene, NH: 1823. 8vo. Dedn, contents, 102 pp. Bds, worn. Ex lib.
(Elgen) **$65 [≃ £36]**
- A descriptive, diagnostic and practical essay on disorders of the digestive organs and general health ... Keene: 1823. 1st Amer edn. Mod bds. *(Scientia)* **$125 [≃ £69]**
- Principles of the theory and practice of medicine. Boston: 1839. 1st Amer edn. 8vo. iv,724 pp. Lea, much scuffed & worn, rear bd detchd, top hinge weak.
(Rittenhouse) **$50 [≃ £27]**

Hall, T.G.

- A treatise on the differential and integral calculus and the calculus of variations. Cambridge: Univ Press, 1841. 3rd edn. xii,380 pp. Figs. Contemp calf, new backstrip & label, jnts strengthened.
(Hinchliffe) **£18 [≃ $32]**

Hall, W.W.

- The guide-board to health, peace and competence; or, the road to happy old age. Springfield: [1869]. 8vo. 752 pp. Port frontis. Sheep, black lea spine labels.
(Elgen) **$35 [≃ £19]**

Haller, Albert

- First lines of physiology. Translated from the third Latin edition. Troy: 1803. 1st Amer edn. 8vo. 2ff,498 pp. Occas spotting. Contemp calf, rubbed.
(Hemlock) **$150 [≃ £83]**
- Pathological observations from dissections of morbid bodes. London: Wilson & Durham, 1756. 1st edn in English. 8vo. viii,iii, [1],197, [3] pp. 3 fldg engvd plates. Title sl foxed. Contemp sheep, front cvr re-hinged.
(Antiq Sc) **$375 [≃ £208]**

Halliwell, James Orchard

- A collection of letters illustrative of the progress of science in England from ... Queen

Elizabeth to ... Charles the Second. Hist Soc of Science, 1841. 8vo. xix,124,9 list of members, [1 advt] pp. Ex lib in orig blue cloth, rebacked. *(Blackwell's)* **£50 [≃ $90]**

Halsted, William S.

- Surgical papers. Balt: 1924. 1st edn. 2 vols. 586; 602 pp. Cloth. *(Scientia)* **$225 [≃ £125]**

Hamilton, Alexander

- A treatise on the management of female complaints and of children in early infancy ... New York: Samuel Campbell, 1795. 8vo. vi,7-304 pp. Contemp calf, dull, cracks in calf. *(Hemlock)* **$100 [≃ £55]**

Hamilton, Alice

- Exploring the dangerous trades. Boston: 1843. 1st edn. 433 pp. Cloth.
(Scientia) **$125 [≃ £69]**
- Industrial poisons in the United States. New York: 1925. 1st edn. 590 pp. Cloth, worn dw.
(Scientia) **$225 [≃ £125]**

Hamilton, Allan

- A manual of medical jurisprudence, with special reference to diseases and injuries of the nervous system. New York: 1883. 1st edn. 380 pp. Orig cloth. *(Fye)* **$50 [≃ £27]**
- Railway and other accidents with relation to injury and diseases of the nervous system. New York: 1904. 8vo. 351 pp. 15 plates. Cloth. *(Goodrich)* **$125 [≃ £69]**

Hamilton, Frank Hastings

- Conversations between Drs. Warren and Putnam on the subject of medical ethics, with an account of the medical empiricisms of Europe and America. New York: 1884. 1st edn. 8vo. 129 pp. Orig cloth, spine ends frayed. *(Elgen)* **$60 [≃ £33]**

Hamilton, Hugh

- Philosophical essays on ... I. The ascent of vapours ... II ... Aurora Borealis ... III On ... mechanicks. London: Nourse, 1767. 1st London edn. 12mo. [iv],177,[1] pp. Engvd fldg plate, half-title to each part. Uncut. Orig wraps, vell backstrip cracked.
(Rootenberg) **$225 [≃ £125]**
- Philosophical essays on ... I. ... vapours ... II ... Aurora Borealis ... III ... mechanicks. London: for J. Nourse, 1772. 3rd edn. 8vo. Fldg frontis, 3 part titles, final blank. Stain to upper marg of most leaves. Contemp mrbld bds, sl worn, mod calf spine.
(Stewart) **£225 [≃ $405]**

Hamilton, J.
- The theory of elementary particles. Oxford: 1959. 1st edn. 8vo. xii,482 pp. Cloth, dw. Ex lib. *(Elgen)* **$35** [≈ £19]

Hamilton, Robert
- Remarks on hydrophobia or the disease produced by the bite of a mad dog or other rabid animal. London: 1798. 2nd edn. 2 vols. 8vo. 297; 590 pp. List of subscribers. New paper-cvrd bds. *(Oasis)* **$200** [≈ £111]

Hamilton, Sir William
- Lectures on logic. Edited by the Rev. H.L. Mansel ... Edinburgh: William Blackwood ..., 1860. 2 vols. 8vo. Prize calf, gilt, gilt crest of Glasgow University on upper cvrs, sl rubbed. *(Hughes)* **£75** [≈ $135]
- Observations on Mount Vesuvius, Mount Etna, and other volcanoes. London: T. Cadell, 1772. 1st edn. 8vo. iv,179 pp. 5 fldg plates, fldg map. Contemp calf, gilt. *(Spelman)* **£240** [≈ $432]
- Observations on Mount Vesuvius, Mount Etna, and other volcanos: in a series of letters addressed to the Royal Society. London: 1773. 2nd edn. 8vo. 179 pp. 5 plates. Contemp calf, rebacked, new endpapers. *(Argosy)* **$250** [≈ £138]

Hamilton, William
- The history of medicine, surgery and anatomy, from the creation of the world, to the commencement of the nineteenth century. London: 1831. 2 vols. 419; 308 pp. Light foxing, some dampstaining. Rec cloth. *(Goodrich)* **$135** [≈ £75]
- The history of medicine, surgery and anatomy ... London: 1831. 2 vols. 419; 308 pp. Light foxing. 3/4 sheep, lightly rubbed. *(Goodrich)* **$175** [≈ £97]

Hamilton, William R.
- Supplement to an essay on the theory of systems of rays. Dublin: R. Graisberry ..., 1830. 1st edn. Lge 4to. Marg tears to 2 leaves. Author's pres copy. *(Minkoff)* **$375** [≈ £208]

Hammond, John
- The practical surveyor. London: T. Heath, 1725. 1st edn. 8vo. viii,112 pp. 7 fldg engvd plates, 2 with mtd flaps. Some spotty browning. Contemp blindstamped cloth, rebacked, gilt spine. *(Antiq Sc)* **$450** [≈ £250]

Hammond, Nathaniel
- The elements of algebra in a new and easy method ... London: for the author, 1752. 2nd edn, crrctd. 8vo. E4 reprd. Rebound in rexine. *(Stewart)* **£30** [≈ $54]

Hammond, Robert
- The electric light in our homes. London: [1884]. 8vo. xii,205 pp. 3 mtd photos, ills. Orig elab pict cloth, gilt. *(Weiner)* **£60** [≈ $108]

Hammond, William A.
- Military medical and surgical essays prepared for the United States Sanitary Commission. Phila: 1864. 1st edn. 552 pp. Bubbling on front cvr. *(Scientia)* **$300** [≈ £166]

Hammond, Wm.
- Treatise on diseases of the nervous system. New York: 1873. 3rd edn. 8vo. 754 pp. 1 leaf loose. Orig cloth. *(Goodrich)* **$95** [≈ £52]

Hancocke, John
- Febrifugum magnum: or, common water the best cure for fevers, and probably for the plague. R. Halsey, 1723. 4th edn. Sm 8vo in 4s. [vi],3-108 pp. New mrbld bds, unlettered. *(Blackwell's)* **£75** [≈ $135]

Hand, William M.
- The house surgeon and physician; designed to assist heads of families, travellers, and sea-faring people ... New Haven: 1820. 2nd edn. 288 pp. Rebound in cloth-backed bds. *(Fye)* **$100** [≈ £55]
- The house surgeon and physician; designed to assist heads of families, travellers, and sea-faring people, in discerning, distinguishing, and curing disease. New Haven: 1820. 8vo. xii,288 pp. Foxing. Calf, rebacked. *(Goodrich)* **$115** [≈ £63]

Handbook of Clinical Neurology
- Handbook of Clinical Neurology. Amsterdam: 1968-82. Vols 1-44, vols 45-47 of new series (1984-85). As issued. *(Elgen)* **$3,500** [≈ £1,944]

Handley, James
- Colloquia chirurgica: or, the whole art of surgery epitomiz'd and made easie, according to modern practice ... London: Bates & Bettesworth, 1705. 1st edn. 8vo. [16],192,[4] pp. Paste-downs detached. Mottled calf. *(Rootenberg)* **$350** [≈ £194]

Handmaid ...
- The new handmaid to arts, sciences, agriculture ... husbandry ... art of painting ... dying silks ... [&c., &c.]. London: for W. Clements & J. Sadler, 1790. 1st edn (?). 8vo. 118 pp. Near-contemp qtr calf, mrbld bds. *(Gough)* **£115** [≈ $207]

Hannover, Adolphe
- On the construction and use of the microscope. Edited by John Goodsir. Edinburgh: 1853. 1st edn in English. 100 pp. 2 plates.   *(Scientia)* **$150 [≃ £83]**

Hanzlik, P.J.
- Actions and uses of the salicyclates and cinchophen. Baltimore: 1927. 1st edn. 200 pp. Orig cloth.   *(Fye)* **$50 [≃ £27]**

Harazthy, A.
- Grape-culture, wines, and wine-making. With notes upon agriculture and horticulture. New York: 1862. 8vo. Orig cloth, spine sunned. Ex lib.   *(Goodrich)* **$1,500 [≃ £833]**

Hardwicke ...
- Hardwicke's Science Gossip. An illustrated medium of interchange and gossip ... London: 1866-1901. Vols 1-29, New Series Vols 1-7. Entire run excepting New Series Vol 8. Old series Vols 1-28 orig blue cloth gilt; Vol 29 & New Series Vols 1-7 bndrs cloth.
            (Pollak) **£200 [≃ $360]**

Hardy, G.H.
- Ramunajan, twelve lectures on subjects suggested by his life and work. Cambridge: 1940. 236 pp. Port. Orig cloth.
            (Weiner) **£40 [≃ $72]**

Harkins, Henry
- The treatment of burns. Springfield: 1942. 1st edn. 457 pp. Cloth, dw.
            (Scientia) **$65 [≃ £36]**

Harley, George Way
- Native African medicine ... its practice in the Mano Tribe of Liberia. Harvard Univ Press, 1941. xvi,294 pp. Frontis, map. Orig gilt-stamped cloth.   *(Karmiole)* **$35 [≃ £19]**

Harper, R.M.J.
- Evolution and illness. A short essay on the clinical significance of evolutionary vestiges. Edinburgh: Livingstone, 1962. 8vo. vii,[i],108 pp. 35 pp. Pub bndg, dw.
            (Pollak) **£20 [≃ $36]**

Harper, Thomas
- The accomptant's companion; or young arithmetician's guide. London: the author, 1765. 2nd edn. 12mo in 6's. [iv],vi, [ii],192 pp. Port frontis. Title cropped at hd. Contemp sheep, worn, backstrip defective.
            (Clark) **£60 [≃ $108]**

Harris, Chapin
- A dictionary of dental science, biography, bibliography, and medical terminology. Phila: 1849. 1st edn. 780 pp. Lea.
            (Scientia) **$225 [≃ £125]**

Harris, Henry F.
- Pellagra. New York: 1919. 1st edn. 421 pp. Cloth, 2 tiny nicks in front cvr.
            (Scientia) **$75 [≃ £41]**

Harris, J.
- Elements of plane and spherical trigonometry ... and several projections of the sphere in plano ... London: 1723. 207 pp. 6 fldg plates, num text diags. Insignificant worming through inner margs. Contemp calf, rebacked, unsuitable new endpapers.
            (Whitehart) **£95 [≃ $171]**

Harris, John
- The description and uses of the celestial and terrestrial globes; and of Collin's pocket-quadrant. London: 1725. 6th edn. Sm 8vo. 62 pp. Frontis. Contemp calf, upper cvr detached.   *(Robertshaw)* **£40 [≃ $72]**
- Lexicon technicum; or, an universal English dictionary of arts and sciences. For Dan Brown ..., 1704. 1st edn. Folio. Red & black title, engvd port, 7 plates (2 fldg), w'cut ills & text diags. Half calf.
            (Halewood) **£325 [≃ $585]**

Harris, Joseph
- The description and use of the globes, and the orrery. London: Wright & Cushee, 1738. 4th edn. 8vo. viii,190 pp. Fldg engvd frontis, 6 fldg engvd plates. Armorial b'plate on title verso (over portion of advt). Contemp panelled calf, jnts cracked.
            (Antiq Sc) **$200 [≃ £111]**
- The description and use of the globes, and the orrery. London: 1745. 6th edn. 8vo. viii,190 pp. 6 plates (1 sl cropped). A few sm stains. Contemp lea, rebacked, spine gilt.
            (Whitehart) **£60 [≃ $108]**
- An essay upon money and coins. Part 1. The theories of commerce, money and exchanges. Part 2. That the established standard of money should not be violated or altered. London: 1757. 1st edn. Demy 8vo. Half calf, rebacked.   *(Halewood)* **£125 [≃ $225]**

Harrison, James Bower
- The medical aspects of death, and the medical aspects of the human mind. London: Longman ..., 1852. 8vo. 165 pp. Orig cloth, uncut. Author's pres copy.
            (Goodrich) **$95 [≃ £52]**

Harrison, John
- The pathology and treatment of stricture of the urethra. London: Churchill, 1852. viii,104 pp. 4 fldg plates. Scattered lib stamps. Orig cloth, little wear to spine. Author's pres inscrptn. *(Pollak)* **£30 [≈ $54]**

Harrison, Sarah
- The house-keeper's pocket book and compleat family cook ... the eighth edition. London: for C. & R. Ware, 1764. Some tables at end shaved at bottom. Contemp sheep, rebacked. *(Waterfield's)* **£195 [≈ $351]**

Harrison, T.R.
- Principles of internal medicine. Phila: December 1950. Cloth.
  (Rittenhouse) **$50 [≈ £27]**

Harrison, W. Jerome
- Geology of the Counties of England and of North and South Wales. London: Kelly ..., 1882. 1st edn. 8vo. xxviii,346 pp. 106 text figs. Orig brown pict cloth, gilt. Pres copy.
  (Gough) **£18 [≈ $32]**

Hart, D. Berry
- Contributions to the topographical and sectional anatomy of the female pelvis. Edinburgh: Johnston, 1885. Folio. [iv],6,[iv] pp. 12 plates. Orig cloth, faded.
  (Pollak) **£20 [≈ $36]**

Hart, D.B. & Barbour, A.H.
- Manual of gynecology. New York: Wood's Library, 1883. 1st Amer edn. 2 vols. 8vo. 313; 366 pp. 9 plates, some cold, 132 text ills. Orig cloth. *(Oasis)* **$75 [≈ £41]**

Harting, James Edmund
- British animals extinct within historic times with some account of British Wild White Cattle. Trubner, 1800. 8vo. x,258 pp. 36 ills in text. Orig olive cloth, b'plate.
  (Blackwell's) **£45 [≈ $81]**

Hartley, David (1705-1757)
- A view of the present evidence for and against Mrs. Stephen's medicines, as a solvent for the stone ... London: for S. Harding, 1739. 1st edn. 8vo. vi,[2],204 (some mispagination),[4] pp. Rec bds. *(Rootenberg)* **$400 [≈ £222]**

Hartley, David (1732-1815)
- An account of the invention and use of fire-plates, for the security of buildings and ships against fire. London: James Cochrane, 1834. 2nd edn. 8vo. 32 pp. Without pp 5 & 6 but apparently complete. Etched frontis.
  (Burmester) **£35 [≈ $63]**

Hartree, D.R.
- Calculating instruments and machines. Cambridge: 1950. 1st edn. ix,138 pp. 68 figs in text including 13 photos.
  (Whitehart) **£25 [≈ $45]**

Hartridge, Gustavus
- The ophthalmoscope. A manual for students. London: Churchill, 1894. 2nd edn. xiii,[i], 156,32 ctlg pp. 4 cold plates, 67 ills. 2 sm marks on title. Orig cloth.
  (Pollak) **£20 [≈ $36]**

Harvey, Gideon
- The art of curing diseases by expectation ... other various discourses in physick ... London: 1689. 1st edn. 12mo. [iv],224 pp. Ink stain on title, some foxing & staining. Contemp mor, gilt, crnrs worn, chipped. Sgntr of Gideon Harvey on endpaper. Wing H1056. *(Pickering)* **$1,250 [≈ £694]**
- Casus medico-chirurgicus, or a most memorable case of a noble-man deceased, wherein is shewed his Lordship's wound ... how his physicians ... treated him ... London: Rooks, 1678. 1st edn. 12mo. 3ff, 160 pp. Lib b'plate, stamp on title. Old calf, rebacked.
  (Hemlock) **$350 [≈ £194]**
- The City Remembrancer: being historical narratives of the Great Plague at London, 1665; Great Fire, 1666 ... reflections on the plague in general ... London: for W. Nicoll, 1769. 1st edn. 2 vols. 8vo. Contemp tree calf, jnts cracked but sound.
  (Quaritch) **$350 [≈ £194]**
- The vanities of philosophy and physick ... London: for A. Roper ..., 1699. 1st edn. 8vo. [viii],184 pp. Early sgntrs on title, some browning & foxing. Contemp speckled sheep, panelled in blind, crnrs sometime reprd, jnts cracked. Wing H1079.
  (Pickering) **$650 [≈ £361]**
- The third edition of the vanities of philosophy and physick: enlarged ... offering moreover ... different hypotheses ... physick ... and other diseases. London: Roper, 1702. [28],381 pp. Some pencilling. Contemp panelled calf, rebacked.
  (Goodrich) **$195 [≈ £108]**

Harvey, William
- The anatomical exercise concerning the motion of the heart and blood ... to which is added, Dr. James de Back, his discourse on the heart. London: R. Lowndes, 1673. 2nd edn in English. 8vo. 12ff, 107 pp; 10 ff, 172 pp. Lacking front free endpapers. Old calf.
  (Hemlock) **$2,250 [≈ £1,250]**
- The anatomical exercise. De Mortu Cordis

1628 ... The first English text of 1653 now newly edited by Geoffrey Keynes. London: Nonesuch Press, 1928. One of 1450, numbered. Orig niger mor, gilt, t.e.g., other edges uncut.   *(Traylen)* **£160 [≈ $288]**
- The anatomical exercise. De Mortu Cordis 1628 ... The first English text of 1653 now newly edited by Geoffrey Keynes. London: Nonesuch Press, 1928. One of 1450, numbered. 8vo. xvi,202 pp. Uncut in crushed mor, gilt, spines sl faded.
        (Frew Mackenzie) **£90 [≈ $162]**
- The anatomical exercise ... Nonesuch Press, 1928. Tercentenary celebration edition. One of 1450, numbered. Post 8vo. Orig niger mor, t.e.g., uncut, a little used.
        (Sotheran) **£135 [≈ $243]**
- The anatomical exercise. London: Nonesuch Press, 1928. One of 1450. xiv,202 pp. Fldg plate. Niger mor.   *(Goodrich)* **$195 [≈ £108]**
- The ear in health and disease. London: Renshaw, 1856. 3rd edn. 8vo. 240 pp. Text ills. 1 page frayed. New qtr calf, orig wrap laid down. Author's pres inscrptn.
        (Oasis) **$85 [≈ £47]**
- The works ... London: Sydenham Soc, 1847. 8vo. 624 pp. Discreet name on title. Orig cloth.   *(Oasis)* **$150 [≈ £83]**
- The works ... translated from the Latin with a life of the author. London: Sydenham Soc, 1847. Thick 8vo. Some occas pencil notes in margs. Rebound qtr red mor.
        (Hughes) **£65 [≈ $117]**
- The works ... translated from the Latin with a life of the author by Robert Willis. London: Sydenham Soc, 1847. 8vo. xcvi,624 pp. Orig cloth.   *(Goodrich)* **$250 [≈ £138]**
- The works translated from the Latin with a life of the author. Sydenham Soc, 1847. 8vo. xcvi,624 pp. Orig cloth, gilt, rebacked preserving orig spine & endpapers.
        (Bickersteth) **£75 [≈ $135]**

Haselden, Thomas
- Euclid's elements ... See Barrow, Isaac

Haskoll, W. Davis
- Land and marine surveying in reference to the preparation of plans for roads and railways; canals ... towns' water supplies ... with description and use of surveying instruments. London: 1868. 8vo. Text ills, fldg maps. Orig cloth, faded.
        (Tooley) **£55 [≈ $99]**

Hasluck, P.N.
- The book of photography, practical, theoretic and applied. London: 1905. Lge 8vo. xl,744 pp. Plates, ills. Name stamp on title & half-

title. Maroon half roan, sl worn.
        (Weiner) **£65 [≈ $117]**

Hasluck, P.N. (ed.)
- Cassell's cyclopaedia of mechanics. 1908-10. 5 vols. 447; 352; 352; 352; 352 pp. Profusely illust. Half mor, rubbed, spines sl worn.
        (Whitehart) **£60 [≈ $108]**

Hassall, Arthur Hill
- Food and its adulterations; comprising the reports of the Analytical Sanitary Commission of "The Lancet" for the years 1851 to 1854 ... revised and extended. London: Longman ..., 1855. Thick 8vo. Ills. Some fraying, fingering & waterstaining. Mod cloth.   *(Hughes)* **£25 [≈ $45]**

Hasse, Charles Ewald
- An anatomical description of the diseases of the organs of circulation and respiration. London: for the Sydenham Soc, 1846. 1st edn in English. 8vo. [xv],[1 blank], 400pp. Orig blindstamped cloth, t.e.g.
        (Taylor) **£26 [≈ $46]**
- An anatomical description of the diseases of the organs of circulation and respiration. London: Sydenham Soc, 1846. 8vo. xvi,400pp. Orig green cloth, blocked in gilt & blind.   *(Blackwell's)* **£30 [≈ $54]**
- An anatomical description of the diseases of the organs of circulation and respiration. London: Sydenham Soc, 1846. 8vo. 400 pp. Orig cloth.   *(Goodrich)* **$35 [≈ £19]**

Hassler, Ferdinand Rudolph
- Elements of the geometry of planes and solids. Richmond: 1828. 4 fldg plates. Stamp on title, foxed. Orig bds, cvrs detchd.
        (Allen) **$50 [≈ £27]**

Haswell, J. Eric
- Horology. The science of time measurement and the construction of clocks, watches and chronometers. London: Chapman & Hall, 1928. 1st edn. 8vo. Plates, ills. Orig blue cloth, gilt, rubbed. Ex lib.
        (Hughes) **£28 [≈ $50]**

Havers, G. & Davies, J.
- Collection of philosophical conferences of the French virtuosi upon questions of all sorts ... London: for Thomas Dring ..., 1665. 4to. [8]ff,496 pp. Browned, title with crnr & sm section missing with loss of 4 letters. Contemp calf, worn, jnts open.
        (Elgen) **$450 [≈ £250]**

Haviland, Alfred
- The geographical distribution of disease in Great Britain. London: Swan Sonnenschein, 1892. 2nd edn. 8vo. 4 cold fldg maps (inc frontis). Orig green cloth, gilt, crnrs sl rubbed.   *(Hughes)* £20 [≈ $36]

Hawkins, B. Waterhouse
- A comparative view of the human and animal frame. London: Chapman & Hall, 1859. Folio. 27 pp. 10 litho plates. Crrctns in text with lengthy ms note on front blank stating it to be the author's proof copy.
                         (Goodrich) $495 [≈ £275]

Hawkins, Francis Bisset
- Elements of medical statistics ... London: for Longman, Rees .., 1829. 1st edn. 8vo. xii,234 pp. Some sl foxing. Uncut in orig grey bds, crnrs worn, new cloth spine.
                      (Pickering) $1,200 [≈ £666]

Hawkins, Thomas
- The book of the great sea-dragons, Ichthyosauri and Plesiosauri, Gedolim Taninim, of Moses. Extinct monsters of the ancient earth. London: Pickering, 1840. 1st edn. Folio. [iv],27 pp. Frontis, 30 litho plates. Orig ptd wraps laid down on later cloth.
                         (Gough) £275 [≈ $495]

Hayes, Charles
- A treatise of fluxions: or an introduction to mathematical philosophy ... London: for Midwinter & Leigh ..., 1704. 1st edn. Folio. [xvi],xii,315,[1 advt] pp. W'cut diag pasted to ft of p 2, num w'cut text diags. Contemp panelled calf, rebacked, crnrs worn.
                     (Pickering) $2,650 [≈ £1,472]

Hayes, Thomas
- A serious address on the dangerous consequences of neglecting common coughs and colds, with ample directions for the prevention and cure on consumptions. Boston: 1796. 1st Amer edn. 12mo. 105 pp. Foxed, stamp on title. New qtr calf.
                       (Goodrich) $325 [≈ £180]
- A serious address on the dangerous consequences of neglecting common coughs and colds ... Boston: 1796. 1st Amer edn. Old sgntr on title. Qtr mor, mrbld bds, upper hinge v sl cracked, crnrs sl wear.
                      (Rittenhouse) $225 [≈ £125]

Haymaker, Webb
- The founders of neurology. Springfield: [1953]. 1st edn. 8vo. 479 pp. Num ports. Cloth, dw.   *(Elgen)* $40 [≈ £22]

Haynes, C.M.
- Elementary principles of electro-therapeutics. Chicago: 1896. Revsd edn. 507 pp. Orig cloth.   *(Fye)* $95 [≈ £52]

Haynes, Thomas
- A treatise on the improved culture of the strawberry, raspberry, and gooseberry. London: for B. & R. Crosby, 1814. 2nd edn. 8vo. 33 pp advts. Orig bds, rebacked.
                       (Traylen) £95 [≈ £171]

Hayward, George
- Surgical reports and miscellaneous papers on medical subjects. Boston: 1855. 1st edn. 452 pp. Hd & tail of spine chipped.
                      (Scientia) $150 [≈ £83]

Hazzard, Charles
- Practice and applied therapeutics of osteopathy. Kirksville, 1905. 3rd edn. 8vo. 442 pp. Half mor, sl wear at top of spine.
                    (Rittenhouse) $35 [≈ £19]

Head, Henry
- Aphasia and kindred disorders of speech. Cambridge: 1926. 1st edn. 2 vols. 549; 430 pp. Cloth.   *(Scientia)* $350 [≈ £194]
- Aphasia and kindred disorders of speech. 1926, reprinted New York: 1963. 2 vols. 8vo. xiv,549; xxxii,430 pp. Ills. Cloth, dws.
                       (Elgen) $175 [≈ £97]
- Studies in neurology, Oxford: 1920. 2 vols. Lge 4to. Orig cloth. *(Goodrich)* $295 [≈ £163]
- Studies in neurology, Oxford: 1920. 1st edn. 2 vols. 862 pp. Orig cloth, bottom of vol 2 rear cvr sl faded.   *(Scientia)* $265 [≈ £147]
- Studies in neurology. London: 1920. 1st coll edn. 2 vols. 8vo. 862 pp. Num ills. Cloth.
                       (Elgen) $275 [≈ £152]

Healde, Thomas
- The new pharmacopoeia of the Royal College of Physicians of London. Translated ... London: for T. Longman, 1788. 2nd edn, crrctd. xvi,350,[i errata],[i blank] pp. Occas marg mark, wanting half-title. New buckram.
                       (Pollak) £60 [≈ $108]
- The pharmacopoeia of the Royal College of Physicians of London ... London: 1793. 6th edn. Lacking front & rear free endpapers. Contemp calf, some wear.
                     (Robertshaw) £36 [≈ $64]

Hearher, J.F.
- A treatise on mathematical instruments, including most of the instruments employed in drawing, for assisting vision, in surveying and levelling ... 1851. 2nd edn. vi,170 pp.

Num ills. Lib stamps on title & elsewhere. Orig blindstamped limp cloth.
(Whitehart) £18 [≈ $32]

Heath, George Yeoman
- Plague and cholera. Two lectures ... Newcastle-upon-Tyne: Richardson, 1850. 8vo. [iv],[52] pp. Contemp notes on last page. Qtr buckram, mrbld sides.
(Frew Mackenzie) £70 [≈ $126]

Heath, T.
- Aristarchus of Samos. The ancient Copernicus. A history of Greek astronomy to Aristarchus together with Aristarchus's treatise on the sizes and distances of the sun and moon. Oxford: 1913. 1st edn. viii,425 pp. Text figs. Cloth sl dust-stained.
(Whitehart) £45 [≈ $81]

Heaton, George
- A review of a report of a Committee of the A.M.A. on the permanent cure of reducible hernia or rupture. Boston: Chadwick, 1853. 8vo. 31 pp. Orig wraps.
(Goodrich) $65 [≈ £36]

Heaviside, Oliver
- Electrical papers. London: Macmillan, 1892. 1st edn. 2 vols. 8vo. xx,560; xvi,587,[i] pp. Text figs. Pub bndg, rear jnt of vol 2 a bit weak. *(Pollak)* £150 [≈ $270]
- Electromagnetic theory. London: The Electrician, 1893-[1912]. 3 vols. xxi,[i], 466,[ii advts]; xvi,[ii], 542,[ii], 32 advts; [iv],519,[i] pp. Num text figs. Orig cloth, rebacked. *(Pollak)* £200 [≈ $360]

Heberden, William
- Commentaries on the history and cure of diseases. Boston: 1818. Orig bds, lea scuffed & somewhat worn. Ex lib with stamps.
(Rittenhouse) $195 [≈ £108]
- An introduction to the study of physic. New York: 1929. 1st trade edn.
(Elgen) $50 [≈ £27]
- An introduction to the study of physic. New York: 1929. 1st edn. Lge paper, one of 230, numbered, sgnd by editor. xi,159 pp. 2 plates, ills. Cloth-backed bds. *(Elgen)* $150 [≈ £83]

Hebra, Ferdinand & Kaposi, Moritz
- Diseases of the skin, including the exanthemata. Translated and edited ... London: New Sydenham Soc, 1866-80. 5 vols. 8vo. A little foxing at front & rear. Orig cloth, sl wear to spine ends.
(Pollak) £75 [≈ $135]

Hecker, J.F.C., et al.
- The epidemics of the Middle Ages. London: 1844. Upper hinge sl weakened.
(Rittenhouse) $50 [≈ £27]

Hedley, John
- A practical treatise on the working and ventilation of coal mines. London: John Weale, 1851. 1st edn. Tall 8vo. 128 pp. 16 fldg plates. Tipped-in drctns to binder. Orig cloth. *(Spelman)* £120 [≈ $216]

Heilprin, Angelo
- The geographical and geological distribution of animals. New York: Appleton, 1887. 1st edn. 12mo. xii,435 pp. Frontis. Orig cloth.
(Antiq Sc) £40 [≈ £22]
- The geological evidences of evolution. Phila: the author, 1888. 1st edn. 12mo. [4],99 pp. 4 plates, text ills. Orig cloth.
(Antiq Sc) $35 [≈ £19]

Heitzmann, C.
- Anatomy, descriptive and topographical. In 625 illustrations. New York: 1887. 1st edn in English. xxii,238, 270,36 pp. Orig cloth.
(Whitehart) £25 [≈ $45]

Helferich, H.
- On fractures and dislocations ... with notes and additional illustrations by J. Hutchinson. New Sydenham Soc, 1899. 8vo. v,162 pp. 68 plates, 126 text figs. Sl foxing at beginning. Orig cloth. *(Blackwell's)* £35 [≈ $63]

Helmholtz, Herman
- On the sensations of tone as a physiological basis for the theory of music ... London: 1912. 4th edn. Lge 8vo. xix,575 pp. Ills, diags. Orig cloth. *(Weiner)* £120 [≈ $216]
- The sensations of tone as a physiological basis for music ... translated ... with additional notes ... London: Longmans, Green, 1875. 1st English edn. 8vo. xxiv,824,44 advts pp. W'engvd ills, typeset musical examples in text. Orig cloth, rebacked, orig spine.
(Pickering) $500 [≈ £277]

Helsham, Richard
- A course of lectures in natural philosophy. Dublin: R.Reilly, at the University Press, 1739. 1st edn. 8vo. viii,404 pp. Red & black title, 11 fldg engvd plates. Contemp calf, worn. *(Bennett)* £250 [≈ $450]

Henderson, William Augustus
- The housekeeper's instructor; or, universal family cook ... to which is added the complete art of carving. London: Stratford, n.d.

[1790?]. 5th edn. 448,15 index, 3 subscribers, 1 advt pp. Frontis, 10 engvd plates (1 fldg). Contemp tree-calf, spine gilt-ruled.
(Gough) £225 [≃ $405]

Henle, G.G. Jacob
- A treatise on general pathology. Translated by Henry Preston. Phila: 1853. 1st edn in English. 391 pp. Lea, scuffed, top of spine frayed, lacking label. *(Scientia)* $350 [≃ £194]

Henney, Keith
- Electron tubes in industry. New York: McGraw-Hill, 1934. 2nd imp. 8vo. ix,[i],490 pp. Num ills. Pub bndg. *(Pollak)* £20 [≃ $36]

Henoch, Edward
- Lectures on children's diseases. A handbook for practitioners and students. Translated ... London: New Sydenham Soc, 1889. 2 vols. 8vo. Orig cloth, spine ends a bit worn, jnts slack. *(Pollak)* £45 [≃ $81]
- Lectures on diseases of children. New York: Wood's Library, March, 1882. 8vo. 357 pp. Orig cloth. *(Oasis)* $100 [≃ £55]

Henry, Edward R.
- Classification and uses of finger prints. London: Routledge, 1900. 1st edn. 8vo. iv,112 pp. 11 plates, text ills. Orig cloth. *(Antiq Sc)* $175 [≃ £97]
- Classification and uses of finger prints. London: 1900. 1st edn. 8vo. iv,112 pp. 11 plates (3 fldg). Sm tear on 1 leaf, not affecting text, sl foxing. Orig green cloth, spine sl marked & discold. *(Whitehart)* £55 [≃ $99]
- Classification and uses of finger prints. London: 1900. 8vo. iv,98 pp. Plates, some fldg, ills, tables. 1 sheet loose. Orig cloth. *(Weiner)* £50 [≃ $90]

Henry, William
- Elements of experimental chemistry. Phila: 1819. 1st Amer edn. 2 vols in 1. Thick 8vo. 13 engvd plates. Contemp calf, worn. Ex lib. *(Argosy)* $75 [≃ £41]

Henson, Wm.
- Great facts of modern astronomy ... the formation of the planets and their satellites ... theory of light, and the sun spots. Newark, NJ: Daily Advertiser, 1871. 29 pp.
(Xerxes) $40 [≃ £22]

Herb, Charles O.
- Machine tools at work. New York: Industrial Press, 1942. 8vo. [viii],552 pp. Many ills. Pub bndg. *(Pollak)* £20 [≃ $36]

Herbal ...
- A new medicinal, economical, and domestic herbal. Blackburn: 1808. 8vo. [2],257 pp. Old bds, rebacked, uncut.
(Goodrich) $195 [≃ £108]
- A new medicinal, economical, and domestic herbal. Blackburn: R. Parker, 1808. 1st edn (?). 8vo. [ii],ii,257,[1] pp. 19th c half mor, rebacked. *(Burmester)* £60 [≃ $108]

Heresbach, Conrad
- Foure bookes of husbandrie ... Newly Englished, and increased by Barnaby Googe. London: John Wright, 1586. Sm 4to. Black letter. W'cut arms on title verso, w'cut in text, final leaf "Olde English Rules", colophon, vignette on verso. Mrbld bds, calf. STC 13198. *(Traylen)* £685 [≃ $1,233]

Hermippus Redivivus ...
- Hermippus redivivus ... See Cohausen, Johann Heinrich

Heron, Robert
- General view of the natural circumstances of those Isles ... distinguished by the common name of ... Hebrides. Edinburgh: 1794. 4to. Bds, calf spine. *(Traylen)* £42 [≃ $75]

Herrell, W.E.
- Penicillin and other antibiotic agents. Phila: 1945. xv,348 pp. 45 text figs. Cloth.
(Whitehart) £25 [≃ $45]

Herrick, C. Judson
- Neurological foundations of animal behavior. New York: 1924. 8vo. 334 pp. Ills. Orig cloth. *(Goodrich)* $25 [≃ £13]

Herschel, Caroline Lucretia
- Catalogue of stars, taken from Mr. Flamsteed's observations ... in ... the Historia Coelestis. With an index ... Sold by Peter Elmsly ..., 1798. 1st edn. Folio. 136 pp. Engvd lf of scales, errata lf. Marg worming throughout, reprd on title. Rec grey bds.
(Pickering) $600 [≃ £333]

Herschel, Clemens
- 115 experiments on the carrying capacity of large, riveted, metal conduits ... New York: 1897. 8vo. vi,122 pp. Plates, graphs. Orig cloth. *(Weiner)* £30 [≃ $54]

Herschel, John Frederick William
- Essays from the Edinburgh and Quarterly Reviews with addresses and other pieces. 1857. 750 pp. Advts at end dated 1867. Orig

blindstamped cloth, sl marked.
(*Whitehart*) **£35 [≈ $63]**

- Observations of the apparent distances and positions of 380 double and triple stars ... 1821 [-] 1823 ... a description of a five-feet equatorial instrument employed in the observations. London: W. Nicol, 1824. 4to. 412 pp. 2 plates. Rebound in buckram.
(*Xerxes*) **$155 [≈ £86]**

- Outlines of astronomy ... London: 1849. 2nd edn. xvi,661 pp. 6 plates. Foxed. Prize calf, worn.   (*Weiner*) **£25 [≈ $45]**

- Outlines of astronomy ... London: for Longman, Brown ..., 1849. 1st edn. 8vo. xiv,[1 errata], 661,32 pub advts pp. 6 engvd plates (1 fldg). Plates foxed. Orig plum cloth, spine faded & sl frayed.
(*Pickering*) **$350 [≈ £194]**

- Outlines of astronomy. London: for Longman ..., 1849. 2nd edn. 8vo. Engvd frontis (sl spotted), 5 plates (1 fldg). Orig cloth, rubbed & faded. Ex lib.   (*Hughes*) **£45 [≈ $81]**

- Preliminary discourse on the study of natural philosophy. London: Longman ..., 1830. 1st edn. 12mo. vii,[1],327 pp. Engvd title. Prize calf, top of spine chipped.
(*Antiq Sc*) **$150 [≈ £83]**

- Results of astronomical observations made during the years 1834,5,6,7,8, at the Cape of Good Hope ... London: Smith, Elder ... 1847. 1st edn. 4to. xx,452,[2 advts] pp. Tinted litho frontis, 17 engvd or litho plates, sev fldg. Contemp cloth, lower jnt reprd.
(*Pickering*) **$700 [≈ £388]**

- Results of astronomical observations made during years 1834-38 at the Cape of Good Hope. London: Smith, Elder, 1847. 1st edn. Lge 4to. xx,452,[4 errata & pub advt] pp. Litho frontis, 17 engvd plates (4 fldg). Light edge browning. Old cloth. Author's pres copy.   (*Antiq Sc*) **$750 [≈ £416]**

Herter, Christian A.

- On infantilism from chronic intestinal infection. New York: 1908. 1st edn. 118 pp. Tears in half-title, title & 1st few pp reprd with tape.   (*Scientia*) **$45 [≈ £25]**

Hertzler, A.E.

- Clinical surgery by case histories. 1921. 2 vols. xvi,546; xii,547-1106 pp. 284; 199 ills. Cloth sl worn, dust-stained, spines faded, top of 1 spine torn & reprd.
(*Whitehart*) **£40 [≈ $72]**

Hertzler, Arthur

- Surgical pathology of the skin, fascia, muscles, tendons, blood and lymph vessels. Phila: Lippincott, 1931. 1st edn. 301 pp. Ills.

Orig cloth. Author's pres inscrptn.
(*Oasis*) **$35 [≈ £19]**

Hess, Alfred F.

- Scurvy past and present. Phila: 1920. 1st edn. 279 pp. Cloth.   (*Scientia*) **$95 [≈ £52]**

Hess, Julius H.

- Premature and congenitally diseased infants. Phila: 1922. 1st edn. 8vo. 397 pp. 189 engvs, fldg forms. Cloth. Author's pres copy.
(*Elgen*) **$65 [≈ £36]**

Heurck, Henri van

- The microscope; its construction and management including technique, photo-micrography, and the past and future of the microscope. London: 1893. 1st edn in English. 4to. 382 pp. 3 plates. Cloth.
(*Scientia*) **$250 [≈ £138]**

Heustis, Jabez W.

- Physical observations, and medical tracts and researches, on the topography and diseases of Louisiana ... New York: Swords, 1817. 1st edn. 4to. 165 pp. Ownership sgntr dated 1818 on title, b'plate removed. Orig bds, paper label, superficial defect to upper cvr.
(*Hemlock*) **$450 [≈ £250]**

Hevesey, George & Paneth, Fritz

- A manual of radioactivity. Translated ... London: OUP, 1926. 8vo. xix,[i],252 pp. 42 ills. Pub bndg.   (*Pollak*) **£25 [≈ $45]**

Hewson, Addinell

- Earth as a topical application in surgery. Phila: 1872. 8vo. 309 pp. 4 Woodburytype relief plates. Cloth. (*Goodrich*) **$125 [≈ £69]**

Hewson, William

- The works ... edited ... by George Gulliver. London: for the Sydenham Soc, 1846. 1st edn. 8vo. lvi,360 pp. Engvd frontis, 8 plates. Orig blindstamped cloth, gilt arms on sides.
(*Pickering*) **$250 [≈ £138]**

- The works ... edited ... by George Gulliver. London: for the Sydenham Soc, 1846. 8vo. lvi,360 pp. Orig blindstamped cloth, spine sl faded & chipped at hd. Ex lib.
(*Rittenhouse*) **$35 [≈ £19]**

Hey, William

- Practical observations in surgery, illustrated with cases. London: for Cadell & Davies, 1803. 1st edn. v pp, 1f, 537 pp, 7ff. 10 copperplates (inc fldg plate). Contemp half calf, back gilt, front hinge beginning to crack.
(*Offenbacher*) **$675 [≈ £375]**

- A treatise on the puerpereal fever. Illustrated by cases, which occurred in Leeds and its vicinity, in the years 1809-1812. Phila: M. Carey, 1817. 1st Amer edn. 8vo. 234,[2] pp. Orig bds, paper label.
(Hemlock) **$200 [≈ £111]**

Heynes, Samuel
- A treatise of trigonometry, plane and spherical, theoretical and practical ... To which is added a correct table of logarithms, sines ... London: 1701. 1st edn. 2 works in 1 vol. 12mo. 16 fldg plates, 2 engvd figs with moveable flaps, fldg table. Lib buckram.
(Argosy) **$200 [≈ £111]**
- A treatise of trigonometry, plane and spherical, theoretical and practical. London: 1701. [2],135, [52],[92], 8 pp. 16 fldg plates. Old panelled calf, edges & front worn, top of spine sl defective. *(Whitehart)* **£150 [≈ $270]**

Higgins, Bryan
- Experiments and observations made with a view of improving ... calcereous cements and of preparing quicklime ... for building, incrustation or stuccoing, and artificial stone. London: T. Cadell, 1780. 1st edn. 8vo. xi,[i],233 pp. Rec half calf, mrbld bds.
(Spelman) **£260 [≈ $468]**

Hildenbrand, Johann von
- A treatise on the nature, cause and treatment of contagious typhus. Translated by Samuel D. Gross. NY & Phila: 1829. 1st edn in English. 175 pp. Lea, rec rebacked.
(Scientia) **$225 [≈ £125]**

Hill, B.
- The essentials of bandaging with directions for managing fractures and dislocations; for administering ether and chloroform ... 1883. 5th edn. xiii,341 pp. 136 figs. Half-title sl dust-stained. Cloth faded, sl marked & worn, edges of spine split. *(Whitehart)* **£18 [≈ $32]**

Hill, John
- Arithmetic both in theory and practice, made plain and easy ... whole numbers and fractions, vulgar and decimal ... extraction of the square and cube roots ... London: 1764. 12th edn. vi,416 pp. Lacking half-title, 1 or 2 pp stained. Contemp calf, rebacked.
(Whitehart) **£55 [≈ $99]**

Hill, Sir John
- The family herbal or an account of those family plants, which are remarkable for their virtues ... Bungay: Brightly & Kinnersley, [1810?]. 8v0. viii,xl,376 pp. 15ff index in ms, 17 blanks. 54 hand-cold plates. Contemp tree calf, endpapers reinforced.
(Rootenberg) **$500 [≈ £277]**

Hill, William H.
- History of the Hospital and School in Glasgow. Founded by George and Thomas Hutcheson ... Glasgow: for the Hospital, 1881. 4to. One of 150. xiii,[iii], 326,[ii] pp. 5 plates, 2 maps, text ills. Orig cloth, a little dusty. Author's pres copy.
(Pollak) **£45 [≈ $81]**

Hillary, William
- Observations on the changes of air, and the concomitant epidemical diseases in the Island of Barbadoes, to which is added, a treatise on the putrid bilious fever ... Phila: 1811. 8vo. xiii,260 pp. Orig bds, scuffed, chip on lower spine, sl damage at hd.
(Rittenhouse) **$275 [≈ £152]**

Hills, Robert
- Elements of cattle, comprising rudiments of drawing and groups for the embellishment of landscape ... London: 1806-09. Folio. Engvd port, engvd title (spotted), 199 engvs on 104 plates. Contemp calf, gilt, rebacked.
(Traylen) **£850 [≈ $1,530]**

Hilton, John
- On rest and pain: a course of lectures ... and on the diagnostic value of pain ... New York: Wood, 1879. 8vo. 299 pp. Cloth, worn.
(Goodrich) **$65 [≈ £36]**
- On the influence of mechanical and physiological rest in the treatment of accidents and surgical diseases ... London: Bell & Daldy, 1863 [1950 edn]. 8vo. xxxiv,[ii], 503,[i] pp. Frontis, plate, 105 ills. Pub bndg, dw. *(Pollak)* **£25 [≈ $45]**

Hilton-Simpson, M.W.
- Arab medicine and surgery. A study of the healing art in Algeria. London: 1922. 8vo. viii,96 pp. Ills. Orig cloth, ex lib.
(Goodrich) **$65 [≈ £36]**

Hind, G.W.
- A series of twenty plates illustrating the causes of displacement in the various fractures of the bones of the extremities. [Date not noted by cataloguer]. 2nd edn. Folio. 52 pp. 20 plates & legend leaves. Lower qtr of final leaves waterstained. Rebacked.
(Goodrich) **$495 [≈ £275]**

Hinde, M., et al.
- A new royal and universal dictionary of arts and sciences ... London: 1772-71. Folio. 2 vols. 1st edn, 2nd ptg & 1st edn. 100 (ex 101)

plates. Vol 2 lacking leaf 4P. Contemp calf, v
worn.   *(Elgen)* **$225 [≈£125]**

Hints ...
- Hints for the table ... See Timbs, John
- Hints respecting the culture and use of
  potatoes. [London?:] 1795. 8vo. 8 pp. Drop-
  head title.   *(C.R. Johnson)* **£120 [≈$216]**

Hippocrates
- The aphorisms of Hippocrates, in the original
  Greek. With an interlineal ... translation... by
  J.W. Underwood. London: for the author,
  1831. 1st edn. 8vo. vii,[1],254 pp. Buckram.
  Ex lib.   *(Elgen)* **$90 [≈£50]**
- The genuine works ... with a preliminary
  discourse and annotations by Francis Adams.
  London: Sydenham Soc, 1849. 2 vols. 8vo. 8
  plates. Orig cloth, worn.
                       (Goodrich) **$175 [≈£97]**
- The genuine works ... with a preliminary
  discourse and annotations by Francis Adams.
  New York: 1929. 2 vols in 1. 8vo. v,390; 366
  pp. 8 plates. Cloth, spine lettering faded.
                       (Elgen) **$85 [≈£47]**
- The genuine works. In two volumes. New
  York: Wood's Library, 1886. Red cloth.
                    (Rittenhouse) **$30 [≈£16]**
- The genuine works. New York: Wood's
  Library, 1886. 2 vols. Orig cloth.
                     (Goodrich) **$125 [≈£69]**

Hirsch, August
- Handbook of geographical and historical
  pathology. Translatad ... London: New
  Sydenham Soc, 1883-86. 1st edn in English.
  3 vols. 8vo. Endpapers foxed. Orig brown
  cloth, gilt, extremities worn some rubbing.
               (Frew Mackenzie) **£60 [≈$108]**
- Handbook of geographical and historical
  pathology. Translated ... London: 1883-86.
  1st edn in English. 3 vols. Orig cloth.
                     (Scientia) **$175 [≈£97]**

Hitt, Thomas
- A treatise on fruit trees. London: For
  Robinson & Roberts, 1768. 8vo. viii,394,[v]
  pp. 7 fldg engvd plates. Contemp polished
  calf.   *(Bickersteth)* **£125 [≈$225]**
- A treatise on fruit trees. London: T. Osborne,
  1755. 1st edn. 8vo. xv,392 pp. 7 fldg plates (2
  reprd, 3 with sl snags in fold).
  Direction/errata leaf present. Contemp
  sprinkled calf, upper jnt tender.
                   (Blackwell's) **£250 [≈$450]**

Hoadly, Benjamin
- Three lectures on the organs of respiration.
  Read at the Royal College of Physicians, A.D.

1737 ... London: for W. Wilkins, 1740. 1st
edn. 8vo. iv,112,20 pp. 3 engvd plates. Cut
close in upper marg & 1st word of title,
headlines & plates shaved. Disbound.
                     (Pickering) **$250 [≈£138]**

Hobson, John Morrison
- Some early and later houses of pity. London:
  Routledge, 1926. 8vo. xi,[i],199,[i] pp.
  Frontis, 20 plates, 4 text ills. Pub bndg.
                        (Pollak) **£25 [≈$45]**

Hodson, F.M.
- Encyclopedia Mancuniensis; or the new
  school of arts, science, and manufactures.
  Manchester: 1813. 2 vols. 8vo. vi,675; iv,702
  pp. 24 plates. Contemp calf.
                       (Spelman) **£120 [≈$216]**

Hoff, E.C. & Fulton, J.F.
- A bibliography of aviation medicine. [With]
  Supplement ... Springfield & Balt: 1942;
  Washington: 1944. 2 vols. Lge 8vo. xv,237;
  xiv,109 pp. Orig cloth, supplement volume ex
  lib with rear endpaper grubby.
                       (Weiner) **£50 [≈$90]**

Hoffman, K.B. & Ultzmann, R.
- Analysis of the urine, with special reference
  to the diseases of the genito-urinary organs.
  New York: 1879. 1st Amer edn. 8vo. 269,10
  pub ctlg pp. 8 cold plates. Orig pebble cloth,
  spine ends with sm tears. *(Elgen)* **$45 [≈£25]**

Hofmann, A.W.
- Introduction to modern chemistry
  experimental and theoretic ... twelve lectures
  delivered in the Royal College of Chemistry,
  London. London: 1865. 1st edn. 8vo. xv,233
  pp. 64 figs. Orig cloth, dull, spine faded.
                   (Bow Windows) **£25 [≈$45]**

Hogg, Jabez
- The microscope: its history, construction and
  application. London: 1854. 1st edn. xvi,440
  pp. 15 plates, 169 diags. V sl foxing. Orig
  cloth, sl worn, spine sl cracked.
                     (Whitehart) **£48 [≈$86]**
- The microscope: its history, construction and
  application. London: Routledge ..., 1861. 5th
  edn. 8vo. xiv,[2],621 pp. 5th edn. 8vo. W'cut
  frontis, text w'cuts. Unif browned. Orig
  cloth, top of spine chipped.
                      (Antiq Sc) **$60 [≈£33]**
- The microscope: its history, construction and
  application. London: 1911. 15th edn. 8vo.
  xxiv,704 pp. 21 plates (some cold), many ills.
  A few early pages loose. Orig cloth.
                       (Weiner) **£25 [≈$45]**

- The microscope: its history, construction and application. London: Routledge, 1911. 15th edn. 8vo. xxiv,704 pp. Frontis, 20 plates (some cold), 445 text ills. Stain at top edge of last few leaves. Orig cloth, front jnt strained. *(Pollak)* £15 [≈ $27]

Hogg, John
- Practical observations on the prevention of consumption. With statistical tables of the prevalence of the disease ... the comparative salubrity of places at home and abroad. Hardwicke, 1860. 1st edn. 8vo. xii,226 pp. Half-title removed. Orig cloth, gilt. *(Fenning)* £32.50 [≈ $57]

Holden, Edgar
- Mortality and sanitary record of Newark, New Jersey. Newark: 1880. 4to. 4 cold maps, sev diags. Contemp qtr mor, rubbed, ex lib. *(Goodrich)* $60 [≈ £33]

Holden, Harold M.
- Noses. Cleveland: [1950]. 1st edn. 8vo. 252 pp. Port frontis, ills, plates. Cloth. *(Elgen)* $35 [≈ £19]

Holins, John
- The reformed botanic practice; and the nature and cause of disease clearly explained. Birmingham: 1855. 8vo. 265 pp. Half calf, a.e.g. *(Goodrich)* $45 [≈ £25]

Holland, G. Calvert
- The philosophy of animated nature; or the laws and action of the nervous system. London: Churchill, 1848. 8vo. 512 pp. Cloth, worn, spotted. *(Goodrich)* $125 [≈ £69]

Holland, G.C.
- The origin and nature of disease. Edinburgh: Jack, 1840. 1st edn. 8vo. 387 pp. Half calf, worn. *(Oasis)* $35 [≈ £19]

Holland, H.
- Chapters on mental physiology. 1858. 2nd edn. xvi,347 pp. A little light foxing. Cloth, spine faded. *(Whitehart)* £25 [≈ $45]

Holland, Sir Henry
- Essays on scientific and other subjects. London: Longman's, 1862. 1st edn. 8vo. 499 pp. Half calf, spine gilt. *(Oasis)* $150 [≈ £83]
- Medical notes and reflections. London: Longman's, 1840. 2nd edn. 638,16 pub ctlg pp. Orig cloth. *(Oasis)* $75 [≈ £41]

Holland, John
- The history and description of fossil fuel, the collieries, and coal trade of Great Britain. London: 1841. 8vo. xvi,485 pp. Few ills & diags. Sm stain in crnr of 1st few leaves. Uncut in orig cloth, spine darkened with ends sl frayed. *(Weiner)* £60 [≈ $108]
- A treatise on the progressive improvement and present state of the manufactures in metal. London: 1831-34. 3 vols. Sm 8vo. Over 1100 pp. Extra engvd titles, num ills & diags. Orig cloth, spines faded. *(Weiner)* £100 [≈ $180]

Hollander, A.R. & Cottle, M.H.
- Physical therapy in diseases of the eye, ear, nose and throat. New York: 1926. xvii,307 pp. Ills. Cloth. *(Rittenhouse)* $35 [≈ £19]

Hollander, B.
- The mental functions of the brain. An investigation into their localisation and their manifestation in health and disease, 1901. xviii,512 pp. Frontis, 37 ills. Foxing on page edges. Cloth, sl worn. *(Whitehart)* £25 [≈ $45]

Holliday, F.
- An introduction to fluxions, designed for the use, and adapted to the capacities of beginners. London: 1777. xx,iv,343 pp. 7 plates. Contemp tree calf, sl worn, sl damage to label. *(Whitehart)* £60 [≈ $108]

Hollins, John
- The reformed botanic practice and the nature and cause of disease. Birmingham: 1852. 8vo. xi,265 pp. Qtr calf. *(Goodrich)* $65 [≈ £36]

Hollopeter, W.C.
- Hay-fever and its successful treatment. Phila: 1898. 1st edn. 8vo. viii,9-137, 30pub ctlg pp. Half-title, frontis. Marg browning. Orig gilt dec cloth, spine edges sl chipped. *(Elgen)* $75 [≈ £41]

Holmes, Alexander
- A brief history of dairy education at home and abroad from 1832 to 1892. Middlesbrough: 1892. 8vo. [vi],74 pp. 13 pp advts. Plates. Orig cloth-backed bds. *(Weiner)* £25 [≈ $45]

Holmes, George W. & Ruggles, Howard E.
- Roentgen interpretation. Phila: 1931. 4th edn. 8vo. xii,339 pp. *(Rittenhouse)* $30 [≈ £16]

Holmes, Oliver Wendell
- Currents and counter-currents in medical science. With other addresses and essays. Boston: Ticknor & Fields, 1861. 1st edn.

12mo. ix,[3], 406,[2 pub advts] pp. Inserted dedn leaf. Orig blindstamped cloth, sl worn, spine faded.   *(Antiq Sc)* **$65 [≃ £36]**
- Homeopathy, and its kindred delusions; two lectures ... Boston: 1842. Some foxing at beginning. Cvrs shelfworn, upper hinge splitting.   *(Rittenhouse)* **$85 [≃ £47]**
- Our hundred days in Europe. Boston: Houghton, Mifflin, 1887. 1st edn, 1st iss. 8vo. 329 pp. 14 pp pub ctlg. Orig cloth. Author's pres copy.   *(Oasis)* **$200 [≃ £111]**

Holmes, T. & Hulke, J.W. (eds.)
- A system of surgery theoretical and practical in treatises by various authors. 1883. 3rd edn. 3 vols. Num ills. Light scattered foxing on half-titles and some plates. 1 contents leaf torn & reprd with some loss. Some inner hinges cracked.   *(Whitehart)* **£25 [≃ $45]**
- A system of surgery theoretical and practical in treatises by various authors. 1870. 2nd edn. 5 vols. 8vo. Num ills. Prize calf, some rubbing.   *(Goodrich)* **$125 [≃ £69]**

Holmes, Timothy
- Sir Benjamin Collins Brodie. London: T. Fisher Unwin, 1898. 1st edn. 8vo. 254 pp. Orig cloth, gilt, somewhat stained.
            (Oasis) **$30 [≃ £16]**

Holt, L. Emmett
- The diseases of infancy and childhood. New York: 1902. 2nd edn, enlgd. 8vo. 1161 pp. A few pages damaged in bottom marg. Orig cloth.   *(Oasis)* **$30 [≃ £16]**
- The diseases of infancy and childhood. New York: 1897. 1st edn. 8vo. 1117 pp. Sheep, front jnt weak, rubbed.
            (Goodrich) **$250 [≃ £138]**

Home, Everard
- A short tract on the formation of tumours. London: Longman, 1830. 1st edn. 8vo. [2],98,[1] pp. 4 engvd plates, 2 fldg. Orig cloth-backed bds, a bit worn & soiled.
            (Antiq Sc) **$375 [≃ £208]**

Home, Francis
- Experiments on bleaching ... added, I. ... the use of leys and sours ... II. ... the effects of lime upon alkaline salts ... by Joseph Black ... III.... Dublin: Ewing, 1771. 1st Dublin edn. 12mo. [iv],295 pp. W'cut ill. Contemp lea, hd of spine discold.   *(Bennett)* **£275 [≃ $495]**
- Medical facts and experiments. London: 1759. 1st edn. 8vo. 288 pp. Mod qtr calf, mrbld bds.   *(Goodrich)* **$495 [≃ £275]**
- The principles of agriculture and vegetation. London: for A. Millar ..., 1759. 2nd edn with

addtns. 8vo. viii,207 pp. 1st 2ff foxed. Orig calf, gilt, back & crnrs sl worn.
            (Titles) **£150 [≃ $270]**

Home, Henry, Lord Kames
- Progress of flax-husbandry in Scotland. Edinburgh: 1766. 1st edn. 8vo. 31,[1] pp. Disbound.   *(Burmester)* **£250 [≃ $450]**

Honig, Pieter & Verdoorn, Frans (eds.)
- Science and scientists in the Netherlands Indies. N.Y.C.: 1945. Roy 8vo. xxiv,491 pp. Ptd in double column. Frontis, 133 text ills & maps. Orig cloth.   *(Orient)* **£45 [≃ $81]**

Hood, Charles
- Practical treatise on warming buildings by hot water; on ventilation ... and the combustion of smoke. London: 1844. 2nd edn. 8vo. Num text w'cuts. Crude cloth-backed bds. Ex lib.   *(Argosy)* **$40 [≃ £22]**

Hood, P.
- The successful treatment of scarlet fever ... 1857. iv,[1],200 pp. Orig blindstamped cloth.
            (Whitehart) **£40 [≃ $72]**

Hooke, Robert
- The diary ... 1672-1680. Edited by Henry W. Robinson. London: Taylor & Francis, 1935. 1st edn. 8vo. Frontis, 10 full-page plates. Orig red cloth.   *(Chaucer Head)* **£55 [≃ $99]**
- Micrographia restaurata: or, the copper-plates of Dr. Hooke's wonderful discoveries by the microscope ... London: John Bowles, 1745. Folio. 33 plates (2 fldg). Contemp calf, rebacked, orig spine laid down.
            (Traylen) **£750 [≃ $1,350]**
- Microscopic observations, or Dr. Hooke's wonderful discoveries by the microscope. London: 1781. Folio. [iv],65,[4] pp. 33 plates. V sl foxed. New mrbld bds, calf back.
            (Wheldon & Wesley) **£750 [≃ $1,350]**
- Philosophical experiments and observations of the late eminent Dr. Robert Hooke... London: Innys, 1726. 1st edn. 8vo. [viii],391,[4] pp. Stamp on title. Old panelled calf, rebacked.   *(Goodrich)* **$695 [≃ £386]**
- Philosophical experiments and observations of the late eminent Dr. Robert Hooke ... and other eminent virtuoso's in his time. London: W. & J. Innys, 1726. 1st edn. 4 engvd plates (2 fldg), w'cut ills in text, leaf of advts at end. Contemp calf, rebacked.
            (Traylen) **£550 [≃ $990]**
- Philosophical experiments and observations of the late eminent Dr. Robert Hooke... London: Printed by W. & J. Innys..., 1726. 1st edn. 8vo. [viii],391,[7],[2 advts] pp. W'cut

headpieces, initials & diags in text. Contemp sprinkled calf, upper jnt cracked.
(Pickering) **$1,500 [≈ £833]**
- The posthumous works ... To these discourses is prefixt the author's life ... London: Sam. Smith & Benj Walford, 1705. 1st edn. Folio. 3ff, xxviii,572 pp, 6ff (pp 210-276 omitted in pagination). 15 copperplates. No half-title. Contemp panelled calf, rubbed.   *(Offenbacher)* **$1,500 [≈ £833]**

Hooker, Joseph Dalton
- The cryptogamic botany of the Antarctic voyage of H.M. discovery ships 'Erebus' and 'Terror' ... London: Reeve, 1845. Slim lge 4to. Vignette title, 52 cold lithos. Half mor.
(Halewood) **£200 [≈ $360]**

Hooper, Robert
- The anatomist's vade-mecum. Containing the anatomy and physiology of the human body. Windsor, Vt: 1809. 2nd Amer edn. 12mo. 264 pp. Paper browning. Lea, rubbed, bottom spine end chipped off.   *(Elgen)* **$50 [≈ £27]**
- Lexicon medicum; or medical dictionary. New York: 1848. 16th Amer edn. 2 vols in 1. A little light foxing & waterstaining. Orig lea, scuffed & somewhat dry.
(Rittenhouse) **$27.50 [≈ £15]**
- The physician's vade-mecum. Revised by W.A. Guy and J. Harley. New York: 1884. 1st Amer edn (10th English). 2 vols. 8vo. xii,338; 358 pp. Ills. Cvrs soiled.
(Elgen) **$30 [≈ £16]**
- The surgeon's vade-mecum: containing the symptoms, causes, diagnosis, prognosis and treatment of surgical diseases ... select formulae of descriptions ... Albany: E.F. Backus, 1813. 12mo. xxviii,[1],275 pp, index. Orig sheep.   *(Hemlock)* **$85 [≈ £47]**

Hooper, William
- Rational recreations, in which the principles of numbers and natural philosophy are clearly and copiously elucidated ... London: 1816. 1st edn. 4 vols. 8vo. 65 fldg plates, w'cut ills in text. Contemp calf, gilt, a little worn.
(Traylen) **£275 [≈ $495]**

Hopkins, A.A.
- The Scientific American Cyclopaedia of receipts, notes and queries. New York: 1892. 675 double-column pp. A few text ills. Orig pict cloth, spine slit at edges without affecting hinges.   *(Whitehart)* **£25 [≈ $45]**

Hopkinson, J.
- The working of the steam engine explained by the use of the indicator ... greatest effect ...

of impulsive power ... with the least expenditure of fuel. 1860. 3rd edn. xii,355,15 advts pp. 4 plates (1 fldg). Orig blindstamped cloth, a few sm stains.
(Whitehart) **£45 [≈ $81]**

Hopkinson, John
- Original papers. Cambridge: Univ Press, 1901. 2 vols. 8vo. Port frontis, another port, num charts & diags. Orig red cloth, gilt.
(Chaucer Head) **£55 [≈ $99]**

Horblit, Harrison
- One hundred books famous in science based on an exhibition held at the Grolier Library. Grolier, 1964. One of 1000. Plates. Orig cloth, slipcase.   *(Goodrich)* **$395 [≈ £219]**

Hornaday, William
- Taxidermy and zoological collecting. A complete handbook for the amateur taxidermist, collector ... sportsman and traveller. London: Kegan, Paul, 1891. 1st edn. 8vo. xix,362 pp. 23 b/w plates, 104 text ills. Orig green cloth, gilt.
(Gough) **£80 [≈ $144]**

Horner, G.R.B.
- Medical and topographical observations upon the Mediterranean; and upon Portugal, Spain, and other countries. Phila: 1839. 210 pp. Errata page. 8 plates. New buckram.
(Rittenhouse) **$35 [≈ £19]**

Horner, William
- A treatise on special and general anatomy. Phila: 1830. 2nd edn. 2 vols. 535; 528 pp. Orig lea, both front bds detchd, lacking labels, lacking endpapers vol 2.
(Fye) **$75 [≈ £41]**

Horsley, V. & Sturge, M.D.
- Alcohol and the human body. An introduction to the study of the subject ... 1908. 2nd edn. xxvii,374 pp. 14 plates, 21 figs. A few pencil underlinings, endpapers foxed. Cloth dust-stained, spine faded.
(Whitehart) **£15 [≈ $27]**

Horsley, Victor
- The cerebellum: its relation to spatial orientation and to locomotion. Being the Boyle lecture for 1905. London: 1905. 4to. 37 pp. Frontis. Ills. Orig wraps.
(Goodrich) **$195 [≈ £108]**
- The structure and functions of the brain and spinal cord. New York: 1892. 1st Amer edn. 223 pp. Cloth.   *(Scientia)* **$200 [≈ £111]**

Hosack, David

- An inaugural discourse delivered at the opening of Rutgers Medical College ... New York: Seymour, 1826. 8vo. 176 pp. Engvd frontis. Light foxing. Orig bds, worn.
(Goodrich) **$195 [≈ £108]**
- Lectures on the theory and practice of physic, delivered in the College of Physicians and Surgeons of the University of the State of New York. Phila: 1838. 8vo. xvi,699 pp. Frontis. Minimal foxing. Orig lea, worn.
(Rittenhouse) **$135 [≈ £75]**
- Lectures on the theory and practice of physic, delivered in the College of Physicians and Surgeons of the University of the State of New York. Phila: 1838. 1st edn. 8vo. xvi,[17]-699 pp. Port frontis, errata leaf. Orig sheep, sl rubbed. *(Elgen)* **$275 [≈ £152]**
- Observations of the medical character. Addressed to the Graduates of the College of Physicians and Surgeons. New York: 1826. 8vo. 38 pp. Antique bds.
(Goodrich) **$125 [≈ £69]**
- A system of practical nosology: to which is prefixed, A synopsis of the systems of ... Linnaeus ... Cullen, Darwin ... New York: 1821. 2nd edn. 8vo. xix, [20-23], 24-386 pp. Half calf, mrbld bds, hinges rubbed & partially split, sm defect to hd of spine.
(Hemlock) **$125 [≈ £69]**

Hotson, W.C.

- The principles of arithmetic. Cambridge: 1840. 2nd edn. [2],96 pp. [With] The principles of algebra. Cambridge: 1842. 2nd edn. viii,184 pp. Contemp polished calf, rebacked, spine gilt. *(Whitehart)* **£38 [≈ $68]**

Hough, Walter

- Cotton fabrics. A book of reference for those who are engaged in the cotton industry ... Supplemented March, 1924, by the addition of several cloths. Manchester: the author, 1924. 4to. Typed title & text. Leaves of fabric samples with descriptions. Mor.
(Chaucer Head) **£55 [≈ $99]**

Houghton, Henry C.

- Lectures on clinical otology delivered ... in the New York Homoepathic Medical College ... Boston: 1885. 1st edn. 8vo. xiv,260 pp. 2 chromolitho plates, text w'cuts. Cloth. Ex lib.
(Elgen) **$75 [≈ £41]**

Houghton, John

- Husbandry and trade improv'd ... Revised, corrected, and published ... by Richard Bradley. London: Woodman & Lyon, 1727-29. 4 vols. 8vo. Contemp speckled calf,

gilt, mor labels. Vol IV not quite uniform.
(Traylen) **£350 [≈ $630]**

Houghton, Thomas

- Royal institutions: being proposals for articles to establish ... laws, liberties and customs of silver and gold mines ... in Africa and America ... London: Daniel Poplar, [1694]. 1st edn. 126 pp. 2 leaves cut short, a few sl browned. Orig sheep, crnrs worn.
(Pirages) **$1,500 [≈ £833]**

Housekeeper ...

- The housekeeper and butler's guide; or, a system of cookery, and making of wines. Glasgow: n.d. [ca 1830's?]. 12mo. 24 pp. Last leaf torn without loss. Disbound, sewn as issued. *(Weiner)* **£30 [≈ $54]**

Howard, George Selby

- The New Royal Cyclopaedia and Encyclopaedia; or, complete modern and universal dictionary of arts and sciences ... London: Alex Hogg, [1788]. 1st edn. 3 vols. Folio. 161 engvd plates, 4 pp subscribers' list. Contemp half calf, mrbld sides, rubbed & worn. *(Traylen)* **£330 [≈ $594]**

Howard, Richard Baron

- Report on the prevalence of diseases ... amongst the labouring classes in Manchester. London: HMSO, 1840. 8vo. Pamphlet, disbound. *(Marlborough)* **£50 [≈ $90]**

Howard, Thomas

- On the loss of teeth and loose teeth; and on the best means of restoring them. London: Simpkin & Marshall, 1860. 12mo. [i],61,[i advt] pp. Port frontis, 2 cold plates, 1 with overflap. Orig dark green cloth, gilt-lettered, a.e.g. *(Frew Mackenzie)* **£68 [≈ $122]**
- On the loss of teeth; and on the best means of restoring them. 1857. Sm 8vo. 61 pp. Cold frontis with overlay slip. Orig cloth, sl worn & marked. *(Whitehart)* **£35 [≈ $63]**

Howard-Flanders, L. & Carr, C.F.

- Gliding and motorless flight. London: Pitman, 1932. 2nd edn. 8vo. xiii,[i], 145,[i],20, [iv advts] pp. 29 plates, 22 text figs. Pub bndg. *(Pollak)* **£25 [≈ $45]**

Howarth, Sir Henry H.

- The glacial nightmare and the Flood. A second appeal to common sense from the extravagance of some recent geology. 1893. 1st edn. 2 vols. 8vo. Blind lib stamp on each title. Orig cloth, sm white lib number on each upper cvr. *(Bickersteth)* **£45 [≈ $81]**

Howe, Joseph
- Emergencies and how to treat them. The etiology, pathology and treatment of the accidents, diseases, and cases of poisoning, which demand prompt action. New York: 1871. 1st edn. 265 pp. Orig cloth.
(Fye) **$75 [≃ £41]**

Howe, Joseph W.
- The breath, and the diseases which give it a fetid odor. New York: 1885. 3rd edn. 8vo. 108 pp. Advts. Ex lib.
(Rittenhouse) **$50 [≃ £27]**

Howell, H.H.
- The geology of the Warwickshire coal-field ... London: for HMSO, 1859. 1st edn. 57,[3] pp. Interleaved. Hand-cold map, lge fldg plate. Orig limp mor, rebacked, edge of upper cvr reprd.
(Claude Cox) **£28 [≃ $50]**

Howell, J.W. & Schroeder, H.
- The story of the incandescent lamp. Schenectady: 1927. 8vo. 208 pp. Ills. Orig cloth.
(Weiner) **£30 [≃ $54]**

Hoyle, F. & Narlikar, J.V.
- Action at a distance in physics and cosmology. San Francisco: 1974. 1st edn. 8vo. x,266 pp. Cloth.
(Elgen) **£35 [≃ £19]**

Hrdlicka, Ales.
- Physiological and medical observations among the Indians of Southwestern United States and Northern Mexico. Washington: 1908. 1st edn. 450 pp. Num ills. Orig cloth.
(Fye) **$50 [≃ £27]**

Huarte Navarro, Juan de Dios
- Examen de ingenios: or, the tryal of wits. Discovering the great difference of wits among men ... ... made English ... London: for Richard Sare, 1698. 8vo. [40],502 pp, leaf of advts. A few pp with reprd tears. Contemp calf, worn, hinges cracking. Wing H3205.
(Karmiole) **$250 [≃ £138]**

Hubble, Edwin
- The realm of the nebulae. London: 1936. 8vo. xiii,210 pp. Plates. Some pencil markings. Orig cloth. *(Weiner)* **£40 [≃ $72]**

Hudson, Thomas Jay
- The law of physic phenomena ... study of hypnotism, spiritism, mental therapeutics, etc. London: Putnam .. Chicago, 1893. 1st edn. 8vo. 409 pp. Orig blue cloth, upper cvr trifle marked.
(Burmester) **£20 [≃ $36]**

Hufeland, C.W.
- The art of prolonging human life ... a new edition, with notes by an English physician. London: 1829. 8vo. xxxix,328 pp. Uncut, in new buckram.
(Weiner) **£40 [≃ $72]**

Huggins, William
- The Royal Society or, science in the state and in the schools. New York: 1906. 8vo. 131 pp. Orig cloth.
(Goodrich) **$35 [≃ £19]**

Hughes, Robert
- A catalogue of the genuine and most curious collection of Sardonyx's ... and other oriental stones, antique cameo's and intaglia's in rings, pictures ... curious mathematical and optical instruments ... London: Bastin, 1770. 4to. 9 pp. Stitched.
(Marlborough) **£300 [≃ $540]**

Hull, Edward
- The coal-fields of Great Britain: their history, structure, and resources. London: Edward Stanford, 1861. 2nd edn, revsd & enlgd. 8vo. xx,[1], 277,[3] pp. Lge fldg map, plate, other ills. Contemp half calf. *(Fenning)* **£35 [≃ $63]**
- The physical geology and geography of Ireland. London: Stanford, 1878. 1st edn. 8vo. xvi,291 pp. Cold map, 24 text ills. Orig green cloth, gilt.
(Gough) **£18 [≃ $32]**

Hulls, Jonathan
- A description and draught of a new-invented machine ... for carrying vessels or ships ... London: for the author, 1737. 1st edn. 12mo. 48 pp. Fldg engvd frontis (dustsoiled, tear reprd, cropped with loss of imprint). Title & last leaf soiled. 19th c calf.
(Pickering) **$4,000 [≃ £2,222]**

Humane Industry ...
- Humane industry ... See Powell, Thomas

Humber, William
- A comprehensive treatise on the water supply of cities and towns ... Chicago: 1879. Lge 4to. xiv,298 pp. Cold litho frontis, 50 double-page plates with num ills, 258 ills, tables. Pub half mor, worn, reprd. *(Weiner)* **£150 [≃ $270]**

Humboldt, Alexander von
- Aspects of nature, in different lands and different climates; with scientific elucidations. London: 1849. 1st edn in English. 2 vols. Sm 8vo. xix,301; 347 pp. Orig cloth, spines ends worn.
(Weiner) **£30 [≃ $54]**
- Aspects of nature, in different lands and different climates; with scientific elucidations. London: Longman ..., 1849. 1st

edn in English. 2 vols. 8vo. xv,[iii],301; [vi],347 pp. Owner's inscrptn on half-titles, some spotting. Orig cloth, spines faded.
(Frew Mackenzie) **£68 [≃ $122]**

- A geognostical essay on the superposition of rocks, in both hemispheres. Translated ... London: Longman, 1823. 8vo. viii,482 pp. Some light foxing. Uncut & lgely unopened in new half calf, mrbld sides.
(Frew Mackenzie) **£130 [≃ $234]**

- Views of nature: or contemplations on the sublime phenomena of creation, with scientific illustrations. London: 1850. 1st English edn. Sm 8vo. xxx,452 pp. Col ptd frontis by Baxter. Polished calf, gilt, by Westerton's.   *(Bow Windows)* **£65 [≃ $117]**

- Views of nature: or contemplations on the sublime phenomena of creation ... London: Bohn, 1850. Cr 8vo. xxx,452 pp. Cold Baxter frontis. Orig cloth.   *(Taylor)* **£25 [≃ $45]**

Hunt, Charles
- A history of the introduction of gas lighting. London: 1907. Lge 8vo. viii,150 pp. 3 fldg plans, port, ills. Orig gilt-lettered blue cloth.
(Weiner) **£75 [≃ $135]**

Hunt, H.C.
- A retired habitation: a history of the Retreat, York. London: 1932. 1st edn. Sq 8vo. xvi,144 pp. 21 ills. Orig half linen, dec paper sides.
(Bow Windows) **£20 [≃ $36]**

Hunt, Harrit K.
- Glances and glimpses; or fifty years social including twenty years professional life. Boston: 1856. 1st edn. 418 pp. Cloth, crnrs worn, hd & ft of spine frayed.
(Scientia) **$225 [≃ £125]**

Hunt, James
- A treatise on the cure of stammering ... With memoir of the late Thomas Hunt. London: Longman ..., 1854. 1st edn. 8vo. Frontis. A little spotting. Orig blindstamped cloth.
(Chaucer Head) **£80 [≃ $144]**

Hunt, Robert
- Researches on light ... molecular changes produced by the influence of the solar rays ... London: Longman, 1844. 1st edn. vii,[1], 303,[1] pp, 32 pp pub advts. Errata slip. Hand-cold fldg frontis. Lib stamps on title & p 303. Orig cloth, hd & ft spine chipped.
(Rootenberg) **$500 [≃ £277]**

Hunt, Thomas
- Practical observations on the pathology and treatment of certain diseases of the skin

generally pronounced intractable. London: Churchill, 1847. xii,156,[xxxii ctlg] pp. Orig cloth, working copy.   *(Pollak)* **£20 [≃ $36]**

Hunter, Alexander
- Culina famulatrix medicinae: or, receipts in cookery, worthy of the notice of those medical practitioners, who ride in their chariots ... and who receive two-guinea fees from their rich and luxurious patients. York: 1804. Frontis. 119 pp. Qtr roan.   *(Goodrich)* **$495 [≃ £275]**

- Georgical essays. York: 1803-04. 6 vols. 8vo. 14 plates (12 fldg), fldg table. Contemp half calf, gilt.   *(Traylen)* **£160 [≃ $288]**

Hunter, J.
- Essays and observations on natural history, anatomy, physiology, psychology and geology ... edited by R. Owen. London: 1861. 2 vols. 8vo. Port, plate. A little minor foxing. Orig cloth, trifle worn at hd & ft of spines.
(Wheldon & Wesley) **£60 [≃ $108]**

Hunter, John
- The natural history of the human teeth ... structure, use, formation, growth and diseases. London: J. Johnson, 1771. 16 plates. [with] A practical treatise on the diseases of the teeth ... a supplement ... London: 1778. 1st edns. 4to. Half-title to pt 2. Half calf.
(Halewood) **£850 [≃ $1,530]**

- A treatise on the blood, inflammation, and gunshot wounds ... Phila: James Webster, 1817. 4to. viii,xii, 514 pp. 8 litho plates. Minimal foxing 1st few pages, sgntr on title. Contemp calf, sm cracks in hinges.
(Hemlock) **$150 [≃ £83]**

- A treatise on the blood, inflammation, and gunshot wounds. Phila: 1823. 2nd Amer edn. 480 pp. 8 engvd plates. Lea, front hinge cracked.   *(Fye)* **$400 [≃ £222]**

- A treatise on the blood, inflammation, and gunshot wounds. Phila: 1840. 8vo. 611,32 pub ctlg (dated Sept 1850) pp. 5 engvd plates. Foxed, some marg staining. Contemp lea, jnts tender, spine ends chipped.
(Elgen) **$135 [≃ £75]**

- A treatise on the venereal disease. London: 1786. 1st edn. 4to. [6],395 pp. 7 engvd plates. Contemp calf, rebacked, preserving orig spine. Author's pres copy.
(Goodrich) **$1,295 [≃ £719]**

- A treatise on the venereal disease. London: 1786. 1st edn. 4to. 7 engvd plates. Contemp calf, rebacked, orig spine laid down. Author's pres copy.   *(Traylen)* **£550 [≃ $990]**

Hunter, William
- The anatomy of the human gravid uterus

exhibited in figures ... London: for the Sydenham Soc, 1851. Folio. [vi],16 pp. 34 litho plates (18 double-page), notice to members slip bound in. Sev plates foxed. Orig green cloth, spine & crnrs reprd.

(Pickering) **$600 [≈ £333]**

Hurd-Mead, Kate Campbell
- A history of women in medicine from the earliest times to the beginning of the nineteenth century. Haddam, Ct: 1938. 1st edn. Author's sgntr on front endpaper.

(Rittenhouse) **$97.50 [≈ £53]**
- A history of women in medicine ... Haddam: 1938. 1st edn. 569 pp. Cloth.

(Scientia) **$125 [≈ £69]**

Hurry, Jamieson B.
- The woad plant and its dye. London: 1930. 8vo. xxvii,328 pp. Port, 17 plates, some cold, few ills. Orig cloth.   *(Weiner)* **£30 [≈ $54]**

Hurst, Arthur F. & Stewart, M.J.
- Gastric and duodenal ulcer. Oxford: 1929. 1st edn. 544 pp. Stamp on title. Cloth.

(Scientia) **$75 [≈ £41]**

Hurst, C.C.
- The mechanism of creative evolution. Cambridge: 1933. 8vo. xxi,365 pp. Text figs. Cloth.   *(Bickersteth)* **£22 [≈ $39]**

Hurtley, Thomas of Malham
- A concise account of some natural curiosities in the environs of Malham, in Craven, Yorkshire. London: Logographic Press, 1786. 1st edn. 8vo. 3 fldg plates, subscribers' list, 199 pp appendix. Calf.

(Halewood) **£98 [≈ $176]**

Husbandman ...
- The good husbandman's jewel ... to know the means whereby horses, sheep, &c. come to have ... diseases; the way to cure them perfectly ... Preston: W. Smith, n.d. [ca 1750]. 12mo. W'cuts on title & last page. A bit dog-eared & dust-marked. Mod qtr calf.

(Charles Cox) **£105 [≈ $189]**

Husbandry ...
- Select essays on husbandry, extracted from the Museum Rusticum, and foreign essays on agriculture. Edinburgh: for John Balfour, 1767. 8vo. x,408 pp. Advt leaf, 2 engvd plates, fldg table. Contemp calf, jnts partly cracked, minor wear. *(Pirages)* **$300 [≈ £166]**

Husmann, George
- American grape growing and wine making ...

the grape industries of California. New York: Orange Judd, 1883. New & enlgd edn. 310 pp. 7 plates, text ills. Gilt pict cloth, somewhat spotted. *(Argonaut)* **$125 [≈ £69]**

Husson, Henri
- Report on the magnetical experiments made by the Commission of the Royal Academy of Medicine of Paris, read in the meetings of June 21 & 28, 1831. Translated ... Boston: 1836. 1st edn in English. 172 pp. Embossed stamp on title. Mod bds, new endpapers.

(Scientia) **$200 [≈ £111]**

Hutchinson, B.
- Biographia medica; or, historical and critical memoirs of the lives and writings of the most eminent medical characters ... London: 1799. 1st edn. 2 vols. 8vo. Marg repr on 1 leaf. Half niger mor.   *(Halewood)* **£150 [≈ $270]**

Hutchinson, Jonathan
- A clinical memoir on certain diseases of the eye and ear, consequent on inherited syphilis. London: 1863. 1st edn. 8vo. xii,259 pp. Half-title. Orig cloth, sunned, uncut. Author's pres copy.   *(Goodrich)* **$450 [≈ £250]**
- The pedigree of disease being six lectures on temperament, idiosyncracy and diathesis. New York: [1881]. 1st Amer edn. 113 pp. Orig cloth.   *(Fye)* **$75 [≈ £41]**
- Syphilis. London: 1887. 1st edn. Sm 8vo. xii,532 pp. 8 chromolitho plates. Some spotting. Orig cloth, front inner hinge torn.

(Bow Windows) **£48 [≈ $86]**
- Syphilis. London: Cassell, 1887. 1st edn. 8vo. 532 pp. 8 chromolitho plates, 8 pp pub ctlg. Orig cloth, string-marked.

(Oasis) **$85 [≈ £47]**

Hutchinson, P.O.
- A guide to the land-slip, near Axmouth, Devonshire: together with a geological and philosophical enquiry into its nature and causes ... Sidmouth: 1840. 2nd edn. Sm 8vo. 24 pp. 2 extndg engvd plates. Orig ptd wraps a little dust marked, spine fragile.

(Bow Windows) **£40 [≈ $72]**

Hutchinson, R.W.
- Television up-to-date. London: 1937. 2nd edn. 8vo. xii,211 pp. Frontis, ills, diags. Orig embossed cloth, sl worn pict dw.

(Weiner) **£25 [≈ $45]**

Hutchinson, Thomas Joseph
- Impressions of Western Africa ... the diseases of the climate and a report on the peculiarities of trade ... London: Longman ..., 1858. 1st

edn. 8vo. xvi,313,[6 advts] pp. Title vignette. Orig blindstamped cloth, sl rubbed.
(Morrell) **£135 [≈ $243]**

Hutton, Charles

- The compendious measurer; being a brief, yet comprehensive treatise of mensuration and practical geometry adapted for the use of schools and practice. London: 1790. 2nd edn. xii,323 pp. Num text diags. Contemp lea bds, rebacked. *(Whitehart)* **£40 [≈ $72]**

- A course of mathematics in three volumes composed for the use of the Royal Military Academy ... London: 1810-11. 6th edn. 3 vols in 2. viii,384; 420; vii,[1],379 pp. Some minor staining, lib stamps on titles. Ex lib in mod cloth. *(Whitehart)* **£35 [≈ $63]**

- A course of mathematics. Vol I ... Vol II ... for the use of gentlemen cadets ... London: 1806-05. 5th, 4th edns. vii,388; iv,415 pp. Text diags. Unif sprinkled calf, spines gilt & sl rubbed, cvrs sl stained.
(Whitehart) **£40 [≈ $72]**

- A mathematical and philosophical dictionary. London: 1795-96. 1st edn. 2 vols. 4to. viii,650; 756 pp. 37 engvd plates, num text ills. Contemp calf, rebacked.
(Frew Mackenzie) **£275 [≈ $495]**

- A mathematical and philosophical dictionary containing an explanation of the terms, and an account of ... mathematics, astronomy ... London: Johnson, 1796-95. 1st edns. 2 vols. 4to. viii,650; ii,756 pp. 17 & 20 engvd plates. Tree calf, rebacked, crnrs reprd.
(Pollak) **£175 [≈ $315]**

- A mathematical and philosophical dictionary containing mathematics, astronomy ... London: J. Johnson, 1796-95. 1st edn. 2 vols. 4to. viii,650; ii,756 pp. 12 & 25 engvd plates. Contemp sgntr of Thos. Maugham on titles. Contemp tree sheep, gilt sides, rebacked.
(Pickering) **$800 [≈ £444]**

- A mathematical and philosophical dictionary. London: for J. Johnson ..., 1795-96. 1st edn. 2 vols. 4to. 37 engvd plates. New half antique calf, gilt, mor labels, gilt.
(Traylen) **£190 [≈ $342]**

- Mathematical tables ... common, hyperbolic, and logistic logarithms ... to which is prefixed a large and original history of the discoveries and writings relating to those subjects ... London: 1801. 8vo. Contemp calf, hinges reprd. *(Argosy)* **£100 [≈ $55]**

- Mathematical tables ... to which is prefixed a large and original history of the discoveries and writings ... 1811. 5th edn. vii,179,344 pp. Contemp lea, rebacked, edges worn, spine sl defective. *(Whitehart)* **£28 [≈ $50]**

- Tracts on mathematical and philosophical

subjects ... theory of bridges ... gunpowder ... modern practice of artillery. London: Rivington ..., 1812. 1st edn. 3 vols. x,[2],485,[1]; [2],383,[1]; pp. Engvd frontis, 10 fldg engvd plates. Light browning. Cloth.
(Antiq Sc) **$225 [≈ £125]**

- A treatise on mensuration, both in theory and practice. Newcastle-upon-Tyne: for the author, 1770. 1st edn. 4to. Engvd plate, num figs (by Thomas Bewick), list of subscribers, errata leaf. Half crimson mor, gilt.
(Traylen) **£330 [≈ $594]**

Huxham, John

- An essay on fevers, and their various kinds, as depending on different constitutions of the blood ... London: for S. Austen, 1750. 2nd edn. 8vo. xvi,288 pp. 1st gathering springing. Contemp calf, lightly rubbed.
(Frew Mackenzie) **£140 [≈ $252]**

- Medical and chemical observations upon antimony. John Hinton, 1756. 1st edn. 8vo. [iv],78,[ii] pp. Dedn leaf sgnd 'A', half-title, advt leaf at end, interleaved copy. Inscrptn on title. New qtr calf over orig mrbld bds.
(Blackwell's) **£100 [≈ $180]**

Huxley, Leonard

- Life and letters of Thomas Henry Huxley. London: 1900. 1st edn. 2 vols. 8vo. 11 plates. Some foxing & other marks, endpapers dust soiled. Orig cloth, spines faded, ends a little worn, inner hinges a little cracked.
(Bow Windows) **£48 [≈ $86]**

Huxley, Thomas Henry

- Collected essays. London: Macmillan, 1893-1904. Various edns inc some 1sts. 9 vols. Orig cloth. *(Pollak)* **£60 [≈ $108]**

- The crayfish. London: Kegan Paul, 1880. 1st edn, 1st iss. 8vo. One of 250 lge paper, sgnd by printer. xiv,371 pp. W'cut frontis, 81 w'cut figs. Armorial b'plate. Orig cloth, uncut, t.e.g. *(Antiq Sc)* **$175 [≈ £97]**

- Diary of the voyage of H.M.S. 'Rattlesnake'. Edited ... by Julian Huxley. London: Chatto & Windus, 1935. 1st edn. 8vo. viii,372 pp. Half-title, cold frontis, 12 plates, fldg map. Orig blue cloth. *(Morrell)* **£50 [≈ $90]**

- Essays ... London: 1901-04. 9 vols. Sm 8vo. Random spotting & other marks. Orig matching cloth, some spines lightly faded.
(Bow Windows) **£85 [≈ $153]**

- Evidence as to man's place in nature. London: Williams & Norgate, 1863. 1st edn, 1st iss. 8vo. [viii],159,8 advts dated Feb 1863, ptd advt endpapers. Orig dark green mor-grained cloth, gilt, b'plate.
(Blackwell's) **£250 [≈ $450]**

- Evidence as to man's place in nature. London: 1863. 1st edn. 8vo. [3],159 pp. Frontis, 8 pp pub ctlg dated Feb 1863. Ink inscrptns on front endpaper. Orig blindstamped cloth, dust-stained & worn. *(Whitehart)* **£50 [≈ $90]**
- Evidence as to man's place in nature. London: 1863. 1st edn. 8vo. [viii],159 pp inc w'engvd frontis. 8 pp advts dated Feb 1863, further advts on endpapers. W'engvd text ills. Orig turquoise cloth, jnts rubbed, upper hinge cracked. *(Pickering)* **$500 [≈ £277]**
- Evidence as to man's place in nature. New York: 1863. 1st Amer edn. 8vo. 184 pp. Frontis, 32 ills. Orig cloth, sl worn, signs of use. *(Wheldon & Wesley)* **£30 [≈ $54]**
- An introduction to the classification of animals. 1st edn. 8vo. London: John Churchill, 1869. Ills. Orig cloth.
  (Chaucer Head) **£110 [≈ $198]**
- A manual of the anatomy of invertebrated animals. London: Churchill, 1877. 1st edn. 8vo. 596 pp. Num text ills. Polished prize calf, spine gilt. *(Karmiole)* **$100 [≈ £55]**
- On our knowledge of the causes of the phenomena of organic nature, being six lectures ... London: 1863. 8vo. 156 pp. Orig dec green cloth, little shaken & worn.
  (Weiner) **£85 [≈ $153]**
- On the origin of species. New York: 1863. 1st Amer edn. 8vo. 150,6 pub ctlg pp. Text w'cuts. Orig pebble cloth, spine edges chipped. *(Elgen)* **$80 [≈ £44]**
- On the origin of species. New York: D. Appleton, 1863. 1st Amer edn. 150 pp. Advts. 5 text figs. Owner's sgntr on title. Orig brown cloth, soiled, spine extremities sl frayed. *(Karmiole)* **$150 [≈ £83]**
- Science and culture and other essays. London: 1882. 1st edn. 8vo. 349 pp. Lib cloth. *(Argosy)* **$50 [≈ £27]**
- The scientific memoirs ... Edited by Professor Michael Foster ... London: 1898-1903. 1st edn. 5 vols (inc Supplement). 4to. 4 ports, 140 plates (many fldg), 2 maps. Orig red cloth, gilt. *(Traylen)* **£260 [≈ $468]**
- Selected works. New York & London: n.d. [ca 1930]. Westminster Edition, one of 1,000, numbered. 9 vols. 8vo. Orig blue buckram, gilt, t.e.g., other edges uncut.
  (Traylen) **£180 [≈ $324]**

Hydrotherapy ...
- A few pages on hydrotherapy, or the water cure. Written for the benefit of those suffering under severe acute or chronic diseases. W.E. Painter, 1843. 1st edn. 8vo. 16 pp. Wraps. *(Fenning)* **£35 [≈ $63]**

Hymers, J.
- The elements of the theory of astronomy. Cambridge: 1840. vii,354 pp. 4 lge fldg plates. Orig bds, linen spine, bds worn.
  (Whitehart) **£25 [≈ $45]**

Hymers, J.A.
- A treatise on analytical geometry of three dimensions. Cambridge: Deighton ..., 1848. 3rd edn. Med 8vo. Half-title, 6 fldg plates. Orig qtr cloth, paper bds worn, spine split & cracked. E.J. Stone's copy with his sgntr.
  (Taylor) **£29 [≈ $52]**

Ihde, Aaron J.
- The development of modern chemistry. New York: [1964]. 1st edn. 8vo. xii,851 pp. Ills. Cloth, dw. *(Elgen)* **$35 [≈ £19]**

Ilavater, John Caspar
- Essays on physiognomy, designed to promote the knowledge and the love of mankind ... Translated ... London: for John Murray ..., 1789-98. 5 vols. 4to. 4to. Num engvd plates, vignettes & ills in text. Contemp diced calf, gilt, v sl worn. *(Traylen)* **£595 [≈ $1,071]**

Ince, Joseph
- A few papers on foreign pharmacy and other subjects. London: C. Whiting, 1859. 1st edn. 8vo. [iv],124 pp. Orig blue limp cloth, a little rubbed, lower cvr a bit marked.
  (Burmester) **£30 [≈ $54]**

Inder, W.S.
- On active service with the St. John Ambulance Brigade in the South African War, 1899-1902. Kendal: 1903. 25 ills. Cloth.
  (Halewood) **£28 [≈ $50]**

Inebriate Asylum ...
- The history of the first inebriate asylum in the world ... See Turner, J. Edward

Infantile Paralysis ...
- Infantile paralysis in Vermont 1894-1922. Burlington: 1924. *(Rittenhouse)* **$35 [≈ £19]**

Ingen-Housz, John
- Experiments upon vegetables, discovering their great power of purifying the common air in the sun-shine, and of injuring it in the shade and at night. London: for P. Elmsly & H. Payne, 1779. 1st edn. 8vo. Fldg engvd plate. Contemp calf, rebacked.
  (Traylen) **£850 [≈ $1,530]**

Inglis, John
- Bible illustrations from the New Hebrides.

With notices of the progress of the Mission.
London: Nelson, 1890. xi,[i],356 pp. Orig
cloth. Author's inscrptn. (Natural history of
the New Hebrides included).
(Pollak) £25 [≃ $45]

Inglis, K.
- Paget's disease of the nipple and its relation to
surface cancers and precancerous states in
general. 1936. xii,233 pp. 237 text diags.
Light ink & pencil anntns on 2 pp. Cloth,
edges of spine sl worn.
(Whitehart) £18 [≃ $32]

Ingram, A.
- A concise system of mensuration, adapted to
the use of schools. Edinburgh: 1822. x,vi,324
pp. Text diags. Contemp tree calf, rebacked,
spine gilt.   *(Whitehart)* £40 [≃ $72]

Innes, John
- A short description of the human muscles,
arranged as they appear on dissection. New
York: Collins, 1818. 2nd Amer edn, 1st illust.
12mo. x,140,[34] pp. 17 engvd plates. Minor
foxing. Orig bds, uncut, spine chipped,
extremities rubbed.   *(Karmiole)* $85 [≃ £47]

Instructions ...
- Instructions for collecting and preserving
insects ... See Curtis, William

Invalid ...
- The invalid ... See Graves, Richard

Irish, C.W.
- An account of the detonating meteor, of
February 12, 1875. Iowa City: 1875. Lge 4to.
16,11 pp. Lge fldg map, plate. Orig ptd
wraps, rear bottom crnr chewed, sunned,
flaking at spine.   *(Reese)* $100 [≃ £55]

Jaccoud, S.
- The curability and treatment of pulmonary
phthisis. Translated ... New York: 1885. 8vo.
407 pp. Contemp sheep, spine label damaged.
(Rittenhouse) $30 [≃ £16]

Jack, Richard
- Elements of conic section in three books.
Edinburgh: Tho. Wal & Tho. Ruddimans,
1742. 1st edn. 8vo. [iv],xi,331 pp. 9 fldg
engvd plates. Mrbld bds, calf spine.
(Burmester) £85 [≃ $153]

Jackson, Charles T.
- A manual of etherization, containing
directions for the employment of ether,
chloroform and other anaesthetic agents.

Boston: 1861. Lacking front endpaper.
Blindstamped cloth, crnrs worn, hd of spine
chipped.   *(Rittenhouse)* $145 [≃ £80]

Jackson, Chevalier
- Bronchoscopy and esophagoscopy. Phila:
1922. 1st edn. 8vo. 346 pp. 5 plates (4 cold),
over 100 text ills. Cloth. *(Elgen)* $65 [≃ £36]
- Diseases of the air and food passages of
foreign-body origin. Phila: 1936. 1st edn. 4to.
636 pp. 3 cold plates. 2000 ills. Cloth.
(Elgen) $75 [≃ £41]
- The larynx and its diseases. Phila: 1937. 1st
edn. 8vo. 555 pp. 11 cold plates, 210 ills.
Cloth.   *(Elgen)* $60 [≃ £33]
- The life ... an autobiography. New York:
1938. 1st edn, 3rd ptg. x,229 pp. Port frontis,
80 pp plates. Cloth. Author's pres copy, sgnd.
(Elgen) $45 [≃ £25]

Jackson, Clarence M.
- The effects of inanition and malnutrition
upon growth and structure. Phila: [1925]. 1st
edn. Lge 8vo. xii,616 pp. 117 ills. Cloth.
(Elgen) $55 [≃ £30]

Jackson, James
- Essays on various agricultural subjects, and
an account of the Parish of Penecuik ...
Edinburgh: 1833. 1st coll edn. 8vo.
Interleaved with blanks. Contemp calf, spine
gilt. Author's pres copy to his daughter with
inscrptn & a.l.s. from Robt. Scott Moncrieff.
(Hughes) £245 [≃ $441]

Jackson, James C.
- Consumption: how to prevent it, and how to
cure it. Boston: 1862. 8vo. vii,400 pp. Advts.
Orig bds.   *(Rittenhouse)* $35 [≃ £19]

Jackson, James
- Letters to a young physician just entering
upon practice. Boston: 1855. 1st edn, 1st iss.
8vo. iv,344 pp. Errata tipped-in. Orig
embossed cloth, spine ends frayed. Ex lib.
(Elgen) $65 [≃ £36]
- Letters to a young physician just entering
upon practice. Boston: 1855. 1st edn, 2nd iss,
with errata corrected. 8vo. iv,344 pp. Orig
embossed cloth.   *(Elgen)* $50 [≃ £27]
- Memoirs of James Jackson, Jr., M.D. Written
by his father ... Boston: 1841. xi,228 pp.
Some light foxing. Orig blindstamped bds, sl
chipping at hd of spine.
(Rittenhouse) $50 [≃ £27]

Jackson, John Hughlings
- Neurological fragments. London: 1925. 1st
edn. 227 pp. Sgntr on title, sl pencilling.

Cloth.   *(Scientia)* **$250** [≃ £138]
- Selected writings. New York: [1958]. 1st Amer edn. 2 vols. 8vo. 500; 510 pp. 2 frontis. Cloth, dws.   *(Elgen)* **$125** [≃ £69]

Jackson, Robert (1750-1827)
- A systematic view of the formation, discipline, and economy of armies. London: for the author. 1804. 4to. xxxi,347 pp. Contemp bds, rebacked, uncut.
                (Goodrich) **$325** [≃ £180]
- A treatise on the fevers of Jamaica, with some observations on the intermitting fever of America, and an appendix ... on the means of preserving the health of soldiers in hot climates. Phila: 1795. 1st Amer edn. 12mo. Contemp calf, worn. Ex lib.
                (Argosy) **$200** [≃ £111]
- A view of the formation, discipline. and economy of armies. London: Parker ..., 1845. 3rd edn. 8vo. cxxxv,[i], 425,[i] pp. Errata slip. Port frontis (foxed). Half mor, a bit rubbed.
                (Pollak) **£55** [≃ $99]

Jackson, Robert
- The crime doctors. London: [1966]. 1st edn. 8vo. 237 pp. 7 photos. Orig cloth.
                (Argosy) **$30** [≃ £16]

Jacob, Giles
- The compleat court-keeper; or, land-steward's assistant ... London: for B. Lintot ..., 1715. 2nd edn. 8vo. viii,480,[21 index],[3 advts] pp. Sm name stamp on title. Contemp calf.
                (Fenning) **£85** [≃ $153]

Jacob, J.
- Observations on the structure and draught of wheel-carriages. London: 1773. 1st edn. 4to. Half-title, 14 fldg plates. Contemp half calf, mrbld bds, jnts sl cracking.
                (Halewood) **£375** [≃ $675]
- Observations on the structure and draught of wheel-carriages. London: E. & C. Dilly, 1773. 1st edn. 4to. 14 fldg plates. Contemp half calf, respined, orig label.
                (Spelman) **£550** [≃ $990]

Jacobi, Abraham
- Infant diet. New York: 1873. 1st edn. 50 pp. Orig ptd wraps.   *(Scientia)* **$150** [≃ £83]
- The intestinal diseases of infancy and childhood. Detroit: Davis, 1887. 1st edn. 8vo. xv,[1], 301,[3] pp. Stamp on title. Orig cloth.
                (Rootenberg) **$350** [≃ £194]
- A treatise on diphtheria. New York: 1880. 8vo. 252 pp. Orig cloth.
                (Goodrich) **$95** [≃ £52]

Jacobi, Mary Putnam
- Lectures on hysteria, brain-tumor and some other cases of nervous disease. New York: 1888. 1st edn. 216 pp. Sgntr on title. Cloth.
                (Scientia) **$200** [≃ £111]

Jacobs, W.S.
- The student's chemical pocket companion. Phila: for the author, 1802. 1st edn. 12mo. [2],ii, 114,[2] pp. Some scattered staining, perf lib stamp on title. Mod calf. Author's pres inscrptn.   *(Antiq Sc)* **$350** [≃ £194]

Jacoby, George W. & Ralph, J.
- Electricity in medicine. Phila: [1919]. Lge 8vo. xxii,612 pp. 262 ills. Cloth.
                (Elgen) **$50** [≃ £27]

Jaffe, Bernard
- Crucibles. The lives and achievements of the great chemists. New York: Simon & Schuster, 1930. viii,[ii],377,[i] pp. 24 plates. Pub bndg, spine faded.   *(Pollak)* **£20** [≃ $36]

James, Prosser
- The therapeutics of the respiratory passages. New York: 1884. 1st Amer edn. 8vo. vii,316 pp. Text ills. Cloth, sl soiled.
                (Elgen) **$40** [≃ £22]

James, Robert
- A dissertation on fevers, and inflammatory distempers. The eighth edition ... now first added ... a vindication of the fever powder. London: for Francis Newbery, jnr, 1778. 8vo. Engvd port frontis. Contemp polished calf.
                (Quaritch) **$975** [≃ £541]
- A medicinal dictionary. London: 1743-45. 1st edn. 3 vols. Thick folio. Unpaginated, ptd in double column. 63 plates. 3 leaves with sm loss of text, replaced in facsimile on old paper. Mod lea.   *(Scientia)* **$2,000** [≃ £1,111]
- Pharmacopoiea universalis: or, a new universal English dispensatory. London: for J. Hodges, 1747. 8vo. xxxi,[i], 836,[xlviii] pp. Later half calf, 2 lower crnrs with marg tears, half-title & last leaf with some old splashes & some v sm holes. Later half calf.
                (Pollak) **£75** [≃ $135]
- A treatise on canine madness. London: Newberry, 1760. 8vo. vi,264 pp. Light foxing. Old calf, rebacked, crude endpapers.
                (Goodrich) **$495** [≃ £269]

James, William
- The principles of psychology, New York: Henry Holt, 1890. 1st edn. 2 vols. 8vo. xii,689; vi,704 pp. 8 pp pub advts. Num text figs. Previous owners' sgntrs. Orig cloth,

edges sl worn.   *(Rootenberg)* **$650 [≈ £361]**

Jameson, Horatio G.
- A treatise on epidemic cholera. Phila: 1855.
8vo. xvi,286 pp. 19th c cloth, worn.
(Goodrich) **$65 [≈ £36]**

Jameson, Robert
- A mineralogical description of the County of
Dumfries. Edinburgh: 1805. 1st edn. 8vo.
Fldg engvd map, 4 plates. Orig bds, paper
spine, worn, uncut edges.
(Traylen) **£110 [≈ $198]**
- Mineralogy of the Scottish Isles ... and
dissertations upon peat and kelp. Edinburgh:
C. Stewart, 1800. 1st edn. 2 vols. 4to. 2 fldg
engvd maps (1 part cold in outline), 11 engvd
maps & plates (1 fldg), errata leaf. Contemp
mrbld bds, calf spines, gilt.
(Traylen) **£240 [≈ $432]**
- Mineralogy of the Scottish Isles; with
mineralogical observations made in a tour
through ... parts of ... Scotland. Edinburgh:
1800. 2 vols in 1. 4to. 13 maps & plates (3
supplied in Xerox facs). Margs at end of vol
1 weakened by damp. New half calf.
(Wheldon & Wesley) **£195 [≈ $351]**
- An outline of the mineralogy of the Shetland
Isles, and of the Island of Arran. With an
appendix ... observations on peat, kelp, and
coal. Edinburgh: for William Creech, 1798.
Roy 8vo. Engvd plate, 2 maps (1 fldg).
Contemp half calf, gilt spine.
(Traylen) **£150 [≈ $270]**
- Outline of the mineralogy of the Shetland
Islands and the Islands of Arran, with an
appendix on peat, kelp and coal ...
Edinburgh: Creech, 1798. Lge 8vo. 2 engvd
maps, engvd plate. Final leaf stained.
Contemp mrbld bds, uncut, spine renewed.
(Marlborough) **£210 [≈ $378]**

Jameson, Robert, et al.
- Narrative of discovery and adventure in
Africa, from the earliest ages ... with ... the
geology, mineralogy and zoology. Edinburgh:
Cabinet Lib, 1830. 1st edn. Sm 8vo. xv,[1],
492,[4 advts] pp. Addtnl title, fldg map, 7
plates. Contemp roan-backed bds.
(Fenning) **£48.50 [≈ $86]**

Janet, Pierre
- Psychological healing. A historical and
clinical study. Translated from the French ...
London: Allen & Unwin, 1925. 2 vols. 8vo.
698,[ii]; [iv],705-1265, [iii] pp. Pub bndg,
dws.   *(Pollak)* **£60 [≈ $108]**
- Psychological healing. A historical and
clinical study. Translated by E. & C. Paul.

London: 1925. 1st edn in English. 2 vols.
1265 pp. Sm tears in top of spine of each vol.
(Scientia) **$150 [≈ £83]**

Janossy, L.
- Cosmic rays. Oxford: Clarendon Press, 1950.
454 pp. 10 photos. Orig cloth.
(Xerxes) **$35 [≈ £19]**

Jeans, J.H.
- The dynamical theory of gases. Cambridge:
Univ Press, 1904. 1st edn. Tall 8vo.
vi,[2],352 pp. Half-title. Lacking front flyleaf,
lightly browned. Orig cloth.
(Antiq Sc) **$90 [≈ £50]**
- Report on radiation and the quantum theory.
London: 1914. 1st edn. 90 pp. Binder's cloth.
(Weiner) **£60 [≈ $108]**

Jeans, Sir James
- Astronomy and cosmogony. Cambridge:
1928. 1st edn. Lge 8vo. x,420 pp. 16 plates,
diags. Orig cloth, spine & part of back cvr
faded.   *(Weiner)* **£35 [≈ $63]**
- Astronomy and cosmogony. Cambridge:
1929. 2nd edn. 4to. Orig cloth.
(Xerxes) **$30 [≈ £16]**
- Mathematical theory of electricity and
magnetism. Cambridge: 1941. 5th edn. 4to.
652 pp. Orig cloth.   *(Xerxes)* **$35 [≈ £19]**
- Problems of cosmogony and stellar dynamics
... an essay to which the Adams Prize ... for
1917 was adjudged. Cambridge: 1919. Lge
8vo. viii,293 pp. 4 plates, diags. Orig cloth.
(Weiner) **£50 [≈ $90]**
- Science and music. New York & Cambridge:
1937. 1st edn. 8vo. Frontis, ills. Orig cloth.
(Argosy) **$40 [≈ £22]**

Jeffery, Alfred
- Notes on the marine glue. J. Teulon, 1843.
1st edn. 8vo. 16 pp. 4 plates inc frontis.
Disbound.   *(Spelman)* **£60 [≈ $108]**

Jeffries, David
- A treatise on diamonds and pearls in which
their importance is considered; and plain
rules are exhibited for ascertaining the value
of both; and the true method of
manufacturing diamonds. London: 1800. 3rd
edn. xiv,[2],118 pp. 30 plates. Contemp 3/4
calf.   *(Hemlock)* **$300 [≈ £166]**

Jennings, I.H.
- How to photograph microscopic objects. A
manual ... New York: E. & H.T. Anthony,
[1886]. 32,[1] pp. Text half tones & w'cuts.
(Antiq Sc) **$100 [≈ £55]**

Jenyns, L.
- Observations in meteorology ... Being chiefly the results of a meteorological journal kept for 19 years at Swaffham Bulbeck in Cambridgeshire ... 1858. ix,415 pp. New cloth. *(Whitehart)* **£25 [.≈ $45]**

Jervis, W.P.
- The mineral resources of Central Italy ... mines and marble quarries ... mineral springs ... 1868. 8vo. vi,132 pp. Frontis, 3 full-page text ills, 12 fldg tables. Cancelled blind lib stamp on title. Orig cloth, top of spine worn. *(Bickersteth)* **£22 [≈ $39]**

Jesse, George R.
- Evidence. Given before the Royal Commission on Vivisection.L: 1875, preface dated 1876. xii,156 p. Title sl soiled. Cloth, discold. *(Weiner)* **£25 [≈ $45]**

Jevons, William Stanley
- The principles of science: a treatise on logic and scientific method. London: Macmillan, 1874. 1st edn. 2 vols. 8vo. xiv,463; vii,[1],480 pp. Engvd frontis, text diags. Lib stamp & owner's sgntr on titles, lib labels on pastedowns. Orig cloth, faded. *(Rootenberg)* **$550 [≈ £305]**
- The principles of science: a treatise on logic and scientific method. New York: 1874. Special Amer edn. 8vo. 463; 480 pp. Buckram. Ex lib. *(Goodrich)* **$35 [≈ £19]**
- The principles of science: a treatise on logic and scientific method. London: Macmillan, 1877. 2nd edn revsd. Thick 8vo. Frontis. Orig cloth, spine sl soiled. *(Chaucer Head)* **£180 [≈ $324]**
- Studies in deductive logic. A manual for students ... London: Macmillan, 1880. 1st edn. 8vo. xxviii,304,4 advts, 34 advts, [2 advts] pp. Occas pencil anntns. Orig mor-grained cloth, lower inner hinge cracked, spine & crnrs rubbed. *(Pickering)* **$400 [≈ £222]**

Johnson, Charles Pierpoint
- The useful plants of Great Britain ... capable of application as food, medicine, or in the arts and manufactures. London: Robert Hardwicke, n.d. [ca 1862]. Lge 8vo. 324 pp. 25 hand-cold plates. 19th c half green mor, rebacked, orig backstrip laid down. *(Karmiole)* **$200 [≈ £111]**

Johnson, E.C.
- An inquiry into the musical instruction of the blind, in France, Spain and America. London: 1855. 1st edn. 8vo. [iv],42 pp. 6 plates (1 fldg). Some dust marks or spotting. Author's inscrptn on title. Orig cloth, cvrs dull & marked. *(Bow Windows)* **£50 [≈ $90]**

Johnson, James
- The economy of health or the stream of human life from the cradle to the grave ... S. Highley, 1836. 1st edn. 8vo in 4s. viii,220 pp. Plate. Sl discolouration throughout. Orig drab bds, sometime rebacked in green suede, crnrs strengthened. *(Blackwell's)* **£60 [≈ $108]**

Johnson, Theodora
- The Swedish system of physical education: its medical and general aspects. Bristol: John Wright, 1899. 8vo. 79,[i advts] pp. Frontis, 4 plates, 23 text figs. Orig cloth. *(Pollak)* **£25 [≈ $45]**

Johnson, W.B.
- History of the progress and present state of animal chemistry. London: 1803. 3 vols. Ca 1300 pp. Uncut in later lib cloth. Uncut edges of paper a little brittle *(Weiner)* **£160 [≈ $288]**

Johnston, A.K.
- Atlas of astronomy, comprising in 18 plates, a complete set of illustrations of the heavenly bodies ... in attractive colours ... Blackwood: 1856. Sm folio. Orig bds, rebacked. *(Halewood)* **£45 [≈ $81]**

Johnston, James F.W.
- The chemistry of common life. Edinburgh & London: 1854-55. 1st edn. 2 vols. Sm 8vo. viii,352; vi,466 pp. Num ills. 1 or 2 short tears, minor spotting. Orig cloth, dull, inner hinges torn. *(Bow Windows)* **£36 [≈ $64]**
- Experimental agriculture being the results of past and suggestions for future experiments in scientific and practical agriculture. Edinburgh: Blackwood, 1849. 1st edn. 8vo. xvi,266 pp. Advt 1f. Lacking front & rear endpapers. Orig cloth, some sl soiling. *(Karmiole)* **$100 [≈ £55]**
- Experimental agriculture ... Edinburgh: Blackwood, 1849. 1st edn. 8vo. xvi,265 pp. Advt 1f. Orig cloth, backstrip faded. *(Claude Cox)* **£30 [≈ $54]**
- Lectures on agricultural chemistry and geology. With an appendix ... experiments in practical agriculture ... Edinburgh & London: Blackwood, 1844. 3 vols. 8vo. Contemp half calf, mrbld bds, jnts of 1 vol reprd. *(Traylen)* **£50 [≈ $90]**
- Lecture on agricultural chemistry and geology. Blackwood, 1847. 2nd edn. 8vo.

Orig green cloth, faded. *(Gough)* **£30 [≃$54]**

Johnston, Thomas
- General view of the agriculture of the county of Selkirk, with observations. London: W. Bulmer, 1794. 1st edn. 4to. 50 pp, final blank. Half-title. Disbound.
(Claude Cox) **£30 [≃$54]**

Johnston-Lavis, Henry James
- Bibliography of the geology and eruptive phenomena of the more important volcanoes of Southern Italy ... London: 1918. 4to. xxiv,3774 pp. 2 ports. Ex lib.
(Weiner) **£150 [≃$270]**

Johnstone, John
- An account of the most approved method of draining land; according to the system practised by Mr. Joseph Elkington in the County of Warwick. Edinburgh: 1797. 1st ed. 4to. 16 plates. Later bds, cloth spine, uncut.
(Robertshaw) **£40 [≃$72]**
- An account of the mode of draining land, according to the system practised by Mr. Joseph Elkington. London: 1801. 2nd edn, crrctd & enlgd. 8vo. 19 fldg plans. Half lea, gilt back. *(Argosy)* **$150 [≃£83]**

Jokl, Ernst
- The medical aspect of boxing. Pretoria: 1941. 251 pp. 4 plates, 55 ills. Orig pict cloth, rebacked, orig spine laid down.
(Whitehart) **£35 [≃$63]**
- The medical aspect of boxing. Pretoria: 1941. 8vo. 251 pp. 4 plates, ills. Orig pict cloth, rebacked, orig spine laid down.
(Weiner) **£75 [≃$135]**

Jones, C.H.
- Clinical observations on functional nervous disorders. Phila: Lea, 1867. 8vo. 348 pp. Qtr sheep, mrbld bds, rubbed, ex lib.
(Goodrich) **$95 [≃£52]**

Jones, Charles W.
- A series of lectures, on the most approved principles and practice of modern surgery, principally derived from the lectures delivered by Astley Cooper. Boston: 1823. 1st Amer edn. 456 pp. Lea.
(Scientia) **$135 [≃£75]**

Jones, David
- On diseases of the bladder and the prostate, and obscure affections of the urinary organs ... London: 1883. 5th edn. 8vo. xiv,ii,200, [4],[3 advts] pp. Sev text figs. Sl spotting. Orig cloth. *(Bow Windows)* **£48 [≃$86]**

Jones, E. Parry
- Kielland's forceps. 1952. x,212pp. Over 100 text diags. Orig cloth, dw.
(Whitehart) **£30 [≃$54]**

Jones, Ernest
- The life and work of Sigmund Freud. New York: [1953-57]. 1st edn. 3 vols. 8vo. Ports, ills. Cloth, dws. *(Elgen)* **$65 [≃£36]**
- The life and work of Sigmund Freud. New York: 1953-57. One of 250, sgnd. 1st edn. 3 vols. 428; 512; 537 pp. Cloth.
(Scientia) **$250 [≃£138]**
- On the nightmare. London: Hogarth Press, 1931. 1st edn. 8vo. 374 pp. Orig cloth. Ex lib.
(Oasis) **$40 [≃£22]**
- Treatment of the neuroses. London: Bailliere, 1920. 1st edn. 8vo. 288 pp. Some pencilling. Orig cloth. *(Oasis)* **$35 [≃£19]**

Jones, F.W.
- The principles of anatomy as seen in the hand. 1946. 2nd edn. vii,418 pp. Frontis, 144 ills. *(Whitehart)* **£20 [≃$36]**
- Structure and function as seen in the foot. 1943, repr 1946. iv,329 pp. 150 text ills. Cloth marked & sl worn.
(Whitehart) **£20 [≃$36]**

Jones, George Ellis
- Hygiene and war. Washington: Carnegie, 1917. 207,[iii] pp. Wraps.
(Pollak) **£15 [≃$27]**

Jones, Robert
- Artificial fire-works, improved to the modern practice, from the minutest to the higher branches. London: J. Millan, 1766. 2nd edn. 8vo. xxvi, errata, 262 pp. 8 fldg plates. Some faint waterstaining to early lower margs. Rec half calf. *(Spelman)* **£420 [≃$756]**

Jones, W.H.S.
- Malaria and Greek history. To which is added the history of Greek therapeutics ... by E.T. Withington. Manchester: 1909. 8vo. 175 pp. Cloth. *(Goodrich)* **$110 [≃£61]**
- Malaria and Greek history ... the history of Greek therapeutics ... by E.T. Withington. Manchester: Univ Press, 1909. 1st edn. 8vo. Orig blue cloth, spine snagged at hd.
(Chaucer Head) **£40 [≃$72]**
- The medical writings of Anonymus Londinensis. Cambridge: Univ Press, 1947. 8vo. viii,168 pp. Pub bndg.
(Pollak) **£25 [≃$45]**

Jones, William
- An essay on the first principles of natural philosophy ... in four books. Oxford: 1762. 4to. 3ff, 281 pp. 3 plates (2 fldg). Old polished calf, worn, lacking label, front jnt cracked.
(Weiner) **£250 [≈ $450]**

Jordan, R.J.
- Skin diseases and their remedies. London: 1860. xi,283 pp. Rear free endpaper missing, front free endpaper replaced. Orig cloth, spine sl defective at hd & ft.
(Whitehart) **£35 [≈ $63]**

Jordan, W.L.
- The ocean. A treatise on ocean currents and tides, and their causes, demonstrating the system of the world. 1885. 2nd edn. 8vo. Charts, diags, w'cuts. Orig cloth, a little worn.
(Halewood) **£30 [≈ $54]**

Jorpes, J.E.
- Heparin. Its chemistry, physiology and application in medicine. 1939. xi,87 pp. Port frontis, cold plate, 12 text ills. Sgntr on title. Cloth sl worn, binding sl loose at bottom.
(Whitehart) **£18 [≈ $32]**

Joule, James Prescott
- The scientific papers. London: Physical Society of London, 1884-87. 1st edn. 2 vols. 8vo. xix,657; xii,391 pp. Port frontis, num fldg plates, tables, figs, text ills. B'plate on paste-down, previous owner's sgntr. Orig cloth.
(Rootenberg) **$500 [≈ £277]**

Joyce, Frederick
- Practical chemical mineralogy ... methods ... for readily ascertaining the nature and value of ... metallic ores ... London: 1825. 1st edn. 12mo. xii,376 pp, 6,2 pub ctlg ff. Engvd frontis, extra engvd title, errata slip. Contemp bds, rebacked, uncut.
(Offenbacher) **$275 [≈ £152]**

Joyce, Rev. J.
- Letters on nature and experimental philosophy, addressed to a youth settling in the metropolis. London: for Baldwin, Cradock ..., 1821. 2nd edn. Sm 8vo. Fldg engvd frontis, 15 plates. Contemp half russia, mrbld bds.
(Chaucer Head) **£55 [≈ $99]**

'Jude' (pseud.)
- Medicinal and perfumery plants and herbs of Ireland. Dublin: M.H. Gill, 1933. 1st edn. 8vo. xxiii,124 pp. 10 plates (7 cold). Orig cloth, dw.
(Gough) **£35 [≈ $63]**

Jukes, Joseph Beete
- Narrative of the surveying voyage of H.M.S. 'Fly' ... in Torres Strait, New Guinea ... London: Boone, 1847. 1st edn. 2 vols. 8vo. [ii],xii,[ii], 423, 8 advts; 8 advts, vi,[ii], 362 pp. 19 engvd plates, 2 fldg charts. Orig cloth, spines sl faded & rubbed.
(Morrell) **£1,100 [≈ $1,980]**
- The student's manual of geology. Edinburgh: 1857. 1st edn. 8vo. [2],xiii,607 pp. Errata leaf. Some ills. Orig cloth. Author's pres copy to his wife.
(Fenning) **£55 [≈ $99]**
- The student's manual of geology. Edinburgh: 1862. New edn. Thick 8vo. [xx],764,[4 advts] pp. 124 text figs. Sgntr on title, some spotting. Orig embossed cloth, rebacked, orig faded spine laid down.
(Bow Windows) **£45 [≈ $81]**

Justice, J.
- The British gardener's new director. Dublin: 1765. 4th edn. 8vo. [xvi],443,[12] pp. 4 plates. Upper marg of title cut away with loss of 1st line of title. Contemp calf, trifle worn, jnts cracked.
(Wheldon & Wesley) **£40 [≈ $72]**

Kagan, Solomon R.
- Jewish contributions to medicine in America (1656-1934). Boston: 1934. 1st edn. 8vo. xxxi,549 pp. Ports. Cloth.
(Elgen) **$145 [≈ £80]**

The Kaleidoscope
- The Kaleidoscope: or Literary and Scientific Mirror. Liverpool: Egerton Smith, 1818-20. 104 weekly numbers in 2 vols. Folio. All published in folio, after 1820 being in 4to. Contemp qtr calf, mrbld bds.
(C.R. Johnson) **£240 [≈ $432]**

Kanavel, Allen
- Infections of the hand; a guide to the surgical treatment of acute and chronic suppurative processes in the fingers, hand, and forearm. Phila: 1912. 1st edn. 447 pp. Ink underlining on 10 pp. Cloth.
(Scientia) **$150 [≈ £83]**
- Infections of the hand. Phila: 1914. 2nd edn. 8vo. 463 pp. 147 engvs. Cloth.
(Goodrich) **$65 [≈ £36]**
- Infections of the hand. Phila: 1933. 6th edn. Cloth.
(Rittenhouse) **$37.50 [≈ £20]**

Kane, R.
- Elements of chemistry, theoretical and practical, including the most recent discoveries and applications of the science to medicine and pharmacy ... Dublin: 1849. 2nd edn. xx,1069 pp. 230 text ills. Orig cloth,

rebacked, orig spine preserved.
(Whitehart) **£40 [≈ $72]**

Karman, Theodore von
- The collected works. London: Butterworth Scientific, 1956. 4 vols. Lge 8vo. x,531; vi,436; vi,391; vi,480 pp. Num tables, graphs, equations, photo ills. Port frontis vol 1. Orig red cloth, spine gilt.
(Karmiole) **$100 [≈ £55]**

Karpinski, L.C.
- The history of arithmetic. Chicago & New York: 1925. 8vo. 200 pp. Occas anntns in ink. Orig cloth.   *(Weiner)* **£40 [≈ $72]**

Kater, H. & Lardner, D.
- A treatise on mechanics. [L: Lardner's Cabinet Encyc, 1830]. Sm 8vo. ix,342 pp. Engvd vignette title, 21 engvd plates (foxed). Calf, spine gilt dec, mrbld endpapers & edges.
(Bow Windows) **£48 [≈ $86]**

Kato, Genichi
- The further studies on decrementless conduction. Tokyo: 1926. 1st edn. 163 pp. Cvrs somewhat warped.
(Scientia) **$125 [≈ £69]**

Kauffman, Edward
- Pathology for students and practitioners. Translated ... London: Lewis, 1920-29. 3 vols. 8vo. 2452 pp. 1072 pp. Pub bndg, frayed dws.   *(Pollak)* **£35 [≈ $63]**

Kay, William
- Report on the sanitary conditions of Bristol and Clifton. Clifton: January 22, 1844. Folio. 32 pp. Half calf. Author's pres copy.
(Goodrich) **$65 [≈ £36]**

Kaye, G.W.C.
- High vacua. London: Longmans, Green, 1927. 8vo. xii,175.[i] pp. Frontis, 91 ills. Pub bndg.   *(Pollak)* **£30 [≈ $54]**
- The practical applications of X-rays. London: Chapman & Hall, 1922. 8vo. viii,135,[i] pp. 96 ills. Pub bndg.   *(Pollak)* **£25 [≈ $45]**

Kazanjian, V.H. & Coverse, J.M.
- The surgical treatment of facial injuries. Balt: Williams & Wilkins, 1949. 1st edn. 8vo. 574 pp. Num ills. Orig cloth. *(Oasis)* **$60 [≈ £33]**

Keating, John
- Cyclopaedia of the diseases of children, medical and surgical. Phila: 1889. 4 vols. 992; 1066; 1371; 1128 pp. Vol 1 orig cloth; vols 2, 3 & 4, orig lea.   *(Fye)* **$150 [≈ £83]**

Keating, John M. & Coe, Henry C. (eds.)
- Clinical gynecology, medical and surgical for students and practitioners by eminent American teachers. Phila: 1896. Lge thick 8vo. xviii,994 pp. Orig lea.
(Rittenhouse) **$25 [≈ £13]**

Keen, W.W.
- Surgery. Its principles and practice. Phila: 1910-26. 8 vols. Red cloth.
(Goodrich) **$150 [≈ £83]**
- The treatment of war wounds. Phila: 1917. 169 pp. Bds soiled. *(Goodrich)* **$30 [≈ £16]**

Keen, William W.
- Animal experimentation and medical progress. Boston: 1914. 1st edn. 8vo. xix,312 pp. Text ills. Cloth. Ex lib.
(Elgen) **$45 [≈ £25]**

Keill, James
- The anatomy of the humane body abridged. London: Keblewhite, 1698. 1st edn. 12mo. xxii,[ii errata 1f, recto blank],328,[6 table],[2 advts] pp. Sm waterstain in crnr of 1st few gatherings, sev sgntrs on title & verso. Contemp sheep, jnts splitting. Wing K131.
(Pickering) **$450 [≈ £250]**
- Essays on several parts of the animal oeconomy. Fourth edition, to which is added, a dissertation concerning the force of the heart, by James Jurin ... London: for George Strahan, 1738. 8vo. 16 pp pub advts. Antique calf.   *(Traylen)* **£38 [≈ $68]**

Keill, John
- An introduction to the true astronomy. London: J. Buckland, 1769. 6th edn, crrctd. 8vo. [6],xiv,[4], 396,[10] pp. Advt leaf. 28 fldg plates (2 not called for). Contemp calf, sm crack to upper jnt. *(Spelman)* **£95 [≈ $171]**

Keith, Sir Arthur
- The antiquity of man. London: 1925. 2 vols. 8vo. Num ills. Orig cloth. Author's sgnd inscrptn to Dr. Albert Wilson in vol 1, Wilson's sgntr vol 2.
(Bow Windows) **£52 [≈ $93]**
- The antiquity of man. London: Williams & Norgate, 1915. 8vo. xx,519,4 advts pp. Frontis, 189 figs. Pub bndg.
(Pollak) **£25 [≈ $45]**
- The engines of the human body ... Christmas lectures given at the Royal Institution ... 1916-1917. London: Williams & Norgate, 1919. 8vo. xii,284 pp. 2 plates, 47 figs. Pub bndg.   *(Pollak)* **£20 [≈ $36]**
- New discoveries relating to the antiquity of man. Williams & Norgate, 1931. 8vo. 512 pp.

Frontis, 186 ills. Pub bndg.
(Pollak) £16 [≈ $28]

Keith, George Skene
- Tracts on weights, measures and coins. London: Murray, 1791. 4to. Sewn as issued, edges frayed. *(Marlborough)* £85 [≈ $153]

Keith, T.
- An introduction to the theory and practice of plane and spherical trigonometry ... including the theory of navigation. London: Longman, Orme ..., 1839. 7th ed, crrctd & imprvd. xxx,442 pp. 5 fldg plates, tables, 16 pp ctlg. A little pencilling. Contemp cloth.
(Hinchliffe) £35 [≈ $63]

Keith, Thomas
- A new treatise on the use of the globes ... designed for the instruction of youth. London: Longman, Hurst, 1815. 4th edn, crrctd. 8vo. 24,359 pp. Calf, jnts worn.
(Tara) £30 [≈ $54]

Kelland, P.
- Algebra; being a complete and easy introduction to analytic science. Edinburgh: Black, 1871. 1st edn. v,454 pp. Calf, gilt, crnrs a little rubbed. *(Hinchliffe)* £18 [≈ $32]

Kellog, Oliver
- Foundations of potential theory. Murray Unger, 1929. 384 pp. Orig cloth.
(Xerxes) $45 [≈ £25]

Kelly, Howard A.
- Gynecology. New York: 1928. 8vo. 1042 pp. Light dampstaining. Orig cloth.
(Goodrich) $35 [≈ £19]
- Operative gynecology. New York: 1899. 1st edn, 2nd iss. 2 vols. 8vo. Orig cloth, light wear. *(Goodrich)* $75 [≈ £41]

Kelly, Howard A. & Ward, Grant E.
- Electrosurgery. Phila: 1932. 382 ills. A few water spots on front cvr. B'plate.
(Rittenhouse) $50 [≈ £27]

Kelvin, William Thomson, Lord
- Baltimore lectures of molecular dynamics and the wave theory of light ... C.J. Clay, 1904. 8vo. xxi,[1],703 pp. Errata slip. Num diags. Orig cloth. Ex lib. *(Fenning)* £28.50 [≈ $50]
- Popular lectures and addresses. London: 1889-94. 3 vols. 8vo. xi,460; x,599; x,511 pp. Plates, diags. Ex lib, stamp on titles.
(Weiner) £75 [≈ $135]

Kelvin, William Thomson, Lord & Tait, P.G.
- Elements of natural philosophy. Cambridge: 1894. 8vo. vii,295 pp. Diags. Orig cloth.
(Weiner) £20 [≈ $36]

Kempton, P.H.S.
- The industrial application of X-rays. An introduction to the apparatus and methods used ... London: Pitman, 1922. 8vo. xiii,[i],112, [xiv advts] pp. 35 ills. Pub bndg.
(Pollak) £15 [≈ $27]

Kendall, Francis
- A descriptive catalogue of the minerals, and fossil organic remains of Scarborough, and the vicinity. Scarborough: J. Coutas, 1816. Sole edn. 8vo. Cold illust on engvd title, 5 hand-cold plates, fldg engvd plate, half-title, subscribers' list. Orig bds.
(Chaucer Head) £550 [≈ $990]

Kendall, P.F. & Wroot, H.E.
- Geology of Yorkshire. An illustration of the evolution of Northern England. 1924. 1st edn. 3 pts in 1. Thick 8vo. xxii,995 pp. Num ills. A few finger marks & dust spots. Orig cloth, a little faded, sl rubbed.
(Bow Windows) £60 [≈ $108]

Kendo, T.A.
- Treatise on silk and tea culture and other Asiatic industries adapted to the soil and climate of California. San Francisco, Roman, 1870. 11st edn. Sm 8vo. 74,[4 pub advts] pp. Rubber stamp on title. Orig green gilt-stamped cloth. *(Karmiole)* $100 [≈ £55]

Kennedy, John
- A treatise upon planting, gardening. London: 1777. 2nd edn. 2 vols. 8vo. Orig bds, spine worn.lf. *(Wheldon & Wesley)* £35 [≈ $63]
- A treatise upon planting, gardening, and the management of the hot-house ... Dublin: for W. Wilson, 1784. 1st Dublin edn. 8vo. xvi,462,[ii advts] pp. Contemp calf.
(Gough) £125 [≈ $225]

Kennedy, R.
- The book of electrical installations. London: 1914-15. 3 vols. 254; 276; 235 pp. 24 plates, num diags, 3 sectional models. Orig pict cloth, sl waterstain on lower edges.
(Whitehart) £45 [≈ $81]
- Modern engines and power generators. [1905]. 6 vols. Many full-page plates. Orig cloth. *(Whitehart)* £35 [≈ $63]

Kent, N.
- General view of the agriculture of the County of Norfolk. 1794. 1st edn. 4to. Half-title, title, advt leaf, [56] pp. 2 hand-cold aquatint plates. Mod bds, lower crnrs bumped.
(Edwards) **£100 [≈ $180]**

Kentish, T.
- A treatise on a box of instruments and the slide rule, with the theory of trigonometry and logarithms ... Relfe & Fletcher, 1839. 1st edn. iv,100 pp. Fldg frontis, text figs. Paper bds, rebacked with new calf, new endpapers.
(Hinchliffe) **£20 [≈ $36]**

Kerley, Charles G.
- The practice of pediatrics. Phila: 1914. 8vo. 878 pp. Orig cloth. Author's pres copy.
(Goodrich) **$35 [≈ £19]**

Kerr, Richard
- Wireless telegraphy popularly explained. London: 1898. Sm 8vo. xv,111 pp. Port, ills, diags. Orig cloth. A few cuttings tipped-in.
(Weiner) **£50 [≈ $90]**

Kersey, John
- The elements of that mathematical art commonly called algebra ... R.& W. Mount ..., 1717. Folio. [ii],24,323 pp. Engvd port, sl defective at 1 crnr, occas rubber stamps. Ex lib in contemp panelled calf, rec rebacked.
(Blackwell's) **£160 [≈ $288]**

Kettilby, Mary
- A collection of above three hundred receipts in cookery, physick and surgery ... the second edition, to which is added, a second part ... London: for Mary Kettilby, 1719. 2 pts in 1. Half-title. Light marg staining. Contemp panelled calf. *(Traylen)* **£390 [≈ $702]**
- A collection of above three hundred receipts in cookery, physick and surgery ... to which is added, a second part ... London: for Mary Kettilby, 1724. 3rd edn. 2 pts in 1. 8vo. Advt leaf. Contemp panelled calf, rebacked.
(Traylen) **£195 [≈ $351]**

Keyes, A.M.
- The venereal disease including stricture of the urethra. New York: Wood's Library, 1880. 1st edn. 8vo. 348 pp. Text ills. Orig cloth. *(Oasis)* **$45 [≈ £25]**

Keynes, Geoffrey
- A bibliography of Sir Thomas Browne. Oxford: 1968. 2nd edn. 4to. 292 pp. Ills. Orig cloth, stains on top bd, dw.
(Goodrich) **$135 [≈ £75]**

- A bibliography of the writings of William Harvey. Cambridge: 1928. 1st edn. One of 300. Cloth. *(Goodrich)* **$175 [≈ £97]**

Keynes, John Maynard
- The general theory of employment, interest and money. London: 1936. 1st edn. 8vo. A few minor marg finger or other marks, endpapers & edges a little dusted. Orig cloth, d.w. worn. *(Bow Windows)* **£275 [≈ $495]**
- A treatise on money. London: 1935-34. 2 vols. 8vo. prize labels in both volumes. Orig cloth cvrs dull. *(Bow Windows)* **£48 [≈ $86]**
- A treatise on probability ... London: Macmillan & Co ..., 1921. 1st edn. 8vo. [iv],xi,[i],466,[2 advts] pp. Errata slip tipped-in. Sm tear in inner marg of 1 leaf. Ownership inscrptn & pencil anntns of Maurice Cornforth. Orig brown cloth.
(Pickering) **$550 [≈ £305]**
- A treatise on probability. London: Macmillan, 1921. 1st edn. 8vo. Orig brown cloth, sl snag to top of rear hinge, spine sl rubbed. *(Chaucer Head)* **£375 [≈ $675]**
- A treatise on probability. 1921, reprinted 1929. xi,466 pp. Orig cloth, full & sl marked, spine torn. *(Whitehart)* **£35 [≈ $63]**

Kick, Friedrich
- Flour manufacture, a treatise on milling science and practice [with] Recent progress in flour manufacture, supplement to the treatise. London: 1888. 2 vols in 1. 8vo. xvi,191; 76 pp. 28 fldg plates, diags, fldg table. Orig cloth. *(Weiner)* **£50 [≈ $90]**

Kinahan, G. Henry
- Manual of the geology of Ireland. London: Kegan Paul, 1878. 8vo. 444 pp. Ills, map. Orig cloth. *(Emerald Isle)* **£65 [≈ $117]**

King, Henry C.
- The history of the telescope. London: Griffin, 1955. Cr 4to. xvi,456 pp. Author's pres copy. *(Taylor)* **£43 [≈ $77]**

King, Lester S.
- The medical world of the eighteenth century. [Chicago: 1958]. 1st edn. 8vo. xvii,346 pp. Ills. Cloth, dw. *(Elgen)* **$30 [≈ £16]**

Kingdon, J.A.
- Applied magnetism, an introduction to the design of electromagnetic apparatus. London: Alabester, n.d. [late 19th c.]. 292 pp. Line drwngs. Orig cloth. *(Xerxes)* **$40 [≈ £22]**

Kingsbury, J.E.
- The telephone and telephone exchanges, their

invention and development. London: 1915. Thick 8vo. x,558 pp. Plates, ills, diags, tables. Orig cloth. Inscrbd by author.

(Weiner) £75 [≃$135]

Kingsley, C.
- Scientific lectures and essays. London: 1885. 1st edn thus. Sm 8vo. 336 pp. Polished tree calf by Bickers, Banstead School insignia on cvr, jnts just beginning to crack.

(Bow Windows) £35 [≃$63]

Kinns, Samuel
- Moses and geology; or, the harmony of the Bible with science. London: 1882. 2nd edn. 8vo. xxiv,508 pp. Cold frontis, 110 ills (sev full-page). A few ginger marks or spots. Contemp qtr roan, jnts v sl rubbed, t.e.g.

(Bow Windows) £52 [≃$93]

Kirby, Thomas
- Essay on criticism in the course of which the theory of light and the gravity of the earth are particularly considered. London: W. Owen, 1757. 32 pp. Rebound in wraps.

(Xerxes) $150 [≃£83]

Kirby, William
- On the power, wisdom and goodness of God as manifested in the creation of animals ... London: Pickering, 1835. 1st edn. 2 vols. 8vo. cv,406; viii,542 pp. 20 plates. Half lea.

(Weiner) £40 [≃$72]
- On the power, wisdom and goodness of God as manifested in the creation. London: Pickering, 1835. 2nd edn. 2 vols. 8vo. cv,412; viii,542,[2] pp. 20 plates (some foxed). Random spotting. Prize calf, little scraped, hd of spines a little rubbed, 1 jnt cracking.

(Bow Windows) £60 [≃$108]
- On the power, wisdom and goodness of God ... London: Pickering, 1835. 2nd edn. 2 vols. 8vo. cv,412; viii,542 pp. 20 plates. Orig cloth. Generally a bit soiled & worn.

(Weiner) £35 [≃$54]

Kirchhoff, Gustav
- Researches on the solar spectrum, and the spectra of the chemical elements. Cambridge & London: Macmillan, 1862-63. 1st edn in English. 4to. iv,36; 16 pp. 4 double-page cold litho plates, engvd plate. B'plates removed. Orig ptd bds.   *(Antiq Sc)* $900 [≃£500]

Kirkbride, Thomas
- On the construction, organization and general arrangements of hospitals for the insane. With some remarks on insanity and its treatment. Phila: 1880. 2nd edn, 320 pp. 23 plates.

Cloth, spine extremities rubbed.

(Scientia) $300 [≃£166]

Kirkpatrick, James
- The analysis of inoculation: comprizing the history, theory, and practice of it ... The second edition corrected, J. Buckland ..., 1761. xii,xxxii, 429,[i errata],xv pp. Some dampstaining & foxing throughout. Contemp sprinkled calf.   *(Blackwell's)* £180 [≃$324]

Kirwan, Richard
- An essay on the analysis of mineral waters. London: for D. Bremner, 1799. 1st edn. 8vo. viii,279 pp. 7 fldg tables. Contemp calf, rebacked. Franklin Institute Lib b'plate.

(Offenbacher) $450 [≃£250]
- The manners most advantageously applicable to the various sorts of soils ... London: for Vernor & Hood, 1796. 4th edn. 8vo. Title sl soiled. New wraps.   *(Stewart)* £75 [≃$135]

Kitchiner, William
- The cook's oracle. Containing receipts for plain cookery ... containing also a complete system of cookery for Catholic families. London: for Cadell, 1829. 12mo. xix,512,[1], [6 advts] pp. Orig bds, uncut, spine badly chipped.   *(Karmiole)* $125 [≃£69]
- The traveller's oracle; or, maxims for locomotion containing precepts for ... preserving the health of travellers ... London: Henry Colburn, 1827. 2nd edn. 2 vols. 8vo. viii,264; viii,336 pp. Engvd plates of music. Contemp calf, rebacked, crnrs reprd.

(Claude Cox) £90 [≃$162]

Kitto, John
- The lost senses. Deafness. Blindness. London: Charles Knight, 1845. 1st edn. 2 series in 1 vol. 12mo. 206; 254 pp. Half calf.

(Oasis) $50 [≃£27]

Kleen, Emil A.G.
- Massage and medical gymnastics. Translated ... London: Churchill, 1918. xiv,618 pp. 182 ills. Orig cloth, front hinge weak.

(Pollak) £20 [≃$36]

Klein, E. & Smith, E. Noble
- Atlas of histology. London: 1880. 1st edn. 4to. 448 pp. 48 cold plates. Sm stamp on each plate verso & title verso. Half lea, mrbld bds.

(Scientia) $275 [≃£152]
- Atlas of histology. London: Smith, Elder, 1880. Folio. x,iv, 448,[ii advts] pp. 48 cold plates. Occas faint foxing, 1 plate loose & a little dusty at edges. Half calf, a little rubbed, front bd marked.   *(Pollak)* £40 [≃$72]

Klein, M.
- The psycho-analysis of children. London: Intnl Psycho-Anal Lib, 1932. 1st edn in English. 8vo. 396 pp. Orig green cloth, a little marked & cockled.
(Bow Windows) £48 [≃ $86]

Knight, E.H.
- The practical dictionary of mechanics .... [with] Supplement. London: [1877-84]. 4 vols. 8v0. viii,2831; viii,960 pp. 129 plates (sev fldg, 1 cropped), num ills. Occas light foxing. Orig cloth.   *(Weiner)* £150 [≃ $270]

Knott, C.G.
- Life and scientific work of Peter Guthrie Tait. Supplementing the two volumes of Scientific Papers published in 1898 and 1900. Cambridge: 1911. Lge 4to. ix,379 pp. 5 plates. Orig cloth, front cvr sl stained.
(Whitehart) £35 [≃ $63]
- The physics of earthquake phenomena. London: 1908. 8vo. xii,283 pp. Plates, diags. Ex lib with stamps, cloth sl discold.
(Weiner) £30 [≃ $54]

Knowles Middleton, W.E.
- A history of the thermometer and its use in meteorology. Balt: John Hopkins Press, 1966. 1st edn. 4to. Frontis, plates, text figs. Pict dw.
(Chaucer Head) £32 [≃ $57]

Knox, Robert
- Great artists and anatomists; a biographical and philosophical study. London: 1852. 8vo. 213 pp. Cloth.   *(Goodrich)* $95 [≃ £52]
- A manual of artistic anatomy, for the use of sculptors, painters, and amateurs. London: 1852. xxv,175 pp. Ills. Orig cloth, shaken.
(Weiner) £40 [≃ $72]
- Radiography and radio-therapeutics. New York: 1919. 3rd edn. 2 vols. 606 pp. 93 plates (mainly X-rays), num text ills. Orig cloth.
(Oasis) $50 [≃ £27]

Knox, Robert (1791-1862)
- The anatomy of the bones of the human body ... a new edition, by R. Knox, M.D. ... Edinburgh: Edward Mitchell, 1829. 4to. Title, advt leaf, 32 plate, each with explanatory text. Orig cloth, rebacked preserving orig spine & endpapers.
(Bickersteth) £115 [≃ $207]
- Engravings of the cardiac nerve ... with descriptions ... translated by ... Dr. Knox. Edinburgh: for Maclachlan & Stewart, 1832. 3rd edn. 4to. 4 pp. 23 engvd plates, many part cold, each with explanatory text. Light spotting. Orig cloth, spine worn.

(Bickersteth) £135 [≃ $243]
- Plates of the arteries of the human body ... translated by Dr Knox. Edinburgh: for Maclachlan & Stewart, 1831. 2nd edn. 4to. 32 engvd plates, part cold, each with letterpress. Light spotting. Uncut in orig cloth, defective at hd & ft of spine.
(Bickersteth) £125 [≃ $225]

Kobell, Franz von
- Instructions for the discrimination of minerals by simple chemical tests. Glasgow: Griffin, 1841. 1st edn in English. 8vo. 51 pp. Mod half calf.   *(Oasis)* $40 [≃ £22]

Koch, Robert
- Investigations into the etiology of traumatic infective diseases. London: 1880. 1st English translation. 101 pp. Orig cloth.
(Fye) $250 [≃ £138]

Kohlrausch, F.
- An introduction to physical measurements. With appendices on absolute electrical measurements. Translated ... London: Churchill, 1883. 2nd edn. 8vo. xi,[ii],344, xvi ctlg pp. 36 text figs. Orig cloth.
(Pollak) £45 [≃ $81]
- An introduction to physical measurements. Translated ... London: 1873. 8vo. xii,249 pp. A few outer leaves foxed. Contemp prize calf, gilt, by Maclehose, emblem of University of Glasgow on cvr & spine.
(Bow Windows) £45 [≃ $81]

Kolmer, John
- Infection, immunity and specific therapy, with special reference to immunological technic. Phila: Saunders, 1915. 1st edn. 8vo. 899 pp. 143 ills, many in color. Orig cloth.
(Oasis) $35 [≃ £19]

Kolmer, John A.
- Penicillin therapy including tyrothricin and other antibiotic therapy. New York: 1945. 8vo. xv,302 pp. Ills. Orig cloth.
(Weiner) £25 [≃ $45]

Koning, D.A. Wittop
- Art and pharmacy. A collection of plates from the Netherlands Pharmaceutical Calendar. Deventer: Ysel Press, 1952-58. 2 vols. 4to. 84 cold plates with explanatory text. Vol 2 title sl creased. Orig cloth, spiral bndg.
(Pollak) £45 [≃ $81]

Kopetsky, Samuel J.
- Otologic surgery. New York: 1925. 1st edn. Lge 8vo. xvi,539 pp. 4 cold plates, num ills,

charts. Cloth. Author's pres copy.
(Elgen) **$40 [≈ £22]**

Krafft-Ebing, R. von
- Psychopathia sexualis, with especial reference to contrary sexual instinct ... Phila & London: 1893. 8vo. xiv,436,[32 advts] pp. Some foxing. Orig cloth, cvrs a little rubbed & marked. *(Bow Windows)* **£40 [≈ $72]**
- Psychopathia sexualis, with especial reference to contrary sexual instinct ... Phila: 1893. 1st edn in English. 8vo. xiv,435 pp. 2 leaves loose, blank crnr of 1 torn away. Orig cloth.
(Weiner) **£50 [≈ $90]**

Kramers, H.A. & Holst, Helge
- The atom and the Bohr theory of its structure ... with a foreword by Sir Ernest Rutherford. London: Gyldendal, 1923. 8vo. xii,210,[ii] pp. 2 cold plates, 34 text figs. Pub bndg.
(Pollak) **£30 [≈ $54]**
- The atom and the Bohr theory of its structure. An elementary presentation. 1923. xiii,210 pp. Frontis, 2 cold plates, 34 text figs. Cloth. *(Whitehart)* **£35 [≈ $63]**

Kreig, Margaret B.
- Green medicine. The search for plants that heal. Chicago: Rand McNally, 1964. 8vo. 462,[ii] pp. 24 plates. Pub bndg, dw.
(Pollak) **£25 [≈ $45]**

Krogh, August
- The anatomy and physiology of capillaries. New Haven: 1922. 1st edn. 276 pp. Cloth.
(Scientia) **$100 [≈ £55]**
- The anatomy and physiology of capillaries. New Haven: 1922. 1st edn. 8vo. xvii,276 pp. Ills. Cloth. *(Elgen)* **£85 [≈ £47]**
- The anatomy and physiology of capillaries. New Haven: 1929. Revsd & enlgd edn. 8vo. xiii,422 pp. Ills. Cloth. *(Elgen)* **£55 [≈ £30]**
- The respiratory exchange of animals and man. London: 1916. 1st edn. 173 pp. Ex lib, perf stamp on title, white ink on front bd.
(Scientia) **$50 [≈ £27]**

Kronfeld, Robert
- Kronfeld on gliding and soaring. The story of motorless human flight. Translated ... London: Hamilton, n.d. [ca 1932]. 8vo. xiv,[ii],379, [i] pp. Frontis, 93 plates, 31 text figs. Pub bndg. *(Pollak)* **£30 [≈ $54]**

Kuchenmeister, F.
- On animal and vegetable parasites of the human body. Translated ... London: Sydenham Soc, 1857. 2 vols. 8vo. Orig cloth, worn. *(Goodrich)* **$85 [≈ £47]**

Kuhne, Frederick, N.Y. Police Department
- The finger print instructor. New York: 1916. 8vo. vii,155 pp. Frontis, 11 fldg plates in pocket, plates, ills, diags. Orig gilt-dec green cloth. *(Weiner)* **£18 [≈ $32]**

Kyan, John Howard
- On the elements of light, and their identity with those of matter, radiant and fixed. London: Longman ..., 1838. 1st edn. 8vo. xiv,130 pp. Hand-cold engvd frontis, 3 engvd plates (1 hand-cold). Orig cloth.
(Rootenberg) **$250 [≈ £138]**

Kyle, Thomas
- Treatise on the management of peach and nectarine trees; either in forcing houses, or on hot and common walls. Edinburgh: for the author, 1787. 2nd edn, enlgd & imprvd. 128 pp. Fldg plate. lea. *(Xerxes)* **$175 [≈ £97]**

La Wall, C.H.
- The curious lore of drugs and medicines. Garden City, New York: 1927. 1st edn. Thick 8vo. Frontis, plates. Orig cloth, gilt. Ex lib.
(Hughes) **£16 [≈ $28]**
- The curious lore of drugs and medicines. Garden City, New York: 1927. Orig cloth.
(Weiner) **£30 [≈ $54]**
- Four thousand years of pharmacy, an outline history of pharmacy and the allied sciences. Phila & London: 1927. Thick 8vo. xv,665 pp. 64 plates. Lacking front endpaper. Orig cloth.
(Weiner) **£30 [≈ $54]**

Labaraque, A.G.
- Instructions and observations concerning the use of the chlorides of soda and lime. New Haven: Storer, 1840. 3rd edn. Translated. 30 pp. Sm piece torn from lower crnr last 2 leaves. Orig wraps. *(Oasis)* **$35 [≈ £19]**

Labat, Gaston
- Regional anesthesia: its technic and clinical application. Phila: Saunders, 1922. 1st edn. 496 pp. Ills. Orig cloth. *(Oasis)* **$100 [≈ £55]**

Lacroix, S.F.
- An elementary treatise on the differential and integral calculus. Translated from the French. Cambridge: for J. Deighton, 1816. 1st English edn. 8vo. 5 fldg plates. Contemp half calf, gilt, gilt spine.
(Traylen) **£450 [≈ $810]**
- An elementary treatise on the differential and integral calculus. Translated from the French. Cambridge: 1816. 1st English edn. Thick 8vo. viii,720 pp. 5 fldg plates. Occas

old ink anntns, a few leaves sl foxed. Contemp half calf, worn, front jnt cracked.
(Weiner) **£100 [≈ $180]**

Ladenburg, A.
- Lectures on the history of the development of chemistry since the time of Lavoisier. Translated ... Edinburgh: 1900. 8vo. xvi,373 pp. A few marg pencil anntns. Orig cloth, v sl wear.   *(Weiner)* **£25 [≈ $45]**

Ladies' Indispensable Assistant ...
- Ladies' indispensable assistant ... a companion for the sister, mother, and wife ... a great variety of valuable recipes, forming a complete system of family medicine ... New York: 1851. 2 parts in 1. vi,72; [vi],48, [121]-136 pp. Old waterstaining. Orig cloth.
(Karmiole) **$65 [≈ £36]**

Laennec, R.T.H.
- A treatise on diseases of the chest, and on mediate auscultation. Translated ... by John Forbes ... New York: 1823. 1st Amer edn. 8vo. 8 plates. Orig lea cvrs scuffed, hinges weakening.   *(Rittenhouse)* **$600 [≈ £333]**
- A treatise on diseases of the chest ... described according to their anatomical characters, and their diagnosis established ... by means of acoustick instruments ... Phila: James Webster, 1823. 1st Amer edn. 8vo. 319 pp. 8 plates. Contemp calf.
(Hemlock) **$400 [≈ £222]**
- A treatise on diseases of the chest ... London: Underwood, 1827. 2nd English edn, greatly enlgd. 8vo. Engvd frontis (sl discold), 8 plates. Contemp half calf, mrbld bds, rebacked.   *(Chaucer Head)* **£350 [≈ $630]**
- A treatise on diseases of the chest ... Translated ... by John Forbes ... New York: 1838. 8vo. xlviii,782 pp. Some foxing inc on title. Orig lea cvrs worn, rear cvrs almost detchd.   *(Rittenhouse)* **$175 [≈ £97]**

Lakin, Thomas
- The valuable receipts of ... in the manufacture of porcelain earthenware and iron stone china ... improvements in ... glass staining and painting. Leeds: 1824. 4to. vii,86 pp. Title grubby & partly detached, margs grubby. Old cloth-backed mrbld bds.
(Weiner) **£325 [≈ $585]**

Lamb, Horace
- The dynamics theory of sound. London: Arnold, 1910. 1st edn. 8vo. viii,303 pp. Text figs. Orig cloth.   *(Antiq Sc)* **$100 [≈ £55]**
- Hydrodynamics. Cambridge: Univ Press, 1895. 1st edn. 8vo. xviii,[1 errata],604 pp. Orig cloth.   *(Antiq Sc)* **$225 [≈ £125]**

Lambe, William
- Water and vegetable diet in consumption, scrofula, cancer, asthma, and other chronic diseases ... showing the superiority of the farinacea and fruits to animal food ... New York: Fowlers & Wells, [1850]. 8vo. viii, 9-258, 8 ctlg pp. Light staining. Ptd wraps.
(Hemlock) **$70 [≈ £38]**

Lamme, Benjamin G.
- Electrical engineering papers. East Pittsburgh: Westinghouse, 1919. 8vo. 773 pp, ills, diags. Cloth.   *(Weiner)* **£40 [≈ $72]**

Lancereaux, E.
- A treatise on syphilis: historical and practical. Translated ... London: 1868. 2 vols. 8vo. 405; 379 pp. Blindstamped cloth.
(Rittenhouse) **$50 [≈ £27]**

Lanchester, F.W.
- The flying-machine from an engineering standpoint. London: 1916. 8vo. viii,135 pp. Diags. Orig cloth. Pres copy.
(Weiner) **£60 [≈ $108]**

Landolt, H.
- Handbook of the polariscope and its practical applications. Translated ... 1882. 1st edn. xvi,262 pp. 57 ills. Endpapers & half-title sl holed. Orig cloth.   *(Whitehart)* **£38 [≈ $68]**

Langford, T.
- Plain and full instructions to raise all sorts of fruit-trees that prosper in England. London: 1696. 2nd edn, revsd & enlgd. 8vo. [xxx],220,[6] pp. 2 plates. Contemp calf, trifle worn.   *(Wheldon & Wesley)* **£140 [≈ $252]**

Langham, William
- The garden of health: containing the sundry rare and hidden vertues and properties of all kinds of simples and plants. London: Thomas Harper, 1633. 2nd edn. 4to. Title strengthened, lacking final blank, final leaf of index & fldg table. Contemp calf, rebacked.
(Stewart) **£225 [≈ $405]**

Langie, A.
- Cryptography. London: 1922. viii,192 pp. Fldg chart, diags. Orig cloth, stabmarks on front cvr.   *(Weiner)* **£25 [≈ $45]**

Langley, Samuel Pierpont
- The 1900 Solar Eclipse Expedition of the Astrophysical Observatory of the Smithsonian Institution. Washington: 1904. Folio. 26 pp text. 22 plates. Later qtr cloth.
(Argosy) **$100 [≈ £55]**

- Experiments in aerodynamics. Washington: 1902. 2nd edn. Folio. 115 pp. 10 full-page plates. Orig cloth, sl worn.
(Whitehart) **£40 [≈ $72]**
- Researches on solar heat and its absorption by the earth's atmosphere, a report of the Mount Whitney expedition. Washington: 1884. 4to. 242 pp. Frontis, map, 21 plates (some fldg), diags. Orig cloth.   *(Weiner)* **£40 [≈ $72]**

Lankester, E. Ray
- The advancement of science. Occasional essays and addresses. London: Macmillan, 1890. 1st edn. 8vo. vi,[2],387 pp. Lib blindstamp on title. Orig cloth.
(Antiq Sc) **$45 [≈ £25]**
- The advancement of science. Occasional essays and addresses. London: Macmillan, 1890. 8vo. vi,[2],387, [iv],59,[i] pp. 23 figs. Pub bndg.   *(Pollak)* **£25 [≈ $45]**

Lankester, Edwin (ed.)
- The correspondence of John Ray: consisting of selections from the philosophical letters ... and original letters ... in the British Museum. London: Ray Soc, 1848. 8vo. xvi,502 pp. Frontis, plate. Orig cloth, faded, rebacked, old spine relaid.   *(Pollak)* **£60 [≈ $108]**
- Memorials of John Ray. Consisting of his life ... biographical and critical notices ... With his itineraries. London: Ray Soc, 1846. 8vo. xii,220 pp. Tinted litho frontis. Orig cloth, faded, recased.   *(Pollak)* **£50 [≈ $90]**

Laplace
- Elementary illustrations of the celestial mechanics ... See Young, Thomas

Lardner, Dionysius
- Popular lectures on science and art: delivered in the principal cities and towns of the United States. 1846. 2 vols. Stamp on a few pages & edges. Old sheep, rubbed. *(Allen)* **$50 [≈ £27]**
- Popular lectures on science and art. New York: Greeley, 1846. 1st edn. 2 vols. 568; 806 pp (erratic pagination but complete). half calf, sl worn.   *(Oasis)* **$50 [≈ £27]**
- The steam engine familiarly explained and illustrated ... London: for Taylor & Walton, 1836. 6th edn, crrctd & enlgd. Cr 8vo. 12 plates, many text cuts. Contemp mor.
(Stewart) **£120 [≈ $216]**

Larmor, Joseph
- Aether and matter. A development of the dynamical relations of the aether to material systems on the basis of the atomic constitution of matter. Cambridge: Univ Press, 1900. 8vo. xxviii,365,[i] pp. Text figs.

Orig cloth.   *(Pollak)* **£100 [≈ $180]**
- Aether and matter. A development of the dynamical relations of the aether to material systems ... Cambridge: 1900. 8vo. xxviii,365 pp. Diags. Orig cloth, uncut.
(Weiner) **£50 [≈ $90]**

Larner, E.T.
- Practical television. With a foreword by John L. Baird. London: Benn, 1928. 8vo. xiv,[ii], 18-175,[i] pp. Frontis, 97 ills. Pub bndg.
(Pollak) **£45 [≈ $81]**

Larrey, Dominique
- Memoirs of military surgery, and campaigns of the French Army, on the Rhine, in Corsica, Catalonia ... Poland, Spain and Austria. Balt: Joseph Cushing, 1814. 1st Amer edn, sole edn in English. 2 vols. 8vo. 8ff, xxiii,415 pp; 4ff,434 pp. Contemp calf.
(Hemlock) **$750 [≈ £416]**

Lashley, K.S.
- Brain mechanism and intelligence. Chicago: 1929. 8vo. 186 pp. 11 plates. Text dampstained. Cloth. *(Goodrich)* **$55 [≈ £30]**

Lassek, A.M.
- Human dissection. Its drama and struggle. Springfield: 1958. 8vo. 312 pp. Lacking front blank. Orig cloth. *(Goodrich)* **$45 [≈ £25]**

Latham, John
- Facts and opinions concerning diabetes. London: for John Murray, 1811. 1st edn. 8vo. Lge uncut copy in later half calf.
(Quaritch) **$350 [≈ £194]**

Lathrop, W.G.
- The brass industry in Connecticut ... Shelton, Conn: 1909. 8vo. 143 pp. Ports. One page of index torn out. Orig cloth.
(Weiner) **£25 [≈ $45]**

Laundry, Samuel Linn
- Table of quarter-squares of all integer numbers, up to 100,000 by which the product of two factors may be found ... London: C. & E. Layton, 1856. Lge 8vo. xxviii,214 pp. Orig cloth, rebacked. *(Spelman)* **£30 [≈ $54]**

Laurence, John
- The fruit-garden kalendar ... the art of managing the fruit-garden ... appendix on the usefulness of the barometer. London: for Bernard Lintot, 1718. 1st edn. 8vo. Fldg frontis, half-title, 3 pp ctlg. Mod wraps.
(Stewart) **£85 [≈ $153]**
- A new system of agriculture ... a complete

body of husbandry and gardening ... Tho. Woodward, 1726. 1st edn. Folio. [xxiv],456 pp. Engvd frontis, 2 plates. Occas light soiling. Contemp panelled calf, rubbed, jnts beginning to split.
(Frew Mackenzie) **£250 [≃ $450]**

- A new system of agriculture ... Tho. Woodward, 1726. Folio. [xxiv],456 pp. Frontis, 2 plates. Contemp panelled calf, rubbed, crnrs worn newly rebacked.
(Blackwell's) **£135 [≃ $243]**

- A new system of agriculture ... in five books ... Dublin: 1727. Folio. Engvd frontis, 2 plates. Old calf, new spine.
(Halewood) **£150 [≃ $270]**

Laurie, J.
- Homeopathic domestic medicine. New York: 1846. 3rd Amer edn. 8vo. xxx,438 pp. Title foxed & partly detchd. Half mor, mrbld bds, upper hinge a little loose, sides & edges v worn.   *(Rittenhouse)* **$35 [≃ £19]**

Lavater, Johann Caspar
- Essays on physiognomy. London: 1789. 1st English translation. 3 vols. 241; 324; 314 pp. 360 engvs. Lea, rebacked.
(Fye) **£500 [≃ £277]**

- Essays on physiognomy. Boston: Spotswood & West, [1794]. 1st Amer edn. 12mo. [4],272 pp. Engvd title, 7 engvd plates. Light browning. Contemp calf, front jnt cracked, rear jnt partially so. *(Antiq Sc)* **$140 [≃ £77]**

- Essays on physiognomy. London: H.D. Symonds, 1797. 4 vols. 8vo. Num plates. Some stamps. Contemp calf, rec rebacked.
(Waterfield's) **£250 [≃ $450]**

- Essays on physiognomy. London: Tegg, 1855. 9th edn. 508 pp. 80 engvd plates. Contemp calf, rebacked, orig spine laid down.   *(Oasis)* **$100 [≃ £55]**

- Physiognomy: or the corresponding analogy between the conformation of the features and the ruling passions of the mind. London: n.d. [ca 1795]. 8vo. [10],280 pp. Frontis. 4 engvd plates. Calf, worn. *(Goodrich)* **$55 [≃ £41]**

Laveran, A.
- Paludism. London: New Sydenham Soc, 1893. 1st English edn. 8vo. 197 pp. 6 plates (4 cold, all with minimal dampstaining on lower edge). Orig cloth. *(Oasis)* **$30 [≃ £16]**

- Paludism. London: New Sydenham Soc, 1893. 1st English edn. 8vo. 197 pp. 6 plates. Orig cloth. *(Goodrich)* **$95 [≃ £52]**

Lavoisier, Antoine
- Elements of chemistry in a new systematic order ... Edinburgh: Creech, 1799. 4th edn in

English. 8vo. 592 pp. 13 fldg engvd plates (moderately foxed). New polished mor. Addtnl 19th c engvd port of Lavoisier, 2 b'plates inc 1 armorial. *(Oasis)* **$600 [≃ £333]**

Lawrence, Charles
- History of the Philadelphia almshouses and hospitals from the beginning of the eighteenth to the end of the nineteenth centuries ... 1905. 1st edn. Lge 8vo. 398 pp. Frontis, 20 plates. Cloth.   *(Elgen)* **$125 [≃ £69]**

Lawrence, D.H.
- Psychoanalysis and the unconscious. New York: 1921. 1st edn. 8vo. 120 pp. Orig paper-cvrd bds, 1 inch section of back jnt chewed.
(Elgen) **$50 [≃ £27]**

Lawrence, J. & Potts, G.
- Aneurysms and arteriovenous anomalies of the brain. Diagnosis and treatment. New York: 1965. 8vo. 463 pp. Orig cloth.
(Goodrich) **$75 [≃ £41]**

Lawrence, John
- The clergy-man's recreation: shewing the pleasure and profit of the art of gardening. London: B. Lintott, 1714. 1st edn. 8vo. [12],83,1 pub advts pp. Engvd frontis, w'cut diag in text. Light offsetting on title. Mod calf.   *(Rootenberg)* **$750 [≃ £416]**

Lawrence, Richard
- The complete farrier, and British sportsman ... structure and animal economy of the horse ... diseases ... dogs ... For Thomas Kelly, [1816]. 1st edn. 4to. 518,[6] pp. Addtnl engvd title, 14 engvd plates. Contemp half calf.
(Fenning) **£75 [≃ $135]**

Lawrence, Thomas
- Mercurius centralis: or, a discourse of subterranel cockle, muscle, and oyster-shels ... London: for J. Collins ..., 1664. 1st edn. 12mo. [x],94 pp. Some side-notes cropped. 18th c calf, rather rubbed. The Britwell Court copy. Wing L689D.
(Pickering) **$850 [≃ £472]**

Lawrence, Sir William
- A treatise on the diseases of the eye. Bohn, 1844. 3rd edn, revsd, crrctd & enlgd. 8vo. xv,820 pp. Sl spotting. Uncut & partly unopened in orig blind-dec cloth, lettered in gilt.   *(Frew Mackenzie)* **£85 [≃ $153]**

- A treatise on the diseases of the eye. Phila: 1843. 2nd Amer edn. 778 pp. Lea.
(Scientia) **$95 [≃ £52]**

Lawrence, William
- Lectures on physiology, zoology and the natural history of man, London: Benbow, 1822. 1st edn, 2nd printing. 8vo. 500 pp. 12 engvd plates (some fldg with sm marg tears). Qtr calf, mrbld bds. *(Oasis)* **$200 [≈£111]**
- Lectures on physiology, zoology and the natural history of man, London: 1822. 1st edn. 8vo. 500 pp. 7 engvd plates. Rec cloth. *(Goodrich)* **$150 [≈£83]**
- A treatise on hernia. London: for J. Callow, 1807. 1st edn. 8vo. xvi,314,[1] pp. 3 fldg engvd plates. Paper browned & brittle with tears in 6 or 7 leaves, 1 reprd, with loss of a few letters on 3 leaves. Uncut in contemp mrbld bds, rebacked. *(Pickering)* **$200 [≈£111]**

Lawson, George
- Diseases and injuries of the eye: their medical and surgical treatment. London: Renshaw, 1877. 3rd edn. xii,412 pp. 97 w'engvs plus test types. Contemp half calf. *(Pollak)* **£50 [≈$90]**

Laycock, Thomas
- Lectures on the principles and methods of medical observation and research. Phila: 1857. 8vo. 209 pp. Bds rubbed. *(Goodrich)* **$75 [≈£41]**

Le Clerc, S.
- Practical geometry: or, a new and easy method of treating that art. London: T. Bowles, 1727. 3rd edn. Sm 8vo. [2],195,6 index pp. 82 engvd plates. Front endpaper stained. Rebound in calf. *(Spelman)* **£220 [≈$396]**

Leadbetter, Charles
- Mechanick dialling: or, the new art of shadows ... added ... best and most approved methods of painting sun dials. London: Edward Wicksteed, 1737. 1st edn. 8vo. xvi,193,[i] pp. 12 fldg plates. Contemp calf, rebacked, crnrs reprd. *(Spelman)* **£280 [≈$504]**
- The Royal gauger; or gauging made perfectly easy ... London: 1755. 4th edn. 8vo. xviii,218; 209-446, 481-510 pp (without apparent loss). 2 cold plates (1 fldg to 3 ft), 5 other fldg plates, 2 fldg vouchers. Dust marks. Sm paper fault in 3 ff. Rec half calf. *(Bow Windows)* **£110 [≈$198]**

Leaming, James R.
- Contributions to the study of the heart and lungs. New York: 1887. 8vo. vi,300 pp. Ex lib. *(Rittenhouse)* **$20 [≈£11]**

Lean, Thomas
- Historical statement of the improvements made in the duty performed by the steam engines in Cornwall. London: Camborne printed, 1839. 8vo. vii,152 pp. Tables, 1 fldg. Orig cloth, paper label. *(Weiner)* **£60 [≈$108]**

Lectures on Chemistry ...
- Outlines of the lectures on chemistry delivered in the College of Physicians and Surgeons ... See Torrey, John

Lee, Edwin
- Observations on the principal medical institutions and practice of France, Italy, Germany ... cases from hospital practice ... an appendix on animal magnetism and homoeopathy. Phila: 1837. 1st Amer edn. 8vo. 102 pp. New cloth. *(Goodrich)* **$85 [≈£47]**
- Observations on the principal medical institutions and practice of France, Italy, Germany ... Phila: 1837. 8vo. 102 pp. Occas v light foxing. New buckram. *(Rittenhouse)* **$35 [≈£19]**

Lee, George J.
- The voice: its artistic production, development, and preservation. Dublin: 1870. 2nd edn. 4to. [2],iv,[6], [2 blank],130,[2 blank] pp. Frontis, 4 plates. Contemp green mor, gilt, a.e.g., heavily rubbed. *(Fenning)* **£85 [≈$153]**

Lee, James
- An introduction to botany, an explanation of the theory of that science ... London: J. & R. Tonson, 1765. 2nd edn. 8vo. xv,iv,479, [12] pp. 12 engvd plates. Contemp gilt-panelled calf. Ex lib William Constable with his b'plate. *(Gough)* **£115 [≈$207]**
- An introduction to botany ... the second edition, to which is added, a glossary. London: J. & R. Tonson, 1765. 8vo. xvi,iv, 1-331; 449-479 pp. Contemp sprinkled calf, backstrip gilt, jnts beginning to crack. *(Blackwell's)* **£55 [≈$99]**
- An introduction to botany ... London: 1794. 5th edn, crrctd. 8vo. xxiv,434 pp. 12 copper plates, 2 tables. Contemp calf, upper front hinge split. *(Hemlock)* **$150 [≈£83]**

Lee, John Edward
- Note-book of an amateur geologist. London: 1881. 1st edn. v,90 pp. Mtd photo frontis, 209 plates, 17 figs. Name on half-title, endpapers dampmarked, some finger marks. Orig cloth, a little dull, tiny hole in spine, t.e.g. *(Bow Windows)* **£55 [≈$99]**

- Note-book of an amateur geologist. London: Longmans ..., 1881. 1st edn. 8vo. v,90 pp. Woodburytype frontis, 208 plates, 17 text ills. Occas light foxing. Orig pict green cloth.
(Gough) **£50 [≈ $90]**

Lefeure, Sir G.W.
- The life of a travelling physician ... including twenty years' wanderings through the greater part of Europe. 1843. 1st edn. 3 vols. Sm 8vo. xvi,312; viii,304; viii,294 pp. 3 hand-cold frontis, each with sm stamp. Mod cloth-backed mrbld bds.
(Old Cinema) **£75 [≈ $135]**
- The life of a travelling physician ... London: 1843. 3 vols. 8vo. Cold frontis. Orig cloth.
(Goodrich) **$75 [≈ £41]**

Lefevre, N.
- A compleat body of chymistry. London: Pulteyn, 1670. 2nd English edn. 4to. 2 pts in 1. [x],286; [vi],320 pp. 2 titles, 6 fldg plates, 2 full-page ills. Contemp calf, 1 rear crnr missing. Wing L926. *(P & P)* **£105 [≈ $189]**

Leibnitz, G.W. von & Clarke, Samuel
- A collection of papers which passed between ... Mr. Leibnitz and Dr. Clarke ... Relating to ... natural philosophy ... London: for James Knapton, 1717. 1st edn. xiii,[iii], 416,46 pp. Advt leaf. Worming in margs of 2 gatherings. Contemp calf, rebacked & reprd.
(Bickersteth) **£385 [≈ $693]**

Leidy, Joseph
- An elementary treatise on human anatomy. Phila: 1861. 8vo. 663 pp. 392 ills. Sheep, rubbed.   *(Goodrich)* **$95 [≈ £52]**

Leigh, Charles
- The natural history of Lancashire, Cheshire ... Oxford: for the author, 1700. Folio. Errata, postscript & inserted pp at V2. Port (reprd), 2 plates of arms, map, 22 plates. Title dusty, frayed at edges, few tears in marg. Contemp calf, rebacked, reprd.
(Bow Windows) **£240 [≈ $432]**
- The natural history of Lancashire, Cheshire ... Oxford: for the author, 1700. 1st edn. Folio. 26 copper engvd plates inc port frontis & double-page cold map. Port title & front free endpaper damaged in crnr sl affecting ptd area. Mod qtr calf. Wing L975.
(Blackwell's) **£170 [≈ $306]**
- The natural history of Lancashire, Cheshire and the Peak, in Derbyshire. Oxford: 1700. Folio. Port (crnr defective), cold map, 24 plates. New half calf.
(Wheldon & Wesley) **£225 [≈ $405]**

Lemery, M.L.
- A treatise of all sorts of foods, both animal and vegetable; also of drinkables ... how to choose the best sort of all kinds. Translated ... London: 1745. 12mo. 396 pp. Red & black title, approbation leaf. Contemp bds, new spine.   *(Halewood)* **£115 [≈ $207]**

Lemery, N.
- A course of chymistry, containing an easie method of preparing those chymical medicins which are used in physick ... London: for Kettilby, 1698. 3rd edn. 8vo. [xxii],815, [xvi] pp. 7 full-page plates. Rebound calf, old spine laid down, new endpapers. Wing L1040.
(P & P) **£340 [≈ $612]**

Lemnius, Levinus
- An herbal for the Bible ... Drawen into English by Thomas Newton. London: E. Bollifant, 1587. 1st edn. Sm 8vo. W'cut initials. Mod mor. STC 15454.
(Traylen) **£490 [≈ $882]**

Lempriere, William
- Report on the medicinal effects of an aluminous chalybeate water ... discovered ... in the Isle of Wight. Newport, I of W: Musson & Taylor, [1811]. 1st edn. Roy 8vo. Vignette title, litho frontis (a little browned), errata leaf. Mrbld bds, new calf spine.
(Traylen) **£75 [≈ $135]**

Leslie, John
- Elements of geometry, geometrical analysis, and trigonometry. Edinburgh: 1811. 2nd edn, imprvd & enlgd. ix,500 pp. Many text diags. Contemp sheep, rebacked, spine gilt.
(Whitehart) **£50 [≈ $90]**
- The philosophy of arithmetic; exhibiting a progressive view of the theory and practice of calculation. Edinburgh: Tait, & Longman ..., 1820. 2nd edn, imprvd & enlgd. [2],258 pp. Extra lge fldg table, text w'cuts. Contemp 3/4 calf.   *(Antiq Sc)* **$250 [≈ £138]**

Letchworth, William Pryor
- Care and treatment of epileptics. New York: Putnams, 1900. 8vo. xiii,244 pp. Num plates. Cloth, inner hinge split, uncut, ex lib.
(Goodrich) **$75 [≈ £52]**

Letter ...
- Letter to ... Viscount Palmerston ... on the ... diseases prevention act ... See Burnell, G.R.

Letterman, Jonathan
- Medical recollections of the army of the Potomac. New York: 1866. 1st edn. 194 pp. Sl mottling of spine. *(Scientia)* **$250 [≈ £138]**

Letters ...
- Letters and essays on the small-pox ... See Quier, John
- Letters to married women ... See Smith, Hugh

Lettsom, John Coakley
- The naturalist's and traveller's companion containing instructions for collecting and preserving objects of natural history ... London: 1774. 2nd edn. 8vo. xvi,89,[9] pp. Engvd title & frontis, each with hand-cold ills. Rec half calf by Bernard Middleton.
  (Burmester) **£90 [≃ $162]**
- Some account of the late John Fothergill, M.D. London: Dilly, 1783. 8vo. 193 pp. Qtr calf, rebacked.   *(Goodrich)* **$125 [≃ £69]**

Levi, Leoni
- On the metric system of weights and measures. London: reprinted from "The Exchange", n.d. [ca 1863]. 15 pp. Disbound.
  (C.R. Johnson) **£20 [≃ $36]**

Levinson, Abraham
- Pioneers of pediatrics. New York: 1936. 8vo. 112 pp. Bds stained. Ex lib.
  (Goodrich) **$39 [≃ £21]**

Levy, L.A. & Willis, H.G.
- Radium and other radio-active elements. A popular account treated experimentally. [1904]. 105 pp. 20 plates, other text ills. Orig cloth, dull, spine faded.
  (Whitehart) **£40 [≃ $72]**

Lewes, G.H.
- Comte's philosophy of the sciences. London: 1897. 8vo. viii,351,40 pub ctlg pp. Uncut & unopened. Cloth.   *(Elgen)* **$25 [≃ £13]**

Lewes, George Henry
- The physiology of human life. 1859-60. 1st edn. 2 vols. 8vo. Text figs. Contemp half calf, a little rubbed.   *(Bickersteth)* **£28 [≃ $50]**

Lewis, Henry Carvill
- Papers and notes on the glacial geology of Great Britain and Ireland. London: Longmans ..., 1894. 1st edn. 8vo. lxxxi,469,32 pub advts pp. 10 fldg cold maps, 82 text figs. Orig cloth, spine faded.
  (Gough) **£35 [≃ $63]**

Lewis, Sir Thomas
- Diseases of the heart. London: Macmillan, 1937. 2nd edn. 8vo. Orig tan cloth.
  (Chaucer Head) **£30 [≃ $54]**

Lewis, William
- A course of practical chemistry ... with many new, and several uncommon processes. J. Nourse, 1746. 1st edn. 8vo. [xx],432,ii advts,xx index,ii advts,vii explanation of plates pp. 9 copper engvs. Foxing or browning throughout. Amateur calf, hinge cracked.   *(Blackwell's)* **£125 [≃ $225]**
- A course of practical chemistry ... with many new, and several uncommon processes. London: J. Nourse, 1746. 8vo. 10ff, 432 (i.e. 422) pp, 21ff. 9 copperplates. Contemp calf, back gilt, hinges cracked. Franklin Institute Lib b'plate.
  (Offenbacher) **$500 [≃ £277]**

Lewis, William C. McC.
- A system of physical chemistry. London: Longmans, 1919. 2nd edn. 3 vols. 8vo. 494; 403; 209 pp. Orig cloth. *(Oasis)* **$30 [≃ £16]**

Leybourn, William
- The art of dialling performed geometrically ... arithmetically ... instrumentally ... London: 1669. 1st edn, 2nd iss. Sm 4to. 4ff, 175 pp. W'cut port, fldg plate, num w'cut diags. Ink inscrptns at beginning, prelims a little grubby & stained. Old calf, worn.
  (Weiner) **£750 [≃ $1,350]**
- Compleat surveyor: or, the whole art of surveying of land, by a new instrument lately invented. London: 1722. 5th edn. Folio. [12],166, 155 pp. Advt. Engvd port, 14 fldg plates. Old stamps on title, frontis & elsewhere. Some browning. Contemp calf, rebacked.   *(Spelman)* **£180 [≃ $324]**
- Dialing ... shewing how to make all such dials, and to adorn them with all useful furniture ... London: Churchill, 1682. 1st edn. Folio. [20],76; 89-187; [12],189-192; 12; 181-226; 273-330 pp. Frontis, 23 engvd plates (10 fldg), Old calf, rebacked. Wing L1912.
  (Rootenberg) **$1,800 [≃ £1,000]**
- The line of proportion of numbers, commonly called Gunter's Line made easie. London: for Hannah Sawbridge, 1684. Sm 8vo. 2 pp bookseller's ctlg. Lacking fldg plate, lib stamp on title verso. Contemp calf, jnts reprd. Wing 1921. *(Stewart)* **£250 [≃ $450]**

Liebig, Justus von
- Animal chemistry, or organic chemistry in its application to physiology and pathology. Edited by William Gregory. 1842. Top of spine sl chipped.   *(Allen)* **$75 [≃ £41]**
- Animal chemistry, or organic chemistry in its application to physiology and pathology. London: 1842. 1st edn in English. 8vo. 354,8 pub ctlg pp. Orig bds, rebacked, orig spine laid down.   *(Oasis)* **$250 [≃ £138]**

- Animal chemistry, or organic chemistry in its application to physiology and pathology. London: 1842. 1st English edn. Orig cloth, sl rubbed & stained. Ex lib with stamp on title.
(*Robertshaw*) £24 [≈ $43]
- Chemistry in its application to agriculture and physiology. London: for Taylor & Walton, 1842. 2nd English edn, edited by Lionel Playfair. 8vo. Contemp half calf.
(*Chaucer Head*) £60 [≈ $108]
- Familiar letters on chemistry ... Third edition, revised and much enlarged. London: 1851. Sm 8vo. xx,536 pp. Orig dec cloth, hd of spine defective.   (*Weiner*) £25 [≈ $45]
- Familiar letters on chemistry ... London: 1851. 3rd edn. Sm 8vo. xx,536 pp. Sl foxing, some ms notes on front endpaper. New cloth, sl marked.   (*Whitehart*) £25 [≈ $45]
- Familiar letters on chemistry, and its relation to commerce, physiology and agriculture ... [with] Familiar letters ... second series ... London: 1843-44. 2 vols. Sm 8vo. xii,179; xi,218 pp. Lib stamp on vol 1 title. Orig dec blindstamped cloth, minor wear.
(*Weiner*) £100 [≈ $180]
- Instructions for the chemical analysis of organic bodies. Glasgow: 1839. 8vo. iv,59 pp. Ills, tables. New buckram.
(*Weiner*) £50 [≈ $90]
- The natural laws of husbandry, edited by John Blyth. London: 1863. 1st English edn. 8vo. xx,416 pp. Orig dec cloth, spine torn.
(*Weiner*) £40 [≈ $72]
- Researches on the chemistry of food, and the motion of juices in the animal body. Lowell: Bixby, 1848. 1st Amer edn. 12mo. xxx,219 pp. W'cuts in text. Contemp 3/4 lea, rubbed. Ex lib.   (*Antiq Sc*) $85 [≈ £47]

Lieutard, Joseph
- Synopsis of the universal practice of medicine. Translated ... Phila: 1816. 1st edn in English. 8vo. [6],viii, 641,[1] pp. browning, sl foxing. Contemp calf, hinges rubbed.   (*Elgen*) $225 [≈ £125]

Lilly, William
- Christian astrology. London: Partridge, 1647. Sm 4to. Engvd port frontis (backed). Margs thumbed. Old calf, garish reback. Wing P2215.   (*Halewood*) £350 [≈ $630]
- An easie and familiar method whereby to judge the effects depending on eclipses, either of the sun or moon. London: 1652. 1st edn. Slim 4to. Qtr calf, mrbld bds. Lea b'plate of the 'Plesch' Library.
(*Halewood*) £145 [≈ $261]
- An introduction to astrology ... being the whole of that celebrated author's rules for the

practice of horary astrology ... adapted to ... the present day by Zadkiel. 1835. xvi,342 pp. Text figs. Orig cloth.
(*Whitehart*) £30 [≈ $54]

Limbeck, Rud. R. v.
- The clinical pathology of the blood. Translated ... London: New Sydenham Soc, 1901. 8vo. ix,[i],338 pp. 37 figs. Pub bndg.
(*Pollak*) £20 [≈ $36]

Lind, James
- An essay on diseases incidental to Europeans in hot climates with the means of preventing their fatal consequences. London: Becket & de Hondt, 1771. 2nd edn, enlgd. 8vo. xv,375 pp, 4ff. Marg staining to 1st few leaves. Contemp calf, dull, hinges rubbed.
(*Hemlock*) £250 [≈ £138]
- An essay on diseases incidental to Europeans in hot climates ... London: Becket, 1776. 3rd edn, enlgd. 387 pp. Inked names on title, tiny piece torn from blank crnr of 13 leaves. Contemp calf, rebacked.
(*Oasis*) £350 [≈ £194]
- An essay on the most effectual means of preserving the health of seamen in the Royal Navy. London: Millar, 1757. 1st edn. Sm 8vo. xxiv,119 pp. Lacking half-title, contemp sgntrs on title & another page. Contemp bds, crnrs reprd, rebacked in calf.
(*Oasis*) $2,750 [≈ £1,527]
- A treatise on the scurvy ... the nature, causes, and cure of that disease ... London: A. Millar, 1757. 2nd crrctd edn. 8vo. xvi pp, 2ff, 476 pp. Ownership stamp on title, medical ex lib inside front cvr. Contemp half calf.
(*Hemlock*) $1,875 [≈ £1,041]

Linnaeus, Carl
- Miscellaneous tracts relating to natural history, husbandry, and physic. Translated from the Latin ... by Benj. Stillingfleet. London: R. & J. Dodsley ..., 1759. 1st edn. 8vo. xxx,[i],230 pp. Contemp qtr calf, mrbld bds, spine worn at hd & ft, jnts cracked.
(*Bickersteth*) £285 [≈ $513]

Lister, Joseph
- Collected papers. Oxford: 1909. 1st edn. 2 vols. 4to. 429; 689 pp. 14 plates. Cloth, bottom of vol 1 spine lightly frayed.
(*Scientia*) £350 [≈ £194]

Liston, R.
- Memoir on the formation and connexions of the Crural Arch and other parts connected in inguinal and femoral hernia. Edinburgh: 1819. 22 pp. 3 plates. Some sl foxing. Later mrbld bds, calf spine. (*Whitehart*) £55 [≈ $99]

Liston, Robert
- Elements of surgery. With copious notes and additions by Samuel D. Gross. Phila: 1846. 4th Amer edn. 664 pp. Foxed. Lea. *(Scientia)* **$95 [≈£52]**
- Practical surgery; with one hundred and fifty engravings on wood. London: 1840. 3rd edn. 8vo. Title, 2ff, 592 pp. 16 pp pub ctlg at end. Some ills heightened in red. Uncut & partially unopened, in cloth. *(Hemlock)* **$100 [≈£55]**

Littell, Squier
- A manual of the diseases of the eye; or, a treatise on ophthalmology. Phila: 1846. 2nd edn, revsd & enlgd. 372 pp. Cloth, crnrs worn, sm piece lacking from top of spine. *(Scientia)* **$150 [≈£83]**

Little, Ernest Muirhead
- History of the British Medical Association. London: 1932. 8vo. 341 pp. Plates. Orig cloth, faded,   *(Goodrich)* **$75 [≈£41]**
- History of the British Medical Association, 1832-1932. London: B.M.A., [1932]. 8vo. [x],342 pp. Frontis, 42 plates, some cold. Pub bndg.   *(Pollak)* **£25 [≈$45]**

Little, W.J.
- On spinal weakness and spinal curvatures: their early recognition and treatment. London: Longmans, 1868. 8vo. xi,121 pp. Text engvs. Orig cloth, worn. *(Goodrich)* **$150 [≈£83]**

Livermore, Mary L.
- My story of the war. A woman's narrative of four years' personal experience as a nurse in the Union Army ... Hartford: 1889. 8vo. 700 pp. Port frontis, engvs (some cold), ports. Cloth, gilt back.   *(Elgen)* **$40 [≈£22]**

Liversidge, Archibald
- The minerals of New South Wales, etc. London: Trubner, 1888. 3rd edn. 8vo. viii,326,[2 advts] pp. Fldg map. Orig olive cloth, t.e.g., lower cvr dampstained. *(Morrell)* **£55 [≈$99]**

Livingston, William K.
- The clinical aspects to visceral neurology with special reference to the surgery of the sympathetic nervous system. Springfield: 1935. 1st edn. 254 pp. Cloth. *(Scientia)* **$65 [≈£36]**

Lizars, A. Jardine
- Elements of anatomy intended as a textbook for students. Edinburgh: 1844. 1st edn. Lge 12mo. 900 pp. Half calf. Author's pres

inscrptn on title.   *(Oasis)* **$50 [≈£27]**

Lizars, John
- A system of anatomical plates of the human body. Accompanied with descriptions ... Edinburgh: Lizars ..., [1840?]. 2nd edn. Folio. Engvd title vignette, 103 hand-cold engvd plates. Little light soiling, 2 plates sl shaved. Contemp half calf, spine reprd. *(Quaritch)* **$650 [≈£361]**

Lloyd, Humphrey
- Elementary treatise on the wave-theory of light. London: Longmans, Green, 1873. 3rd edn, revsd & enlgd. xi,247,24 ctlg pp. Text figs. Pub bndg, spine ends bumped. *(Pollak)* **£25 [≈$45]**
- Miscellaneous papers connected with physical science. 1877. v,509 pp. 3 plates. Orig cloth, marked & sl worn, tear on spine reprd, inner hinges sl cracked. *(Whitehart)* **£25 [≈$45]**
- Miscellaneous papers connected with physical science. London: 1877. 8vo. vii,511 pp. 7 plates. Unopened in orig cloth, dusty, worn, closed tear on spine. *(Weiner)* **£65 [≈$117]**

Lobb, Theophilus
- A compendium of the practice of physick, or, the heads of a system of practical physick contained in 24 lectures ... London: 1747. 8vo. 11,9,103,4 advts pp. Contemp calf. *(Halewood)* **£120 [≈$216]**
- Medical practice in curing fevers. John Oswald, 1735. 1st edn. 8vo. xxxii,431,[xxii pp. Contemp sprinkled calf, sometime rebacked, crnrs reprd. *(Blackwell's)* **£140 [≈$252]**
- Medical practice in curing fevers. Correspondent to rational methods ... which arise from the sebrile symptoms of the patient. London: 1735. 1st edn. Thick 8vo. Errata/advt leaf. Contemp calf. *(Halewood)* **£115 [≈$207]**
- Medicinal letters. In two parts ... for removing various disorders ... II ... on the most frequent and dangerous diseases ... John Buckland, 1765. 3rd edn. 12mo. [vii],92,viii advts pp. Title stained in margs. Contemp sheep, jnts cracked, lacking f.e.p. *(Blackwell's)* **£50 [≈$90]**
- A practical treatise of painful distempers, with some effectual methods for curing them ... James Buckland, 1739. 1st edn. 8vo. xxxii, 320,[xiv] pp. Some marg foxing throughout. Contemp sprinkled calf, rec rebacked, gilt, crnrs worn. *(Blackwell's)* **£100 [≈$180]**

Lock, Alfred G & Lock, Charles. G.
- A practical treatise on the manufacture of sulphuric acid. London: Sampson, Low, 1879. 1st edn. Lge roy 8vo. [2],vii,[1 list of plates], 247,[1 advt] pp. 77 plates & figs. Orig cloth, a little worn, edges uncut & little spotted.   *(Taylor)* **£55 [≈ $99]**
- A practical treatise on the manufacture of sulphuric acid. London: 1879. 8vo. ciii,247 pp. Plates (some fldg), num ills & diags. Orig bevelled cloth, crnrs & spine edges a little worn.   *(Weiner)* **£50 [≈ $90]**

Locke, John
- The [philosophical] works. With a preliminary essay and notes by J.S. St. John. London: Bohn, 1854. 2 vols. 8vo. iv,541,[iii]; vii,[i],527, [iii] pp. Fldg chart. Contemp mor, gilt extra, a.e.g., a little rubbing.
                                 (Pollak) **£40 [≈ $72]**

Lockyer, J. Norman
- The chemistry of the sun. London: Macmillan, 1887. 8vo. xix,[i],257, [iii] pp. 134 ills. Orig cloth, jnts weak, shabby.
                                 (Pollak) **£25 [≈ $45]**
- Contributions to solar physics. London: Macmillan, 1874. 1st edn. 8vo. xxi,[1 errata],[2],676 pp. 7 plates (some cold), num text ills. Orig dec cloth laid down on matching blue cloth, t.e.g.
                                 (Antiq Sc) **£150 [≈ £83]**
- Contributions to solar physics. London: 1874. Thick 8vo. Cold & litho plates, num w'cuts. Calf.   *(Halewood)* **£58 [≈ $104]**
- The meteoritic hypothesis - a statement of the results of a spectroscopic inquiry into the origin of the cosmical systems. London: Macmillan, 1890. 8vo. xvi,560 pp. 7 plates. Pub bndg, jnts weak, a little wear to spine ends.   *(Pollak)* **£50 [≈ $90]**
- The meteoritic hypothesis ... London: Macmillan, 1890. 1st edn. 8vo. xvi,560 pp. 7 plates (6 photographic), text w'cuts. Lib marks. Orig cloth, uncut, unopened.
                                 (Antiq Sc) **$90 [≈ £50]**
- The spectroscope and its applications. London & New York: Macmillan, 1873. 12mo. 117 pp. Fldg cold frontis, ills. A few ink notes & lib stamps on front blank.
                                 (Xerxes) **$65 [≈ £36]**

Locy, W.A.
- The growth of biology. Zoology ... botany ... physiology from Harvey to Bernard. New York: 1925. 8vo. 474 pp. Orig cloth.
                                 (Goodrich) **$45 [≈ £25]**

Lodge, Sir Oliver
- Atoms and rays. An introduction to modern views on atomic structure and radiation. London: Benn, 1924. 1st edn. 8vo. 208pp. Plate, 8 figs. Pub bndg. *(Pollak)* **£25 [≈ $45]**
- Pioneers of science, London: Macmillan, 1893. 8vo. xv,[i],404 pp. Port frontis, 120 ills. Pub bndg.   *(Pollak)* **£20 [≈ $36]**

Loeb, Jacques
- Artificial parthogenesis and fertilization. Chicago: 1913. 1st edn. 312 pp. Cloth.
                                 (Scientia) **$85 [≈ £47]**
- The biological basis of individuality. Springfield: 1945. 1st edn. Lge 8vo. xiii,711 pp. Cloth. Ex lib.   *(Elgen)* **$75 [≈ £41]**
- Comparative physiology of the brain and comparative psychology. London: 1901. 8vo. 309 pp. Orig cloth.   *(Goodrich)* **$75 [≈ £41]**
- Comparative physiology of the brain and comparative psychology. New York: 1900. 1st edn in English. 309 pp. Cloth.
                                 (Scientia) **$85 [≈ £47]**
- The dynamics of living matter. New York: 1906. 1st edn. 233 pp. Sgntr on title. Cloth.
                                 (Scientia) **$75 [≈ £41]**
- Forced movements, tropisms, and animal conduct. Phila & London: Lippincott, [1918]. 1st edn. 8vo. 209 pp. 4 plates, text figs. B'plate removed. Orig cloth.
                                 (Antiq Sc) **$85 [≈ £47]**
- Forced movements, tropisms, and animal conduct. Phila & London: 1918. 1st edn. 209 pp. Cloth.   *(Scientia)* **$60 [≈ £33]**
- The mechanistic conception of life; biological essays. Chicago: 1912. 1st edn. 232 pp. Cloth.
                                 (Scientia) **$100 [≈ £55]**
- Studies in general physiology. Chicago: 1905. 1st edn. 2 vols. 782 pp. Cloth.
                                 (Scientia) **$175 [≈ £97]**

Lommius, Jodocus
- A treatise of continual fevers ... to which are added medicinal observations. London: for J. Brotherton, 1732. 1st edn in English. 8vo. xvi,452,iv pp. Marg dampstain in early sgntrs. Contemp sprinkled calf, bds & extremities a bit worn & scuffed, in fldg box.
                                 (Pirages) **$250 [≈ £138]**

London ...
- London's dreadful visitation ... all the bills of mortality for this present year ... London: sold by E. Cotes, 1665. 1st edn. 4to. 55ff. Fldg table (torn in folds affecting sev letters without loss). Title sl soiled. Contemp panelled calf, worn, jnts cracked.
                                 (Pickering) **$2,400 [≈ £1,333]**

Long, Esmond R.
- Selected readings in pathology from Hippocrates to Virchow. Springfield: 1929. 1st edn. 301 pp. Ills. Some pencilling. Orig cloth. *(Goodrich)* **$60 [≃ £33]**

Longmate, Norman
- King Cholera. The biography of a disease. London: Hamilton, 1966. xii,271,[v] pp. 32 ills, 2 maps. Pub bndg, dw.
(Pollak) **£20 [≃ $36]**

Longmore, Thomas
- A treatise on gunshot wounds. Phila: Lippincott, 1862. 1st Amer edn. 12mo. 132 pp. Orig cloth, sl wear to hd & ft of backstrip.
(Antiq Sc) **$125 [≃ £69]**

Longstreth, Morris
- Rheumatism, gout and some allied disorders. New York: Wood, 1882. 8vo. 280 pp. Orig cloth. dampmarked, spine chipped.
(Goodrich) **$35 [≃ £19]**
- Rheumatism, gout and some allied disorders. New York: 1882. 1st edn. 280 pp. Orig cloth.
(Fye) **$60 [≃ £33]**

Lonsdale, H.
- A sketch of the life and writings of Robert Knox, the anatomist. London: 1876. 8vo. 420 pp. Waterstained. Orig binding.
(Goodrich) **$30 [≃ £16]**
- A sketch of the life and writings of Robert Knox, the anatomist. London: 1870. 8vo. xx,420 pp. Orig cloth-backed bds, spine worn & torn at hd, crnrs worn, hinges weak.
(Rittenhouse) **$50 [≃ £27]**

Loomis, A.L.
- Lectures on fevers. New York: 1877. 8vo. 433 pp. pencilling. Cloth. *(Goodrich)* **$25 [≃ £13]**

Lorand, Arnold
- The ultra-violet rays: their action on internal and nervous diseases and use in preventing loss of color and falling of the hair. Phila: 1928. 8vo. 257 pp. *(Rittenhouse)* **$20 [≃ £11]**

Lorentz, H.A.
- The theory of electrons and its applications to the phenomena of light and radiant heat. Laipzig: 1909. 332 pp. Name on title. Later cloth, lea label. *(Whitehart)* **£55 [≃ $99]**

Loriot, Monsieur
- A practical essay on a cement, and artificial stone ... lately discovered ... for ... all manner of buildings and ... all kinds of ornaments of architecture ... London: Cadell, 1774. 1st

English edn. [4],51 pp. Title soiled & marked. Faded contemp wraps.
(Spelman) **£240 [≃ $432]**

Loudon, J.C.
- An encyclopaedia of agriculture. London: Longman, Rees ..., 1831. 2nd edn. 8vo. xl,1282 pp. Num text ills. 16 pp advts tipped-in at beginning. Uncut in orig qtr parchment, mrbld sides, rebacked with orig spine laid down. *(Frew Mackenzie)* **£110 [≃ $198]**

Louis, H.
- The dressing of minerals. 1909. ix,544 plates. 18 plates, 398 text ills. Orig cloth, sl worn, new endpapers. *(Whitehart)* **£25 [≃ $45]**

Louis, Pierre Charles Alexandre
- Anatomical, pathological and therapeutic researches upon the disease known under the name of gastro-enterite. Boston: 1836. 1st edn in English. 2 vols. 8vo. xxiii,395; xi,462 pp. Orig embossed pebbled cloth. Ex S.F. Purple coll with his sgntrs. *(Hemlock)* **$200 [≃ £111]**
- Pathological researches on phthisis. London: 1835. li,388 pp. Sl foxing. Orig cloth, crnrs sl worn, rebacked. *(Whitehart)* **£40 [≃ $72]**
- Pathological researches on phthisis. Translated ... Washington: 1836. 293 pp. Foxing. Qtr calf, mrbld bds.
(Goodrich) **$125 [≃ £69]**

Love, E.A.H.
- A treatise on the mathematical theory of elasticity. Cambridge: 1892-93. 2 vols. xv,354; xi,327 pp. 58 text figs. A little foxing on endpapers, half-title, & at end. Orig cloth. *(Whitehart)* **£35 [≃ $63]**
- A treatise on the mathematical theory of elasticity. New York: Dover, 1944. 8vo. xviii,643,[iii] pp. 74 figs. Pub bndg, sl wear to hd of spine. *(Pollak)* **£20 [≃ $36]**

Love, John
- Geodaesia: or the art of surveying and measuring of land made easy ... also, how to lay out new lands in America, or elsewhere ... London: Betteworth ..., 1731. [20],196,[16], 4,[18],[8] pp. W'cut diags, tables. Rec calf.
(Karmiole) **$150 [≃ £83]**

Lovell, Robert
- Sive pammineralogicon. Or an universal history of mineralls containing the summe of all authors ... Oxford: 1661. 1st edn. Sm 8vo. Title, 103 pp. Some dust marks & light stains. Rec half calf. Wing L3245.
(Bow Windows) **£125 [≃ $225]**

Lovett, Richard
- The electrical philosopher ... new system of physics ... upon the principle of a universal plenum of elementary fire ... Worcester: 1774. 8vo. 2ff,xvi pp,3ff [5]-290 pp, 5ff. 2 fldg plates. Num lib stamps in margs. Contemp bds, spine damaged, uncut.
(Offenbacher) **$450 [≃ £250]**

Low, David
- Elements of practical agriculture ... the cultivation of plants, the husbandry of domestic animals ... Edinburgh: for Bell & Bradfute, 1834. 1st edn. 8vo. 236 ills in text. Contemp diced calf, rebacked, gilt.
(Traylen) **£35 [≃ $63]**

Lowe, Gavin
- An essay on the method of determining the difference of longitude between places at land from the observed transits of the moon over their meridiens ... London: 1803. 8vo. 8pp. Ill. Stitched.
(Argosy) **$50 [≃ £27]**

Lowe, William Robinson
- Lectures on popular and scientific subjects. Wolverhampton & London: 1857. 8vo. iv,437 pp. Errata slip at beginning, inscrptn on title. Orig cloth, sl soiled, stitching a little strained.
(Blackwell's) **£40 [≃ $72]**

Lowry, T.M.
- Historical introduction to chemistry. London: 1926. xv,581 pp. Few ills & diags. Orig cloth.
(Weiner) **£20 [≃ $36]**

Lubbock, John
- On the senses, instincts, and intelligence of animals with special reference to insects. London: Kegan Paul ..., 1888. 8vo. xxix,292,[iv], 42,[vi advts] pp. 118 figs. Orig cloth, mostly unopened. Author's pres inscrptn.
(Pollak) **£20 [≃ $36]**

Lucas, A.
- Ancient Egyptian materials and industries. London: Arnold, 1948. 3rd edn. 8vo. x,[ii],570 pp. Pub bndg, dw.
(Pollak) **£30 [≃ $54]**

Lucas, E.W.
- The book of receipts containing a veterinary materia medica ... a pharmaceutical formulary ... London: 1907. Sm 8vo. x,451 pp. Figs. Red sgntr on half-title, sl foxing. Orig cloth.
(Bow Windows) **£15 [≃ $27]**

Luckett, William & Horn, Frank
- Paraffin in surgery; a critical and clinical study. New York: 1907. 1st edn. 118 pp. Cloth. Sgnd by Horn. *(Scientia)* **$85 [≃ £47]**

Luckiesh, M.
- Light and health. A discussion of light and other radiations in relation to life and to health. Baltimore: Williams & Wilkins, 1926. 1st edn. 302 pp. Ills. Cloth.
(Xerxes) **$45 [≃ £25]**
- Light and work. A discussion of quality and quantity of light in relation to effective vision and efficient work. New York: Van Nostrand, 1924. 1st edn. 296 pp. Ills. Cloth.
(Xerxes) **$45 [≃ £25]**

Ludlam, W.
- Mathematical essays. Cambridge: 1787. 2nd edn, with addtns. 97 pp. Sm 8vo. 3 fldg plates of diags. Cropped by binder with some loss of sgntrs. Later 3/4 lea, mrbld bds.
(Whiteheart) **£50 [≃ $90]**

Lugol, J.G.A.
- Researches on scrofulous diseases. New York: 1847. 2nd Amer edn. 8vo. 325 pp. Addtnl 50 pp essay and formulae on the treatment of scrofula. 10 pp pub ctlg. Lacking front endpaper, mild dampstaining. Orig cloth.
(Oasis) **$75 [≃ £41]**

Luke, T.D.
- A pocket guide to anaesthetics for the student and general practitioner. Edinburgh: 1902. xi,148 pp. 43 ills. Orig limp cloth, rather worn at edges, rebacked, orig spine laid down.
(Whiteheart) **£25 [≃ $45]**

Lunge, Georg
- Coal-tar and ammonia. being the second ... edition of 'A treatise on the distillation of coal-tar ...' 1887. 8vo. xvi,739,[4 advts] pp. 191 full-page & other ills. Orig cloth.
(Fenning) **£32.50 [≃ $57]**

Lunt, Mrs. George
- Behind the bars. Boston: 1871. 1st edn, 356 pp. Cloth. *(Scientia)* **$95 [≃ £52]**

Lupton, Thomas
- A thousand notable things, on various subjects, disclosed from the secrets of nature and art ... London: for T. French, 1795. 12mo. A bit grubby with browning at edges & some fingering. Rec calf.
(Hughes) **£25 [≃ $45]**

Lusk, William Thompson
- The science and art of midwifery. New York: 1896. 4th edn. 8vo. xix,797 pp. Pub ctlg. Ex lib. *(Rittenhouse)* **$25 [≃ £13]**

Luys, J.
- The brain and its functions. 1883. 2nd edn. xix,327 pp. 6 ills. Light scattered foxing. Orig cloth, bottom of spine sl defective.
(Whitehart) **£18 [≈ $32]**

Lydston, G. Frank
- Panama and the Sierras: a doctor's wander days. Chicago: 1900. 1st edn. 8vo. 283 pp. Frontis, num photo plates. Orig cloth, gilt, torn dw. *(Elgen)* **$25 [≈ £13]**

Lyell, Sir Charles
- Elements of geology. London: 1865. 6th edn. 8vo. xvi,794 pp. 769 text figs. Prize calf.
(Wheldon & Wesley) **£40 [≈ $72]**
- The geological evidences of the antiquity of man. London: 1863. 1st edn. 8vo. xii,520 pp. 32 pp advts dated January 1863 at rear. 2 plates, 58 figs. Some minor spots & finger marks. Orig cloth, jnts & spine a little worn.
(Bow Windows) **£150 [≈ $270]**
- The geological evidences of the antiquity of man ... London: Murray, 1863. 1st edn. 8vo. W'engvd frontis, text ills, Some minor marg staining at edge of frontis, title, last 2 leaves. Rebound qtr red mor. *(Hughes)* **£65 [≈ $117]**
- The geological evidences of the antiquity of man ... London: 1873. 4th edn, revsd. 8vo. xix,572 pp. 2 plates, 56 text figs. Orig cloth.
(Wheldon & Wesley) **£70 [≈ $126]**
- A manual of elementary geology. London: Murray, 1851. 3rd, revsd, edn. Demy 8vo. 16,512, advts, 12 pp. 500 w'cuts. Orig embossed cloth, uncut.;
(Halewood) **£85 [≈ $153]**
- Principles of geology, being an attempt to explain the former changes of the earth's surface ... London: Murray, 1830-33. 1st edn. 3 vols. 8vo. 3 engvd frontis (2 cold), 3 maps (2 fldg), 8 engvd plates. Previous owner's inscrptn. Mostly uncut. Rec bds.
(Rootenberg) **$1,800 [≈ £1,000]**
- Principles of geology ... London: Murray, 1832-33. 2nd, 2nd, 1st edn. 3 vols. 8vo. 8 plates (2 cold), 3 maps (2 fldg), w'cut ills. Contemp polished calf, gilt. B'plate of Lord Leigh. *(Traylen)* **£400 [≈ $720]**
- Principles of geology ... London: Murray, 1830-33. 1st edn. 3 vols. 8vo. 8 plates (2 cold), 3 maps (2 fldg, 1 cold), 135 w'cut ills. Contemp half calf, mrbld bds, some jnts reprd. *(Traylen)* **£650 [≈ $1,170]**
- Principles of geology ... London: Murray, 1853. 9th edn. 8vo. 835 pp, 32 pp pub ctlg. maps, plates, w'cuts. Orig gilt cloth, partly unopened, short tear at hd of spine.
(Oasis) **$100 [≈ £55]**

Lyman, Henry M.
- A textbook of the principles and practice of medicine. Phila: 1892. 8vo. 923 pp. Orig cloth, rubbed, inner hinges cracked.
(Goodrich) **$75 [≈ £41]**

McAdam, John Loudon
- Remarks on the present system of road making, with observations, deduced from practice and experience ... Bristol: Gutch, 1816. 1st edn. 8vo. 32 pp. New wraps. Preserved in a fitted case.
(Marlborough) **£1,000 [≈ $1,800]**
- Remarks on the present system of road making ... 1822. 6th edn, revsd. vii,96 pp. Contemp bds, rebacked.
(Whitehart) **£40 [≈ $72]**

Macalpine, Jas. B.
- Cystoscopy: a theoretical and practical handbook containing chapters on separate renal function and pyelography. New York: 1927. 1st Amer edn. 8vo. xvi,284 pp. 12 cold plates, num text ills. Cloth.
(Elgen) **$35 [≈ £19]**

McAulay, A.
- Utility of quaternions in physics. London: 1893. 8vo. xiv,107 pp. Orig cloth.
(Weiner) **£30 [≈ $54]**

McCarrison, Robert
- The thyroid gland in health and disease. Bailliere, Tindall ..., 1917. 1st edn. 8vo. xvii,286 pp. 82 figs in text. Orig pale blue cloth, gilt faded, sm snag in backstrip.
(Blackwell's) **£45 [≈ $81]**

McClellan, George
- Regional anatomy in its relation to medicine and surgery. Edinburgh: Pentland, 1891. 2 vols. 4to. xiv,436; xvi,414 pp. 96 cold plates from photos. Title vol II loose & frayed. Orig cloth, gilt, hinges weak.
(Blackwell's) **£35 [≈ $63]**
- Regional anatomy in its relation to medicine and surgery. Phila: 1891-92. 2 vols. Lge 4to. xxii,436; xvi,414 pp. 97 hand-cold photo plates. Orig cloth, lightly shaken, hinges weak. *(Goodrich)* **$125 [≈ £69]**
- Regional anatomy in its relation to medicine and surgery. Phila: 1894. 2nd edn. 2 vols. 4to. 436; 414 pp. Cold plates, many with ms notations. Half lea, backstrips worn, rubbed, some tears. *(Fye)* **$100 [≈ £55]**

MacCormac, W.
- Surgical operations. Part I. The ligature of arteries. Part II. Amputations ... 1891-89. 2

vols. 2nd & 1st edns. xiii,152; xv,135-480 pp.
Num ills. Light scattered foxing. Orig cloth,
sl worn.   *(Whitehart)* **£38 [≃ $68]**

MacCulloch, John
- Malaria: an essay on the production and
propagation of this poison ... with ... the
means of preventing or diminishing them,
both at home and in the naval and military
service. London: 1727. 1st edn. 8vo.
vi,[2],480 pp. Contemp 3/4 calf, mrbld bds.
        (Hemlock) **$225 [≃ £125]**
- Remarks on the art of making wine ...
London: Longman ..., 1816. 1st edn. 12mo.
[2],vi,261,[1] pp. Rec half calf over mrbld
bds.   *(Rootenberg)* **$550 [≃ £305]**

Macdonald, D.G.F.
- Hints on farming. 1868. 10th edn. 8vo. 3 vols
inc appendix vol. xxiii,760,cclxviii pp. Engvd
port frontis. Prelims sl spotted. Half calf,
mrbld bds, spines gilt.
        (Edwards) **£150 [≃ $270]**

Macdonald, G.
- A treatise on diseases of the nose and its
accessory cavities. 1892. 2nd edn. xix,381 pp.
69 ills. V light foxing on half-title & final
page. Cloth, front inner hinge v sl cracked.
        (Whitehart) **£18 [≃ $32]**

Macdonald, G.W.
- Historical papers on modern explosives.
London: 1912. 8vo. xi,192 pp. Orig cloth, a
bit worn & shaken.   *(Weiner)* **£25 [≃ $45]**

M'Dowell, William A.
- A demonstration of the curability of
pulmonary consumption in all its stages ...
Louisville: 1843. 1st edn. 8vo. 269 pp.
Foxing, partic at beginning. Cvrs & spine
faded, spine label imperfect.
        (Rittenhouse) **$60 [≃ £33]**

MacEwen, William
- Atlas of head sections. Fifty-three engraved
copperplates ... and fifty-three key plates with
descriptive texts. Glasgow: James Maclehose.
1893. 1st edn. 4to. xiii pp, 53 photogravure
plates with key plates, 4 pp index at end.
Later blue cloth.   *(Pickering)* **$400 [≃ £222]**
- The growth of bone. Observations on
osteogenesis. An experimental inquiry into
the development and reproduction of
diaphyseal bone. Glasgow: Maclehose, 1912.
1st edn. 8vo. Ills. Orig cloth, front bd frayed
at top edge.   *(Chaucer Head)* **£60 [≃ $108]**

McGarrison, R.
- The simple goitres. 1928. xi,106 pp. 143
diags & ills on plates. *(Whitehart)* **£18 [≃ $32]**

MacGillivray, W.
- Lives of eminent zoologists, from Aristotle to
Linnaeus. Edinburgh: Oliver & Boyd, 1834.
8vo. 391,[i], 12,4 advts pp. Frontis. Orig
cloth, spine splitting along 1 side.
        (Pollak) **£25 [≃ $45]**

MacIlwain, George
- Memoirs of John Abernethy ... his lectures,
his writings and his characters. London:
Hatchard, 1856. 3rd edn. 8vo. xv,396 pp.
Engvd frontis, text engv. Orig cloth.
        (Goodrich) **$75 [≃ £41]**

McIvor, W.G.
- Notes on the propagation and cultivation of
the medicinal cinchonas or Peruvian bark
trees. Madras: 1867. 8vo. Title, ii,33 pp. 9
fldg litho plates. Contemp linen, lacking rear
cvr.   *(Hemlock)* **$200 [≃ £111]**

Mackay, Andrew
- The new complete navigator... To which is
added, a concise system of calculations for
finding the longitude at sea ... Phila:
Hopkins. 1807. 1st Amer edn. 8vo. xxiii,[1],
276, 40,220,[4 advts] pp. 7 engvd plates.
Spotty foxing. Contemp calf, spine chipped.
        (Antiq Sc) **$200 [≃ £111]**

MacKee, George M.
- X-rays and radium in the treatment of
diseases of the skin. Phila: 1927. 8vo. xii,788
pp. 354 engvs, 31 charts.
        (Rittenhouse) **$35 [≃ £19]**

Mackenzie, Andrew
- A treatise of maritime surveying, in two parts;
with a prefatory essay on draughts and
surveys. London: Dilly, 1774. 1st edn. Sm
4to. xxiii,[1], 119,[1 errata] pp. 6 fldg engvd
plates. Contemp 3/4 calf.
        (Antiq Sc) **$850 [≃ £472]**

Mckenzie, Dan.
- The infancy of medicine. An enquiry into the
influence of folk-lore upon the evolution of
scientific medicine. London: Macmillan,
1927. 8vo. xiii,[i],421,[iii] pp. Pub bndg.
        (Pollak) **£30 [≃ $54]**
- The infancy of medicine. London: 1927. 1st
edn. 8vo. xiii,421 pp. Cloth. Ex lib.
        (Elgen) **$55 [≃ £30]**

Mackenzie, James

- Diseases of the heart. London: OUP, 1908. 1st edn. 8vo. 386 pp, 32 pp pub ctlg. Orig cloth, spine dulled. *(Oasis)* **$300 [≃ £166]**
- Diseases of the heart. London: 1913. 3rd edn. 8vo. 502 pp. Ills. Orig cloth, sl worn & faded. *(Oasis)* **$40 [≃ £22]**
- Diseases of the heart. London: 1921. 3rd edn. 502 pp. Orig cloth. *(Fye)* **$75 [≃ £41]**
- The study of the pulse. Arterial, venous and hepatic and of the movements of the heart. 1902. 1st edn. Demy 8vo. Ills. Orig cloth. *(Halewood)* **£95 [≃ $171]**

Mackenzie, Sir James

- Angina pectoris. London: OUP, 1923. 1st edn. 8vo. 253 pp. 77 ills. Orig cloth. Ex lib with stamps. *(Oasis)* **$125 [≃ £69]**
- The future of medicine. London: OUP, 1919. 1st edn. 8vo. 238 pp. Orig cloth, spine dulled. *(Oasis)* **$30 [≃ £16]**

Mackenzie, James (1680?-1761)

- The history of health and the art of preserving it. Edinburgh: William Gordon, 1758. 1st edn. 8vo. xii,436 pp. Calf, front jnt tender, hd of spine worn. *(Elgen)* **$225 [≃ £125]**

Mackenzie, Morell

- Diseases of the pharynx, larynx, and trachea. New York: Wood's Library, 1880. Cloth. *(Rittenhouse)* **$25 [≃ £13]**
- The use of the laryngoscope in diseases of the throat; with an essay on hoarseness, loss of voice ... With additions ... by J. Solis-Cohen. Phila: 1869. 2nd Amer edn. 289 pp. 2 plates. Cloth, top of spine chipped. *(Scientia)* **$125 [≃ £69]**

Mackintosh, T.S.

- The "Electrical Theory" of the universe. Boston: Josiah P. Medum, 1846. 1st Amer edn. 12mo. xii,423 pp. Fldg table, text figs. Orig brown gilt-stamped cloth. *(Karmiole)* **$75 [≃ £41]**

Mackness, James

- Hastings considered as a resort for invalids ... temperature, salubrity ... suitability in various pulmonary diseases ... London: Churchill, 1842. 1st edn. 8vo. xii,151 pp. Half-title lightly spotted. Contemp half calf. *(Frew Mackenzie)* **£48 [≃ $86]**

MacLagan, T.

- The germ theory applied to the explanation of the phenomena of disease. The specific fevers. London: 1876. 8vo. viii,258,8 pub ctlg pp. Orig pebble cloth, bottom spine edge frayed, sl soiled. *(Elgen)* **$65 [≃ £36]**

MacLagan, T.J.

- Rheumatism. Its nature, its pathology and its successful treatment. 1896. 2nd edn. xiii,324 pp. pencil anntns in text. Orig cloth, dust-stained, spine faded. *(Whitehart)* **£18 [≃ $32]**

Maclaurin, Colin

- An account of Sir Isaac Newton's philosophical discoveries, in four books. For the author's children, 1748. 1st edn. 4to. [viii],[xx subscribers], xx,392 pp. 6 fldg plates. Lightly browned throughout. New panelled calf. *(Frew Mackenzie)* **£275 [≃ $495]**
- An account of Sir Isaac Newton's philosophical discoveries, in four books. London: 1750. 2nd edn. 8vo. Half-title, 6 fldg plates. Qtr calf. *(Halewood)* **£125 [≃ $225]**
- A treatise of algebra, in three parts ... London: A. Millar ..., 1748. 1st edn. 8vo. xiv,366, [ii],65,i errata pp. 12 fldg engvd plates. Calf, worn. *(Pollak)* **£85 [≃ $153]**
- A treatise of algebra, in three parts ... London: A. Millar ..., 1748. 1st edn. 8vo. xiv,366; i,65,i pp. 12 fldg engvd plates of diags, num diags in text. Contemp polished sprinkled calf, engvd b'plate. *(Blackwell's)* **£200 [≃ $360]**

Maclean, Charles

- A view of the science of life ... elements of medicine of John Brown ... epidemics and pestilential diseases ... Phila: 1797. 8vo. 232 pp. Foxing. Antique bds. *(Goodrich)* **$75 [≃ £41]**

McLean, F.K., et al.

- Report of the Solar Eclipse Expedition to Port Davey, Tasmania, May 1910. N.d. [1910?]. [3],42 pp. 5 full-page plates, 2 fldg maps in pocket. Orig bds, rebacked, orig backstrip preserved. *(Whitehart)* **£35 [≃ $63]**

Maclean, John

- Two lectures on combustion. Phila: Dobson, 1797. 1st edn. 8vo. 71 pp. Last leaf with old reprd tear, some staining. Linen-backed blue bds, antique style. *(Antiq Sc)* **$500 [≃ £277]**

Maclean, L.

- An inquiry into the nature, causes, and cure of hydrothorax; illustrated by interesting cases ... Hartford: 1814. 1st Amer edn. 8vo. xiii,176. Contemp bds, worn & loose, lacking cloth on spine. *(Rittenhouse)* **$125 [≃ £69]**

Maclure, William
- Opinions on various subjects, dedicated to the industrious producers. New Harmon, In: 1831-37-38. [4],483; [8],556; [6],321 pp. Sl foxed. Old half lea & bds, somewhat scuffed & worn.   *(Reese)* **$3,500 [≃ £1,944]**

McMahon, Percy A.
- Combinatory analysis. Cambridge: 1915-16. 1st edn. 2 vols. xix,300; xix,340 pp. Ex lib, stamps on titles, lib nos on cvrs, cancellation stamps.   *(Whitehart)* **£50 [≃ $90]**
- Combinatory analysis. Cambridge: 1915-16. 2 vols. 8vo. Cancelled blind lib stamps on title. Orig cloth.   *(Bickersteth)* **£30 [≃ $54]**

Macmichael, William
- The goldheaded cane. London: 1828. 2nd edn. 8vo. 267 pp. Engvs. Bds, rebacked, uncut.   *(Goodrich)* **$110 [≃ £61]**

MacMunn, C.A.
- The spectroscope in medicine. 1880. xiv,198 pp. 3 chromolithos, 13 w'cuts. Orig blindstamped cloth. *(Whitehart)* **£40 [≃ $72]**

MacNair, Peter
- The geology and scenery of the Grampians and the Valley of Strathmore. Glasgow: 1908. One of 480. 2 vols. 8vo. 10 maps, some fldg, 164 plates from photos. Orig blue cloth, gilt, t.e.g.   *(Traylen)* **£65 [≃ $117]**

MacNair, Peter and Mort, Frederick (eds.)
- History of the Geological Society of Glasgow, 1858-1908. Glasgow: 1908. 8vo. 303 pp. Ports. Orig cloth.   *(Weiner)* **£30 [≃ $54]**

Macneven, William James
- Exposition of the atomic theory of chymistry ... New York: Grattan & Banks, 1819. 1st edn. 8vo. vii,74 pp, 2ff, 29 pp. Errata slip. Paper stains. Franklin Institute Lib b'plate, perf stamp on title. Green lib buckram.
(Offenbacher) **$350 [≃ £194]**

Macnevin, Malcolm G. & Vaughan, Harold S.
- Mouth infections and their relation to systemic diseases. A review of the literature. New York: 1930-33. 2 vols. 8vo. xvii,390; xxvi,395 pp. Fldg graph. Cloth.
(Elgen) **$30 [≃ £16]**

Macnish, Robert
- The philosophy of sleep. Glasgow: W.R. M'Phun, 1830. 1st edn. Sm 8vo. xi,268,8 advts pp. Orig brown silked cloth, dampstain on upper cvr, rec recased.

(Blackwell's) **£85 [≃ $153]**
- The philosophy of sleep. New York: 1834. 1st Amer edn. Sm 8vo. 296 pp. Occas light foxing. Mod cloth.   *(Weiner)* **£50 [≃ $90]**

Macrery, Joseph
- An inaugural dissertation on the principle of animation. Submitted ... to the University of Pennsylvania, for the Degree of Doctor of Medicine. Wilmington: 1802. Some cropping. Disbound.
(Rittenhouse) **$125 [≃ £69]**

McVail, John C.
- Vaccination vindicated; being an answer to the leading anti-vaccinators. New York: 1887. 8vo. 176 pp. Fldg tables. Orig cloth.
(Goodrich) **$75 [≃ £41]**

McWilliam, Robert
- An essay on the origin and operation of the dry rot. London: J. Taylor ..., 1818. 1st edn. 4to. xx,420 pp. Errata leaf, 3 engvd plates (a little browned & some offsetting). Contemp speckled gilt-dec calf. *(Gough)* **£295 [≃ $531]**

Maddock, Alfred Beaumont
- Practical observations on the efficacy of medicated inhalations in the treatment of pulmonary consumption, asthma, bronchitis ... London: 1844. 1st edn. 4to. [8],121 pp. Cold fldg frontis, sev full-page ills. Sgntr on title. Orig blindstamped cloth.
(Hemlock) **$400 [≃ £222]**

Magendie, Francois
- An elementary compendium of physiology; for the use of students. Translated from the French ... Edinburgh: John Carfrae, 1823. 1st English edn. 8vo. Orig bds, rebacked, orig ptd label.   *(Traylen)* **£250 [≃ $450]**
- Physiological and chemical research on the use of the prussic or hydro-cyanic acid in the treatment of the breast and particularly in phthisis pulmonale. New Haven: 1820. 1st Amer edn. 8vo. xv-89 pp. Old bds, rebacked, uncut.   *(Goodrich)* **$150 [≃ £83]**

Magie, William Francis
- A source book in physics. New York: 1935. 1st edn. 8vo. xiv,620 pp. Ills. Cloth.
(Elgen) **$35 [≃ £19]**

Magnus, Hugo
- Superstition in medicine. New York: 1905. 1st edn in English. Sm 8vo. ix,205 pp. Cloth.
(Elgen) **$50 [≃ £27]**

Mahfouz, N.P.
- Atlas of Mahfouzz's obstetric and gynaecological museum. 1949. Sm 4to. 3 vols. 1276 pp. 713 figs on plates, many cold.
(Whitehart) **£65 [≃ $117]**

Mahoney, Jas. W.
- The Cherokee physician, or Indian guide to health, as given by Richard Foreman, a Cherokee doctor ... Ashville, N.C.: Edney & Dedman, 1849. 1st edn. 308,5 pp. Some foxing. Orig calf, sl worn.
(Jenkins) **$1,250 [≃ £694]**

Major, Ralph H.
- Classic descriptions of disease. Springfield: 1955. 3rd edn. 8vo. 571 pp. Ills. Cloth.
(Goodrich) **$45 [≃ £25]**
- Classic descriptions of disease. Springfield: 1932. 1st edn. 8vo. xxviii,630 pp. Ills, ports. Cloth.
(Elgen) **$80 [≃ £44]**
- A history of medicine. Oxford: Blackwell, 1954. 2 vols. 8vo. xxv,[i], 563,[iii]; xii,[ii], 564-1155,[iii] pp. Many ills. Pub bndg.
(Pollak) **£50 [≃ $90]**
- A history of medicine. Springfield: [1954]. 1st edn. 2 vols. 8vo. xxv,563; xii,564-1155 pp. Num ills, ports. Cloth, dws.
(Elgen) **$100 [≃ £55]**

Makemson, Maud Worcester
- The morning star rises. An account of Polynesian astronomy. Yale: 1941. 1st edn. 8vo. xii,301 pp. Orig blue cloth, dw.
(Pacific) **$75 [≃ £41]**

Malcolm, Alexander
- A new system of arithmetick ... for the purposes of men of science ... for men of business. London: for J. Osborn ..., 1730. 4to. 4,v-xx, 623,[i errata] pp. Contemp calf, rebacked, crnrs reprd, new endpapers.
(Pollak) **£150 [≃ $270]**

Malgaigne, Joseph F.
- A treatise on fractures. With notes and additions by John H. Packard. Phila: 1859. 1st edn in English. 683 pp. 16 plates. Lea, rec rebacking.
(Scientia) **$275 [≃ £152]**

Mallik, D.N.
- Optical theories, based on lectures delivered before the Calcutta University. Cambridge: 1917. 181 pp. Inscrbd by author to R.T. Glazebrook. Orig cloth. *(Weiner)* **£30 [≃ $54]**

Mallory, Frank B.
- The principles of pathological histology. Phila: 1914. 1st reprinting. 8vo. 677 pp. Orig

cloth, worn, ex lib. *(Goodrich)* **$45 [≃ £25]**

Malthus, Thomas R.
- An essay on the principle of population; or a view of its past and present effects on human happiness ... A new edition, very much enlarged. London: 1803. 2nd edn. 4to. 610 pp. Qtr lea, rec rebacking, contemp mrbld bds. *(Scientia)* **$1,850 [≃ £1,027]**

Man's Power ...
- On man's power over himself to prevent or control insanity ... See Barlow, John

Manilius (fl. ca B.C. 60)
- Astronomicon. London: Woodfall, 1739. 4to. Port frontis, lge fldg engvd plate (remargined). Contemp calf, spine gilt, short split at hd of 1 jnt.
(Marlborough) **£190 [≃ $342]**

Mann, Gustav
- Physiological histology; method and theory. Oxford: 1902. 1st edn. 488 pp. Fldg table. Staining in upper marg. Cloth.
(Scientia) **$85 [≃ £47]**

Mann, Ida
- Development abnormalities of the eye. Cambridge Univ Press, 1937. 1st edn. 8vo. 444 pp. Cold plates. Orig cloth.
(Oasis) **$85 [≃ £47]**

Mann, Matthew D. (ed.)
- A system of gynecology. Phila: 1887. 1st edn. 2 vols. Lge 8vo. 789; 1180 pp. 7 cold plates, 562 w'cuts. Contemp sheep.
(Elgen) **$150 [≃ £83]**

Manson, Patrick
- Tropical disease. London: Cassell, 1898. 1st edn, 2nd printing. 8vo. xvi,607,[1],[8 pub ctlg] pp. 2 cold plates, text figs. Orig cloth.
(Antiq Sc) **$225 [≃ £125]**

Mantell, Gideon Algernon
- The fossils of the South Downs, or illustrations of the geology of Sussex. London: Relfe, 1822. 1st edn. 4to. 327 pp. 42 litho plates inc cold map. Edges of prelims & title fragile & sl frayed. Rebound in cloth-backed mrbld bds. *(Oasis)* **$150 [≃ £83]**
- Geological excursions round the Isle of Wight, and along the adjacent coast of Dorsetshire ... London: Bohn, 1847. 1st edn. Sm 8vo. 428,[2 advts] pp. Cold fldg map, 19 plates in text. Some spots & dustmarks, sgntr on half-title. Orig cloth, inner hinges torn.
(Bow Windows) **£90 [≃ $162]**

- The geology of the South-East of England. London: 1833. 8vo. xix,415 pp. Frontis, 5 plates, cold map. Trifle foxed at beginning. Half calf. *(Wheldon & Wesley)* **£90 [≈ $162]**
- The medals of creation; or, first lessons in geology ... London: 1844. 1st edn. 2 vols. Post 8vo. 6 plates (4 cold), 167 w'engvs. Orig dec cloth, reprd.
(Wheldon & Wesley) **£50 [≈ $90]**
- A pictorial atlas of fossil remains ... selected from Parkinson's "Organic Remains ..." and Artis's "Antediluvian Phytology". London: Bohn, 1850. 1st edn. 4to. 74 cold plates (1 fldg), text ills. Cloth, mor spine, gilt.
(Traylen) **£160 [≈ $288]**

Manzolli, Pietro Angelo
- The zodiake of life. London: Robert Robinson, 1588. 3rd edn. [viii],242,[xix] pp. Sm hole mended in marg of 1st 2 gatherings. Rec calf. *(Pirages)* **$1,250 [≈ £694]**

Maple, William
- A method of tanning without bark. Dublin: A. Rhames, 1729. 1st edn. 8vo. [6],35,[5] pp. Engvd hand-cold plate. Front paste-down detached & partially lacking. Mottled gilt-dec calf. *(Rootenberg)* **$950 [≈ £527]**

Marbarger, John
- Space medicine. The human factor in flights beyond the earth. Urbana: Univ Illinois Press, 1951. 1st edn. 8vo. Ills. Orig cloth, sl worn dw. *(Oasis)* **$75 [≈ £41]**

Marcet, Jane
- Conversations on chemistry ... Phila: Carey, 1818. 2 vols. 8vo. Plates. Old calf, v worn, lacking 1 cvr. *(Oasis)* **$25 [≈ £13]**
- Conversations on chemistry ... London: 1825. 10th edn. 2 vols. 12mo. 18 engvd plates of figs (lightly browned with some foxing). Sm pieces torn from tips of fore-edges & crnrs of some leaves, 2 outer margs cut close. Contemp half calf, edges & crnrs sl rubbed. *(Bow Windows)* **£60 [≈ $108]**
- Conversations on mineralogy. London: 1822. 2 vols in 1. 12mo. [xvi],259; iv,282 pp. Hand-cold extndg frontis, 11 other extndg plates, mostly foxed. Sm piece torn from upper crnr of title, tip of lower crnr reprd. Old half calf, a little rubbed, gilt spine.
(Bow Windows) **£135 [≈ $243]**
- Conversations on natural philosophy ... London: Longman, Rees ..., 1827. 5th edn. 8vo. x,[ii],429 pp. 23 engvd plates (rather browned). Contemp polished calf, gilt, a.e.g., crnrs a little rubbed.
(Claude Cox) **£25 [≈ $45]**

Marcet, William
- An experimental inquiry into the action of alcohol on the nervous system. London: J.E. Adlard, 1860. 1st edn. 8vo. 20 pp. Rec bds. *(Rootenberg)* **$150 [≈ £83]**

Marchiafava, E., et al.
- Two monographs on malaria and the parasites of malarial fevers. London: New Sydenham Soc, 1894. 1st edn in English. 428 pp. 6 cold litho plates. Orig cloth.
(Oasis) **$50 [≈ £27]**

Marey, Etienne Jules
- Animal mechanism. A treatise on terrestrial and aerial locomotion. London: Henry S. King, 1874. 1st edn in English. 8vo. xvi,283 pp. 32 pp pub advts, 117 w'engvs. Orig red cloth. *(Rootenberg)* **$250 [≈ £138]**

Mariani, Angelo
- Coca and its therapeutic application. New York: 1892. 2nd edn. 78 pp. Sev w'cuts.
(Fye) **$150 [≈ £83]**

Marinet, Johannes Florentina
- The catechism of nature. For the use of children. Boston: David West, 1795. 12mo. 99,[1],[3 advts] pp. Contemp calf over bds, a bit rubbed & soiled. *(Karmiole)* **$75 [≈ £41]**

Mark, Leonard P.
- Acromegaly; a personal experience. London: 1912. 1st edn. 160 pp. Cloth.
(Scientia) **$100 [≈ £55]**

Markham, Gervase
- Cheap and good husbandry for the well-ordering of all beasts and fowles, and for the generall cure of their diseases. London: for E. Brewster ..., 1657. 4to. W'cut & sev decorative head & tail-pieces. Half calf. Wing M613. *(Traylen)* **£65 [≈ $117]**
- Markham's farewell to husbandry: or, the enriching of all sorts of barren and sterile grounds in our nation ... London: for E. Brewster ..., 1656. 4to. W'cut ills in text. Calf-backed mrbld bds. Wing M650.
(Traylen) **£75 [≈ $135]**

Marks, A.A.
- A treatise on artificial limbs with rubber hands and feet. New York: A.A. Marks, 1903. 8vo. 503 pp. Frontis, num text ills. Orig ptd wraps. *(Oasis)* **$75 [≈ £41]**

Marsh, George P.
- Man and nature; or, physical geography as modified by human action. New York:

Scribner, 1864. 1st edn. 8vo. xix,[1],560 pp.
Orig cloth, rebacked. *(Antiq Sc)* **$175 [≃ £97]**

Marsh, Howard

- Diseases of the joints. London: Cassell, 1886.
x,461,[i] pp. Cold frontis, 64 text figs. Orig
cloth, new lea spine.   *(Pollak)* **£40 [≃ $72]**

Marshall, A.

- The Black Musketeers, the work and
adventures of a scientist on a South Sea Island
at war and in peace. London: 1937. 8vo. 329
pp. Ills, maps. Orig cloth, dw.
(Bonham) **£45 [≃ $81]**

Marshall, A.W.

- Flying machines: past, resent and future.
London: n.d. [ca 1909]. 3rd edn. 8vo. 135 pp.
23 plates, diags. Orig pict wraps, worn.
(Weiner) **£20 [≃ $36]**

Marshall, Arthur

- Explosives. History, manufacture, properties
and tests. 1917. 2 vols. Roy 8vo. 155 ills. Orig
cloth.   *(Halewood)* **£40 [≃ $72]**

Marshall, John

- Practical observations on diseases of the
heart, lungs, stomach, liver ... occasioned by
spinal irritation ... Phila: 1837. 8vo. 111 pp.
Some foxing & browning. Rec rebound.
(Rittenhouse) **$25 [≃ £13]**

Marshall, William

- The rural economy of Norfolk. London: T.
Cadell, 1787. 1st edn. 8vo. xix,400;
[xvi],392,[iv] pp. Fldg map. Sl worming in
gutters vol I & some margs vol II, signtr Cc
vol II misfolded. Orig grey bds, untrimmed.
(Blackwell's) **£160 [≃ $288]**
- The rural economy of the Midland Counties
... management of livestock in Leicestershire
... Dublin: J. Moore, 1793. 2 vols. 8vo.
[8],280; [8],287,[8] pp. Vol 1 endpapers
removed & sl wormed in marg. Contemp tree
calf.   *(Spelman)* **£95 [≃ $171]**
- The rural economy of the West of England:
including Devonshire; parts of Somersetshire,
Dorsetshire, and Cornwall. London: G. Nicol
..., 1796. 1st edn. 2 vols. 8vo. 34,332; 24,358
pp. Engvd fldg frontis map. Inscrptns cut
from endpapers. Mottled calf, gilt.
(Tara) **£95 [≃ $171]**

Martel, Th. & Chatelin, Ch.

- Wounds of the skull and brain ... London:
1918. 1st English translation. 8vo. 313 pp.
Cloth, dw.   *(Goodrich)* **$95 [≃ £52]**

Marti-Ibanez, Felix

- Ariel. Essays on the arts and the history and
philosophy of medicine.. New York: MD
Publications, 1962. xiii,[i],292, [vi] pp. paper
flaw in 1 leaf. Pub bndg, dw.
(Pollak) **£20 [≃ $36]**

Martin, B.

- The philosophical grammar: being a view of
the present state of experimental physiology,
or natural philosophy. In 4 parts ... London:
1762. 6th edn. 368 pp. 26 fldg plates.
Contemp lea, rebacked.
(Whitehart) **£80 [≃ $144]**

Martin, Benjamin

- The new art of surveying by the goniometer.
London: for the author, 1766. 1st edn. 8vo.
ii,36 pp. Red & black title. 2 fldg engvd
plates. Old lea-backed mrbld bds.
(Antiq Sc) **£475 [≃ £263]**
- A new compleat and universal system or body
of decimal arithmetick ... London: for George
Keith, 1763. 2nd edn. 8vo. [xiv],403 pp.
Prelim advt leaf, num diags & tables.
Contemp calf, rebacked, orig spine preserved,
(Burmester) **£90 [≃ $162]**

Martin, John H.

- Microscopic objects figured and described.
London: Van Voorst, 1870. vi,114,20 advts
pp. 97 plates, each with 2 figs. Cloth, shabby,
hinges weak.   *(Pollak)* **£25 [≃ $45]**
- Microscopic objects figured and described.
London: Van Voorst, 1870. 8vo. vi,114 pp.
97 plates. Orig cloth.   *(Weiner)* **£25 [≃ $45]**

Martin, P.I.

- A geological memoir on a part of Western
Sussex; with some observations upon chalk-
basins ... London: 1828. 1st edn. 4to. x,100
pp. Table, lge cold fldg map, 3 cold plates.
Some foxing & other marks. Orig cloth,
recased.   *(Bow Windows)* **£145 [≃ $261]**

Martin, S.A.

- The parlour book: or familiar conversations,
on science and the arts, for the use of schools
and families. William Darton, [1835?]. Sole
edn. 16mo. 16 plates. Partly hand-cold
frontis, half-title. Late 19th c binder's cloth,
mrbld edges.   *(Blackwell's)* **£55 [≃ $99]**

Martin, T.C. & Wetzler, Joseph

- The electric motor and its applications. New
York: 1887. 4to. viii,208 pp. Fldg plate, num
ills (many full-page). Cloth, worn. Ex lib.
(Weiner) **£85 [≃ $153]**

Martineau, James
- A word for scientific theology in appeal from the men of science and the theologians. An address at ... Manchester New College. London: Williams & Norgate, 1868. 32 pp. Disbound.   *(C.R. Johnson)* **£15 [≈ $27]**

Martyn, Thomas
- Thirty-eight plates, with ·explanations; intended to illustrate Linnaeus's system of vegetables ... London: for J. White, 1799. 8vo. Advt leaf. Some light foxing. Mod bds.   *(Stewart)* **£90 [≈ $162]**
- Thirty-eight plates, with explanations; intended to illustrate Linnaeus's system of vegetables ... London: J. White, 1799. 8vo. vi,72 pp. 38 plates. Some minor foxing. 19th c half calf, spine gilt. *(Spelman)* **£70 [≈ $126]**

Maseres, Francis
- Tracts on the resolution of affected algebraick equations ... London: ... soldby J. White ..., 1800. 1st edn. 8vo. lxxviii,[2],479 pp. Contemp tree calf, rebacked. Maseres' copy, sgnd & dated, with ms additions on endleaves.   *(Pickering)* **$1,000 [≈ £555]**

Maskeleyne, Nevil
- Tables requisite to be used with the Nautical Ephemeris, for finding the latitude and longitude at sea. London: 1802. 3rd edn. v,206,61, 106 appendix pp. Sl worming & dampstaining to prelim margs, lacking last endpapers. Contemp calf, gilt-dec spine.   *(Gough)* **£65 [≈ $117]**

Mason, John J.
- Minute structure of the central nervous system of certain reptiles and batrachians of America. Newport: Author's edition, 1879-82. 1st edn. Lge 4to. One of 100. 24,[9] pp. 113 microphoto plates. Contemp 3/4 lea, mrbld bds, rebacked, orig spine laid down.   *(Antiq Sc)* **$650 [≈ £361]**

Mason, Otis
- A treatise of the physiological and therapeutic action of the sulphate of quinine. Phila: 1882. 1st edn. 164 pp. Orig cloth. Inscrbd by author.   *(Fye)* **$75 [≈ £41]**

Massy, R. Tuthill
- Mild medicine in contradistinction to severe medicine. London: Sanderson, 1859. 2nd edn. Sm 8vo.. Dusty, lacking front free endpaper. Cloth. *(Marlborough)* **£45 [≈ $81]**

Masters, Walter E.
- A physician's autobiography of travel and adventure. Clearwater, Fl: privately printed, 1954. 1st edn. 8vo. 299 pp. 42 pp ills, ports. Cloth.   *(Elgen)* **$40 [≈ £22]**

The Mathematician
- The Mathematician. Numbers 1-4 [of 6 published]. Containing articles on: the rise, progress and improvement of geometry; chief properties of the parabola; conic sections ... London: 1745. viii,259 pp. Diags. 1st title grubby. New 3/4 lea.   *(Whitehart)* **£150 [≈ $270]**

Mather, W.
- The young-man's companion: or, arithmetick made easy ... London: 1734. 14th edn. 8vo. Frontis loose. Contemp calf.   *(Robertshaw)* **£30 [≈ $54]**
- The young-man's companion: or, the several branches of useful learning made perfectly easy ... London: 1764. 22nd edn. 8vo. Frontis, 4 plates. Contemp sheep.   *(Robertshaw)* **£30 [≈ $54]**

Mathieu, Albert
- Treatment of the diseases of the stomach and intestines. New York: 1894. 8vo. viii,294 pp. Sgntr on front endpaper. Cloth.   *(Rittenhouse)* **$30 [≈ £16]**

Matho ...
- Matho: or, the cosmotheoria puerilis ... See Baxter, Andrew

Matthew, Patrick
- On naval timber and arboriculture; with critical notes on authors who have recently treated the subject of planting. Edinburgh: Adam Black, 1831. 1st edn. 8vo. Half-title, 6 ills in text. Owner's stamp on title. Orig cloth, ptd paper label, uncut edges.   *(Traylen)* **£650 [≈ $1,170]**

Matthews, C.G. & Lott, F.E.
- The microscope in the brewery and malt-house. 1889. Lge 8vo. xxi,198 pp. Frontis, 21 plates, 30 text figs. Some plates foxed & offset. New endpapers.   *(Whitehart)* **£25 [≈ $45]**

Matthews, Henry
- The diary of an invalid being the journal of a tour in pursuit of health in Portugal, Italy, Switzerland and France ... 1818 and 1819. London: John Murray, 1820. 2nd edn. 8vo. xv,[1],515 pp. Title foxed. Contemp half calf. B'plate.   *(Claude Cox)* **£25 [≈ $45]**

Matthews, L.G.
- The Royal apothecaries. London: 1967. 8vo. 191 pp. Cloth, dw. Pres copy.
(Goodrich) **$65 [≈£36]**

Mauriceau, A.M.
- The married woman's private medical companion ... menstruation ... pregnancy. and how it may be determined ... discovery to prevent pregnancy ... New York: 1847. 1st edn. 238 pp. Foxed. Binding sl stained.
(Scientia) **$275 [≈£152]**

Mauriceau, Francois
- The diseases of women with child, and in child-bed: as also the best means of helping them in ... labours ... London: Andrew Bell, 1710. 4th edn. 8vo. xliv,373,[11] pp. 10 plates, most fldg. Browning & spotting, stamps on title & plates. Contemp calf.
(Hemlock) **$275 [≈£152]**

Maury, M.F.
- The physical geography of the sea. New York: Harper, 1855. 1st edn. 8vo. xxiv,274 pp. 12 plates (8 fldg). Orig blue gilt-stamped cloth, cvrs faded, extremities rubbed & chipped. *(Karmiole)* **$250 [≈£138]**
- The physical geography of the sea, and its meteorology. London: 1874. 15th edn. 8vo. xx,487 pp. 15 plates & diags (2 bound in upside down). Contemp polished calf, gilt spine. *(Bow Windows)* **£45 [≈$81]**

Mawe, John
- A descriptive catalogue of minerals, intended for the use of students ... the new invented blow-pipe ... the lapidary's apparatus. London: the author ..., 1816. 2nd edn. 8vo. xiv,94,[2 errata] pp. Inserted leaf *ix/*x, engvd frontis. Contemp half-calf, worn.
(Burmester) **£120 [≈$216]**
- Familiar lessons in mineralogy and geology ... London: 1820. 2nd edn. 12mo. vi,[ii],96 pp. 2 hand-cold plates (1 a little cropped) & 2 others. Some foxing. Rec qtr calf.
(Bow Windows) **£95 [≈$171]**
- Familiar lessons in mineralogy and geology ... to which is added a practical description of the use of the lapidary's apparatus. London: for the author, 1822. 4th edn. Cr 8vo. 4 aquatint plates. Rec half mor, mrbld bds.
(Stewart) **£100 [≈$180]**
- Familiar lessons in mineralogy and geology ... a practical description of the use of the lapidary's apparatus. London: 1828. 10th edn. Sm 8vo. 5 plates (4 cold). Mod half calf.
(Wheldon & Wesley) **£65 [≈$117]**
- The mineralogy of Derbyshire, with a

description of the most interesting mines in the North of England, in Scotland, and in Wales ... London: 1802. 1st edn. 8vo. Engvd frontis. Orig grey bds, paper spine (worn), uncut edges. *(Traylen)* **£105 [≈$189]**

Mawe, Thomas & Abercrombie, J.
- Every man his own gardener, being a new and much more complete gardener's calendar and general directory. London: 1803. 17th edn. Lge 12mo. vii,758, [96 index],[2 blank] pp. Engvd frontis. Rec half calf.
(Bow Windows) **£75 [≈$135]**
- Every man his own gardener, with a new complete gardener's calendar and general directory. London: 1805. 18th edn, crrctd & enlgd. Thick 12mo. About 850 pp. Port. Old lea, gilt back. *(Argosy)* **$150 [≈£83]**

Mawley, Edward
- The weather of 1879. As observed in the neighbourhood of London ... with tables of daily observations and a diagram. London: Bemrose, [1880]. Orig ptd wraps. Author's sgnd pres copy. *(C.R. Johnson)* **£18 [≈$32]**

Maxim, Sir Hiram S.
- Artificial and natural flight. London: 1909. 2nd edn. 8vo. xv,176 pp. Ills. Cloth, ft of cvr with sm tears & sev heavy indents.
(Elgen) **$85 [≈£47]**
- Artificial and natural flight. London: 1908. 1st edn. 8vo. xv,166 pp. Num ills & diags. Orig gilt-lettered cloth, faded.
(Weiner) **£75 [≈$135]**

Maxwell, James Clerk
- An elementary treatise on electricity. Oxford: Clarendon Press, 1888. 2nd edn. 8vo. xvi,208 pp. 6 plates, 53 text figs. Orig cloth, trifling wear to spine ends. *(Pollak)* **£40 [≈$72]**
- An elementary treatise on electricity. Oxford: Clarendon Press, 1881. 1st edn. xvi,208 pp. 6 litho plates, 39 pp pub advts, text ills. Orig cloth. *(Rootenberg)* **$350 [≈£194]**
- The scientific papers ... Edited by W.D. Niven. Cambridge: University Press, 1890. 1st edn. 2 vols. Lge 4to. xxix,[3],607; vii,[1], 806 pp, 2 pp pub advts. Port frontis, 2 ports, 14 litho plates, num ills. Uncut in orig cloth, cvrs lightly discold.
(Rootenberg) **$850 [≈£472]**
- Theory of heat. London: Longmans, Green, 1872. 2nd edn. 8vo. xii,312 pp. 40 text figs. Foxed at ends. Orig cloth, faded.
(Pollak) **£40 [≈$72]**
- A treatise on electricity and magnetism. Oxford: Clarendon Press, 1873. 1st edn. 2 vols. 8vo. 20 plates & an un-numbered plate,

2 half-titles, errata slip in vol 1. Contemp calf, gilt arms on sides, rebacked.
(Chaucer Head) **£1,100 [≃ $1,980]**
- A treatise on electricity and magnetism. Oxford: Clarendon Press, 1881. 2nd edn. 2 vols. 8vo. Orig cloth.
(Chaucer Head) **£175 [≃ $315]**
- A treatise on electricity and magnetism. Oxford: Clarendon Press, 1881. 2nd edn. 2 vols. 8vo. xxxi,[i],464; xxiii,[i],456, 32 ctlg pp. 20 plates, 104 text figs. Marg pencilled notes. Orig cloth, recased.
(Pollak) **£250 [≃ $450]**
- A treatise on electricity and magnetism. Oxford: Clarendon Press, 1904. 3rd edn. 2 vols. 8vo. Orig cloth, gilt.
(Traylen) **£130 [≃ $234]**

Maxwell, Robert, of Arkland
- The practical husbandman; being a collection of miscellaneous papers on husbandry, &c. Edinburgh: for the author, 1757. 1st edn. xii,432,[4] pp. Contemp half calf, upper hinge broken, lower hinge cracked.
(Claude Cox) **£100 [≃ $180]**

May, W.
- The Queen's closet opened. Incomparable secrets in physic, chirurgery, preserving ... Part II ... making perfumes ... Part III The compleat cook ... London: Blagrave, 1683. 12mo. [10],190,[8]; 106,[4]; 123,[7]. Pp 95-102 in pt III in facs. Mod calf. Wing M104.
(Hemlock) **£550 [≃ £305]**

Mayer, Edgar
- Clinical application of sunlight and artificial radiation. Balt: Williams & Wilkins, 1926. 1st edn. 468 pp. Ills. Orig cloth.
(Oasis) **$25 [≃ £13]**
- Clinical application of sunlight and artificial radiation ... Balt: 1926. 1st edn. xiv,468 pp. Ills. Orig cloth. *(Rittenhouse)* **$37.50 [≃ £20]**

Maynwaring, Everard
- Tutela sanitatis ... the protection of long life, and detection of its brevity ... London: Peter Lillicrap, 1664. 1st edn (?). 8vo. [24],118,[2] pp. Red & black title. Sm hole B5 affecting 1 letter, possibly lacking last leaf. Contemp calf, rebacked, recrnrd.
(Rootenberg) **£500 [≃ £277]**

Mayo, Herbert
- A series of engravings ... the structure of the brain and spinal chord in man. London: 1827. 1st edn. Folio. 7 engvd plates on india paper, 7 outline plates (outer marg of 1 reprd, some spotting & soiling). Stamp on title. Contemp

bds, rebacked in cloth.
(Quaritch) **$650 [≃ £361]**

Mayow, John
- Medico-physical works. Being a translation of Tractatus Quinque Medico-Physici. Edinburgh: 1907. 8vo. 331 pp. Plates. Cloth.
(Goodrich) **$75 [≃ £41]**

Mead, Kate Campbell
- Medical women of America. A short history of the pioneer medical women of America and a few of their colleagues in England. Froben Press, 1933. 95 pp. Ports. Cloth, ex lib.
(Goodrich) **$75 [≃ £41]**

Mead, Richard
- A discourse concerning the action of the sun and the moon on animal bodies ... London: 1708. 1st edn. 8vo. 32 pp. Sl foxed. A lge copy in rec mor-backed bds.
(Pickering) **$800 [≃ £444]**
- A discourse on the plague ... the ninth edition corrected and enlarged. London: for A. Millar ..., 1744. Lge paper. 8vo. [viii],xl,164 pp. Inscribed 'From the author' on blank facing title. Polished calf, gilt, rebacked, orig spine laid down, 2 crnrs reprd.
(Pickering) **$450 [≃ £250]**
- A mechanical account of poisons. In several essays. London: 1702. 1st edn. 175 pp. Plate. Stamp on title. Lea, rebacked, new endpapers. *(Scientia)* **$250 [≃ £138]**
- A mechanical account of poisons in several essays. London: for Ralph Smith, 1708. 2nd edn, revsd. 8vo. [xvi],189,[2 explanation],[1 blank] pp. Fldg engvd plate. Contemp polished calf, jnts cracked.
(Pickering) **$250 [≃ £138]**
- A mechanical account of poisons in several essays. London: for Ralph Smith, 1702. 1st edn. Sm 8vo. [xvi],183,[i] pp. Contemp sprinkled calf, sl rubbed, rec rebacked.
(Blackwell's) **£160 [≃ $288]**
- A mechanical account of poisons in several essays. London: 1708. 2nd edn. Rebound in stiff mrbld wraps.
(Rittenhouse) **$195 [≃ £108]**
- Medical precepts and cautions ... Translated from the Latin by Thomas Stack. London: 1755. 2nd edn. 8vo. xvi,311,[1] pp. Inscrptn on flyleaf. Contemp calf.
(Hemlock) **$240 [≃ £133]**
- Medical precepts and cautions. Translated by Thomas Stack. London: J. Brindley, 1755. 2nd edn. 8vo. xvi,311 pp. Advt leaf. Orig lea bds, rebacked, crnrs bumped, hd of spine chipped. *(Elgen)* **$250 [≃ £138]**
- The medical works. London: 1762. 1st edn.

4to. 662 pp. 6 fldg plates. Rec half lea.
(Fye) **$400 [≃ £222]**

- The medical works ... with an account of the life and writings of the author ... Edinburgh: Alexander Donaldson, 1765. 1st edn of this coll. 3 vols. 8vo. 18,272; viii,255; 213,[73 index] pp. Contemp polished calf, hd of 1 spine nicked, jnts of 1 vol weak.
(Pickering) **$600 [≃ £333]**

- The medical works. Dublin: Thomas Ewing, 1767. 8vo. 5 plates. Contemp calf, worn, spine broken. *(Robertshaw)* **£25 [≃ $45]**

- A short discourse concerning pestilential contagion, and the methods to be used to prevent it ... Dublin: George Grierson, 1720. 4th edn. Portions of lower marg cut away & replaced. Mod mrbld bds.
(Emerald Isle) **£125 [≃ $225]**

- A short discourse concerning pestilential contagion, and the methods to be used to prevent it ... London: Sam. Buckley ..., 1722. 8th edn, with lge addtns. Lge paper. 8vo. [viii], xxxvi,150 pp. Contemp red mor, spine & sides gilt. *(Pickering)* **$400 [≃ £222]**

Meager, Leonard
- The English gardener or a sure guide to your planters and gardeners ... For P. Parker ..., 1670. 1st edn. Sm 4to. 24 engvs. Lower portion of 1 plate torn away with some loss, sm piece cut out of the middle of 3 plates. Early calf, rebacked, new endpapers.
(Sotheran) **£585 [≃ $1,053]**

Meigs, Charles D.
- Obstetrics, the science and the art. Phila: 1849. 1st edn. Lge 8vo. 685,32 pub ctlg pp. Num ills. Sheep. *(Elgen)* **$110 [≃ £61]**

Meigs, J. Forsyth
- A practical treatise on the diseases of children. Phila: 1853. 2nd edn. 711 pp. Lea.
(Fye) **$75 [≃ £41]**

- A practical treatise on the diseases of children. Phila: 1858. 3rd edn. 8vo. 724 pp. Orig cloth, rubbed. *(Goodrich)* **$25 [≃ £13]**

Melville, Henry, First Viscount
- A letter ... to ... Spencer Perceval, on the subject of naval timber. London: S. Bagster, 1810. 44 pp. Stabbed & uncut as issued.
(C.R. Johnson) **£75 [≃ $135]**

Memoirs ...
- Memoirs of diphtheria. From the writings of Bretonneau, Guersant, Thousseau ... and Daviot. New Sydenham Soc, 1859. 8vo. Orig cloth. *(Halewood)* **£30 [≃ $54]**
- Memoirs of diptheria from the writings of

Bretonneau, Guersant, Trousseau ... and Daviot. London: New Sydenham Soc, 1859. Orig cloth. *(Rittenhouse)* **$37.50 [≃ £20]**

Mendeleeff, Dmitry I.
- The principles of chemistry. London: Longmans, Green, 1891. 1st edn in English. 2 vols. 8vo. xvi,611; vi,487.[1] pp. Fldg table, text figs. Some cloth dye staining to margs of some pp vol I. Lib stamps on titles. Orig cloth, rear cvrs waterstained.
(Antiq Sc) **$300 [≃ £166]**

Mendelsohn, Simon
- Embalming fluids: their historical development and formulation ... New York: 1940. 8vo. ix,166 pp. Frontis. Cloth. Ex lib.
(Elgen) **$25 [≃ £13]**

Merle, William
- Merle's ms 'Consideraciones Temperiei pro 7 Annis ...'; the earliest known journal of the weather, kept ... 1337-1344, reproduced and translated ... London: 1891. Folio. Not paginated. One of 100, of which 20 for sale. Orig ptd parchment-cvrd bds, bowed.
(Weiner) **£50 [≃ $90]**

Merrill, A.P.
- Lectures on fever delivered in the Memphis Medical College, 1853-56. New York: 1865. 8vo. 236 pp. Orig cloth.
(Goodrich) **$60 [≃ £33]**

Merriman, Samuel
- A synopsis of the various kinds of difficult parturition, with practical remarks on the management of labours. Phila: Thomas Dobson, 1816. 1st Amer edn. 8vo. viii,9-297 pp. 5 engvd plates, fldg table. Contemp calf, hd of spine bruised, hinges rubbed.
(Hemlock) **$175 [≃ £97]**

Metchnikoff, Elie
- Immunity in infective diseases. Translated ... Cambridge Univ Pres, 1905. 1st edn in English. 8vo. xvi,591 pp. Text ills. Orig cloth, jnts started, crnrs bumped. Ex lib.
(Elgen) **$250 [≃ £138]**

Method of Tanning ...
- A method of tanning without bark ... See Maple, William

Methods ...
- Sure methods of improving health and prolonging life ... by regulating the diet and regimen ... rules for reducing corpulence ... illustrated by cases. London: 1828. 3rd edn, revsd & enlgd. Sm 8vo. xii,394,[2] pp.

Contemp cloth, minor bruises to end of spine.
(Hemlock) **$100 [≈ £55]**

Mettler, Cecilia
- History of medicine. A correlative text, arranged according to subjects. Phila: Blakiston, 1947. 8vo. 1215 pp. Ills. Cloth.
(Goodrich) **$150 [≈ £83]**

Meyer, Ernst von
- A history of chemistry ... translated with the author's sanction. London: 1891. 8vo. xiii,556 pp. Orig cloth, spine a little worn.
(Weiner) **£25 [≈ $45]**

Meyer, Oskar Emil
- The kinetic theory of gases. Translated ... London: Longmans, Green, 1899. 1st English edn. 8vo. xvi,[ii],472, 32 ctlg pp. 4 text figs. Pub bndg, a little faded.
(Pollak) **£80 [≈ $144]**

Meyer, W. & Schmieden, V.
- Bier's hyperemic treatment in surgery, medicine and the specialities. A manual of its practical application. Phila: 1908. 209 pp. 95 diags. Light foxing on endpapers. Cloth, dust-stained, spine faded, inner hinges sl cracked.
(Whitehart) **£25 [≈ $45]**

Meyrick, W.
- The new family herbal; or, domestic physician. Birmingham: Pearson, 1790. xxiv,498,[vi advts] pp. Engvd frontis (sl waterstained), 14 plates. Calf, rebacked.
(P & P) **£98 [≈ $176]**

Michelson, Albert A.
- On the application of interference methods to spectroscopic measurements. Washington: Smithsonian, 1892. 1st edn. Folio. 24 pp. 5 litho plates (4 double-page). Orig ptd wraps, a bit frayed at edges. Rubber stamp on front wrap & title.
(Antiq Sc) **$100 [≈ £55]**

Mickle, Wm. Julius
- General paralysis of the insane. London: 1880. 1st edn. 8vo. vi,246,16 pub ctlg pp. Orig cloth, spine edges sl frayed, some spotting on cvrs.
(Elgen) **$90 [≈ £50]**

Miles, A.
- Surgical ward work and nursing. A handbook for nurses and others. London: 1899. 2nd edn. viii,288 pp. 333 ills. Orig cloth, marked, spine badly defective, front inner hinge cracked.
(Whitehart) **£25 [≈ $45]**

Miles, Alexander
- The Edinburgh School of Surgery before Lister. Edinburgh: Black, 1918. viii,220 pp. Frontis, 7 plates. Pub bndg.
(Pollak) **£20 [≈ $36]**

Miles, W.J.
- Modern practical farriery. London: n.d. [ca 1840]. 4to. 536; 96 pp. Full-page cold plates. Uncut in new cloth. *(Goodrich)* **$75 [≈ £41]**
- Modern practical farriery, a complete system of the veterinary art. 1868-69. 4to. 20 cold, 28 plain plates, other ills in text. Victorian half calf. *(Sotheran)* **£88 [≈ $158]**
- Modern practical farriery. London: n.d. [post 1886]. 4to. vii,vi,538, 96 pp. 46 plates (20 cold). Red half mor, trifle rubbed.
(Bow Windows) **£105 [≈ $189]**

Mill, James
- Analysis of the phenomena of the human mind. A new edition with notes illustrative and critical ... London: Longmans, 1869. 2 vols. 8vo. xxiv,453; vi,403,24 advts pp. Occas foxing. Uncut in orig brown cloth.
(Frew Mackenzie) **£120 [≈ $216]**

Mill, John Stuart
- A system of logic ... being a connective view of the principles of evidence, and the methods of scientific investigation. London: John W. Parker, 1856. 4th edn. 2 vols. 8vo. Mod half mor, cloth bds.
(Chaucer Head) **£130 [≈ $234]**
- A system of logic ... being a connective view of the principles of evidence, and the methods of scientific investigation. London: Parker ..., 1862. 5th edn. 2 vols. xvi,536; xii,550 pp. Endleaves dampstained. 19th c prize calf.
(Frew Mackenzie) **£98 [≈ $176]**

Millard, John
- The new art of memory, founded upon the principles taught by Feinagle; with some account of the principal systems of artificial memory. London: 1812. 408 pp. 5 fldg plates. Orig bds, lacking backstrip, front cvr detached. *(Argosy)* **$75 [≈ £41]**

Miller, Edward
- The medical works. New York: 1814. 1st edn. 384 pp. Waterstain affecting sev leaves, final leaf torn without loss. Half lea, backstrip rubbed, hinges cracked. *(Fye)* **$200 [≈ £111]**

Miller, Hugh
- The cruise of the 'Betsey'; or, a summer ramble among the fossiliferous deposits of the Hebrides. With rambles of a geologist ...

Edinburgh: 1858. 1st edn. 8vo. [iv],486,[5 advts] pp. Some spots & dust marks. Rec half calf, mrbld sides, new endpapers.
(Bow Windows) £65 [≈ $117]
- Edinburgh and its neighbourhood geological and historical, with the geology of the Bass Rock. Edinburgh: 1864. 8vo. xi,313 pp. 3 plates, errata leaf. Orig cloth, front inner jnt loose, sl wear. *(Weiner)* £40 [≈ $72]
- The old red sandstone; or new walks in an old field. Edinburgh: John Johnstone, 1841. 1st edn. Cold fldg frontis, 9 engvd plates, 3pp pub ctlg. Ink name on title. Half mor, gilt, by Ramage. *(Cooper Hay)* £85 [≈ $153]
- The testimony of the rocks: or geology in its bearings on the two theologies, natural and revealed. London: 1857. 1st edn. 8vo. xii,500 pp. Ills. Orig cloth, a little loose & worn.
(Weiner) £30 [≈ $54]
- The testimony of the rocks; or, geology in its bearings on the two theologies, natural and revealed. Edinburgh: 1857. 1st edn. 8vo. [xii],500 pp. Frontis, 152 figs. Light damp mark on lower marg through sev sgntrs, other spots & marks. Rec half calf.
(Bow Windows) £55 [≈ $99]

Miller, Philip
- The abridgement of the gardeners dictionary. London: 1771. 6th edn. 4to. Engvd frontis, 12 fldg plates. Plate 5 defective, last few leaves heavily stained, inscrptn cut from title marg. Half calf, worn.
(Wheldon & Wesley) £65 [≈ $117]
- The abridgement of the gardeners dictionary. For the author, 1771. 6th edn. 4to. [vii,920] pp. Frontis, 10 fldg plates, ptd in double column. Sl foxing & soiling. New qtr brown mor. *(Blackwell's)* £85 [≈ $153]
- The gardener's and botanist's dictionary. Ninth edition, edited by T. Martyn. London: 1807. 2 vols in 4. Folio. 20 engvd plates. Half russia. *(Wheldon & Wesley)* £150 [≈ $270]
- The gardeners dictionary ... cultivating and improving the kitchen ... flower-garden ... the physick garden ... London: 1731. 1st edn. Folio. Engvd frontis, 4 fldg plates. Title a bit stained & dusty, some minor staining & worming. Contemp calf, rebacked.
(Clark) £250 [≈ $450]
- The gardeners dictionary ... kitchen, fruit and flower-garden ... physick garden ... London: 1731. 1st edn. Folio. Unpaginated. Engvd frontis, 4 engvd plates. Trivial soiling. Conte,mp panelled calf, rebacked, sides rubbed. *(Frew Mackenzie)* £290 [≈ $522]
- The gardeners dictionary ... the kitchen, fruit and flower garden ... London: 1731. 1st edn. Folio. xvi,[841] pp. Frontis, 4 plates. Mod

buckram, crnrs trifle bumped.
(Wheldon & Wesley) £200 [≈ $360]
- The gardeners dictionary ... as also, the physick garden ... London: for the author, 1733. 2nd edn crrctd. [with] An appendix to ... 1735. Folio. Unpaginated. Engvd frontis, 4 engvd plates. text figs. Contemp calf.
(Frew Mackenzie) £265 [≈ $477]
- The gardeners kalendar; directing what works are to be performed every month in the kitchen, fruit and pleasure gardens ... 1762. 13th edn. Engvd frontis, 4 fldg plates. Contemp calf, rebacked.
(Halewood) £58 [≈ $104]
- The gardeners kalendar. London: 1769. 15th edn. 8vo. lxvi,382,[21] pp. Frontis, 5 plates. New half calf.
(Wheldon & Wesley) £45 [≈ $81]

Miller, W.H.
- A treatise on crystallography. Cambridge: Deighton, 1839. 1st edn. 8vo. 10 plates. Uncut. Mod bds, qtr cloth, a little worn.
(Taylor) £23 [≈ $41]

Millikan, Robert A.
- The electron: its isolation and measurement and the determination of some of its properties. Chicago: Univ of Chicago Press, [1917]. 1st edn, 1st imp. 12mo. xii,[268],[1 pub advt] pp. 5 plates, ills in text. Orig cloth, spine faded, hinges reprd.
(Antiq Sc) $125 [≈ £69]

Millikan, Robert Andrew
- Evolution in science and religion. New Haven: 1935. 7th ptg. 95 pp. Uncut & unopened. Cloth. *(Elgen)* $25 [≈ £13]

Millingen, J.G.
- Curiosities of medical experience. London: 1839. 2nd edn. 8vo. xvi,566 pp. Occas light foxing. Cloth, spine worn & reglued.
(Weiner) £20 [≈ $36]

Milne, David
- Essay on comets. Edinburgh: 1828. Lge paper. 4to. 189 pp. Uncut in contemp cloth-backed bds. *(Argosy)* $75 [≈ £41]

Milne, E.A.
- Kinematic relativity. Oxford: 1948. vii,238 pp. Dw. *(Whitehart)* £35 [≈ $63]
- Relativity, gravitation and world structure. Oxford: 1935. 1st edn. ix,365 pp. Frontis, 3 other plates. Torn dw.
(Whitehart) £40 [≈ $72]

Milton, John Laws
- The treatment of syphilis. London: [1875].
1st edn. 8vo. 151,16 pub ctlg pp. Text w'cuts.
Orig cloth, gilt, front cvr detchd.
(Elgen) **$50 [≃£27]**

Minto, Walter
- An inaugural oration, on the progress and
importance of the mathematical sciences.
Trenton [N.J.]: Isaac Collins, 1788. 1st edn.
8vo. 51 pp. Brown staining. Mod blue wraps.
(Antiq Sc) **$350 [≃£194]**
- Researches into some parts of the theory of
the planets ... to determine the circular orbit
of a planet ... London: C. Dilly, 1783. 8vo.
xviii,72 pp. Orig bds, uncut, new paper
backstrip, paper label.
(Cooper Hay) **£35 [≃$63]**

Mitchel, O.M.
- The astronomy of the Bible. New York: 1867.
Sm 8vo. 322 pp. Port frontis. Scattered
foxing. Cloth, spine ends frayed.
(Elgen) **$40 [≃£22]**

Mitchell, Edward
- Engravings of the muscles, carefully copied
from the folio plates of Jules Cloquet.
Edinburgh: Maclachlan & Stewart, 1832. 1st
edn. 4to. Title, advt leaf, 24 engvd plates,
each with explanatory text. Orig watered
cloth.   *(Bickersteth)* **£110 [≃$198]**

Mitchell, James
- The portable encyclopaedia: or, a dictionary
of the arts and sciences ... Thomas Tegg,
1839. 8vo. iv,710 pp. 51 engvd plates. Foxed.
Contemp calf, rec rebacked.
(Blackwell's) **£55 [≃$99]**

Mitchell, Joseph
- Practical suggestions for relieving the over-
crowded thoroughfares of London   ...
improved ... locomotion; diverting the sewage
from the Thames ... London: Stanford, 1857.
1st edn. 8vo. 26 pp. Fldg map, 4 lithos (2
fldg). Some browning. Orig ptd wraps.
(Frew Mackenzie) **£220 [≃$396]**

Mitchell, S. Weir
- Fat and blood and how to make them.
London: 1878. 1st English edn from 2nd
Amer. 8vo. 109 pp. Rubbed.
(Goodrich) **$125 [≃£69]**
- Lectures on diseases of the nervous system,
especially in women. Phila: 1881. 1st edn.
238 pp. Orig cloth.   *(Fye)* **$275 [≃£152]**
- Lectures on diseases of the nervous system,
especially in women. Phila: 1885. 2nd edn,

revsd & enlgd. 8vo. xii,287 pp. Ex lib, with
stamps.   *(Rittenhouse)* **$50 [≃£27]**

Mitchell, Samuel Alfred
- Eclipses of the sun. New York: Columbia
Univ Press, 1923. 1st edn. 8vo. xvii,425 pp.
Frontis, 58 plates (3 cold or partly cold). Orig
dark green cloth, gilt.
(Blackwell's) **£45 [≃$81]**
- Eclipses of the sun. New York: Columbia
Univ Press, 1923. 1st edn. Thick 8vo. 425 pp.
Cold frontis, photo plates. Orig cloth.
(Xerxes) **$75 [≃£41]**

Mitchell, Thomas
- Hints on the connexions of labour with study,
as a preventive of diseases peculiar to students
... Cincinnati: 1832. 12mo. 85 pp. Foxed. Old
bds, rebacked.   *(Goodrich)* **$65 [≃£36]**

Mitscherlich, E.
- Practical and experimental chemistry,
adapted to arts and manufactures. London:
1838. xii,316 pp. 104 text engvs. New cloth.
(Whitehart) **£40 [≃$72]**

Moffatt, J.M.
- The book of science; a familiar introduction
... natural philosophy, adapted to the
comprehension of young people. 1834. 2nd
edn. Sm 8vo. Frontis, vignette title, ills. Orig
cloth, g.e.   *(Halewood)* **£25 [≃$45]**

Molesworth, Caroline
- The Cobham Journals: abstracts and
summaries of the meteorological and
phenological observations made by ... at
Cobham Surrey in the years 1825 to 1850.
London: Edward Stanford, 1880. Orig cloth.
(Waterfield's) **£20 [≃$36]**

Moller, F.P.
- Cod liver oil and chemistry. 1895. 4to.
cxxiii,508 pp. 2 fldg tables, num text diags.
Marg notes on some pp. New cloth.
(Whitehart) **£35 [≃$63]**
- Cod liver oil and chemistry. London: 1895.
Lge 8vo. cxxii,508 pp. Frontis, cold chart,
fldg table, diags. Orig pict cloth, gilt. Inscrbd
by author.   *(Weiner)* **£50 [≃$90]**

Molyneux, Thomas
- A concise introduction to the knowledge of
the globes ... London: Longman, Rees, 1829.
9th edn. 8vo. iv,130,[i] pp. Frontis with
moving dial, plate, full-page ill. Contemp tree
calf, gilt, crnrs lightly bumped.
(Frew Mackenzie) **£60 [≃$108]**

Monell, S.H.
- Thirty chapters on static electricity selected from the original manual of static electricity in X-ray and therapeutic uses. New York: 1903. Ltd edn with author's notes.
(Rittenhouse) **$45** [≈ £25]

Money, Edward
- Essay on the cultivation and manufacture of tea. Calcutta: 1872. 1st edn. 8vo. 156 pp. Cvrs dampmarked. Pres copy.
(Robertshaw) **£20** [≈ $36]

Monro, Alexander
- A description of all the bursae mucosae of the human body ... Edinburgh: for C. Elliot ..., 1788. 1st edn. Folio. 10 engvd plates (1 fldg), extra-illust with 4 plates (margs of some frayed), some spotting. Lge uncut copy in orig bds, soiled, rebacked.
(Quaritch) **$575** [≈ £319]

Monro, Alexander Primus
- The anatomy of the humane bones ... an anatomical treatise of the nerves ... description of the humane lacteal sac and duct ... Edinburgh: for William Munro, 1732. 2nd edn, 1st with treatise on nerves. 8vo. viii,iv, 41,[2 advts] pp. Contemp calf, rebacked.
(Pickering) **$750** [≈ £416]
- The anatomy of the humane bones ... an anatomical treatise of the nerves ... Edinburgh: for Wm Munro, 1732. 2nd edn. 8vo. viii,344, iv,41, [i blank],[ii advts] pp. Occas foxing, early names on prelims, lacking rear free endpaper. Contemp calf, sl worn.
(Pollak) **£125** [≈ $225]

Monteath, Robert
- The forester's guide and profitable planter ... to which is added the prevention and cure of dry rot. Edinburgh: Stirling & Kenney, 1824. 2nd edn. 8vo. 15 engvd plates. Orig bds, new cloth spine. *(Traylen)* **£50** [≈ $90]
- The forester's guide and profitable planter ... to which is added the prevention and cure of dry rot. 1836. 3rd edn. xi,500 pp. Fldg table, 16 plates (1 sl foxed). Contemp half calf, rebacked. *(Whitehart)* **£42** [≈ $75]

Montfaucon de Villars, Abbe de
- The diverting history of the Count de Gabalis ... the nature and advantages of studying the occult sciences ... the carnal knowledge of women to be renounc'd ... London: 1714. 2nd edn. 88 pp. Mod half calf.
(Robertshaw) **£130** [≈ $234]

Monti, Achille
- The fundamental data of modern pathology, history ... applications. Translated ... New Sydenham Soc, 1900. 8vo. viii,266 pp. Orig brown cloth, stain on upper cvr.
(Blackwell's) **£21** [≈ $37]

Moon, R.O.
- Hippocrates and his successors in relation to the philosophy of their time. The Fitzpatrick Lectures for 1921-1922. London: Longmans, Green, 1923. 8vo. ix,[iii],171,[i] pp. Pub bndg. *(Pollak)* **£25** [≈ $45]
- The relation of medicine to philosophy. London: Longmans, Green, 1909. 8vo. xiv,221, [iii] pp. Pub bndg. Ex lib.
(Pollak) **£20** [≈ $36]

Moore, F.J.
- A history of chemistry. New York: 1939. 3rd edn. 8vo. xxi,447 pp. Ports, diags. Orig cloth.
(Weiner) **£20** [≈ $36]

Moore, George
- The use of the body in relation to the mind. London: 1847. 2nd edn. 8vo. 433 pp. Name on title. Calf, spine sl rubbed.
(Oasis) **$75** [≈ £41]

Moore, Isabella
- The useful and entertaining family miscellany. Palmer, 1766. 1st edn. 8vo. vii,[i],112 pp. A few sl marks & creases. New half mor. *(Ash)* **£500** [≈ $900]

Moore, John
- An inaugural dissertation on digitalis purpurea, or fox-glove; and its use in some diseases ... submitted to the ... University of Pennsylvania ... for the Degree of Master of Medicine. Phila: 1800. Without plates. Cropped, disbound.
(Rittenhouse) **$150** [≈ £83]

Moore, John Hamilton
- The new practical navigator. London: B. Law ... and the author, 1796. 12th edn. 8vo. viii,309,[1],[222 tables].[6] pp. Engvd frontis, 8 engvd plates, text w'cuts. Scattered spotting, tear to 1 lf. Contemp calf, old rebacking. *(Antiq Sc)* **$175** [≈ £97]
- The new practical navigator. London: 1814. 19th edn, enlgd ... by Joseph Dessiou. 8vo. Port, xvi,336, [218 tables] pp. 11 plates (2 fldg), many text diags. Rec bds.
(Fenning) **£55** [≈ $99]

Moore, Sir Jonas
- A mathematical compendium ... arithmetick,

geometry, astronomy ... dyalling ... application of pendulums ... London: for J. Philips ..., 1705. 4th edn. 12mo. [24],120,[174] pp. 4 engvd tables (1 fldg), sev tables in text. 19th c calf, rebacked.
(Burmester) **£40 [≃ $72]**

Moore, Norman

- An essay on the history of medicine in Ireland. Dublin: 1910. Sm 8vo. 36 pp. Wraps. *(Weiner)* **£15 [≃ $27]**
- The history of St. Bartholemew's Hospital. London: 1918. 2 vols. 4to. xxii,614; xiii,992 pp. Plates. Orig cloth, dws.
(Weiner) **£85 [≃ $153]**
- The history of the study of medicine in the British Isles ... Oxford: 1908. 8vo. vii,202 pp. 11 plates. Orig cloth. *(Weiner)* **£50 [≃ $90]**
- The history of the study of medicine in the British Isles. The Fitzpatrick Lectures for 1905-1906. Oxford: Clarendon Press, 1908. 8vo. vi,[ii],202 pp. Frontis, 10 plates. Pub bndg. *(Pollak)* **£30 [≃ $54]**
- The physician in English history. Linacre Lecture, 1913. Cambridge: 1913. 8vo. 57 pp. *(Weiner)* **£15 [≃ $27]**

Moorhead, John J.

- Traumatic surgery. Phila: 1917. 1st edn, 3rd ptg. Lge 8vo. 760,14 pub ctlg pp. Num ills, plates. Cloth. *(Elgen)* **$40 [≃ £22]**

Moral Philosophy ...

- Outlines of moral philosophy ... See Stewart, Dugald

Morewood, Samuel

- A philosophical and statistical history of ... the manufacture and use of inebriating liquors ... practice of distillation ... consumption and effects of opium ... Dublin: William Curry ..., 1838. 8vo. W'engvs in text. Half calf, gilt panelled spine.
(Traylen) **£135 [≃ $243]**

Morfitt, Campbell

- A treatise on chemistry applied to the manufacture of soap and candles. Phila: 1860. New imprvd edn. 8vo. 599 pp. Num text ills. Orig cloth. *(Oasis)* **$50 [≃ £27]**

Morgagni, Giovanni Battista

- The seats and causes of diseases investigated by anatomy: in five books ... from the Latin. London: A. Millar ..., 1769. 1st edn in English. 3 vols. 4to. xxxii,[4], 3-868; vi,[2],3-770; 3-604,[152] pp. Lightly browned. Contemp calf, 19th c rebacking.
(Rootenberg) **$2,000 [≃ £1,111]**

Morgan, George T.

- An outline of inflammation and its effects: being first principles of surgery. Phila: 1838. 8vo. viii,134 pp. Foxed. Half lea, mrbld bds, rubbed & scuffed. Ex lib. *(Elgen)* **$40 [≃ £22]**

Morgan, John

- The journal of Dr. John Morgan of Philadelphia from the City of Rome to the City of London 1764 ... Phila: for private circulation, 1907. 1st edn. One of 165. Orig cloth, spine mottled, paper labels v worn.
(Scientia) **$150 [≃ £83]**

Morgan, Sir T.C.

- Sketches of the philosophy of life. London: 1819. 8vo. x,[ii],466 pp. Contemp calf, spine gilt, crnrs sl worn & 1 bumped.
(Bow Windows) **£45 [≃ $81]**

Morgan, Thomas

- Philosophical principles of medicine, in three parts ... a demonstration of the general laws ... the more particular laws ... chief intentions of medicine ... London: 1725. 8vo. lviii,440 pp. Fldg plate. Contemp panelled calf, spine edges & crnrs sl worn. *(Pollak)* **£250 [≃ $450]**

Morgan, Thomas Hunt

- A critique of the theory of evolution. Princeton Univ Press, 1916. 1st edn. x,197 pp. Text figs. Orig cloth. Author's sgnd pres inscrptn. *(Antiq Sc)* **$275 [≃ £152]**
- A critique of the theory of evolution. Princeton Univ Press, 1916. 1st edn. x,197 pp. Text figs. Orig cloth. Lib shelf number removed from spine. *(Antiq Sc)* **$75 [≃ £41]**
- A critique of the theory of evolution. Princeton: 1916. 1st edn. 197 pp. Orig cloth.
(Scientia) **$65 [≃ £36]**
- Embryology and genetics. New York: Columbia Univ Press, 1934. 1st edn. 8vo. vii,[3],258,[1] pp. Text figs. Orig cloth.
(Antiq Sc) **$50 [≃ £27]**
- Evolution and genetics. Princeton: 1925. 8vo. ix,211 pp. 77 text figs. Orig cloth.
(Wheldon & Wesley) **£55 [≃ $99]**
- Experimental embryology. New York: 1927. 1st edn. 766 pp. Sm piece cut from single leaf with loss of text. Orig cloth.
(Scientia) **$85 [≃ £47]**
- Heredity and sex. New York: 1913. 1st edn. 282 pp. Cloth. *(Scientia)* **$125 [≃ £69]**
- The physical basis of heredity. Phila & London: Lippincott, [1919]. 1st edn. 8vo. 305 pp. Text figs. Orig cloth.
(Antiq Sc) **$75 [≃ £41]**
- The physical basis of heredity. Phila: 1919.

1st edn. 305 pp. Orig cloth.
(Scientia) **$85 [≃£47]**
- The physical basis of heredity. Phila: 1919. 1st edn. 8vo. 305 pp. Plates, diags. Some pencil underlining. Orig cloth.
(Weiner) **£25 [≃$45]**
- The theory of the gene. New Haven: 1926. 1st edn. 343 pp. Embossed stamp on title. Orig cloth. *(Scientia)* **$75 [≃£41]**
- The theory of the gene. Yale Univ Press, 1926. 1st edn. 8vo. xvi,343 pp. Text figs. Orig cloth. *(Antiq Sc)* **$75 [≃£41]**
- The theory of the gene. New Haven: 1928. Enlgd & revsd edn. 8vo. xviii,358 pp. Num ills. Cloth. *(Elgen)* **$45 [≃£25]**

Morgan, Thomas Hunt, et al.
- The mechanism of Mendelian heredity. New York: H. Holt, 1915. 1st edn. 8vo. xiii,[1], 62 pp. Text figs. Blindstamp on title. Orig cloth, a little soiled, label removed from spine.
(Antiq Sc) **$175 [≃£97]**
- The mechanism of Mendelian heredity. New York: 1915. 1st edn. 262 pp. Orig cloth, spine faded. *(Scientia)* **$250 [≃£138]**

Morley, Edward W.
- On the densities of oxygen and hydrogen, and the ratio of their atomic weights. Washington: Smithsonian, 1895. 1st edn. Folio. xi,117 pp. Orig ptd wraps, stamps on front wrap & title, wraps a bit soiled. *(Antiq Sc)* **$85 [≃£47]**

Morley, Henry
- The life of Bertrand Palissy of Saintes. Boston: Ticknor, Reed ..., 1853. 1st Amer edn. 2 vols. 8vo. 303: 347 pp. Orig cloth, spines sl worn. *(Oasis)* **$85 [≃£47]**

Morley, John
- Diderot and the Encyclopaedists. London: Macmillan, 1886. 2 vols. 8vo. xv,[i], 365,[iii]; xii,351,[v advts] pp. Pub bndg.
(Pollak) **£30 [≃$54]**

Morrice, Alexander
- A treatise on brewing: wherein is exhibited the whole process of the art and mystery ... For the author, 1802. 2nd edn. 8vo. [vi],180,[xii]pp. Fldg engvd plate. Contemp half calf, mrbld sides, jnts cracked, generally rubbed. *(Frew Mackenzie)* **£130 [≃$234]**

Morris, Caspar
- An essay on the pathology and therapeutics of scarlet fever. Phila: 1858. 2nd edn. 8vo. 192 pp. Orig cloth. *(Goodrich)* **$65 [≃£36]**

Morris, Corbyn
- An essay towards illustrating the science of insurance ... to fix, by precise calculation, several important maxims ... to solve various problems ... London: 1747. 1st edn. 8vo. xvi,[i],61 pp. Lacking half-title. Disbound.
(Burmester) **£350 [≃$630]**

Morris, George W.
- The early history of medicine in Philadelphia. Phila: privately printed, 1886. One of 125. 4to. 232 pp. Hand-made paper, plates. Orig cloth, rubbed.
(Goodrich) **$295 [≃£163]**

Morris, John
- A catalogue of British fossils ... with references to their geological distribution ... London: the author, 1854. 2nd edn, enlgd. 8vo. viii,372 pp. Cancelled blind lib stamp on title. Mod buckram. *(Bickersteth)* **£48 [≃$86]**

Morrison, John
- Medicine no mystery; being a brief outline of the principles of medical science ... London: 1829. 8vo. 165 pp. Orig bds, rebacked, uncut.
(Goodrich) **£65 [≃$36]**

Morse, John T.
- Life and letters of Oliver Wendell Holmes. Boston: Houghton, Mifflin, 1896. 1st edn. 2 vols. 8vo. 358; 335 pp. 2 engvd frontis. Orig cloth, t.e.g. *(Oasis)* **$60 [≃£33]**

Mortenson, O.
- Jen Olsen's clock. A technical description. Copenhagen: 1957. 4to. 156 pp. Port frontis, 83 text ills. *(Whitehart)* **£25 [≃$45]**

Mortimer, John
- Cotton spinning: the story of the spindle. Manchester: Palmer Howe, 1895. 49 ills. Orig red cloth. *(C.R. Johnson)* **£38 [≃$68]**

Mortimer, W. Golden
- Peru. History of coca "The Divine Plant" of the Incas. With an introductory account of the Incas, and of the Andean Indians. New York: J.H. Vail, 1901. 1st edn. 8vo. xxxi,576 pp. Line drawings throughout. Staining to front endpapers. Orig maroon cloth, gilt.
(Frew Mackenzie) **£135 [≃$243]**

Morton, A. Stanford
- Refraction of the eye. Its diagnosis and the correction of its errors. London: Lewis, 1897. 6th edn. viii,74,32 ctlg pp. 4 text plates, 9 figs. Orig cloth. *(Pollak)* **£20 [≃$36]**

Morton, Edward

- Remarks on the subject of lactation ... the disorders produced in mothers by suckling ... proving ... it is a common cause, in children, of hydrencephalus ... London: 1831. 1st edn. 8vo. ix,63 pp. Half-title. Interleaved with blanks (ms notes). Cloth, v worn.
(Elgen) **$175 [≈ £97]**

Morton, John

- On the nature and property of soils: their connexion with the geological formation on which they rest ... Second edn with an appendix. London: 1840. 2 vols. 12mo. Fldg cold plan. Contemp half calf, gilt.
(Traylen) **£30 [≈ $54]**

Morton, Richard

- Phthisiologia: or, a treatise of consumptions ... three books. I. Of original consumptions ... II. ... III. Of symptomatical consumptions ... London: for Sam. Smith ..., 1694. 1st edn in English. 8vo. Port frontis. Contemp panelled calf, rebacked. Wing M2830.
(Traylen) **£375 [≈ $675]**

Morton, Samuel G.

- Illustrations of pulmonary consumption, its anatomical characters, causes, symptoms and treatment. Phila: 1834. 1st edn. 8vo. xiii,183 pp. 12 cold plates. Occas light foxing. Orig calf, sl worn.   *(Rittenhouse)* **$195 [≈ £108]**
- Illustrations of pulmonary consumption, its anatomical characters, causes, symptoms and treatment. Phila: 1834. 1st edn. 183 pp. 12 plates (11 hand-cold). Lea, scuffed.
(Scientia) **$350 [≈ £194]**
- Illustrations of pulmonary consumption ... some remarks on the climate of the United States, the West Indies, &c. Phila: 1837. 2nd edn. 349 pp. 13 hand-cold engvd plates. Rec leatherette.   *(Fye)* **$200 [≈ £111]**

Morton, T. & Cadge, W.

- The surgical anatomy of the principal regions of the human body. 1850. ix,371,24 pp. 25 cold plates, some fldg (sev torn & reprd), text figs. New cloth.   *(Whitehart)* **£55 [≈ $99]**

Morton, Thomas

- Engravings illustrating the surgical anatomy of the head and neck, axilla, bend of elbow, and wrist, with descriptions. London: Taylor & Walton, 1845. 1st edn. 8vo. 1f, 24,8 pub ctlg pp. 8 lge fldg hand-cold copperplates. Orig cloth, sl damaged.
(Offenbacher) **$300 [≈ £166]**
- The surgical anatomy of the perinaeum, Taylor & Walton, 1838. Lge 8vo. [iv],80,[i advt] pp. 4 cold lithos & figs in the text. Orig green cloth, rebacked.
(Blackwell's) **£50 [≈ $90]**

Morton, William J.

- The X-ray or photography of the invisible and its value in surgery. New York: 1896. 1st edn. 196 pp. [with] "List of Radiographs, all life-sized, handsomely mounted." 53 line drawings, 30 repros of x-rays.
(Rittenhouse) **$300 [≈ £166]**

Moseley, H.

- A treatise on hydrostatics and hydrodynamics; for the use of students in the university. Cambridge: 1830. 1st edn. xii,290 pp. 4 fldg plates. Lib label, contemp ink sgntr on endpaper. 3/4 roan, badly rubbed, mrbld bds.   *(Whitehart)* **£28 [≈ $50]**

Moseley, Sydney A. & Chapple, H.J. Barton

- Television today & tomorrow. With a foreword by John L. Baird. London: Pitman, 1931. 2nd edn. 8vo. xxvii,163, 20,[iv advts] pp. Frontis, 64 plates, 44 figs. Pub bndg.
(Pollak) **£35 [≈ $63]**

Mosely, Henry Nottidge

- Notes by a naturalist on the 'Challenger' being an account of various observations made during the voyage ... Macmillan, 1879. 1st edn. 8vo. xvi,620 pp. Half-title, 2 plates, fldg map in colour, num text w'cuts. Sl foxing. Orig brown cloth.
(Blackwell's) **£100 [≈ $180]**
- Notes by a naturalist ... observations during the voyage of H.M.S. 'Challenger' ... 1892. New & revsd edn. 8vo. xxiv,540 pp. Port frontis, num w'cuts, fldg map. Orig cloth, sl soiled, upper hinge tender.
(Old Cinema) **£25 [≈ $45]**

Mosso, A.

- Fatigue. Translated by M. & W.B. Drummond. 1906. 2nd edn. xiv,334 pp. 30 diags. Cloth sl worn, inner hinges cracked but firm.   *(Whitehart)* **£35 [≈ $63]**

Mott, R.A.

- The history of coke making and of the Coke Oven Managers' Association. Cambridge: 1936. 8vo. 139 pp. Plates, ills. Orig cloth.
(Weiner) **£20 [≈ $36]**

Motte, Andrew

- A treatise of the mechanical powers, wherein the laws of motion ... are explained and demonstrated ... London: Benj. Motte, 1727. 1st edn. 8vo. [6],222,[2] pp. Errata, advt leaf,

3 engvd plates, text w'cuts (1 full-page). Contemp panelled calf, rebacked.
(Rootenberg) **$950 [≃ £527]**

Motte, Benjamin
- The philosophical transactions from the year MDCC (where Mr. Lowthorp ends) to the year MDCCXX. London: for R. Wilkin ..., 1721. 2 vols. 4to. 53 plates or diags (some fldg). Contemp panelled calf, rebacked.
(Waterfield's) **£300 [≃ $540]**

Moxon, Joseph
- A tutor to astronomy and geography ... London: for Joseph Moxon, 1674. 3rd edn, crrctd & enlgd. 4to. Engvd frontis, text figs. Paper flaw on M4 without loss of text. New grey bds. Wing 3024.
(Stewart) **£175 [≃ $315]**

Moyes, J.
- Medicine and kindred arts in the plays of Shakespeare. Glasgow: 1896. 8vo. 123 pp. Orig cloth, uncut. *(Weiner)* **£30 [≃ $54]**

Moyniham, Sir Berkeley
- Essays on surgical subjects. Phila: 1921. 1st Amer edn. 8vo. 253 pp. Ills. Cloth, sm stain on cvr. *(Elgen)* **$60 [≃ £33]**
- Gall-stones and their surgical treatment. Phila: 1904. 1st Amer edn. Lge 8vo. 386,16 pub ctlg pp. Cold frontis, 71 ills, plates. Cloth, inner hinges cracked.
(Elgen) **$85 [≃ £47]**
- Gall-stones and their surgical treatment. Phila: 1905. 1st edn, 2nd iss. 8vo. 385 pp. Cloth. *(Goodrich)* **$50 [≃ £27]**

Mudie, R.
- The air. 1835. viii,280 pp. Col ptd frontis & cold vignette title (both by Baxter). Sm piece cut from title. Mod cloth.
(Whitehart) **£20 [≃ $36]**

Muir, M.M. Pattison
- A history of chemical theories and laws. New York: 1907. 8vo. xx,555 pp. Title re-margined & tissued on verso, New buckram.
(Weiner) **£50 [≃ $90]**

Muirhead, James Patrick
- Correspondence of the late James Watt on his discovery of the theory of the composition of water. 1846. Lge paper. Lge 4to. cxxviii,264 pp. Contemp polished calf gilt, rebacked, orig spine laid on. *(Whitehart)* **£125 [≃ $225]**
- The life of James Watt with selections from his correspondence. London: 1858. 1st edn. 8vo. xvi,580 pp. Port (a little dampmarked),

plates, figs. Foxing on plates & adjacent leaves. Orig cloth, hinges a little strained, hd of spine trifle fingered.
(Bow Windows) **£140 [≃ $252]**
- The origin and progress of the mechanical inventions of James Watt. London: Murray, 1854. 1st edn. 3 vols. 8vo. 3 frontis, 60 w'cut ills, 34 lge fldg plates. Full polished calf, gilt, gilt panelled spines, mrbld edges.
(Traylen) **£330 [≃ $594]**

Muller, John, Professor of Artillery ...
- Elements of mathematics ... for the use of the Royal Academy of Artillery at Woolwich. London: 1765. 3rd edn, imprvd. 8vo. xxxvi,312 pp. 28 fldg plates. Cloth-backed mrbld bds, worn. *(Weiner)* **£45 [≃ $81]**

Munde, Paul F.
- Minor surgical gynecology. New York: Wood's Library, 1880. 1st edn. 381 pp. 300 text ills. Orig cloth. *(Oasis)* **$75 [≃ £41]**

Munk, William
- The Roll of the Royal College of Physicians of London ... from 1518 to 1825. London: 1878. 2nd revsd edn. 3 vols. 8vo. B'plates.
(Rittenhouse) **$75 [≃ £41]**

Munro, Robert
- The lake-dwellings of Europe. 1890. Roy 8vo. xl,600,16 pub ctlg pp. Many ills inc some fldg. Endpapers foxed. Orig cloth, spine sl faded. *(Old Cinema)* **£45 [≃ $81]**
- Palaeolithic man and Terramara settlements in Europe. Edinburgh; 1912. 1st edn. Lge 8vo. [xxiv],507 pp. 75 plates. 174 text figs. Orig cloth. *(Bow Windows)* **£30 [≃ $54]**

Murchison, Sir Roderick Impey
- Siluria. The history of the oldest known rocks containing organic remains. London: Murray, 1854. 1st edn. Roy 8vo. Hand-cold fldg engvd map, 37 litho plates (3 fldg), w'cut diags in text. Half calf.
(Traylen) **£85 [≃ $153]**

Murchisonn, Charles
- A treatise on the continued fevers of Great Britain. London: 1862. 1st edn. 638 pp. Pub ctlg dated 1865. Mod half lea, mrbld bds.
(Scientia) **$300 [≃ £166]**

Murray, John
- A treatise on pulmonary consumption. Its prevention and remedy. London: Whittaker ..., 1830. 8vo. x,156,[ii] pp. Orig cloth, faded, spine ends worn. Author's pres copy.
(Pollak) **£30 [≃ $54]**

Murray, John
- A system of chemistry. Edinburgh: 1809. 2nd edn. 4 vols. Thick 8vo. Nearly 3000 pp in total. 8 plates. Contemp cloth-backed bds.
  (Weiner) £100 [≃ $180]

Museum Rusticum ...
- Museum rusticum et commerciale: or, select papers on agriculture, commerce, arts, and manufactures ... London: 1764-66. 1st edn. 6 vols. 8vo. 14 engvd plates (7 fldg), 9 tables (7 fldg), other ills. Contemp speckled calf, gilt, mor labels (1 lacking).
  (Traylen) £280 [≃ $504]

Musgrave, Samuel
- An essay on the nature and cure of the (so-called) worm-fever. London: sold by T. Payne ..., 1776. 8vo. Light staining on title. Mod bds.   *(Stewart)* £75 [≃ $135]

Muspratt, Sheridan
- Chemistry theoretical, practical and analytical, as applied and relating to the arts and manufactures. William Mackenzie, [1860]. 1st edn. 2 vols. 835,9 index; [iv],1186, 10 index pp. 32 engvd ports, 1007 w'engvs in text. 2 engvd titles, ptd title vol II.
  (Blackwell's) £75 [≃ $135]
- Chemistry theoretical, practical and analytical ... London: 1860. 2 vols. Lge thick 8vo. 9,836; 1186,10 pp. Extra engvd titles (with lib stamps), 32 engvd ports, text ills. Orig gilt-dec cloth, a little faded, short tear at ft of vol 2 spine, hinge sl shaken.
  (Weiner) £100 [≃ $180]

Muybridge, Eadweard
- The human figure in motion; an electrophotographic investigation of consecutive phases of muscular actions. London: 1931. 7th imp. 277 pp. Cloth, spine faded & with sm tears at hd & ft.
  (Scientia) $85 [≃ £47]
- See also Stillman, J.D.B.

Myer, Jesse S.
- Life and letters of Dr. William Beaumont. St. Louis: 1912. 1st edn. Tattered dw.
  (Rittenhouse) $45 [≃ £25]

Myers, Charles S.
- A text-book of experimental psychology. New York: Longmans, & London: Arnold, 1909. 1st edn. 8vo. xvi,432 pp. Num figs in text. Orig cloth.   *(Antiq Sc)* $75 [≃ £41]

Myrtle, A.S.
- Practical observations on the Harrogate

mineral waters with cases. London: Bailliere ..., 1874. 3rd edn. 8vo. Orig cloth, gilt.
  (Cooper Hay) £24 [≃ $43]

Naismith, John
- General view of the agriculture of the county of Clydesdale. Brentford: 1794. 1st edn. 4to. 82 pp. Half-title. Disbound, final leaf almost detchd.   *(Claude Cox)* £30 [≃ $54]
- General view of the agriculture of the county of Clydesdale. Glasgow: J. Mundell ..., 1798. 8vo. Fldg engvd map. 19th c half calf, mrbld sides, lightly rubbed. *(Hughes)* £75 [≃ $135]

Napier, James
- A manual of dyeing and dyeing receipts, comprising a system of elementary chemistry ... with coloured pattern of cloth of each fabric. Charles Griffin, 1875. 3rd edn. 8vo. xxviii,420,32 advts pp. Text ills, 57 mtd cloth samples. Orig cloth, reprd.
  (Fenning) £65 [≃ $117]

Nascher, I.L.
- Geriatrics: the diseases of old age and their treatment. Phila: Blakiston, 1914. 1st edn. 8vo. 517 pp. 50 plates. Orig cloth.
  (Oasis) $45 [≃ £25]

Nash, E.B.
- Leaders in typhoid fever. Phila: 1900. 1st edn. Sm 8vo. 135 pp. Cloth. Ex lib.
  (Elgen) $30 [≃ £16]

Nasmyth, James & Carpenter, James
- The moon: considered as a planet, a world, and a satellite. London: Murray, 1874. 1st edn. xvi,189 pp. 24 plates, inc Woodburytypes, heliotypes, engvs & a litho, text w'cuts. Orig dec cloth, rebacked.
  (Antiq Sc) $600 [≃ £333]
- The moon: considered as a planet, a world, and a satellite. London: 1885. 3rd edn. 26 plates, mostly mtd Woodburytypes. Orig dec cloth, sl rubbed.   *(Oasis)* $120 [≃ £66]

Nature & Place of Hell ...
- An enquiry into the nature and place of hell. London: W. Bowyer. for W. Taylor, 1714. 2 fldg plates, errata. Contemp calf, rebacked. (Situated in the sun, with supporting astronomical arguments).
  (C.R. Johnson) £75 [≃ $135]

Neale, Richard
- The medical digest, or busy practitioner's vade-mecum. Ledger, Smith, 1882. 2nd edn. 8vo. [xvi],643, lxxxii pp. Orig cloth.
  (Blackwell's) £25 [≃ $45]

- The medical digest, or busy practitioner's vade-mecum. London: 1882. 2nd edn. 8vo. 643 pp. 82 pp index. Crnr of title torn away. Cloth. Ex lib with some defects.
(Rittenhouse) **$30 [≃ £16]**

Needham, John Turbeville
- An account of some new microscopical discoveries founded on an examination of the calamary ... London: for F. Needham, 1745. 1st edn. 8vo. viii,126,[2 advts] pp. Contemp calf, gilt spine, new label, rubbed, crnrs worn.
(Pickering) **$450 [≃ £250]**

Needham, Joseph
- Biochemistry and morphogenesis. Cambridge Univ Press, 1942. 1st edn. 8vo. xvi,785 pp. Cold frontis, 35 plates (4 cold), num ills. A little pencil underlining & marg notes. Cloth, sl shaken, inner hinges cracked.
(Elgen) **$60 [≃ £33]**

Negretti & Zambra
- A treatise on meteorological instruments. London: Negretti & Zambra, 1864. 1st edn. Roy 8vo. xii,152 pp. 8 pp pub ctlg, 98 text w'cuts. Orig cloth, spine faded.
(Rootenberg) **$425 [≃ £236]**

Neidhard, C.
- Pathogenetic and clinical repertory of the most prominent symptoms of the head. With their concomitants and conditions. Phila: 1888. 1st edn. 8vo. 188 pp. Pub ctlg.
(Rittenhouse) **$35 [≃ £19]**

Neligan, J. Moore
- Atlas of cutaneous diseases. Phila: 1857. 16 cold plates. Orig cloth, extremities worn.
(Scientia) **$135 [≃ £75]**
- Atlas of cutaneous diseases. Phila: 1859. 1st Amer edn, later ptg. 4to. 16 plates (15 chromolithos), all with tissue gds & explanatory leaves. Orig blindstamped cloth, spine edges & crnrs frayed, inner hinges cracked, shaken.   *(Elgen)* **$150 [≃ £83]**

Neri, A.
- The art of glass wherein are shown the wayes to make and colour glass, pastes, enamels ... London: 1662. Sole English trans. 11ff (ex 12), 352 pp (ex 362, lacking 10,[4] at end although final leaf has 'Finis'). 6 plates from another work. Mod half lea.
(Whitehart) **£200 [≃ $360]**

Nernst, Walter
- Theoretical chemistry from the standpoint of Avogadro's Rule and thermodynamics. London: Macmillan, 1916. 4th English edn

(with addtnl material). 8vo. 853 pp. Orig cloth, spine sl snagged.   *(Oasis)* **$50 [≃ £27]**

Neuberger, Albert
- The technical arts and sciences of the ancients. Translated ... London: Methuen, 1930. xxxii,518,[i] pp. 676 figs. Pub bndg, a trifle slack.   *(Pollak)* **£45 [≃ $81]**

Neumann, Caspar
- The chemical works ... Abridged and methodized. With large additions ... by William Lewis ... London: Johnston ..., 1759. 1st edn in English. 4to. [xvi],586, [xxxviii index] pp. Contemp calf, sl rubbed, spine reprd at hd & ft.
(Frew Mackenzie) **£575 [≃ $1,035]**
- The chemical works ... Abridged and methodized. With large additions ... by William Lewis ... London: Johnston ..., 1759. 1st edn. 4to. [28],586, [76] pp. Contemp lea, jnts cracked.   *(Antiq Sc)* **$350 [≃ £194]**

Neumann, John von & Morganstern, Oscar
- Theory of games and economic behavior ... Princeton: Univ Press, 1944. 1st edn. 8vo. xviii,625,[1]pp. Orig cloth, corrigenda laid in.
(Rootenberg) **$400 [≃ £222]**

Newcastle, William Cavendish, Duke of
- A new method, and extraordinary invention, to dress horses, and work them according to nature. London: 1667. 1st edn. Lge paper. Folio. [xxii],40, 352,[iv] pp. 1 leaf with minor tear, another ragged at ft, occas light foxing& staining. Contemp calf, rebacked.
(Pirages) **$650 [≃ £361]**

Newenham, Thomas
- A statistical and historical inquiry into the progress and magnitude of the population of Ireland. For C. & R. Baldwin, 1805. 1st edn. 8vo. vi,xix,360 pp. Final advt leaf, 3 fldg tables. Without the errata. Contemp half calf, jnts weak, headbands worn.
(Fenning) **£185 [≃ $333]**

Newlands, J.A.R. & B.E.R.
- Sugar. A handbook for planters and refiners. 1909. New edn. xxxvi,876, [48,32] pp. Plates & num ills. Orig pict cloth, sl marked.
(Whitehart) **£18 [≃ $32]**

Newman, Sir George
- The rise of preventative medicine. The Health Clark Lectures for 1931. London: OUP, 1932. vi,[vi], 270,[ii] pp. 8 plates. Pub bndg.   *(Pollak)* **£30 [≃ $54]**

Newman, George, et al.
- Prize essays on leprosy. New Sydenham Soc, 1895. 8vo. v,227,37 ctlg pp. Orig brown cloth.   *(Blackwell's)* **£21 [≃ $37]**

Newsholme, Sir Arthur
- Fifty years in public health. A personal narrative with comments. London: 1935. 8vo. 415 pp. Ports, graphs (some fldg). Orig cloth.   *(Weiner)* **£21 [≃ $37]**

Newton, Herbert C.
- Harmonic vibrations and vibration figures. London: [1909]. 8vo. 215 pp. 28 plates (most cold with overlays), diags, ills. Orig cloth, marked.   *(Weiner)* **£25 [≃ $45]**

Newton, Sir Isaac
- The chronology of ancient kingdoms amended ... London: for J. Tonson ..., 1728. 1st edn. xiv,[2],376 pp. 3 fldg plans. 1st half of text v sl mottled, tear in 1 marg. Contemp Cambridge calf, jnts cracked, spine worn & darkened.   *(Pirages)* **$200 [≃ £111]**
- Mathematical elements of natural philosophy ... 1720. 1st English edn. xxii,259,[2] pp. 33 fldg plates (2 loose). Marg of title & following page reprd. Contemp lea, spine & edges sl worn, new endpapers.
                            (Whitehart) **£180 [≃ $324]**
- The mathematical principles of natural philosophy ... laws of the moon's motion ... London: Motte, 1729. 1st edn in English. 2 vols. 8vo. [xxxviii],320; [ii],393,[13 index], viii appendix,71,[1 errata] pp. 2 engvd frontis, 32 fldg engvd plates. Mod calf, gilt.
                        (Pickering) **$6,000 [≃ £3,333]**
- The mathematical principles of natural philosophy ... Translated into English by Andrew Motte. London: Benjamin Motte, 1729. Vol 1 only. 1st edn in English. 8vo. [xxxviii],320 pp. Title reprd. Contemp calf, jnts cracking.   *(Halewood)* **£500 [≃ $900]**
- Observations upon the prophecies of David and the Apocalypse of St. John. In two parts. J. Darby & T. Browne, 1733. 1st edn. 4to. vi,[i],323 pp. Title lightly spotted & sm piece torn from crnr without loss. Contemp half calf, extremities worn, rebacked.
                        (Frew Mackenzie) **£175 [≃ $315]**
- Opticks: or a treatise on the reflections, refractions, inflections and colours of light. London: Innys, 1721. 3rd edn. 8vo. 382 pp. 12 fldg plates. Advt leaf at end. Contemp name on title. Contemp calf, sl worn, rec rebacked.   *(Oasis)* **$750 [≃ £416]**
- The system of the world demonstrated in an easy and popular manner ... London: for J. Robinson, 1740. 2nd edn, crrctd & imprvd.

8vo. 2 plates, cancel title. Contemp calf, front jnt cracked.   *(Waterfield's)* **£400 [≃ $720]**
- A treatise of the system of the world. London: for F. Fayram, 1728. 1st edn in English. 8vo. 2 engvd plates, errata leaf. Mod polished calf.
                    (Chaucer Head) **£1,100 [≃ $1,980]**

Newton, John
- Trigonometria Britannica: or, the doctrine of triangles in two books ... London: R. & W. Leybourn, 1658. 1st edn. Folio. [4]ff,96 pp, [94]ff, [46]ff, [12 of 14]ff. Title laid down (v worn with some segments missing). Browning, ms notes & scribbles. Lib buckram.   *(Elgen)* **$650 [≃ £361]**

Neymann, Clarence A.
- Artificial fever produced by physical means; its development and application. Springfield: [1938]. 8vo. xv,294 pp. Ills, plates. Cloth.
                            (Elgen) **$75 [≃ £41]**

Nias, J.B.
- Dr. John Radcliffe, a sketch of his life, with an account of his Fellows and Foundations. Oxford: 1918. 1st edn. 8vo. 147 pp. Port, 12 ills. Orig cloth. *(Bow Windows)* **£36 [≃ $64]**

Nichols, R.H. & Wray, F.A.
- The history of the Foundling Hospital. London: OUP, 1935. 4to. xiv,422 pp. Frontis, 61 plates. Endpapers spotted. Orig cloth, spine sl damaged.
                            (Whitehart) **£25 [≃ $45]**
- The history of the Foundling Hospital. London: OUP, 1935. 1st edn. 4to. xiv,422 pp. Num ills. Orig cloth.
                        (Bow Windows) **£42 [≃ $75]**

Nicholson, William (1753-1815)
- The first principles of chemistry. London: for G.G.J. & J. Robinson, 1790. 1st edn. Fldg plate. Contemp half calf.
                    (Chaucer Head) **£120 [≃ $216]**
- The first principles of chemistry ... London: for G.C.J. & J. Robinson ..., 1790. 1st edn. 8vo. xxviii,532,[5 index] pp. Fldg engvd plate. Sm wormhole in marg of 1st few leaves, title a little dust soiled. Early notes on endpaper. Contemp calf, little rubbed.
                        (Pickering) **$1,000 [≃ £555]**
- The first principles of chemistry. London: 1790. 1st edn. 8vo. xxvii,532,[5] pp. Fldg engvd plate. Calf, worn. Ex lib.
                            (Elgen) **$300 [≃ £166]**
- The first principles of chemistry. London: Robinson, 1790. 1st edn. xxvii,[1], 532,[5] pp. Fldg engvd plate. Contemp tree calf, ends of spine sl chipped, rubbed.

(Antiq Sc) **$300 [≈ £166]**
- The first principles of chemistry. London: Robinson, 1796. 3rd edn. xxi,[3], 564,[4] pp. Fldg engvd plate. Light unif browning. Contemp tree calf, lightly worn.
(Antiq Sc) **$85 [≈ £47]**
- An introduction to natural philosophy. London: for J. Johnson, 1782. 1st edn. 2 vols. 8vo. xx,383,[1 blank],[12 index]; xi,[1 blank],441,[14 index] pp. 25 fldg engvd plates. Contemp speckled half calf, mrbld bds, hds of spines chipped. The Westport House copy. *(Pickering)* **$1,000 [≈ £555]**

Nicol, Walter
- The planter's kalendar; or the nurseryman's and forester's guide in the operations of the nursery, the forest and the grove. Edinburgh: 1812. 1st edn. 596 pp. 3 plates (2 cold). Pub calf, sl worn. *(Edwards)* **£110 [≈ £198]**
- The practical planter, or, a treatise on forest planting ... London: Whittingham, 1803. 2nd edn. 8vo. Half polished calf, gilt, jnts worn.
(Traylen) **£45 [≈ £81]**

Nierenstein, M.
- Incunabula of tannin chemistry, a collection of some early papers ... reproduced in facsimile. 1932. Lge sq 8vo. 167 pp. Fldg map. Orig cloth. *(Weiner)* **£30 [≈ £54]**

Nightingale, Florence
- Florence Nightingale to her nurses. A selection from Miss Nightingale's address to probationers and nurses ... 1914. x,147 pp. Port frontis. Ink inscrptn on endpaper. Cloth, sl marked. *(Whitehart)* **£18 [≈ £32]**
- Notes on nursing: what it is and what it is not ... London: [December 1859 - January 1860]. 1st edn. 8vo. Yellow cold endpapers with advts. Orig limp black cloth.
(Traylen) **£105 [≈ £189]**
- Notes on nursing. London: [1860]. 1st edn. 8vo. Yellow cold endpapers with advts dated 1860. Orig limp black cloth, rebacked.
(Traylen) **£75 [≈ £135]**
- Notes on nursing. London: Harrison, [1860]. 1st edn, 1st iss, 1st state. 8vo. 79,[1] pp. Advts ptd on yellow coated endpapers. Orig black cloth, gilt lettering on upper cvr, rebacked, cloth a little faded.
(Pickering) **$1,000 [≈ £555]**
- Notes on nursing ... With some account of her life. Boston: William Carter, 1860. Pirated edn (?). Gilt embossed cloth, some rubbing.
(Goodrich) **$295 [≈ £163]**
- Notes on nursing. London: 1860. New edn, revsd & enlgd. 222 pp. Cloth, rebacked, new endpapers. *(Scientia)* **£165 [≈ £91]**

- Organization of nursing ... Liverpool & London: Longman ..., 1865. 1st edn. 8vo. [8],102 pp. Frontis (lightly foxed). Qtr mor over cloth. *(Rootenberg)* **$550 [≈ £305]**
- Statements exhibiting the voluntary contributions received by Miss Nightingale, for the use of the British War Hospitals in the East ... London: 1857. Sole edn. 8vo. Fldg litho frontis, lge fldg map, leaf 'additional list of subscribers' tipped-in. Orig wraps.
(Chaucer Head) **£220 [≈ $396]**

Nihell, James
- New and extraordinary observations concerning prediction by various crises of the pulse ... London: ... sold by James Crokatt, 1741. 1st edn. 8vo. xxviii,[xii], 154,[14 index] pp. Contemp sprinkled calf, spine gilt; Hopetoun b'plate.
(Pickering) **$1,000 [≈ £555]**

Niktalopsia ...
- Niktalopsia ... See Lynn, Walter

Noad, Henry M.
- A course of eight lectures; on electricity, galvanism, magnetism, and electro-magnetism. 1839. x,382 pp. 110 diags in text. Orig cloth, sl dust-stained, Author's pres copy. *(Whitehart)* **£40 [≈ £72]**
- Lectures on chemistry; including its applications in the arts and the analysis of organic and inorganic compounds. 1855. [6],505 pp. Errata leaf. Lge fldg chart, 106 text figs. Orig watered silk, marked & sl dust-stained, a little worn. *(Whitehart)* **£40 [≈ £72]**
- Lectures on electricity, comprising galvanism, magnetism ... thermo-electricity. London: 1844. New edn. 8vo. vi,457 pp. Extra engvd title. Orig binding.
(Weiner) **£50 [≈ $90]**

Noble, Sir Andrew
- Artillery and explosives. London: John Murray, 1906. 1st edn. Lge 8vo. Plates, diags. Orig gilt-lettered cloth.
(Chaucer Head) **£85 [≈ $153]**

Noble, Benjamin
- Geodaesia Hibernica, or an essay on practical surveying ... useful improvements ... Dublin: for the author, 1768. Errata slip tipped-in, fldg figs. Some fore-edge reprs. Contemp calf.
(Emerald Isle) **£165 [≈ $297]**

Noguchi, Hideyo
- Serrum diagnosis of syphilis and the butyric acid test for syphilis. Phila: 1910. 8vo. 173 pp. Owner's stamp on title. Cloth.
(Rittenhouse) **$45 [≈ £25]**

- Serrum diagnosis of syphilis and the butyric acid test for syphilis. Phila: 1910. 1st edn. 173 pp. Cloth.   (*Scientia*) **$100 [≃ £55]**

Nomenclature of Disease ...
- The nomenclature of disease drawn up by ... the Royal College of Physicians of London, reprinted by order of the American Medical Association. Phila: 1869. 99 pp. Orig ptd wraps bound in mod card wraps.
                (*Weiner*) **£100 [≃ $180]**

Noorden, Carl von
- Metabolism and practical medicine. London: 1907. 1st English edn. 3 vols. Roy 8vo. Orig cloth, gilt.   (*Traylen*) **£55 [≃ $99]**

Normandy, A.
- The commercial hand-book of chemical analysis ... determination of the intrinsic or commercial value of substances ... 1850. 12mo. xii,640 pp. Text figs. Cancelled blind lib stamp on title. Mod cloth.
                (*Bickersteth*) **£38 [≃ $68]**

Norris, H.S.
- Electric gas lighting. How to install ... systems for use in houses, churches, theatres, halls, schoole ... New York: Spon & Chamberlain, 1901. 12mo. viii,97,[19] advts pp. 57 text ills. Green cloth, stamped in gold & white.19   (*Karmiole*) **$30 [≃ £16]**

Norris, Richard
- The physiology and pathology of the blood. London: 1882. 1st edn. xlv,274 pp. 23 plates (part cold), 2 fldg tables. Cloth. Author's pres copy.   (*Elgen*) **$40 [≃ £22]**

Northcote, William
- A concise history of anatomy, from the earliest ages to antiquity. London: 1772. 1st edn. 8vo. Pencilled notes in text & on rear endpaper. Half calf, rear jnt reprd.
                (*Argosy*) **$150 [≃ £83]**

Norton, Geo S.
- Ophthalmic therapeutics. New York: 1882. 2nd edn. 8vo. 342 pp. Errata leaf, 20 pp pub ctlg. Cloth.   (*Elgen*) **$35 [≃ £19]**

Nothnagel, Hermann
- Diseases of the intestines and peritoneum. Phila: 1904. 1st edn in English. 8vo. 1032,16 pub ctlg pp. 20 plates. Some underlining in pink marker. Cloth, inner hinges cracked.
                (*Elgen*) **$30 [≃ £16]**

O'Malley, C.D., et al.
- Harvey's lectures on the whole of anatomy. Los Angeles: 1961. 239 pp. Orig cloth, dw.
                (*Goodrich*) **$35 [≃ £19]**

O'Neill, Charles
- A dictionary of calico printing and dyeing ... arts of printing and dyeing textile fabrics; with practical receipts ... London: Simpkin, Marshall ..., 1862. 1st edn. 8vo. [iv],215,xv pp. Some sl soiling, crnr torn from flyleaf. Orig cloth, spine rubbed.
                (*Burmester*) **£78 [≃ $140]**

O'Reilly, John
- The placenta, the organic nervous system, the blood, the oxygen ... physiologically examined. New York: 1861. 2nd edn. 8vo. 204,4 pp. 2 plates. Orig blindstamped pebbled cloth. Author's pres copy.
                (*Elgen*) **$200 [≃ £111]**

Observations ...
- Observations on modern gardening ... See Whately, T.
- Some observations concerning the plague ... occasioned by ... discourse of the learned Dr. Mead ... by a well wisher to the public. Dublin: George Grierson, 1721. Sm triangular piece cut from lower marg & replaced. Mod mrbld bds.
                (*Emerald Isle*) **£85 [≃ $153]**

Oeconomy of Human Life ...
- The oeconomy of human life ... See Dodsley, Robert

Oefele, Felix von
- History of chiropody. New York: n.d. [ca 1900]. 65 pp.   (*Goodrich*) **$25 [≃ £13]**

Oertel, Max J.
- Therapeutics of circulatory derangements. London: 1887. 1st edn in English. 276 pp. Cloth, rebacked, orig spine laid down, new endpapers.   (*Scientia*) **$150 [≃ £83]**

Oesterlen, F.
- Medical logic. London: Sydenham Soc, 1855. 8vo. 435 pp. Orig cloth, faded, hd of spine worn.   (*Goodrich*) **$35 [≃ £19]**

Oettingen, W.F. von
- Poisoning, a guide to clinical diagnosis and treatment. New York: 1952. 8vo. x,524 pp. Lib stamp on title. Cloth.
                (*Rittenhouse*) **$75 [≃ £41]**

Ohm, G.S.
- The galvanic circuit investigated mathematically. Translated ... New York: 1891. 12mo. 269 pp. Cloth. Ex lib.
(Elgen) **$30 [≈£16]**

Okell, Bateman
- A short treatise of the virtues of Dr. Bateman's pectoral drops: the nature of the distempers they cure, and the manner of their operation. [1726]. Sm 8vo. vii,48 pp. Mor-backed bds. *(Rootenberg)* **$350 [≈£194]**

Oliver, George
- Plain facts on vaccination. Simpkin, Marshall, 1871. Sm 8vo. 74 pp. Contemp green calf. mrbld endpapers.
(Blackwell's) **£75 [≈$135]**

Oliver, Henry K.
- An elementary treatise on the construction and use of the mathematical instruments usually put into portable cases. Boston: Perks & Marvin, 1830. 1st edn. 8vo. 68 pp. Errata slip. 6 fldg engvd plates, 1 sl torn, Unif light browning. Orig cloth-backed bds.
(Antiq Sc) **$110 [≈£61]**

Oliver, William
- A practical dissertation on Bath-waters ... to which is added a relation of a very extraordinary sleeper near Bath. Printed for Samuel Leake, bookseller in Bath ..., 1764. Contemp sheep, rebacked.
(Waterfield's) **£65 [≈$117]**

Olmsted, Denison
- An introduction to astronomy, designed ... for the students of Yale College. New York: 1846. 288 pp. Ills. Top edges stained. Orig calf. *(Jenkins)* **$45 [≈£25]**

Olmsted, J.M.D.
- Francois Magendie, pioneer in experimental physiology and scientific medicine in XIX century France. New York: 1944. 1st edn. 8vo. xvi,290 pp. Ills, ports. Cloth.
(Elgen) **$50 [≈£27]**

Opera Mineralia Explicata ...
- Opera mineralia explicata ... See Stringer, Moses

Oppenheim, H.
- Diseases of the nervous system. Phila: Lippincott, 1900. 1st edn in English. 8vo. 899 pp. Text ills. Orig cloth.
(Oasis) **$175 [≈£97]**

Oracle ...
- Oracle of the arts; or entertaining expounder ... A series of amusing experiments, useful receipts ... on popular arts and sciences. London: J. Bumpus, 1824. 12mo. 3 engvd plates. Contemp calf, gilt.
(Traylen) **£20 [≈$36]**

Orcutt, William Dana
- Wallace Clement Sabine. A study in achievement. Norwood, MA: privately printed, 1933. Lge 8vo. xiv,376 pp. 9 plates. 3/4 red mor, gilt spine.
(Karmiole) **$50 [≈£27]**

Ordinaire, Cluade Nicolas, Abbe
- The natural history of volcanoes: including submarine volcanoes, and other analogous phenomena. H. Baldwin, 1801. 8vo. xxiv,328 pp. Light browning throughout. Mod half tan, gilt, backstrip faded, mrbld bds & endpapers. *(Blackwell's)* **£150 [≈$270]**

Ordronaux, John
- Code of health of the School of Salerno. Translated into English verse ... Phila: 1870. Lge 8vo. 167 pp. Sgntr, & tear, on title. cvrs worn. *(Rittenhouse)* **$27.50 [≈£15]**

Orr, H. Winnett
- On the contributions of Hugh Owen Thomas ... Sir Robert Jones ... [et al.] to modern orthopedic surgery. With a supplement ... Springfield: [1949]. 1st edn. 8vo. xiv,253 pp. Frontis, ills, drwngs. Cloth, dw.
(Elgen) **$50 [≈£27]**

Orth, Johannes
- A compend of diagnosis in pathological anatomy. Translated ... Sole authorized English edition. New York: 1878. 8vo. 440 pp. Plates. Orig cloth. *(Goodrich)* **$75 [≈£41]**

Orton, J.W.
- The miner's guide and metallurgist's directory. New York: & Cincinnati: 1849. 1st edn. 12mo. 86,[9 advts] pp. Frontis chart. Occas minor foxing. Orig cloth, crnrs bumped, somewhat rubbed.
(Heritage) **$200 [≈£111]**

Orton, Job
- Discourses to the aged; on several important subjects. Shrewsbury: Eddowes, 1805. 8vo. 6,[ii],278, [ii] pp. Lge private lib stamp on f.e.p. Contemp tree calf, rebacked, crnrs reprd. *(Blackwell's)* **£45 [≈$81]**

Oschner, Albert J. & Thompson, Ralph L.

- The surgery and pathology of the thyroid and parathyroid glands. St. Louis: 1910. 1st edn. 8vo. 391 pp. 40 plates (4 cold), 57 text ills. Cloth.   *(Elgen)* **$50 [≃ £27]**

Oschner, Albert J. (ed.)

- Surgical diagnosis and treatment by American authors. Phila: 1920-22. 1st edn. 4 vols. 8vo. 46 cold plates, num engvs. Orig cloth.
  (Elgen) **$125 [≃ £69]**

Osler, Sir William

- An Alabama student and other biographical essays. Oxford: Clarendon Press, 1908. 1st edn. 8vo. [viii],334 pp. Frontis, 3 plates. Occas dusty marg. Orig cloth, spine faded & beginning to wear at ends.
  (Pollak) **£55 [≃ $99]**
- An Alabama student and other biographical essays. Oxford: 1929. Orig cloth, dw.
  (Goodrich) **$75 [≃ £41]**
- The evolution of modern medicine. New Haven: 1923. Lge 8vo. xv,243 pp. Ills. Orig cloth, spine ends & crnrs a little worn.
  (Weiner) **£50 [≃ $90]**
- The evolution of modern medicine. New Haven: 1935. 4to. Num ills. Cloth.
  (Halewood) **£48 [≃ $86]**
- The evolution of modern medicine. New Haven: Yale Univ Press, 1935. 5th printing. 4to. xiv,[1],243 pp. 107 ills. Orig cloth.
  (Hemlock) **$100 [≃ £55]**
- Incunabula medica. A study of the earliest printed medical books 1467-1480. Oxford: Biblio Soc., 1923. 4to. Engvd frontis. Orig qtr linen, soiled, bds rubbed.
  (Goodrich) **$425 [≃ £236]**
- Incunabula medica. A study of the earliest printed medical books 1467-1480. Oxford: 1923. 4to. 137 pp. 16 plates. Orig cloth.
  (Weiner) **£150 [≃ $270]**
- Lectures on angina pectoris and allied states. New York: 1897. 1st edn. 160 pp. Cloth.
  (Scientia) **$375 [≃ £208]**
- Lectures on the diagnosis of abdominal tumors. New York: 1899. Later iss. 192 pp. Orig cloth.   *(Goodrich)* **$75 [≃ £41]**
- Lectures on the diagnosis of abdominal tumors. New York: 1901. Cloth. Ex lib with stamps.   *(Rittenhouse)* **$35 [≃ £186]**
- The old humanities and the new science. Boston & New York: Houghton Mifflin, 1920. 8vo. xxii,64,[ii] pp. Frontis. Orig paper bds, sl wear to spine ends.
  (Pollak) **£30 [≃ $54]**
- The old humanities and the new science. Boston: 1920. 8vo. 64 pp. Cloth, worn dw.

(Goodrich) **$65 [≃ £36]**
- The principles and practice of medicine ... New York: 1892. 1st edn, 2nd iss. Rebound in full blue panelled calf. ₋ The principles and practice of medicine ... New York: Appleton, 1895. 2nd edn. Orig cloth, some wear.   *(Goodrich)* **$150 [≃ £83]**
  (Goodrich) **$575 [≃ £319]**
- The principles and practice of medicine ... New York: Appleton, 1899. 3rd edn. 3/4 calf, worn, jnts weak.   *(Goodrich)* **$125 [≃ £69]**
- The principles and practice of medicine ... NY & London: 1930. 11th edn, revsd. Thick 8vo. xxviii,[ii],1237 pp. Sgntr on flyleaf. Orig cloth.   *(Bow Windows)* **£60 [≃ $108]**
- Science and immortality. London: 1904. 12mo. 94 pp. Cloth, worn.
  (Goodrich) **$45 [≃ £25]**
- The student life and other essays. London: Constable, 1928. 1st coll edn. 8vo. xxxvi,145, [iii] pp. Frontis. Orig cloth, spine & rear cvr faded.   *(Pollak)* **£25 [≃ $45]**

Osmer, William

- A treatise on the diseases and lameness of horses. London: for T. Waller ..., 1761. 2nd edn. 8vo. [ii][2],300 pp. Half mor.
  (Pickering) **$150 [≃ £83]**

Ostrander, Tobias

- The planetarium, and astronomical calculator. Lyons [New York]: Western Argus, 1832. 1st edn. 8vo. Errata leaf. Mod half leà.   *(Argosy)* **$150 [≃ £83]**

Ostwald, Wilhelm

- Colour science ... authorised translation with introduction and notes. London: Winsor & Newton, [1931-33]. 2 vols. 8vo. xviii,141; xii,173 pp. Ports, plates (sev with mtd colour samples), 1 with volvelle), diags. Orig cloth.
  (Weiner) **£65 [≃ $117]**
- Manual of physico-chemical measurements. Translated ... London: Macmillan, 1894. 1st English edn. 8vo. xii,255,[i] pp. 188 text figs, 3 sets of tables in rear pocket. Pub bndg.
  (Pollak) **£30 [≃ $54]**
- The principles of inorganic chemistry. Translated ... London: 1914. 4th English edn. 8vo. xxxiii,836 pp. Ills. Cloth.
  (Elgen) **$30 [≃ £16]**
- The scientific foundations of analytical chemistry treated in an elementary manner. 1895. 1st English edn. xviii,207 pp. Orig cloth, v sl worn.   *(Whitehart)* **£25 [≃ $45]**

Ott, Isaac

- The action of medicines. Phila: 1878. 1st edn.

168 pp. Orig cloth. *(Fye)* **$75 [≈£41]**

Ottley, D.

- Observations of the surgical diseases of the head and neck. London: 1848. 8vo. 294 pp. Cloth, rebacked. *(Goodrich)* **$95 [≈£52]**

Owen, Charles

- An essay towards a natural history of serpents: in two parts ... London: for the author, 1742. 1st edn. 4to. 7 engvd plates. Contemp calf, gilt, rebacked, jnts cracking. *(Traylen)* **£420 [≈$756]**
- An essay towards a natural history of serpents: in two parts ... to which is added a third part ... London: 1742. xxiii,240,[12] pp. Pp 49-56 misbound. Various pp of related ms material bound in. Later half calf. *(Whitehart)* **£285 [≈$513]**

Owen, David Dale

- Report of a geological survey of Wisconsin, Iowa, and Minnesota; and ... a portion of Nebraska Territory ... Phila: 1852. 2 vols. 4to. 638,[1] pp text & frontis; atlas vol. Lge cold map, 2 other maps, 27 litho plates, 19 sections (18 cold). Orig cloth. *(Bow Windows)* **£235 [≈$423]**
- Report of a geological survey of Wisconsin, Iowa, and Minnesota; and ... a portion of Nebraska Territory ... Phila: 1852. 1st edn. 2 vols. 4to. xxxviii,637 pp. 119 engvs (72 w'cut, 2 copper, 36 steel, 9 stone), 3 maps (1 fldg & cold. Cvrs worn & rubbed. *(Edwards)* **£125 [≈$225]**
- Report of the geological survey in Kentucky. Made during the years 1854 and 1855. Kentucky: 1856. 1st edn. 3 vols, fldr of plates & maps. Lge 8vo. 416; 391; 589 pp. Orig cloth. Ex lib. *(Edwards)* **£125 [≈$225]**

Owen, Richard

- Descriptive and illustrated catalogue of the fossil reptilia of South Africa in ... the British Museum. London: 1876. Lge 4to. Title, xii,88 pp. 70 litho plates (some foxed). Some text leaves spotted. Orig cloth, jnts a little torn, inner hinges cracked. *(Bow Windows)* **£255 [≈$459]**
- Odontography; or a treatise on the comparative anatomy of the teeth ... London: Bailliere, 1840-45. 1st edn. 2 vols. Lge 8vo. xix,[3], lxxiv,655, [3]; 37,[1] pp. 168 litho plates numbered 1-150. Perf lib stamps on titles, some light foxing. Orig red half mor. *(Rootenberg)* **£750 [≈£416]**
- On parthenogenesis, or the successive production of procreating individuals from a single ovum. London: van Voorst, 1849. 1st

edn. 8vo. Litho frontis. Title spotted. Orig cloth. *(Quaritch)* **$350 [≈£194]**

- On the anatomy of vertebrates. London: Longmans, Green, 1866-68. 1st edn. 3 vols. 8vo. xlii,650; viii,592; x,915 pp. 2 fldg tables, num w'cuts. Orig cloth, rebacked, orig spines laid down. *(Antiq Sc)* **£285 [≈£158]**
- On the classification and geographical distribution of the mammalia ... To which is added an appendix On the gorilla, and On the extinction and transmutation of species. London: Parker, 1859. 1st edn. 8vo. Orig gilt-lettered brown cloth. *(Chaucer Head)* **£190 [≈$342]**
- The principle forms of the skeleton and of the teeth. Phila: 1854. 1st Amer edn. 329 pp. Pub ctlg. Cloth, spine lettering rubbed. *(Scientia)* **$75 [≈£41]**

Oxford University Expedition ...

- Scientific results of the Oxford University Expedition to Sarawak in 1932. Oxford Univ Press, 1952. 1st edn. 48 papers in 1 vol, as issued. Lge thick 8vo. Frontis, 34 half-tone ills, 20 plates, 2 sketch maps. Orig buckram. *(Halewood)* **£65 [≈$117]**

Ozanam, J.

- Recreations in mathematics and natural philosophy ... a new edition ... now translated into English ... by Charles Hutton. London: 1814. 4 vols. 8vo. 97 engvd plates. Contemp diced calf, rebacked. *(Traylen)* **£160 [≈$288]**

Pack, George T., et al.

- Burns; types, pathology and management. Phila: 1930. 1st edn. 364 pp. Cloth. *(Scientia)* **$75 [≈£41]**

Packard, F.R.

- Guy Patin and the medical profession in Paris in the XVIIth century. Oxford: 1924. xxii,334 pp. 17 ills inc 9 full-page plates. Cloth. *(Whitehart)* **£25 [≈$45]**

Packard, Francis R.

- History of medicine in the United States. New York: 1931 [2nd edn, i.e. 1932]. 2 vols. 8vo. xxv,656; xi,657-1323 pp. 103 ills, ports. 1 sgntr bound upside-down. Cloth. *(Elgen)* **$200 [≈£111]**
- Some account of the Pennsylvania Hospital from its first rise to the beginning of the year 1938. Phila: 1938. 1st edn. 8vo. xii,133 pp. Num ills, plates, facs. Orig cloth-backed bds, uncut & unopened. *(Elgen)* **$75 [≈£41]**
- Some account of the Pennsylvania Hospital ... Second printing, with a continuation of the account to the year 1956 ... Phila: 1957. 8vo.

xii,163 pp. Num ills, plates. Cloth, dw.
(Elgen) **$50 [≈ £27]**

Packard, John H.
- A manual of minor surgery. Phila: 1863. 1st edn. 288 pp. 145 ills. Front cvr stained.
(Scientia) **$175 [≈ £97]**

Paget, Sir James
- Medical classics. Balt: 1936. 8vo. Orig cloth.
(Goodrich) **$35 [≈ £19]**

Paget, Stephen
- Essays for students. London: Bailliere ..., 1899. 8vo. [iv],177,[i] pp. faded buckram.
(Pollak) **£20 [≈ $36]**
- Experiments on animals. With an introduction by Lord Lister. London: 1906. 3rd, revsd, edn. xii,387 pp. Frontis. Orig cloth, rather rubbed. *(Weiner)* **£25 [≈ $45]**

Pais, Abraham
- Developments in the theory of the electron, containing also an abstract of 'Field and Charge Measurements ...' a paper by N. Bohr and L. Rosenfeld. Princeton, NJ: 1948. 45 pp. Orig ptd wraps. *(Weiner)* **£50 [≈ $90]**

Paley, William
- Natural theology; or, evidences of the existence and attributes of the Deity. Collected from the appearance of nature. A new edition. London: 1817. 8vo. 468 pp. Some printer's smudges & other marks. Old half calf, a little rubbed.
(Bow Windows) **£55 [≈ $99]**

Pananicolau, George & Traut, H.F.
- Diagnosis of uterine cancer by the vaginal smear. New York: 1947. 3rd printing. Roy 8vo. 46 pp. 11 cold plates. Orig cloth, worn.
(Goodrich) **$50 [≈ £27]**

Pancoast, Joseph
- A treatise on operative surgery ... Phila: 1844. 1st edn. 4to. 380 pp. 80 plates (1 sl browned). Sl foxed. Cloth, spine edge reprd.
(Scientia) **$800 [≈ £444]**

Paneth, F.
- Radio-elements as indicators and other selected topics in inorganic chemistry. New York: 1928. 1st edn. ix,164 pp. Port frontis, text figs. Sgntr on title. Cloth.
(Whitehart) **£25 [≈ $45]**

Papin, Denis
- A new digester or engine for softening bones. London: H. Bonwicke, 1681. 1st edn. Sm 4to.

[4],52,[2 blank] pp. License lf, fldg engvd plate. Early lower margins worn, license lf backed & foremargin strengthened, a few dampstains. Old calf-backed mrbld bds.
(Antiq Sc) **$1,500 [≈ £833]**

Paris, John Ayrton
- Memoirs of the life and labours of the late Rev. William Gregor ... London: 1818. 8vo. 37 pp. Disbound. Author's pres copy.
(Goodrich) **$65 [≈ £36]**
- A treatise on diet ... for the prevention and cure of the diseases incident to a disordered state of the digestive functions. New York: 1828. 8vo. 210 pp. Uncut, cloth, stained & worn. Ex lib with sgntr & date on title, labels, b'plate. *(Rittenhouse)* **$170 [≈ £94]**
- A treatise on diet: with a view to establish ... a system of rules for the prevention and cure of the diseases incident to the disordered state of the digestive functions. London: Underwood, 1828. 3rd edn. 8vo. vii,439 pp. Advt leaf. 3/4 polished calf, gilt.
(Elgen) **$200 [≈ £111]**

Park, Roswell
- An epitome of the history of medicine. Phila: 1899. 2nd edn. 8vo. 360 pp. Orig cloth.
(Goodrich) **$35 [≈ £19]**
- A treatise on surgery by American authors. Condensed edition. New York: Lea Bros, 1899. 8vo. 1262 pp. 37 plates (sev in color), 625 text ills. Orig cloth, sl worn & shaken.
(Goodrich) **$50 [≈ £27]**

Parke, Thos Heazle
- My personal experiences in Equatorial Africa as medical Officer of the Emin Pasha Relief Expeditions. London: 1891. 8vo. 526 pp. Map, ills. Orig cloth. Shaken.
(Goodrich) **$35 [≈ £19]**

Parker, G.
- The early history of surgery in Great Britain, its organisation and development. London: 1920. 204 pp. Plates. Orig cloth.
(Weiner) **£20 [≈ $36]**
- The early history of surgery in Great Britain. Its organisation and development. London: 1920. 8vo. 204 pp. Orig cloth.
(Goodrich) **$35 [≈ £19]**

Parkes, Edmund
- A manual of practical hygiene ... for use in the medical service of the army, London: Churchill, 1866. 2nd edn. 8vo. 624 pp. Ills. Orig cloth. *(Oasis)* **$80 [≈ £44]**
- A manual of practical hygiene ... New York: Wood's Library, 1883. 6th edn. 2 vols. 8vo.

368; 556 pp. Ills. Orig cloth.
                    (Oasis) **$50 [≃ £27]**

Parkes, Samuel
- A chemical catechism for the use of young
  people ... London: 1806. 1st edn. 8vo. xi pp,
  [2]ff, 607,[1] pp. Frontis. Lib buckram. Ex
  lib.   *(Elgen)* **$125 [≃ £69]**
- The chemical catechism with notes,
  illustrations and experiments. London: 1818.
  8th edn. 8vo. 622 pp. Fldg frontis, plate. Half
  maroon calf, spine gilt, mrbld bds.
                    (Oasis) **$200 [≃ £111]**
- Chemical essays, principally relating to the
  arts and manufactures of the British
  Dominions. London: for the author, 1823.
  2nd edn. 2 vols. 8vo. 24 plates (some
  offsetting). Contemp half calf, rebacked.
                    (Chaucer Head) **£180 [≃ $324]**

Parkinson, J.
- Theatrum botanicum. The theater of plantes
  or, an universall and compleate herball.
  London: 1640. Folio. [xx],1756 (i.e. 1746),[1]
  pp. Errata leaf at end. W'cut tile, letterpress
  title, 2714 w'cuts. Contemp calf, rebacked.
                    (Wheldon & Wesley) **£1,500 [≃ $2,700]**

Parkinson, James
- Organic remains of a former world. London:
  1804-11. 1st edn. 3 vols. 4to. 2 cold & 1 plain
  frontis, plate of strata, 50 hand-cold plates.
  Contemp Spanish calf, gilt, gilt panelled
  spines.   *(Traylen)* **£595 [≃ $1,071]**

Parkyns, Sir Thomas
- (Greek title, then) The inn-play: or Cornish-
  hugg wrestler ... a method which teacheth to
  break all holds, and throw most falls
  mathematically ... For tho. Weekes ..., 1727.
  3rd edn crrctd. 4to. W'cuts in text. Sl
  browned. Contemp sheep, worn & rubbed.
                    (Charles Cox) **£225 [≃ $405]**

Parnell, Edward Andrew
- Elements of chemical analysis. London: 1845.
  New edn. 8vo. xiv,520 pp. Diags, tables. Orig
  dec blindstamped cloth. *(Weiner)* **£40 [≃ $72]**

Parr, Bartholomew
- The London medical dictionary; including,
  under distinct heads, every branch of
  medicine ... Phila: Mitchell et al., 1819. 1st
  Amer edn. 2 vols. Lge thick 4to. 57 engvd
  plates, some fldg. Foxed, with some
  dampstaining. Contemp calf, rebacked.
                    (Goodrich) **$395 [≃ £219]**
- The London medical dictionary; including,
  under distinct heads, every branch of

medicine ... Phila: 1819. 2 vols. 1020;
512,157 appendix, [15 index] pp. Plates.
Browned. Rebound.
                    (Rittenhouse) **$55 [≃ £30]**

Parry, John George
- Substitutes for wheaten flour. A treatise on
  rice and potatoes, as far as it related to the use
  of them in pastry ... London: for J. Bell, 1801.
  1st edn. 8vo. Disbound.
                    (Minkoff) **$375 [≃ £208]**

Parsons, J. Herbert
- Diseases of the eye. A manual for students
  and practitioners. J. & A. Churchill, 1907. 1st
  edn. 8vo. x,664,16 ctlg pp. 14 cold plates, 308
  figs in text. Orig red cloth, gilt, backstrip
  faded.   *(Blackwell's)* **£30 [≃ $54]**
- An introduction to the study of colour vision.
  Cambridge: 1915. viii,308 pp. Cold frontis,
  75 text diags. Foxing on endpapers & half-
  title. Cloth.   *(Whitehart)* **£18 [≃ $32]**

Parsons, James
- A mechanical and critical enquiry into the
  nature of hermaphrodites. London: for J.
  Walthoe, 1741. 1st edn. 8vo. 2ff, liv,[2],156
  pp. Advt leaf before p 1, 3 fldg engvd plates.
  2 short tears. Rec polished calf.
                    (Pirages) **$450 [≃ £250]**
- Philosophical observations on the analogy
  between the propagation of animals and that
  of vegetables. London: C. Davis, 1752. 1st
  edn. 8vo. xvi,276,[12] pp. Fldg engvd plate.
  Lightly browned. Contemp calf, jnts lightly
  cracked.   *(Antiq Sc)* **$275 [≃ £152]**
- Philosophical observations on the analogy
  between the propagation of animals and that
  of vegetables. London: 1752. 8vo.
  xvi,276,[12] pp. Fldg plate. Title & plate
  somewhat foxed. 1 or 2 pp torn without loss,
  few lib stamps. Contemp half calf, rebacked.
                    (Wheldon & Wesley) **£100 [≃ $180]**

Parsons, Usher
- Directions for making anatomical
  preparations formed on the basis of Pole,
  Marjolin ... and including the new method of
  Mr. Swan. Phila: 1831. 8vo. xxvi,316 pp. 4
  plates. Foxed. Old calf, rebacked.
                    (Goodrich) **$85 [≃ £47]**
- On the comparative influence of vegetable
  and animal decomposition as a cause of fever
  ... Phila: Skerrett, 1830. 8vo. 36 pp. Orig
  wraps.   *(Hemlock)* **$50 [≃ £27]**

Parsons, William
- The scientific papers of William Parsons,
  third Earl of Rosse 1800-1867. London: 1926.

1st edn. Lge 4to. Plates, ills in text. Orig black buckram. *(Chaucer Head)* **£90 [≈ $162]**

Particulars ...
- Some particulars of the Royal indisposition of 1788-1789 [George III], and of its effects upon illustrious personages and opposite parties interested in it. London: for the editor, 1804. 8vo. iv,111,[i advt] pp. Later cloth.
(Pollak) **£75 [≈ $135]**

Partington, C.F.
- An historical and descriptive account of the steam engine. London: 1822. xvi,187,90 pp. 8 fldg plates inc frontis. Orig bds, new cloth spine, a little dust-stained & browned.
(Whitehart) **£80 [≈ $144]**

Partington, J.R.
- A history of Greek fire and gunpowder. Cambridge: 1960. Lge 8vo. xvi,381 pp. Frontis, ills. Orig cloth, dw.
(Weiner) **£45 [≈ $81]**
- Origins and development of applied chemistry. London: 1935. Lge thick 8vo. xii,597 pp. Orig cloth.
(Weiner) **£100 [≈ $180]**
- Origins and development of applied chemistry. London: [1935]. 1st edn. 8vo. xii,597 pp. Orig cloth, sl marked, lib stamp on front endpaper. *(Whitehart)* **£85 [≈ $153]**
- A short history of chemistry. London: 1939. 8vo. xiv,386 pp. Ports, diags. Orig cloth.
(Weiner) **£25 [≈ $45]**

Partridge, William
- A practical treatise on dyeing of woollen, cotton and skein silk ... also a correct description of sulphuring woollens and chemical bleaching of cottons. New York: H. Wallis, 1823. 1st edn. 8vo. Plate. Orig calf, front hinge weakened.
(Minkoff) **$295 [≈ £163]**

Pasley, C.W.
- Observations on limes, calcereous cements, mortars ... numerous experiments for making an artificial water cement ... London: John Weale, 1838. 1st edn. 8vo. [76],288, 124 pp. Errata, ills in text. Rebacked pub cloth retaining orig spine, cvrs marked & faded.
(Spelman) **£70 [≈ $126]**

Pasley, Sir Charles W.
- Observations on the expediency and practicability of simplifying and improving the measures, weights, and money, used in this country ... Egerton's Military Lib., 1834. 1st edn. 8vo. xxx,176 pp. Sm stamp on title. Orig cloth. *(Fenning)* **£45 [≈ $81]**

Pasteur, Louis
- Studies on fermentation. The diseases of beer, their causes and means of preventing them. 1879. 1st English edn. xv,418 pp. 12 plates, 85 text ills. Light dampstain on a few pp at front & end, mostly marg. New cloth.
(Whitehart) **£85 [≈ $153]**
- Studies on fermentation. The diseases of beer, their causes and means of preventing them. London: Macmillan, 1879. 1st English edn. 8vo. 12 plates, text ills. Name stamp on title, w'cut port of Pasteur placed as frontis. Orig cloth.   *(Chaucer Head)* **£140 [≈ $252]**

Paterson, John
- The calculus of operations. Albany: Gray & Sprague, 1850. 1st edn. 8vo. viii,184 pp. 6 fldg charts. Orig cloth, extremities a little chipped.   *(Karmiole)* **$50 [≈ £27]**

Paul, C. Norman
- The influence of sunlight in the production of cancer of the skin. London: 1918. 1st edn. Sm 4to. 57 pp text, 44 full-page plates.
(Elgen) **$40 [≈ £22]**

Paulus, Aeginata
- The seven books. Trans. from the Greek ... by Francis Adams. London: Sydenham Soc, 1844-48. 3 vols. 8vo. xxviii,683; xi,[1],511; viii,653 pp. Ex lib Fisher collection. Orig cloth.   *(Hemlock)* **$300 [≈ £166]**

Pavlov, Ivan Petrovich
- Conditioned reflexes, an investigation of the physiological activity of the cerebral cortex ... Oxford: 1927. 1st English edn. 8vo. Small stain on fore-edge. Orig cloth.
(Sotheran) **£135 [≈ $243]**
- Conditioned reflexes. An investigation of the physiological activity of the cerebral cortex. Translated & edited ... Oxford: 1928. 2nd imp. 8vo. 430 pp. ills. Orig cloth.
(Goodrich) **$75 [≈ £41]**
- Conditioned reflexes, an investigation of the physiological activity of the cerebral cortex ... 1927, reprinted 1946. 8vo. xv,430 pp. Plate, diags. Orig cloth, dw. *(Weiner)* **£21 [≈ $37]**
- Lectures on conditioned reflexes. New York: 1928. 8vo. 414 pp. Ports. Orig cloth.
(Weiner) **£75 [≈ $135]**
- Lectures on conditioned reflexes and conditioned reflexes and psychiatry. New York: 1941. 2 vols, 3rd printing & 1st edn in English respectively. 414; 199 pp. Orig cloth, chipped dws.   *(Oasis)* **$60 [≈ £33]**
- The work of the digestive glands. London: 1902. 1st English edn. 8vo. xii,196 pp. Advts. Orig cloth, ex lib. *(Goodrich)* **$295 [≈ £163]**

- The work of the digestive glands. London: 1910. 2nd English edn. 8vo. 266 pp. Orig cloth. *(Fye)* **$150 [≈ £83]**
- The work of the digestive glands. London: 1910. 2nd English edn. 8vo. Orig cloth. E.A. Schafer's copy with his b'plate & sgntr. *(Goodrich)* **$135 [≈ £75]**

Payne, John
- Tables for valuing labor and stores, by weight or number. London: 1811. Folio. Contemp polished calf, upper jnt sl cracked. *(Spelman)* **£200 [≈ $360]**

Payne, Joseph Frank
- Thomas Sydenham. London: T. Fisher Unwin, 1900. 1st edn. 8vo. 264 pp. Orig cloth, gilt, sl stained. *(Oasis)* **$35 [≈ £19]**

Peacock, George
- A treatise on algebra. Cambridge: Deighton, 1842-45. 2 vols. 8vo. xvi,399; x,455 pp. 19th c calf, tops of both spines a bit chipped. *(Karmiole)* **$150 [≈ £83]**

Peacock, John
- Observations upon the medical properties of the Sulphur Spring, Dinsdale. The second edition ... also a new and complete analysis of the above water. 1829. Slim 8vo. Mod cloth. *(Deighton Bell)* **£40 [≈ $72]**

Pearce, Charles
- Vaccination. Its tested effects on health, mortality, and population. An essay ... London: 1868. 8vo. 120 pp. Orig cloth, gilt. *(Goodrich)* **$75 [≈ £41]**

Pearl, Raymond
- The biology of death. Phila: 1922. 1st edn. 275 pp. Cloth. *(Scientia)* **$50 [≈ £27]**
- Constitution and health. London: 1933. 8vo. 97 pp. Orig cloth. Author's pres copy to Fielding H. Garrison. *(Goodrich)* **$45 [≈ £25]**
- The natural history of population. New York: 1939. 1st Amer edn. 416 pp. Cloth, dw worn. *(Scientia)* **$60 [≈ £33]**

Pearson, Karl
- The chances of death and other studies in evolution. London: 1897. 2 vols. xi,388; ii,460 pp. Plates, graphs, diags. Titles, frontis & last leaves foxed. Unopened in orig cloth. *(Weiner)* **£75 [≈ $135]**
- The chances of death and other studies in evolution. London: 1897. 1st edn. 2 vols. 388; 460 pp. Cloth, cvrs bubbled. *(Scientia)* **$165 [≈ £91]**
- The life, letters and labours of Francis

Galton. Cambridge: 1914-30. 1st edn. 3 vols in 4. 4to. Orig cloth. *(Scientia)* **$400 [≈ £222]**
- The life, letters and labours of Francis Galton. Cambridge: Univ Press, 1914-30. 1st edn. 3 vols in 4. Folio. Orig gilt-stamped blue buckram. *(Chaucer Head)* **£250 [≈ $450]**

Peaslee, E. Randolph
- Ovarian tumors: their pathology, diagnosis, and treatment, especially by ovariotomy. New York: 1872. 1st edn. xxvii,551,24 pub ctlg pp. Half-title, 56 w'cuts. Orig pebble cloth, edges sl frayed. Cloth. *(Elgen)* **$275 [≈ £152]**
- Ovarian tumors: their pathology, diagnosis, and treatment, especially by ovariotomy. New York: 1872. 1st edn. 551 pp. Cloth, hd & ft of spine chipped or frayed, spine cracking at ft. *(Scientia)* **$175 [≈ £97]**

Pemberton, Henry
- A view of Sir Isaac Newton's philosophy. London: S. Palmer, 1728. 1st edn. 4to. [1],407 pp. 12 fldg engvd plates, sev engvd decorations. Minor waterstaining. Uncut in 19th c half vell. Stamp of Royal Society of Edinburgh on title. *(Pickering)* **$1,000 [≈ £555]**
- A view of Sir Isaac Newton's philosophy. Dublin: reprinted by & for John Hyde, 1728. 8vo. 12 fldg engvd plates. Contemp calf, spine rubbed, lacks label. *(Marlborough)* **£190 [≈ $342]**

Pemberton, Oliver
- Clinical observations of various forms of cancer, and of other diseases likely to be mistaken for them, with especial reference to their surgical treatment. London: 1867. Folio. 128 pp. 12 full-page plates (1 cold), 27 w'cut ills. Some waterstaining. New cloth *(Goodrich)* **$175 [≈ £97]**
- Clinical observations of various forms of cancer, and of other diseases likely to be mistaken for them ... London: 1867. 1st edn. Folio. 128 pp. 12 plates (mostly cold). Cloth, rebacked. *(Scientia)* **$175 [≈ £97]**

Pemberton, Ralph
- Arthritis and rheumatoid conditions, their nature and treatment. Phila: 1929. 1st edn. 8vo. xii,354 pp. *(Rittenhouse)* **$30 [≈ £16]**

Pengelly, William
- A memoir of ... of Torquay, F.R.S., geologist ... Edited ... With a summary of his scientific work ... London: 1897. 1st edn. 8vo. x,341 pp. Port (spotted & with short tear), 10 ills. Orig cloth, marked. Pres inscrptn from the editor. *(Bow Windows)* **£60 [≈ $108]**

Pennsylvania Hospital
- History of the Pennsylvania Hospital Unit (Base Hospital Number 10, U.S.A.) in the Great War. New York: 1921. Sl shelfwear, sl weakness in upper hinge.
(Rittenhouse) **$50 [≈ £27]**

Pepper, John Henry
- The playbook of metals ... experiments relating to alchemy and the chemistry of the fifty metallic elements ... London: Routledge ..., 1861. 1st edn. 8vo. viii,504 pp. Frontis, 265 w'engvd ills. Orig gilt dec cloth, sides lightly marked, backstrip faded.
(Claude Cox) **£45 [≈ $81]**

Pepper, William
- An American text-book of the theory and practice of medicine. Phila: 1893-94. 2 vols. 8vo. Lea.
(Goodrich) **$125 [≈ £69]**

Pepper, William (ed.)
- A system of practical medicine by American authors. Phila: 1885-86. 1st edn. 5 vols. 8vo. Full sheep, sl edge wear.
(Elgen) **$275 [≈ £152]**
- A system of practical medicine by American authors. Phila: 1885-86. 1st edn. 5 vols. 8vo. Full lea, cvrs of vol 1 lightly stained.
(Scientia) **$150 [≈ £83]**
- A system of practical medicine by American authors. Phila: 1885. 5 vols. 8vo. Lea.
(Fye) **$250 [≈ £138]**

Percival, Thomas
- Medical ethics; or, a code of institutes and precepts, adapted to the professional conduct of physicians and surgeons ... added an appendix containing a discourse of hospital duties ... Manchester: 1803. 1st pub edn. 246 pp. Half lea, top of spine worn.
(Scientia) **$450 [≈ £250]**
- Percival's medical ethics. Edited by Chauncey D. Leake. Baltimore: 1927. 8vo. ix,291 pp. Ills, ports. Half cloth, dw.
(Elgen) **$55 [≈ £30]**

Percy, John
- Metallurgy: the art of extracting metals from their ores, and adapting them to various purposes of manufacture. [Part 2] Iron and Steel. London: Murray, 1864. 1st edn. 8vo. xvi,934,[2 advts] pp. 4 fldg plates, 223 full-page & other ills. Rebound in cloth.
(Fenning) **£65 [≈ $117]**
- Metallurgy: the art of extracting metals from their ores, Silver and Gold. [Part 1]. London: 1880. Thick 8vo. xii,698 pp. Ills, diags. Orig cloth, rebacked, old spine laid on.

(Weiner) **£75 [≈ $135]**

Pereira, Jonathan
- The elements of materia medica and therapeutics. London: Longmans, 1849-50. 3rd edn. 2 vols in 3. 8vo. 2316 pp. Num text ills. Polished calf, spines gilt, spine of vol I rubbed & labels chipped.
(Oasis) **$100 [≈ £55]**
- Lectures on polarized light, together with a lecture on the microscope. London: Longman ..., 1854. 2nd edn. 8vo. xxviii,311 pp. Text figs. Orig cloth.   *(Antiq Sc)* **$85 [≈ £47]**
- Manual of materia medica and therapeutics. Abridgement ... by Frederic John Farre et al. Phila: 1866. 1st Amer edn. Lge 8vo. 1030,34 pub ctlg pp. 236 w'cuts. Some marg staining. Orig cloth, spine sunned. *(Elgen)* **$55 [≈ £30]**

Periam, Jonathan
- The American encyclopaedia of agriculture ... useful information for the farm and household. Chicago: Rand, McNally, 1881. Lge 8vo. 1085 pp. Full-page plates, w'engvs. Orig gilt-stamped green cloth, a bit rubbed.
(Karmiole) **$60 [≈ £33]**

Pering, Richard
- A brief enquiry into the causes of premature decay, in our wooden bulwarks, with an examination of the means ... to prolong their duration. Plymouth-Dock, 1812. 1st edn. 8vo. Half-title (soiled), title, 78 pp, errata lf, Uncut & unopened in mod bds.
(Bickersteth) **£145 [≈ $261]**

Perry, Charles
- A disquisition on the stone and gravel; together with strictures on the gout, when combined with these disorders. By S. [sic] Perry ... London: for T. Becket, 1779. 6th edn. Sm 8vo. Minor marg dampstaining, sm tear to hd of 1 leaf with sl loss. Mod qtr calf.
(Hughes) **£24 [≈ $43]**

Petit, Robert
- How to build an aeroplane, translated from the French ... London: 1910. 8vo. xiii,118 pp. Ills, diags. Orig cloth, sl grubby.
(Weiner) **£40 [≈ $72]**

Pettigrew, J.B.
- Animal locomotion or walking, swimming and flying with a dissertation on aeronautics. London: Intnl Science Series, 1873. 1st edn. 8vo. 264 pp. Text ills, 37 pp pub ctlg. Orig cloth, v worn & stained. *(Oasis)* **$60 [≈ £33]**
- Design in nature, illustrated by spiral and other arrangement ... London: 1908. 3 vols.

4to. 3 ports, 182 plates, 581 text figs. Orig cloth, trifle faded. Ex lib.
(Wheldon & Wesley) **£75 [≈ $135]**

Pettigrew, T.J.
- On superstitions connected with the history and practice of medicine and surgery. Phila: 1844. 8vo. 239 pp. half-title, plate. Waterstained. new cloth.
(Goodrich) **$65 [≈ £36]**

Pfaundler, M. & Schlossman, A.
- The diseases of children. Phila: 1908. 1st English translation. 4 vols. 440; 619; 552; 543 pp. Num photos ills, cold plates. Orig cloth.
(Fye) **$100 [≈ £55]**

Pharmacopoeia ...
- The British dispensatory, containing a faithful translation of the New London Pharmacopoeia ... the whole contents of the Edinburgh Pharmacopoeia. London: Edward Cave, 1747. 8vo. xii,136, 83,[i] pp. Some foxing & old ink marks. New qtr calf.
(Pollak) **£50 [≈ $90]**
- British pharmacopoeia 1858. 1864. xxii,[1],444 pp. Endpapers waterstained, dec inscrptn on half-title. Cloth, waterstained, hinges cracked but firm.
(Whitehart) **£35 [≈ $63]**
- British pharmacopoeia 1858. London: Spottiswoode, 1864. 1st edn. 8vo. xxii,[ii], 444 pp. Lacking front free endpaper, occas foxing. Orig cloth, front hinge weak.
(Pollak) **£60 [≈ $108]**
- Pharmacopoeia of the Massachusetts Medical Society. Boston: E. & J. Larkin, 1808. Orig edn. 8vo. x,[4],272 pp. Moderate foxing. Orig bds, front cvr loose, rear hinge rubbed.
(Hemlock) **$425 [≈ £236]**
- The pharmacopoiea of the United States of America. Boston: 1820. 1st edn. 272 pp. Edges of title worn, stamps on title. Mod cloth.
(Scientia) **$275 [≈ £152]**
- The pharmacopoiea of the United States of America. Boston: 1820. 1st edn. Lea, rebacked, front bd detchd.
(Fye) **$350 [≈ £194]**

Phelps, Charles
- Traumatic injuries of the brain and its membranes; with a special study of pistol-shot wounds of the head in their medico-legal and surgical relations. New York: 1897. 1st edn. 582 pp. Stamp on title. Cloth.
(Scientia) **$125 [≈ £69]**

Philalethes, Eugenius
- Long livers: a curious history of such persons of both sexes who have liv'd several ages, and grown young again. 1st English edn of Robert Samber's translation. 8vo. [2],lxiv, 199,viii,[3] pp. Index & errata. Little light browning. Full calf.
(Rootenberg) **$350 [≈ £194]**

Philanthropos (pseud.)
- Physiological cruelty; or, fact and fancy. An inquiry into the vivisection question. New York: Wiley, 1883. 1st edn. 156 pp. Cloth. Ex lib.
(Xerxes) **$95 [≈ £52]**

Philip, A.P.W.
- A treatise on febrile diseases ... With notes and additions by Nathan Smith. Hartford: 1816. 2nd Amer edn. 2 vols. Some browning throughout, vol 1 title dampstained. Orig lea, scuffed & stained.
(Rittenhouse) **$37.50 [≈ £20]**

Phillips, B.
- Scrofula; its nature, its causes, its prevalence, and the principles of treatment. 1846. v,379 pp. Plate. Light scattered foxing, lib stamp on title. Later cloth. *(Whitehart)* **£35 [≈ $63]**

Phillips, H.
- History of cultivated vegetables ... botanical, medicinal, edible and chemical qualities, and relation to art, science and commerce. London: 1822. 2nd edn. 2 vols. Roy 8vo. Orig bds, uncut.
(Wheldon & Wesley) **£80 [≈ $144]**

Phillips, John
- Geology of Oxford and the valley of the Thames. Oxford: Clarendon Press, 1871. 1st edn. 8vo. xxiv,523,44 advts pp. 17 plates (4 cold), num text diags. Orig cloth, inner hinges cracked, spine sl faded, extremities rubbed.
(Frew Mackenzie) **£55 [≈ $99]**
- Illustrations of the geology of Yorkshire. Part I. The Yorkshire Coast [all published]. London: John Murray, 1875. 3rd edn. 4to. xii,354 pp. 28 plates (7 hand-cold), fldg cold map. Orig blue cloth, spine gilt.
(Gough) **£120 [≈ $216]**
- Manual of geology: practical and theoretical. London: 1855. 8vo. xii,669 pp. Cold map, 376 text figs. Occas minor foxing, light stain on 2 leaves. Old sgntr on half-title. Rec half calf.
(Bow Windows) **£68 [≈ $122]**
- The rivers, mountains and sea-coast of Yorkshire, with essays on the climate, scenery ... London: 1853. 8vo. xv,302 pp. 36 plates (1 few sl foxed). Inscrptn on dedn leaf. Orig cloth.
(Weiner) **£60 [≈ $108]**

Phillips, Sir Richard

- An easy grammar of natural and experimental philosophy. For the use of schools. Phila: Conrad, 1818. 4th edn. 12mo. 160,[2 advts] pp. 10 engvd plates (2 fldg). Contemp mottled calf, spine chipped, outer hinges cracking.
(Karmiole) **£40 [≈ £22]**

Phillips, Robert

- A dissertation concerning the present state of the high roads of England ... wherein is proposed a new method of repairing and maintaining them. London: L. Gilliver, 1737. 1st edn. 8vo. [16],62 pp, advt leaf. 8 plates. Sm repr to title marg. Rec qtr calf.
(Spelman) **£280 [≈ $504]**

Phillips, William

- An elementary treatise on mineralogy comprising an introduction to the science. Boston: 1844. 8vo. [2]ff, cl,662 pp. Errata slip tipped-in, 600 w'cuts. Lacking front flyleaf, a few pp foxed. Orig embossed cloth.
(Elgen) **£50 [≈ £27]**

Physicians ...

- The physicians of Myddvai; meddygon Myddvai, or the medical practice of the celebrated Rhiwallon and his sons ... with an English translation ... Llandovery: Welsh Mss Soc, 1861. 8vo. xxx,469 pp. Orig cloth, sl wear.
(Weiner) **£50 [≈ $90]**

Physik ...

- Primitive physik ... See Wesley, J.

Pickering, E.C.

- Elements of physical manipulation. 1876-83. 2 vols. xii,225; x,316 pp. 114 text figs. Orig cloth, faded, spine & edges worn.
(Whitehart) **£25 [≈ $45]**

Piesse, Septimus

- The art of perfumery, and the methods of obatining the odours of plants ... manufacture of perfumes ... scented powders, odorous vinegars ... London: Longman ..., 1855. 1st edn. 8vo. xiv,287,22 pub advts pp. Vignette, 3 plates. Orig pict cloth, gilt.
(Gough) **£65 [≈ $117]**

Pike, Nicolas

- A new and complete system of arithmetic, composed for the use of citizens of the United States. Worcester: Isaiah Thomas, 1797. 2nd edn. Thick 8vo. 516 pp. Orig calf, worn.
(Argosy) **$100 [≈ £55]**

Pilcher, Lewis

- The treatment of wounds. New York: Wood's Library, 1883. 1st edn. 8vo. 391 pp. 116 text ills. 2 pp sl torn without loss. Orig cloth.
(Oasis) **$45 [≈ £25]**
- The treatment of wounds. New York: Wood, 1883. 1st edn. 8vo. xii,391 pp. 116 w'cuts. Orig cloth.
(Elgen) **$50 [≈ £27]**
- The treatment of wounds. New York: Wood, 1889. 8vo. xiii,453 pp. 142 w'cuts. Orig cloth.
(Elgen) **$40 [≈ £22]**

Pilon, H.

- The Coolidge tube. Its scientific applications, medical and industrial. London: Bailliere ..., 1920. [viii],95,[i] pp. 59 ills. Pub bndg.
(Pollak) **£30 [≈ $54]**

Piney, A.

- Diseases of the blood. Phila: 1932. 2nd edn. 8vo. viii,310 pp. Num ills, plates (some cold), ports. Cloth.
(Elgen) **$30 [≈ £16]**

Pinncok, Wm.

- A catechism of mineralogy; or, an introduction to the knowledge of the mineral kingdom. Adapted to the capacities of youth ... London: for Pinnock & Maunder, 1820. 1st edn. 12mo. 72 pp. Frontis. Light foxing in places, Orig ptd paper wraps, worn, sl defective.
(Fenning) **£35 [≈ $63]**

Planck, M.

- A survey of physics. A collection of lectures and essays. Translated ... 1925. 1st edn. vii,184 pp. Spine sl faded, cloth sl marked, rather worn dw.
(Whitehart) **£18 [≈ $32]**

Plat, Sir Hugh

- Delights for ladies, to adorne their persons, tables, closets ... with beauties, banquets, perfumes, and waters. London: R.Y., 1632. 12mo. Text within typographical borders. A little light waterstaining. Full blue mor, gilt. STC 19985.
(Traylen) **£975 [≈ $1,755]**
- The Garden of Eden ... all fruits and flowers now growing in England ... advance their nature and growth ... seeds and hearbes ... London: Leake, 1660. 5th edn. 2 pts in 1. 1st edn 2nd part. 12mo. Contemp calf, rebacked, crnrs reprd. Wing 2387A.
(Spelman) **£420 [≈ $756]**
- The Garden of Eden. or ... all fruits and flowers now growing in England ... how to advance their nature and growth ... London: for William Leake, 1660. 5th edn. [bound with] The second part ... 1660. 2 vols in 1. Contemp calf, recased, rebacked. Wing 2387A,
(Stewart) **£250 [≈ $450]**

Plate-Glass Book ...

- The plate-glass book ... authentic tables ... glass-house table ... grinding, polishing, silvering ... London: Wicksteed, 1757. 4to. [with, as issued] The compleat appraiser ... London: 1756. 1st edn. Title & 1st few leaves frayed. Contemp sheep, jnts cracked.
(Marlborough) **£750 [≈ $1,350]**

Plattner, Charles

- The use of the blowpipe, in the examination of minerals, ores, furnace-products, and other metallic combinations. Translated ... London: Taylor & Walton, 1845. 1st edn in English. 8vo. Text ills. Orig cloth.
(Chaucer Head) **£120 [≈ $216]**

Playfair, John

- Elements of geometry ... the first six books of Euclid ... plane and spherical trigonometry. Edinburgh: 1795. 1st Playfair edn. 8vo. xvi,400, 16 advts pp. Sep title to 2nd part. W'cut diags in text. Text sl soiled. Contemp sheep, jnts cracked, crnrs worn.
(Pickering) **$250 [≈ £138]**
- Illustrations of the Huttonian Theory of the Earth. Edinburgh: 1802. 8vo. xx,528 pp. Some ltd foxing, partic of title. Half calf, gilt.
(Wheldon & Wesley) **£500 [≈ $900]**

Pleasonton, A.J., et al.

- Influence of the blue ray of the sunlight, and of the blue colour of the sky. Phila: Claxton, Remsen, 1877. Roy 8vo. 185 pp. Ptd on blue paper. Frontis. Orig cloth, back cvr & spine sl wrinkled.
(Xerxes) **$55 [≈ £30]**
- Influence of the blue ray of the sunlight, and of the blue colour of the sky, in developing animal and vegetable life; in arresting disease ... Phila: 1877. 2nd edn. 185 pp. Ptd on blue paper. Orig cloth.
(Fye) **$75 [≈ £41]**

Ploss, H.H., et al.

- Woman: an historical, gynaecological and anthropological compendium. 1935. 1st English edn. 3 vols. Roy 8vo. Num ills. Orig cloth.
(Halewood) **£78 [≈ $140]**
- Woman: an historical, gynaecological and anthropological compendium. London: 1935. 1st edn in English. 3 vols. Lge 8vo. More than 2000 pp, over 1000 ills, 7 cold plates. Minor foxing. Orig buckram, slipcase.
(Bow Windows) **£105 [≈ $189]**

Plot, Richard

- The natural history of Oxfordshire, being an essay towards the natural history of England. Oxford: for Charles Brome, 1705. 2nd edn. Folio. Lge fldg map, 16 engvd plates. 19th c half mor, gilt, t.e.g. *(Traylen)* **£330 [≈ $594]**

Pohl, John F. & Kenney, Sister Elizabeth

- The Kenney concept of infantile paralysis and its treatment. Minneapolis: Bruce, 1943. 1st edn. 8vo. 366 pp. Ills. Orig cloth. Sgnd by both authors.
(Oasis) **$45 [≈ £25]**

Poincare, H.

- Science and hypothesis. London & Newcastle: 1905. 8vo. xxvii,244 pp. Orig cloth.
(Weiner) **£20 [≈ $36]**
- Science and method, translated ... with a preface by the Hon. Bertrand Russell. London: [1914]. 8vo. 288 pp. Orig cloth.
(Weiner) **£20 [≈ $36]**

Pointer, John

- A rational account of the weather, shewing signs of its several changes and alterations, together with the philosophical reasons for them. Oxford: for S. Wilmot ..., 1723. 76 pp. Rebound in panelled calf.
(C.R. Johnson) **£260 [≈ $468]**

Pole, Thomas

- The anatomical instructor; or, an illustration of the modern and most approved methods of preparing the different parts of the human body and of quadrupeds ... London: 1790. 8vo. lxxx,[6],304,[7] pp. 10 plates. Calf, jnts split.
(Goodrich) **$125 [≈ £69]**

Pomet, Pierre

- A compleat history of druggs ... added, what is further observable on the same subject, from Messrs. Lemery, and Tournefort ... London: for R. Bonwicke, 1712. 1st English edn. 2 vols in 1. Red & black title, 86 engvd plates, advt leaf. Contemp calf, rebacked.
(Traylen) **£350 [≈ $630]**

Pomey, F.

- Indiculus universalis; or, the universe in epitome wherein the names of almost all the works of nature, or all the arts and sciences ... are in English, Latine and French ... London: 1679. 1st edn. 8vo. Later half calf, rubbed, hd of spine chipped. *(Robertshaw)* **£40 [≈ $72]**

Pontey, William

- The forest pruner; or, timber owner's assistant ... the management of oak woods. London: 1808. 2nd edn. 8vo. 8 plates (3 fldg). Orig bds, cloth spine, uncut edges.
(Traylen) **£55 [≈ $99]**
- The profitable planter. A treatise on the theory and practice of planting forest trees ... the planting and management of permanent screens ... London: for J. Harding, 1814. 4th edn, enlgd. Frontis, advt leaf. Half calf, mor

label, gilt, uncut edges. *(Traylen)* **£48 [≈ $86]**

Pool, E.H. & McGowan, F.J.

- Surgery at the New York Hospital one hundred years ago. New York: 1929. Deluxe ltd edn, 1 of 250, sgnd by both authors. 188 pp. 24 plates.   *(Goodrich)* **$75 [≈ £41]**
- Surgery at the New York Hospital one hundred years ago. New York: 1930.
(Rittenhouse) **$35 [≈ £19]**

Porter, Henry H.

- Porter's health almanac for 1832; calculated generally for all parts of the U.S. ... the calculations by Wm. Collum. Phila: Porter, 1832. 3-78 pp (ex 80). W'cut ill. Browning, edges bumped. Sewn. *(Hemlock)* **$50 [≈ £27]**

Portlock, Joseph E.

- Report on the geology of the County of Londonderry, and of parts of Tyrone and Fermanagh. Dublin: 1843. 8vo. xxx,[1],784 pp. Lge fldg cold map, 9 fldg (mostly cold) plates, 45 litho plates, 26 text ills. Orig cloth, a little wear to handband.
(Fenning) **£95 [≈ $171]**
- Report on the geology of the County of Londonderry, and of parts of Tyrone and Fermanagh. Dublin: Milliken, 1843. Thick 8vo. Maps, cold plates. Orig cloth.
(Emerald Isle) **£85 [≈ $153]**

Potter, Francis

- An interpretation of the number 666 ... how this number ought to be interpreted ... an exquisite and perfect character ... Oxford: L. Litchfield ..., 1647. 2nd edn. 4to. [xvi],214 pp. Engvd title, architectural border. Old calf, rebacked.   *(Young's)* **£150 [≈ $270]**

Pottery Industry ...

- A history of the pottery industry and its evolution as applied to sanitation ... [Trenton, NJ:] Thomas Maddock's Sons, 1910. Sq 8vo. 224 pp. Cold frontis, num ills & diags. Title almost detached. Cloth rather worn & shaken.
(Weiner) **£40 [≈ $72]**

Pottle, Frederick A.

- Stretchers: the story of a hospital unit on the Western Front. New Haven: 1929. 8vo. xvi,366 pp. Ills, plates. Cloth.
(Elgen) **$30 [≈ £16]**

Poulet, Alfred

- A treatise on foreign bodies in surgical practice. New York: Wood's Library, 1880. 1st edn. 8vo. 271; 320 pp. Text ills. Orig cloth.   *(Oasis)* **$60 [≈ £33]**

Powell, Baden

- Natural philosophy: an historical view of the progress of the physical and mathematical sciences ... to the present times. London: 1834. Sm 8vo. xvi,396 pp. Extra engvd title. Orig cloth, sl wear.   *(Weiner)* **£25 [≈ $45]**

Powell, H.J.

- Glass-making in England. Cambridge: 1923. 4to. x,183 pp. Frontis, fldg map, 106 ills. Orig cloth.   *(Weiner)* **£60 [≈ $108]**

Powell, Thomas

- Humane industry: or, a history of most manual arts, deducing the original progress and improvement of them ... London: Herringman, 1661. 1st edn. 8vo. xvi,188 pp. Prelims lightly browned. Contemp anntns. Contemp calf, rebacked. Wing P3072.
(Rootenberg) **$950 [≈ £527]**

Power, Henry

- Experimental philosophy in three books; containing new experiments ... London: 1664. 1st edn. 4to. [xxiv],193,[1 blank] pp. Errata lea Fldg engvd plate. Title & prelims dust soiled, sm wormhole in title. Contemp calf, chipped, worn, jnts weak. Wing P3099.
(Pickering) **$3,500 [≈ £1,944]**

Poynton, Frederick J.

- Heart disease and thoracic aneurysm. London: 1907. 1st edn. 8vo. x,310 pp. 19 plates, text ills. Limp cloth.
(Elgen) **$30 [≈ £16]**

Prandtl, L. & Tietjens, O.G.

- Applied hydro- and aero-mechanics. Translated ... New York: 1934. 1st edn, 5th imp. 8vo. xvi,311 pp. Ills, 27 plates. Cloth.
(Elgen) **$35 [≈ £19]**

Pratt, John Henry

- The mathematical principles of mechanical philosophy and their application to the theory of universal gravitation. Cambridge: 1836. xxvi,[1],616 pp. 5 fldg plates. Light scattered foxing. Half calf, edges sl worn.
(Whitehart) **£35 [≈ $63]**
- The mathematical principles of mechanical philosophy ... Cambridge: 1841. 2nd edn. xxvi,598 pp. 5 fldg plates. Old half calf, mrbld bds.   *(Weiner)* **£40 [≈ $72]**

Prescott, George

- History, theory, and practice of the electric telegraph. Boston: Ticknor & Fields, 1860. 1st edn. 8vo. [3],xii, 468,[2] pp. Engvd frontis, 98 text w'cut ills. Orig cloth, gilt spine, worn.   *(Rootenberg)* **$150 [≈ £83]**

Prestwich, A.
- The young man's assistant to cotton spinning. Revised and enlarged. Containing a collection of useful and practical calculations. Manchester: John Heywood, 1883. Orig cloth. *(C.R. Johnson)* **£25 [≈ $45]**

Prestwich, J.
- Geology, chemical, physical, and stratigraphical. London: 1886-88. 2 vols. Roy 8vo. 5 maps (4 cold), 19 plates (2 cold), 474 text figs. Inscrptn on half-title. Orig cloth, trifle worn. *(Wheldon & Wesley)* **£35 [≈ $63]**

Price, Frederick W.
- Diseases of the heart. Their diagnosis, prognosis and treatment by modern methods. 1918. xiv,472 pp. 245 text figs. Scattered foxing. Cloth marked & dust-stained.
(Whitehart) **£18 [≈ $32]**

Prichard, James Cowles
- The natural history of man ... London & Paris, Bailliere, 1843. 1st edn. 8vo. xvi,556,[1] pp inc 2 pp pub advts. Hand-cold engvd frontis, 40 engvd plates (on 39ff), 36 hand-cold), num text w'cuts. Occas light foxing. Half calf over mrbld bds. B'plate.
(Rootenberg) **£550 [≈ £305]**
- The natural history of man ... London: 1848. 8vo. xvii,677 pp. 50 cold & 5 plain ills on 52 plates. Num w'engvs in text. Minor dust or other marks. Contemp calf, crnrs worn, resewn & rebacked with cloth, orig calf spine laid down over cloth.
(Bow Windows) **£185 [≈ $333]**
- The natural history of man ... London: 1855. 2 vols. 8vo. xxiv,343; vii,343-720 pp. 62 plates (57 cold), num text ills. Some finger & dust marks, sev gatherings a little loose. Orig cloth, faded, hd of spines a trifle fingered.
(Bow Windows) **£225 [≈ $405]**
- Researches into the physical history of mankind ... London: Houlston & Stoneman ..., [1836-47]. 3rd edn. 5 vols. 8vo. xx,376; iii-xiv,373; xxiv,507; xvi,631; xvi,570 pp. 20 litho plates (sev hand-cold), fldg map. Orig cloth, a little rubbed.
(Pickering) **£450 [≈ £250]**
- Researches into the physical history of mankind ... London: J. & A. Arch, 1826. 2nd edn. 2 vols. 8vo. xxxii,544; [ii],623 pp. 10 stipple engvd plates (6 cold). 19th c polished calf, rebacked, orig backstrips laid down, a little rubbed. Armorial b'plate.
(Morrell) **£210 [≈ $378]**
- A treatise on insanity and other disorders affecting the mind. Phila: 1837. 1st Amer edn. viii,339 pp. Half-title. Foxed. Calf, rear jnt open, scuffed. *(Elgen)* **$250 [≈ £138]**

Priestley, Joseph
- Directions for impregnating water with fixed air; in order to communicate to it the peculiar spirit and virtues of Pyrmont Water, and other mineral waters ... London: J. Johnson, 1772. 1st edn. 8vo. [2],iii,22, [3] advts pp. Frontis. Rec qtr calf.
(Spelman) **£280 [≈ $504]**
- Experiments and observations on different kinds of air ... the second edition. London: for J. Johnson, 1775-77. 3 vols. 8vo. 5 engvd plates. Contemp calf, backstrips a little rubbed, red mor labels.
(Waterfield's) **£350 [≈ $630]**
- Experiments and observations on different kinds of air. London: 1781-84-77. 3rd, 2nd, 1st edns. 3 vols. [With] Experiments ... relating to various forms of natural philosophy. 1779-81-86. 1st edns. 3 vols. Browning & foxing. Vols 1-5, worn calf; vol 6 cloth. *(Elgen)* **$1,500 [≈ £833]**
- Experiments and observations on different kinds of air, and other branches of natural philosophy connected with the subject. Birmingham: Thomas Pearson, 1790. 3 vols. 8vo. Fldg engv frontis, 8 fldg engvd plates, 6 pp advts vol III. Contemp speckled calf.
(Traylen) **£330 [≈ $594]**
- Heads of lectures on a course of experimental philosophy particularly including chemistry delivered at the New College in Hackney, London: for J. Johnson, 1794. Contemp calf, rebacked. *(Waterfield's)* **£300 [≈ $540]**
- The history and present state of discoveries relating to vision, light, and colours. London: 1772. 1st edn. 2 vols. 4to. v,[1],xvi, 422; 423-812,[20] pp. Frontis, 25 plates, errata leaf, subscr list, pub advts. Lib stamps on 1st title. Contemp calf, rebacked.
(Rootenberg) **$1,500 [≈ £833]**
- The history and present state of electricity, with original experiments. London: for J. Dodsley ..., 1767. 1st edn. 4to. [iv],xxxi,736,[2 biblio],[5 index],[1 advt] pp. Advt plate, 7 fldg engvd plates. Some foxing & soiling. Contemp sprinkled calf, rebacked. *(Pickering)* **$1,800 [≈ £1,000]**
- Memoirs ... to the year 1795, written by himself: with a continuation ... by his son ... London: reprinted from the American edition by the several Unitarian Societies in England ..., 1809. Untrimmed in orig bds.
(Chaucer Head) **£140 [≈ $252]**
- Memoirs ... to the year 1795, written by himself: with a continuation ... by his son ... London: J. Johnson, 1806. [viii],v,[i], 469 (i.e. 481),[i errata] pp. Some foxing & browning at end, a few pencil notes. Contemp speckled calf, jnts worn. *(Pollak)* **£65 [≈ $117]**

Priestley, Sir R., et al. (eds.)
- Antarctic research. A review of British scientific achievement in Antarctica. 1964. 4to. Ills, portfolio of maps. Slip-case.
(Halewood) **£38 [≃ $68]**

Principles ...
- First principles of the differential and integral calculus, or the doctrine of fluxions ... taken chiefly from the mathematics of Bezout ... Cambridge: Hilliard & Metcalf, 1824. 195 pp. 2 fldg plates. lea, front hinge cracked.
(Xerxes) **$80 [≃ £44]**
- The principles of mechanics ... See Emerson, William
- Principles of penal law ... See Eden, William

Pringle, Andrew
- Practical photo-micrography. Iliffe: [1893]. 1st edn. Sm 4to. 159,[1], iv,[6 advts] pp. 29 ills. Orig cloth, gilt. *(Fenning)* **£18.50 [≃ $32]**

Pringle, Sir John
- Observations on the diseases of the army. London: A. Millar ..., 1768. 6th edn, crrctd. 8vo. xxiv,345, appendix, cxx [28 index] pp. Errata leaf. Occas light foxing, stain on title, sm burn hole in front flyleaf. Contemp calf, rubbed, crnrs bumped, jnts tender.
(Elgen) **$275 [≃ £152]**
- Observations on the diseases of the army. With notes by Benjamin Rush. Phila: 1810. 1st Amer edn. xlvii,411 pp. Stamp, & sm tear, on title. Lea, rebacked.
(Scientia) **$275 [≃ £152]**
- Observations on the diseases of the army. London: Stockdale, 1810. New edn. 8vo. 471 pp. Rec qtr calf. *(Oasis)* **$200 [≃ £111]**
- Observations on the diseases of the army. With notes by Benjamin Rush. Phila: Finlay, 1812. 8vo. xlvii,411 pp. Contemp calf, some scuffing & chipping, rebacked. Ex lib.
(Elgen) **$225 [≃ £125]**

Prinz, Hermann & Greenbaum, Sigmund S.
- Diseases of the mouth and their treatment. Phila: [1944]. 2nd edn, revsd. 8vo. 670 pp. 12 cold plates, 324 engvs. Cloth.
(Elgen) **$45 [≃ £25]**

Prioleau, Philip G.
- An inaugural dissertation on the use of nitric and oxigenated muriatic acids, in some diseases. Phila: J. Bioren, 1798. 1st edn. 8vo. 72 pp. Title foxed, spotty foxing throughout. Mod linen-backed bds.
(Antiq Sc) **$175 [≃ £97]**

Prior, Thomas
- An authentick narrative of the success of tar-water ... London: Innys, 1746. 8vo. 192 pp. Mod half calf, mrbld sides.
(Emerald Isle) **£100 [≃ $180]**
- An authentick narrative of the success of tar-water ... See also Berkeley, George

Pritchard, Andrew
- Microscopic illustrations of living objects with memoirs on the new microscopes. London: 1843. New edn. 8vo. 248 pp. 4 plates (2 hand-cold, 1 foxed), ills. Half calf, worn. *(Weiner)* **£85 [≃ $153]**
- Microscopic illustrations of living objects with researches concerning the methods of constructing microscopes ... London: 1845. 3rd edn. 295 pp. 4 plates.
(Scientia) **$100 [≃ £55]**
- The natural history of animalcules ... London: Whittaker ..., 1834. 1st edn. 8vo. [iv],194 pp. Fldg litho frontis, 6 plates (damp-mark in top crnrs). Orig cloth backed bds, paper label chipped. *(Pollak)* **£250 [≃ $450]**
- The natural history of animalcules ... London: Whittaker ..., 1834. 1st edn. 8vo. [iv],196 pp. Fldg litho frontis, 6 engvd plates (somewhat foxed). Orig bds, rebacked with cloth. *(Pickering)* **$1,000 [≃ £555]**

Prochaska, G.
- A dissertation on the functions of the nervous system. See Unzer, J.A. - The principles of physiology ...

Proctor, R.A.
- Old and new astronomy. 1892. 1st edn. Lge 4to. viii,816 pp. 31 plates, 472 text figs. A little scattered foxing. Orig pict gilt cloth, t.e.g., hd & ft of spine a little worn.
(Whitehart) **£40 [≃ $72]**

Proctor, Richard A.
- Other worlds than ours: the plurality of worlds studied under the light of recent scientific researches. New York: Appleton, 1871. 334 pp. 4 cold, 9 sm b/w ills. Orig cloth, spine ends worn & torn.
(Xerxes) **$75 [≃ £41]**

Projection ...
- The projection of the sphere ... See Emerson, William

Proposal for Uniformity ...
- A proposal for uniformity of weights and measures in Scotland ... See Swinton, John

Prout, William

- Chemistry, meteorology and the function of digestion considered with reference to natural theology. London: Pickering, 1834. 1st edn. 8vo. xxviii,565 pp. Fldg map. Orig cloth. *(Weiner)* £50 [≃ $90]
- Chemistry, meteorology and the function of digestion considered with reference to natural theology. London: 1834. [8 advts], xxviii,564 pp. Fldg cold map, a few tables. A little foxing on title & preceding page. Contemp lea, worn. *(Whitehart)* £28 [≃ $50]
- Chemistry, meteorology and the function of digestion considered with reference to natural theology. Phila: Carey, Lea ..., 1834. 306 pp. Some foxing. Orig cloth, cvrs worn, cracking along outer hinges. *(Xerxes)* $80 [≃ £44]
- An inquiry into the nature and treatment of diabetes, calculus, and other affections of the urinary organs. Phila: Towar & Hogan, 1826. 1st Amer edn. xi,308 pp. Hand-cold fldg frontis. Waterstain to upper edge of final 100 pp. Contemp calf, sl rubbed. *(Karmiole)* $150 [≃ £83]

Pryce, William

- Mineralogia cornubiensis; a treatise on minerals, mines, and mining ... with the methods of ... working of tin, copper, and lead mines. London: for the author, 1778. 1st edn. Folio. Port, 7 plates, 2 fldg tables. Half calf, rebacked, orig spine laid down. *(Traylen)* £485 [≃ $873]

Pulley, John

- An essay on the proximate cause of animal impregnation ... London: for the author ..., 1801. 1st edn. 4to. 31 pp. Ms ex lib of Medical Society of Edinburgh on title. Disbound. *(Pickering)* $385 [≃ £213]

Pullin, V.E. & Wiltshire, W.J.

- X-rays past and present. London: Benn, 1927. 8vo. 229,[iii] pp. 43 ills. Pub bndg, front jnt a little weak. *(Pollak)* £30 [≃ $54]

Pulteney, Richard

- A general view of the writings of Linnaeus. London: for T. Payne ..., 1781. 1st edn. 8vo. iv,425 pp. Contemp calf, spine a bit rubbed, sl wear at ft. *(Burmester)* £200 [≃ $360]

Punnett, R.C.

- Mendelism. Cambridge: 1905. 1st edn. Sm 8vo. vii,63 pp. A little foxing. Orig cloth. *(Wheldon & Wesley)* £40 [≃ $72]

Purdy, Charles W.

- Practical uranalysis and urinary diagnosis.

Phila: 1895. 1st edn. 8vo. 357 pp. 5 cold plates, 44 ills. Cloth. *(Elgen)* $40 [≃ £22]

Pusey, William Allen

- The history of dermatology. Springfield: Charles C. Thomas, 1933. 1st edn. 223 pp. Ills. Orig cloth, sl chipped dw. *(Oasis)* $60 [≃ £33]
- The principles and practice of dermatology. New York: 1907. 1st edn. 8vo. xxiv,1021,2 advts pp. Errata tipped-in. Cold plates, 367 text ills. 3/4 lea, rubbed, piece torn out at hd of spine. *(Elgen)* $60 [≃ £33]
- Syphilis as a modern problem. Chicago: 1915. 1st edn. 8vo. 129 pp. Cloth. *(Elgen)* $30 [≃ £16]

Putzel, L.A.

- A treatise on common forms of functional nervous diseases. New York: Wood's Library. 1880. 1st edn. 256,46 pub ctlg pp. Orig cloth. *(Oasis)* $50 [≃ £27]

Quain, Jones

- Elements of anatomy. 1837. 4th edn. xl,910 pp. 4 plates, num engvs. Orig blindstamped cloth, worn, dust-stained, top & bottom of spine defective. *(Whitehart)* £18 [≃ $32]
- Elements of anatomy. New York: 1882. 9th edn. 2 vols. 747; 947 pp. 380 engvs (78 cold). Rebound, orig spines laid down. *(Fye)* $75 [≃ £41]

Quain, Jones & Wilson, W.J.E.

- The nerves of the human body. London: for Taylor & Walton, 1839. 1st edn. Folio. 38 hand-cold litho plates. Very minor occas spotting. Green mor prize binding. Armorial b'plate. Pres inscrptn from co-author. *(Quaritch)* $850 [≃ £472]
- A series of anatomical plates with references and physiological comments illustrating the structure of the different parts of the human body. Phila: 1846. 3rd edn, revsd. 4to. Some foxing, partic on title, some pages loose. Lea spine & crnrs, worn. *(Rittenhouse)* $65 [≃ £36]

Quain, Richard & Sharpey, William (eds.)

- Human anatomy. Phila: 1849. 1st Amer edn. 2 vols. 638; 639 pp. Lea. *(Fye)* $75 [≃ £41]

Quain, Richard (ed.)

- A dictionary of medicine including general pathology, general therapeutics, hygiene and the diseases peculiar to women and children. New York: 1885. 8th edn. xviii,1816,8 pub ctlg pp. Text w'cuts. Half mor. *(Elgen)* $50 [≃ £27]

- A dictionary of medicine including general pathology, general therapeutics, hygiene and the diseases peculiar to women and children. 13th thousand. 1886. 2 vols. xviii,1816 pp. 138 figs in text. 3/4 roan, sl rubbed & worn. *(Whitehart)* **£18 [≃ $32]**

Quatrefages, A.
- The human species. International Scientific series. New York: Appleton, 1879. 8vo. 498 pp. Orig cloth. *(Oasis)* **$75 [≃ £41]**

Quay, George H.
- A monograph of diseases of the nose and throat. Phila: Boericke, 1897. 1st edn. 8vo. 214 pp. Ills. Orig cloth. *(Oasis)* **$20 [≃ £11]**

Queen's Closet ...
- The Queen's closet ... See May, W.

Quekett, John
- A practical treatise on the use of the microscope. London: 1848. 8vo. xxi,464 pp. 9 plates, 241 ills. Some light foxing. Orig cloth, a little worn & shaken. *(Weiner)* **£75 [≃ $135]**
- A practical treatise on the use of the microscope. London: 1852. 2nd edn. 8vo. xxii,515 pp. 12 plates(1 fldg), 270 ills. A few sm lib stamps. Orig dec cloth, rebacked, old spine laid down. *(Weiner)* **£75 [≃ $135]**

Quier, John
- Letters and essays on the small-pox and inoculation, the measles, the dry belly-ache and ... the fevers ... of the West Indies ... London: for J. Murray, 1778. 1st edn. 8vo. Half-title. Contemp calf, gilt spine, mor label, gilt, front jnt cracking.
(Traylen) **£375 [≃ $675]**

Quinan, John R.
- Medical annals of Baltimore from 1608 to 1880. Baltimore: 1884. 8vo. 275 pp. Port frontis. 1st few pages crudely rebound. Half roan, chipped, v worn, crudely rebacked with cloth. *(Weiner)* **£45 [≃ $81]**
- Medical annals of Baltimore from 1608 to 1880. Baltimore: 1884. 8vo. Paper cvrs.
(Rittenhouse) **$35 [≃ £19]**

Quincy, John
- Lexicon physico-medicum: or, a new medical dictionary ... London: for T. Longman, 1757. 7th edn. 8vo. Contemp calf, rebacked.
(Traylen) **£40 [≃ $72]**
- Lexicon physico-medicum: or, a new medical dictionary ... London: for J. Osborn & T. Longman, 1730. 4th edn. 8vo. Contemp sgntr

on title. Contemp panelled calf, lower jnt cracked. *(Stewart)* **£120 [≃ $216]**
- Pharmacopoea officinalis et extemporanea, or a complete English dispensatory. London: 1724. 5th edn. 8vo. xvi,674,[62] pp. Inner blank marg of title restored. Contemp calf, worn, cvrs detchd.
(Wheldon & Wesley) **£45 [≃ $81]**
- Pharmacopoea officinalis et extemporanea, or a complete English dispensatory, in four parts. London: 1736. 10th edn. 8vo. xvi,700, lx pp. Advt leaf. Some foxing. Newly rebound in calf. *(Spelman)* **£120 [≃ $216]**

Rabies ...
- See Canine Madness

Radcliff, Thomas
- A report on the agriculture of Eastern and Western Flanders; drawn up at the desire of the Farming Society of Ireland. London: for John Harding, 1819. 8vo. Fldg cold map, 11 fldg plates. Half calf, upper jnt cracked.
(Stewart) **£100 [≃ $180]**

Radcliffe, Charles B., et al.
- On diseases of the spine and of the nerve. Phila: Lea, 1871. 8vo. 196 pp. Uncut in new cloth. *(Goodrich)* **$85 [≃ £47]**

Raffald, Elizabeth
- The experienced English housekeeper ... London: 1794. 11th edn. Port, 3 plates. Author's sgntr on p 1. Contemp calf, rebacked. *(Robertshaw)* **£125 [≃ $225]**
- The experienced English housekeeper ... London: for R. Baldwin, 1806. 13th edn. 8vo. viii,397 pp. Engvd port, 3 engvd fldg plates. Tiny hole at top of title. Contemp tree sheep, early 20th c rebacking, spine gilt.
(Gough) **£145 [≃ $261]**

Ralphson, Joseph
- A mathematical dictionary ... use of the principal mathematical instruments ... London: for J. Nicholson, 1702. [vi],40, [lxxvii], 26,18 pp. 3 fldg plates. Gutter & lower edge of title reprd, lacking final blank. Contemp calf gilt, rebacked, old spine relaid.
(Pollak) **£200 [≃ $360]**

Ramadge, Francis Hopkins
- Asthma, its species and complications, or researches into the pathology of disordered respiration ... in connection with disease of the heart, catarrh, indigestion ... London: 1835. 1st edn. 4to. vii,[1],380 pp. 6 cold lithos. Uncut in orig bds, crnrs scuffed.
(Chaucer Head) **$275 [≃ £152]**

- Consumption curable; and the manner in which nature ... operates in effecting a healing process ... added, a mode of treatment ... London: Longman, 1834. 2nd edn. 8vo. 6 engvd plates (5 hand-cold). Some waterstaining. Orig bds, rebacked. Author's pres copy.   *(Chaucer Head)* **£55 [≈$99]**

Ramchundra

- A treatise on problems of maxima and minima, solved by algebra ... London: Wm. H. Allen, 1859. 2nd edn. [xxiii],[v],185 pp. 8 plates. Orig pub blindstamped cloth, spine faded. Author's pres copy.
(Karmiole) **$175 [≈£97]**

Ramsay, Sir William

- Essays, biographical and chemical. London: 1908. 1st edn. 8vo. Sev ills. Orig cloth. "Presentation copy" embossed stamp on title.
(Argosy) **$50 [≈£27]**

Ramsay, William

- A course of mathematics composed for the use of the Royal Military Academy by Charles Hutton. Tegg, 1833. vii,522 pp. Figs. Mod qtr paper bds, cloth spine, new endpapers.
(Hinchliffe) **£27.50 [≈$48]**
- The gases of the atmosphere. The history of their discovery. London: Macmillan, 1896. 1st edn. viii,240 pp. Frontis, 7 plates. Pub bndg.   *(Pollak)* **£30 [≈$54]**

Ramsbotham, Francis H.

- Obstetric medicine and surgery. London: Churchill, 1856. 4th edn. 8vo. 762 pp. 90 full-page litho plates (2 cold). Calf, richly gilt.   *(Oasis)* **£150 [≈$83]**
- The principles and practice of obstetric medicine and surgery in reference to the process of parturition. London: John Churchill, 1844. 2nd edn. 8vo. xxiv,732 pp. 90 engvd plates. Half-title, title & p 1 fingered, some odd foxing. Old half calf, somewhat used.   *(Taylor)* **£75 [≈$135]**
- The principles and practice of obstetric medicine and surgery. London: 1844. Thick 8vo. xxiv,732 pp. 92 plates (1 cold), ills. Half calf, worn.   *(Weiner)* **£50 [≈$90]**

Ranby, John

- A narrative of the last illness of the Right Honourable the Earl of Orford ... 4ff,47 pp. Fldg copperplate. [With] An appendix to the narrative. 43 pp. London: John & Paul Knapton, 1745. 1st edn. 2 pts in 1. Main tract lge margs, appendix cut down. Mod cloth.
(Offenbacher) **$300 [≈£166]**

Randall, John

- The semi-Virgilian husbandry, deduced from various experiments ... a new discourse of national farming ... with the philosophy of agriculture ... London: for B. Law, 1764. 1st edn. 8vo. 3 engvd plates (2 fldg). Contemp calf, gilt spine, jnts reprd.
(Traylen) **£150 [≈$270]**

Rank, B.K. & Wakefield, A.R.

- Surgery of repair as applied to hand injuries. Edinburgh: 1953. 1st edn. 8vo. xiv,256 pp. Cold frontis, num ills. Cloth.
(Elgen) **$125 [≈£69]**

Rankine, W.J.M.

- A manual of applied mechanics. London: 1870. 5th edn, revsd. 8vo. xvi,648 pp. Some spotting, inscrptn on endpaper. Contemp polished calf, full gilt spine a little rubbed at ends, lower jnt cracked.
(Bow Windows) **£45 [≈$81]**

Ranney, Ambrose

- Lectures on nervous diseases from the standpoint of cerebral and spinal localization. Phila: 1888. 8vo. xiv,778 pp. Num plates, some photo engvs. Orig cloth.
(Goodrich) **$65 [≈£36]**

Ranney, Ambrose L.

- Practical suggestions respecting the varieties of electrical currents and the uses of electricity in medicine. New York: Appleton, 1885. 1st edn. 8vo. ix,[1],147 pp. 14 plates, text w'cuts (1 fldg). Orig cloth.
(Antiq Sc) **$100 [≈£55]**

Raspe, Rudolph Eric

- An account of some German volcanos, and their productions ... London: Lockyer Davis, 1776. 1st edn. 8vo. xix,[1],140 pp inc 4 pp pub advts. Half-title, 2 engvd fldg plates. Contemp calf, rebacked.
(Rootenberg) **$525 [≈£291]**

Ray, John

- A collection of English words not generally used ... with an account of the preparation and refining of such metals as are gotten in England. London: for Christopher Williams, 1691. 2nd edn. 12mo. 5 pp ctlg at end. Sl browned. Contemp sheep rubbed. Wing R389.   *(Charles Cox)* **£125 [≈$225]**
- A collection of English words not generally used ... in two alphabetical catalogues ... with an account of the preparation and refining of such metals as are gotten in England. London: 1691. 11ff, 211,[5] pp. Lacking A1

blank. Contemp lea, rebacked, edges worn.
(Whitehart) **£120 [≈ $216]**
- Observations topographical, moral and physiological; made in a journey through part of the Low-Countries, Germany ... and France. London: for John Martyn, 1673. [xvi],499, [i],[viii], 115,[i] pp. 4 engvd plates, 3 text w'cuts. New half calf, old mrbld bds.
(Pollak) **£250 [≈ $450]**
- Observations topographical, moral and physiological; made in a journey through part of the Low-Countries, Germany ... and France. London: 1673. [16],499 pp, 4 plates, [8],115 pp. Lea, spine cracking.
(Scientia) **$600 [≈ £333]**
- Observations topographical, moral and physiological; made in a journey through part of the Low-Countries, Germany ... and France. London: for John Martyn, 1673. 1st edn. 8vo. [xvi],499 pp. Port, 3 plates, text figs. Title sl soiled. Old calf, old rebacking.
(Frew Mackenzie) **£135 [≈ $243]**
- Select remains. With his life, by the late William Derham. London: Dodsley, 1760. 1st edn. 8vo. vii,336 pp. Engvd port frontis (sl offsetting to title), text engv. Lacking errata leaf. Contemp mottled calf, spine richly gilt. *(Frew Mackenzie)* **£180 [≈ $324]**
- The wisdom of God manifested in the works of creation. In two parts ... London: for Sam. Smith ..., 1704. 4th edn. 8vo. Port frontis. Sm lib stamp on title. Rebound in qtr calf.
(Hughes) **£85 [≈ $153]**
- The wisdom of God manifested in the works of creation. London: for W. Innys, 1743. 11th edn, crrctd. 8vo. [xxiv],[17]-405 pp. 3 pp advts. Orig calf, short cracks at hd & ft of jnts, a little spine wear. *(Bickersteth)* **£75 [≈ $135]**
- The wisdom of God manifested in the works of creation. London: 1762. 8vo. [xx],259 pp. Fldg engvd frontis. Half calf, rebacked.
(Wheldon & Wesley) **£120 [≈ $216]**

Ray, P. (ed.)
- History of chemistry in ancient and medieval India. Calcutta: 1956. 8vo. 14,[ii],494 pp. Port, plates, ills, fldg chart. Orig cloth, dw.
(Weiner) **£30 [≈ $54]**

Rayer, Pierre
- A theoretical and practical treatise on the diseases of the skin. London: for Bailliere, 1835. 2nd edn. 8vo. lxiv,1238 pp. Without half-title. Contemp prize calf of St. Bartholemew's Hospital, rebacked, old spine relaid. *(Pollak)* **£120 [≈ $216]**
- A theoretical and practical treatise on the diseases of the skin ... With notes and other additions by John Bell. Phila: 1845. 4to. 449

pp. 40 cold plates (dusky). Mod qtr cloth, mrbld bds, new endpapers.
(Scientia) **$225 [≈ £125]**

Rayleigh, Lord & Ramsey, Sir W.
- Argon: a new constituent of the atmosphere. Washington: Smithsonian, 1896. 1st edn. Folio. iv,43 pp. Orig cloth.
(Whitehart) **£65 [≈ $117]**

Rayleigh, Lord [Strutt, John William]
- Scientific papers. Cambridge: Univ Press, 1899-1920. 6 vols. 8vo. Orig cloth, ex lib with stamps, some cvrs dampstained. A working set. *(Pollak)* **£150 [≈ $270]**
- The theory of sound. London: 1894-96. 2nd edn, revsd & enlgd. 2 vols. 8vo. xiv,480; xvi,504 pp. Diags. Name clipped from vol 1 title. Orig cloth, vol 1 crnrs & hd of spine worn. *(Weiner)* **£75 [≈ $135]**
- The theory of sound. London: Macmillan, 1894-96. 2nd edn, revsd & enlgd. 2 vols. 8vo. xiv,480; xvi,504 pp. Num text ills. Orig cloth.
(Pollak) **£150 [≈ $270]**
- The theory of sound. London: Macmillan, 1894. 2nd edn, revsd & enlgd. 2 vols. 8vo. Orig brown cloth, gilt. *(Traylen)* **£38 [≈ $68]**

Read, John
- Humour and humanism in chemistry. London: Bell, 1947. 1st edn. 8vo. 388 pp. Cold frontis, plates, text ills. Orig cloth.
(Oasis) **$60 [≈ £33]**

Ready Reckoner ...
- The ready reckoner; or, trader's sure guide ... by exact tables, ready cast up. Edinburgh: 1778. 8vo. Contemp calf, rubbed.
(Stewart) **£75 [≈ $135]**

Record, Robert
- The castle of knowledge. London: Reginalde Wolfe, 1556. Sm folio. [8] ff, 287 pp. W'cut title, ills & figs. Extensive reprs, marg strengthening & recrnring to title & elsewhere, minor worming, staining. Lacking endpapers. Old vell, soiled. New STC 20796.
(Bow Windows) **£3,000 [≈ $5,400]**
- Record's arithmetick: or, the ground of arts ... afterwards augmented by Mr. Dee. And since enlarged ... by John Mellis ... London: E. Flesher, 1673. Sm 8vo. 536 pp. Text figs & tables. Mod 3/4 calf. Wing R648.
(Argosy) **$350 [≈ £194]**

Recreative Science
- Recreative Science: A record and a remembrancer of intellectual observation. : Groombridge, 1860-63. 3 vols. Sm 4to.

[iv],367,[i]; [iv],364; [i],359,[iii] pp. Num text w'cuts. Orig cloth, faded, a little wear to spine ends. *(Pollak)* **£40 [≃ $72]**

Redgrove, H. Stanley
- Alchemy: Ancient and modern. London: 1922. 8vo. 16 full-page ills. Orig cloth. *(Argosy)* **$35 [≃ £19]**
- Alchemy: Ancient and modern. London: William Rider, 1922. 2nd revsd edn. 8vo. xx,141,[i advt] pp. 16 plates, table. Orig sl faded red cloth, gilt. *(Gough)* **£20 [≃ $36]**

Reece, R.
- The medical guide, for the use of clergy, junior practitioners in medicine and surgery. 1824. 14th edn, 8vo. Calf. *(Halewood)* **£30 [≃ $54]**

Reece, Richard
- The chemical guide, or complete companion to the portable chest of chemistry. London: 1814. 1st edn. 12mo. xxiv,335,[1] pp. Lib binding. Ex lib. *(Elgen)* **$80 [≃ £44]**

Reed, Thomas E.
- Sex, its origin and determination. A study of the metabolic cycle ... New York: [1913]. 1st edn. 8vo. 313,4 advts pp. Orig cloth, sl soiled. *(Elgen)* **$35 [≃ £19]**

Reed, Walter
- Yellow fever; a compilation of various publications. Washington: 1911. 1st edn. One of 1000. 250 pp. Orig ptd wraps, worn. *(Scientia)* **$100 [≃ £55]**

Reed, William H.
- Hospital life in the army of the Potomac. Boston: 1866. 1st edn. 199 pp. Spine faded, some bubbling on front cvr. *(Scientia)* **$85 [≃ £47]**

Rees, Abraham
- The Cyclopaedia: or, universal dictionary of arts, sciences and literature. London: for Longman, Hurst ..., 1819-20. 45 vols. 4to. Port, 62 maps, 8 leaves type specimens, num engvd plates. Contemp str-grained calf, gilt panelled borders, mrbld edges. *(Traylen)* **£1,600 [≃ $2,880]**

Reese, David M.
- Observations on the epidemic of 1819, as it prevailed in a part of city of Baltimore. Balt: the author, 1819. 1st edn. 12mo. 114,[1] pp. Contemp calf, dull, front hinge splitting. Dr. Willard Parker's copy. *(Hemlock)* **$150 [≃ £83]**

Regimen ...
- Regimen sanitatis Salerni. This booke teachinge all people to governe them in healthe ... translated out of the Latyne tongue ... by Thomas Paynell. London: Thomas Berthelot, 1541. 4to. Black letter. Title within w'cut border. Mor gilt. STC 21599. *(Traylen)* **£1,100 [≃ $1,980]**

Reid, David B.
- Ventilation in American dwellings with a series of diagrams ... to which is added a an introductory outline of the progress of improvement in ventilation by Elisha Harris. New York: 1858. 8vo. 124 pp. Num plates, some cold. Orig cloth. *(Goodrich)* **$150 [≃ £83]**

Reid, David Boswell
- Elements of practical chemistry, comprising a series of experiments ... Edinburgh: 1830. 1st edn. 8vo. xxx,511 pp. Diags, fldg table. 2 leaves marg frayed. Later cloth. *(Weiner)* **£40 [≃ $72]**

Reid, Douglas A.
- Soldier-surgeon, the Crimean War letters ... Edited by Joseph O. Baylen ... Knoxville: [1968]. 1st edn. 158 pp. Ills. Cloth, dw. *(Elgen)* **$35 [≃ £19]**

Reid, E.G.
- The great physician. A life of Sir William Osler. Oxford: 1931. 3rd imp. 8vo. Cloth, dw. *(Goodrich)* **$35 [≃ £19]**

Reid, James D.
- The telegraph in America: Morse memorial (second edition). New York: 1886. Lge thick 8vo. xv,894 pp. Engvd title, num plates & ills. New buckram. *(Weiner)* **£75 [≃ $135]**

Reid, Thomas
- An inquiry into the human mind, on the principles of common sense. Edinburgh: Anderson & Macdowall, 1818. 8vo. xvi,400 pp. Some foxing at front & damp marks at top edge of 1st few leaves. New paper bds. *(Pollak)* **£40 [≃ $72]**
- An inquiry into the human mind, on the principles of common sense. London: for T. Cadell ..., 1769. 3rd edn, crrctd. Mod bds. *(Waterfield's)* **£125 [≃ $225]**

Reid, W.
- An attempt to develop the law of storms ... and hence to point out a cause for the variable winds ... London: John Weale, 1850. 3 rd edn. Roy 8vo. Half-title, 11 fldg charts, 3

engvd plates, text ills. Orig cloth, spine faded, new ptd paper label. *(Traylen)* **£75 [≈ $135]**

- The progress of the development of the law of storms and of the variable winds ... 1849. iv,424 pp. 2 compass card plates, 3 fldg plates, 2 other plates, sev ills. Orig watered silk binding, rebacked.
(Whitehart) **£40 [≈ $72]**

Reik, Theodor
- From thirty years with Freud. New York: Farrar & Rinehart, [1940]. xi,241 pp. Frontis. Black cloth, gilt. Author's pres copy.
(Karmiole) **$75 [≈ £41]**

Reinhold, August F. (trans.)
- Louis Kuhme's facial diagnosis. New York: 1897. 8vo. 106 pp. 52 figs. Bds, sl soiled.
(Rittenhouse) **$35 [≈ £19]**

Remarks ...
- Remarks on the art of making wine ... See MacCulloch, John

Renaud, F.
- A short history of the rise and progress of the Manchester Royal Infirmary ... 1752 to 1877. Manchester: Cornish, 1898. 8vo. 152 pp. Orig cloth-backed bds. *(Pollak)* **£30 [≈ $54]**

Rennie, Robert
- Essays on the natural history of peat moss ... Edinburgh: George Ramsay, 1807. 1st edn. 8vo. Contemp half calf, rebacked, gilt.
(Traylen) **£42 [≈ $75]**

Renouard, P.V.
- History of medicine from its origin to the nineteenth century, with an appendix ... to the present time, translated from the French ... Cincinnati: 1856. 8vo. xvi,[ix-719] pp (apparently correct thus). Old calf, worn, jnts cracked. *(Weiner)* **£60 [≈ $108]**

Reuss, August Ritter von
- The diseases of the new born. New York: 1922. 8vo. 622 pp. 1 leaf reprd. Orig cloth,sl shaken. *(Goodrich)* **$65 [≈ £36]**

Reyner, J.H.
- Television: theory and practice. London: 1937. 2nd revsd edn. 8vo. xi,224 pp. Plates, diags, advts. Orig cloth. *(Weiner)* **£25 [≈ $45]**

Reynolds, Sir J. Russell
- Essays and addresses. London: 1896. 1st edn. 8vo. xxiv,307,4 advts pp. Half-title, port frontis. Cloth, inner hinge raced, uncut.
(Elgen) **$85 [≈ £47]**

- Vertigo. A paper read ... [at the] London Medical Society. London: 1854. 8vo. 46 pp. New bds. Author's pres copy.
(Goodrich) **$75 [≈ £41]**

Reynolds, Sir J. Russell (ed.)
- A system of medicine. With numerous additions and illustrations by Henry Hartshorne. Phila: 1880. 1st Amer edn. 3 vols. Text engvs. Orig full sheep, black labels. *(Elgen)* **$175 [≈ £97]**

Reynolds, S.R.M.
- Physiology of the uterus. New York: 1965. 2nd edn. 8vo. xxvi,619 pp. Ills. Cloth, dw.
(Elgen) **$40 [≈ £22]**

Rhazes
- A treatise on the small-pox and measles ... Translated ... London: 1848. 8vo. 212 pp. Cloth. *(Goodrich)* **$125 [≈ £69]**
- A treatise on the small-pox and measles. Translated by W.A. Greenhill. London: Sydenham Soc, 1848. 212 pp. Orig cloth.
(Scientia) **$100 [≈ £55]**

Rhind, William
- A treatise on the nature and cure of intestinal worms of the human body arranged according to the classification of Rudolphi and Bremser ... London: 1829. 8vo. 152 pp. 6 engvd plates. Rec cloth, uncut. *(Goodrich)* **$105 [≈ £58]**

Rhodes, Frederick Leland
- Beginnings of telephony. New York: 1929. 8vo. xvii,261 pp. Num plates, ills. Orig cloth.
(Weiner) **£45 [≈ $81]**

Ricci, James V.
- One hundred years of gynaecology, 1800-1900. Phila: [1945]. 1st edn. Lge 8vo. xiv,649 pp. Cloth. Ex lib. *(Elgen)* **$90 [≈ £50]**

Ricci, James V. & Marr, James Pratt
- Principles of extraperitoneal casarean section. Phila: [1942]. 1st edn. 8vo. 224 pp. Num ills. Cloth. *(Elgen)* **$75 [≈ £41]**

Rice, Nathan P.
- Trials of a public benefactor, as illustrated in the discovery of etherization. New York: 1859. 1st edn. 12mo. xx,[13]-460 pp. Port frontis, 4 ills. Orig cloth, hd of spine sl chipped. Pres copy from Wm. T.G. Morton.
(Hemlock) **$250 [≈ £138]**

Richards, J.M.
- A chronology of medicine. London: 1880. 8vo. 314 pp. Port frontis. Mod buckram.

(Weiner) £25 [≃ $45]

Richards, Vyvyan

- From crystal to television ... with a foreword by J.L. Baird. London: 1928. 8vo. x,116 pp. Frontis, diags. Orig cloth.
(Weiner) £25 [≃ $45]

Richardson, Sir Benjamin Ward

- Biological experimentation, its functions and limits ... London: 1896. 8vo. 170 pp. Orig cloth. *(Weiner)* £35 [≃ $63]
- Disciples of Aesculapius. With a life of the author by his daughter ... London: Hutchinson, 1900. 2 vols. 8vo. vii,424; viii, 425-827 pp. 2 frontis, 47 plates, 16 text w'cuts. Orig cloth, gilt, t.e.g.
(Pollak) £125 [≃ $225]
- A Ministry of Health and other addresses. London: Chatto & Windus, 1879. 8vo. ix,[iii],354, [ii],32 ctlg pp. Lacking front free endpaper. Orig cloth, sl wear to spine ends, part unopened. *(Pollak)* £35 [≃ $63]
- Vita medica: chapters of medical life and work. London: 1897. 1st edn. 8vo. xvi,496,32 pub ctlg pp. Half-title. A little pencil underlining. Cloth, sm tear at hd of spine. Uncut & unopened. *(Elgen)* $80 [≃ £44]

Richerand, A.

- Elements of physiology ... Translated from the French ... with notes by N. Chapman. Phila: 1823. 8vo. viii,621,xvi pp. Foxing. Orig sheep, rubbed. *(Goodrich)* $75 [≃ £41]

Richter, August G.

- Medical and surgical observations. Translated from the German. Edinburgh: 1794. 1st edn in English. 336 pp. Mod qtr lea, cloth bds. *(Scientia)* $225 [≃ £125]

Ricketson, Shadrach

- Means of preserving health, and preventing diseases. New York: Collins, Perkins ..., 1806. 1st edn. 12mo. [2],x,298,[2 advts] pp. Inserted 'Recommendations' leaf. Occas light foxing. Contemp mottled calf, extremities lightly rubbed. *(Heritage)* $250 [≃ £138]

Ricord, Philippe

- Letters on syphilis addressed to the Chief Editor of l'Union Medicale. Translated ... Boston: 1853. 1st edn in English 404 pp. Piece torn from front blank. Half lea, scuffed.
(Scientia) $150 [≃ £83]
- Letters on syphilis. Phila: Blanchard & Lea, 1854. 8vo. 270 pp, 32 pp pub ctlg. Orig cloth, extremities sl worn. *(Oasis)* $35 [≃ £19]

Ridley, Humphrey

- The anatomy of the brain. London: for Sam. Smith & Benj. Walford, 1695. 1st edn. 8vo. [12],200,[24] pp. Dedn leaf, 5 engvd fldg plates, errata, lacking imprim leaf. Wellcome Lib stamp & withdrawal on title verso, sgntr on 1st free endpaper. Russia. Wing R1449.
(Rootenberg) $6,000 [≃ £3,333]

Rigby, Edward

- On the constitutional treatment of female diseases. Phila: 1857. 8vo. xv,256,12 pub ctlg pp. Half-title. Orig blindstamped pebble cloth. *(Elgen)* $45 [≃ £25]
- On the constitutional treatment of female diseases. Phila: 1857. 8vo. xv,256 pp. Orig cloth, spine v faded.
(Rittenhouse) $35 [≃ £19]

Righi, Augusto

- Modern theory of physical phenomena - radio-activity, ions, electrons. New York: Macmillan, 1904. 1st edn in English. 8vo. xiii,[1],165 pp. Text figs. Orig cloth.
(Antiq Sc) $65 [≃ £36]

Riley, Henry Alsop

- An atlas of the basal ganglia, brain stem and spinal cord. Balt: Williams & Wilkins, 1943. 1st edn. Obl 4to. 708 pp. Photo ills throughout. Orig cloth, sl worn.
(Oasis) $125 [≃ £69]

Rindfleisch, Edward

- A manual of pathological histology to serve as an introduction to the study of morbid anatomy. London: New Sydenham Soc, 1872-73. 2 vols. xiii,464; vii,410 pp. Num ills. Orig cloth. *(Whitehart)* £18 [≃ $32]
- A textbook of pathological histology. Translated ... Phila: 1872. 1st edn in English. 8vo. 695,44 pub ctlg pp. 208 text engvs. Sheep, rubbed. *(Elgen)* $50 [≃ £27]
- A textbook of pathological histology. Phila: 1872. Cvrs faded & shelfworn.
(Rittenhouse) $37.50 [≃ £20]

Ring, John

- A treatise on the cow-pox; containing the history of vaccine inoculation ... London: 1801-03. 1st edn. 2 vols. 8vo. [ii],ii,528; [ii],vi,529-1037,[1],xxi,[1 errata] pp. 2 hand-cold engvd plates. Contemp str-grained mor, richly gilt. Ex Wellcome collection.
(Pickering) $1,500 [≃ £833]

Riseman, David

- The story of medicine in the Middle Ages. New York: 1935. 8vo. xii,402 pp. Many ills.

Orig cloth.   *(Weiner)* **£40 [≈ $72]**

Risteen, A.D.
- Molecules and the molecular theory of matter. Boston: 1895. viii,223 pp. Text figs. Sgntr on title. Orig cloth, sl dust-stained.
          (Whitehart) **£25 [≈ $45]**

Ritchie, David G.
- Darwinism and politics. London: Swan Sonnenschein, 1889. 8vo. [viii],101,[iii] pp. Orig buckram, sm mark on rear cvr.
          (Pollak) **£25 [≈ $45]**

Riverius, Lazarus
- The secrets of the famous Lazarus Riverius ... newly translated from the Latin. London: for Daniel Brown ..., 1685. 8vo. 1st English trans. 124 pp. Browning. Old calf, rebacked.
          (Goodrich) **$295 [≈ £163]**

Rivers, Henry
- Accidents. Popular directions for their immediate treatment; with observations on poisons and their antidotes. Boston: 1845. 8vo. 108 pp. Cloth, spine sunned & worn.
          (Goodrich) **$85 [≈ £47]**

Riviere, Lazare
- The practice of physick. London: Sawbridge, 1688. 6th edn. Folio. [xii],645 (pagination errors); [xii],463, [1],[32] pp. Sm worm holes through some margs, paper flaw in M3 with sl loss, title & frontis soiled. Contemp calf, rebacked, crnrs reprd. Wing R1564.
          (Pickering) **$550 [≈ £305]**

Rivington, Walter
- The medical profession ... the essay awarded the First Carmichael Prize ... 1879. Dublin: 1879. 8vo. xii,477 pp. Orig cloth.
          (Weiner) **£50 [≈ $90]**

Roberts, William
- Homoeopathy as practised in Manchester, contrasted with its alleged principles. London: 1862. 8vo. 84 pp. New bds.
          (Goodrich) **$60 [≈ £33]**

Robertson, J. Drummond
- The evolution of clockwork with a special section on the clocks of Japan ... comprehensive bibliography of horology ... London: 1931. 8vo. xvi,358 pp. Num ills. Orig cloth.   *(Weiner)* **£50 [≈ $90]**

Robinson, Nicholas
- A treatise on the virtues and efficacy of a crust of bread, eat early in a morning fasting ... by a physician. London: E. Robinson ..., 1756. 1st edn. Half-title, title, v,[7]-76 pp. Orig wraps, backstrip partly off.
          (Elgen) **$275 [≈ £152]**

Robinson, Samuel
- A catalogue of American minerals, with their localities ... Boston: Cummings, Hilliard, 1825. 1st edn. 8vo. [viii],316 pp. Orig brown gilt-stamped cloth, spine & cvr extremities faded.   *(Karmiole)* **$60 [≈ £33]**

Robinson, Victor
- The life of Jacob Henle. New York: 1921. One of 500. 8vo. Frontis. 115 pp. Orig cloth. Author's pres copy. *(Goodrich)* **$70 [≈ £38]**
- Pathfinders in medicine. New York: 1929. 2nd edn. 8vo. xvii,810 pp. Plates, ports. Cloth.   *(Elgen)* **$75 [≈ £41]**
- Pathfinders in medicine. New York: Medical Life Press, 1929. 2nd edn. 8vo. 810 pp. Num plates. Orig cloth, spine sl worn.
          (Oasis) **$40 [≈ £22]**

Robson, A.W. Mayo & Moynihan, Berkeley
- Diseases of the stomach and their surgical treatment. New York: 1901. 1st Amer edn. 308 pp. Pub ctlg. Cloth, 2 sm nicks on front cvr.   *(Scientia)* **$75 [≈ £41]**

Roddis, Louis
- A short history of nautical medicine. New York: 1941. 2nd printing. 8vo. 359 pp. Orig cloth.   *(Goodrich)* **$35 [≈ £19]**

Rodger, Ella Hill Burton
- Aberdeen doctors at home and abroad. The narrative of a medical school. Edinburgh: Blackwood, 1893. 8vo. xv,355 pp. Orig cloth gilt, spine faded.   *(Pollak)* **£30 [≈ $54]**

Roesslin, Eucharius
- The birth of man-kinde otherwise named the womans booke ... London: for A.H., 1626. 4to. 204 pp. Black letter. 9 copperplates, initials. Insignificant reprs to outer margs prelims, minimal soiling. Lge paper copy in full mor by Sangorski.
          (Rootenberg) **$2,500 [≈ £1,388]**

Rogers, A.W.
- An introduction to the geology of Cape Colony. London: 1905. 1st edn. 8vo. [xviii], 463,[40 advts] pp. Cold fldg map, 21 plates, 27 figs. Orig cloth.
          (Bow Windows) **£24 [≈ $43]**

Roget, Peter Mark

- Animal and vegetable physiology considered with reference to natural theology. London: Pickering, 1834. 1st edn. 2 vols. Demy 8vo. xxxvii, 593; vii,661 pp. Some occas sparse foxing. Half mor, a little rubbed at extremities.   *(Taylor)* £45 [≈$81]
- Animal and vegetable physiology ... London: Pickering, 1834. 1st edn. 2 vols. 8vo. xxxvii,593; vii,661 pp. 463 text figs. Contemp calf, gilt, rebacked with orig spines laid on, t.e.g.   *(Whitehart)* £40 [≈$72]
- Animal and vegetable physiology ... London: Pickering, 1834. 2nd edn. 2 vols. 8vo. Occas spots or other minor marks. Contemp prize calf, gilt (Trinity College, Dublin), ends of spines & crnrs rubbed.
                (Bow Windows) £85 [≈$153]
- Animal and vegetable physiology ... London: Pickering, 1834. 2nd edn. 2 vols. 8vo. xxxvi,524; vii,598 pp. Num ills. Half calf, vol 1 front bd loose. Ex lib. *(Weiner)* £35 [≈$63]

Rohde, Eleanour Sinclair

- A garden of herbs. London: 1921. 1st edn. 8vo. 232 pp. Ills. Orig cloth.
                (Goodrich) $35 [≈£19]
- The old English herbals. London: Longmans, 1922. 1st edn. Lge 8vo. Cold frontis, plates. Orig cloth.   *(Hughes)* £65 [≈$117]

Rokitansky, Carl

- A manual of pathological anatomy. London: 1854. 4 vols. Cvrs sl worn. Ex lib.
                (Rittenhouse) $120 [≈£66]
- A manual of pathological anatomy. London: Sydenham Soc., 1849-54. 4 vols. 8vo. 8 figs on 2 plates. Orig blindstamped cloth, t.e.g.
                (Hemlock) $275 [≈£152]

Rolleston, H.D.

- The Cambridge Medical School, a biographical history. Cambridge: 1932. 8vo. 235 pp. Ports. Orig cloth, stained. Author's inscrptn to K.J. Franklin.
                (Weiner) £25 [≈$45]

Rolleston, Humphry

- Diseases of the liver, gall-bladder and bile-ducts. Phila: 1905. 1st Amer edn. 794 pp. Num photo-micrographs & other plates. Orig cloth, inner hinges cracked.
                (Fye) $125 [≈£69]

Rolnick, Harry C.

- The practice of urology. Phila: [1949]. 1st edn, 2nd ptg. 2 vols. Lge 8vo. xviii,1245 pp. 9 cold plates, over 1300 ills. Cloth, dw.
                (Elgen) $50 [≈£27]

Romanes, G.J.

- The scientific evidences of organic evolution. 1882. 1st edn. vii,88 pp. Orig cloth, sl marked.   *(Whitehart)* £25 [≈$45]

Romer, Ferd.

- The bone caves of Ojcow in Poland. London: Longmans ..., 1884. 1st English edn. 4to. xii,41 pp. Woodburytype frontis, 12 plates, map. Orig pict cloth, gilt. Translator's pres copy.   *(Gough)* £38 [≈$68]

Ronayne, Philip

- Treatise of algebra in two books. London: W. & J. Innys, 1727. 461 pp. A few minor spots & stains. Gilt dec lea, a.e.g., a bit worn.
                (Xerxes) $200 [≈£111]

Roscoe, H.E.

- Spectrum analysis. Six lectures delivered in 1868, before the Society of Apothecaries of London. 1869. 1st edn. xv,348 pp. 4 plates, 72 ills. Sl foxing. Orig pict cloth, marked.
                (Whitehart) £25 [≈$45]

Rose, H.

- A manual of analytical chemistry, translated from the German ... London: 1831. 1st edn in English. 8vo. xvi,454 pp. Few w'cuts. Lib stamp on title. Half calf, rebacked.
                (Weiner) £50 [≈$90]

Rosen van Rosenstein, Nicholas

- The diseases of children and their remedies. Translated by Andrew Sparrman. London: 1776. 1st edn in English. 364 pp plus index. Lea, rebacked.   *(Scientia)* $1,000 [≈£555]

Rosen, George

- A history of public health. New York: [1958]. 1st edn. 8vo. 551 pp. Cloth, dw.
                (Elgen) $30 [≈£16]

Rosenbaum, Julius

- The plague of lust, being a history of venereal disease in classical antiquity. Translated ... Paris: Charles Carrington, 1901. One of 500. 2 vols. 8vo. Red & black titles. Orig half parchment, gilt, sl spotted.
                (Hughes) £65 [≈$117]

Ross, Hugh Campbell

- Induced cell-reproduction and cancer. The isolation of the chemical causes of normal and of augmented asymmetrical human cell-division. Phila: 1911. 8vo. xxx,423 pp. 129 ills. Cloth.   *(Elgen)* $85 [≈£47]

Ross, James
- Handbook of the diseases of the nervous system. Phila: 1885. 1st Amer edn. 8vo. 723 pp. 184 ills. Sheep. *(Goodrich)* **$95 [≃£52]**
- A treatise on the diseases of the nervous system. New York: 1883. 2nd edn. 2 vols. 1047 pp. Orig photographic plates. Lea.
  (Fye) **$100 [≃£55]**

Ross, Ronald
- Studies on malaria. London: 1928. 8vo. xi,196 pp. 4 plates. Author's inscrptn on flyleaf "Advance copy ...".
  (Weiner) **£60 [≃$108]**

Rousseau, Jean Jacques
- Letters on the elements of botany. Addressed to a lady ... and twenty-four additional letters, fully explaining the system of Linneaus. By Thomas Martyn. London: White, 1787. 2nd edn. xxvi,500,[28] pp. Orig bds, uncut, later paper spine, a little chipped.
  (Karmiole) **$100 [≃£55]**
- Letters on the elements of botany. Addressed to a lady ... and twenty-four additional letters, fully explaining the system of Linneaus. By Thomas Martyn. London: 1787. 2nd edn. xxv,[i],500,[28] pp. Contemp calf, rebacked, gilt spine. *(Whitehart)* **£85 [≃$153]**
- Letters on the elements of botany. London: for B. & J. White, 1794. 4th edn. 8vo. xxiv,503,[28 indices] pp. Fldg chart. Occas spotting. 19th c half calf, rebacked with orig worn backstrip. *(Claude Cox)* **£20 [≃$36]**

Rowbotham, G.F.
- Acute injuries of the head. Edinburgh: 1942. 4to. 288 pp. Cloth, worn, jnts split.
  (Goodrich) **$45 [≃£25]**

Rowe, John
- An introduction to the doctrine of fluxions. London: J. & J. March, 1767. 3rd edn. 8vo. xii,218,[ii errata] pp. 13 plates. Contemp sheep, rebacked, crnrs worn.
  (Pollak) **£100 [≃$180]**

Royal College of Physicians
- Historical sketch and laws of the Royal College of Physicians of Edinburgh from its institution to 1891. Edinburgh: 1891. 4to. 214 pp. Orig cloth. *(Goodrich)* **£35 [≃£19]**

Royal College of Surgeons
- A descriptive and illustrated catalogue of the calculi and other animal concretions contained in the Museum [of the Royal College of Surgeons]. London: Taylor, 1842. 1st edn. 4to. 138 pp. 12 cold litho plates.

Anntns. Orig cloth, rebacked.
  (Oasis) **$200 [≃£111]**

Royal Hospitals ...
- Memoranda, references, and documents relating to the Royal Hospitals of the City of London ... London: Arthur Taylor, 1836. xii,107, [i],167,[i] pp. Occas foxing. Orig cloth, new spine. *(Pollak)* **£50 [≃$90]**

Royle, J. Forbes
- Materia medica and therapeutics: Including the preparation of the Pharmacopeias of London, Edinburgh ... Phila: 1847. 1st Amer edn. 8vo. xii,[2], [17]-689,32 pub ctlg pp. Half-title. 98 w'cuts. Prelims marg stained, marg foxing, browning. Lea, sl scuffed.
  (Elgen) **$65 [≃£36]**

Royle, J.F.
- An essay on the antiquity of Hindoo medicine ... London: Allen, 1837. 8vo. 196 pp. Advts. Orig bds, worn, uncut. Author's pres copy.
  (Goodrich) **$295 [≃£163]**

Rubin, I.C.
- Collected papers, 1910-1954. [1954]. 1st coll edn. Lge v thick 8vo. 132 sep papers, sep paginations. Ills. Cloth. Ex lib. Author's sgnd pres copy. *(Elgen)* **$95 [≃£52]**
- Uterotubal insufflation: a clinical diagnostic method of determining the tubal factor in sterility ... St. Louis: 1947. 1st edn. 8vo. 453 pp. Frontis, 5 cold plates, num ills & other plates. Cloth. *(Elgen)* **$45 [≃£25]**

Ruffer, Marc
- Studies in the paleopathology of Egypt. Edited by R.L. Moodie. Chicago: 1921. 1st edn. 372 pp. Cloth. *(Scientia)* **$175 [≃£97]**

Ruhrah, John
- Pediatrics of the past. An anthology ... New York: 1925. 8vo. 592 pp. 18 plates, 54 text ills. Orig cloth. *(Goodrich)* **$145 [≃£80]**

Rundell, Maria Eliza
- A new system of domestic cookery ... a new edition, corrected. London: Murray .., 1829. Engvd frontis (loose), 9 plates (foxed). Orig cloth, ptd spine label v worn, front inner hinge cracked. *(Sanders)* **£32 [≃$57]**
- A new system of domestic cookery ... with the addition of numerous new receipts ... London: for T. Allman, n.d. [ca 1850]. Sm 8vo. Engvd frontis, addtnl title with vignette, 11 plates. Orig cerise cloth, blocked in blind & gilt, jnts sl worn. *(Sanders)* **£25 [≃$45]**

Rundle, J.F.
- Joll's disease of the thyroid gland. 1951. 2nd edn. x,520 pp. Frontis, 164 diags & ills. Cloth, dust-stained dw.
(Whitehart) **£25 [≈ $45]**

Rural Improvements ...
- Rural improvements ... See Wimpey, Joseph

Rusby, H.H.
. - Jungle memories. New York: 1933. 8vo. xiii,388 pp. 16 plates. Orig cloth.
(Wheldon & Wesley) **£30 [≈ $54]**

Rush, Benjamin
- An account of the bilious remitting yellow fever, as it appeared in the City of Philadelphia, in the year 1793 ... Phila: Thomas Dobson, 1794. 1st edn. 8vo. x,363 pp. Sgntr on flyleaf. Contemp calf. Ex lib Fisher collection. *(Hemlock)* **$625 [≈ £347]**
- Essays, literary, moral and philosophical. Phila: 1806. 2nd edn. Title & following pp sl creased. Orig cvrs, top cvr almost detchd.
(Rittenhouse) **$150 [≈ £83]**
- Medical inquiries and observations upon the diseases of the mind. Phila: 1830. 4th edn. V light foxing on title & elsewhere. Cvrs sl worn. Ex lib. *(Rittenhouse)* **$175 [≈ £97]**
- Medical inquiries and observations. Vol. 2. Phila: 1793. 1st edn. 321,[1] pp. Lea, rec rebacked. *(Scientia)* **$325 [≈ £180]**
- The works of Thomas Sydenham ... See Sydenham, Thomas

Russell, Bertrand
- The ABC of relativity. London: 1925. 1st edn. Sm 8vo. 231 pp. Inked marginalia, spotting here & there, stain on fore-edge. Orig cloth, faded. *(Bow Windows)* **£32 [≈ $57]**
- The ABC of relativity. New York: Harper, 1925. 1st Amer edn. 231 pp. Blue cloth, sl chipped dw. *(Karmiole)* **$40 [≈ £22]**

Russell, E.S.
- The interpretation of development and heredity. A study in biological method. Oxford: 1930. [vii],312 pp. A few light pencil anntns, mostly marginal. Cloth, sl marked.
(Whitehart) **£18 [≈ $32]**

Russell, J. Rutherford
- The history and heros of the art of medicine. London: 1861. 8vo. x,491 pp. Frontis loose. Binding shelfworn, hinge cracked, spine chipped, shaken. *(Rittenhouse)* **$35 [≈ £19]**

Russell, K.
- British anatomy. 1525-1800. A bibliography. Melbourne Univ Press, [1963]. Lge 8vo. xviii,254 pp. Frontis, 52 plates. Orig cloth, acetate wrapper, slipcase. One of 750, numbered, sgnd by author.
(Karmiole) **$75 [≈ £41]**
- British anatomy. 1525-1800. A bibliography. Melbourne: 1963. 8vo. One of 750, sgnd by author. Slipcase, orig plastic cvrs.
(Rittenhouse) **$50 [≈ £27]**

Russell, Richard
- A dissertation on the use of sea-water in the diseases of the glands. London: for the translator, 1752. 1st English edn. Engvd frontis, engvd plate. Contemp polished calf. *(Quaritch)* **$400 [≈ £222]**
- A dissertation on the use of sea-water in the diseases of the glands ... Translated from the Latin ... London: W. Owen ..., 1752. 1st edn in English. 12mo. xii,204 pp. Engvd frontis, double-page plate. Orig calf, sl rubbed.
(Elgen) **$275 [≈ £152]**
- A dissertation on the use of sea-water in the diseases of the glands ... Also an account of the nature ... of mineral waters in Great Britain. London: for W. Owen, 1760. [with] A treatise ... a proper supplement ... Owen, 1762. 2 plates. Contemp calf, rubbed.
(Waterfield's) **£125 [≈ $225]**

Rutherford, Ernest
- The collected papers ... published under the scientific direction of Sir James Chadwick. London: 1962-65. 3 vols. 8vo. Plates, diags. Orig cloth, dws. *(Weiner)* **£75 [≈ $135]**
- The collected papers. London: Allen & Unwin, 1962-65. 3 vols. 8vo. 931,[v]; 590,[ii]; 428,[iv] pp. 32 plates, num text figs. Pub bndg, dws. *(Pollak)* **£55 [≈ $99]**
- The natural and artificial disintegration of the elements. Phila: Franklin Institute, 1924. 1st edn. 8vo. 24 pp. Orig ptd stiff wraps.
(Antiq Sc) **$60 [≈ £33]**
- Radio-activity. Cambridge Univ Press, 1904. 1st edn. 8vo. 399 pp. Ills. Lacking front free endpaper. Orig cloth. *(Oasis)* **$450 [≈ £250]**
- Radio-activity. Cambridge: Univ Press, 1904. 1st edn. 8vo. viii,[2],399 pp. Plate, text figs. Orig cloth. *(Antiq Sc)* **$475 [≈ £263]**
- Radio-activity. Cambridge: 1905. 2nd edn. xi,580 pp. Plate, 108 text figs. Orig cloth, marked. *(Whitehart)* **£100 [≈ $180]**
- Radio-activity. Cambridge: 1905. 2nd edn. 8vo. xi,580 pp. Plate, diags. Orig cloth.
(Weiner) **£50 [≈ $90]**
- Radioactive substances and their radiations.

Cambridge: 1913. 1st edn. 8vo. 699 pp. Ills. Discreet name on title. Orig cloth.
(Oasis) **$150 [≃ £83]**

- Radioactive substances and their radiations. Cambridge: 1913. 1st edn. 8vo. viii,699 pp. Green cloth, a bit rubbed.
(Karmiole) **$175 [≃ £97]**

- Radioactive transformations. 1912. 2nd edn. [3],287 pp. 53 text figs. Orig cloth, dull, spine sl nicked at top.   *(Whitehart)* **£60 [≃ $108]**

Rutherford, Ernest, et al.
- Radiations from radioactive substances. Cambridge: 1930. 1st edn. x,588 pp. 12 plates, 140 text diags. Ink sgntr on endpaper. Orig cloth, spine sl worn.
(Whitehart) **£40 [≃ $72]**

- Radiations from radioactive substances. Cambridge: 1930. 8vo. xi,588 pp. 12 plates, diags. Ex lib with stamps.
(Weiner) **£38 [≃ $68]**

Rutter, J.
- Delineations of the North Western Division of the County of Somerset, and of the antediluvian bone caverns ... London: 1829. Imp 4to, lge paper. xxiv,336 pp. 2 ff advts at front. Cold map, 12 engvd & litho plates. Some spotting on frontis & plates. Qtr mor.
(Bow Windows) **£110 [≃ $198]**

Rutty, John
- A methodical synopsis of mineral waters, comprehending the most celebrated medicinal waters ... of Great-Britain, Ireland, France, Germany ... London: for William Johnston, 1757. 1st edn. Thick 4to. Tables. Title spotted & frayed. Calf, rebacked.
(Chaucer Head) **£220 [≃ $396]**

Rutty, John, et al.
- The argument of sulphur or no sulphur in waters discussed ... annexed, two tracts. ... analysis of milk ... on the uses of goat's whey. Dublin: Alex M'Culloh, 1762. 1st edn. vii,109; [ii],v,3-19; 21 pp. Fldg table, addtnl leaf between pp 94/5. Disbound.
(Burmester) **£75 [≃ $135]**

Rutty, William
- A treatise of the urinary passages ... their description, powers and uses ... London: for Tho. Worrall, 1726. 4to. [viii],54,[vi] pp. 4 plates. Occas foxing, sm tear in fore-edge of title & half-title, 1st plate trimmed a little close. New paper bds. *(Pollak)* **£150 [≃ $270]**

Ryan, James
- Elementary treatise on algebra. New York:

Collins & Hannay, 1824. 12mo. 511 pp. pencil notes at end, heavily foxed. Cloth, outer hinges split.   *(Xerxes)* **$45 [≃ £25]**

- A treatise on the art of measuring ... New York: Collins ... & the author, 1831. 1st edn. 12mo. 344 pp. Text figs. Spotty foxing. Lib buckram with stamps & shelf marks.
(Antiq Sc) **$65 [≃ £36]**

Sabine, Edward
- Report on the variations of the magnetic intensity observed at different points of the earth's surface. London: Taylor, 1838. 1st sep edn. [1],85,[1 blank],[1] pp. 2 full-page plates in text, 3 fldg plates at rear. Contemp bds, sl wear. "From the author".
(Karmiole) **$250 [≃ £138]**

Sabine, John
- The practical mathematician. London: T. Jones, [1811]. 2nd edn. Sm 8vo. iv,[ii],358 pp. 22 engvd plates, fldg table. Outer edges of a few plates trimmed. Contemp half calf, rebacked.   *(Burmester)* **£38 [≃ $68]**

Sabine, W.C.
- Collected papers on acoustics. Cambridge, Mass: 1927. ix,283 pp. Port frontis, num diags & ills. Cloth worn & dust-stained.
(Whitehart) **£35 [≃ $63]**

Sachs, Bernard & Hausman, Louis
- Nervous and mental disorders from birth through adolescence. New York: 1926. 1st edn. 861 pp. Cloth, top of spine sl frayed, spine lettering dull.   *(Scientia)* **$75 [≃ £41]**

Sadger, Dr. J.
- Sleep walking and moon walking. A medico-literary study. New York & Washington: 1920. 8vo. x,140,[2] pp. A few leaves carelessly opened. Orig paper wraps, spine chipped at ends. *(Bow Windows)* **£15 [≃ $27]**

Saks, Stanislaw
- Theory of the integral. New York: Hafner, 1937. 2nd edn, revsd. 347 pp. Orig cloth.
(Xerxes) **$70 [≃ £38]**

Salisbury, J.H.
- The relation of alimentation and disease. New York: 1888. 1st edn. 8vo. xi,332 pp. 19 plates. Light marg browning. Cloth.
(Elgen) **$50 [≃ £27]**

Salmon, G.
- Lessons introductory to the modern higher algebra. Dublin: 1859. xii,147 pp. Author's inscrptn on title. Orig blindstamped cloth, spine faded.   *(Whitehart)* **£25 [≃ $45]**

Salmon, William
- Doron medicum: or, a supplement to the New London Dispensatory, in III books ... completed with the Art of Compounding Medicines. London: 1683. 1st edn. 8vo. xvi,720, [60 index], [4 author's books] pp. Old calf, hinges rubbed, sm repr to hinge. Wing S426. *(Hemlock)* **$475 [≈£263]**
- Pharmacopoeia Londinensis: or, the new London dispensatory. In VI books ... As also the praxis of chymistry. London: for R. Chiswell, 1707. 7th edn. Sm 8vo. Most pp browned. Contemp panelled calf, rebacked. *(Chaucer Head)* **£120 [≈$216]**

Salusbury, Thomas
- Mathematical collections and translations. In two parts. London: ... George Sawbridge, 1667. 2 pts in 1. Folio. 4 fldg plates. Title & last page soiled, sm reprs at crnrs & inner margs, tear in A2, sm tear in dedn leaf reprd, some staining. Old calf, rebacked. *(Traylen)* **£1,100 [≈$1,980]**
- Mathematical collections and translations. In two tomes. [L:1661 & 1665]. Reprinted in facsimile 1967. One of 200. 2 vols. Folio. Full calf by Zaehnsdorf. *(Bow Windows)* **£150 [≈$270]**

Sampson, R.A.
- Tables of the four great satellites of Jupiter. Univ of Durham Observatory, 1910. Lge 4to. xlviii,300 pp. Errata booklet & explanatory offprint. *(Whitehart)* **£25 [≈$45]**

Sanctorius
- Medicina statica: being the aphorisms of Sanctorius. Translated ... added, Dr. Keil's Medicina Statica Britannica ... As also Medico-Physical Essays ... London: 1723. 3rd edn. 8vo. vii,344, [18],[4], 116 pp. Frontis, fldg plate. Contemp calf, hinges cracked. *(Hemlock)* **$150 [≈£83]**

Sappington, John
- The theory and treatment of fevers. Revised and corrected by Ferdinando Stith. Arrow Rock: 1844. 1st edn. 8vo. 216 pp. Foxing. New qtr calf. *(Goodrich)* **$175 [≈£97]**

Sargant, William
- Battle for the mind. A physiology of conversion and brain-washing. London: Heinemann, 1957. xxiv,248 pp. Frontis, 24 plates. Pub bndg, dw. *(Pollak)* **£20 [≈$36]**

Sarkar, Benoy Kumar
- Hindu achievements in exact science. New York: 1918. 1st edn. Sm vo. xiii,82,[2] pp. A

few marks in margs. Cloth.
(Elgen) **$35 [≈£19]**

Sarsfield, L.G.H.
- Electrical engineering in radiography ... X-ray work in medicine and industry. London: Chapman & Hall, 1936. 8vo. xiii,[i],284 pp. Pub bndg, dw. *(Pollak)* **£30 [≈$54]**

Sarton, George
- From magic to science. Essays on the scientific twilight. 1928. 8vo. xix,253 pp. Many plates inc 14 tipped-in cold, ills. Orig cloth, dampstained. *(Weiner)* **£35 [≈$63]**
- A history of science. Cambridge, Mass: 1952. 2 vols. 8vo. xxvi,646; xxvi,554 pp. Cloth, front cvrs somewhat waterstained. *(Elgen)* **$55 [≈£30]**
- A history of science: ancient science through the golden age of Greece; Hellenistic science and culture ... 1959. 2 vols. Orig cloth. *(Allen)* **$50 [≈£27]**

Saul, Edward
- An historical and philosophical account of the barometer ... reason and use of that instrument, the theory of the atmosphere ... probable judgement of the weather. London: A. Bettesworth ..., 1730. 100 pp. Contemp panelled calf, rebacked. *(C.R. Johnson)* **£260 [≈$468]**

Saunders, John Cunningham
- The anatomy of the human ear, illustrated by a series of engravings, of the natural size ... London: E. Cox, 1817. 2nd edn. 8vo. viii,112 pp. Half-title, 4 fldg engvd plates (lightly foxed). Rebound in half-cloth, bds. Ex lib. *(Elgen)* **$150 [≈£83]**

Saunders, William
- A treatise on the chemical history and medical powers of some of the most celebrated mineral waters. London: William Phillips, 1800. 1st edn. 8vo. New half antique calf, gilt. *(Traylen)* **£48 [≈$86]**
- A treatise on the structure, economy and diseases of the liver; together with an enquiry into the ... bile and biliary concretions. Boston: 1797. 1st Amer from 2nd London edn. Sm 8vo. 231 pp. Name excised from top of title, mild browning. Calf, v worn. *(Oasis)* **$85 [≈£47]**
- A treatise on the structure, economy, and diseases of the liver; together with an enquiry into ... the bile, and biliary concretions. Boston: W. Pelham, 1797. 1st Amer edn. 12mo. xx,231 pp. Contemp tree calf, lea label. *(Antiq Sc)* **$100 [≈£55]**

Saunderson, Nicholas

- The elements of algebra, in ten books. Cambridge: University Press, 1740. 1st edn. 4to. [xx],[ii errata],xxvi, [iv],360; [ii],363-748 pp. Port frontis, engvd plate vol I, 8 fldg engvd plates vol II. Without the addtnl title vol I. Rebound in grey bds.
  (Pickering) **$450** [≃ £250]
- The method of fluxions applied to a select number of useful problems ... London: for A. Millar ..., 1756. 1st edn. xxiv,309,[1 errata] pp. 12 fldg engvd plates. Some browning in margs. Rebound in calf-backed bds.
  (Pickering) **$850** [≃ £472]

Saunier, C.

- The watchmaker's handbook ... for those engaged in watchmaking and the allied mechanical arts. 1891. 3rd edn, revsd. xiv,498 pp. 14 fldg plates, 36 text figs. Orig cloth, inner hinges cracked.
  (Whitehart) **£25** [≃ $45]

Savage, G.C.

- New truths in ophthalmology. Nashville: 1896. 3rd edn. 8vo. viii,270 pp. Text ills. Orig cloth, edges rubbed, front inner hinge cracked.
  (Elgen) **$25** [≃ £13]
- New truths in ophthalmology. Nashville: the author, 1893. 1st edn. 8vo. 152 pp. Orig cloth.
  (Oasis) **$45** [≃ £25]
- Ophthalmic neuro-myology. Nashville: the author, [1905]. 1st edn. 8vo. vii,221 pp. 39 plates, 12 text ills. Orig cloth, sl soiled. Author's pres inscrptn. *(Elgen)* **$35** [≃ £19]

Savage, Henry

- The surgery, surgical pathology and surgical anatomy of the female pelvic organs. New York: Wood's Library, 1880. 3rd edn. 136 pp. 60 pp pub ctlg, 32 plates. Orig cloth.
  (Oasis) **$85** [≃ £47]
- The surgery, surgical pathology and surgical anatomy of the female pelvic organs. New York: 1880. 3rd edn. 8vo. 129,[8] pp. 60 pp pub ctlg. 32 litho plates, 22 text w'cuts. Orig embossed cloth. *(Elgen)* **$75** [≃ £41]

Savery, Thomas

- The miner's friend; or, an engine to raise water by fire, described ... London: for S. Crouch, 1702. Reprinted 1827, republished 1829. 12mo. 53,[i blank] pp. Port frontis, port, 4 engvd plates. Orig dec yellow glazed bds, rebacked, new front pastedown.
  (Pollak) **£75** [≃ $135]
- The miner's friend; or, an engine to raise water by fire, described ... London: for S. Crouch, 1702. Reprinted 1827, republished 1829. Sm 8vo. 53 pp. Port, 4 plates, w'cuts. Orig dec paper wraps. *(Weiner)* **£35** [≃ $63]

Sawer, J. Ch.

- Odorographia; a natural history of raw materials and drugs used in the perfume industry ... London: Gurney ..., 1892. 8vo. xxiv,383,4 pub advts pp. 13 ills, sketch map. General foxing. Orig brown cloth, gilt, a little worn at jnts. *(Gough)* **£85** [≃ $153]

Scarpa, Antonio

- Engravings of the cardiac nerves, the nerves of the ninth pair ... copied from the "Tabulae Neurologicae" ... Edinburgh: 1832. 3rd edn. 4to. [84] pp. 30 plates, most cold. Inscrptn of Alexander Fleming on title. Light foxing. New cloth-backed mrbld bds.
  (Weiner) **£200** [≃ $360]

Schacht, Hermann

- The microscope and its application to vegetable anatomy and physiology. London: 1855. 2nd edn. 202 pp. Cloth.
  (Scientia) **$65** [≃ £36]

Schall, W.E.

- X-rays: their origin, dosage, and practical application. Bristol: John Wright, 1940. 5th edn. 8vo. xi,[i],252 pp. 248 ills. Pub bndg.
  (Pollak) **£25** [≃ $45]

Scheele, Carl Wilhelm

- The chemical essays ... Translated ... with additions ... With a sketch of the life ... London: Scott, Greenwood, 1901. 1st edn thus (with the Life). 8vo. Orig gilt-lettered cloth. *(Chaucer Head)* **£90** [≃ $162]

Scheppegrell, William

- Hayfever and asthma: care, prevention and treatment. Phila: Lea & Febiger, 1922. 1st edn. 274 pp. Cold frontis, 107 text ills. Orig cloth. *(Oasis)* **$45** [≃ £25]

Schindler, Robert

- Mechanics of the Moon. Lucerne: the author, 1912. English edn ltd to 300. 12mo. 69 pp. Photos, inc 1 fldg plate. Orig gilt illust cloth. Author's pres copy, unsgnd.
  (Xerxes) **$55** [≃ £30]

Schlick, Moritz

- Space and time in contemporary physics. An introduction to the theory of relativity and gravitation. New York: 1920. 89 pp. Cloth.
  (Xerxes) **$35** [≃ £19]

Schorlemmer, Carl
- Chemistry in America. Chapters from the history of the science in the United States. New York: 1914. 8vo. xiii,356 pp. Frontis (detchd), ports, ills. Cloth. Ex lib.
(Weiner) **£35 [≃ $63]**
- Old chemistries. New York: 1927. 4to. xi,89 pp. 32 plates. Uncut, cloth. Ex lib.
(Weiner) **£30 [≃ $54]**
- The rise and development of organic chemistry. 1894. Revsd edn. 8vo. xxvii,280 pp. Port. Orig cloth.   *(Weiner)* **£30 [≃ $54]**

Schott, Theodor
- The balneo-gymnastic treatment of chronic diseases of the heart. Phila: [1914]. 1st edn in English. 8vo. xi,191 pp. Ills, plates. Cloth.
(Elgen) **$40 [≃ £22]**

Schoute, D.
- Occidental therapeutics in the Netherlands East Indies during three centuries of Netherlands settlement (1600-1900). Batavia: 1937. Lge 8vo. iv,214 pp. Orig cloth.
(Weiner) **£38 [≃ $68]**

Schouten, J.
- The Rod and Serpent of Asklepios. Symbol of Medicine. Amsterdam: Elzevier, 1967. ix,[i],260 pp. 76 ills. Pub bndg, dw.
(Pollak) **£30 [≃ $54]**

Schrader, Frank C. & Brooks, Alfred H.
- Preliminary report on the Cape Nome Gold Region, Alaska. Washington, 1900. 56 pp. Num ills, maps (2 fldg). Ptd wraps.
(Argonaut) **$75 [≃ £41]**

Schrader, Frank C. & Spencer, Arthur Coe
- The geology and mineral resources of a portion of the Copper River District, Alaska. Washington: 1901. 94 pp. Num ills from photos, 2 lge fldg maps. Ptd wraps, worn at spine.   *(Argonaut)* **$75 [≃ £41]**

Schroeder van der Kolk
- On the minute structure and functions of the spinal cord and medulla oblongata & on ... treatment of epilepsy. Translated ... London: 1859. 8vo. ix,291 pp. Sl chipped at hd & tail of spine. Ex lib, b'plates.
(Rittenhouse) **$45 [≃ £25]**

Schroeder van der Kolk, J.L.C.
- The pathology and therapeutics of mental diseases. Melbourne: S. Mullen, 1869. 1st edn in English. 8vo. xii,158 pp. Stamps on title, scattered underlining, unif light

browning. Orig cloth, sl worn. Translator's pres copy.   *(Antiq Sc)* **$275 [≃ £152]**

Schuster, Arthur
- The progress of physics during 33 years [1875-1908], four lectures delivered ... 1908. Cambridge: 1911. 8vo. x,164 pp. Port. Orig cloth.   *(Weiner)* **£35 [≃ $63]**

Schwann, Th.
- Microscopical researches into the accordance of the structure and growth of animals and plants. Translated ... London: 1847. 8vo. xx,268 pp. Orig cloth, hinge split at top. Ex lib.   *(Rittenhouse)* **$125 [≃ £69]**

Scofield, Samuel
- A practical treatise on vaccina or cowpock. New York: 1810. 8vo. xvi,139 pp. Cold plate. Foxing. Contemp calf.
(Goodrich) **$195 [≃ £108]**

Scoresby, William
- Journal of a voyage to Australia and around the world for magnetical research. London: 1859. 1st edn. 8vo. 96; 315 pp. Frontis, fldg map, ills. Orig cloth, unopened.
(Bonham) **£280 [≃ $504]**
- Journal of a voyage to Australia ... for magnetical research. London: 1859. 1st edn. 8vo. xlviii,315,22 pub ctlg pp. Port frontis, fldg map, a few text ills. Lib b'plate, stamp on title. Orig blue embossed cloth, sl worn, spine chipped, lower jnt split.
(Edwards) **£200 [≃ $360]**

Scot, Reginald
- The discoverie of witchcraft. London: William Brome, 1548. 1st edn. 560 pp, 8ff. 12 charts & diags (2 full-page). 2 leaves reprd at inner margs, title & a few leaves stained, soiled or inked, 2 leaves sl trimmed. Rec calf.
(Pirages) **$3,900 [≃ £2,166]**

Scott, Alexander
- An introduction to chemical theory. London: A. & C. Black, 1891. 1st edn. 8vo. 266 pp. 2 fldg tables. Prize calf.   *(Oasis)* **$30 [≃ £16]**

Scott, George
- Select remains of the learned John Ray ... with his life ... London: Ja. Dodsley, 1760. 8vo. vii,[i],336 pp. Port, 3 text engvs. Errata slip pasted to ft of last page. Antique style calf, orig spine label. *(Pollak)* **£80 [≃ $144]**

Scott, H. Harold
- A history of tropical medicine. London: Edward Arnold, 1939. 1st edn. 2 vols. 8vo.

Plates. Orig blue cloth, gilt, sl rubbed, sl marked, 1 inner hinge reprd.
(Hughes) **£45 [≈ $81]**

Scott, H.H.
- Some notable epidemics. 1934. xix,272 pp. Cloth. *(Whitehart)* **£18 [≈ $32]**

Scott, R.E.
- Inquiry into the limits and peculiar objects of physical and metaphysical science ... nature of causation ... Edinburgh: A. & J. Aikman ..., 1810. 1st edn. 8vo. Title spotted & sl dusty, some spotting, ex lib with stamps on title & verso. Mod qtr calf. *(Hughes)* **£65 [≈ $117]**

Scott, Robert F.
- A treatise on the theory of determinants and their applications in analysis and geometry. Cambridge: Univ Press, 1880. 1st edn. 8vo. xi,[1],251 pp. Orig cloth, a bit worn.
(Antiq Sc) **$60 [≈ £33]**

Scott, Robert H.
- Instructions in the use of meteorological instruments. London: HMSO, 1875. 8vo. 118 pp. Ills, fldg cold plate, fldg table. Orig binding. *(Weiner)* **£30 [≈ $54]**

Scott, William
- Report of the epidemic cholera as it has appeared in the territories subject to the Presidency of Fort St. George. Edinburgh: 1849. 8vo. 212 pp. Fldg map. Orig cloth, uncut & unopened. Author's pres copy.
(Goodrich) **$85 [≈ £47]**

Scoville, Wilbur
- Extracts an perfumes. A treatise on the most practical method for the manufacture by the retail or wholesale pharmacist. Boston: Spatula, n.d. [ca 1915]. Narrow sm 8vo. 112 pp. Cloth, a bit soiled. *(Xerxes)* **$25 [≈ £13]**

Scripture, E.W.
- The new psychology. New York: Scribner's, 1897. 1st edn. 8vo. 500 pp. 124 ills. Sm tear in title. Orig cloth, spine sl snagged.
(Oasis) **$85 [≈ £47]**
- Thinking, feeling, doing. New York: Flood & Vincent, 1895. 1st edn. 8vo. 304 pp. Cold frontis, num text ills. Orig cloth.
(Oasis) **$35 [≈ £19]**

Scroggie, M.G.
- Television. London: 1935. 8vo. ix,68 pp. 7 plates, diags. Orig cloth, dw.
(Weiner) **£35 [≈ $63]**

Scudder, Charles Locke
- Tumors of the jaws. Phila: 1912. 1st edn. 8vo. 391,16 pub ctlg pp. Profusely illust inc cold frontis. Cloth. *(Elgen)* **$65 [≈ £36]**

Seale, Robert F.
- The geognosy of the Island of St. Helena, illustrated in a series of views. London: Ackerman, 1834. 1st edn. Obl folio. 24ff. 11 hand-cold aquatints (10 called for), hand-cold vignette, 7 other vignettes. Occas light foxing. Orig half mor, spine restored.
(Gough) **£525 [≈ $945]**

Searle, A.B.
- The chemistry and physics of clays and other ceramic materials. 1924. 1st edn. Thick roy 8vo. 693 pp. Ills. Orig cloth.
(Halewood) **£25 [≈ $45]**

Seaward, John
- Observations on the re-building of London Bridge ... with an examination of the Arch of Equilibrium proposed by ... Dr. Hutton; and ... a new method for forming an arch of that description. London: 1824. 1st edn. 8vo. 143 pp. 7 fldg plates. Contemp qtr cloth.
(Argosy) **$300 [≈ £166]**

Sebright, John Saunders
- The art of improving the breeds of domestic animals. In a letter addressed to ... Sir Joseph Banks. London: for John Harding, 1809. 1st edn. 8vo. 31 pp. Author's pres inscrptn in pencil on title. Orig plain green wraps, uncut.
(Burmester) **£120 [≈ $216]**

Secrets ...
- Valuable secrets concerning arts and trades; or approved directions ... engraving ... varnishes ... gilding ... making wines ... preparing snuff ... London: Will. Hay, 1775. 1st edn. F'cap 8vo. [8],xxiv,312 pp. Contemp calf, hd & tail of spine chipped.
(Spelman) **£450 [≈ $810]**
- Valuable secrets in arts, trades, etc. Selected from the best authors, and adopted to the situation of the United States. New York: Edward Duyinck, 1809. 1st edn. 8vo. Contemp calf, rebacked.
(Minkoff) **£550 [≈ $305]**

Seguin, Edouard
- Idiocy; and its treatment by the physiological method. New York: 1866. 1st edn. 457 pp. Cloth, hd & ft of spine sl chipped.
(Scientia) **$175 [≈ £97]**
- Medical thermometry and human temperature. New York: 1876. 2nd edn. 8vo.

xxii,446 pp. Ills. Orig cloth, spine ends frayed.   *(Elgen)* **$75 [≃ £41]**
- Medical thermometry and human temperature. New York: 1876. 1st edn. 446 pp. Orig cloth.   *(Fye)* **$85 [≃ £47]**

Seligmann, G.
- Snow structure and ski fields. being an account of snow and ice forms in nature and a study of avalanches and snowcraft. 1936. xii,555 pp. 371 text figs.
                    (Whitehart) **£25 [≃ $45]**

Selwyn-Brown, Arthur
- The physician through the ages: a record of the doctor from the earliest historical period ... New York: 1928. 1st edn. 4to. 2 vols. 848; 854,26 pub ctlg pp. Errata leaf tipped-in. Num ills. Cloth.   *(Elgen)* **$95 [≃ £52]**
- The physician through the ages: a record of the doctor from the earliest historical period ... New York: 1938. Folio. 2 vols. Orig cloth, jnts split.   *(Goodrich)* **$35 [≃ £19]**

Sendivogius, Michael
- A new light of alchymy: taken out of the fountain of nature and manual experience ... a treatise of sulphur ... a chymical dictionary. London: Tho. Williams, 1674. 8vo. Title & final leaf sl soiled, some headlines cropped. New calf, old top cvr. Wing 2507A.
                    (Stewart) **£600 [≃ $1,080]**

Sennert, Daniel
- Practical physick: or five distinct treatises of the most predominant diseases of these times [scurvey, dropsie, feavers, agues, French pox, gout]. London: for W. Whitwood, 1676. 1st edn in English. 8vo. [xiv],151, [xii],176, 179 pp. Mod half mor. Wing S2542.
                    (Bickersteth) **£550 [≃ $990]**

Seward, A.C.
- Darwin and modern science. Essays in commemoration of the centenary of the birth of Charles Darwin ... Cambridge: Univ Press, 1909. 1st edn. 8vo. [xviii],595 pp. 5 plates (1 cold). Name stamp on endpaper, occas pencil marginalia. Orig buckram, faded.
                    (Bow Windows) **£45 [≃ $81]**
- Darwin and modern science. Essays ... Cambridge: 1909. 8vo. 595 pp. Orig cloth, faded.   *(Goodrich)* **$35 [≃ £19]**

Seymer, L.R.
- A general history of nursing. 1932. 1st edn. xi,307 pp. 37 ills. Cloth.
                    (Whitehart) **£18 [≃ $32]**
- A general history of nursing. London: 1932.

xi,307 pp. Plates. Orig cloth.
                    (Weiner) **£18 [≃ $32]**
- A general history of nursing. London: 1932. 8vo. 307 pp. Ills. Orig cloth.
                    (Goodrich) **$35 [≃ £19]**

Shackleton-Rowett
- Report made on the geological collections, made during the voyage of the 'Quest' on the Shackleton-Rowett Expedition to the South Atlantic ... in 1921-1922. 1930. Lge 8vo. xi,161 pp. Frontis, 2 plates, 26 text figs. Orig cloth, gilt.   *(Old Cinema)* **£55 [≃ $99]**

Shaffer, Newton
- Selected essays on orthopaedic surgery ... New York: 1923. 1st edn. 636 pp. Orig cloth.
                    (Fye) **$100 [≃ £55]**

Sharp, Samuel
- A treatise on the operations of surgery, with a description and representation of the instruments used in performing them ... London: J. & R. Tonson, 1751. 8vo. [8]ff, lii,236 pp. 14 engvd plates. Sl marg browning. Contemp lea bds, rebacked.
                    (Elgen) **$450 [≃ £250]**
- A treatise on the operations of surgery ... London: Tonson, 1761. 8vo. 234 pp. 12 (ex 14) plates. Final leaf torn with loss of 3 inch of text at ft. Calf, worn spine defective.
                    (Goodrich) **$65 [≃ £36]**

Sharpe, William
- Neurosurgery. Principles, diagnosis and treatment. Phila: 1928. 8vo. 762 pp. Cold frontis. Light shelf wear.
                    (Goodrich) **$45 [≃ £25]**
- Neurosurgery. Principles, diagnosis and treatment. Phila: 1928. 8vo. 762 pp. Cold frontis. Orig ptd wraps. Author's pres copy.
                    (Goodrich) **$65 [≃ £36]**

Sharpey-Schafer, Sir E.
- The endocrine organs, an introduction to the study of internal secretion. London: 1924-26. 2nd edn. 2 vols. Lge 8vo. xxii,418 pp. Ills. Orig cloth.   *(Weiner)* **£40 [≃ $72]**

Shattuck, Lemuel, et al.
- Report ... for the promotion of public and personal health, devised ... by the Commissioners ... of Massachusetts, relating to a sanitary survey of the State. Boston: 1850. 1st edn. 544 pp. 5 plates, 2 maps. Orig wraps, worn & mtd, cloth spine.
                    (Scientia) **$350 [≃ £194]**

Sheehan, J. Eastman
- Plastic surgery of the orbit. New York: 1927. Cloth.   *(Rittenhouse)* **$55 [≃ £30]**

Sheldon, H. Horton & Grisewood, Edgar Norman
- Television. Present methods of picture transmission. London: Library Press, 1930. 2nd printing. 8vo. x,194 pp. 129 ills. Pub bndg.   *(Pollak)* **£35 [≃ $63]**

Shepherd, A.
- Tables for correcting the apparent distance of the moon and a star from the effects of refraction and parallax. Cambridge: 1772. 1st edn. Lge thick 4to. [2]ff, xii pp, [556] pp. 3 other tables pasted onto last blank leaf. Cloth.   *(Elgen)* **$150 [≃ £83]**

Sherlock, S.
- Diseases of the liver and biliary system. Oxford: 1955. xv,720 pp. 188 diags & ills. Dw.   *(Whitehart)* **£25 [≃ $45]**

Sherrington, Sir Charles
- The integrative action of the nervous system. New York: 1906. 1st edn (Amer iss). 411 pp. 2 stamps on title. Cloth, lightly rubbed.   *(Scientia)* **$750 [≃ £416]**
- The integrative action of the nervous system. New Haven: 1911. 2nd printing. 8vo. 411 pp. Front endpaper renewed. Orig cloth, some spotting & wear.   *(Goodrich)* **$395 [≃ £219]**
- The integrative action of the nervous system. New Haven: Yale Univ Press, 1916. 1st edn, 4th printing. 8vo. 411 pp. Ills. Orig cloth, hd & tail of spine worn.   *(Oasis)* **$250 [≃ £138]**
- The integrative action of the nervous system. Cambridge: Univ Press, 1947. 8vo. xxiv,[ii], 433,[iii] pp. Frontis, 85 figs.   *(Pollak)* **£30 [≃ $54]**
- Mammalian physiology; a course of practical exercises. London: 1919. 1st edn. 4to. 156 pp. 9 plates, 48 figs. Cloth, cvrs bubbling.   *(Scientia)* **$150 [≃ £83]**

Sherwood, H.H.
- The motive power of the human system, with the symptoms and treatment of chronic disease. New York: J.W. Bell, 1840. 1st edn. 8vo. 120 pp. Text w'cuts. Lacking front flyleaf. Contemp lea-backed mrbld bds, a bit worn.   *(Antiq Sc)* **$100 [≃ £55]**

Sherwood, Mary M.
- An introduction to astronomy. Intended for little children. Wellington, Salop: for F. Houlston, 1818. 12mo. 54 pp. Initial blank leaf. Orig ptd blue wraps, a little worn.

(Fenning) **£21.50 [≃ $37]**

Shew, Joel
- Hydropathy; or, the water-cure ... New York: 1844. 1st edn. 8vo. xv,304 pp. Half-title, engvd frontis. Light foxing. Orig embossed cloth, chipped along jnt & crnrs.   *(Elgen)* **$65 [≃ £36]**

Shoemaker, John V.
- A practical treatise on diseases of the skin. New York: Appleton, 1892. 2nd edn, enlgd. 8vo. 878 pp. 8 chromogravure plates. Orig half mor, worn.   *(Oasis)* **$35 [≃ £19]**

Short, Thomas
- Discourses on tea, sugar, milk, made-wines ... with plain and useful rules for gouty people. London: for T. Longman ..., 1750. 1st edn. 8vo. Advt leaf as frontis, 2 pp advts at end. Contemp calf, 2 line gilt border, gilt panelled spine, mor label, gilt.   *(Traylen)* **£720 [≃ $1,296]**
- A general chronological history of the air, weather, seasons, meteors, etc ... London: for T. Longman ..., 1749. 1st edn. 2 vols. 8vo. [xxxii],494; [ii],536,[8] pp. Errata leaf. 1st & last few leaves spotted, sm chip in marg of both titles. Rec half calf.   *(Pirages)* **$450 [≃ £250]**
- The natural, experimental, and medicinal history of the mineral waters of Derbyshire, Lincolnshire, and Yorkshire. London: 1734 [and] ... Cumberland ... Westmoreland, Sheffield: 1740. 1st edns. 2 vols. 4to. 5 engvs (4 fldg). Vol 2 sl browned. Mottled calf.   *(Rootenberg)* **$475 [≃ £263]**
- The natural, experimental, and medicinal history of the mineral waters of Derbyshire, Lincolnshire, and Yorkshire. London: 1734 [and] ... Cumberland ... Westmoreland, Sheffield: 1740. 1st edns. 2 vols. 4to. 4 fldg plates. Mod mrbld bds.   *(Chaucer Head)* **£220 [≃ $396]**

Shrady, John (ed.)
- The College of Physicians and Surgeons, New York ... A history. New York: n.d. [ca 1903]. 2 vols. xii,640; vii,533 pp. 207 ports. 3/4 mor, a.e.g.   *(Elgen)* **$250 [≃ £138]**

Shrewsbury, J.F.D.
- A history of bubonic plague in the British Isles. Cambridge: 1970. xi,661 pp. 2 double-sided plates.   *(Whitehart)* **£25 [≃ $45]**

Sibly, E.
- Illustration of the occult sciences: or the art of foretelling future events and contingencies by

the ... heavenly bodies. N.d. [ca 1813-17]. 2 vols. 8vo. 1130 pp. 29 plates. Mor, shaken, crnrs bumped, spines worn.
(Edwards) **£175 [≃ $315]**

Sidgwick, N.V.
- The electronic theory of valency. Oxford: 1927. xii,3100 pp. Pencil anntns in margs. Cloth, sl worn, front inner hinge cracked. Sgnd by author.   *(Whitehart)* **£35 [≃ $63]**

Siegbahn, Manne
- The spectroscopy of X-rays. Translated ... London: OUP, 1925. 8vo. xii,287,[i] pp. 118 figs. Pub bndg.   *(Pollak)* **£30 [≃ $54]**

Siemens, C. William
- On the conservation of solar energy - a collection of papers ... London: Macmillan, 1883. 1st edn. 8vo. xx,111 pp. Text figs. Orig cloth, top of spine chipped.
(Antiq Sc) **$125 [≃ £69]**
- On the conservation of solar energy. A collection of papers and discussions. London: 1883. Orig cloth, bottom of spine sl worn. Author's pres copy. *(Whitehart)* **£50 [≃ $90]**
- The scientific works ... edited by E.F. Bamber. London: Murray, 1889. 3 vols. 8vo. 95 plates (2 fldg). Contemp polished calf, gilt, gilt panelled spines. *(Traylen)* **£125 [≃ $225]**

Sigerist, Henry E.
- American medicine. 1934. 8vo. xix,316 pp. Plates. Orig cloth.   *(Weiner)* **£30 [≃ $54]**
- The great doctors: a biographical history of medicine. New York: [1933]. 1st Amer edn. 8vo. 436 pp. Num ills, ports. Cloth.
(Elgen) **$75 [≃ £41]**
- A history of medicine. New York: 1951-61. 1st edn. 2 vols. 8vo. xxi,564; xvi,352 pp. Num ills, plates. Cloth, dws.
(Elgen) **$95 [≃ £52]**
- A history of medicine. Primitive and archaic medicine; early Greek, Hindu and Persian medicine. New York: 1951-61. 2 vols (all published). 8vo. Orig cloth, dws.
(Goodrich) **$85 [≃ £47]**
- Landmarks in the history of medicine. London: 1956. 1st edn. 8vo. viii,78 pp. 4 plates. Cloth.   *(Elgen)* **$35 [≃ £19]**

Sigmond
- A practical and domestic treatise on the diseases and irregularities of the teeth and gums; with the methods of treatment. Bath: Wood & Cunningham, 1825. 1st edn. 8vo. Untrimmed in orig bds.
(Chaucer Head) **£180 [≃ $324]**

Silliman, Benjamin, Jr. (1816-1885).
- First principles of chemistry. Phila: Loomis & Peck, 1847. 1st edn. Sm 8vo. 492 pp. Num w'cuts in text. Contemp sheep, hd of spine very chipped, jnts cracked.
(Antiq Sc) **$85 [≃ £47]**

Simmons, James Stevens, et al.
- Global epidemiology. A geography of disease and sanitation. Volume I: India and the Far East; the Pacific Area. London: Heinemann, 1944. 8vo. xxvi,504,[ii] pp. Sev maps. Pub bndg. Frayed dw.   *(Pollak)* **£25 [≃ $45]**

Simmons, Samuel
- Elements of anatomy and the animal economy. From the French of M. Person ... London: Wilie, 1775. 1st edn. 8vo. xii,396 pp. Errata leaf. 3 engvd plates. Light penciling. Old qtr calf, worn.
(Goodrich) **$75 [≃ £41]**

Simms, F.W.
- Practical tunnelling ... setting out of the works, shaft sinking ... levelling ... construction of brickwork ... particulars of Blechingley and Saltwood tunnels. 1860. 2nd edn, revsd. 4to. Frontis, lge fldg plates. Some foxing. Cloth.   *(Halewood)* **£58 [≃ $104]**
- A treatise on the principal mathematical instruments employed in surveying, levelling and astronomy ... Baltimore: [1836]. 1st Amer edn. 8vo. 109,[15] pp. W'cuts. Some foxing. Cloth. Ex lib.   *(Elgen)* **$90 [≃ £50]**

Simms, William
- The achromatic telescope and its various mountings, especially the equatorial. 1852. [iv],74,16 pp. 56 diags. Orig blindstamped cloth, worn, spine defective at hd & ft, inner hinge cracked.   *(Whitehart)* **£40 [≃ $72]**
- The achromatic telescope and its various mountings, especially the equatorial ... some hints on private observatories. London: 1852. 8vo. 74 pp. Ills, 16 pp ctlg of instruments. Orig cloth.   *(Weiner)* **£65 [≃ $117]**

Simon, John
- English sanitary institutions, reviewed in their course of development, and in some of their political and social relations. London: 1897. 2nd edn. 516 pp. Cloth, inner hinges cracked.   *(Scientia)* **$175 [≃ £97]**
- Public health reports. Edited for the Sanitary Institute of Great Britain by Edward Seaton. London: 1887. 2 vols. xix,554,[ii]; xiii,618 pp. 2 frontis. Orig cloth.
(Pollak) **£250 [≃ $450]**

Simpson, James Y.

- Anaesthesia or the employment of chloroform and ether in surgery, midwifery. Phila: 1849. 1st edn. 248 pp. Top & bottom of spine reprd.
(Scientia) **$750 [≈ £416]**

Simpson, Sir James Young

- Acupressure a new method of arresting surgical haemorrhage and of accelerating the healing of wounds. Edinburgh: Black, 1864. 1st edn. 8vo. [5],xiv,580 pp. Half-title, over 40 text w'cuts. Orig cloth. Uncut.
(Rootenberg) **$350 [≈ £194]**

- Notes on some ancient Greek medical vases for containing lykion; and on the modern use of the same drug in India. Edinburgh: 1856. 1st edn. 8vo. 12 pp. Plate. Wraps.
(Fenning) **£16.50 [≈ $28]**

Simpson, T.

- Trigonometry, plane and spherical; with the construction and application o of logarithms. Phila: 1810. 125 pp. 7 fldg plates. Some browning throughout. Contemp calf, rebacked. *(Whitehart)* **£35 [≈ $63]**

Simpson, Thomas

- The doctrine and application of fluxions ... to which s prefixed an account of his life, the whole revised ... by William Davis. [1805]. xxiv,442 pp. Text diags. pp xv-xviii defective with sl loss of text. Reversed calf, lea label, spine sl worn. *(Whitehart)* **£55 [≈ $99]**

- The doctrine and application of fluxions ... And the solution of a variety of new ... problems in different branches of the mathematicks. London: for J. Nourse, 1750. 8vo. 2 pts in 1 vol. xi,274; [iv],275-576 pp. Contemp calf, reprd, new back, crnrs worn.
(Pollak) **£100 [≈ $180]**

- Select exercises for young proficients in the mathematics ... new edition ... An account of the life and writings of the author, by Charles Hutton. For F. Wingrave, 1792. 8vo. [4],iv,xxiii, [1 list of books], 252 pp. Ink splashes on 4pp. Contemp calf.
(Fenning) **£45 [≈ $81]**

Sims, J. Marion

- Clinical notes on uterine surgery. With special reference to the management of the sterile condition. New York: 1866. 1st Amer edn. 8vo. xi,401 pp. 142 w'cuts. Rec rebound in cloth on orig bds. *(Elgen)* **$350 [≈ £194]**

- Clinical notes on uterine surgery. With special reference to the management of the sterile condition. New York: 1866. 1st Amer edn. 401 pp. Sgntr & stamp on title. Orig cloth, recased. *(Scientia)* **$325 [≈ £180]**

Simson, Robert

- Elements of the conic sections. The first three books translated from the Latin original. Edinburgh: Elliott, 1775. 1st edn. [vi],255 pp. 24 fldg plates. Lacking both free endpapers. Orig qtr calf, a little wear to ft of spine, crnr bent, uncut.
(Hinchliffe) **£70 [≈ $126]**

- Elements of the conic sections ... translated from the Latin original, for the use of students of mathematics. New York: W. Falconer, 1804. 278 pp. 14 fldg plates. Contemp tree calf, top of spine a bit chipped, front hinge starting. *(Karmiole)* **$150 [≈ £83]**

Sinclair, George

- The hydrostaticks; or, the weight, force, and pressure of fluid bodies ... Edinburgh: 1672. 1st edn. 4to. x,319,[1 blank] pp plus engvd title. Fldg engvd coat of arms, 7 fldg engvd plates. Contemp sgntr on title. Contemp calf, jnts cracking. Wing S3854.
(Pickering) **$2,000 [≈ £1,111]**

Sinclair, Sir John

- The code of agriculture; including observations on gardens, orchards, woods, and plantations. London: for Sherwood, Neely ..., 1817. 1st edn. 8vo. 4 pp advts. Port frontis, 10 engvd plates, tables & charts in the text. Orig bds, new paper spine, uncut edges.
(Traylen) **£350 [≈ $630]**

- General view of the agriculture of the Northern Counties and Islands of Scotland ... London: 1795. 4to. Half-title, 2 fldg cold maps, fldg engvd plate, appendix. Bds, calf spine. *(Traylen)* **£55 [≈ $99]**

Sinclair, M.

- The Thomas splint and its modifications in the treatment of fractures. 1927. xiv,168 pp. Num ills, 3 charts. Cloth, ex lib with stamps.
(Whitehart) **£18 [≈ $32]**

Singer, Charles

- The evolution of anatomy. A short history of anatomical and physiological discovery to Harvey ... London: 1925. 8vo. xii,209 pp. Extra engvd title, 22 plates. Orig cloth.
(Weiner) **£40 [≈ $72]**

- The evolution of anatomy. A short history of anatomical and physiological discovery to Harvey ... London: 1925. 8vo. 209 pp. Orig cloth. *(Goodrich)* **$115 [≈ £63]**

- From magic to science: essays on the scientific twilight. 1928. xix,253 pp. 14 cold plates, 108 b/w plates & ills. Orig cloth, spine faded. *(Whitehart)* **£38 [≈ $68]**

- From magic to science: essays on the

scientific twilight. New York: 1928. Lge 8vo. 14 mtd cold plates, 108 other ills. Orig cloth. *(Argosy)* **$50 [≈ £27]**

- A history of technology. Oxford: 1957-59. 5 vols. Later reprinting. Orig blue cloth. *(Goodrich)* **$250 [≈ £138]**

- A history of technology. Oxford: Clarendon Press, 1958-57. 5 vols. 4to. Orig cloth, dws. *(Chaucer Head)* **£180 [≈ $324]**

- Science, medicine and history. Essays on the evolution of scientific thought and practice written in honour of Charles Singer ... Oxford: 1953. 2 vols. Roy 8vo. Orig cloth. *(Goodrich)* **$225 [≈ £125]**

- A short history of medicine ... Oxford: Clarendon Press, 1928. 8vo. xxiv,368 pp. 147 ills. Orig cloth. *(Pollak)* **£20 [≈ $36]**

- A short history of medicine. Oxford: 1928. 8vo. xxiv,368 pp. Ills. Orig cloth. *(Weiner)* **£30 [≈ $54]**

- A short history of science in the nineteenth century. Oxford: 1941. 8vo. 399 pp. Orig cloth, dw. *(Goodrich)* **$30 [≈ £16]**

- The story of living things. A short account of the evolution of the biological sciences. New York: 1931. 8vo. 572 pp. Orig cloth, dw. *(Goodrich)* **$35 [≈ £19]**

Singer, Charles & Rabin, C.

- A prelude to modern science. Being a discussion of the history, sources and circumstances of the Tabulae Anatomicae Sex of Vesalius. London: 1946. 8vo. Ills. Orig cloth. *(Goodrich)* **$195 [≈ £108]**

- A prelude to modern science ... the Tabulae Anatomicae Sex of Vesalius. Cambridge: 1946. 1st edn. 4to. lxxxvi,58 pp. 6 plates. *(Scientia)* **$195 [≈ £108]**

Singer, George John

- Elements of electricity and electro-chemistry. London: 1814. 1st edn. 8vo. 4 engvd plates, errata leaf. Contemp half calf, mrbld bds, rebacked, orig spine laid down. *(Traylen)* **£90 [≈ $162]**

Sisley, R.

- Epidemic influenza: notes on its origin and method of spread. 1891. xi,150 pp. 17 diags. Cloth, worn, Author's inscrptn. *(Whitehart)* **£25 [≈ $45]**

Skelton, Dr.

- Dr. Skelton's botanic record and family journal. Leeds: 1855. 8vo. 640 pp. Plates. Qtr roan. *(Goodrich)* **$125 [≈ £69]**

Skene, Alexander J.C.

- A treatise on the diseases of women. New York: 1889. 8vo. xiv,966 pp. Orig cloth, worn, rear hinge loosened, cloth separated at spine. *(Rittenhouse)* **$35 [≈ £19]**

Slack, David B.

- An essay on the human colour. In three parts. Providence: J.F. Moore, printer, 1845. 1st complete edn. Lge 12mo. vi,[2 blank],[5]-100 pp. (Complete thus?). A few light fingermarks. Orig cloth-backed paper bds. *(Fenning)* **£145 [≈ $261]**

Slater, J.W.

- Handbook of chemical analysis for practical men ... London: 1861. xvi,384 pp. 17 text diags. Sgntr on title & endpaper. 3/4 roan, mrbld bds, rubbed. *(Whitehart)* **£35 [≈ $63]**

Smeaton, John

- A narrative of the building and a narrative of the construction of the Eddystone Lighthouse ... London: T. Davidson, 1813. 2nd edn. Folio. Lge engvd vignette on title (with sm lib stamp), 23 engvd plates. Contemp cloth, rebacked, gilt. *(Traylen)* **£330 [≈ $594]**

Smedley, Edward, et al.

- Encyclopaedia metropolitana; or, universal dictionary of knowledge. London: 1845. 29 vols. 4to. 65 maps. 532 engvd plates. Contemp polished calf, gilt, gilt panelled spines, some jnts a little worn. *(Traylen)* **£1,100 [≈ $1,980]**

Smee, Alfred

- Elements of electro-metallurgy. London: 1843. 2nd edn. 8vo. xxx,338 pp. Electrotype title & frontis, ills. Contemp half calf, worn. Author's pres inscrptn. *(Weiner)* **£50 [≈ $90]**

Smellie, William

- The philosophy of natural history. Edinburgh: 1790. 4to. Contemp speckled calf, sl rubbing on jnts & wear on lower crnrs. *(Waterfield's)* **£80 [≈ $144]**

- The philosophy of natural history. Edinburgh: 1790. 1st edn. 4to. Contemp half calf, gilt, mrbld bds. *(Traylen)* **£85 [≈ $153]**

- The philosophy of natural history. Edinburgh: 1790-99. 2 vols. 4to. Vol 1 calf, vol 2 orig bds, spine sl defective. *(Wheldon & Wesley)* **£195 [≈ $351]**

- The philosophy of natural history. Edinburgh: 1790-99. 1st edn. 2 vols (inc the 2nd vol, published posthumously). 4to. xiii,547, errata leaf; xii,515 pp. Old tree calf, worn. A non-matching set, vol I with larger

margins.   *(Weiner)* **£175** [≈ **$315**]
- The philosophy of natural history. Dublin: for Chamberlaine & Rice ..., 1790. Piracy but 2nd edn. 2 vols. 8vo. Some light dust-soiling, 1 leaf in vol 2 reprd, final leaf of index torn with sl loss. Contemp half calf, sl rubbed & worn, mrbld bds.   *(Stewart)* **£250** [≈ **$450**]
- A set of anatomical tables ... and an abridgement, of the practice of midwifery. London: [for subscribers], 1754. 1st edn. Lge folio. 39 engvd plates. Light spotting, mainly marg. Ownership inscrptn & ptd stamp on title. Orig mrbld bds, rebacked.
                 (Quaritch) **$3,750** [≈ **£2,083**]
- A set of anatomical tables, with explanations, and an abridgement, of the practice of midwifery. London: 1754. Atlas folio. 39 copperplates. Some marg dustiness & fingerprints. Orig panelled calf, crnrs & headpiece worn.
                 (Goodrich) **$4,250** [≈ **£2,361**]
- A set of anatomical tables, with explanations, and an abridgement of the practice of midwifery. Worcester, Mass: I. Thomas, 1793. 2nd Amer edn. 8vo. 84 pp. 40 engvd plates. Spotty foxing, light browning. Mod half calf.   *(Antiq Sc)* **$500** [≈ **£277**]
- A treatise on the theory and practice of midwifery. London: 1762. 4th edn [with] A collection of cases and observations ... London: 1764. 3rd edn [with] A collection of preternatural cases ... London: 1764. 1st edn. 3 vols. 1st complete edn. Some browning. Contemp calf.   *(Oasis)* **$450** [≈ **£250**]
- A treatise on the theory and practice of midwifery. London: for D. Wilson, 1752. 1st edn. 8vo. Title dust-soiled & rubbed (without loss), some spotting & soiling. Contemp calf, rebacked & recrnrd.
                 (Quaritch) **$1,600** [≈ **£888**]

Smethurst, G.
- Tables of time: whereby the day and the month ... Manchester: 1749. Sm 8vo. viii,132,48 pp. Embossed stamp on title & a few other pp. Later lib cloth, sl dust-stained.
                 (Whitehart) **£40** [≈ **$72**]

Smiles, Samuel
- Industrial biography: iron workers and tool makers. London: Murray, 1863. 15th thousand. 8vo. xiv,342,4 advts pp. A little foxing. Orig cloth, recased.
                 (Pollak) **£30** [≈ **$54**]
- Lives of the engineers, with an account of their particular works. London: 1857-65. 4 vols. 8vo. 8 ports, 268 ills. Uniform half polished calf, fully gilt spines, mor labels, gilt, mrbld edges.   *(Traylen)* **£150** [≈ **$270**]

- Robert Dick: Baker, of Thurso, geologist and botanist. London: 1878. 1st edn. 8vo. x,[ii],436,[6 advts] pp. Errata slip. Etched port, 15 plates & other ills. Foxing & some marks, some crnrs folded. Rec qtr calf, new endpapers.   *(Bow Windows)* **£40** [≈ **$72**]

Smilie, E.R.
- An address delivered before the class of the Castleton Medical College, on the history of the original application of anaesthetic agents, May 17, 1848. Boston: 1848. 1st edn. 23 pp. Orig ptd wraps.   *(Scientia)* **$275** [≈ **£152**]

Smith, A. Hopewell
- Dental microscopy. London: Dental Manufacturing Co., 1899. 2nd edn, revsd & enlgd. 8vo. xxxiii,[i],206,[ii] pp. Cold frontis, 8 plates, 67 text figs. Sm tear on 1 leaf. Orig cloth, spine ends a bit worn.
                 (Pollak) **£25** [≈ **$45**]
- The histology and patho-histology of the teeth and associated parts. 1903. 1st edn. xxix,633 pp. 2 cold plates, 493 text ills.
                 (Whitehart) **£15** [≈ **$27**]

Smith, David Eugene
- History of Japanese mathematics. Chicago: Open Court, 1914. 288 pp. Ills. Cloth. Ex lib.
                 (Xerxes) **$80** [≈ **£44**]
- History of mathematics. Boston: 1923-25. 2 vols. xxii,596; xii,725 pp. Num ills.
                 (Whitehart) **£25** [≈ **$45**]
- Rara arithmetica. A catalogue of the works written before the year MDCI ... Boston: Gin & Co., 1908. 1st edn. Tall 8vo. xiii,508 pp. 9 photo plates. Blue cloth, a bit discold.
                 (Karmiole) **$75** [≈ **£41**]

Smith, E.
- Clinical studies of disease in children. Disease of the lungs. Acute tubercolosis. 1876. xv,303 pp. Light scattered foxing. B'plate. Cloth dust-stained.   *(Whitehart)* **£18** [≈ **$32**]

Smith, E. Noble
- The surgery of deformities. London: Smith, Elder, 1882. 1st edn. 8vo. 280 pp. Text ills. Orig cloth.   *(Oasis)* **$50** [≈ **£27**]

Smith, Edgar
- Old chemistries. New York: McGraw-Hill, 1927. 1st edn. 4to. 89 pp. Ills. Orig cloth.
                 (Xerxes) **$100** [≈ **£55**]

Smith, Emily A.
- The life and letters of Nathan Smith. New Haven: 1914. 1st edn. One of 1000. 8vo. xiv,185 pp. 23 plates. Half calf, paper-cvrd

bds, spine ends sl chipped, t.e.g.
(Elgen) **$50 [≈ £27]**

Smith, Eustace
- A practical treatise on disease in children. London: 1884. 1st edn. 8vo. xxiv,844 pp. Cloth, spine ends sl torn. *(Elgen)* **$55 [≈ £30]**

Smith, Henry H.
- Anatomical atlas illustrative of the structure of the human body. Phila: Lea & Blanchard, 1847. 1st edn. Tall 8vo. 200 pp. Frontis, vignette title, 634 engvd figs. Old sheep, worn. *(Oasis)* **$100 [≈ £55]**

Smith, Henry John Stephen
- The collected mathematical papers ... Edited by J.W.L. Glaisher. Oxford: 1894. Lge 4to. 2 vols. xcv,603; vii,719 pp. Orig cloth. Ex lib with perf stamps on title, lib marks on spine. *(Whitehart)* **£80 [≈ $144]**

Smith, Hugh
- Formulae medicamentorum concinnatae: or, elegant medical prescriptions for various disorders. Translated ... To which is prefixed a sketch of his life. London: J.S. Barr, 1791. 12mo. viii,131 pp. Disbound.
(Burmester) **£45 [≈ $81]**
- Letters to married women. London: G.K. Kearsley, 1767. 1st edn. 1st edn. Sm 8vo. viii,246 pp. Browning at extreme margs of title. Mod bds. *(Hemlock)* **$950 [≈ £527]**
- Letters to married ladies. To which is added a letter on corsets, and copious notes by an American physician. New York: 1827. 8vo. xix,283 pp. Browning. Half calf, rubbed, mrbld bds. *(Elgen)* **$150 [≈ £83]**

Smith, J. Greig
- Abdominal surgery. London: Churchill, 1887. xii,608,14, [ii advts] pp. 45 figs. Occas foxing. Orig cloth, front hinge a bit weak, sl wear to hd of spine. Author's inscrptn on title. *(Pollak)* **£30 [≈ $54]**

Smith, J. Lewis
- A treatise on the diseases of infancy and childhood. Phila: 1872. 2nd edn. 8vo. xvi,741 pp. Pub ctlg. Orig lea, some scuffing. *(Rittenhouse)* **$35 [≈ £19]**
- A treatise on the diseases of infancy and childhood. Phila: 1886. 6th edn. 8vo. 870 pp. Lea. *(Fye)* **$50 [≈ £27]**

Smith, James
- The panorama of science and art ... in two volumes ... Thirteenth edition. Caxton Press, n.d. [ca 1837]. Engvd frontis, 49 plates (5

fldg). Some dampstaining. Contemp half calf, sl worn. *(Sanders)* **£40 [≈ $72]**

Smith, James E.
- An introduction to physiological and systematical botany. Phila: Finlay, 1814. 1st Amer edn. 415 pp. Pict title, 15 engvd plates. Foxing. Rec qtr calf. *(Goodrich)* **$125 [≈ £69]**

Smith, James, of Jordanhill
- Researches in New Pilocene and Post-tertiary geology. Glasgow: 1862. 1st edn. 8vo. xi,191 pp. Text figs. 4 tinted litho plates. Cancelled blind lib stamp on title. Orig cloth, rebacked.
(Bickersteth) **£35 [≈ $63]**

Smith, John (1630-1679)
- The pourtract of old age ... a sacred anatomy both of soul and body. And a perfect account of the infirmities of age ... London: for Walter Kettilby, 1676. 2nd edn, crrctd. 8vo. Fldg table, imprimatur, title-page in duplicate. Contemp calf. Wing S4116.
(Traylen) **£295 [≈ $531]**

Smith, John Pye.
- The relation between the Holy Scriptures and some part of geological science. London: Jackson & Walford, 1840. 2nd edn. 8vo. xv,525,[ii advts] pp. Orig cloth, faded, spine worn at hd. *(Gough)* **£35 [≈ $63]**
- The relation between the Holy Scriptures and some part of geological science. London: 1852. 5th edn. Sm 8vo. lxviii,468 pp. Polished calf, gilt, by Westerton's.
(Bow Windows) **£65 [≈ $117]**

Smith, Lawrence W. & Gault, Edwin S.
- Essentials of pathology. New York: [1938]. 1st edn. 4to. xxi,886 pp. 160 plates. Cloth. *(Elgen)* **$75 [≈ £41]**

Smith, Maurice
- A short history of dentistry. London: Allan Wingate, 1958. 8vo. 120 pp. 12 ills. Pub bndg, dw. *(Pollak)* **£20 [≈ $36]**

Smith, Nathan
- Surgical anatomy of the arteries. Balt: 1830. 1st edn. 4to. 104,iv pp. 18 hand-cold plates. Foxed. Mod qtr lea, mrbld bds, new endpapers. *(Scientia)* **$650 [≈ £361]**
- Medical and surgical memoirs ... Edited, with addenda ... Baltimore: W.A. Francis, 1831. 1st edn. 8vo. 374,[1 errata] pp. Engvd frontis, 44 lithos, 2 w'cut plates. Contemp tree calf. *(Antiq Sc)* **$175 [≈ £97]**

Smith, Robert
- The universal directory for taking alive and detroying rats, and all other kinds of four-footed and winged vermin ... London: for J. Walker, 1812. 4th edn. Cr 8vo. 6 engvd plates (4 fldg). Mod wraps, uncut edges.
(Traylen) £55 [≃ $99]

Smith, Sir S. & Fiddes, F.S.
- Forensic medicine. A textbook for students and practitioners. 1955. Demy 8vo. 173 ills. Cloth, dw.   *(Halewood)* £20 [≃ $36]

Smith, Samuel Stanhope
- An essay on the causes of the variety of complexion and figure in the human species. New Brunswick: 1810. 2nd enlgd edn. 8vo. 411 pp. Contemp mottled calf, hinges mended. Ex lib.   *(Argosy)* $125 [≃ £69]

Smith, T. & Walsham, W.J.
- A manual of operative surgery on the dead body. London: 1876. 2nd edn. 8vo. xiv,255,[43 advts] pp. 46 ills in text. 1 or 2 leaves finger-marked, editors' inscription on title. Orig cloth, cvrs mottled.
(Bow Windows) £40 [≃ $72]

Smith, Thomas
- Evolution: or, the power and operation of numbers ... London: Longman, Rees ..., 1835. 8vo. iv,158,[2 advts] pp. Text figs. Orig blue cloth over ptd bds, extremities rubbed, bds somewhat soiled. *(Karmiole)* $50 [≃ £27]

Smith, Willoughby
- The rise and extension of submarine telegraphy. Lge 8vo. xii,390 pp. Plates (some cold), ills, diags. Qtr mor.
(Weiner) £50 [≃ $90]

Smoke ...
- May young England smoke? A modern question. Medically and socially considered. London: S.W. Partridge, n.d. [ca 1880]. 32 pp. Ptd wraps.   *(C.R. Johnson)* £25 [≃ $45]

Smyth, Charles Piazzi
- Madeira meteorologic. Being a paper on the above subject read before the Royal Society, Edinburgh, 1st May, 1882. Edinburgh: 1882. viii,83 pp. Frontis, plates, 3 ills. Cloth, v sl stained.   *(Whitehart)* £25 [≃ $45]
- Teneriffe, an astronomer's experiment. London: Lovell Reeve, 1858. 1st edn. 8vo. xvi,451 pp. Advts. Map, 20 mtd stereo photos. Orig dec cloth, gilt, rebacked.
(Morrell) £195 [≃ $351]

Smyth, J.C.
- A description of the jail distemper ... amongst the Spanish prisoners at Winchester ... And: An account of the experiment made ... to determine the effect of nitric acid in destroying contagion. 1803. 2 pts in 1 vol. Pt 2 2nd edn. 8vo. Lea cloth.
(Halewood) £95 [≃ $171]

Smyth, R.B.
- Geological survey of Victoria. Report of progress ... with reports on the geology, mineralogy ... of various parts of the Colony ... London: n.d. [ca 1875]. Lge 8vo. vi,141 pp. 6 fldg plates. Some finger & dust marks. Orig paper wraps frayed & detchd.
(Bow Windows) £40 [≃ $72]

Snape, Andrew
- The anatomy of a horse. London: for the authour, 1683, 1st edn. Folio. [xii],237,45 appendix, [iv table] pp. Engvd port, 48 (ex 49) engvd plates (missing plate 1 supplied in facs). Plate 13 restored, without loss. Wide-margined copy in early 20th c half calf.
(Gough) £325 [≃ $585]

Snow, John
- On chloroform and other anesthetics: their action and administration. [1950] Facs edn. One of 1000. Simulated mor, gilt.
(Oasis) $75 [≃ £41]
- On the inhalation of the vapour of ether in surgical operations. London: J. Churchill, 1847. Sole edn. Tall 8vo. viii,88. Sm tear in 1 leaf. Orig gilt-stamped green cloth, 2 sm splits in upper jnt.
(Hemlock) $2,500 [≃ £6,944]

Social Evil ...
- The social evil [prostitution] with special reference to conditions existing in the City of New York. New York: Putnam's, 1902. 8vo. Orig cloth, gilt, t.e.g.
(Cooper Hay) £30 [≃ $54]

Solis-Cohen, Myer
- Woman: in girlhood, wifehood, motherhood. her responsibilities. And her duties at all periods of life. Phila: 1906. 8vo. xxii,469 pp. man ills.   *(Rittenhouse)* $27.50 [≃ £15]

Solly, Samuel
- Surgical experiences: the substance of clinical lectures. London: Hardwicke, 1865. 8vo. 656 pp. New cloth. Author's pres copy.
(Goodrich) $125 [≃ £69]

Somerville, Alexander
- The whistler at the plough: containing travels, statistics and descriptions of scenery and agricultural customs in most parts of England ... Manchester: James Ainsworth, 1852. 1st edn. 8vo. Port, engvd title. Orig cloth, rebacked, orig spine laid down.
(Traylen) £175 [≃ $315]

Somerville, M.
- On molecular and microscopic science. 1869. 1st edn. 2 vols. xi,432; viii,320 pp. 2 frontis, 180 figs, many on plates. Light scattered foxing, light waterstaining in crnrs of some plates. Orig cloth, new endpapers.
(Whitehart) £48 [≃ $86]

Somerville, Martha
- Personal recollections, from early life to old age, of Mary Somerville. London: Murray, 1873. 8vo. vi,377,[i] pp. Port frontis. Half mor over mrbld bds. *(Pollak)* £30 [≃ $54]

Sommerfeld, Arnold
- Atomic spectra and spectral lines. 1923. 1st edn in English. xiii,625 pp. 124 text diags. Contemp ink sgntr on endpaper. Orig cloth.
(Whitehart) £25 [≃ $45]
- Three lectures of atomic physics, translated ... London: 1926. 8vo. 70 pp. Diags. Few pencil markings. Orig cloth, dw.
(Weiner) £30 [≃ $54]
- Wave-mechanics. 1930. 1st edn in English. xii,304 pp. 33 text diags. Sm contemp ink sgntr on endpaper. Orig cloth.
(Whitehart) £35 [≃ $63]
- Wave-mechanics. London: 1930. 8vo. xii,304 pp. Diags. Orig cloth. *(Weiner)* £35 [≃ $63]

Sonntag, C.F.
- The morphology and evolution of the apes and man. 1924. xi,364 pp. 57 ills. Cloth, dull, ex lib with stamps. *(Whitehart)* £18 [≃ $32]

Sopwith, Thomas
- Treatise on isometrical drawings as applicable to geological and mining plans ... London: 1838. 2nd edn. 8vo. 224 pp. Engvd frontis, extra engvd title, 33 plates. Ex lib, rebacked. *(Weiner)* £60 [≃ $108]

Sorsby, A.
- A short history of opthalmology. London: 1933. Sm 8vo. vii,103 pp. 2 plates, diags. Orig cloth-backed bds. *(Weiner)* £30 [≃ $54]

South, J.F.
- Household surgery; or, hints on emergencies. 1847. xvi,340 pp. Frontis, sev ills. Orig blindstamped & gilt cloth, rebacked, orig spine laid down, sl worn.
(Whitehart) £35 [≃ $63]

South, James
- Observations on the apparent distances and positions of 458 double and triple stars ... 1823, 1824 and 1825 ... London: Nicol, 1825. 4to. 391 pp. Rebound with new endpapers.
(Xerxes) $200 [≃ £111]

Spalding, James Alfred
- Dr. Lyman Spalding, the originator of the United States Pharmacopoeia ... Boston: 1916. 1st edn. 8vo. viii,380 pp. Port frontis, facs. Sm lib stamp. Uncut & unopened. Cloth, t.e.g. *(Elgen)* $40 [≃ £22]

Spalding, Lyman
- An inaugural dissertation on the production of animal heat. Walpole, NH: D. Carlisle, 1797. 1st edn. 8vo. 30 pp. Uncut, stitched as issued. *(Antiq Sc)* $185 [≃ £102]

Spallanzani, Lazzaro
- Tracts on the nature of animals and vegetables. Edinburgh: 1799. 1st edn. 394 pp. 6 plates. Title re-cornered. Mod qtr lea, mrbld bds, new endpapers.
(Scientia) $250 [≃ £138]

Speculations ...
- Speculations on the mode and appearances of impregnation ... See Couper, Robert

Spence, J.
- Lectures on surgery. Edinburgh: 1882. 3rd edn. xxvii,510; xxiv,513-1226 pp. 39 plates, 245 ills. A few pencil & ink underlinings & anntns, sl foxing. Cloth, sl worn at edges & dust-stained. *(Whitehart)* £40 [≃ $72]

Spencer, Herbert
- The principles of psychology. London: 1855. 1st edn. 620 pp. Orig cloth, rebacked, orig spine laid down, spine lettering dull.
(Scientia) $250 [≃ £138]
- The principles of psychology. London: 1899. 4th edn. 2 vols. 8vo. xiv,640; viii,762 pp. Sgntr of C.P. Blacker on endpapers & num marginal notes throughout. Some sl foxing. Orig cloth, a little rubbed, some crnrs bumped. *(Bow Windows)* £44 [≃ $79]

Spitta, Edmund J.
- Microscopy. The construction, theory and use of the microscope. London: Murray, 1920. 3rd edn. 8vo. xxviii,534 pp. Frontis, 28 plates, 25 text figs. Pub bndg.
(Pollak) £30 [≃ $54]

- Microscopy. The construction, theory and use of the microscope. London: 1920. 3rd edn. xxviii,537 pp. Plates, ills.
(Whitehart) £35 [≈ $63]

Spooner, W.C.A.
- A treatise on the structure, functions, and diseases of the foot and leg of the horse. London: Longman, 1840. 1st edn. F'cap 8vo. Subscribers' leaf, 16 pp pub list. 1 or 2 minor faults. Uncut. Orig cloth, spine sl faded.
(Taylor) £35 [≈ $63]

Sprat, Thomas
- The history of the Royal Society of London. London: Scott, 1702. 2nd edn. 4to. [7],438 pp. Plate. Old calf, rebacked.
(Goodrich) $150 [≈ £83]

Spratt, G.
- The medico-botanical pocket-book. Comprising a compendium of vegetable toxicology. London: for the author, n.d. [ca 1850]. 1st edn. Sm 8vo. x,118 pp. Hand-cold title vignette, 15 hand-cold plates, 6 hand-cold text figs. Orig cloth, recased & rebacked.
(Gough) £185 [≈ $333]

Spratt, George
- Flora medica ... delineations of the various medicinal plants admitted into the London .... and Dublin pharmacopoeias. [L: 1829-30]. 2 vols. 8vo. Marg cut into title & 1st few leaves, without loss. 184 hand-cold plates. Contemp half calf, sl rubbed.
(Traylen) £420 [≈ $756]
- Obstetric tables; comprising graphic illustrations, with descriptions and practical remarks. Phila: 1848. 1st Amer edn. 21 plates, mostly cold. Lightly foxed. Cloth, crnrs worn, sm section missing at top of spine.
(Scientia) $375 [≈ £208]

Sprengel, Kurt
- An introduction to the study of cryptogamous plants. London: J. White, 1807. 1st edn in English. 8vo. viii,411 pp. 10 fldg engvd plates. Contemp 3/4 lea, mrbld bds, front jnt cracked, lacking label, a bit rubbed.
(Antiq Sc) $100 [≈ £55]

Sprengell, Conrad Joachim
- The Aphorisms of Hippocrates, and the Sentences of Celsus ... Aphorisms upon the smallpox, measles ... London: for R. Bonwick ..., 1708. 1st edn of this trans. 8vo. 2 engvd ports. Red & black title. Contemp panelled calf, Constable b'plate.
(Quaritch) $525 [≈ £291]

Spurgin, John
- The physician for all; his philosophy, his experience, and his mission. London: 1855. 8vo. 226 pp. Orig cloth. Author's pres copy.
(Goodrich) $55 [≈ £30]

Spurr, J.A.
- Features of the moon. Geology applied to selenology. The Imbrian Plain region of the moon. [Lancaster, Pa:] 1945. 2nd printing. x,318 pp. 4 plates, 23 text figs. Cloth, sl marked & faded. *(Whitehart)* £25 [≈ $45]

Spurzheim, Johann Caspar
- Observations on the deranged manifestations of the mind, or insanity. Boston: 1833. 1st Amer edn. 8vo. viii,260 pp. 4 plates, errata slip. Some foxing, back endpapers a little wormed. Orig pub cloth, ends of spine sl worn, label missing.
(Bow Windows) £125 [≈ $225]
- The physiognomical system of Drs. Gall and Spurzheim; founded on an anatomical and physiological examination of the nervous system in general ... London: Baldwin, 1815. 2nd edn. 8vo. xvii,581 pp. Engvd frontis, 18 engvd plates. Qtr calf, jnts weak.
(Goodrich) $125 [≈ £69]
- A view of the elementary principles of education founded on the study of the nature of man. Edinburgh: for Archd. Constable. 1821. 1st edn. 12mo. Contemp tree calf, gilt brdrs & spine. *(Quaritch)* $550 [≈ £305]

Stanley, John Thomas
- An account of the hot springs in Iceland; with an analysis of their waters. [Edinburgh?:] n.d. [ca 1793]. 8vo. Title (loose), 100 pp. Last page soiled, title a little so, marg stains at beginning & end, short tear in last leaf. Sewn (as issued?). *(Weiner)* £300 [≈ $540]

Starling, Ernest
- Mercers' Company lectures on recent advances in the physiology of digestion. Chicago: 1906. 1st edn. 156 pp. Cloth.
(Scientia) $100 [≈ £55]

Starr, Arnold
- Organic and functional nervous diseases. New York: 1907. 2nd edn. 8vo. 818 pp. 282 engvs, 26 cold plates. Orig cloth.
(Goodrich) $35 [≈ £19]

Starr, L. (ed.)
- An American text-book of the diseases of children. 1898. 2nd edn, revsd. xvi,604 pp. 13 plates, num diags, text ills. Inscrptn on front endpaper. Cloth, sl worn, spine faded.
(Whitehart) £25 [≈ $45]

Starr, Louis
- Diseases of the digestive organs in infancy and childhood, with chapters on the investigation of disease, and of the general management of children. Phila: 1886. 1st edn. 385 pp. Orig cloth. *(Fye)* **$100 [≈ £55]**

Starr, M. Allen
- Familiar forms of nervous disease. New York: 1890. 1st edn. 339 pp. Orig cloth.
(Fye) **$75 [≈ £41]**

Steel, J.H.
- A treatise on the diseases of the ox. Being a manual of bovine pathology. 1881. xxii,498 pp. 2 plates, 117 ills. Foxing at beginning & end. Orig cloth. *(Whitehart)* **£25 [≈ $45]**

Steel, John H.
- An analysis of the Congress Spring, with practical remarks on its medical properties. New York: William W. Rose, 1856. Later edn, revsd & crrctd. 35 pp. Engvd frontis. Sm portion cut from last leaf. Orig gilt & blindstamped cloth. *(Argonaut)* **$45 [≈ £25]**
- An analysis of the mineral waters of Saratoga and Baliston ... observations on the geology and mineralogy of the surrounding country. Saratoga Springs: G.M. Davison, 1838. Sm 8vo. 203,[1 blank], 205-208 [appendix] pp. Tipped in final advt. Contemp cloth.
(Antiq Sc) **$85 [≈ £47]**

Steinmetz, Charles Proteus
- Elementary lectures on discharges, waves and impulses, and other transients. New York: [1911]. 8vo. 149 pp. Ills. Cloth, sl worn. Ex lib. *(Elgen)* **$25 [≈ £13]**
- Theory and calculation of electrical apparatus. New York: 1917. 1st edn, 2nd imp. 8vo. 480 pp. Ills. Cloth, inner jnts cracked. *(Elgen)* **$25 [≈ £13]**
- Theory and calculation of transient electrical phenomena and oscillatiors. New York: 1920. 3rd edn, revsd & enlgd. 8vo. 696 pp. Ills. Cloth. *(Elgen)* **$25 [≈ £13]**
- Theory and calculation of transient electrical phenomena and oscillations. New York: 1909. 1st edn. 8vo. 556 pp. 84 text ills & charts. Orig cloth. *(Argosy)* **$150 [≈ £83]**

Stellatus, Marcellus Palingenious (pseud?)
- See Manzolli, Pietro Angelo

Stelwagon, Henry W.
- Treatise on diseases of the skin. Phila: 1903. 2nd edn. Lge 8vo. 1115,16 pub ctlg pp. 26 full-page cold litho & h/t plates, 220 text ills. Orig cloth, very rubbed, shaken.

(Elgen) **$40 [≈ £22]**

Stephenson, J. & Churchill, J.M.
- Medical botany ... new edition by G.T. Burnett. London: 1834-36. 3 vols. Roy 8vo. 187 (i.e. 1-185, 75, 106). Hand-cold plates. A little offsetting in text. Contemp diced calf, trifle rubbed, rebacked.
(Wheldon & Wesley) **£750 [≈ $1,350]**

Sternberg, George
- Infection and immunity with special reference to the prevention of infectious diseases. New York: 1903. 1st edn. 293 pp. Cloth, sl snag in spine. *(Scientia)* **$85 [≈ £47]**

Sternberg, Martha L.
- George Miller Sternberg, a biography. Chicago: 1920. 1st edn. 8vo. 331 pp. Port frontis, ills, ports. Cloth, t.e.g.
(Elgen) **$50 [≈ £27]**

Sternberg, S.
- Lectures on differential geometry. New Jersey: Prentice Hall, 1964. 1st edn. xi,390 pp. Orig cloth, dw. *(Hinchliffe)* **£25 [≈ $45]**

Stetson, Harland T.
- Sunspots and their effects from the human point of view. New York: McGraw-Hill, 1937. 2nd edn. 201 pp. Drawings, photos. Orig cloth. *(Xerxes)* **$50 [≈ £27]**

Steuart, Sir Henry
- The planter's guide ... method of giving immediate effect to wood ... to place the art on fixed principles ... useful and ornamental ... Edinburgh: 1828. 1st edn. 8vo. xxii,473 pp. Double-page frontis, 4 plates (foxed). Contemp calf, spine sl split.
(Edwards) **£125 [≈ $225]**
- The planter's guide ... the best method of giving immediate effect to wood, by the removal of large trees ... chiefly intended for the climate of Scotland. Edinburgh: Blackwood, 1828. 1st edn. 8vo. Double-page frontis, 3 plates (edges foxed). Qtr calf.
(Hughes) **£75 [≈ $135]**
- The planter's guide; or, a practical essay on the best method of giving immediate effect to wood ... 1828. 2nd edn, enlgd. 8vo. Plates. Grey bds. *(Halewood)* **£48 [≈ $86]**

Steven, John
- The pathology of mediastinal tumours with special reference to diagnosis. London: 1892. 1st edn. 100 pp. Orig cloth. *(Fye)* **$75 [≈ £41]**

Stevens, William
- Observations on the healthy and diseased properties of the blood. London: 1832. 1st edn. 8vo. xx,504 pp. Rec cloth.
(Elgen) **$75 [≈ £41]**

Stevenson, David
- The principles and practices of canal and river engineering. Edinburgh: Black, 1872. 2nd edn. Tall 8vo. xv,339 pp. Advts, fldg plan frontis, 15 plates (some fldg). Orig cloth, sl shaken, backstrip faded with sm splits, crnrs sl bumped. *(Edwards)* **£100 [≈ $180]**
- A treatise on the application of marine surveying and hydrometry to the practice of civil engineering. Edinburgh: A. & C. Black, 1842. 1st edn. Roy 8vo. xiii,173,[1], [2 blank] pp. 14 plates (2 fldg, 1 cold), 16 other ills. Orig cloth, spine worn.
(Fenning) **£75 [≈ $135]**

Stevenson, Edward Luther
- Terrestrial and celestial globes: their history and construction ... value as aids in the study of geography and astronomy. New Haven: Hispanic Soc of Amer, 1921. One of 1000. 2 vols. 8vo. xxvi,218; xi,291 pp. 166 plates. Orig cloth, faded. *(Weiner)* **£180 [≈ $324]**
- Terrestrial and celestial globes: their history and construction ... New Haven: Hispanic Soc of Amer, 1921. One of 1000. 2 vols. 8vo. 218; 291 pp. Num photo ills, 5 orig photos laid-in. Orig cloth. *(Xerxes)* **$175 [≈ £97]**

Stewart, A.P. & Jenkins, E.
- The medical and legal aspects of sanitary reform. London: 1867. 8vo. 100 pp. Bds. Authors' pres copy to Lord Houghton with a.l.s. (by Stewart) to Houghton tipped-in.
(Goodrich) **$75 [≈ £41]**

Stewart, D.
- Elements of the philosophy of the human mind. London: 1837. New edn. 8vo. 6,xii,447 pp. Half calf, gilt. *(Halewood)* **£75 [≈ $135]**

Stewart, Dugald
- Outlines of moral philosophy. For the use of students in the University of Edinburgh. Edinburgh: for William Creech ..., 1793. 1st edn. 8vo. Half-title. Contemp calf, edges a bit worn, rebacked. Sgntr of James Smith Kidston (Edinburgh 1796) on half-title.
(Hughes) **£165 [≈ $297]**
- Philosophical essays. Edinburgh: Creech, 1810. 1st edn. 4to. lxxvi,591,[i] pp. Errata slip tipped-in at end. Traces of foxing. 19th c diced russia, gilt, mrbld edges.
(Frew Mackenzie) **£325 [≈ $585]**
- Philosophical essays. Edinburgh: 1816. 2nd edn. 8vo. Occas spotting. Contemp half calf, rebacked. *(Robertshaw)* **£40 [≈ $72]**

Stewart, Dugald, et al.
- Dissertations on the history of metaphysical and ethical, and of mathematical and physical science. London: 1835. Thick 4to. viii,711 pp. Old half calf, worn.
(Weiner) **£100 [≈ $180]**

Stewart, F. Campbell
- Eminent French surgeons, with a historical and statistical account of the hospitals of Paris. Buffalo: n.d. [ca 1845]. 8vo. 432 pp. Dampstained. Orig bds, worn.
(Goodrich) **$135 [≈ £75]**

Still, Andrew T.
- Autobiography ... with a history of the discovery and development of the science of osteopathy. Kirksville, Mo: the author, 1897. 1st edn. 8vo. 460 pp. Ills, ports. Cloth, hinges cracked. *(Elgen)* **$85 [≈ £47]**
- Autobiography ... with a history of the ... development of the science of osteopathy. Kirksville: 1897. 8vo. 460 pp. Cloth. Pres copy. *(Goodrich)* **$60 [≈ £33]**

Still, George Frederick
- Common disorders and diseases of childhood. 1918. 3rd edn. Half-title discold. Orig cloth, spine faded. *(Whitehart)* **£18 [≈ $32]**
- Common disorders and diseases of childhood. London: [1920]. 8vo. xvi,845 pp. Ills. Orig cloth. *(Elgen)* **$25 [≈ £13]**
- The history of paediatrics ... up to the end of the XVIIIth century, London: Dawsons, reprinted 1965. 8vo. Plates. Orig green cloth, gilt, sl faded. *(Hughes)* **£24 [≈ $43]**

Stille, Alfred & Maisch, John M.
- The national dispensatory. Phila: 1879. 2nd edn revsd. 8vo. xi,1680 pp. 32 pp pub ctlg. Num text engvs. Sheep, scuffed, inner hinges starting. *(Elgen)* **$75 [≈ £41]**

Stille, Charles J.
- History of the United States Sanitary Commission; being the General Report of its work during the War of the Rebellion. Phila: 1866. 1st edn. 553 pp. Stamp on title, Cvrs stained. *(Scientia)* **$150 [≈ £83]**

Stillingfleet, B.J.
- Miscellaneous tracts relating to natural history, husbandry, and physick. To which is added the calendar of flora. London: 1762. 2nd edn. xxxi,391 pp. 11 plates. Contemp

sprinkled calf, spine gilt, sl rubbed.
(Whitehart) **£110 [≃ $198]**

Stillman, J.D.B.
- The horse in motion, as shown by instantaneous photography [by E. Muybridge]; with a study on animal mechanics ... in which is demonstrated the theory of quadrupedal locomotion. Boston: 1882. 1st edn. Sm folio. 107 plates. Orig cloth, rubbed. *(Argosy)* **$400 [≃ £222]**

Stillman, J.M.
- The story of early chemistry. New York: 1924. 8vo. xiii,566 pp. Orig cloth, dw.
(Weiner) **£25 [≃ $45]**

Stimson, Lewis A.
- A practical treatise on fractures and dislocations. New York: 1905. 4th edn, revsd & enlgd. Lge 8vo. xxii,844 pp. 46 plates, 331 ills. Orig sheep. *(Elgen)* **$50 [≃ £27]**

Stinchfield, S.M.
- Speech disorders. A psychological study of the various defects of speech. London: 1933. 8vo. xii,341 pp. 8 plates, other ills. Some spotting, sgntr on flyleaf. Orig cloth.
(Bow Windows) **£18 [≃ $32]**

Stirling, William
- Some apostles of physiology being an account of their lives. London: 1902. Sm folio. Orig cloth, a bit worn. *(Goodrich)* **$95 [≃ £52]**

Stockton, Charles
- Diseases of the stomach and their relation to other diseases. New York: 1914. xix,774 pp. Index, 5 plates, 22 radiograms & 65 ills in text. Cloth. *(Rittenhouse)* **$25 [≃ £13]**

Stoddart, Richard
- Tables for computing the solid contents of timber ... scantling, deals, planks ... Leith: for the author, 1818. Tall sm 8vo. Early leaves sl soiled, some notes on endpapers. Contemp calf. *(Stewart)* **£45 [≃ $81]**

Stokes, William
- The diseases of the heart and the aorta. Phila: 1855. 2nd ptg. 8vo. xvi,710 pp. Lea, jnts tender, scuffed, spine ends sl frayed.
(Elgen) **$300 [≃ £166]**
- An introduction to the use of the stethoscope with its application to the diagnosis in diseases of the thoracic viscera. Edinburgh: 1825. 1st edn. Title browned, index misbound at beginning. Bds soiled, spine much frayed. *(Rittenhouse)* **$2,300 [≃ £1,277]**

- Lectures on the theory and practice of physic. Phila: 1837. 1st Amer edn. 8vo. x,406,[1] pp. Scattered foxing. Contemp lea, scuffed.
(Elgen) **$55 [≃ £30]**
- Lectures on the theory and practice of physic. Phila: 1837. 1st edn. 8vo. 408 pp interleaved with contemp blanks. New mor.
(Oasis) **$200 [≃ £111]**
- A treatise on the diagnosis and treatment of diseases of the chest. Part I. Diseases of the lung and windpipe. [All published]. London: New Sydenham Soc, 1882. 8vo. 596 pp. Port frontis. Orig cloth. *(Oasis)* **$200 [≃ £111]**

Stone, Edward
- A new mathematical dictionary. London: 1743. 2nd edn. 8vo. xii,[278] pp. Num text w'cuts. Old calf, jnts reprd, new labels.
(Pollak) **£85 [≃ $153]**

Stone, William L.
- Letter to Doctor A. Brigham, on animal magnetism. New York: George Dearborn, 1837. 8vo. 72 pp. Stabbed & tied at inner marg. Lacking orig wraps (?).
(Karmiole) **$35 [≃ £19]**
- Letter to Doctor A. Brigham, on animal magnetism being an account of a remarkable interview between the author and Miss Loraina Brackett while in a state of somnambulism. New York: 1837. 2nd edn. 8vo. 75 pp. New bds. *(Goodrich)* **$90 [≃ £50]**

Stookey, Byron
- A history of Colonial medical education in the province of New York [1767-1830]. Springfield: 1962. 8vo. 286 pp. Ills. Orig cloth. Author's pres copy.
(Goodrich) **$75 [≃ £41]**

Stopes, H.
- Malt and malting. An historical, scientific and practical treatise ... London: 1885. 8vo. xiv,662,xxiv advts pp. Engvd title, plates (some fldg), ills, tables. Binder's cloth.
(Weiner) **£65 [≃ $117]**

Stopes, Marie C.
- Change of life in men and women. London: Putnam [1936]. 1st edn. 8vo. xvi,282,6 advts pp. Orig maroon cloth, sl worn.
(Pickering) **$65 [≃ £36]**
- Contraception. London: Bale & Danielsson, 1923. 1st edn, 1st printing June 27th, 1923. 8vo. 418 pp. 4 plates. Some adhesive marks on prelims. Orig cloth. *(Oasis)* **$85 [≃ £47]**

Store-house ...
- A rich storehouse, or treasury of the diseased

... many approved medicines ... for ... poorer sort of people. By G.W. London: 1650. 274 pp. Calf, rebacked, some scuffing.
(Rittenhouse) **$775 [≃ £430]**

Storer, Horatio R.

- The causation, course, and treatment of reflex insanity in women. Bolton: 1871. 1st edn in book form. 236 pp. Cloth.
(Scientia) **$75 [≃ £41]**

Stowell, C.H. & L.R.

- Microscopical diagnosis. Detroit: 1882. 8vo. viii,93,118, 32,[3] pp. 10 plates, ills. Orig cloth. *(Weiner)* **£20 [≃ $36]**

Strait, N.A.

- Roster of Regimental Surgeons and Assistant Surgeons in the late war, with their service and last-known post-office address. 1882. 1st edn. 320 pp. *(Scientia)* **$95 [≃ £52]**

Straker, Ernest

- Wealden iron, a monograph on the former ironworks in the Counties of Sussex, Surrey and Kent ... a history of the industry ... to its cessation ... London: 1931. 8vo. xiv,487 pp. Num maps, plates & ills. Orig cloth.
(Weiner) **£50 [≃ $90]**

Straub, George F.

- Surgery of the chest. Springfield: 1932. 1st edn. 8vo. xvii,475 pp. 68 cold plates, num ills. Cloth. *(Elgen)* **$35 [≃ £19]**

Streeter, Edwin W.

- Precious stones and their gems. Their history and distinguishing characteristics. London: Chapman & Hall, 1879. 2nd edn, with addtns. 8vo. Frontis, 13 plates (7 cold & inc 2 mtd photos). Contemp half red mor, gilt, gilt panelled spine. *(Traylen)* **£175 [≃ $315]**

Stricker, Solomon

- Manual of human and comparative histology. Translated ... London: New Sydenham Soc, 1870. 3 vols. 8vo. Orig cloth, worn.
(Goodrich) **$75 [≃ £41]**

Strickland, F.

- A manual of petrol motors, and motor cars. Comprising the designing, construction and working of petrol motors. London: 1907. viii,376 pp. 329 ills, 15 tables. Sl grubby in places. Orig cloth, sl stained, new endpapers.
(Whitehart) **£40 [≃ $72]**

Stringer, Moses

- Opera mineralia explicata: or, the mineral

kingdom, within the dominions of Great Britain, dislay'd. London: n.d. [ca 1713]. Sm 8vo. 4ff,xii, 7-308, 16 ctlg pp. Staining to lower part, sm hole in 1 leaf. Ctlg cropped. Contemp calf, v worn, rebacked.
(Weiner) **£210 [≃ $378]**

Strother, Edward

- An essay on sickness and health ... for the regulation of diseas'd and healthy persons ... Dr. Cheyne's mistaken opinions ... H.P. for Charles Rivington, 1725. 1st edn. 8vo. lxviii,64, 64 bis-79, 81-463, [1 advts] pp. Contemp panelled calf, reprd.
(Fenning) **£165 [≃ $297]**

Strumpfell, Adolf

- A textbook of medicine ... translated ... notes by Frederick C. Shattuck. New York: 1891. 8vo. 981 pp. Ills. Orig sheep, worn, jnts weak.
(Goodrich) **$950 [≃ £527]**

Strutt, John William

- See Rayleigh, Lord

Struve, Christian Augustus

- Asthenology; or, the art of preserving feeble life; and of supporting the constitution under the influence of incurable diseases. London: Murray ..., 1801. 1st edn in English. 8vo. xxxiii,431 pp. Advt leaf. Lacking front free flyleaf. Contemp calf, scuffed.
(Elgen) **$135 [≃ £75]**

Stuart, Robert

- Descriptive history of the steam engine. New edition, with a supplement ... to the year 1829. London: 1829. 8vo. viii,249 pp. 52 w'cut plates, text w'cuts. New buckram.
(Weiner) **£75 [≃ $135]**

Stubbs, S.G.B. & Bligh, E.W.

- Sixty centuries of health and physick: the progress of ideas from primitive medicine magic to modern medicine. London: [1931]. 1st edn. 8vo. xvi,253 pp. Errata leaf tipped-in. Cold frontis, 64 plates. Cloth.
(Elgen) **$50 [≃ £27]**

Sturgeon, William

- Scientific researches, experimental and theoretical, in electricity, magnetism, galvanism ... and electro-chemistry. Bury: Thomas Crompton, 1850. 1st edn. Lge 4to. 19 engvd plates. Orig blindstamped cloth, spine reprd. *(Chaucer Head)* **£220 [≃ $396]**

Summers, John

- A short account of the success of warm bathing in paralytic disorders. London: 1751.

2nd edn. 8vo. 38 pp. Rec calf.
(Goodrich) **\$125 [≈£69]**

Surgeon ...
- The surgeon's vade-mecum ... See Hooper, Robert

Sutherland, Alexander
- The nature and qualities of Bristol-water; illustrated by experiments and observations ...Bristol: E. Farley, 1758. 1st edn. 8vo. Half mor, gilt.   *(Traylen)* **£85 [≈\$153]**

Sutton, Samuel
- An historical account ... for extracting the foul air out of ships ... annexed two relations ... and A discourse on the scurvy by Dr. Mead. London: Brindley, 1749. 1st edn of the Mead. 8vo. viii,120 pp. Fldg engvd plate. Lge copy in contemp calf, sl rubbed.
(Pickering) **£850 [≈£472]**

Sutton, Thomas
- A practical account of a remittant fever, frequently occurring among the troops in this climate. Canterbury: James Simmons, 1806. 1st edn. 8vo. 42 pp. Title sl spotted & with old stamp. Disbound.
(Burmester) **£110 [≈\$198]**

Sutton, W.L.
- A history of the disease usually called typhoid fever, as it has appeared in Georgetown and its vicinity; ... reflections as to its causes and nature. Louisville: 1850. iv,127 pp. Orig blindstamped cloth, rebacked, orig spine & label preserved. Ex lib.
(Whitehart) **£45 [≈\$81]**

Svedberg, T., et al.
- The ultracentrifuge. Oxford: 1940. 1st edn. x,478 pp. 15o figs. Orig cloth, sl marked.
(Whitehart) **£40 [≈\$72]**

Swan, Joseph
- Illustrations of the comparative anatomy of the nervous system. London: Longman ..., 1835. 4to. xxxii,311 pp. 35 plates. Stamp on title verso & some plates. Rec cloth.
(Goodrich) **\$750 [≈£416]**

Swan, Joseph P.
- The vaccination problem. London: C.W. Daniel, 1936. 8vo. 346 pp. Advts. Sl soiled dw.   *(Taylor)* **£20 [≈\$36]**

Swedenborg, Emanuel
- The brain considered anatomically, physiologically and philosophically. London:

1882-87. 1st edn in English. 2 vols. 794; 645 pp. Cloth, sm tear at top of spine reprd.
(Scientia) **\$375 [≈£208]**
- Concerning the earths in our solar system which are called planets. London: Hindmarsh, 1787. 212 pp. Some spotting throughout. New lea spine.
(Xerxes) **\$100 [≈£55]**

Swinton, John
- A proposal for uniformity of weights and measures in Scotland ... With tables of the English and Scottish standards ... Edinburgh: for Charles Elliot ..., 1779. 1st edn. 8vo. Half-title, Some minor marg staining. Uncut in orig bds, spine defective.
(Hughes) **£65 [≈\$117]**

Switzer, Stephen
- An introduction to a general system of hydrostaticks and hydraulicks, philosophical and practical. London: for T. Astley ..., 1729. 1st edn. 2 vols. 4to. Engvd frontis, 61 plates (60 fldg). 20th c half calf, bds.
(Chaucer Head) **£1,000 [≈\$1,800]**
- The nobleman, gentleman, and gardener's recreation: or, an introduction to gardening, planting, agriculture ... London: 1715. 1st edn. 8vo. Frontis. Contemp calf.
(Robertshaw) **£150 [≈\$270]**
- The nobleman, gentleman, and gardener's recreation: or, an introduction to gardening, planting, agriculture ... London: B. Barker, 1715. 1st edn. 8vo. [8],xxxiv, 266,[16] pp. Engvd frontis. Contemp calf, sm repr on upper jnt. Ex lib Colquhoun of Luss.
(Spelman) **£420 [≈\$756]**

Sydenham, Thomas
- Dr. Sydenham's compleat method of curing almost all diseases ... To which are now added, five discourses by the same author ... London: for J. Hodges, 1737. 7th edn. 12mo. [viii],202,[6] pp. 18th c cloth.
(Burmester) **£45 [≈\$81]**
- The entire works ... Third edition with all the notes inserted by John Swan, M.D. London: 1753. 8vo. 692 pp. Old calf.
(Halewood) **£85 [≈\$153]**
- The whole works. London: for Richard Wellington ..., 1696. 1st edn in English. [xxiv],592 (i.e. 488) pp. 1st 2 leaves a little chipped, some browning. Mod half calf.
(Ash) **£250 [≈\$450]**
- The whole works. London: for Richard Wellington ..., 1696. 1st edn in English. 8vo. [24],592 pp. Pagination error but complete. Sgntr on title. Mod calf, gilt. Wing 6305.
(Hemlock) **\$575 [≈£319]**

- The works ... on acute and chronic diseases ...
With notes, intended to accomodate them ...
to the climate and diseases of the United
States, by Benjamin Rush. Phila: 1809. 1st
edn. Orig bds, hinges a little weak, sl scuffed.
(Rittenhouse) **$1,500 [≃ £833]**
- The works ... Translated ... With a life of the
author by R.G. Latham. London: 1848. 2
vols. Ex lib, with b'plates.
(Rittenhouse) **$40 [≃ £22]**
- The works ... Translated from the Latin
edition of Dr. Greenhill, with a life of the
author ... London: Sydenham Soc, 1848-50. 2
vols. 276; 395 pp. Orig cloth.
(Scientia) **$125 [≃ £69]**

Sykes, John F.J.
- Public health problems. London: 1892. 8vo.
370 pp. Half calf, mrbld bds.
(Goodrich) **$50 [≃ £27]**

Syme, James
- The principles of surgery. Edinburgh:
Maclachlan, 1832. 1st edn. 8vo. 716 pp. 2
plates. Title sl soiled. New half calf.
(Oasis) **$250 [≃ £138]**
- The principles of surgery. Phila: 1832. 1st
Amer edn. 8vo. 375,[1] pp. 12 pp pub ctlg.
Engvd frontis. Very foxed. Lea, worn, jnt
cracked. Ex lib. *(Elgen)* **$90 [≃ £50]**
- The principles of surgery. Edinburgh: 1837.
2nd edn. 8vo. 460 pp. Stamps on title. Later
half cloth. *(Goodrich)* **$95 [≃ £52]**

Symington, Johnson
- The topographical anatomy of the child.
Edinburgh: Livingstone, & London: Bailliere
..., 1887. 1st edn. Folio. 14 chromolitho
plates (13 life-sized), 2 fldg, 1 cleanly torn &
reprd, 33 w'cut ills. Occas light soiling. Orig
cloth. 3 pres inscrptns.
(Quaritch) **$350 [≃ £194]**

System of Arithmetic ...
- A short system of practical arithmetic
compiled from the best authorities ...
Hallowell, Maine: Dec, 1807. 12mo. 173 pp.
Waterstained throughout. Lea.
(Xerxes) **$100 [≃ £55]**

System of Magick ...
- A system of magick ... See Defoe, Daniel

Systema Agriculturae ...
- Systema agriculturae ... See Worlidge, John

T.M.
- See Moffett, Thomas

Tables ...
- Tables for correcting the apparent distance of
the moon ... See Shepherd, A.

Tait, Lawson
- Diseases of women. Birmingham: 1887. 2nd
edn. xii,192 pp. Title & following 4 pp
affected by damp along edges, title reprd.
Victorian style cloth. *(Whitehart)* **£35 [≃ $63]**
- Diseases of women. New York: Wood's
Library, 1879. 2nd edn. 8vo. 192 pp. Orig
cloth. *(Oasis)* **$30 [≃ £16]**

Tait, P.G.
- An elementary treatise on quaternions.
Cambridge: [1873]. 2nd edn. Some scattered
browning, crude repr to tear in 1 leaf. Later
amateur cloth. *(Whitehart)* **£18 [≃ $32]**
- Newton's laws of motion. London: A. & C.
Black, 1899. 8vo. vii,[i], 53,[iii] pp. Orig
cloth. *(Pollak)* **£25 [≃ $45]**

Talbot, Eugene S.
- Interstitial gingivitis; or, so called pyorrhea
alveolaris. Phila: 1899. 1st edn. 8vo. viii,192
pp. Frontis, ills, plates. Cloth, sl shaken, sm
tear in backstrip. *(Elgen)* **$45 [≃ £25]**

Tamplin, Richard W.
- Lectures on the nature and treatment of
deformities. Phila: 1846. 1st Amer edn. 8vo.
216 pp. 60 text w'cuts. Foxed. Cloth-backed
pts bds, worn. *(Elgen)* **$30 [≃ £16]**

Tanner, Fred W.
- Bacteriology. A text-book of micro-
organisms. New York: Wiley, 1933. 2nd edn.
8vo. xvii,[i], 548,[vi] pp. 138 ills. Pub bndg.
(Pollak) **£20 [≃ $36]**

Tanner, John
- The hidden treasures of the art of physick;
fully discovered in four books. London:
George Sawbridge, 1659. 1st edn. Thick sm
8vo. Errata at end. Old calf, jnts reprd. Wing
T138. *(Traylen)* **£675 [≃ $1,215]**

Tanner, T.H.
- The practice of medicine. 1875. 7th edn.
xix,642; 675 pp. Sm hole in 1 half-title, sl
foxing vol II. Cloth, worn, sl marked, nw
endpapers.i *(Whitehart)* **£25 [≃ $45]**

Taplin, William
- The gentleman's stable directory, or modern
system of farriery; all the most valuable
prescriptions and remedies, etc. Dublin:
Wogan, 1793. 2 vols in 1. 8vo. Contemp calf,
crack in 1 spine. *(Emerald Isle)* **£65 [≃ $117]**

- The gentleman's stable directory, or modern system of farriery, prescriptions and approved remedies ... London: 1796. 13th edn. Thick 8vo. 504 pp. Frontis. Bds, uncut.
(Halewood) £65 [≈ $117]

Tarbell, John A.
- Homeopathy simplified; or, domestic practice made easy ... Boston: 1859. 4th edn. 8vo. 360 pp. Some light waterstaining throughout. Blindstamped cloth, bottom & edge of spine chipped.   *(Rittenhouse)* $22.50 [≈ £12]

Tardieu, Ambroise
- Treatise on epidemic cholera. Translated ... Boston: 1849. 1st edn in English. 8vo. xi,286,8 pub ctlg pp. Orig blindstamped cloth, lower qtr of spine torn.
(Elgen) $175 [≈ £97]

Taussign, Helen
- Congenital malformations of the heart. New York: 1948. 2nd printing. 8vo. 618 pp. Orig cloth.   *(Goodrich)* $75 [≈ £41]

Tauvry, Daniel
- A new rational anatomy ... made English ... London: for D. Midwinter ..., 1701. 1st English edn. [xvi],301 pp. Engvd frontis, 21 plates. 2 leaves of table misbound, dustsoiled & dampstained in places, short tear in 1 leaf. Contemp calf, jnts reprd.
(Pickering) $650 [≈ £361]

Taylor, Alfred S.
- A manual of medical jurisprudence. London: 1846. 2nd edn. Sm thick 8vo. xvi,704 pp. Few stains. Binder's cloth, soiled.
(Weiner) £40 [≈ $72]
- The principles and practice of medical jurisprudence. 1883. 3rd edn. 2 vols. xx,727; xiv,657 pp. 188 text figs. New cloth.
(Whitehart) £18 [≈ $32]

Taylor, C.
- Elements of algebra, compiled from Garnier's French translation of Leonard Euler. London: 1824. iv,338 pp. Scattered foxing on title & endpapers. Contemp 3/4 lea, sl worn, mrbld bds & edges. *(Whitehart)* £35 [≈ $63]

Taylor, Fanny M.
- Eastern hospitals and English nurses. The narrative of twelve months' experience in the hospitals of Koulali and Scutari. London: Hurst & Blackett, 1857. 3rd edn, revsd. 2 tinted lithos. Orig gilt dec cloth.
(Chaucer Head) £120 [≈ $216]

Taylor, Frederick W.
- Principles of scientific management. NY & London: Harper & Bros, 1911. 1st edn. 8vo. 144 pp. Front flyleaf renewed. Orig cloth.
(Antiq Sc) $150 [≈ £83]

Taylor, J.
- The complete weather guide; a collection of practical observations for prognosticating the weather. 1814. 2nd edn. viii,160 pp. Fldg frontis. Orig sheep, rubbed, spine sl cracked.
(Whitehart) £45 [≈ $81]

Taylor, Michael
- A sexagesimal table, exhibiting at sight, the result of any proportion, where the terms do not exceed sixty minutes ... London: 1780. 1st ed. 8vo. xlv,[i errata],[2],316 pp. Fldg table. Contemp tree calf, spine gilt, jnts cracked.
(Pickering) $350 [≈ £194]
- Tables of logarithms ... sines and tangents ... with a preface ... by Neville Maskelyne ... London: 1792. Folio. Folio. [xiv], 64 pp. The text only, lacking the tables. A few contemp anntns. Old mrbld bds, mod calf spine.
(Weiner) £50 [≈ $90]

Taylor, R.C.
- Statistics of coal, the geographical and geological distribution of mineral combustibles ... in all parts of the world ... Phila: 1848. 8vo. cxlviii,754 pp. 6 fldg cold maps (2 creased & a little torn), w'cuts. Orig pict dec cloth, gilt, worn, rebacked.
(Weiner) £85 [≈ $153]

Taylor, Robert W.
- The pathology and treatment of venereal diseases. Phila: 1895. 1st edn. 8vo. 1002 pp. 230 ills, 7 cold plates. Orig binding, sl scuffed.   *(Rittenhouse)* $55 [≈ £30]

Taylor, Samuel
- An essay intended to establish a standard for an universal system of stenography or shorthand writing ... London: for the author, 1786. [18],98,x pp. Engvd title, 11 engvd plates (as called for). Old tree calf, crnrs bumped.   *(Karmiole)* $175 [≈ £97]
- An essay intended to establish a standard for an universal system of stenography or shorthand writing ... London: privately printed, 1786. 1st edn. 8vo. Engvd title, 11 engvd plates. Contemp tree calf, 19th c rebacking, gilt, 2 sm wormholes, crnrs frayed.
(Chaucer Head) £200 [≈ $360]

Taylor, W.E.
- Geology: its facts and fictions: or, the modern

theories of geologists ... London: 1855. 1st edn. Sm 8vo. [xvi],270,[2 advts] pp. Frontis, num text ills. Random dust marks. Orig cloth, inner hinges strained, jnts & crnrs a little rubbed.   *(Bow Windows)* **£25 [≃$45]**

Teacher, John H.
- A manual of obstetrical and gynaecological pathology. Oxford: 1935. 4to. 407 pp. Ills. Orig cloth, worn.   *(Goodrich)* **$65 [≃£36]**

Telescope, Tom (pseud.)
- The Newtonian system of philosophy; explained by familiar objects in an entertaining manner for the use of young ladies and gentlemen. London: Ogilvy ..., 1798. 2ff, 137,[ii] pp. Engvd frontis, 4 plates, final advt leaf. Orig sprinkled sheep, jnts cracked.   *(Pirages)* **$150 [≃£83]**

Tesla, Nikola
- Experiments with alternate currents of high potential and high frequency. New York: Johnston, 1892. 1st edn. 8vo. ix,146 pp. Frontis, text figs. Orig cloth.
        (Antiq Sc) **$285 [≃£158]**

Teste, Alphonse
- A homoeopathic treatise on the diseases of children. Translated ... Cincinnati: 1854. 1st edn in English. 8vo. 342.14 pub ctlg pp. Scattered foxing. Cloth. *(Elgen)* **$95 [≃£52]**

Testelin, A. & Warlomont, E.
- Glaucoma and its cure by iridectomy. Translated ... Albany: J. Munsell, 1866. 1st edn in English. 8vo. 40 pp. Disbound.
        (Antiq Sc) **$85 [≃£47]**

Thacher, James
- American medical biography, or memoirs of eminent physicians who have flourished in America ... Boston: 1828. 1st edn. 2 vols in 1. Orig bds, cloth torn along upper hinge.
        (Rittenhouse) **$150 [≃£83]**
- American medical biography, or memoirs of eminent physicians who have flourished in America ... A succinct history of medical science in the United States. Boston: 1828. 2 vols in 1. 8vo. 14 engvd plates. Contemp calf, spine reprd.   *(Goodrich)* **$225 [≃£125]**
- The American new dispensatory. Boston: 1813. 2nd edn. 732 pp. Sm piece torn from bottom of title & intro leaf without loss of text. Lea.   *(Fye)* **$125 [≃£69]**
- The American new dispensatory. Boston: 1821. 4th edn. 736 pp. Lea.
        (Fye) **$100 [≃£69]**
- Observations on hydrophobia, produced by

the bite of a mad dog, or other rabid animal ... Plymouth: 1812. 8vo. 302 pp. Hand-cold plate. Foxed. New qtr calf.
        (Goodrich) **$375 [≃£208]**

Thackrah, C. Turner
- The effects of the principal arts, trades, and professions, and of civic states and habits of living on health and longevity. Phila: 1831. '2nd' edn. 180 pp. Lea.
        (Scientia) **$350 [≃£194]**

Thames Tunnel ...
- An explanation of the works of the tunnel under the Thames from Rotherhithe to Wapping. London: W. Warrington ..., 1837. Obl 12mo. 16 pp,17-24ff. 10 engvd plates inc tinted aquatint, sev fldg or double-page, 1 with overlay. Orig drab wraps, ptd paper labels.   *(Pickering)* **$250 [≃£138]**
- Sketches of the works for the tunnel under the Thames from Rotherhithe to Wapping. Harvey & Darton, 1829. Obl 12mo. 30 pp. 14 plates in aquatint, line engvd & litho, sev double-page or fldg. 2 plates a little frayed, blindstamp on title. Orig mrbld wraps.
        (Pickering) **$350 [≃£194]**

Thayer, Gerald H.
- Concealing-coloration in the animal kingdom ... the laws of disguise through color and pattern ... New York: 1909. 1st edn. 4to. xix,260 pp. 16 cold plates, 58 other plates. Cancelled blind lib stamp on title. Orig cloth, a.e.g., top of spine sl worn.
        (Bickersteth) **£85 [≃$153]**
- Concealing-coloration in the animal kingdom ... the laws of disguise through color and pattern ... New York: Macmillan, 1918. New edn. 4to. xix,260 pp. 16 cold plates, 140 photos & diags. Blue cloth, spotted, inner hinge reprd.   *(Karmiole)* **$50 [≃£27]**

Thayer, William Sydney
- Osler and other papers. Balt: 1931. 8vo. 386 pp. Orig cloth.   *(Goodrich)* **$35 [≃£19]**
- Osler and other papers. Balt: John Hopkins Press, 1931. 8vo. [viii],386 pp. Orig cloth.
        (Pollak) **£25 [≃$45]**

Theory ...
- A theory of the universe ... See Case, Robert Hope

Thermometrical Navigation ...
- Thermometrical navigation ... See Williams, Jonathan

Thirring, J.H.
- The ideas of Einstein's theory. London: 1921. 1st edn in English. 8vo. 167 pp. Orig cloth.
(Oasis) **$50** [≃ £27]
- The ideas of Einstein's theory. London: Methuen, 1922. 2nd edn, revsd. 8vo. 168,8 pub ctlg pp. Orig cloth, dw.
(Oasis) **$30** [≃ £16]

Thomas, K.B.
- Curare. Its history and usage. 1964. 144 pp. Frontis, 11 plates, 4 text diags. Sgnd by author. *(Whitehart)* **£18** [≃ $32]

Thomas, Robert
- The modern practice of physic ... New York: 1813. 2nd Amer edn. Lea, scuffed.
(Rittenhouse) **$125** [≃ £69]
- The modern practice of physic, exhibiting the characters, causes, symptoms, prognostics ... diseases of all climates. New York: 1817. 4th Amer edn. 8vo. xvi,915 pp. Browning. Lea, scuffed, rubbed. *(Elgen)* **$85** [≃ £47]
- The modern practice of physic ... New York: 1824. 7th Amer edn. 1058 pp. Lea, half inch chipped from spine. *(Fye)* **$85** [≃ £47]

Thomas, T. Gailliard
- Abortion and its treatment ... From notes by P. Brynberg Porter, M.D., revised by the author. New York: 1892. 112,6 pub ctlg pp. Cloth. *(Elgen)* **$45** [≃ £25]
- A practical treatise on the diseases of women. Phila: 1868. 1st edn. 625 pp. Pub ctlg. Cloth.
(Scientia) **$200** [≃ £111]

Thompson, C.J.S.
- The lure and romance of alchemy. London: 1932. 1st edn. 8vo. 249 pp. Plates, text ills. Orig cloth. *(Oasis)* **$100** [≃ £55]
- The lure and romance of alchemy. London: 1932. 1st edn. Sm 8vo. 249 pp. Plates, ills. Orig cloth, marked in spots.
(Elgen) **$30** [≃ £16]
- The mystery and art of the apothecary. Phila: 1929. 1st Amer edn. 8vo. 287 pp. Plates. Orig cloth. *(Oasis)* **$50** [≃ £27]
- The mystery and art of the apothecary. Phila: Lippincott, 1929. 8vo. x,287 pp. Frontis, 8 plates, 18 text ills. Black cloth, spine gilt.
(Karmiole) **$30** [≃ £16]
- The mystery and art of the apothecary. London: John Lane, 1929. 1st edn. 8vo. Frontis, plates, text ills. Orig cloth.
(Hughes) **£20** [≃ $36]
- The mystic mandrake. London: 1934. 1st edn. 8vo. 253 pp. Plates. Orig cloth, dw.
(Oasis) **$60** [≃ £33]

Thompson, Sir Henry
- Clinical lectures on diseases of the urinary organs. London: 1879. 5th edn. 8vo. xii,355,16 pub ctlg pp. 2 plates, 71 text ills. Light foxing. Cloth, spines ends sl frayed.
(Elgen) **$45** [≃ £25]
- The diseases of the prostate, their pathology and treatment. London: Churchill, 1861. 2nd edn. 364,32 pub ctlg pp. 13 litho plates (2 cold). Orig cloth. *(Oasis)* **$175** [≃ £97]
- The diseases of the prostate, their pathology and treatment. London: Churchill, 1866. 6th edn. xii,237, [iii],14,[ii] pp. 39 figs. Orig cloth, mostly unopened, a little wear to spine ends. *(Pollak)* **£25** [≃ $45]
- The pathology and treatment of stricture of the urethra and urinary fistulae. London: Churchill, 1858. 2nd edn. 8vo. 426,32 pub ctlg pp. 4 plates (1 cold). 1 page torn without loss. New cloth. *(Oasis)* **$100** [≃ £55]
- Practical lithotomy and lithotrity or an enquiry into the best modes of removing stone from the bladder. London: Churchill, 1880. 3rd edn. 8vo. xvi,304,24 ctlg pp. 87 figs. Orig cloth. Author's pres inscrptn.
(Pollak) **£50** [≃ $90]

Thompson, Reginald E.
- The physical examination of the chest in health and disease. London: 1879. 260 pp. Hinges somewhat weak, spine damaged at hd. Ex lib with b'plates, &c.
(Rittenhouse) **$25** [≃ £13]

Thompson, Silvanus P.
- Cantor lectures on dynamo-electric machinery. London: William Trounce, 1883. 1st edn. 8vo. 54 pp. Text ills & diags throughout. Lacks wraps.
(Rootenberg) **$150** [≃ £83]
- Michael Faraday. His life and work. London: Cassell, 1901. 8vo. ix,[iii], 308,[xvi advts] pp. Frontis, 22 ills. Orig cloth.
(Pollak) **£25** [≃ $45]
- Treatise on light in which are explained the causes of that which occur in reflexion, & in refraction. London: Macmillan, 1912. 4to. xii,128,[1] pp. Red & black title. Uncut in orig bds. Author's pres copy.
(Rootenberg) **$275** [≃ £152]

Thompson, Theophilus
- Annals of influenza or epidemic catarrhal fever in Great Britain from 1510 to 1837. London: Sydenham Soc, 1852. 8vo. xvi,406 pp. New buckram. *(Weiner)* **£38** [≃ $68]
- Annals of influenza or epidemic catarrhal fever in Great Britain from 1510 to 1837. London: 1852. 8vo. xvi,406 pp. Orig cloth,

piece torn from upper spine, sm dent in lower back cvr.   *(Rittenhouse)* **$40 [≃ £22]**

Thompson, Thomas

- An enquiry into the origin, nature and cure of the small-pox ... added, a prefatory address to Dr. Mead concerning the present discipline in the general administration of physic in this kingdom. London: Millar, 1752. 8vo. 134 pp. Errata leaf. Rec qtr mor.
        (Goodrich) **$125 [≃ £69]**

Thompson, W. Gilman

- The occupational diseases: their causations, symptoms, treatment and prevention. New York: 1914. 1st edn. 724 pp. Cloth, spine faded & rubbed at hd & ft.
        (Scientia) **$85 [≃ £47]**
- The occupational diseases: their causations, symptoms, treatment and prevention. New York: 1914. Ist edn. Lge 8vo. xxvi,724 pp. 118 ills. Cloth, inner hinges cracked.
        (Elgen) **$75 [≃ £41]**
- Practical diatetics. With special reference to diet in disease. New York: Appleton, 1913. 4th edn. 8vo. 928 pp. Ills. Orig cloth.
        (Oasis) **$30 [≃ £16]**
- Practical diatetics. With special reference to diet in disease. New York: 1905. 3rd edn. xxiii,846 pp. Lacking front free endpaper, sm stain on edges at beginning. Cloth, sl marked, spine worn at hd & ft, front inner hinge cracking.   *(Whitehart)* **£18 [≃ $32]**

Thoms, H.

- Classical contributions to obstetrics and gynecology. Springfield & Balt: 1935. 8vo. xxiii,265 pp. Ports. Orig cloth.
        (Weiner) **£38 [≃ $68]**

Thoms, William

- Human longevity: its facts and its fictions. London: Murray, 1873. 1st edn. 8vo. 320 pp. Diced calf, spine gilt.   *(Oasis)* **$75 [≃ £41]**
- Human longevity: its facts and its fictions. London: Murray, 1873. 1st edn. 8vo. xii,320 pp. Orig cloth, tiny defect to spine, crnrs bumped.   *(Hemlock)* **$85 [≃ £47]**

Thomson, A.T.

- A conspectus of the pharmacopoeia of the London, Edinburgh and Dublin Colleges of Physicians. 1841. 13th edn. Sm 8vo. xxiv,203 pp. Front blank torn out, many notes in a contemp hand. Orig linen wraps.
        (Whitehart) **£25 [≃ $45]**

Thomson, Anthony Todd

- Some observations on the preparation and

medicinal employment of the iodurate and hydroiodate of iron. London: 1834. 8vo. 64 pp. Title lightly spotted, few leaves sl dog-eared. Sewing broken, disbound.
        (Weiner) **£30 [≃ $54]**

Thomson, Sir Charles Wyville

- The Atlantic. A preliminary account of the general results of the exploring voyage of H.M.S. 'Challenger' during the year 1873 and ... 1876. New York: Harper, 1878. 2 vols. xxix,424; 396 pp. Num plates, maps, charts, ills. Cloth. Ex lib.   *(Xerxes)* **$175 [≃ £97]**
- The depths of the sea ... the general results of the dredging cruises of ... 'Porcupine' and 'Lightning' during ... 1868 and 1870. London: Macmillan, 1873. 8vo. xxiii,521,61 pp pub ctlg. 8 double-page maps & charts (7 cold). Orig pict cloth, spine darkened.
        (Gough) **£55 [≃ $99]**
- The voyage of the 'Challenger' ... 1873 and the early part of 1876. 1877. 1st edn. 2 vols. 8vo. xxx,424; xiv,396 pp. Port frontis, 168 ills, 42 plates (mainly cold, 15 fldg, 23 double-page), fldg cold frontis map. Orig dec cloth, spines chipped.
        (Edwards) **£140 [≃ $252]**
- The voyage of the 'Challenger' ... during the year 1873 and the early part of 1876. London: 1877. 1st edn. 2 vols. 8vo. Port, lge cold fldg map, 42 plates, maps, tables & diags, most extndg. Orig gilt illust cloth, recased with new endpapers, sl marked.
        (Bow Windows) **£150 [≃ $270]**
- The voyage of the 'Challenger' ... during the year 1873 and the early part of 1876. 1877. 2 vols. 42 maps, charts & plates, some fldg. Orig pict cloth, gilt, some sl wear.
        (Farahar) **£100 [≃ $180]**

Thomson, J.J.

- Applications of dynamics to physics and chemistry. London: 1888. 8vo. viii,312 pp. Orig cloth, little worn & shaken. C.T.R. Wilson's copy with his initials on endpaper.
        (Weiner) **£50 [≃ $90]**
- Applications of dynamics to physics and chemistry. London: Macmillan, 1888. 1st edn. 8vo. viii,312,[ii] pp. Orig cloth.
        (Pollak) **£80 [≃ $144]**
- Beyond the electron. A lecture given at Girton Collage on 8 March 1928. Cambridge: Univ Press, 1928. [ii],43,[iii] pp. Orig wraps.
        (Pollak) **£45 [≃ $81]**
- Conduction of electricity through gases. Cambridge: 1903. 1st edn. 8vo. 8vo. vii,566 pp. Diags. Orig cloth. *(Weiner)* **£60 [≃ $108]**
- Conduction of electricity through gases [Joint author: G.P. Thomson]. Cambridge:

1928-33. 3rd edn. 2 vols. 491; vi,608 pp. 7 plates, 353 text figs. A few pencil markings in margins of vol I. Orig cloth, vol II spine nicked at hd & ft. *(Whitehart)* £60 [≃ $108]
- The corpuscular theory of matter. London: 1907. 8vo. vii,172 pp. Diags. Orig cloth.
          (Weiner) £40 [≃ $72]
- The corpuscular theory of matter. 1907. 1st edn. vi,172 pp. 29 text figs. Sl foxing on half-title & endpapers, ink sgntrs on title & endpapers. Orig cloth, traces of label removed from spine. *(Whitehart)* £50 [≃ $90]
- The corpuscular theory of matter. New York: 1907. 1st Amer edn. 8vo. vi,[2],172 pp. Ills. The English sheets with a cancel title. Cloth.
          (Elgen) $80 [≃ £44]
- The discharge of electricity through gases. 1908. x,203 pp. 41 text figs. Endpapers sl discold. Orig cloth, sl marked, spine sl worn.
          (Whitehart) £40 [≃ $72]
- Electricity and matter. 1904. 1st edn. [3],162 pp. 18 text figs. Orig cloth, dull, spine sl rubbed & worn. *(Whitehart)* £35 [≃ $63]
- The electron in chemistry, being five lectures delivered at the Franklin Institute. Phila: 1923. 1st edn. 8vo. 144 pp. Diags. Ex lib, with blindstamp at ft of title & another page.
          (Weiner) £25 [≃ $45]
- Rays of positive electricity and their application to chemical analyses. London: Longmans, Green, 1913. 1st edn. 8vo. vii,[i], 132 pp. 50 ills. Orig cloth, a little rubbed at spine ends. *(Pollak)* £60 [≃ $108]
- Rays of positive electricity and their application to chemical analyses. London: 1913. 1st edn. 8vo. vii,132 pp. Plates, diags. Orig cloth. *(Weiner)* £40 [≃ $72]
- Recent researches in electricity and magnetism. Oxford: 1893. 1st edn. 8vo. 578 pp. Text ills. Orig cloth, sl worn.
          (Oasis) $150 [≃ £83]
- Recollections and reflections. New York: 1937. 8vo. 451 pp. Port frontis, ills, ports. Cloth. *(Elgen)* $35 [≃ £19]
- A treatise on the motion of vortex rings ... Adams Prize ... 1882. London: 1883. 8vo. xix,124 pp. Diags. Lgely unopened in orig cloth, spine faded & torn at hd.
          (Weiner) £120 [≃ $216]
- A treatise on the motion of vortex rings. An essay ... London: Macmillan, 1883. 1st edn. 8vo. xix,[1],124 pp. Orig maroon cloth.
          (Pickering) $400 [≃ £222]

Thomson, John
- Historical sketch of the opinions entertained by medical men respecting the varieties ... of small-pox; with observations on   ...

vaccination against attacks of that disease. London: 1822. 8vo. viii,400, 43 appendix pp. Mor, gilt, spine & edges worn.
          (Rittenhouse) $375 [≃ £208]

Thomson, John (1765-1846)
- Lectures on inflammation, exhibiting a view of the general doctrines, pathological and practical, of medical surgery. Phila: 1831. 2nd Amer edn. 8vo. viii,526 pp. Scattered light foxing. Lea, rubbed.
          (Elgen) $185 [≃ £102]

Thomson, R.W.
- Ben Rhydding, the Asceplion of England. Ilkley: 1862. 12mo. viii,92,3 pub ctlg pp. Frontis, 6 plates. Cloth. *(Elgen)* $25 [≃ £13]

Thomson, Spencer
- Health resorts in Britain; and how to profit by them. London: Ward & Lock, 1860. 1st edn. Demy 8vo. xii,330 pp. Pull-out frontis map, full-page & engvd text vignettes. Orig blindstamped cloth gilt, upper inner hinge tender. *(Taylor)* £29 [≃ $52]
- Health resorts in Britain; and how to profit by them. London: Ward & Lock, 1860. 1st edn. 8vo. 12,330 pp. Fldg frontis map, num ills. Orig cloth, lower cvr sl defective.
          (Tara) £35 [≃ $63]

Thomson, Thomas
- An attempt to establish the first principles of chemistry by experiment. London: Baldwin, Cradock, & Joy, 1825. 1st edn. 2 vols. 8vo. xxiii,[1],532 pp. Half-title, imprint lf. Contemp half calf, jnt cracked, bds a bit rubbed. *(Antiq Sc)* $400 [≃ £222]
- The history of chemistry. London: 1830-31. 1st edn. 2 vols. Sm 8vo. ix,349; 325 pp. Port in vol I. New buckram.
          (Weiner) £75 [≃ $135]
- History of the Royal Society ... to the end of the eighteenth century. London: 1812. 1st edn. 4to. viii,552,xci pp. Half calf, jnts strengthened, inner hinge open (title tenderly attached). Ex lib. *(Elgen)* $175 [≃ £97]

Thorek, Max
- The face in health and disease. Phila: 1946. 1st edn. 781 pp. Cloth, spine edges rubbed.
          (Scientia) $75 [≃ £41]
- Plastic surgery of the breast and abdominal wall. Springfield: 1942. 1st edn. 446 pp. Cloth. *(Scientia)* $150 [≃ £83]

Thorley, John
- The female monarchy. London: for the author, 1744. 1st edn. 8vo. Engvd frontis, 4

plates. Contemp calf.
(Marlborough) £300 [≈ $540]

Thorndike, Lynn
- A history of magic and experimental science during the first thirteen centuries of our era. London: 1923. 1st edn. 2 vols. 8vo. Orig green cloth, gilt.   *(Traylen)* £65 [≈ $117]

Thorner, W.E.
- Lessons in practical anatomy, for the use of dissectors. Phila: 1827. 8vo. 500 pp. Foxing. Sheep.   *(Goodrich)* $35 [≈ £19]

Thornton, J.H.
- Memories of seven campaigns. Record of 35 years' service in the Indian Medical Department in India, China, Egypt and the Sudan. 1895. Demy 8vo. Ills. Uncut. Cloth.
(Halewood) £45 [≈ $81]

Thornton, Robert J.
- A family herbal: or familiar account of the medical properties of British and foreign plants ... London: 1814. 2nd edn. 8vo. 902 pp (irregular pagination). Port, 258 w'cuts by T. Bewick. Inscrptn on title, piece cut from upper blank marg. Half calf, rebacked.
(Wheldon & Wesley) £120 [≈ $216]
- A family herbal: or familiar account of the medical properties of British and foreign plants ... uses in dying and the various arts. 1814. 2nd edn. 900 pp. Port frontis, num hand-cold engvs. Title sl soiled. Contemp calf, hinges tender. *(Edwards)* £250 [≈ $450]
- A new family herbal ... of the natures and properties of the various plants used in medicine, diet, and the arts. London: for Richard Phillips, 1810. 1st edn. Roy 8vo. Half-title, 283 w'engvs by T. Bewick, 3 pp advts. Some foxing of prelims. Half mor, gilt.
(Traylen) £95 [≈ $171]

Thornton, T.C.
- The new cabinet of arts: a series of entertaining experiments in various branches of science, numerable valuable recipes, and useful facts. London: J.S.Pratt, 1846. 12mo. 252 pp. Frontis. Contents rather dusty. Orig cloth, worn at hd & tail of spine.
(Spelman) £20 [≈ $36]

Thorpe, T.E.
- Humphry Davy, poet and philosopher. London: Cassell, 1896. 8vo. 240,[xvi ctlg] pp. Frontis. Pub bndg.   *(Pollak)* £20 [≈ $36]

Thousand notable things ...
- A thousand notable things ... from the secrets of nature and art ... See Lupton, Thomas

Thudichum, J.L.W.
- A treatise on the pathology of the urine ... a complete guide to its analysis. London: 1877. 2nd edn. 8vo. 577 pp. Orig cloth, sunned, inner hinges cracked.
(Goodrich) $100 [≈ £55]
- A treatise on wines. Their origins, nature and varieties. London: 1894. 8vo. 387 pp. Orig gilt dec cloth.   *(Goodrich)* $195 [≈ £108]

Thurlow, S.
- The land surveyor's ready reckoner, or gentleman and farmer's guide to land measure ... Dean & Mundy, [1810]. 12mo. 142 pp. Fldg plate. Lacking last leaf & endpaper. Contemp roan.   *(Hinchliffe)* £25 [≈ $45]

Tibbits, Herbert
- A handbook of medical electricity. Phila: 1873. 1st Amer edn. 8vo. xii,164 pp. Num ills. Cloth, spine ends sl frayed.
(Elgen) $75 [≈ £41]

Tidy, C.M.
- Legal medicine. New York: Wood's Library, 1882. 2 vols. 8vo. 314; 298 pp. Cold frontis. Orig cloth.   *(Oasis)* $60 [≈ £33]

Tilney, Frederick
- The brain from ape to man. A contribution to the study of the evolution and development of the human brain. New York: 1928. 1st edn. 2 vols. 1120 pp. Cloth.
(Scientia) $200 [≈ £111]
- Contribution to the study of hypophysis cerebri with especial reference to its comparative histology. Phila: 1911. 8vo. 92 pp. 12 plates, 2 text ills, fldg table. Orig ptd wraps, some chipped edges, uncut & unopened.   *(Elgen)* $65 [≈ £36]

Tiltman, R.F.
- Television for the home, the wonders of "Seeing by Wireless". London: [1927]. 8vo. xix,106 pp. Plates. Orig cloth.
(Weiner) £50 [≈ $90]

Timbs, John
- Hints for the table: or, the economy of good living. London: Kent & Co., 1859. 1st edn. 8vo. W'engvd frontis, title vignette. Orig cloth, blocked in blind & gilt, backstrip faded.
(Sanders) £100 [≈ $180]

Tinney, J.
- A compendious treatise of anatomy. Adapted to the arts of designing, painting, and sculpture ... in which the external muscles of the human body are ... represented. London:

for R. Sayer, n.d. [ca 1762]. Folio. 4 ff, 8 plates. Occas foxing. Contemp wraps. Used.
(Pollak) **£175 [≈ $315]**

Tissandier, Gaston

- Popular scientific recreation in natural philosophy, astronomy, geology, chemistry, etc. [1881-82]. 1st English edn. Roy 8vo. 781 pp. Many wood engvs. Victorian half green calf, upper jnt cracked.
(Sotheran) **£68 [≈ $122]**

- Popular scientific recreation. A storehouse of instruction and amusement. [1890-91]. New & enlgd edn. x,884 pp. Frontis, 1021 text ills. Orig pict cloth, sl worn, new endpapers.
(Whitehart) **£35 [≈ $63]**

Tissot, S.A.D.

- Advice to people in general, with respect to their health ... Translated ... Edinburgh: A. Donaldson, 1766. 2 vols. Contemp calf, red labels. From the library of Colquhoun of Luss. *(C.R. Johnson)* **£250 [≈ $450]**

- Advice to people in general with regard to their health ... Translated ... London: 1768. 3rd edn. 8vo. 620 pp. Jnts weak.
(Goodrich) **£60 [≈ $33]**

- An essay on diseases to literary and sedentary persons. Notes by J. Kirkpatrick. London: 1769. 2nd edn. 12mo. [Bound with] Tissot: Onanism: or a treatise upon the diseases ... 1766. 12mo. Contemp calf.
(Robertshaw) **£136 [≈ $244]**

- The life of M. Zimmermann ... Translated ... London: 1797. 8vo. 154,2 pub list pp. Half-title, port frontis. Lea, front cvr detaching, spine gilt. *(Elgen)* **$75 [≈ £41]**

- Onanism: or, a treatise upon the disorders produced by masturbation ... Translated ... London: for the translator, 1766. 1st English edn (?). 12mo. xii,184 pp. Mod qtr calf.
(Hannas) **£140 [≈ $252]**

Todd, Robert B.

- Clinical lectures on certain acute diseases. London: 1860. 8vo. xl,487 pp. Orig cloth, soiled. *(Goodrich)* **$150 [≈ £83]**

Todhunter, Isaac

- A history of the mathematical theory of probability from the time of Pascal to that of Laplace. London: Macmillan, 1865. 1st edn. 8vo. xvi,624 pp. Binder's cloth, lea label.
(Pollak) **£60 [≈ $108]**

- A history of the mathematical theories of attraction and the figure of earth from the time of Newton to that of Laplace. London: 1873. 1st edn. 2 vols. 8vo. xxxvi,476; 508 pp. Tear in vol 2 title. Cloth. Ex lib.

(Elgen) **$185 [≈ £102]**

- A history of the progress of the calculus of variations during the nineteenth century. Cambridge: 1861. 8vo. xii,532 pp. Fldg plate. Orig cloth, ex lib. Pres copy.
(Weiner) **£60 [≈ $108]**

- Researches in the calculus of variations. Principally on the theory of discontinuous solutions. 1871. viii,278 pp. Text figs. Orig cloth, sl stained. *(Whitehart)* **£35 [≈ $63]**

- Researches in the calculus of variations, principally on the theory of discontinuous solutions. London: 1871. 8vo. viii,278 pp. Diags. Orig cloth, a little worn & soiled.
(Weiner) **£50 [≈ $90]**

Tolman, Richard

- Relativity, thermo-dynamics and cosmology. Oxford: Clarendon, 1924. Sm 4to. 502 pp. Orig cloth. *(Xerxes)* **$40 [≈ £22]**

Tomes, C.S., et al.

- A manual of dental anatomy, human and comparative. 1914. 7th edn. vi,616 pp. 300 ills. Cloth dull & faded.
(Whitehart) **£18 [≈ $32]**

Tomes, Sir John

- A system of dental surgery. London: Churchill, 1887. 3rd edn. 8vo. x,772 pp. 292 text figs. Orig cloth, rubbed. Ex Lewis Library. *(Pollak)* **£45 [≈ $81]**

Tomlinson, Charles

- Cyclopaedia of useful arts and manufactures. Mechanical and chemical, manufactures, mining and engineering. 1852-54. 9 vols. 1052 pp. 40 engvs (some foxing), 2477 w'engvs, 10 pp pub advts. Pub cloth, gilt, sl rubbed & bumped. *(Edwards)* **£100 [≈ $180]**

- Cyclopaedia of useful arts, mechanical and chemical, manufactures, mining and engineering [complete with the Appendix]. London: [1854]. 3 vols. 4to. 3 sep titles, 63 engvd plates, 3,063 w'engvs in text. Contemp half calf, gilt. *(Traylen)* **£150 [≈ $270]**

- Illustrations of the useful arts. No. I. The manufacture of a needle, illustrated ... by specimens of wire in its various stages ... 1855. 1st edn. Sq 12mo. 38,[1],19,[1] pp. 7 ills. Lacking the wire samples. Orig cloth, slip-case. *(Fenning)* **£28.50 [≈ $50]**

Tompkins, B.

- The theory of water finding by the diving rod: its history, method, utility and practice. Private printed, 1899. 2nd edn, enlgd. ix,128 pp. Ills. Orig stiff wraps, later linen spine.
(Whitehart) **£25 [≈ $45]**

Topham, J.

- An epitome of chemistry wherein the principles of the science are illustrated in one hundred entertaining and instructive experiments. 1824. 3rd edn. iv,146 pp. Some scattered light foxing. Orig bds, spine sl defective.   *(Whitehart)* £35 [≈ $63]

Torrey, John

- Outlines of the lectures on chemistry delivered in the College of Physicians and Surgeons of the University of the State of New York. New York: 1929. 2nd edn. 114ff ptd one side only. Cloth-backed bds, bds detchd.   *(Elgen)* $150 [≈ £83]

Totten, J.G.

- Essays on hydraulic and common mortars and on limeburning. Translated ... and an account of some experiments made therewith at Ford Adams, New Port Harbour, R.I. ... Phila: 1838. 1st edn. 256,24 pub ctlg pp. 2 engvd plates. Cloth, spine sunned.
        (Elgen) $100 [≈ £55]

Tow, Abraham

- Diseases of the newborn. Oxford Univ Press, 1937. 8vo. 477 pp. Orig cloth, worn.
        (Goodrich) $50 [≈ £27]

Townsend, Peter

- An account of the yellow fever as it prevailed in the city of New York, in the summer and autumn of 1822. New York: Halsted, 1823. 8vo. 383 pp. Orig bds, rebacked, uncut.
        (Goodrich) $125 [≈ £69]

Townsend, Richard

- Chapters on the modern geometry of the point, line and circle. Dublin: Smith, 1863. 1st edn. 2 vols. 8vo. 300; 400 pp. Half calf by Bickers, rather worn.   *(Oasis)* $50 [≈ £27]
- Chapters on the modern geometry of the point, line and circle. Dublin: 1863-65. 2 vols. xx,300; xx,400 pp. Foxing on half-titles. Contemp blindstamped cloth, rebacked,
        (Whitehart) £35 [≈ $63]

Townshend, Chauncy Hare

- Facts in mesmerism, with reasons for a dispassionate inquiry into it. London: 1844. 2nd edn, revsd & enlgd. 8vo. Orig cloth, short tear in upper jnt, lacking front free endpaper.
        (Robertshaw) £36 [≈ $64]
- Mesmerism proved true, and the quarterly reviewer reviewed. London: Thomas Bosworth, 1854. 1st edn. Lge 12mo. xii,216,[ii] pp. Orig cloth, rebacked preserving spine.   *(Bennett)* £40 [≈ $72]

Tracts ...

- Miscellaneous tracts relating to natural history ... See Linnaeus, Carl

Trade catalogue

- Allen & Hanburys Ltd: General list of drugs, pharmaceuticals and the Allenbury's Specialities. February, 1911. 431 pp. Sev plates & ills. Orig cloth, spine sl marked.
        (Whitehart) £18 [≈ $32]
- Bailey, W.H. & Sons: Surgical instruments and appliances. Illustrated price list. N.d. [ca 1895]. ix,170 pp. Num ills. Orig cloth, badly stained & marked, front inner hinge cracked, 1 gathering a little loose.
        (Whitehart) £45 [≈ $81]
- Baker, C.: Microscopes and accessories. N.d. [ca 1913-14]. 8vo. 76 pp. 89 ills. Orig wraps.
        (Pollak) £35 [≈ $63]
- Barbour, J. & E.R.: Mechanical rubber goods, engineer specialities, steamboat, railroad and mill supplies ... Mechanic Falls, Maine: Poole Bros, n.d. [ca 1890]. 4to. 244,[10] pp. Frontis, 100's of w'cuts. Black cloth, extremities a bit rubbed & frayed.
        (Karmiole) $50 [≈ £27]
- Bausch & Lomb: Microscopy catalogue. N.d. [ca 1910]. 70 pp. Ills. 12 pp supplementary ctlg loosely inserted. Orig ptd wraps.
        (Oasis) $60 [≈ £33]
- Brady & Martin Ltd: Current wholesale prices of drugs and medical sundries and surgical instruments and appliances. October, 1935. vi,201 pp. Num ills. 2 or 3 pp sl torn & creased in outer marg. Cloth sl dust-stained.   *(Whitehart)* £18 [≈ $32]
- Cassala, London: An illustrated and descriptive catalogue of surveying, philosophical, mathematical ... instruments ... Holborn: 1871. 8vo. viii,260 pp. Orig cloth, inner hinge tender.
        (Taylor) £28 [≈ $50]
- Clarke & Page: A catalogue of high-class microscopical preparations, microscopes, objectives, general accessories, &c. N.d. [ca 1890's]. 11,[i] pp. Orig wraps.
        (Pollak) £20 [≈ $36]
- Cooke, Troughton & Simms Ltd: Microscopes developed and manufactured by ... N.d. [ca 1945]. 173 pp. Num plates & ills.
        (Whitehart) £35 [≈ $63]
- Down Bros. Ltd: A catalogue of surgical instruments and appliances, also of aseptic hospital furniture. 1906. iv,2247 pp. 8455 ills. A little foxing. Orig cloth, marked & dust-stained.   *(Whitehart)* £55 [≈ $99]
- General Electric: Equipment and accessories for physical therapy. Chicago: n.d. [ca 1930]. Roy 8vo. 110 pp. Ills. *(Xerxes)* $35 [≈ £19]

- Hearson, Chas. & Co: General and industrial laboratory apparatus. 1930. 4to. xxiv,584 pp. Num ills. Jnts a little weak.
  (Pollak) £40 [≃ $72]
- Hearson, Chas. & Co: The problem solved. [1896]. 21st edn. 148 pp. many text w'engvs. New front bd & spine. (Agricultural equipment). *(Pollak)* £25 [≃ $45]
- Krohne & Sesemann: Illustrated catalogue of surgical instruments and appliances. [1909]. xl,544 pp. Profuse illust. Orig cloth, front hinge weak. *(Pollak)* £100 [≃ $180]
- Leitz, Ernst: Catalogue No. 43 G. Photomicrographic apparatus. [1910]. 28 pp. 2 real photo plates, 10 text ills. Wraps.
  (Pollak) £40 [≃ $72]
- Levi, Joseph & Co: Price list of nautical and surveying instruments ... etc. etc. London: 1891. Sm cr 4to. 76 pp. 125 figs. Orig ptd wraps, spine worn. *(Taylor)* £18 [≃ $32]
- Mappin & Co.: Illustrated catalogue of surgical instruments, appliances, &c. Birmingham: [April, 1891]. 4to. xviii,401 pp. Orig cloth, recased.
  (Bickersteth) £85 [≃ $153]
- Mathews, A.I. & Co: Hints on various subjects connected with our business [Druggists]. Buffalo: 1856. 8vo. 151 pp. Some marg foxing. Limp cloth. *(Elgen)* $55 [≃ £30]
- May & Baker: Price list of chemicals and pharmaceutical specialities. April, 1938. 301 pp. 4 cold, 1 plain plate. Orig paper wraps.
  (Pollak) £30 [≃ $54]
- Rouse Bros: Rouse's dictionary of synonyms for the use of chemists, their assistants and apprentices. London: 1898. 224 pp. Orig limp cloth. *(Pollak)* £25 [≃ $45]
- Standley, Belcher & Mason: Price list of chemical and general scientific apparatus and chemicals. Birmingham: 1927. 4to. [iv],413,[iii] pp. *(Pollak)* £40 [≃ $72]
- Stedall & Co: General catalogue for builders, engineers and contractors No. 20. London: 1946. 4to. xvi,[496] pp. Many ills.
  (Pollak) £25 [≃ $45]
- The Surgical Manufacturing Co: Surgical and scientific instruments and appliances. Hospital and invalid furniture. London: n.d. [ca 1920]. 1312 pp. Ills throughout. Orig cloth, marked, sl worn & dust-stained, new endpapers. *(Whitehart)* £50 [≃ $90]
- Swift, James & Son: Catalogue of microscopes, objectives, oculars and microscope apparatus. 1913. 25th edn. 72 pp. Num ills. Lacking the order form before title. Stiff cvrs. *(Pollak)* £40 [≃ $72]
- Swift, James & Son: Catalogue of microscopes, objectives ... [1910]. 28 pp. 2 real photo plates, 10 text ills. Wraps.
  (Pollak) £40 [≃ $72]
- Thackray, C.F.: A catalogue of surgical instruments, surgical appliances ... Leeds & London: n.d. [ca 1935]. Cr 4to. xxxvii pp prelims, 472 illust pp. Some sl spotting. Orig cloth. *(Bow Windows)* £55 [≃ $99]
- The Unexcelled Fireworks Co.: Unexcelled fireworks of New York and St. Louis. N.d. [ca 1880]. Obl 12mo. B/w ills. 1st & last page worn & torn. Lacking front wrap.
  (Xerxes) $40 [≃ £22]
- The Unexcelled Fireworks Co.: Illustrated catalogue of exhibition [firework] pieces. New York: n.d. [ca 1888]. 63 pp. 55 cold plates. Orig cold wraps. *(Xerxes)* $95 [≃ £52]
- Weller Manufacturing Co: Elevating, conveying and power transmitting machinery for cement mills ... tanneries, brickyards ... paper mills, &c. No. 30. Chicago: 1919. 432 pp. Many ills. Cvrs faded.
  (Pollak) £30 [≃ $54]
- Wooley, James, Sons & Co: Catalogue of surgical instruments and appliances. Manchester: [August, 1931]. xxviii,392 pp. Num ills. Scattered foxing. Cloth, dust-stained. *(Whitehart)* £35 [≃ $63]
- Zeiss, Carl: Microscopes and microscope accessories. 1902. 32nd edn. ;viii],162 pp. 65 figs. Orig bds. (With 2 leaflets, also from Zeiss, on other microscope accessories, and a covering letter from Zeiss, London).
  (Pollak) £60 [≃ $108]

Traill, Thomas Stewart

- Outlines of a course of lectures on medical jurisprudence. Phila: 1841. 1st Amer edn. 8vo. 234,22 pub ctlg pp. Sgntr clipped off front flyleaf, lower marg waterstained through half of book. Cloth.
  (Elgen) $75 [≃ £41]

Trall, Russell T.

- The hydropathic encyclopedia ... New York: 1873. 2 vols in 1. 8vo. 463; 504 pp. 5 cold plates, num text w'cuts. Orig purple cloth, front jnt cracked, spine ends sl frayed.
  (Elgen) $30 [≃ £16]

Travelling Physician ...

- The life of a travelling physician ... See Lefeure, Sir G.W.

Travers, Benjamin

- A further inquiry concerning irritation, and the pathology of the nervous system. London: Longman, Rees ..., 1835. 8vo. viii,444 pp. Contemp half calf, spine rubbed & splitting at hd. *(Pollak)* £50 [≃ $90]

Travers, M.W.
- The discovery of the rare gases. 1928. 4to.
vii,128 pp. Frontis, 21 text ills. Dw sl torn.
Pres copy from Lady Ramsay.
(Whitehart) **£45 [≈ $81]**

Treasure of Poore Men ...
- Here begynneth a good boke of medycynes:
called the Treasure of Poore Men. London: ...
by Thomas Petyt, 1539. 2nd or 3rd edn. Sm
8vo. [iv],44 ff. Title within w'cut border.
Some old anntns on a few leaves. Mor by
Riviere, upper jnt reprd, g.e. STC 24201.
(Pickering) **$3,500 [≈ £1,944]**

Treatise ...
- An elementary treatise on the construction
and use of the mathematical instruments ...
See Oliver, Henry K.
- Treatise of algebra in two books. London: J.
Nourse, 1780. 2nd edn. 531 pp. Many fldg
plates. Lacking bds & endpapers.
(Xerxes) **$100 [≈ £55]**
- A treatise on the arts, manufactures ... of the
Greeks and Romans ... See Fosbrooke, T.D.
- A treatise on the progressive improvement ...
of the manufactures in metal ... See Holland,
John
- A treatise on the virtues and efficacy of a crust
of bread ... See Robinson, Nicholas

Treeby, S.
- The elements of astronomy ... for the use of
schools and junior students. London:
Longman, 1821. 1st edn. 12mo. 204 pp. 8
engvd plates inc fldg frontis. Lacking front
endpaper, sl soiled. Contemp mor, rather
worn.   *(Oasis)* **$45 [≈ £25]**

Treves, F.
- The tale of a field hospital. London: 1901
(later printing). 4to. Red & black text. Mor.
(Goodrich) **$45 [≈ £25]**

Treves, Frederick
- The influence of clothing on health. London:
Cassell, [1886]. 8vo. vi,7-112 pp. 15 text figs.
Many pencil notes in margs & on endpapers.
Orig cloth, shabby, working copy.
(Pollak) **£15 [≈ $27]**

Treves, Sir Frederick
- Scrofula and its gland diseases. New York:
1882. 1st Amer edn. 8vo. 181 pp. Cloth, some
shelf wear.   *(Elgen)* **$45 [≈ £25]**

Tripler, Charles & Blackman, George
- Hand-book for the military surgeon ...
Cincinnati: 1861. 1st edn. 121,xlii pp. Cloth,

front edge of upper cvr worn.
(Scientia) **$225 [≈ £125]**

Trist, Sidney (ed.)
- The under dog, a series of papers by various
authors on the wrongs suffered by animals at
the hand of man. London: "The Animals'
Guardian", 1913. 2nd edn. xx,203,v pp.
Cold frontis, many plates. Orig wraps.
(Weiner) **£40 [≈ $72]**

Trotter, Thomas
- Medicina nautica: an essay on the diseases of
seamen. Comprehending the history of health
in his majesty's fleet ... London: 1797. 1st
edn. 8vo. viii,487 pp. Title sl foxed. Contemp
cloth-backed bds, cvrs loose, spine defective
at hd & ft.   *(Hemlock)* **$400 [≈ £222]**
- A view of the nervous temperament. Troy,
New York: Wright, Goodenow, & Stockwell,
1808. 1st Amer edn. 12mo. 338,[1] pp. Light
browning. Contemp tree calf.
(Antiq Sc) **$275 [≈ £152]**

Trousseau, Armand
- Lectures on clinical medicine ... Translated
and edited. New Sydenham Soc, 1869-82. 3rd
revsd & enlgd edn. 5 vols. 8vo. Some foxing
chiefly to prelims. Orig brown cloth, spines
chipped at hds.
(Frew Mackenzie) **£75 [≈ $135]**
- Lectures on clinical medicine ... Translated
and edited. London: New Sydenham Soc,
1868-72. 1st edn in English. 5 vols. 8vo. Orig
brown cloth, 1 or 2 inner hinges strained, hd
of 1 spine fingered.
(Bow Windows) **£72 [≈ $129]**
- Lectures on clinical medicine, delivered at the
Hotel-Dieu, Paris. Translated ... London:
New Sydenham Soc, 1868-72. 5 vols. Orig
cloth.   *(Scientia)* **$125 [≈ £69]**

Trowbridge, John
- What is electricity? New York: Appleton,
1896. 1st edn. 8vo. vi,[2],315 pp. Frontis, text
figs. Orig cloth.   *(Antiq Sc)* **$75 [≈ £41]**

Trowell, Samuel
- The farmer's instructor; or, the husbandman
and gardener's useful and necessary
companion ... now completed ... by William
Ellis. London: for J. Hodges ..., 1747. 1st
edn. [xiv],276 pp. Engvd frontis. Bottom crnr
shaved without loss. New bds.
(Young's) **£98 [≈ $176]**

Trueta, J., et al.
- Studies of the renal circulation. Oxford: 1947.
1st edn. xix,187 pp. 83 ills. Sgntr on

endpaper. Cloth, spine faded.
(Whitehart) **£25 [≈ $45]**

Trueta, Joseph
- The principles and practice of war surgery. St. Louis: 1943. 1st edn. 8vo. 441 pp. 144 ills. Cloth. *(Elgen)* **$40 [≈ £22]**
- Treatment of war wounds and fractures, with special reference to the closed method as used in the war with Spain. New York: [1940]. 1st Amer edn. 8vo. xiii,146 pp. 48 ills. Cloth, soiled. Ex lib. *(Elgen)* **$35 [≈ £19]**

Truran, William
- The iron manufacture of Great Britain theoretically and practically considered. London: 1855. 4to. x,176 pp. 23 plates (many fldg). Orig dec blindstamped cloth, worn, crnrs bumped, spine torn.
(Weiner) **£95 [≈ $171]**

Tryon, Thomas
- Some memoirs of the life ... written by himself: together with some rules ... in cleanness, temperance, and innocency. London: T. Sowle, 1705. st edn. 12mo. 128 (i.e. 146) pp. Epitaph, 1f, 2 advts pp. Fldg engvd frontis. Calf, sl shelf wear.
(Elgen) **$500 [≈ £277]**
- Wisdom's dictates: or, aphorisms and rules, physical ... divine. For preserving the health of the body ... added, a bill of fare of seventy five noble dishes of excellent food. London: Salusbury, 1696. 12mo. 3ff,144 pp. Browned. Polished calf, gilt, by Bliss.
(Elgen) **$500 [≈ £277]**

Tucker, James
- The reformed Roman or Oriental baths, reviewed as thermo-electrical temples of health; with medical remarks on the nature and scientific treatment of cattle distempers by the hot air bath. Dublin: McGee, 1860. 1st edn. 8vo. 36 pp. Wraps.
(Fenning) **£35 [≈ $63]**

Tucker, Wright
- An inaugural dissertation on the operation of cold: submitted ... to the University of Pennsylvania, for the Degree of Doctor of Medicine. Phila: 1906. Dampstain on title & another page. Disbound.
(Rittenhouse) **$125 [≈ £69]**

Tuke, Daniel H.
- Illustrations on the influence of the mind upon the body in health and disease, designed to elucidate the action of the imagination. Phila: 1884. 2nd Amer edn. 8vo. xviii,482 pp.

Cloth, upper hinge sl weak.
(Rittenhouse) **$85 [≈ £47]**

Tuke, Samuel
- Description of the Retreat, an institution near York, for insane persons of the Society of Friends. York: for W. Alexander ..., 1813. 1st edn. 4to. Lge paper. Engvd frontis, 2 plans. Some offsetting from frontis & title. Contemp half russia, mrbld bds.
(Chaucer Head) **£900 [≈ $1,620]**

Tull, Jethro
- The horse-hoing husbandry; or, an essay on the principles of tillage and vegetation. London: for the author, 1733. 1st edn. Sm folio. 6 fldg plates, imprim lf. Contemp calf, gilt, rebacked. *(Traylen)* **£330 [≈ $594]**
- The horse-hoing husbandry; complete in four parts; or, an essay on the principles of tillage and vegetation ... London: for A. Millar, 1743. 2nd edn [with] A Supplement. 2 pts in 1. Sm folio. 7 fldg engvd plates. Contemp calf, rebacked. *(Traylen)* **£265 [≈ $477]**
- The horse-hoing husbandry ... London: A. Millar, 1762. 8vo. 7 fldg plates. A few crnrs lightly stained. Contemp calf.
(Emerald Isle) **£165 [≈ $297]**

Tully, William
- Materia medica; or, pharmacology and therapeutics. Springfield: J. Church, 1857-58. 2 vols. 8vo. xi,778; 779-1534, viii pp. Mod blue buckram. *(Elgen)* **$165 [≈ £91]**

Turck, Fenton B.
- The action of the living cell. Experimental researches in biology. New York: 1933. 1st edn. 8vo. Ills. Orig cloth.
(Argosy) **$45 [≈ £25]**

Turnbull, A.A.
- Treatise on painful and nervous diseases. London: Churchill, 1837. 3rd edn. 8vo. 162 pp. Plate (stained). Rebound in buckram. Ex lib with stamps. *(Oasis)* **$30 [≈ £16]**

Turnbull, Laurence
- The advantages and accidents of artificial anaesthesia; being a manual of anaesthetic agents, and their modes of administration. Phila: 1878. 1st edn. 210 pp.
(Scientia) **$175 [≈ £97]**
- The advantages and accidents of artificial anaesthesia; being a manual of anaesthetic agents, and their modes of administration. Phila: 1879. 2nd edn, revsd & enlgd. 322 pp. Top & bottom of spine chipped.
(Scientia) **$100 [≈ £55]**

Turner, Daniel
- De morbis cutaneis. A treatise of diseases incident to the skin. London: 1714. 1st edn. 8vo. Advt leaf. Some foxing & age stains. Old calf.   *(Halewood)* £185 [≃ $333]
- Syphilis. A practical dissertation on the venereal disease, in two parts. The fifth edition, still farther improved ... London: for R. Wilkin ..., 1737. 8vo. [xxviii],476 pp. Title laid down, lacking A1 (half-title?). Contemp calf, rebacked.   *(Pollak)* £100 [≃ $180]

Turner, Edward
- Elements of chemistry, including the recent discoveries and doctrines of the science. 1834. 5th edn, revsd & enlgd. xx,1065 pp. A few text figs. A little light foxing. New cloth. Author's pres copy. *(Whitehart)* £55 [≃ $99]
- Elements of chemistry, including the actual state and prevalent doctrines of the science. London: for Taylor & Walton, 1842. 7th edn. Thick 8vo. Orig gilt & blindstamped cloth.
                    (Chaucer Head) £38 [≃ $68]

Turner, J. Edward
- The history of the first inebriate asylum in the world ... also a sketch of the Woman's National Hospital ... New York: the author, 1888. 1st edn. 8vo. 503 pp. Plates, ports, facs. Cloth, sl shelf wear.   *(Elgen)* $120 [≃ £66]

Turner, Richard
- An easy introduction to the arts and sciences ... the present state of electricity, Galvanism &c. London: Rivington ..., 1816. 17th edn. 12mo. xii,276 pp. 3 maps, many text figs. Contemp half calf, mrbld sides, backstrip gilt.
                    (Claude Cox) £20 [≃ $36]

Turnor, Edmund
- Collections for the history of ... Grantham ... memoirs of Sir Isaac Newton ... London: for W. Miller, 1806. 1st edn. Lge 4to. xvi,200 pp. Engvd hand-cold frontis map, 8 engvd plates, 2 engvs in text. Some foxing & offsetting. Contemp half sheep, jnts cracked.   *(Pickering)* $850 [≃ £472]
- Collections for the history of ... Grantham. Containing authentic memoirs of Sir Isaac Newton ... London: 1806. xvi,200 pp. Cold frontis map, 2 engvd plates (ex 8), 2 vignettes. Sm wormhole in map & title. New cloth spine, mrbld bds. *(Whitehart)* £200 [≃ $360]

Turnor, Hatton
- Astra castra. Experiments and adventures in the atmosphere. 1865. 1st edn. 4to. xxiii,530,44 subscribers pp. W'cut vignette frontis, 31 photozincographs, many ports,

num vignettes. Orig bds, worn & rubbed, mor rebacking.   *(Edwards)* £175 [≃ $315]

Tusser, Thomas
- Five hundred points of good husbandry, united to as many of good husswiferie ... now lately augmented ... London: ... Richard Tottell, 1574. Sm 4to. Black letter. W'cut title (mtd). Contemp calf, mor label. STC 24378.   *(Traylen)* £1,600 [≃ $2,880]
- Five hundred points of good husbandry [in verse] ... London: for the Company of Stationers, 1630. 4to. 164 pp. Old calf, respined. STC 24390.
                    (C.R. Johnson) £385 [≃ $693]
- Five hundred points of good husbandry ... A new edition with notes ... and other improvements by William Mavor. London: 1812. 4to. Engvd title, red & black title. Mod cloth-backed bds.   *(Argosy)* $150 [≃ £83]
- Five hundred points of good husbandry ... together with a book of good huswifery ... New edition, with improvements by William Mavor. Lackington, Allen, 1812. 338 pp. Contemp half green calf, gilt-ruled.
                    (Gough) £115 [≃ $207]
- Five hundred points of good husbandry ... London: for Lackington ..., 1812. 2 pts. 4to. Lge paper. Ptd red & black throughout. Contemp calf, rebacked & crnrd in roan.
                    (Hannas) £120 [≃ $216]
- Five hundred points of good husbandry. With an introduction by Sir Walter Scott and a benediction by Rudyard Kipling. London: James Tregaskis, 1931. 4to. xiv,336 pp. One of 500. Hand-made paper. Brown polished calf in orig box. *(Karmiole)* $200 [≃ £111]

Tweedie, Mrs. Alec
- George Harley, F.R.S. The life of a London physician. London: 1899. xii,360 pp. Port frontis. Orig cloth, gilt. Author's pres copy, sgnd.   *(Elgen)* $45 [≃ £25]

Tweedie, Alexander
- Clinical illustrations of fever ... the cases treated at the London Fever Hospital 1828-1829. London: Whittaker ..., 1830. 1st edn. [4],204 pp. Orig cloth.
                    (Claude Cox) £38 [≃ $68]
- The library of medicine. London: 1840. 5 vols. 8vo. Prize calf, gilt, with pres slip (of St. Bart's) sgnd by the faculty.
                    (Goodrich) $150 [≃ £83]

Tweedie, Alexander (ed.)
- Dissertations on nervous diseases by James Hope, J.C. Prichard ... Theophilus Thomson. With American notes and

additions by W.W. Gerhard. Phila: 1840. 1st
Amer edn. 551 pp. lea, scuffed, crnrs worn,
gouge in front cvr. *(Scientia)* **$275 [≈£152]**

Twining, Thomas
- Science for the people: a memorandum on
various means for propagating scientific and
practical knowledge among the working
classes ... London: 1870. 8vo. vii,[i], [9]-136
pp. Orig cloth, spine ends a little worn.
(Pollak) **£25 [≈$45]**

Tyndall, John
- Contributions to molecular physics in the
domain of radiant heat. 1872. 1st edn. xiv,446
pp. 2 fldg plates, 32 text figs. Orig cloth,
spine sl faded & worn at top.
(Whitehart) **£40 [≈$72]**
- Essays on the floating-matter of the air in
relation to putrefaction and infection.
London: Longmans. Green, 1881. xix,338,[1]
pp. 24 text w'cuts. 20th c half calf over mrbld
bds. *(Karmiole)* **$150 [≈£83]**
- Essays on the floating-matter of the air in
relation to putrefaction and infection.
London: 1881. 1st edn. 8vo. xix,338 pp. Ills.
Orig cloth, discold, spine faded & sl frayed at
hd. Lib stamp on front flyleaf, sm blindstamp
on title. *(Weiner)* **£150 [≈$270]**
- Essays on the floating-matter of the air ...
New York: 1884. 338 pp. Orig cloth.
(Fye) **$60 [≈£33]**
- The forms of water in clouds, rivers, ice,
glaciers. London: 1872. 1st edn. 8vo. Orig
cloth, somewhat marked.
(Wheldon & Wesley) **£20 [≈$36]**
- The glaciers of the Alps being a narrative of
excursions and ascents ... the origin ... of
glaciers. London: 1860. 1st edn. 8vo. 444 pp.
Engvd frontis, 5 tinted diags, many diags in
text. Orig maroon cloth, hd & tail chipped,
jnts & crnrs rubbed. *(Bonham)* **£125 [≈$225]**
- The glaciers of the Alps, a narrative of
excursions and ascents. London: 1906. New
edn. 8vo. xxvi,445 pp. Frontis, 61 text figs.
Orig cloth, sl soiled & faded.
(Wheldon & Wesley) **£20 [≈$36]**
- The glaciers of the Alps, being a narrative of
excursions and ascents. London: Longmans
Green, 1911. 8vo. Prize calf.
(O'Reilly) **£30 [≈$54]**
- Heat considered as a mode of motion.
London: Longman ..., 1863. 1st edn. 8vo.
xix,[1],468 pp. Fldg engvd plate, text w'cuts.
Orig cloth, rebacked with orig spine (faded)
laid down, *(Antiq Sc)* **£125 [≈£69]**
- Heat. A mode of motion. London: 1880.
Thick cr 8vo. Fldg frontis, text diags.
Contemp half calf. *(Halewood)* **£35 [≈$63]**

- Lectures on light. New York: Appleton,
1873. 1st Amer edn. 194,[10 advts] pp. Text
w'cuts & line drwngs. Orig brown cloth,
stamped in gold & black.
(Karmiole) **$75 [≈£41]**
- On radiation. the Rede Lecture delivered in
the Senate-House ... May 16th, 1865.
London: Longman, Green ..., 1865. 8vo.
[vi],62,[ii] pp. Frontis. Orig cloth, recased.
(Pollak) **£75 [≈$135]**
- Researches on diamagnetism and magne-
crystallic action ... London: Longmans,
Green, 1870. 1st edn. 8vo. x,361,[2] & 24
advts. Frontis, 9 plates. Orig maroon cloth, a
little worn. *(Pickering)* **$200 [≈£111]**
- Six lectures on light delivered in America in
1872-1873. London: Longmans, Green,
1873. 1st English edn. 8vo. xiv,277 & [2],32
advts. W'cut text ills. Uncut in orig purple
cloth, spine & upper bd faded, inner hinge
split. *(Pickering)* **$150 [≈£83]**
- Six lectures on light. Delivered in the United
States in 1872-3. 1895. 5th edn. 8vo. Frontis,
text ills. prize tree calf, gilt, a.e.g.
(Halewood) **£45 [≈$81]**

Tyson, Edward
- Orang-utang sive homo sylvestris, or the
anatomie of a pygmie compared with that of
an ape and a man. London: Bennet, 1699. 1st
edn. 4to. 2 pts in 1 vol. 108,58 pp. 8 fldg
plates (marg tears), advt leaf at end. Imprim
leaf in photo facs. Rec half calf.
(Oasis) **$2,750 [≈£1,527]**
- A philological essay concerning the pygmies
of the ancients ... Now edited ... by Bertram
C.A. Windle. London: David Nutt, 1894. 1st
edn thus. One of 60 lge paper. 8vo. civ,103
pp. Endpapers browned. Orig parchment-
backed bds, crnrs worn.
(Bow Windows) **£120 [≈$216]**

Tyson, James
- A treatise on Bright's disease and diabetes.
Phila: 1881. 1st edn. 312 pp. Orig cloth.
(Fye) **$100 [≈£55]**

Tyson, James L.
- Diary of a physician in California ... New
York: Appleton, 1850. 1st edn. 92 pp.
Lacking 4 pp advts. Ptd wraps supplied in
facsimile. *(Argonaut)* **$325 [≈£180]**
- Diary of a physician in California ...
including notes of the journey by land and
water ... New York: 1850. 92,[4 advts] pp.
Contemp lib stamp. Later cloth, mor label.
(Reese) **$325 [≈£180]**
- Diary of a physician in California ... New
York & Phila: Appleton, 1850. 1st edn. 8vo.

92.[2 advts] pp. Unif light to moderate foxing, lacking 1 leaf of terminal advts. 3/4 polished calf, sl worn at extremities.
(Heritage) **$250 [≈£138]**

Tyson, Philip T.
- Geology and industrial resources of California. Baltimore: 1851. 2nd edn. 127,37 pp. 3 lge fldg maps, 9 fldg plates. Cloth, in slipcase.
(Reese) **$225 [≈£125]**

Underwood, Michael
- A treatise on the diseases of children with directions for the management of infants ... Phila: 1818. 3 vols in 1. 8vo. Sheep, jnts weak, worn.
(Goodrich) **$105 [≈£58]**

United States Army Base Hospital ...
- The story of U.S. Army Base Hospital No. 5 ... See Cushing, Harvey

United States Sanitary Commission
- The United States Sanitary Commission. A sketch of its purposes and its work. Compiled from documents and private papers. Boston: 1863. 1st edn. 299 pp.
(Scientia) **$85 [≈£47]**

Universal Library ...
- The universal library: or, compleat summary of science ... See Curzon, H.

Unzer, J.A.
- The principles of physiology [with] Prochaska, G. A dissertation on the functions of the nervous system. London: Sydenham Soc, 1851. 8vo. 463 pp. Lacks front blank. Cloth.
(Goodrich) **$75 [≈£41]**

Upham, Thomas C.
- Outlines of imperfect and disordered mental action. New York: 1841. 1st edn. Sm 8vo. 399 pp. Orig mor.
(Oasis) **$100 [≈£55]**
- Outlines of imperfect and disordered mental action. New York: 1855.
(Rittenhouse) **$35 [≈£19]**

Ure, Andrew
- A dictionary of arts, manufactures and mines. New York: Appleton, 1844. V thick sm 4to. 1340 pp. Lea, back hinge cracked.
(Xerxes) **$75 [≈£41]**
- A dictionary of arts, manufactures and mines. London: 1843. 3rd edn. 8vo. vii,1334 pp. Num ills. Half mor, worn.
(Weiner) **£45 [≈$81]**
- A dictionary of arts, manufactures and mines, edited by Robert Hunt. London: 1867-78. 3 vols. 6th, 6th, 7th edns. 8vo. Approx 3000 pp. Orig cloth, lightly worn & discold, 1 jnt

shaken.
(Weiner) **£50 [≈$90]**
- A dictionary of arts, manufactures and mines. New York: 1843. 3rd Amer edn. 2 vols. 8vo. 732; 607 pp. Many ills. Some foxing. Contemp sheep, scuffed. *(Elgen)* **$60 [≈£33]**
- A dictionary of arts, manufactures and mines. 1839. 1st edn. vii,1334 pp. 1241 text engvs. Light scattered foxing. Contemp 3/4 lea, rather worn, top of spine defective & sl waterstained.
(Whitehart) **£90 [≈$162]**
- A dictionary of chemistry ... principles of the science examined anew ... London: 1823. 2nd edn. 8vo. 15 engvd plates (3 fldg). Contemp half vellum, gilt.
(Traylen) **£50 [≈$90]**
- A dictionary of chemistry, on the basis of Mr. Nicholson's; in which the principles of the science are investigated anew ... London: for Thomas Tegg ..., 1824. 8vo. 14 engvd plates (3 fldg). Some spotting. Contemp calf, rebacked.
(Chaucer Head) **£55 [≈$99]**

Urquhart, J.W.
- Electro-motors: a treatise ... For the use of engineers and others. Manchester: 1882. xii,178 pp. 30 text figs. Sgntr in biro on half-title. Gilt-stamped cloth, hd & ft of spine sl defective.
(Whitehart) **£20 [≈$36]**

Useful Arts ...
- A history of useful arts and manufactures. Dublin: 1822. 18mo. 175 pp. W'cut frontis, 6 other full-page ills. Contemp calf, upper spine torn.
(Argosy) **$85 [≈£47]**

Uspensky, J.V.
- Introduction to mathematical probability. New York: 1937. 1st edn. ix,411 pp. 19 text diags.
(Whitehart) **£25 [≈$45]**

Uwins, David
- A treatise on those disorders of the brain and nervous system, which are usually considered and called mental. London: Renshaw & Rush, 1833. 1st edn. 8vo. iv,235 pp. Orig bds, recased, untrimmed.
(Elgen) **$50 [≈£27]**

Vail, Alfred
- The American electro magnetic telegraph: with the reports of Congress, and a description of all telegraphs known ... Phila: Lea & Blanchard, 1845. 1st edn. 8vo. 208 pp. 81 text w'cuts. Light spotty foxing. Orig ptd wraps. Pres copy from Vail & Morse.
(Antiq Sc) **$185 [≈£102]**
- Description of the American electro magnetic telegraph: now in operation between the cities of Washington and Baltimore. Washington: 1845. 24 pp. W'cut ills.
(Jenkins) **$85 [≈£47]**

Valentin, G.

- A text book of physiology. Translated and edited ... London: [1853]. 1st English edn. 8vo. [ii],xxii,684 pp. 5 engvd plates (1 cold), 403 text figs. Short tear in 1 leaf reprd. Rec half calf, mrbld sides.
(Bow Windows) £60 [≈ $108]

Vallory-Radot, R.

- Louis Pasteur, his life and labours by his son-in-law. Translated ... New York: 1885. 1st edn in English. 8vo. xliii,300,6 pub ctlg pp. Ex lib, number on spine. *(Elgen)* $45 [≈ £25]

Van Butchell, S.J.

- Facts and observations relative to a successful mode of treating piles, fistula ... without cutting or confinement. London: Henry Renshaw, 1847. 10th edn. [iv],iv,192, [8] pp. 2 prelim leaves reprd in marg. Orig blindstamped cloth, upper cvr marked.
(Claude Cox) £30 [≈ $54]

Van der Heyden, Hermannus

- Speedy help for rich and poor. or, certain physicall discourses touching the vertue of whey, in the cure of the griping flux of the belly. London: 1653. Lea.
(Rittenhouse) $900 [≈ £500]

Van Dyke, Harry B.

- The physiology and pharmacology of the pituitary body. Chicago: 1936-39. 1st edn. 2 vols. 577; 402 pp. Cloth, vol 2 with dw.
(Scientia) $85 [≈ £47]

Van Heurck, Henri

- The microscope: its construction and management. Including technique, photo-micrography, and the past and future of the microscope. London: Lockwood, 1893. 1st edn in English. Sm folio. xv,[i],382 pp. Frontis, num w'cuts. Orig cloth, gilt, sl worn at edges. *(Antiq Sc)* $250 [≈ £138]

Van Kampen, N. & Son

- The Dutch florist: or, true method of handling all sorts of flowers with bulbous roots ... the particular method of treating the Guernsey Lily. London: 1764. 2nd edn. 8vo. [viii],104 pp. Paper a trifle .browned, a few minor stains. Half calf, rebacked.
(Wheldon & Wesley) £85 [≈ $153]

Van Rensselaer, Jeremiah

- Lectures on geology. New York: E. Bliss ..., 1825. 1st edn. 8vo. 358 pp. Text w'cuts. Some spotty foxing. Uncut in orig bds, front jnt cracked. *(Antiq Sc)* $225 [≈ £125]

Van Swieton, Gerard

- The commentaries upon the aphorisms of Dr. Herman Boerhaave ... concerning the knowledge and cure of the several diseases incident to the human body. London: Knapton, 1759-54-65. 14 vols. Foxing. Contemp calf, rebacked.
(Goodrich) $995 [≈ £552]

Vaquez, H. & Bordet, E.

- The heart and the aorta: studies in clinical radiology. Translated ... New Haven: 1920. 1st edn in English. 8vo. xvii,256 pp. 181 ills, plates. Orig paper-cvrd bds.
(Elgen) $35 [≈ £19]

Varlo, Charles

- The guide of reason, or floating ideas of nature, suited to the philosopher, farmer, and mechanic ... London: 1798. 2 vols. Orig calf, gilt extra, wear to headbands & hinges.
(Reese) $300 [≈ £166]

Vaughan, Victor C. & Novy, Frederick G.

- Ptomaines and leucomaines: or, the putrefactive and physiological alkaloids. Phila: 1888. 1st edn. 8vo. viii,316,16 pub ctlg pp. Fldg chart. Cloth, inner hinges cracked. Ex lib. *(Elgen)* $45 [≈ £25]

Vaux, George

- Mathesis juvenilis: or a course of mathematicks for young students ... Made English from the Latin of Jo. Christopher Sturmius ... London: for Dan. Midwinter, 1708-09. 1st edn. 3 vols. 8vo. 111 engvd plates, some fldg. Contemp panelled calf, a little worn. *(Traylen)* £225 [≈ $405]

Veitch, James

- A fasciculus including a letter to ... Lords Commissioners of the Admiralty on the assimilation of medical departments of the army and navy, in respect of pay ... description of the medico-chirurgical ambulance ... London: W.N. Wright, 1847. 35 pp. Disbound. *(C.R. Johnson)* £30 [≈ $54]

Velpeau, Alfred Armand L.M.

- A treatise on diseases of the breast. Translated from the French. Phila: 1840. 8vo. 83 pp. New bds. *(Goodrich)* $65 [≈ £36]
- A treatise on surgical anatomy or the anatomy of regions ... Translated from the French. New York: 1830. 2 vols. 8vo. 14 plates. Foxed. Sheep, worn. *(Goodrich)* $95 [≈ £52]
- A treatise on the diseases of the breast and mammary region. Translated from the French. London: Sydenham Soc, 1856. 8vo.

xxxii,608 pp. Uncut & partially unopened in orig green cloth, t.e.g., spine faded & torn at hd.   *(Frew Mackenzie)* **£145** [≃ **$261**]

Venn, John
- The logic of chance. An essay on the foundations and province of the theory of probability ... London: Macmillan 1888. 3rd edn. 8vo. xxix,508 pp. A few crnrs creased. Orig cloth, front hinge tender.
          (Pollak) **£50** [≃ **$90**]

Venner, Tho.
- Via recta ad vitam longam. Or a treatise ... for attaining to a long and healthy life clearly demonstrated ... famous waters of Bathe ... concerning tobacco ... London: Flesher, 1650. 8vo. [12],417 pp. Sep titles. Light foxing. Mod calf, orig dec panels laid down.
          (Elgen) **$450** [≃ **£250**]

Ventilation of Mines ...
- On the ventilation of mines ... See Gibbons, Benjamin

Vesling, Johann
- The anatomy of the body of man ... Englished by N. Culpeper. London: Peter Cole, 1653. 1st English edn. Sm folio. xii,192 pp. 24 anatomical plates. Lacking engvd frontis. Contemp panelled calf, rubbed.
          (Goodrich) **$595** [≃ **£330**]

Vestiges
- Vestiges of the natural history of creation ... See Chambers, Robert

View ...
- A view of the general sea-bathing infirmary, in a walk from Margate. Margate: G. Witherden, 1817. 1st edn. 8vo. [ii],16 pp. Possibly wanting half-title. Disbound.
          (Burmester) **£90** [≃ **$162**]

Vince, S.
- A complete system of astronomy. London: 1814-23. 2nd edn. 3 vols 4to. 19 engvd plates. Contemp half calf, gilt, mor labels, gilt.
          (Traylen) **£120** [≃ **$216**]

Vincent, Thomas
- Gods terrible voice in the city ... London: for George Calvert, 1668. 6th edn. Browned. Early 19th c polished calf, snagged at inside front cvr.   *(Waterfield's)* **£60** [≃ **$108**]

Virchow, Rudolph
- A description and explanation of the method of performing examinations in the dead-

house. Phila: 1877. 1st English translation. 86 pp. Orig cloth, top of spine chipped.
          (Fye) **$100** [≃ **£55**]
- Post-mortem examinations [as performed] in the dead-house of the Berlin Charite Hospital. London: Churchill, 1880. 2nd English edn. 12mo. 124 pp. 4 litho plates. 16 pp pub ctlg. Stamp on title. Orig cloth.
          (Oasis) **$60** [≃ **£33**]

Vogel, Hermann
- The chemistry of light and photography in its application to art, science and industry. London: King, 1875. 1st edn. 8vo. 288 pp. 100 ills inc 5 mtd photos. 35 pp pub ctlg. Orig cloth.   *(Oasis)* **$20** [≃ **£11**]

Vries, Hugo de
- Species and varieties. Their origin by mutation. London: 1905. Thick 8vo. xviii,847 pp. Pub list. Cloth, a little worn at hd & tail.   *(Taylor)* **£28** [≃ **$50**]

Wadd, William
- Comments on corpulency, lineaments of leanness ... diets and dietetics. London: John Ebers, 1829. 8vo. Etched frontis, 5 etched plates. Rebound in qtr calf.
          (Hughes) **£85** [≃ **$153**]

Wainwright, John W.
- The medical and surgical knowledge of William Shakespeare ... New York: for the author, 1907. One of 200. Tall 8vo. 81 pp. Port frontis. Bds, t.e.g., upper crnrs & tip of spine bumped.   *(Hemlock)* **$125** [≃ **£69**]

Wakeley, Andrew
- The mariner's compass rectified; containing tables, shewing the true hour of the day, the sun being upon any point of the compass ... London: J. Mount, 1765. 12mo. Foxed. Lea, worn.   *(Argosy)* **$125** [≃ **£69**]
- The mariner's compass rectified. With the description and use of those instruments most in use in the art of navigation. London: J. Mount, 1767. 8vo. 272 pp. W'cuts in text, 1 with moveable dial. Contemp calf.
          (Spelman) **£160** [≃ **$288**]

Waksman, Seman A.
- My life with the microbes. New York: [1954]. 1st edn. 8vo. xii,364 pp. Port frontis. Cloth-backed bds.   *(Elgen)* **$35** [≃ **£19**]
- Streptomycin, nature and practical applications. Baltimore: 1949. 8vo. ix,618 pp. Ills. Cloth. Ex lib, stamp on title, number on spine.   *(Elgen)* **$50** [≃ **£27**]

Waksman, Seman A. & Davison, Wilburt C.
- Enzymes: properties, distribution, methods ... Baltimore: 1926. 1st edn. 8vo. xii,364 pp. Cloth.   *(Elgen)* **$50** [≃ £27]

Waksman, Seman A. & Starkey, Robert L.
- The soil and the microbe. New York: 1931. 1st edn. 8vo. xi,260 pp. Ills. Cloth.
                              (Elgen) **$75** [≃ £41]

Walker, Adam
- A system of familiar philosophy: in twelve lectures. London: 1799. 1st edn. 4to. xviii,571 pp. 47 copper plates. Occas spotting & offsetting. Contemp polished calf, mrbld edges, jnts reprd.
              (Frew Mackenzie) **£180** [≃ $324]
- A system of familiar philosophy: in twelve lectures. London: for the author ..., 1799. 1st edn. 4to. xviii,571 pp. 48 fldg plates on 47 leaves. Orig half calf, a little rubbed, sl worn at top of spine. *(Bickersteth)* **£185** [≃ $333]

Walker, Alexander
- Beauty illustrated by an analysis and classification of beauty in woman ... illustrated by drawings from life ... London: 1852. 1st edn. Frontis, 22 cold lithos. Some spotting. Contemp half calf, sl rubbed.
                          (Robertshaw) **£45** [≃ $81]
- Physiognomy founded on physiology and applied to various countries, professions and individuals. London: 1834. 1st edn. 8vo. 286 pp. 23 plates. Some foxing. Contemp qtr mor.
                          (Goodrich) **£125** [≃ $80]

Walker, George Alfred
- Gatherings from grave yards; particularly those of London: with a concise history of the modes of interment ... from the earliest periods. London: 1839. 8vo. 215 pp. Cloth, spine defective. Author's pres copy.
                          (Goodrich) **£125** [≃ £69]
- Gatherings from grave yards; particularly those of London: with a concise history of the modes of interment ... London: Longman, Nottingham printed, 1839. 1st edn. 8vo. xvii,258 pp. Addtnl engvd title. Orig blindstamped cloth, lightly dampstained.
                          (Claude Cox) **£45** [≃ $81]

Walker, James
- The analytical theory of light. Cambridge: 1904. xv,416 pp. 64 text figs. Orig cloth, marked, back cvr sl defective.
                          (Whitehart) **£25** [≃ $45]

Walkingame, Francis
- The tutor's assistant being a compendium of arithmetic; and a complete question book. London: for the author, 1757. 3rd edn. 12mo. Contemp calf, worn, poorly rebacked.
                      (Waterfield's) **£60** [≃ $108]

Wall, E.J.
- The history of three-color photography. Boston, Mass: 1925. Lge 8vo. [x],747 pp. Num ills & diags. Orig cloth.
                      (Weiner) **£125** [≃ $225]

Wallace, Alfred Russel
- Contributions to the theory of natural selection. A series of essays. London: Macmillan, 1870. 1st edn. 8vo. Orig green cloth.   *(Chaucer Head)* **£120** [≃ $216]
- Contributions to the theory of natural selection. London: Macmillan, 1870. 1st edn. 8vo. xvi,384 pp. Title soiled with lib stamp verso & recto. Rec bds, new endpapers.
                      (Rootenberg) **$250** [≃ £138]
- Darwinism. An exposition of the theory of natural selection ... London: Macmillan, 1889. 1st edn. 8vo. xvi,494 pp. Photogravure frontis, cold fldg map, text figs. Orig cloth.
                          (Antiq Sc) **£125** [≃ £69]
- Darwinism. An exposition of the theory of natural selection ... London: 1889. 2nd edn. 8vo. xvi,494,[2 advts] pp. Port, extndg map, other ills. Orig cloth, extreme edges of spine v sl fingered. *(Bow Windows)* **£70** [≃ $126]
- Darwinism: an exposition of the theory of natural selection ... London: Macmillan, 1889. 8vo. Orig green diaper-grain cloth, sl shaken.   *(Waterfield's)* **£75** [≃ $135]
- Darwinism. An exposition of the theory of natural election ... London: Macmillan, 1890. 8vo. [5],494,[2] pp. Port frontis, text ills. Orig green cloth, recased. 8 line holograph letter, sgnd by Wallace, tipped onto front flyleaf.
                      (Rootenberg) **$400** [≃ £222]
- The geographical distribution of animals. London: Macmillan, 1876. 1st edn. 2 vols. 8vo. xxi,[2],503; viii,[4],607 pp. 7 cold maps (some fldg), text ills. Orig cloth.
                      (Rootenberg) **$750** [≃ £416]
- Is Mars habitable? London: 1907. 1st edn. 8vo. xii,110,[2 advts] pp. 2 plates. Sgntr on flyleaf. Orig cloth, cvrs v sl marked.
                      (Bow Windows) **£85** [≃ $153]
- Is Mars habitable? London: Macmillan, 1907. 1st edn. 8vo. xii,110,[2] pp. Frontis, plate. Orig cloth, dampstain to rear cvr & gutter margins of endpapers.
                          (Antiq Sc) **$75** [≃ £41]
- Island life. London: 1880. 1st edn. 8vo. xix,526 pp. 26 maps & ills. A little foxing.

Recased, with new endpapers, in orig cloth.
(Wheldon & Wesley) **£100 [≃ $180]**
- Island life. London: 1892. 2nd, revsd. edn.
8vo. xx,563 pp. 26 maps & ills, some part
cold. Minor dust marks. Orig cloth.   .
(Bow Windows) **£85 [≃ $153]**
- Island life. New York: Harper & Bros, 1881.
1st Amer edn. 8vo. xvi,522,[4 advts] pp. 3
cold maps, 23 text w'cuts, some full-page.
Stamp on title verso. Orig cloth, label
removed from spine. *(Antiq Sc)* **$75 [≃ £41]**
- Island life. London: Macmillan, 1895. 8vo.
xx,563 pp. 26 maps & ills. Orig green cloth,
spine gilt.   *(Gough)* **£25 [≃ $45]**
- On miracles and modern spiritualism. Three
essays. London: 1875. 1st edn. Sm 8vo.
vii,236,[2 blank],[2 advts] pp. Orig cloth,
spine ends trifle fingered, lower edge rubbed.
(Bow Windows) **£45 [≃ $81]**

Wallace, John
- The farmer's guide in the operations of using
lime, and calcereous substances, as manures,
and in the improvement of texture of soils.
Wigton: for the author, 1826. 8vo. Pub ptd
paper wraps, rebacked, sl soiled & crnrs dog-
eared.   *(Chaucer Head)* **£40 [≃ $72]**

Wallace, William
- The laws which regulate the deposition of
lead ore in veins. Illustrated in colour by an
examination of the geological structure of the
mining districts. 1861. Demy 8vo. Contemp
calf, gilt edged.   *(Halewood)* **£48 [≃ $86]**

Wallace, William Clay
- The structure of the eye, with reference to
natural theology, New York: 1936. 1st edn.
Sm 8vo. 52 pp. 21 w'cuts. Orig cloth, faded.
(Elgen) **$250 [≃ £138]**

Wallis, George
- The art of preventing diseases, and restoring
health ... London: Robinson, 1793. 8vo.
xx,850,[12] pp. Full tree calf, front jnt
cracked.   *(Goodrich)* **$145 [≃ £80]**

Wallis, John
- Cono-cuneus: or, the shipwright's circular
wedge ... a body resembling in part a conus,
in part a cuneus, geometrically considered.
London: for Richard Davis ..., 1684. 4to.
[iv],17,[1] pp. 7 fldg plates. Disbound,
stabbed & tied. Fldg cloth box. Wing W565.
(Karmiole) **$350 [≃ £194]**

Wallis, Thomas
- The farrier's and horseman's complete
dictionary, containing the art or farriery in all

its branches ... London: 1759. Cr 8vo. Calf.
(Halewood) **£45 [≃ $81]**

Walsh, J.H.
- The horse in the stable and the field; his
varieties, management in health and disease,
anatomy and physiology. London: Routledge,
1892. 8vo. x,622 pp. 170 ills. Later half mor,
spine gilt dec.   *(Gough)* **£55 [≃ $99]**

Walsh, James J.
- Makers of modern medicine. Enlarged by ...
the life of Virchow. New York: Fordham
Univ Press, 1915. 3rd edn. 8vo. 441,[[iii] pp.
Frontis. Pub bndg, spine faded.
(Pollak) **£30 [≃ $54]**
- Makers of modern medicine. New York:
1907. 1st edn. 8vo. 362 pp. Port frontis.
Cloth, spine ends sl frayed, untrimmed.
(Elgen) **$35 [≃ £19]**
- Old-time makers of medicine. New York:
1911. 1st edn. 8vo. vi,446,5 list of books pp.
Cloth, untrimmed, cvr spotted. Author's sgnd
pres inscrptn.   *(Elgen)* **$75 [≃ £41]**
- Old-time makers of medicine. New York:
1911. 1st edn. 8vo. vi,446,5 list of books pp.
Cloth, untrimmed.   *(Elgen)* **$60 [≃ £33]**
- Psychotherapy. New York: 1912. 1st edn.
8vo. xv,806 pp. Ills. Cloth.
(Elgen) **$65 [≃ £36]**

Walsh, Michael
- A new system of mercantile arithmetic:
adapted to the commerce of the United States
... Newburyport: Edmund M. Blunt, 1801.
1st edn. 8vo. 252,[4 booksellers' advts] pp.
Crnr of 1 leaf torn away with sl loss. Contemp
tree calf. F. Cabot Lowell's sgnd copy.
(Antiq Sc) **$200 [≃ £111]**

Walshe, Walter H.
- A practical treatise on the diseases of the
lungs and heart, including the principles of
physical diagnosis. Phila: 1851. 8vo. xi,512
pp. Ex lib, sl nick on spine, wear at crnrs.
(Rittenhouse) **$35 [≃ £19]**

Walston, Sir Charles
- Harmonism and conscious evolution ...
London: Murray, 1922. 1st edn. 8vo. xvi,463
pp. Lib stamps. Orig blue cloth. Author's
pres copy to Sir Charles Sherrington.
(Pickering) **$65 [≃ £36]**

Walter, Johann Gottlieb
- Plates of the thoracic and abdominal nerves,
reduced from the original ... London: for
John Murray ..., 1804. 1st English edn. 4to.
50,[2] advts pp. 4 engvd plates, 4 hand-cold

outline plates. Rebound in calf-backed mrbld bds.   *(Pickering)* **$500 [≈ £277]**

Walton, A.J.
- A text-book of the surgical dyspepsias. London: Arnold, 1930. 2nd edn. viii,720,8 advts. Cold frontis, cold plate, 286 ills. Pub bndg, dw.   *(Pollak)* **£25 [≈ $45]**

Walton, R.P.
- A comprehensive survey of starch chemistry. Volume 1 [all published]. New York: 1928. Lge 8vo. 240,iv,360 pp. Ills, diags. Ex lib. Cloth.   *(Weiner)* **£38 [≈ $68]**

Walton, W.
- A collection of problems in illustration of the principles of elementary mathematics. Cambridge: 1858, xii,247 pp. 5 fldg plates. Orig cloth, rebacked, orig spine laid on.
              (Whitehart) **£35 [≈ $63]**

Wanley, Nathaniel
- The history of man; or, the wonders of humane nature, in relation to the virtues, vices and defects of both sexes. London: for R. Basset ..., 1704. 1st edn under this title. 8vo. Final advt leaf. Contemp panelled calf, rebacked.   *(Hannas)* **£45 [≈ $81]**
- The wonders of the little world: or, a general history of man ... collected from the writings of the most approved historians, philosophers, physicians ... and others. London: for T. Basset ..., 1678. 1st edn. Folio. Contemp calf, amateurishly reprd. Wing W709   *(Hannas)* **£95 [≈ $171]**
- The wonders of the little world: or, a general history of man ... A new edition ... London: 1806. 2 vols. 8vo. 7 engvd plates. Contemp speckled calf, spines gilt, extremities rubbed, 1 jnt tender.   *(Clark)* **£40 [≈ $72]**

Warbasse, James Peter
- Surgical treatment: a practical treatise on the therapy of surgical diseases for the use of practitioners and students of surgery. Phila: 1920. 2nd edn, reprint of 1918 1st. 3 vols & index vol. 2700 pp. *(Rittenhouse)* **$55 [≈ £30]**

Ward, Charles H.
- Anatomical laboratory of Charles H. Ward: Human skeletons, anatomical models, anthropology ... Rochester, New York: 1913. 144 pp. Ills. Lower right crnrs of 1st 20 pp sl bent. Orig ptd paper cvrs, lacking lower right crnr without loss of text.
              (Rittenhouse) **$30 [≈ £16]**

Ward, Ernest
- Medical adventures. Some experiences of a general practitioner. London: John Bale ..., 1929. 8vo. xii,291,[i] pp. Frontis, 4 plates, text figs. Orig cloth.   *(Pollak)* **£20 [≈ $36]**

Ward, John
- The young mathematician's guide: being a plain and easy introduction to the mathematics. London: 1734. 6th edn, crrctd. viii,456 pp. Port frontis. A few pp stained at edges & browned. Orig panelled calf, rebacked.   *(Whitehart)* **£50 [≈ $90]**

Ward, Leonard, Electric Company
- Theatre lighting past and present. Mount Vernon, New York: 1923. Lge 8vo. 62 pp. Num ills. Sl loss on 2 pp through damp-adhesion. Stapled (rusty) in orig stylised gilt-embossed pict card cvrs.
              (Weiner) **£40 [≈ $72]**

Ward, Hon. Mary
- Telescope teachings: a familiar sketch of astronomical discovery ... objects coming within the range of a small telescope ... Groombridge: 1859. 1st edn. 8vo. [2],xii,[1], 212,[24 advts] pp. Addtnl cold vignette title, 16 cold plates. Orig cloth, gilt.
              (Fenning) **£55 [≈ $99]**

Ward, Samuel, of Cambridge
- The wonders of the load-stone or, the load-stone newly reduc't ... E.P. for Peter Cole, 1640. 1st edn in English. 12mo. [xxxix],281 pp (pagination erratic). Engvd frontis. Early leaves thumbed. Contemp sheep, jnts splitting. NSTC 25030.
              (Blackwell's) **£475 [≈ $855]**

Ward, William
- The most excellent, profitable, and pleasant book of the famous doctor, and expert astrologian ... to find the fatal destiny ... of every man and child by his birth ... London: for Thomas Vere, 1670. 1 leaf torn at crnr, 2 reprd. Thumbed, worn. Mod calf.
              (Charles Cox) **£145 [≈ $261]**

Wardell, J.R.
- Contributions to pathology and the practice of medicine. 1885. x,807 pp. Cloth, sl marked & worn. Ex lib.   *(Whitehart)* **£35 [≈ $63]**

Warder, Joseph
- The true Amazons; or, the monarchy of bees ... also how to make the English wine or mead, equal, if not superior, to the best of other wines. London: 1742. 7th edn. Sm 8vo.

Armorial b'plate. Calf.
(Halewood) **£95 [≃ $171]**
- The true Amazons; or, the monarchy of bees ... London: for John Pemberton ..., 1720. 4th edn, crrctd. 8vo. xvi,120 pp. Without frontis, title soiled, a little worn at crnrs. Late 18th c calf, rebacked.   *(Claude Cox)* **£75 [≃ $135]**

Wardrop, James
- On aneurism, and its cure by a new operation ... London: for Longman & Co., 1828. 1st edn. 8vo. [xii],117 pp. 3ff explanation. 7 engvd plates (1 with hand-colouring, all detached). Light waterstaining. Uncut in orig cloth-backed bds, worn, inner hinge broken.
(Pickering) **$400 [≃ £222]**
- On aneurism, and its cure by a new operation ... London: Longman & Co., 1828. 1st edn. Lge 8vo. 7 engvd plates (1 hand-cold, 6 tinted). Lge copy in orig cloth-backed bds, spine sl worn. Author's pres inscrptn.
(Quaritch) **$600 [≃ £333]**

Ware, John
- An introductory lecture delivered before the medical class in Harvard University, on the 16th October, 1833. 1st edn. 8vo. 40 pp. Disbound.   *(Antiq Sc)* **$60 [≃ £33]**

Waring, Edward
- Bibliotheca therapeutica, or bibliography of therapeutics ... London: New Sydenham Soc, 1878. 2 vols. 8vo. Orig cloth.
(Goodrich) **$75 [≃ £41]**
- Bibliotheca therapeutica, or bibliography of therapeutics, chiefly in reference to articles of the materia medica. London: 1878. 1st edn. 2 vols. 8vo. 934 pp. Orig cloth.
(Fye) **$100 [≃ £55]**

Warner, John
- On the cultivation of flax; the fattening of cattle with native produce; box-feeding and summer-grazing. 1846. xv,321 pp. A few ills. Cloth dull & dust-stained.
(Whitehart) **£25 [≃ $45]**
- On the cultivation of flax; the fattening of cattle with native produce ... London: W. Clowes, 1846. 1st edn. 8vo. 8 plates. Orig green cloth, gilt.   *(Traylen)* **£30 [≃ $54]**

Warren, Edward
- A doctor's experiments on three continents. Balt: 1885. 613 pp. Stamp on title. Cloth.
(Rittenhouse) **$27.50 [≃ £15]**

Warren, J.C. & Gould, A.P. (eds.)
- The international text-book of surgery by British and American authors. London:

Saunders, 1902. 2nd edn. 2 vols. 8vo. 17 cold plates, num ills. Pub bndg, crnrs & spine ends showing sl wear.   *(Pollak)* **£30 [≃ $54]**

Warren, John Collins
- Address before the American Medical Association at the anniversary meeting in Cincinnati, May 8, 1850. Boston: 1850. 1st edn. 65 pp. Stamp on title. paper cvrs.
(Scientia) **$95 [≃ £52]**
- Effects of chloroform and strong chloric ether. Boston: W.D. Ticknor, 1849. 1st edn. 8vo. 66 pp. Orig blindstamped red silk cloth.
(Hemlock) **$650 [≃ £361]**
- Etherization; with surgical remarks. Boston: Ticknor, 1848. 1st edn. 8vo. [2],v,[3], 100,4 pp. 4 pp pub advts tipped-in. Orig brown cloth.   *(Rootenberg)* **$700 [≃ £388]**
- Surgical observations on tumours, with cases and operations. Boston: 1837. 1st edn. 607 pp. 16 hand-cold plates. Sl foxed. Cloth.
(Scientia) **$1,000 [≃ £555]**

Warthin, Aldred Scott
- Old age, the major involution. The physiology and pathology of the aging process. New York: Hoeber, 1929. One of 230, numbered. 29 plates on japan vell. Beige cloth over purple bds, extremities a bit faded.
(Karmiole) **$30 [≃ £16]**

Wasson, R. Gordon
- Soma: divine mushrooms of immortality. New York: Harcourt, Brace ..., [1968]. One of 680. Folio. xiii,381 pp. 2 pochoir cold plates, 22 cold photo ills tipped-in, 4 cold maps. Qtr blue calf over cloth, spine gilt, slipcase.
(Karmiole) **$500 [≃ £277]**

Waterhouse, Benjamin
- A prospect of exterminating the small pox. Part II, being a continuation of a narrative of facts. Cambridge: 1802. 1st edn. 139 pp. Edges of title worn, old stab holes in gutter. Mod bds, paper spine.
(Scientia) **$600 [≃ £333]**

Waterman, Joseph M.
- With sword and lancet; the life of General Hugh Mercer. Richmond: [1941]. 1st edn. 8vo. xi,177 pp. Port frontis, plates. Cloth, dw.   *(Elgen)* **$45 [≃ £25]**

Wateson, George
- See Whetstone, George

Watson, Alexander
- Compendium of the diseases of the human eye, with practical observations on their

treatment. Edinburgh: Maclachlan ..., 1830. 3rd edn. 8vo. xix,[i],432 pp. 18 plates (10 hand-cold). 2 plates XI, lacking plate IX. Orig cloth, shabby, rear jnt weak.
(Pollak) **£25 [≈ $45]**

Watson, Francis S.
- The operative treatment of the hypertrophied prostate. Boston: 1888. 1st edn. 167 pp. Cloth, extremities worn, inner hinges cracked. Inscrbd "With author's compliments". *(Scientia)* **$95 [≈ £52]**

Watson, Hewett C.
- Statistics of phrenology; being a sketch of the progress and present state of that science in the British Islands. London: 1836. 1st edn. 242 pp. Front cvr lightly stained.
(Scientia) **$275 [≈ £152]**

Watson, James D.
- The double helix. A personal account of the discovery of DNA. London: Weidefeld & Nicolson, 1968. 8vo. xvi,226 pp. 27 plates, 11 text figs. Pub bndg, dw. *(Pollak)* **£30 [≈ $54]**
- The double helix. A personal account of the structure of DNA. London: [1968]. 1st edn. 8vo. xvi,226 pp. 6 pp ills at end, other ills in text. Orig paper bds, dw stained.
(Bow Windows) **£36 [≈ $64]**

Watson, Joseph Y.
- A compendium of British mining ... principal mines in Cornwall ... history and uses of metals ... London: for private circulation, 1843. 8vo. iv,82,2 pp. Subscriber's list. Mod buckram. *(Weiner)* **£75 [≈ $135]**

Watson, Sir Thomas
- Lectures on the principles and practice of physic. London: 1845. 2nd edn. 2 vols. 8vo. Later polished half calf.
(Goodrich) **$45 [≈ £25]**
- Lectures on the principles and practice of physic. London: 1857. 4th edn. 2 vols. 8vo. xvi,871; viii,984 pp. 2 plates. Orig blindstamped cloth, rather worn, spines defective at top & bottom.
(Whitehart) **£25 [≈ $45]**
- Lectures on the principles and practice of physic. London: Longmans, 1871. 5th edn. 2 vols. 8vo. 910; 1040 pp. 2 plates. Contemp prize calf, somewhat rubbed.
(Oasis) **$60 [≈ £33]**

Watson-Jones, R.
- Fractures and joint injuries. Edinburgh: 1943. 3rd edn. 2 vols. xi,960 pp. Num ills. Cloth, sl dust-stained.
(Whitehart) **£40 [≈ $72]**

Watt, George
- The pests and blight of the tea plant, being a report of investigations conducted in Assam. Calcutta: 1898. 8vo. iii,467,xvii pp. Few ills. Orig cloth, crnrs bumped, short tear & ink number on spine. *(Weiner)* **£30 [≈ $54]**

Watt, John James
- Anatomical-chirurgical views of the nose, mouth, larynx, fauces, with appropriate explanations. London: 1809. Folio. [3],34 pp. 4 plates & outline duplicates. Ptd wraps, slipcase, worn. *(Goodrich)* **$495 [≈ £275]**

Watt, John M. & Breyer-Brandwijk, Maria G.
- The medicinal and poisonous plants of Southern Africa ... their medicinal uses ... pharmacological effects and toxicology ... Edinburgh: 1932. 1st edn. Lge 8vo. xx,314 pp. Cold frontis, 25 plates (11 cold). Cloth.
(Elgen) **$50 [≈ £27]**

Watt, Robert
- Cases of diabetes, consumption, &c., with observations on the history and treatment of disease in general. Edinburgh: 1808. 8vo. 328 pp. Foxing. Later half calf.
(Goodrich) **$175 [≈ £97]**

Watts, Isaac
- The improvement of the mind: or, a supplement to the art of logic ... in religion, in the sciences, and in common life. London: for J. Buckland, 1781. 8vo. Contemp calf, worn. *(Stewart)* **£20 [≈ $36]**
- Philosophical essays on various subjects ... with some remarks on Mr. Locke's Essay on the human understanding ... a brief scheme of ontology, or the science of being in general ... London: for R. Ford ..., 1734. 2nd edn. 8vo. Contemp calf, worn. *(Stewart)* **£20 [≈ $36]**
- Philosophical essays on various subjects ... with some remarks on Mr. Locke's essay on the human understanding. London: for Richard Ford ..., 1734. 2nd edn. 8vo. Sgntr cut from title marg. Contemp panelled calf, jnts cracked, hd of backstrip chipped.
(Waterfield's) **£90 [≈ $162]**

Watts, W. Marshall
- Index of spectra. With a preface by H.E. Roscoe. London: Gillman, 1872. 8vo. xvi,74 pp. Cold frontis, 8 plates (1 loose). Some marg pencil notes. Orig cloth. *(Pollak)* **£25 [≈ $45]**

Weatherhead, George Hume
- An account of the Beulah Saline Spa at Norwood, Surrey. London: Hatchard, 1832.

2nd edn. 8vo. Aquatint frontis (offset on title). Orig ptd card wraps, dusty.
(Marlborough) **£70 [≈ $126]**

Weathers, John (ed.)
- Commercial gardening. A practical and scientific treatise ... London: Gresham, 1913. 1st edn. 4 vols. Lge 8vo. Cold & plain plates, 2 cold sectional models. Orig cloth, ornately dec. *(Hughes)* **£30 [≈ $54]**

Webb, Gerald B.
- Rene Theophile Laennec, a memoir. New York: 1928. 1st edn. 8vo. xx,186 pp. 13 plates. Cloth. *(Elgen)* **£35 [≈ £19]**

Webb, Herbert Laws
- The development of the telephone in Europe. London: Electrical Press, 1910. 78 pp. Card bds. Author's pres card bound in.
(Xerxes) **$85 [≈ £47]**

Webb, Marshall H.
- Notes on operative dentistry. Phila: 1883. 1st edn. 8vo. 175 pp. Port frontis, text w'cuts. Cloth. *(Elgen)* **$95 [≈ £52]**

Webb-Johnson, A.E.
- Notes on a tour of the principal hospitals and medical schools of the United States and Canada. Printed and privately circulated by S.G. Asher, Middlesex Hospital Medical School, 1923. 8vo. [ii],87,[i] pp. 4 plates, 1 fldg forms. *(Pollak)* **£30 [≈ $54]**

Weber, Frederick Parkes
- Rare diseases and some debatable subjects. London: Staples Press, 1946. 8vo. 174,[ii] pp. Some ills. Cloth, faded. *(Pollak)* **£25 [≈ $45]**

Weber, Hermann & Weber, F. Parkes
- Climatotherapy and balneotherapy; the climates and mineral water health resorts of Europe and North Africa. London: 1907. 1st edn. 833 pp. Cloth. *(Scientia)* **$125 [≈ £69]**

Webster, Charles
- Facts tending to show the connection of the stomach with life, disease, and recovery. London: for J. Murray ..., 1793. 1st edn. 8vo. [iv],59 pp. Rec cloth.
(Burmester) **£120 [≈ $216]**

Webster, John
- Metallographia; or, an history of metals ... the signs of ores and minerals ... some observations and discoveries of the author himself. London: for Walter Kettilby, 1671. Sole edn. 4to. 388,2 pub advts pp. Wing W1231. *(C.R. Johnson)* **£550 [≈ $990]**

Webster, John W.
- A manual of chemistry ... arranged in the order in which they are discussed at Harvard University ... Boston: 1828. 2nd edn. vi,[iv], 619, [vii-viii] pp. Num figs on 9 plates (8 fldg), few diags. Lightly foxed throughout, sl waterstain. Contemp calf.
(Weiner) **£50 [≈ $90]**

Webster, John
- Elements of chemistry. London: for the author, 1811. 8vo. 245 pp. Old half calf, rebacked, worn. *(Weiner)* **£110 [≈ $198]**

Webster, Noah
- A brief history of epidemic and pestilential diseases; etc. Hartford: 1799. 2 vols. Orig lea, some wear. *(Rittenhouse)* **$375 [≈ £208]**

Webster, Ralph W.
- Legal medicine and toxicology. Phila: Saunders, 1930. 1st edn. 8vo. 862 pp. Ills, inc 4 in color. Orig cloth. *(Oasis)* **$35 [≈ £19]**

Webster, W.H.B.
- Narrative of a voyage to the Southern Atlantic Ocean, in the years 1828, 29, 30, ... in H.M. Sloop 'Chanticleer' ... London: Richard Bentley, 1834. 2 vols. 8vo. xi,399; viii,398 pp. 2 maps (1 fldg), 5 aquatints. 19th c half calf, hinges rubbed.
(Karmiole) **$350 [≈ £194]**
- Narrative of a [scientific] voyage to the Southern Atlantic Ocean, in the years 1828, 29, 30, ... in H.M. Sloop 'Chanticleer' ... 1834. 2 vols. xi,399; viii,398 pp. Half-title in vol 2, 2 maps inc 1 fldg, 5 plates (sl foxed). Half calf, mrbld bds.
(Edwards) **£250 [≈ $450]**

Wedderburn, J.H.M.
- Lectures on matrices. New York: Amer Mathematical Soc., 1934 reprinted 1949. vii,205 pp. Orig cloth.
(Hinchliffe) **£20 [≈ $36]**

Wedgwood, J.J.
- Progress of dentistry and oral surgery. London: 1889. 7th edn. Sm 8vo. [viii],132 pp. 22 figs. Orig cloth.
(Bow Windows) **£36 [≈ $64]**

Wedl, Carl
- Rudiments of pathological histology. London: Sydenham Soc, 1845. 8vo. 637 pp. 172 w'ills. Orig cloth, rubbed.
(Goodrich) **$35 [≈ £19]**
- Rudiments of pathological histology. London: Sydenham Soc, 1855. 8vo. xxvi,637

pp. Orig cloth, t.e.g.
(Rittenhouse) **$35 [≃ £19]**

Weeks, Mary Elvira
- The discovery of the elements. Easton, Pa: 1933. 1st edn. 8vo. 363 pp. Num ills, ports. Orig cloth.   *(Weiner)* **£20 [≃ $36]**

Weiderscheim, Robert
- Elements of the comparative anatomy of vertebrates. London: 1886. 1st English translation. 345 pp. Ex lib. *(Fye)* **$60 [≃ £33]**

Weinberger, B.W.
- Pierre Fauchard, surgeon-dentist. A brief account of the beginning of modern dentistry ... Minneapolis: 1941. One of 100. 8vo. 102 pp.   *(Goodrich)* **$60 [≃ £33]**

Weiner, J.S.
- The Piltdown forgery. London: OUP, 1955. 8vo. xii,214 pp. 9 plates. Orig cloth, dw.
(Pollak) **£25 [≃ $45]**

Weissman, August
- Essays upon heredity and kindred biological problems. London: 1889. 8vo. xii,455 pp. Half-title, diags. Orig cloth, crnrs & spine edges worn. Ex lib.   *(Weiner)* **£50 [≃ $90]**
- Essays upon heredity and kindred biological problems. Oxford: 1891-92. 2 vols. 471: 226 pp. Cloth.   *(Scientia)* **$125 [≃ £69]**
- The evolution theory. London: Arnold, 1904. 1st edn in English. 2 vols. 8vo. xvi,416; [4],405,[10] pp. 3 cold plates, num text figs. Orig cloth. Ex lib with stamps.
(Antiq Sc) **$125 [≃ £69]**
- The evolution theory. Translated ... London: 1904. 1st edn in English. 2 vols. 416; 405 pp. Cloth.   *(Scientia)* **$150 [≃ £83]**
- The germ-plasm; a theory of heredity. Translated ... New York: 1893. 1st edn in English (Amer iss). 477 pp. Cloth.
(Scientia) **$125 [≃ £69]**
- The germ-plasm: a theory of heredity. London: 1893. 1st English edn, 8vo. xxii,477 pp. Diags. Orig cloth. *(Weiner)* **£38 [≃ $68]**

Welch, I.A.
- A popular treatise on tinea capitis, or, ringworm. With a classification of the forms under which it manifests itself ... privately printed, [1837]. Contemp bds, rebacked, remnants of spine preserved.
(Whitehart) **£130 [≃ $234]**

Welch, William Henry
- Papers and addresses. Baltimore: 1920. 1st edn. 3 lge thick 4to vols. 3 port frontis, 3 half-

titles. Cloth, t.e.g., partly uncut & unopened.
(Elgen) **$210 [≃ £116]**
- Papers and addresses. Baltimore: 1920. 1st edn. Numbered edn. 3 vols. Cloth.
(Scientia) **$195 [≃ £108]**

Weld, Charles Richard
- A history of the Royal Society, with memoirs of the Presidents. London: John W. Parker, 1848. 2 vols. 8vo. 8 plates & ills in the text. New half antique calf, orig mrbld bds, mor labels, gilt.   *(Traylen)* **£120 [≃ $216]**

Wells, D.W.
- The stereoscope in ophthalmology with special reference to the treatment of heterophoria and heterotrophia. Boston, Ma: 1928. 4th edn. 107 pp. 34 figs.
(Whitehart) **£18 [≃ $32]**

Wells, E.
- The young gentleman's astronomy, chronology and dialling. 1718-17-17. 2nd edn. 3 parts in 1 vol. [2],148 pp, 19 plates; [3],86 pp; [3],54 pp, 15 plates. Gen title & sep title to each part. Contemp panelled calf.
(Whitehart) **£180 [≃ $324]**

Wells, Samuel R.
- New physiognomy, or, signs of character ... New York: [1866]. 1st edn. 8vo. 768 pp. 1055 ills. Red mor, gilt, gilt spine.
(Argosy) **$150 [≃ £83]**

Wells, William Charles
- An essay on dew, and several appearances connected with it. Phila: 1882. Rec bound.
(Rittenhouse) **$25 [≃ £13]**
- An essay on dew, and several appearances connected with it. Phila: 1838. 8vo. 71 pp. Antique style bds.   *(Goodrich)* **$75 [≃ £41]**
- Two essays: one upon single vision with two eyes; the other on dew ... and an account of a female of the white race ... whose skin resembles that of a negro ... London: 1818. 8vo. 439 pp. Calf, sl cracking.
(Halewood) **£85 [≃ $153]**

Werge, John
- The evolution of photography with a chronological record of discoveries, inventions ... London: 1890. 8vo. viii,312 pp. 4 autotype plates. Orig cloth.
(Weiner) **£150 [≃ $270]**

Wesley, J.
- Primitive physik: or, an easy and natural method of curing most diseases. Bristol: 1755. 5th edn. 122 pp. Sl staining in top of outer

margs. Contemp lea, sl rubbed, spine cracked, inner hinges cracked.
(Whitehart) **£40 [≃ $72]**

- Primitive physik: or, an easy and natural method of curing most diseases. Bristol: 1755. 5th edn. 12mo. xx,[2],25-122 pp. Apparently correct thus. Upper part of margs lightly soiled. Old calf, worn, jnts cracked.
(Weiner) **£100 [≃ $180]**

West, Charles

- Lectures on the diseases of infancy and childhood. London: 1848. 1st edn. 488 pp. Pub ctlg. Cloth, top of spine chipped.
(Scientia) **$275 [≃ £152]**
- Lectures on the diseases of infancy and childhood. Phila: 1854. 2nd Amer edn. 487 pp. Orig cloth.   *(Fye)* **$45 [≃ £25]**

Weston, R.

- Botanicus universalis et hortulanus. The universal botanist and nurseryman. London: 1770-77. 4 vols. 8vo. 17 engvd plates [with] The English flora. 1775. 8vo. [xiii],259 pp. Together, 5 vols. Contemp calf, sl worming.
(Wheldon & Wesley) **£195 [≃ $351]**

Wetherald, R.

- The perpetual calendar ... In three parts ... Chronology ... Solar system ... eclipses ... Pneumatics and hydrostatics ... Newcastle upon Tyne: I. Thompson, 1760. 8vo. viii,150,[2] pp. Title & last leaf trifle soiled. Contemp sheep, rebacked.
(Burmester) **£175 [≃ $315]**

Whately, Thomas

- Observations on modern gardening, illustrated by descriptions. Dublin: James Williams, 1770. F'cap 8vo. [8],207,[24 advts] pp. Contemp tree calf, spine gilt, ornate gilt bands.   *(Spelman)* **£160 [≃ $288]**
- Observations on modern gardening, illustrated by descriptions. London: 1771. 3rd edn. 8vo. [viii],257 pp. Contemp calf.
(Wheldon & Wesley) **£60 [≃ $108]**
- Observations on modern gardening, illustrated by descriptions. London: T. Payne, 1793. 5th edn. 8vo. [8],263 pp. Orig green glazed cloth, some sl wear.
(Spelman) **£95 [≃ $171]**

Wheeler, John Martin

- The collected papers ... on ophthalmic subjects. New York: 1939. xvi,431 pp. 8vo. Port frontis, num ills. Cloth.
(Elgen) **$30 [≃ £16]**

Wheeler, W.H.

- A practical manual of tides and waves. London: 1906. viii,201 pp. Frontis, fldg map, few diags. Orig cloth.   *(Weiner)* **£40 [≃ $72]**

Wheeler, Sir William Ireland de C.

- Selected papers on injuries and diseases of bone. New York: 1928. 1st Amer edn. 8vo. xx,148 pp. Profusely illust. Cloth.
(Elgen) **$30 [≃ £16]**

Whetstone [Watestone], George

- The cures of the diseased in forraine attempts of the English Nation. [L: 1598]. Facsimile edn Oxford: Clarendon Press, 1915. 8vo. [xiv],28,[vi] pp. Orig mock vellum paper cvrs, v sl wear to ft of spine. *(Pollak)* **£45 [≃ $81]**
- The cures of the diseased in forraine attempts of the English Nation. [L: 1598]. Facsimile edn Oxford: 1915. 8vo. [x],28,[5] pp. Orig blindstamped limp paper cvrs.
(Weiner) **£20 [≃ $36]**

Whewell, William

- Astronomy and general physics considered with reference to natural theology. London: William Pickering, 1834. 8vo. [x advts],xv, 381,[3] pp. Some browning & other marks. Orig cloth.   *(Bow Windows)* **£60 [≃ $108]**
- Astronomy and general physics considered with reference to natural theology. William Pickering, 1834. 3rd edn. 8vo. xv,381 pp. Advt leaf. 8 & 2 pp advts tipped in at front. Orig cloth, paper spine label a little rubbed.
(Fenning) **£32.50 [≃ $57]**
- Astronomy and general physics considered with reference to natural theology. London: 1834. 3rd edn. 8vo. xv,381 pp, 1ff. New buckram.   *(Elgen)* **$60 [≃ £33]**
- History of the inductive sciences ... a new edition, revised and continued ... London: John Parker ..., 1847. 2nd edn. 3 vols. 8vo. Without the half-titles in vols II & III. W' engvd text ills. Contemp prize calf, gilt arms on sides, spines gilt.
(Pickering) **$450 [≃ £250]**
- History of the inductive sciences. London: John W. Parker, 1837. 1st edn. 3 vols. 8vo. Contemp tan calf, spines gilt, sides ruled in gilt, spines v lightly rubbed.
(Frew Mackenzie) **£250 [≃ $450]**
- Of the plurality of worlds. An essay. London: Parker, 1853. 1st edn. 8vo. xviii,279 pp. Half calf, gilt coronet & monogram, mrbld bds, sl rubbed. Author's inscrptn to Lord Brougham.
(Titles) **£260 [≃ $468]**

Whiston, William

- An account of the surprizing meteor, seen in

the air, March the 6th, 1715/16, at night. London: Senex, 1716. 1st edn. 8vo. 78 pp. Mod speckled calf. *(Antiq Sc)* **$375 [≈£208]**

- Astronomical principles of religion, natural and reveal'd. London: for J. Senex ..., 1717. 1st edn. 8vo. [iv],xxxii,304, 14,[2 blank],[4 advts] pp. 7 engvd plates. Sgntr clipped from marg of title, staining at beginning. Contemp calf, extremities sl rubbed.
(Pickering) **$500 [≈£277]**

- The calculation of solar eclipses without parallaxes ... some late observations made with dipping needles, in order to discover the longitude and latitude ... London: for J. Senex ..., 1724. 1st edn. 8vo. [iv],94,[2 errata] pp. Half-title, engvd plate. Wraps.
(Burmester) **£80 [≈$144]**

- A new theory of the earth, from the original, to the consummation of all things. For Benj. Tooke, 1696. 1st edn. 8vo. [iv],388,[ii advts],[i errata] pp. Engvd frontis, 7 engvd plates (1 fldg, all foxed), sl marg foxing. Contemp calf, rebacked. Wing W1696.
(Blackwell's) **£220 [≈$396]**

Whitaker, J.R.
- Anatomy of the brain and spinal cord. Edinburgh: 1920. 8vo. xvi,262 pp. 36 full-page plates with color. Sl shelfwear on cvrs, spine lettering much faded.
(Rittenhouse) **$35 [≈£19]**

White, Andrew D.
- A history of the warfare of science with theology in Christendom. London: 1896. 1st edn. 2 vols. 8vo. xxiii,415; xiii,474 pp. Orig cloth, a little worn.   *(Weiner)* **£30 [≈$54]**
- A history of the warfare of science with theology in Christendom. London: 1896. 2 vols. 8vo. Orig cloth. *(Goodrich)* **$45 [≈£25]**

White, Charles
- Cases in surgery, with remarks ... to which is added, an essay on the ligature of arteries by J. Aikin. London: for W. Johnston, 1770. 1st edn. 8vo. xv,198,[4] pp. 7 fldg plates. Light browning throughout. Contemp calf, rebacked. Author's pres inscrptn.
(Rootenberg) **$950 [≈£527]**

- A treatise on the management of pregnant and lying-in women. Worcester: Isaiah Thomas, 1793. 8vo. Foxed. Orig sheep, worn, jnts cracked. *(Goodrich)* **$250 [≈£138]**

- A treatise on the management of pregnant and lying-in women ... the means of curing ... the principal disorders to which they are liable ... Worcester: I. Thomas, 1793. 8vo. [2],vii-xvi, 17-328 pp. 2 plates (1 with marg tear). Title browned. Rec cloth.
(Hemlock) **$250 [≈£138]**

White, Gilbert
- The natural history and antiquities of Selborne. London: T. Bensley for B. White ..., 1789. 1st edn. 4to. [vi],468,[xii index, list of plates],[i errata] pp. Fldg engvd frontis (old reprs to 2 folds), 2 vignette titles, 6 plates. Contemp tree calf, rebacked.
(Bow Windows) **£765 [≈$1,377]**

White, J.S.
- Suggestions to the medical witness. Cambridge: 1891. 1st edn. 228 pp. Orig cloth. *(Fye)* **$50 [≈£27]**

White, James
- Dermatitis venenata; an account of the action of external irritants upon the skin. Boston: 1887. 1st edn. 216 pp. Cloth, inner hinges cracked. *(Scientia)* **$150 [≈£83]**

White, Samuel
- Address on insanity delivered before the New York State Medical Society Feb 5, 1844. New York: 1844. 1st edn 20 pp. Orig ptd wraps, front wrap marg chipped.
(Scientia) **$295 [≈£163]**

White, William
- The story of a great delusion in a series of matter-of-fact chapters. London: 1885. 8vo. 627 pp. Later cloth. Ex lib.
(Goodrich) **$75 [≈£41]**

Whitehead, A.N. & Russell, B.
- Principia mathematica. Cambridge: 1950. 3 vols. Approx 2000 pp. Orig cloth.
(Weiner) **£165 [≈$297]**

Whitehead, Alfred North
- The axioms of descriptive geometry. Cambridge: Univ Press, 1907. 1st edn. 8vo. viii,74 pp. Orig ptd wraps, lightly worn & soiled. *(Antiq Sc)* **$85 [≈£47]**
- A treatise on universal algebra with applications. Cambridge: Univ Press, 1898. Vol 1 (all published). 8vo. xxvi,586,[ii] pp. Orig cloth. Sgntr of John Perry, F.R.S., with his notes in the early part.
(Pollak) **£175 [≈$315]**

Whitehead, James
- On the causes and treatment of abortion and sterility ... London: 1847. 1st edn. 8vo. xxx,426 pp. Errata tipped-in. Plate, text w'cuts. Lacking front free flyleaf. Uncut & part unopened in orig embossed cloth.
(Elgen) **$90 [≈£50]**

Whitehead, T.N.
- The industrial worker. A statistical study of human relations in a group of manual workers. London: OUP, 1938. 1st edn. 2 vols in 1. Lge 8vo. Orig cloth, bit rubbed & chafed. Ex lib with stamps & labels.
(Hughes) £25 [≈ $45]

Whitehurst, John
- An attempt towards obtaining ... measures of length, capacity and weight, from the mensuration of time ... London: for the author, 1787. 1st edn. 4to. [iv],xiv,34, pp. 3 fldg engvd plates. Sm piece cut from crnr of title. Mod mor-backed bds. Author's inscrptn.
(Pickering) £500 [≈ £277]
- An inquiry into the original state and formation of the earth. For W. Bent, 1786. 2nd edn. 4to. [x],233 pp. 7 fldg plates. [with] Observations on the ventilation of rooms ... 1794. 1st edn. 4to. [vi],52 pp. Fldg plate. Contemp calf, rebacked.
(Bickersteth) £250 [≈ $450]
- An inquiry into the original state and formation of the earth; deduced from facts and the laws of nature. London: for W. Bent, 1786. 2nd edn. 4to. Half-title, port frontis (offset to title), 7 plates (6 fldg). Frontis & title waterstained. Mod bds.
(Chaucer Head) £180 [≈ $324]

Whitlaw, Charles
- A treatise on the causes and effects of inflammation, fever, cancer, scrofula. and nervous affections. London: the author, 1831. 1st edn. 8vo. xxxii,304 pp. Contemp ms amendment to imprint. Contemp cloth, new ptd paper label. *(Deighton Bell)* £55 [≈ $99]
- A treatise on the causes and effects of inflammation, fever, cancer, scrofula. and nervous affections. London: 1831. 8vo. [1],xxxii,304 pp. Foxing. Orig bds, recased, spine sunned, uncut. *(Goodrich)* $85 [≈ £47]

Whitley, N.
- The application of geology to agriculture, and to the improvement and valuation of land. 1843. 1st edn. 162,32 pp. Fldg chart, pub ctlg at end. New cloth. *(Whitehart)* £55 [≈ $99]

Whittaker, E.T.
- A course of modern analysis. Cambridge: Univ Press, 1902. 1st edn. Tall 8vo. xvi,378 pp. Orig cloth, spine sl torn at hd.
(Antiq Sc) $100 [≈ £55]
- A treatise on the analytical dynamics of particles and rigid bodies. Cambridge: 1904. 1st edn. Lge 8vo. xiii,414 pp. Orig cloth, discold at fore-edge. *(Weiner)* £30 [≈ $54]

Whittaker, Sir Edmund
- A history of the theories of aether and electricity. London: Nelson, 1962-61. 2 vols. 8vo. xiv,434; xi,319,[i] pp. Pub bndg.
(Pollak) £50 [≈ $90]

Whytt, Robert
- Observations on the nature, causes, and cure of those disorders ... commonly called nervous hypochondriac, or hysteric. Edinburgh: & London: T. Becket ..., 1765. 1st edn. 8vo. [4],viii,[8], 520,[2] pp. Some light browning. Rec bds, half mor slipcase.
(Rootenberg) $1,500 [≈ £833]

Wickes, Stephen
- History of medicine in New Jersey. Newark: 1879. 8vo. 449 pp. Front flyleaf lacking. Orig cloth, worn & soiled. *(Goodrich)* $95 [≈ £52]

Widdess, J.D.H.
- A history of the Royal College of Physicians of Ireland 1654-1963. Edinburgh: 1963. xii,255 pp. 10 plates. Dw.
(Whitehart) £25 [≈ $45]
- The Royal College of Surgeons in Ireland and its Medical School 1784-1966. Edinburgh: 1967. 2nd edn. [viii],152 pp. 21 plates. Dw.
(Whitehart) £18 [≈ $32]

Wiedersheim, R.
- The structure of man. An index to his past history. 1895. xxi,227 pp. 105 ills. Light foxing. *(Whitehart)* £18 [≈ $32]

Wiener, A.S.
- Blood groups and blood transfusions. Springfield: 1935. xiv,220 pp. 41 text figs. Cloth, marked, ex lib.
(Whitehart) £18 [≈ $32]

Wiggers, Carl
- The pressure pulses in the cardiovascular system. London: 1928. 1st edn. 200 pp. Cloth. *(Scientia)* $150 [≈ £83]

Wightman, W.P.D.
- Science and the Renaissance ... emergence of science in the sixteenth century. Edinburgh: for the Univ of Aberdeen, 1962. 1st edn. 2 vols. 8vo. Plates. Orig red cloth, gilt, cvrs sl marked, dws. *(Hughes)* £28 [≈ $50]

Wild, James John
- Thalassa. An essay on the depth, temperature and currents of the ocean. 1877. Roy vo. Cold charts & diags. Orig dec cloth gilt.
(Halewood) £48 [≈ $86]

Wilder, Alexander
- History of medicine. A brief outline of medical history of sects of physicians ... and especially ... the American eclectic practice of medicine ... New Sharon: 1904. 1st edn. 946 pp. Orig cloth. *(Fye)* **$100 [≈£55]**

Wildman, Thomas
- A treatise on the management of bees ... various methods of cultivating them ... London: for the author, 1768. 1st edn. 4to. xx,170 pp. 3 lge fldg copperplates. Some foxing to title & plates. Contemp faded grey bds, spine russia, gilt. *(Gough)* **£435 [≈$783]**
- A treatise on the management of bees ... various methods of cultivating them ... London: for the author, 1768. 1st edn. xx,169 pp, 1f, 5 pp, 3 fldg plates. Some worming, reprd. Calf, rebacked. *(Titles)* **£480 [≈$864]**

Wiles, Philip
- Essentials of orthopaedics. London: Churchill, 1949. 8vo. xv,[i],486 pp. 7 cold plates, 365 ills. Pub bndg, dw. *(Pollak)* **£20 [≈$36]**

Wilkes, M.V.
- Automatic digital computers. New York: Wiley, 1956. Photos, lge fldg chart. Minor underlining in red pencil. *(Xerxes)* **$55 [≈£30]**

Wilkins, John
- Mathematicall magick. or the wonders that may be performed by mechanicall geometry. In two books. London: Sa. Gellibrand, 1648. 1st edn. F'cap 8vo. [14],295 pp. Text ills, 4 full-page. Wide margs. Lacking prelim blank A1. Contemp calf, rebacked. Wing W2198. *(Spelman)* **£600 [≈$1,080]**

Wilkinson, Charles Henry
- Elements of galvanism, in theory and practice ... its history ... London: Murray, 1804. 1st edn. 2 vols. 8vo. xvi,468; xii,[2], 473,[40] pp. Engvd frontis, 12 copperplates (2 fldg, 1 hand-cold). Sporadic browning, marg dampstain to plates vol I. Orig calf. *(Rootenberg)* **£850 [≈$472]**

Wilkinson, G. & Gray, A.A.
- The mechanism of the cochlea. A restatement of the resonance theory of hearing. London: 1924. 1st edn. 253 pp. Cloth. *(Scientia)* **$95 [≈£52]**
- The mechanism of the cochlea. 1924. xx,253 pp. 4 plates, 50 text figs. Cloth sl dust-stained. *(Whitehart)* **£18 [≈$32]**

Wilkinson, George
- Experiments and observations on the cortex salicis latifoliae or broad-leafed willow bark. Newcastle upon Tyne: for the author, [1803]. 1st edn. 8vo. [14],118 pp. Hand-cold engvd frontis. Minor browning throughout. Contemp half calf, spine gilt. *(Rootenberg)* **$400 [≈£222]**

Wilks, Samuel
- Lectures on diseases of the nervous system delivered at Guy's Hospital. Phila: 1883. 2nd edn, much enlgd. 602 pp. Stamp on title. Cloth, edges of spine reprd. *(Scientia)* **$75 [≈£41]**

Willan, Robert
- On cutaneous diseases. Vol I [all published]. Phila: 1809. 1st Amer edn. 422 pp. Foxed, section removed from top of title without loss of text. Lea. *(Scientia)* **$195 [≈£108]**

Williams, C.W.
- The combustion of coal and the prevention of smoke chemically and practically considered. London: John Weale, 1854. 1st edn. Ills. Orig gilt-lettered red cloth. *(Chaucer Head)* **£65 [≈$117]**
- The combustion of coal and the prevention of smoke chemically and practically considered. Part the First [all published]. Liverpool: 1840. 1st edn. 8vo. x,151 pp. 11 plates (some fldg), diags. Orig cloth, reprd. *(Weiner)* **£100 [≈$180]**

Williams, Charles
- Principles of medicine. Phila: 1848. 3rd Amer edn. 440 pp. Lea. *(Fye)* **$40 [≈£22]**

Williams, Charles J.B.
- A practical treatise on the diseases of the respiratory organs ... With additions and notes by Meredith Clymer. Phila: 1845. 8vo. vii,508 pp. Pub ctlg. Some light foxing. Cvrs scuffed, lea spine dry. *(Rittenhouse)* **$35 [≈£19]**
- A rational exposition of the physical signs of the diseases of the lungs and pleura ... Phila: 1830. 1st Amer edn. 4to. xii,13-203, [2] pp. Uncut in orig linen-backed bds. *(Hemlock)* **$250 [≈£138]**

Williams, Henry W.
- Recent advances in ophthalmic science. The Boylston Prize Essay for 1865. Boston: 1866. 1st edn. 166 pp. 6 charts. Perf stamp on title. Cloth, hd of spine chipped. *(Scientia)* **$100 [≈£55]**

Williams, J. Whitridge
- Obstetrics; a text-book for the use of students and practitioners. New York: 1903. 1st edn. 845 pp. Half lea, crnrs worn.
  (Scientia) **$200 [≈£111]**

Williams, J.F. Lake
- An historical account of inventions and discoveries in those arts and sciences which are of utility or ornament to man ... London: 1820. 2 vols. 8vo. vii,387; 500 pp. Frontis to vol I, red & black titles. Orig paper-backed bds, cvrs loose or detchd.
  (Weiner) **£65 [≈$117]**

Williams, Jonathan
- Thermometrical navigation. Phila: R. Aitken, 1799. 1st edn. 8vo. xii,98,[3] pp. Lge fldg engvd chart (short tear at fold), mtd errata slip. Lib perforation on title. Old buckram.
  (Antiq Sc) **$800 [≈£444]**

Williams, Stephen
- American medical biography, or memoirs of eminent physicians ... Greenfield: 1845. 8vo. 664 pp. Plates. Dampstained. Orig binding, rebacked.
  (Goodrich) **$85 [≈£47]**

Williams, W. Roger
- The natural history of cancer, with special reference to its causation and prevention. New York: 1908. 1st Amer edn. Lge 8vo. xiv,519 pp. Text ills. Cloth.
  (Elgen) **$55 [≈£30]**

Williamson, George
- Memorials of the lineage, early life, education and development of the genius of James Watt. Edinburgh: for the Watt Club, 1856. 4to. 3 engvd ports, 8 facs, facs map, 5 ills. Bds, mor label, gilt.
  (Traylen) **£55 [≈$99]**

Williamson, R.T.
- Diseases of the spinal cord. Oxford: 1908. xi,432 pp. 7 plates, 183 text figs. Lib stamp on half-title & title. Orig cloth, spine sl marked.
  (Whitehart) **£25 [≈$45]**

Willich, A.F.M.
- Lectures on diet and regimen ... the most rational means of preserving health and prolonging life ... London: 1800. 3rd edn. Demy 8vo. 674 pp. Advts. Contemp half calf.
  (Halewood) **£65 [≈$117]**

Willius, F.A. & Keys, T.E.
- Cardiac classics. A collection of classic works on the heart and circulation ... St. Louis: 1941. 1st edn. 8vo. 858 pp. Orig cloth.
  (Goodrich) **$90 [≈£50]**
- Cardiac classics. A collection of classic works on the heart and circulation ... St. Louis: 1941. 1st edn. Lge 8vo. xix,858 pp. Num ills, plates. Lib stamps on endpapers. Orig cloth.
  (Elgen) **$90 [≈£50]**

Willius, Fredrick A.
- Clinical electrocardiagrams. Phila: 1929. 1st edn. 4to. 219 pp. Cloth, spine ends frayed, spotted.
  (Elgen) **$35 [≈£19]**

Willson, Robert
- Medical men at the time of Christ. Phila: 1910. 8vo. 157 pp. Orig cloth.
  (Goodrich) **$65 [≈£36]**

Wilmer, B.
- Cases and remarks in surgery to which is subjoined an appendix, containing the method of curing the bronchocele in Coventry. London: 1779. 1st edn. 8vo. 10,260 pp. 2 plates. Half calf.
  (Halewood) **£95 [≈$171]**

Wilmer, William H.
- Atlas fundus oculi. New York: 1934. Lge 8vo. 100 cold plates. Cloth.
  (Rittenhouse) **$95 [≈£52]**

Wilson, Duncan K.
- The history of mathematical teaching in Scotland to the end of the eighteenth century. Univ of London Press, 1935. 8vo. viii,99,[i] pp. 2 plates. Pub bndg, dw.
  (Pollak) **£20 [≈$36]**

Wilson, Edmund B.
- An atlas of the fertilization and karyokinesis of the ovum. New York: 1895. 1st edn. Folio. 32 pp. 10 plates. Cloth, extremities worn white ink number on spine.
  (Scientia) **$275 [≈£152]**
- The cell in development and inheritance. New York: Macmillan, 1896. 1st edn. 8vo. xvi,371,[5 pub advts] pp. Text figs. Orig cloth, sl nick to spine.
  (Antiq Sc) **$275 [≈£152]**
- The cell in development and heredity. New York: 1925. 3rd edn. 1232 pp. Sgntr on title. Cloth, lightly stained. *(Scientia)* **$100 [≈£55]**

Wilson, Erasmus
- On diseases of the skin. London: Churchill, 1851. 3rd edn. 8vo. 519 pp. 15 plates (8 cold). Calf, gilt, spine a little damaged.
  (Oasis) **$85 [≈£47]**
- A system of human anatomy, general and special. Phila: 1853. 4th Amer edn. 8vo.

576,32 pub ctlg pp. Frontis, 251 w'cuts. Sheep, rubbed, lib stamps on endpapers.
(Oasis) **$50 [≈ £27]**

Wilson, Erasmus (ed.)
- Hufeland's Art of Prolonging Life. Phila: 1867. 8vo. xii,298 pp. Cloth, shaken, sl chipping at hd & ft of spine.
(Rittenhouse) **$27.50 [≈ £15]**

Wilson, F.P.
- Plague in Shakespeare's London. Oxford: 1927. 8vo. 228 pp. Orig cloth.
(Goodrich) **$75 [≈ £41]**

Wilson, Frank
- Selected papers ... Edited by Franklin D. Johnston ... Ann Arbor: 1954 [i.e. 1955]. 1st edn, 2nd ptg. xlvi,1090 pp. Port frontis, num ills. Cloth.   *(Elgen)* **$75 [≈ £41]**

Wilson, John M.
- The rural cyclopaedia, or a general dictionary of agriculture, and of the arts, sciences, instruments and practice ... Edinburgh: 1847-49. 6 vols. 4to. 66 engvd plates (7 in col). Contemp half green calf, gilt panelled spines.   *(Traylen)* **£150 [≈ £270]**

Wilson, May G.
- Rheumatic fever. Studies of the epidemiology, manifestations, and treatment of the disease during the first three decades. New York: 1940. 1st edn. Lge 8vo. xiv,595 pp. Port frontis, ills, plates, fldg charts. Cloth.   *(Elgen)* **$40 [≈ £22]**

Wilson, Robert
- A treatise on steam boilers; their strength, construction, and economical working. London: Lockwood, 1879. 5th edn. Cr 8vo. Fldg frontis, advts at beginning, ctlgs at end. Orig cloth.   *(Stewart)* **£25 [≈ $45]**

Wilson, Samuel A. Kinnier
- Modern problems in neurology. New York: 1929. 1st Amer edn. 364 pp. Cloth, spine edges rubbed.   *(Scientia)* **$95 [≈ £52]**
- Neurology. Edited by A.N. Bruce. Balt: 1940. 1st Amer edn. 2 vols. 1838 pp. Cloth.
(Scientia) **$300 [≈ £166]**

Wilson, William
- The philosophy of physic; or, the natural history of diseases and their cure. Dublin: Graisberry & Campbell, 1804. 1st edn. Sm 8vo. vi,xxxiv,329, ii pp. Foxed. Orig wraps, v worn & chipped.   *(Elgen)* **$85 [≈ £47]**

Wilton, George
- Fingerprints: history, law and romance. London: 1938. 8vo. xix,317 pp. Port frontis, ills, ports, facs. Cloth, dw.
(Elgen) **$30 [≈ £16]**

Wimpey, Joseph
- Rural improvements: or, essays on the most rational methods of improving estates; accomodated to the soil, climate, and circumstances of England ... London: for J. Dodsley, 1775. 1st edn. 8vo. Contemp bds, new cloth spine, mor label, gilt, edges uncut.
(Traylen) **£85 [≈ $153]**

Wintringham, Sir Clifton
- An enquiry into the exility of the vessels of the human body: wherein animal identity is explained ... London: for Thomas Osborne, 1743. 1st edn. 8vo. Wellcome Lib release stamp on title verso. Contemp calf.
(Quaritch) **$325 [≈ £180]**

Wirtzung, Christopher
- The general practice of physick. Containing all inward and outward parts of the body ... now translated into English ... London: for J.L. ..., 1654. Folio. [10],818,[37] pp. Lacking final 7 index leaves, foxed & dampstained, early anntns. New half calf.
(Goodrich) **$295 [≈ £163]**

Wiseman, Eugene G.
- A treatise on blood pressure in ocular work ... factors of interest to refractionists. Rochester, New York: [1916]. 8vo. xviii,267 pp. Cold frontis, text ills. Cloth. Author's pres copy.
(Elgen) **$30 [≈ £16]**

Wiseman, Richard
- Severall chirurgicall treatises. London: 1676. 1st edn. Folio. [xvi],498. 79,[15] pp. Contemp mor, gilt panelled sides, a.e.g.
(Fye) **$3,000 [≈ £1,666]**

Wistar, Caspar
- A system of anatomy ... with notes and additions by William E. Horner and Joseph Pancoast. Phila: 1846. 9th edn. 2 vols. 538; 622 pp. 12 partly hand-cold engvd plates, 227 w'cut ills. Lea, scuffed.   *(Fye)* **$100 [≈ £55]**

Witchell, E.
- The geology of Stroud and the area drained by the Frome. Stroud: 1882. 1st edn. 8vo. viii,108 pp. 5 engvd plates. Orig cloth.
(Bow Windows) **£55 [≈ $99]**

Withering, William
- An arrangement of British plants; according to the latest improvement of the Linnean System. Birmingham: for the author, 1796. 3rd edn. 4 vols. All half-titles & 31 plates as called for, 1 cold, some fldg. Contemp sheep, bndgs worn & shabby. *(Pollak)* £35 [≈ $63]

Wittgenstein, Ludwig
- Remarks on the foundations of mathematics. Edited ... Translated ... Oxford: 1967. 2nd edn. 8vo. Parallel English & german text. Orig cloth, dw. *(Bow Windows)* £18 [≈ $32]

Wittman, William
- Travels in Turkey [etc] ... 1799 [-] 1801 ... Observations on the plague, and diseases prevalent in Turkey ... Phillips, 1803. 1st edn. 4to. xvi,595,[1 advt] pp. Frontis (browned), map , 22 plates (16 cold, 1 fldg). Contemp calf, rebacked, crnrs bumped.
  (Frew Mackenzie) £550 [≈ $990]

Wolbach, Simeon B., et al.
- The etiology and pathology of typhus. Cambridge: 1922. 1st edn. 4to. 222 pp. 34 plates. Cloth. *(Scientia)* $150 [≈ £83]

Wolf, A.
- A history of science, technology and philosophy in the 16th and 17th centuries. New York: 1935. 1st edn. 8vo. 692 pp. 316 ills, many plates. Orig cloth.
  (Argosy) $85 [≈ £47]
- A history of science, technology and philosophy in the 16th and 17th centuries. 1935. xxvii,692 pp. 316 ills inc frontis. Lib stamps on frontis verso, title & title verso. Orig cloth, rebacked, orig spine laid on.
  (Whitehart) £35 [≈ $63]

Wollaston, William
- The religion of nature delineated. London: Palmer, 1725. 4to. 219 pp. Old calf, rubbed, rebacked. *(Goodrich)* $150 [≈ £83]

Wolley, Hannah
- The Queen-like closet. or rich cabinet ... rare receipts for preserving, candying and cookery ... a supplement ... London: for R. Chiswel ..., 1681-84. 4th edn. 12mo. Imprim leaf, w'engvd frontis. Lacks A5 (dedn leaf). A little wear to crnrs & margs. Mod calf.
  (Gough) £545 [≈ $981]

Wood, Edward Jenner
- A treatise on pellagra. New York: 1912. 1st edn. xv,377 pp. Port frontis, 38 ills. Cloth.
  (Elgen) $40 [≈ £22]

Wood, George B.
- A treatise on therapeutics, and pharmacology or materia medica. Phila: 1856. 1st edn. 2 vols. Lea, wear to hd of spines. Ex lib.
  (Fye) $75 [≈ £41]

Wood, Horatio
- Thermic fever, or sunstroke. Phila: 1872. 1st edn. 128 pp. Pub ctlg. Cloth.
  (Scientia) $100 [≈ £55]

Wood, William
- The history and antiquities of Eyam; with a minute account of the Great Plague which desolated that village in 1666. 1859. 3rd edn. 8vo. W'engvd plates. Orig cloth, faded.
  (Deighton Bell) £30 [≈ $54]

Woodcroft, B.
- The pneumatics of Hero of Alexandria from the original Greek. 1851. 1st edn. xix,117 pp. Engvd half-title, text ills. Orig blindstamped cloth, rebacked, orig spine laid on.
  (Whitehart) £60 [≈ $108]

Woodhead, W.H.
- Human frailty: or physiological researches into the causes and effects of diseases of the generative system. The author, n.d. [ca 1850]. 17th edn. 117 pp. 2 w'cuts. New qtr calf, orig wraps bound in. *(Oasis)* $50 [≈ £27]

Woodhouse, Robert
- The principles of analytical calculations. Cambridge: 1803. 1st edn. 4to. [3],xxxiv,219 pp. Title sl browned around edges. Contemp tree calf, rebacked, spine gilt.
  (Whitehart) £180 [≈ $324]
- A treatise on isoperimetral problems and the calculus of variations. Cambridge: 1810. 8vo. x,154 pp. Diags. New grey bds.
  (Weiner) £50 [≈ $90]
- A treatise on plane and spherical trigonometry. Cambridge: 1822. 4th edn. v,v,264 pp. Uncut in mod cloth.
  (Whitehart) £25 [≈ $45]

Woodruff, C.E.
- Medical ethnology. [1916]. viii,321 pp. Sl stain in bottom marg of final few pp. Back cvr marked & stained, spine faded, new endpapers. *(Whitehart)* £25 [≈ $45]

Woodville, William
- A history of the inoculation of the smallpox, in Great Britain ... review of all publications on the subject ... experimental inquiry into the relative advantages of every measure ... London: 1796. Vol 1 [all published]. 1st edn.

387 pp. Frontis. Mod qtr lea.
(Scientia) **$295 [≈ £163]**

Woodward, Charles
- A familiar introduction to the study of polarized light; ... using the hydro-oxygen polariscope and microscope. London: for Smith, Beck & Beck, 1861. 3rd edn. 8vo. 54 pp. Text w'cuts (2 cold). Uniform light browning. Orig cloth, bit worn.
(Antiq Sc) **$125 [≈ £69]**

Woodward, H.B.
- The history of the Geological Society of London. London: 1907. 8vo. xix,336 pp. Cold frontis, 27 plates. Uncut. Orig cloth.
(Weiner) **£30 [≈ $54]**

Woodward, J.J., et al.
- The medical and surgical history of the War of the Rebellion, 1861-65. Wash: 1870-88. Lge 4to. 6 vols. All 1st edns (1 vol 2nd iss). Num plates, inc chromolithos, text engvs, maps. Orig green cloth, 2 vols with spine ends frayed & inner hinges cracked.
(Elgen) **$950 [≈ £527]**
- The medical and surgical history of the War of the Rebellion, 1861-65. Wash: 1870-88. Lge 4to. 6 vols. Some vols 2nd iss. Orig green cloth, some vols shaken with wear to extremities. *(Fye)* **$1,000 [≈ £555]**

Woodward, John
- Fossils of all kinds, digested into a method, suitable to their mutual relation and affinity ... London: for William Innys, 1728. 1st edn. 8vo. xvi,56,131 pp with 4 unnumbered pp between pp 92 & 93. 7 plates, some fldg, fldg printed table. Orig calf, rebacked.
(Bickersteth) **£280 [≈ $504]**
- Fossils of all kinds, digested into a method, suitable to their mutual relation and affinity ... London: for William Innys, 1728. 1st edn. 8vo. Fldg table, 7 plates. B'plate removed from title verso. Contemp calf, rebacked, mor label, gilt. *(Traylen)* **£175 [≈ $315]**

Woodward, Samuel
- A synoptical table of British organic remains ... London: 1830. Subscribers' copy, lge paper. 4to. xiii,50 pp. Cold frontis. Old half mor, mrbld bds, a little worn.
(Weiner) **£40 [≈ $72]**

Woodworth, J.M.
- Nomenclature of diseases prepared for the use of the medical officers of the United States Marine-Hospital Service ... Washington: 1874. 8vo. 210 pp. Orig cloth.
(Goodrich) **$45 [≈ £25]**

Wootton, A.C.
- Chronicles of pharmacy. London: 1910. 2 vols. 8vo. xii,428; 332 pp. Ills. Orig cloth.
(Weiner) **£50 [≈ $90]**
- Chronicles of pharmacy. London: Macmillan, 1910. 1st edn. 2 vols. 8vo. 74 ills. Orig cloth, gilt. *(Traylen)* **£20 [≈ $36]**

Worlidge, John
- Dictionarium rusticum ... or, a dictionary of husbandry, gardening, trade, commerce ... London: for J. Nicholson ..., 1717. 2nd edn, revsd, crrctd & imprvd. 8vo. 2 engvd plates (1 fldg), num ills. Half antique calf, mor label, gilt. *(Traylen)* **£85 [≈ $153]**
- Systema agriculturae, the mystery of husbandry discovered ... an account of several instruments ... useful in this profession. London: for T. Johnson ..., 1669. 1st edn. Folio. Explanation of frontis, engvd frontis, text w'cuts. New half calf. Wing M3598.
(Traylen) **£375 [≈ $675]**
- Systema horti-culturae; or, the art of gardening, in three books. London: Tho. Burrel ..., 1677. 1st edn. 8vo. [xxiv],285,[18 table] pp. Engvd title, gen title, 3 engvd plates. Later gilt-panelled tree-calf, spine gilt dec. Wing W3603. *(Gough)* **£450 [≈ $810]**
- Systema agriculturae: or, the art of gardening ... London: Will Freeman, 1700. 4th edn. 8vo. Addtnl engvd title, 3 plates, final advt leaf. Mod calf. Wing W3606A.
(Hannas) **£150 [≈ $270]**

Wormley, Theodore G.
- Micro-chemistry of poisons, including their physiological, pathological and legal relations. New York: 1869. 2nd printing. 702 pp. 13 plates. Cloth. *(Scientia)* **$125 [≈ £69]**

Worth, C.
- Squint: its causes, pathology and treatment. 1903. xii,229 pp. 33 text ills. Orig cloth, v sl worn. *(Whitehart)* **£18 [≈ $32]**

Wrench, G.T.
- Lord Lister. His life and work. London: 1913. 1st edn. 8vo. 383 pp. Frontis, Foxed. Orig cloth, rubbed. *(Goodrich)* **$35 [≈ £19]**

Wright, Almroth
- Studies on immunisation and their application to the diagnosis and treatment of bacterial infections. New York: 1910. 1st Amer edn. 490 pp. Orig cloth, rebacked, orig spine laid down, new endpapers.
(Scientia) **$75 [≈ £41]**

Wright, J.M.F.
- An elementary treatise on the theory of numbers; from the private tutor. Cambridge: W.P. Grant, 1831. 126 pp, leaf pub ctlg. Mod grey paper bds. *(Hinchliffe)* **£30 [≃ $54]**

Wright, L.
- The induction coil in practical work including Roentgen X-rays. 1897. viii,172 pp. 4 plates, 72 text ills. A few pencil underlinings. *(Whitehart)* **£35 [≃ $63]**

Wright, R. Patrick
- The standard cyclopaedia of modern agriculture and rural economy. London: 1908-11. 12 vols. 4to. 313 plates (33 cold). Orig gilt dec cloth. *(Traylen)* **£65 [≃ $117]**

Wright, Thomas
- Popular treatises on science during the Middle Ages in Anglo-Saxon, Anglo-Norman, and English. London: Historical Society of Science, 1841. Red & black title. Orig cloth, gilt, spine faded & sl chipped at hd & tail. *(Sanders)* **£45 [≃ $81]**

Wright, Wilbur
- Some aeronautical experiments. N.p., n.d. [ca 1902]. [16] pp. Plates. later cloth, lea label. (Paper to Western Society of Engineers September 18, 1901). *(Jenkins)* **$225 [≃ £125]**

Wunderlich, C.A.
- On the temperature in diseases: a manual of medical thermometry. Translated ... London: 1871. 8vo. xii,468 pp, errata. 7 fldg charts. Cloth, a.e. red. *(Rittenhouse)* **$175 [≃ £97]**

Wyeth, George A.
- Surgery of neoplastic diseases by electrothermic methods. New York: 1926. 1st edn. 8vo. xvi,298 pp. 137 ills. Cloth. *(Elgen)* **$35 [≃ £19]**

Wyman, Morrill
- Autumnal catarrh (hay fever). New York: 1876. 2nd edn. 221 pp. 4 maps. Cloth, spine extremities frayed. *(Scientia)* **$100 [≃ £55]**
- Autumnal catarrh (hay fever). New York: 1872. 1st edn. 173 pp. 3 partly cold maps. Waterstain affecting top & bottom of front cvr & extreme edge of some leaves. *(Fye)* **$150 [≃ £83]**

Yarnall, M.
- Catalogue of stars observed at the U.S. Naval Observatory during 1845-77. Washington: 1878. 2nd edn, revsd. Lge 4to. Qtr mor,

scuffed. *(Argosy)* **$45 [≃ £25]**

Yates, James
- Hand-book to accompany the synoptic table of measures and weights of the metric system constructed by Charles Dowling. Edinburgh: W. & A.K. Johnston, 1864. 18,2 advts pp. Disbound. *(C.R. Johnson)* **£15 [≃ $27]**

Years ...
- Forty years in the wilderness of pills and powders, or the cogitations and confessions of an aged physician. Boston: 1859. 8vo. 384 pp. Frontis. Orig cloth. Ex lib. *(Goodrich)* **$35 [≃ £19]**

Youatt
- Youatt's complete grazier and farmers' and cattle-breeders' assistant ... a compendium of husbandry ... thoroughly revised by William E. Barr. London: Virtue, [ca 1910]. 4 vols. 8vo. Plates, text ills. 2 cold models. Orig dec cloth, rubbed & dampstained. *(Hughes)* **£25 [≃ $45]**

Youmans, Edward L.
- Chemical atlas, or the chemistry of familiar objects exhibiting the general principles of science in a series of beautifully colored diagrams ... New York: Appleton, 1855. 4to. 106 pp. 13 plates (col ptd or hand-cold). Cloth, rebacked. *(Marlborough)* **£350 [≃ $630]**

Young, Arthur
- The farmer's calendar: containing the business necessary to be performed ... during every month of the year. London: Phillips, 1804. New edn. 8vo. Over 600 pp. Contemp calf. *(Argosy)* **$175 [≃ £97]**
- The farmer's guide in hiring and stocking farms ... also plans of farmyards and sections of the necessary buildings. London: for W. Strahan ..., 1770. 1st edn. 8vo. 10 engvd plates (2 fldg), text ills. Contemp polished calf, gilt, jnts sl worn. *(Traylen)* **£150 [≃ $270]**
- The farmer's kalendar; or, a monthly directory for all sorts of country business ... the oeconomical conduct of the farm. London: for Robinson & Roberts ..., 1771. 1st edn. 8vo. Half-title. Mod calf. *(Chaucer Head)* **£130 [≃ $234]**
- The farmer's tour through the East of England ... to enquire into the state of agriculture. London: 1771, 1st edn. 4 vols. 8vo. 29 engvd plates (mostly fldg), fldg table. Some minor jottings, stains & other marks, Contemp calf, jnts cracked, extremities worn. *(Bow Windows)* **£210 [≃ $378]**

- The farmer's tour through the East of England ... to enquire into the state of agriculture. London: for W. Strahan ..., 1771, 1st edn. 4 vols. 8vo. 29 plates (mostly fldg) on 28 sheets. Half-title vol 1, 2 final advt leaves vol 4. Contemp calf, sl worn.
(Hannas) **£280 [≈ $504]**

- General view of the agriculture of the County of Sussex, with observations on the means of its improvement. London: Nichols, 1793. 1st edn. 4to. half-title, title, 97 pp. Fldg hand-cold map, 2 hand-cold plates, fldg plan. Mod qtr calf.
(P & P) **£70 [≈ $126]**

- General view of the agriculture of the County of Suffolk, with observations on the means of its improvement. London: 1794. 4to. Cold map. Bds, calf spine. *(Traylen)* **£50 [≈ $90]**

- Rural oeconomy: or, essays on the practical parts of husbandry ... London: T. Becket, 1770. 1st edn. 8vo. [i],520 pp. Lacking half-title, sl browning, contemp ownership inscrptn on title. Contemp calf, armorial devices on sides, rebacked, armorial b'plate.
(Frew Mackenzie) **£135 [≈ $243]**

- A six months' tour through the North of England ... the present state of agriculture, manufactures and population ... the second edition, corrected and enlarged. London: for W. Strahan ..., 1771. 4 vols. 8vo. 29 plates, 5 fldg tables. Contemp sheep, rebacked.
(Waterfield's) **£275 [≈ $495]**

- A six months' tour through the North of England ... Dublin: 1770. 1st Irish edn. 3 vols. xvi,297; vi,390; vii,403 pp. 28 plates (15 fldg), 5 fldg tables. 1 leaf torn with loss of sev words. Calf, sl worn, vol 2 split down spine into 3 sections. *(Edwards)* **£125 [≈ $225]**

- A six months' tour through the Southern Counties of England and Wales ... London: Nicoll, 1768. 1st edn. 284 pp. Half-title. Mod calf, gilt. *(P & P)* **£165 [≈ $297]**

- A tour in Ireland, 1776-1779. Edited with introduction and notes by A.W. Hutton ,.. London: Bell, 1892. 2 vols. 8vo. Map. Orig cloth. *(Emerald Isle)* **£55 [≈ $99]**

- A tour in Ireland: with general observations on the present state of that Kingdom; made in the years 1776-1778. London: for T. Cadell ..., 1780. 2nd, 1st 8vo, edn. 2 vols. 4 engvd plates (3 fldg). Contemp calf, rebacked.
(Traylen) **£130 [≈ $234]**

Young, George

- A treatise on opium, founded upon practical observations. London: for A. Millar, 1753. 1st edn. Thick paper. 8vo. xv,182,[2] pp. Advt leaf. Contemp calf, upper jnt cracked, spine rubbed. *(Burmester)* **£160 [≈ $288]**

Young, Hugh

- Hugh Young, a surgeon's autobiography. New York: [1940]. 1st edn. 8vo. xii,554 pp. Cold frontis, 2 cold plates, ills. Cloth. Author's pres copy, sgnd. *(Elgen)* **$50 [≈ £27]**

Young, Hugh H. & Davis, David, M.

- Young's practice of urology. Based on a study of 12,500 cases. Phila: Saunders, 1926. 2 vols. 8vo. vii,746; iii,738 pp. 1003 ills inc 20 cold plates. Orig cloth, a little rubbing.
(Pollak) **£50 [≈ $90]**

- Young's practice of urology. Phila: [1926]. 2 vols. 8vo. vii,746; iii,738 pp. Over 1000 ills inc 20 cold plates. Orig cloth, spine ends sl frayed. *(Elgen)* **$95 [≈ £52]**

Young, Hugh Hampton

- Genital abnormalities, hermaphroditism and related adrenal diseases. Baltimore: 1937. 1st edn. xli,649 pp. 379 plates. Cloth, front inner hinge cracked. *(Elgen)* **$100 [≈ £55]**

Young, J.R.

- Theory and solution of algebraical equations. 1842. 2nd edn, enlgd. xxiii,476 pp. A few pp with red underlining. New cloth.
(Whitehart) **£40 [≈ $72]**

Young, James K.

- A practical treatise on orthopedic surgery. Phila: 1894. 8vo. 446 pp. Pub ctlg. Sl mark on front cvr. *(Rittenhouse)* **$37.50 [≈ £20]**

Young, Joseph

- A new physical system of astronomy ... Sir Isaac Newton ... examined, and ... refuted ... New York: Hopkins, 1800. 1st edn. viii, [8]-188 pp. Errata leaf, 2 plates (1 fldg), 8 text w'cuts. Scattered foxing. Contemp calf, spine ends chipped off, bd detaching.
(Elgen) **$295 [≈ £163]**

- A new physical system of astronomy ... the powers which impel the planets and comments ... Successful methods of curing cancerous ulcers, the ague, putrid fevers ... New York: Hopkins, 1800. 1st edn. 188 pp. Errata leaf, Contemp mottled calf.
(Jenkins) **$150 [≈ £83]**

Young, Matthew

- An enquiry into the principal phenomena of sounds and musical strings. Dublin: Joseph Hill, 1784. 1st edn. 8vo. 2 fldg engvd plates. Contemp red str-grained mor, gilt, gilt borders, fully gilt panelled spine, mrbld edges. *(Traylen)* **£775 [≈ $1,395]**

Young, Thomas
- A course of lectures on natural philosophy and the mechanical arts. London: Joseph Johnson, 1807. 1st edn. 2 vols. Thick 4to. 57 engvd plates (ex 58, 2 hand-cold). Mod cloth.
(Hemlock) **$1,500** [≈ £833]
- A course of lectures on natural philosophy and the mechanical arts. London: for Joseph Johnson, 1807. 1st edn. 2 vols. 4to. 58 engvd plates (2 hand-cold). Some light foxing, sm lib stamp on titles. New half red calf, gilt, mrbld edges.
(Traylen) **£550** [≈ $990]
- A course of lectures on natural philosophy and the mechanical arts. London: Taylor & Walton, 1845. 2nd edn. 2 vols. 8vo. 608 pp. 43 engvd double-page plates (2 in color by Baxter). Half calf.
(Oasis) **$650** [≈ £361]
- Elementary illustrations of the celestial mechanics of Laplace. London: 1832. 8vo. v,344 pp. Diags. Mod mrbld bds.
(Weiner) **£75** [≈ $135]
- An introduction to medical literature, including a system of practical nosology. London: 1823. 2nd edn. 8vo. xxvi,659 pp. Orig cloth-backed bds, a trifle bent, lib ticket on spine.
(Rittenhouse) **$30** [≈ £16]

Zeeman, Pieter
- Researches in magneto-optics. London: Macmillan, 1913. 1st edn. 8vo. xiv,[2], 219,[1] pp. 8 photo plates, text figs. Orig cloth. Pres copy to E.N. da C. Anstrade.
(Antiq Sc) **$135** [≈ £75]

Zeissl, Hermann von
- Outlines of the pathology and treatment of syphilis and allied venereal diseases. Translated by H. Raphael. New York: 1886.

1st edn in English. 402 pp. Sgntr on title. Cloth.
(Scientia) **$75** [≈ £41]

Zemsky, J.L.
- Oral diseases ... diagnostic and therapeutic aid to the practitioner of medicine and dentistry. New York: 1930. 402 pp. 414 ills.
(Whitehart) **£15** [≈ $27]

Zilboorg, Gregory
- History of medical psychology. New York: 1941. 1st edn. 8vo. 606 pp. Cloth, spine faded.
(Rittenhouse) **$37.50** [≈ £20]

Zilboorg, Gregory & Henry, George W.
- A history of medical psychology. New York: 1941. 8vo. Orig cloth, dw.
(Goodrich) **$35** [≈ £19]
- A history of medical psychology. New York: Norton, 1941. 8vo. 606,[ii] pp. 21 ills. Pub bndg.
(Pollak) **£25** [≈ $45]

Zinsser, Hans & Bayne-Jones, Stanhope
- A textbook of bacteriology, with a section on pathogenic protozoa. New York: Appleton-Century, 1934. 7th edn. 8vo. xix,[iii],1226 pp. 174 ills. Pub bndg.
(Pollak) **£20** [≈ $36]

Zirkle, Conway
- Death of a science in Russia. The fate of genetics as described in Pravda and elsewhere. Phila: 1949. 8vo. xiv,319 pp. Cloth, dw.
(Elgen) **$30** [≈ £16]

Zuckerkandl, Otto
- Atlas and epitome of operative surgery. Phila: Saunders medical hand Atlases, 1898. 395 pp. 24 chromo plates, text ills. Orig cloth.
(Oasis) **$35** [≈ £19]

Catalogue Booksellers Contributing to IRBP

The booksellers who have provided catalogues during 1987 specifically for the purpose of compiling the various titles in the *IRBP* series, and from whose catalogues books have been selected, are listed below in alphabetical order of the abbreviation employed for each. This listing is therefore a complete key to the booksellers contributing to the series as a whole; only a proportion of the listed names is represented in this particular subject volume.

The majority of these booksellers issue periodic catalogues free, on request, to potential customers. Sufficient indication of the type of book handled by each bookseller can be gleaned from the individual book entries set out in the main body of this work and in the companion titles in the series.

Allen	=	William H. Allen, 2031 Walnut Street, Philadelphia, PA19103, U.S.A. (215 563 3398)
Allix	=	Charles Allix, Bradbourne Farmhouse, Sevenoaks, Kent TN13 3DH, England (0732 451311)
Allsop	=	Duncan M. Allsop, 26 Smith Street, Warwick CV34 4HS, England (0926 493266)
Ampersand	=	Ampersand Books, P.O. Box 674, Cooper Station, New York City 10276, U.S.A. (212 674 6795)
Antic Hay	=	Antic Hay Rare Books, P.O. Box 2185, Asbury Park, NJ 07712, U.S.A. (201 774 4590)
Antiq Sc	=	The Antiquarian Scientist, P.O. Box 367, Dracut, Mass. 01826, U.S.A. (617 957 5267)
Any Amount	=	Any Amount of Books, 62 Charing Cross Road, London WC2H 0BB, England (01 240 8140)
Appelfeld	=	Appelfeld Gallery, 1372 York Avenue, New York, NY 10021, U.S.A. (212 988 7835)
Argonaut	=	Argonaut Book Shop 786-792 Sutter Street, San Francisco, California 94109, U.S.A. (415 474 9067)
Argosy	=	Argosy Book Store, Inc., 116 East 59th Street, New York, NY 10022, U.S.A. (212 753 4455)
Ash	=	Ash Rare Books, 25 Royal Exchange, London EC3, England (01 626 2665)
Barbary	=	Barbary Books, C.P. Counihan, Fortnight, Wick Down. Broad Hinton, Swindon, Wiltshire SN4 9NR, England (079373 693)
Beasley	=	Beasley Books, Paul & Beth Garon, 1533 W. Oakdale, Chicago, IL 60657, U.S.A. (312 472 4528)
Bennett	=	Stuart Bennett, Rare Books & Manuscripts, 3 Camden Terrace, Camden Road, Bath BA1 5HZ, England (0225 333930)
Between the Covers	=	Between the Covers, Tom & Heidi Congalton, 575 Collings Avenue, Collingswood, NJ 08107, U.S.A.
Bickersteth	=	David Bickersteth, 38 Fulbrooke Road, Cambridge CB3 9EE, England (0223 352291)
Blackwell's	=	Blackwell's Rare Books, B.H. Blackwell Ltd., Fyfield Manor, Fyfield, Abingdon, Oxon OX13 5LR, England (0865 390692)
Black Cat	=	Black Cat Books, Ann Mackenzie, 1 Granby Road, Edinburgh EH16 5NH, Scotland (031 667 6341)

Bonham	=	J. & S.L. Bonham, Flat 14, 84 Westbourne Terrace, London W2 6QE, England (01 402 7064)
Book Block	=	The Book Block, 8 Loughlin Avenue, Cos Cob, Connecticut 06807, U.S.A. (203 629 2990)
Boston Book	=	Boston Book Annex, 906 Beacon Street, Boston, MA 02215, U.S.A. (617 266 1090)
Bow Windows	=	Bow Windows Book Shop, 128 High Street, Lewes, East Sussex BN7 1XL, England (0273 480780)
Braiterman	=	Marilyn Braiterman, Antiquarian Bookseller, 20 Whitfield Road, Baltimore, Maryland 21210, U.S.A. (301 235 4848)
Burmester	=	James Burmester, Manor House Farmhouse, North Stoke, Bath BA1 9AT, England (0272 327265)
Camden	=	Camden Books, 146 Walcot Street, Bath, Avon BA1 5BL, England (0225 61606)
Chaucer Head	=	The Chaucer Head, Daniel McDowell, 41 Low Petergate, York YO1 2HT, England (0904 22000)
Clark	=	Robert Clark, 24 Sidney Street, Oxford OX4 3AG, England (0865 243406)
Clearwater	=	Clearwater Books, 19 Matlock Road, Ferndown, Wimborne, Dorset BH22 8QT, England (0202 893263)
Cooper Hay	=	Cooper Hay Rare Books, 203 Bath Street, Glasgow G2 4HZ, Scotland (041 226 3074)
Cortie	=	R.H. Cortie, 3 Hillway, Highgate, London N6 6QB, England (01 340 3738)
Charles Cox	=	Charles Cox, 20 Old Tiverton Road, Exeter, Devon EX4 6LG, England (0392 55776)
Claude Cox	=	Claude Cox, The White House, Kelsale, Saxmundham, Suffolk IP17 2PQ, England (0728 2786)
Dailey	=	William & Victoria Dailey, 8216 Melrose Avenue, P.O. Box 69160, Los Angeles, California 90069, U.S.A. (213 658 8515)
Dalian	=	Dalian Books, David P. Williams, 81 Albion Drive, London Fields, London E8 4LT, England (01 249 1587)
Darees	=	Darees Books, 22 Wanley Road, London SE5 8AT, England (01 737 4557)
Davis & Schorr	=	Davis & Schorr Art Books, 14755 Ventura Boulevard, Suite 1-747, Sherman Oaks, CA 91403, U.S.A. (818 787 1322)
Deighton Bell	=	Deighton, Bell & Co., 13 Trinity Street, Cambridge CB2 1TD, England (0223 353939)
Edrich	=	I.D. Edrich, 17 Selsdon Road, London E11 2QF, England (01 989 9541)
Edwards	=	Francis Edwards, The Old Cinema, Castle Street, Hay-on-Wye, via Hereford HR3 5DF, England (0497 820071)
Elgen	=	Elgen Books, 336 DeMott Avenue, Rockville Centre, New York 11570, U.S.A. (516 53 6276)
Emerald Isle	=	Emerald Isle Books, 539 Antrim Road, Belfast BT15 3BU, Northern Ireland (0232 771798)
Europa	=	Europa Books, 15 Luttrell Avenue, Putney, London SW15 6PD, England (01 788 0312)
Farahar	=	Clive Farahar, XIV The Green, Calne, Wiltshire SN11 8DG, England (0249 816793)
Fenning	=	James Fenning, 12 Glenview, Rochestown Avenue, Dun Laoghaire, County Dublin, Eire (01 857855)
Fine Art	=	Fine Art Catalogues, The Hollies, Port Carlisle, Near Carlisle, Cumbria CA5 5BU, England (096 55 1398)

Frew Mackenzie	=	Frew Mackenzie plc, 106 Great Russell Street, London WC1B 3NA, England (01 580 2311)
Fye	=	W. Bruce Fye, Antiquarian Medical Books, 1607 North Wood Avenue, Marshfield, Wisconsin 54449, U.S.A. (715 384 8128)
Gant	=	Elizabeth Gant, 52 High Street, Thames Ditton, Surrey KT7 0SA, England (01 398 0962)
Gekoski	=	R.A. Gekoski, 33B Chalcot Square, London NW1 8YA, England (01 722 9037)
Goodrich	=	James Tait Goodrich, Antiquarian Books & Manuscripts, 214 Everett Place, Englewood, New Jersey 07631, U.S.A. (201 567 0199)
Gough	=	Simon Gough Books, 5 Fish Hill, Holt, Norfolk, England (026371 2650)
Green Street	=	Green Street Book Shop, 5 Green Street, Cambridge CB2 3JU, England (0223 68088)
Greyne	=	Greyne House, Marshfield, Chippenham, Wiltshire SN14 8LU, England (0225 891279)
Halewood	=	Halewood & Sons, 37 Friargate, Preston, Lancashire PR1 2AT, England (0772 52603)
Hannas	=	Torgrim Hannas, 29a Canon Street, Winchester, Hampshire SO23 9JJ, England (0962 62730)
Hawthorn	=	Hawthorn Books, 7 College Park Drive, Westbury-on-Trym, Bristol BS10 7AN, England (0272 509175)
Hazeldene	=	Hazeldene Bookshop, A.H. & L.G. Elliot, 61 Renshaw Street, Liverpool L1 2SJ, England (051 708 8780)
Hemlock	=	Hemlock Books, 170 Beach 145th Street, Neponsit, New York 11694, U.S.A. (718 318 0737)
Heraldry Today	=	Heraldry Today, 10 Beauchamp Place, London SW3, England (01 584 1656)
Heritage	=	Heritage Book Store, Inc., 8540 Melrose Avenue, Los Angeles, California 90069, U.S.A. (213 659 3674)
High Latitude	=	High Latitude, P.O. Box 11254, Bainbridge Island, WA 98110, U.S.A. (206 842 0202)
Hinchliffe	=	Hinchliffe Books, 15 Castle Street, Thornbury, Bristol BS12 1HA, England (0454 415177)
Howes	=	Howes Bookshop, Trinity Hall, Braybrooke Terrace, Hastings, East Sussex TN34 1HQ, England (0424 423437)
Hughes	=	Spike Hughes Rare Books, Leithen Bank, Leithen Road, Innerleithen, Peeblesshire EH44 6HY, Scotland (0896 830019)
Ivelet	=	Ivelet Books Ltd., 18 Fairlawn Drive, Redhill, Surrey RH1 6JP, England (0737 64520)
James	=	Marjorie James, Flat 1, 53 Onslow Gardens, London SW7, England (01 373 0614)
Jenkins	=	The Jenkins Company, Box 2085, Austin, Texas 78768, U.S.A. (512 280 2940)
C.R. Johnson	=	C.R. Johnson, 21 Charlton Place, London N1 8AQ, England (01 354 1077)
Johnson Arch	=	Johnson Architectural Books, Tynings House, Sherston, Malmesbury, Wiltshire SN16 0LS, England (0666 840404)
Jolliffe	=	Peter Jolliffe, 2 Acre End Street, Eynsham, Oxon OX8 1PA, England (0865 881095)
Karmiole	=	Kenneth Karmiole, Bookseller, 1225 Santa Monica Mall, Santa Monica, California 90401, U.S.A. (213 451 4342)
Kerr	=	Ewen Kerr, (Brian Peate), 1 New Road, Kendal, Cumbria LA9 4AY, England (0539 20659)

Lewcock	=	John Lewcock, 4 Cobble Yard, Napier Street, Cambridge CB1 1HP, England (0223 312133)
Lewton	=	L.J. Lewton, Old Station House, Freshford, Bath BA3 6EQ, England (022 122 3351)
Lloyd-Roberts	=	Tom Lloyd-Roberts, Old Court House, Caerwys, Mold, Clwyd CH7 5BB, Wales (0352 720276)
Lopez	=	Ken Lopez, Bookseller, 51 Huntington Road, Hadley, MA 01035, U.S.A. (413 584 4827)
Lydian	=	Lydian Bookstore, Bockmer House, Medmenham, near Marlow, Buckinghamshire SL7 2HL, England (0491 571218)
Lyon	=	Richard Lyon, 17 Old High Street, Hurstpierpoint, West Sussex BN6 9TT, England (0273 832255)
McKay	=	Barry McKay Rare Books, 29 Nethercote Road, Tackley, Oxfordshire OX5 3AW, England (086 983 228)
Mansfield	=	Judith Mansfield, Books, 60A Dornton Road, London SW12 9NE, England (01 673 6635)
Marlborough	=	Marlborough Rare Books Ltd., 144-146 New Bond Street, London W1Y 9FD, England (01 493 6993)
Marlborough B'Shop	=	Marlborough Bookshop, 6 Kingsbury Street, Marlborough, Wiltshire, England (0672 54074)
Minkoff	=	George Robert Minkoff Inc., Rare Books, Box 147, Great Barrington, Mass 01230, U.S.A. (413 528 4575)
Monk Bretton	=	Monk Bretton Books, Somerford Keynes House, Cirencester, Gloucestershire GL7 6DN, England (0285 860554)
Moore	=	Peter Moore, P.O. Box 66, 200a Perne Road, Cambridge CB1 3PD, England (02223 411177)
Morrell	=	Nicholas Morrell (Rare Books) Ltd., 77 Falkland Road, London NW5 2XB, England (01 485 5205)
Muns	=	J.B. Muns, Fine Arts Books, 1162 Shattuck Avenue, Berkeley, California 94707, U.S.A. (415 525 2420)
Norton	=	The Norton Bookshop, Christopher Casson, 66 Bishopton Lane, Stockton, Cleveland TS18 2AJ, England (0642 601676)
Nouveau	=	Nouveau Rare Books, Steve Silberman, P.O. Box 12471, 5005 Meadow Oaks Park Drive, Jackson, Mississippi 39211, U.S.A. (601 956 9950)
O'Reilly	=	John O'Reilly, Mountain Books, 85/87 King Street, Derby DE1 3EE, England (0332 365650)
Oasis	=	Oasis Books, P.O. Box 171067, San Diego, CA 92117, U.S.A. (619 272 0384)
Offenbacher	=	Emile Offenbacher, 84-50 Austin Street, P.O. Box 96, Kew Gardens, New York 11415, U.S.A. (718 849 11415)
Old Cinema	=	The Old Cinema, Castle Street, Hay-on-Wye, via Hereford HR3 5DF, England (0497 820071)
Orient	=	Orient Books, Little Blakes, Halse, Taunton, Somerset, England (0823 432466)
Ottenberg	=	Simon Ottenberg, P.O. Box 15509, Wedgwood Station, Seattle, WA 98115, U.S.A.
Pacific	=	Pacific Book House, 1016G Kapahulu Avenue, Honolulu, Hawaii 96816, U.S.A. (808 737 3475)
Palladour	=	Palladour Books, Greenlands, Foot's Hill, Cann, near Shaftesbury, Dorset SP7 0BW, England (0747 3942)
Pharos	=	Pharos Books, P.O. Box 17, Fair Haven Station, New Haven, Connecticut 06513, U.S.A.
Pickering	=	Pickering & Chatto Ltd., 17 Pall Mall, London SW1Y 5NB, England (01 930 2515)

Pirages	=	Phillip J. Pirages, Post Office Box 504, 965 West 11th Street, McMinnville, Oregon 97128, U.S.A. (503 472 5555)
Pollak	=	P.M. Pollak, Ph.D., F.L.S., 'Moorview', Plymouth Road, South Brent, Devon TQ10 9HT, England (036 47 3457)
Polyanthos	=	Polyanthos Books Inc., P.O. Box 343, 8 Green Street, Huntington, NY 11743, U.S.A. (516 673 9232)
Post Mortem	=	Post Mortem Books, Ralph Spurrier, 58 Stanford Avenue, Hassocks, Sussex BN6 8JH, England (07918 3066)
Pye	=	Mr. Pye (Books), M.S. & E.J. Kemp, 47 Hailgate, Howden, Goole DN14 7ST, England (0482 25236)
P & P	=	P & P Books, J.S. Pizey, 27 Love Lane, Oldswinford, Stourbridge, West Midlands DY8, England (0384 393845)
Quaritch	=	Bernard Quaritch Ltd., 5-8 Lower John Street, Golden Square, London W1R 4AU, England (01 734 2983)
Rayfield	=	Tom Rayfield, The Blacksmiths, Radnage Common, Buckinghamshire HP14 4DH, England (024 026 3986)
Reese	=	William Reese Company, 409 Temple Street, New Haven, Connecticut 06511, U.S.A. (203 789 8081)
Rittenhouse	=	Rittenhouse Book Store, 1706 Rittenhouse Square, Philadelphia, Pennsylvania 19103, U.S.A. (215 545 6072)
Robertshaw	=	John Robertshaw, 5 Fellowes Drive, Ramsey, Huntingdon, Cambridgeshire PE17 1BE, England (0487 813330)
Rootenberg	=	B. & L. Rootenberg, P.O. Box 5049, Sherman Oaks, California 91403-5049, U.S.A. (818 788 7765)
Sanders	=	Sanders of Oxford Ltd., 104 High Street, Oxford OX1 4BW, England (0865 242590)
Scientia	=	Scientia, Box 433, Arlington, Mass. 02174, U.S.A. (617 643 5725)
Sherick	=	Michael J. Sherick, Bookseller, P.O. Box 91915, Santa Barbara, CA 93190, U.S.A. (805 966 5819)
Sherington	=	Nick Sherington, 11 Clifton Hill, Exeter, Devon EX1 2DL, England (0392 216532)
Sinclair	=	Iain Sinclair Books, 28 Albion Drive, London E8 4ET, England (01 254 8571)
Sklaroff	=	L.J. Sklaroff, Craiglea, The Broadway, Totland, Isle of Wight PO39 0BW, England (0983 753968)
Alan Smith	=	Alan Smith, 15 Oakland Avenue, Dialstone Lane, Stockport, Cheshire SK2 6AX, England (061 483 2547)
John Smith	=	John Smith & Son (Glasgow) Ltd., 57-61 St. Vincent Street, Glasgow G2 5TB, Scotland (041 221 7472)
Snowden Smith	=	Snowden Smith Books, 41 Godfrey Street, London SW3 3SX, England (01 352 6756)
Sotheran	=	Henry Sotheran Ltd., 2, 3, 4 & 5 Sackville Street, Piccadilly, London W1X 2DP, England (01 734 1150)
Spelman	=	Ken Spelman, 70 Micklegate, York YO1 1LF, England (0904 24414)
Spire	=	Spire Books, 38 Rosebery Avenue, New Malden, Surrey KT3 4JS, England (01 942 2111)
Stewart	=	Andrew Stewart, 11 High Street, Helpringham, Sleaford, Lincolnshire NG34 9RA, England (052 921 617)
Tara	=	Tara Associates Ltd., South End House, Church Lane, Lymington, Hampshire SO41 9RA, England (0590 96848)
Thompson	=	Keith Thompson, 4 Sunset Close, Beachlands, Pevensey Bay, East Sussex BN24 6SA, England (0323 766959)
Titles	=	Titles, 15 Turl Street, Oxford OX1 3DQ, England (0865 727928)

Tooley	=	Tooley, Adams & Co. Ltd., 83 Marylebone High Street, London W1M 4AL, England (01 486 9052)
Traylen	=	Charles W. Traylen, Castle House, 49-50 Quarry Street, Guildford, Surrey GU1 3UA, England (0483 572424)
Typographeum	=	Typographeum Bookshop, The Stone Cottage, Bennington Road, Francestown, New Hampshire 03043, U.S.A.
Upcroft	=	Upcroft Books Ltd., 66 St. Cross Road, Winchester, Hampshire SO23 9PS, England (0962 52679)
Virgo	=	Virgo Books, Mrs. Q.V. Mason, Little Court, South Wraxall, Bradford-on-Avon, Wiltshire BA15 2SE, England (02216 2040)
Waddington	=	Geraldine Waddington, Home Farm Cottage, Knowle, Nr. Braunton, North Devon EX33 2LY, England (0271 815011)
Warnes	=	Felicity J. Warnes, 82 Merryhills Drive, Enfield, Middlesex EN2 7PD, England
Washton	=	Andrew D. Washton, 411 East 83rd Street, New York, New York 10028, U.S.A. (212 751 7027)
Waterfield's	=	Waterfield's, 36 Park End Street, Oxford OX1 1HJ, England (0865 721809)
Weiner	=	Graham Weiner 78 Rosebery Road, London N10 2LA, England (01 883 8424)
Weinreb	=	Weinreb Architectural Books, at Henry Sotheran Ltd., 2 Sackville Street, Piccadilly, London W1V 0AA, England (01 434 2019)
Wheldon & Wesley	=	Wheldon & Wesley Ltd., Lytton Lodge, Codicote, Hitchin, Hertfordshire SG4 8TE, England (0438 820370)
Whitehart	=	F.E. Whitehart, Rare Books, 40 Priestfield Road, Forest Hill, London SE23 2RS, England (01 699 3225)
Whiteson	=	Edna Whiteson, 66 Belmont Avenue, Cockfosters, Hertfordshire EN4 9LA, England (01 449 8860)
Willow	=	Willow House Books, The Cottage Bookshop, 5 Hill Street, Chorley, Lancashire PR7 1AX, England (025 72 69280)
Wolff	=	Camille Wolff, Grey House Books, 12A Lawrence Street, Chelsea, London SW3, England (01 352 7725)
Wood	=	Peter Wood, 20 Stonehill Road, Great Shelford, Cambridge CB2 5JL, England (0223 842419)
Words Etcetera	=	Words Etcetera, Julian Nangle, Hod House, Child Okeford, Dorset DT11 8EH, England (0258 860539)
Xerxes	=	Xerxes, Fine & Rare Books & Documents, Box 428, Glen Head, New York 11545, U.S.A. (516 671 6235)
Young's	=	Young's Antiquarian Books, Tillingham, Essex CM0 7ST, England (062187 8187)
Zeno	=	Zeno, 6 Denmark Street, London WC2H 8LP, England (01 836 2522)

Antiquarian Booktrade
Reference Books from Picaflow

Picaflow's range of annual reference works relating to the antiquarian and collector's book world is made up of *Cole's Register of British Antiquarian & Secondhand Bookdealers* (normally referred to merely as *Cole's Register*), together with five separate titles in the *International Rare Book Prices* series (*IRBP*).

Cole's Register

This volume was recognised, on its first appearance in 1985, as setting a new standard for accuracy of information in its field. The title, completely revised and re-issued each April, provides details of some 1,900 antiquarian and secondhand bookdealers and bookshops in Britain. These details are arranged both alphabetically and geographically. The value of the information is further enhanced by extensive cross-indexing of the specialist fields of individual bookdealers and of bookdealers from whom catalogues are available.

Covering the whole spectrum of book collector, *Cole's Register* enables the librarian or collector to contact specialist bookdealers in practically any subject area at any price level.

International Rare Books Prices

The *IRBP* series, published to the same high standard of accuracy, concentrates on books themselves, rather than bookdealers. The series was established to provide modestly-priced, yet extensive, annual records of the current pricing levels of old, rare, and out-of-print books which come onto the market in Britain and the United States; to draw attention to unusual and infrequently found books which have become temporarily available; and to introduce collectors to dealers.

The subject areas covered by individual volumes of *IRBP* are:

The Arts & Architecture
Books on the fine and applied arts from the 17th century to the 1960s with particular emphasis on the 19th and early 20th century.

Early Printed Books
Concentrating entirely on books, in all subject areas, published prior to 1800. Early books in nearly all disciplines are included. Opportunities to obtain such books are diminishing each year.

Modern First Editions
The most authoritative and extensive annual record available of the demand for literary first editions of this century. Some 8,500 entries appear each year in this particular volume.

Science & Medicine
Books published during the development periods of all major branches of science and medicine form the basis of many developing collections across the world. Such books are found here.

Voyages, Travel & Exploration
Hardly a country or area in the world is not represented in this wide-ranging compilation of long out-of-print and increasingly sought-after titles.

New editions are published in April each year